From Grover Cleveland to Gerald Ford...
THE PRESIDENT SPEAKS OFF-THE-RECORD

From Grover Cleveland to Gerald Ford . . .

THE PRESIDENT SPEAKS OFF-THE-RECORD

HISTORIC EVENINGS WITH AMERICA'S LEADERS,
THE PRESS, AND OTHER MEN OF POWER,
AT WASHINGTON'S EXCLUSIVE GRIDIRON CLUB
  BY

Harold Brayman

DOW JONES BOOKS   Princeton, New Jersey

32757

Published by Dow Jones Books
P.O. Box 300, Princeton, NJ 08540

Printed and bound in the United States of America

10 9 8 7 6 5 4 3 2 1

MANY SPEECHES delivered before the Gridiron Club in person by American Presidents and other public figures appear throughout this book. However, in the songs and skits taking place on the Gridiron stage, these public figures are characterized by Gridiron actors, except when otherwise specifically stated.

Likewise, the song lyrics appearing in these pages are parodies, and should be construed as such, unless otherwise specifically noted.

Dow Jones Books gratefully acknowledges:

Excerpt from *The Constant Circle*, by Sara Mayfield. Copyright © 1968 by Sara Mayfield. Reprinted by permission of Delacorte Press.

Excerpts from *Gridiron Nights*, by Arthur Wallace Dunn. Copyright renewed 1943. Reprinted by permission of Mrs. Virginia McK. Dunn.

Excerpt from *As I Knew Them*, by James E. Watson. Copyright © 1936 by Bobbs-Merrill Company, Inc.; renewed 1964. Reprinted by permission of Bobbs-Merrill Company, Inc.

Excerpt from *Our Times*, Vol 2, by Mark Sullivan. Copyright © 1927 by Charles Scribner's Sons; renewed 1955. Reprinted by permission of Charles Scribner's Sons.

Excerpts from *Presidential Wit*, by Bill Adler. Copyright © 1966 by Bill Adler. Reprinted by permission of Simon and Schuster, Inc., Trident Press Division.

Excerpt from *The Works of Theodore Roosevelt. Memorial Edition*. Volume 18. Reprinted with acknowledgement to Charles Scribner's Sons.

Excerpt from *Presidents I've Known*, by Charles Willis Thompson. Copyright © 1929 by Charles Willis Thompson; renewed 1956. Reprinted by permission of Bobbs-Merrill Company, Inc.

Excerpt from *Twelve against the Gods*, by William Bolitho. Copyright © 1929 by Simon and Schuster, Inc.

Renewed 1956 by Cybil Bolitho Fearnley. Reprinted by permission of the latter.

Excerpts from *Hoover after Dinner*, by Herbert Hoover. Copyright © 1933 by Charles Scribner's Sons; renewed 1961 by author. Reprinted by permission of the Herbert Hoover Foundation and Frank E. Mason, Literary Executor of Herbert Hoover.

Excerpt from *Prejudices: Sixth Series*, by Henry Louis Mencken. Copyright © 1927 by Alfred A. Knopf, Inc.; renewed by author. Reprinted by permission of Alfred A. Knopf, Inc.

Excerpt from *The Public Papers and Addresses of Franklin D. Roosevelt*, Vol. 5. Reprinted with acknowledgement to Random House, Inc.

Excerpts from *The Secret Diary of Harold L. Ickes*, Vols. 1-2, by Harold L. Ickes. Copyright © 1953-54 by Simon and Schuster, Inc. Reprinted by permission of Simon and Schuster, Inc.

Excerpts from *Addresses upon the American Road*, by Herbert Hoover. Copyright © 1955 by the Board of Trustees of the Leland Stanford Junior University. Reprinted by permission of the Herbert Hoover Foundation and Frank E. Mason, Literary Executor of Herbert Hoover.

Photographing of Gridiron Club materials, on location, by Marcus Mason Lipp.

Library of Congress Cataloging in Publication Data

Brayman, Harold.
     The President speaks off-the-record.

     Bibliography: p.
     Includes index.
     1. Gridiron Club, Washington, D.C.—Anecdotes, facetiae, satires, etc.
     2. Statesmen—United States—Anecdotes, facetiae, satire, etc.
     3. United States—Politics and government—Anecdotes, facetiae, satire, etc.
     I. Title.
HS2725.W3G823   320.9'73'090207   76-17358
ISBN 0-87128-519-3

To my wife,
Martha Wood Brayman,
      and our two sons,
      Harold Halliday Brayman
      and
      Walter Witherspoon Brayman

CONTENTS

Preface by Jack Steele, Washington editor,
Scripps-Howard Newspapers and
Gridiron Club secretary   xi

Acknowledgements   xvii

Introduction   1
   "With malice toward none and humor for all. . . ."

  I. Both Sides of the Hot Gridiron   8
         (1885-1975) Good Fellowship and High Drama

 II. Grover Cleveland and Benjamin Harrison   25
         (1885-1897) Earliest Gridiron Bedevilments

III. William McKinley   38
         *(1897-1901) And Gridiron Club members from "the
         tented field and barrooms of New York"*

 IV. Theodore Roosevelt   47
         *(1901-1909) TR Swings His Big Stick at a Gridiron
         Dinner*

  V. William Howard Taft   71
         (1909-1913) "Even the elements protest . . ."

 VI. Woodrow Wilson   89
         *(1913-1921) A vision of "the blue heaven, signs of
         spring, and the movement of free clouds. . . ."*

VII. Warren Gamaliel Harding   136
         (1921-1923) Scandal on the Horizon

VIII. Calvin Coolidge   149
         (1923-1929) "Silent Cal" Maintains His Reputation

IX.   Herbert Hoover   194
      (1929-1933) "King for a Day"

X.   Franklin D. Roosevelt   233
      (1933-1934) FDR and H. L. Mencken Face Each
      Other on the Gridiron

XI.   Franklin D. Roosevelt   264
      (1935-1936) FDR Squares off against His Opposi-
      tion in Business and the Press

XII. Franklin D. Roosevelt   307
      (1937-1938) The Supreme Court Packing Fight and
      White Ties and Tails at the Gridiron Club

XIII. Franklin D. Roosevelt   344
      (1939-1945) "Nine Terms! Gentlemen, it is too
      much!"

XIV. Harry S. Truman   402
      (1945-1947) Truman the Meek

XV.   Harry S. Truman   453
      (1948-1952) Truman the Feisty

XVI. Dwight D. Eisenhower   520
      (1953-1956) Republicans and Democrats Laugh
      and Work Together and the Gridiron Burns Neither

XVII. Dwight D. Eisenhower   569
      (1957-1960) "Just don't disturb the table too
      much. . . ."

XVIII. John F. Kennedy   620
      (1961-1963) Gridiron Wit Meets Its Match—
      and Perhaps Its Master

XIX. Lyndon B. Johnson   661
      (1964-1966) "I am a free man first. . . ."
          And Richard Nixon, Barry Goldwater, and
      Hubert Humphrey Also Speak

XX.   Lyndon B. Johnson   707
      (1967-1968) "We are not going to retreat before the
      future. . . ."
          And Robert Kennedy, Hubert Humphrey,
      Gerald Ford, and Ronald Reagan Also Speak

XXI.   Richard M. Nixon   752
       *(1969-1971) "The primary duty of the President is
       to preserve, bring, and keep the peace. . . . "*
            And Hubert Humphrey, Edward Kennedy,
       George Wallace, Spiro Agnew, Edmund Mus-
       kie, and John Mitchell Also Speak

XXII. Richard M. Nixon   795
       (1972-1974) The Triumph and the Debacle
            Hubert Humphrey, George McGovern, and
       Barry Goldwater Speak

XXIII. Gerald R. Ford   833
       *(1975-   ) "How much of a life-saving medicine a
       little laughter is for Presidents."*

       Source Notes   847

       Bibliography   850

       The Gridiron Club: Membership List   853

       Index   857

Preface

By Jack Steele,
Washington editor,
*Scripps-Howard Newspapers**

The Gridiron Club of Washington, D.C., organized more than ninety years ago by a group of Washington newspaper correspondents, is steeped in traditions.

Many of them stem from the club's annual white-tie dinners, which are attended by perhaps the most prestigious audiences that assemble anywhere. These dinners have become world-famous as vehicles for political satire.

Here are a few of these Gridiron traditions:

—The dinners always open with a "speech in the dark" by the club president, with the Statler Hilton Hotel ballroom in complete darkness and the nearly 550 guests standing at their places.

—The gourmet menu is served over a four-hour span with speeches, skits and songs interspersed with the courses. Terrapin Maryland is invariably a featured course, a tradition since the early days after the Club's founding in 1885 as a dining and drinking society.

---

*Jack Steele was president of the Gridiron Club in 1970 and has been its secretary since 1972.

—All speeches, including those of the President of the United States and a spokesman for the opposition party, are off-the-record, although newsworthy comments and incidents often have been leaked.

—Anything off-color is scrupulously avoided. Long before women were elected members of the club and invited to attend its dinners as guests, the Gridiron president intoned in his speech in the dark that "ladies are always present," as a reminder of the ban on what may not be in good taste.

—The President of the United States (to whom the club offers its only toast) is often ribbed in songs and skits, but never portrayed on the Gridiron stage. No other public figure escapes such direct satire. Club members freely impersonate Vice Presidents, congressmen, Supreme Court justices, cabinet members and many others important in government.

—The roasting of the great and not-so-great is generally good-humored. The speech in the dark concludes with the reminder that: "The Gridiron may singe, but it never burns."

One of the Gridiron Club's other traditions is Harold Brayman, the author of this book. No one else conceivably could have written it.

For more than forty years Brayman has immersed himself in Gridiron history. He has attended every formal dinner of the club since he was elected a member in 1933. He was club president in 1941.

With the never-before-given permission of the Gridiron Club executive committee, Brayman has delved through voluminous club records kept since its earliest days. They include complete scripts of all dinner skits since 1914 and, from the beginning of the club, bound volumes, some as much as six inches thick, containing speeches, newspaper clippings, letters, minutes of club meetings and other materials about the Gridiron Club and its members.

Brayman has also combed Presidential libraries, private collections and the Library of Congress to unearth copies of speeches made at Gridiron dinners but missing from its records. He obtained permission from living Gridiron speakers to remove the off-the-record restriction from their speeches so they could be quoted in this book, and the club recently agreed that speeches of those no longer living need no longer be off the record.

Brayman's other unique qualification for writing this Gridiron history is his lifelong fascination with politics and politicians, stemming from his early years as a newspaperman in Albany, New York and Washington, D.C.

Harold Brayman was born in Schoharie County in upstate New York on March 10, 1900, and he graduated from Cornell University. After a brief fling at high school teaching he got his first journalistic job for an Albany paper in 1922.

As legislative correspondent of the *New York Evening Post,* he attended his first national political conventions in 1928 and, after Alfred E. Smith won the Democratic nomination, was assigned to cover his campaign.

It was a heady experience for the twenty-eight-year-old cub reporter. Smith crisscrossed the country in an eleven-car special train making dozens of speeches daily and drawing the largest crowds ever to turn out for a Presidential candidate up to that time. But Brayman learned, as other reporters have before and since, that crowds do not always translate into votes. Many were drawn by curiosity to see the colorful campaigner from New York's Lower East Side, but later voted for Herbert Hoover.

The Smith campaign started Brayman's lifelong love affair with politics. It also caused him to begin rubbing elbows with the journalistic giants of the day: Henry L. Mencken of the *Baltimore Sun;* James O'Donnell Bennett of the *Chicago Tribune,* with whom he shared a compartment on the Smith train; and many Washington reporters with whom he later became associated in the Gridiron Club, including Charles G. Ross of the *St. Louis Post-Dispatch,* Theodore Joslin of the *Boston Transcript* and Richard V. Oulahan of the *New York Times.*

After the election, Brayman was sent to Washington by the *Post.* When it was sold by the Cyrus H. K. Curtis estate in 1933, he moved to the *Philadelphia Evening Ledger* and later the *Houston Chronicle.* In 1937 he started writing one of Washington's earliest syndicated columns.

In 1942 Brayman gave up newspaper work to serve as assistant director of public relations for E. I. du Pont de Nemours and Company. He became director two years later. Brayman came up with new ideas and concepts in the field of corporate relations which the Du Pont Company then sorely needed. In the mid-thirties, at congressional hearings presided over by Senator

Gerald P. Nye, the Du Ponts had been labeled as "warmongers" and "merchants of death."

His campaign to rebuild the Du Pont Company's image with the public, the press and politicians got its acid test in 1961, when the Supreme Court, in a noted antitrust case, ruled that the company would have to dispose of 63 million shares of General Motors Corporation stock worth about $3 billion.

Du Pont decided it would have to distribute the shares to its stockholders who, under existing law, would have had to pay taxes on most of the stock's value as ordinary income.

Brayman worked closely with Crawford H. Greenewalt, then chief executive of Du Pont, and Irving S. Shapiro, now its chief executive officer, to seek legislation which would permit Du Pont stockholders to treat the GM shares they received on a "return-of-capital" basis to lighten their tax burden. Opponents promptly dubbed the legislation "the Du Pont tax relief bill," and most Washington reporters and observers would not have bet a plugged nickel that it would ever be passed.

But the Du Pont team organized a vast letter-writing campaign by Du Pont and GM stockholders, who protested to newspapers and members of Congress that they were about to be ruined financially for actions over which they had no control and which the government had condoned for thirty-five years. Greenewalt went to Washington to tell Du Pont's side of the story to key Congressmen. As the final Senate action approached, Brayman and his assistant, William H. Mylander, also a former newsman and Gridiron member, set up a hotel office to answer reporters' questions and tell Du Pont's story.

Slowly the tide of opinion changed. The House passed the bill by voice vote. It cleared the Senate after a two-week filibuster, and President Kennedy signed it.

Brayman retired in 1965, giving himself time to write a book about some of his pioneering work in public relations, *Corporate Management in a World of Politics*, published by McGraw-Hill in 1967. At that time, he also began his meticulous research on the Gridiron Club.

Belying the flamboyant image often attributed to reporters and public relations men, Brayman is mild mannered, invariably courteous, and even to his colleagues often seems self-effacing and shy.

But he is no Milquetoast. During his Washington news-gathering days, the National Press Club was more rough and tumble than in later years. Shortly before he became its president in 1938, he lost several teeth in a fracas after breaking up an after-hours crap game in the club's kitchen.

And he recently showed his spunk when a Dow Jones editor demanded the source of a quote in this book. The incident recalled that William Howard Taft, breakfasting with Teddy Roosevelt at the White House the morning of Taft's inauguration as President, looked out the window at a raging blizzard and remarked "Even the elements protest."

Brayman dug up a story published by the *New York Evening Post* on February 8, 1930, relating the incident. He sent it to the editor with this brusque comment: "The source is completely reliable, authoritative and, in fact, unimpeachable. I have great confidence in him." The story carried Brayman's own by-line!

And Brayman, for all his knowledge of Gridiron lore, hasn't always abided by its traditions. The menu of the Gridiron dinner of 1941 at which he presided listed among the wines and other strong drinks served "Cliquot Club Ginger Ale." Or perhaps he was trying to start a new Gridiron tradition. If so, happily, it did not stick.

Acknowledgments

Almost no substantial activity is ever carried on by one person without the help of many others. Certainly the writing of this book is no exception.

Those to whom I am most indebted for help and assistance in its preparation include, first of all, members of the Gridiron Club itself.

From its early days, the club has had as one of its officers a historian, charged with collecting, organizing and preserving its records. Consequently, without the assistance of the club itself; of its files; of its secretary, Jack Steele, Washington editor of the Scripps-Howard Newspapers; of its treasurer, Richard L. Wilson, Washington columnist for the *Des Moines Register* and the *Tribune Syndicate;* and of its current historian, Robert Roth, Washington correspondent of the *Philadelphia Bulletin,* this book would not have been possible.

Also of great value has been the enthusiastic support of the 1975 Gridiron president, Lucian Warren, and his immediate predecessors, Walter T. Ridder, Robert Roth, Edgar A. Poe and the late Jack Bell.

Likewise, I am indebted for numerous recollections of interesting details during the 1915-1930 era to the late Arthur Krock and the late Gould Lincoln, and for photographs of Gridiron dress rehearsals to Marshall McNeil and Glen C. H. Perry.

The book would have been incomplete without the cooperation of the Princeton University Library; Frank E. Mason, literary executor for Herbert Hoover; the Roosevelt Library at Hyde Park, New York; the Truman Library at Independence, Missouri; and the U.S. Library of Congress, all of which made available numerous presidential speeches and other data not in the Gridiron records.

Nor would any list of acknowledgments be complete without expressing my gratitude to President Ford and the more than thirty other distinguished living speakers at the Gridiron Club who graciously gave their permission to quote directly from their off-the-record speeches. However, by agreement between the officers of the Gridiron Club and the author of this book, it has been decided to keep the major portion of the speeches made since 1972 off-the-record.

Furthermore, I am very deeply indebted to my secretary, Lillian W. O'Neill, without whose great help in the research, checking and indexing, and in the prolonged dictation and typing and retyping, this book could not have been written.

Introduction

"With malice toward none and humor for all. . . ."

Nearly four years after he left the Presidency, a feisty Harry S. Truman declined an invitation to a dinner at which Richard M. Nixon, at that time the Vice President, was to be present because "I will not sit at the same table with Nixon. . . . or with his boss either."

But years later, the feud was ended after Nixon, then a New York lawyer, during the cocktail preliminaries to a dinner, went to the bar and graciously brought Truman a bourbon and water. At this dinner, Nixon was a speaker. He told of the incident and commented that love was really busting out all over when Harry Truman takes a drink from Richard Nixon and drinks it without having it tested first.

At a later dinner, John F. Kennedy, after his election as President, was a speaker. He had been criticized for appointing his younger brother, Robert F. Kennedy, as attorney general. He wryly suggested at that dinner that he had good reasons for the appointment.

"Bobby wants to practice law, and I thought he ought to get a little experience first."

At a 1968 dinner, Gerald R. Ford told how he loved the House of Representatives, but said that sometimes late at night on his way home, as he went past 1600 Pennsylvania Avenue, he seemed to hear a little voice saying, "If you lived here, you'd be home now."

These remarks were all made in off-the-record speeches at Gridiron Club dinners.

The Gridiron Club was founded in 1885 by Washington correspondents representing newspapers from all over the nation. Its purpose was primarily amusement and entertainment. Today, it consists of just over fifty active members elected from more than 1,000 Washington correspondents, plus about fifty-five associated members (all of whom are former actives), and about twelve limited members. Although a requirement of membership in this exclusive club has always been high professional attainment, it still remains a purely social organization. Its only activity and its only purpose has always been simply the hosting of at least one or two strictly social dinners each year for its journalistic membership and currently more than 400 guests.

Why then is the Gridiron Club and the history of its dinners so noteworthy? This ninety-year record of speeches, guests and incidents, planned and unplanned, gives some indication.

The guests at these private dinners have included Benjamin Harrison and all the Presidents and Vice Presidents from William McKinley to Gerald Ford, all of the more prominent members of the Senate and House of Representatives, the chief justices and most of the associate justices in more recent years, the members of the cabinet, top officers of the army, navy and air corps, and a substantial number of the ambassadors of foreign countries, frequently including the ambassador of the Soviet Union.

The opposition has always been present too, often including defeated candidates for the Presidency and always including the leaders of the opposition party in Congress, as well as both Republican and Democratic party leaders. James A. Farley, for example, was a guest at practically every dinner for about forty years, right up to the time of his death.

Besides the official guests, there is wide representation of the professions and of business, from J. Pierpont Morgan in his day to David Rockefeller in current times. Editors and publishers of papers whose correspondents are members of the Gridiron Club seem somehow to get invited pretty regularly, and so do a great many other people in the newspaper, magazine and broadcasting fields.

Many of the leaders of the largest and most important businesss in the country are among the guests, and several times some of these people have been speakers. One secretary of the Gridiron Club (who makes up the seating list) derived considerable amusement at one time by seating side by side labor leader John L. Lewis and Ben Fairless of United States Steel.

The speakers at the 1975 dinner were President Ford and Vice President Rockefeller for the administration, and Robert S. Strauss, chairman of the Democratic National Committee, and Governor Ella T. Grasso of Connecticut for the opposition.

Secretary of State Henry Kissinger was absent from this dinner because he was in the Middle East, but Helen Thomas, White House correspondent for United Press International, was there, and she was the first woman to be initiated in the Gridiron Club. Mrs. Ford and Mrs. Rockefeller, the first Presidential and Vice Presidential wives to attend as guests, took part in the initiation ceremony.

Because so many people associate a gridiron with football, it should be pointed out that the origin of the club name had nothing to do with that popular game, but rather arose from the idea of roasting or frying things on a gridiron.

At the 1975 Gridiron dinner, for example, President Ford was "roasted" for, among other things, "his ingenious program to whip the recession so we can afford inflation."

The roasting ranges widely from the skits put on by the club through the speeches of the President and one or more of the other illustrious special guests.

When Vice President Rockefeller was introduced at the conclusion of a song, "If I Were a Poor Man," he countered by wanting everyone to know that his appearance was made possible by "the Ford Foundation." He went on to explain that he'd learned in his confirmation hearings that he would have been better off if, like his grandfather, he'd only given away dimes.

Over the years, Presidents have traditionally closed Gridiron dinners with speeches of approximately ten to fifteen minutes. Usually these speeches start out humorously and wind up on a serious note. They have varied from the light witty speeches of John F. Kennedy to some serious, important ones by Theodore Roosevelt and Woodrow Wilson.

Altogether, *The President Speaks* has the significant portions of four hitherto unpublished Gridiron speeches by Woodrow Wilson, thirteen by Franklin D. Roosevelt, three by Harry S. Truman, two by Dwight D. Eisenhower, four by John F. Kennedy, five by Lyndon B. Johnson, four by Richard Nixon, and one by Gerald Ford. There are also eight by Herbert Hoover, which were published in an edition limited to 620 copies.

Here too are the significant portions of speeches by defeated Presidential candidates Alfred M. Landon, Thomas E. Dewey, Adlai E. Stevenson, Barry M. Goldwater, and Hubert H. Humphrey, and by such other well-known public figures as Robert A. Taft, Arthur H. Vandenberg, and Robert F. and Edward M. Kennedy, likewise hitherto unpublished.

One of the most memorable recent events was not a speech at all. It occurred in 1970, when President Richard M. Nixon and Vice President Spiro T. Agnew both appeared on the Gridiron stage and put on a piano duet, laughing at themselves about their lack of "disagreements" and their "Southern strategy." While Nixon played various favorite songs of previous Presidents, Agnew drowned him out with "Dixie."

From the club's early days, skits and songs have been an important part of Gridiron tradition. Aside from the Nixon-Agnew presentation, all of the skits and song lyrics have been written and staged by the Gridiron members, who themselves portray all the characters. Once Vincent Youmans, a guest at several Gridiron dinners, offered to write some original music and lyrics for the club. While his generosity was much appreciated, the offer was declined. Skits and song lyrics are always set to the music of perennial favorites, or popular songs of the day.

To President John F. Kennedy, the "Wild Irish Prose" song:"

His wild Irish prose,
It sparkles as it glows. . .
His fine Harvard style
Beats FDR a mile. . .

And its sadly mistaken verse:

His wild Irish prose,
It humbles all our foes.
And make no mistake
There's nothing can take
The bloom from that wild Irish prose.

To President Lyndon B. Johnson, after he had been photographed lifting up a dog by the ears on his Texas ranch, they sang:

Brown and white beagles
With big floppy ears,
Depletion allowances, and prize winning steers,
Speed boats and barbecues, Texas oil kings,
These are a few of his favorite things.

Poverty programs, and broadcasting stations,
Tax cuts and price cuts, and budget gyrations,
Something for nothing, tied neatly with strings,
These are a few of his favorite things.

To President Franklin D. Roosevelt, after he took a stinging setback in the 1938 Congressional elections:

Find a brand-new Christmas tree,
Santa Claus has been voted down.

And to President-elect Dwight D. Eisenhower:

This ain't the Army, Mister Ike!

This book contains quotations from ninety years of Gridiron Club skits and songs like these, and from the speeches of Presidents and many others. The skits and songs alone that are interspersed throughout a typical Gridiron dinner would run close to two hours if done continuously, only a little shorter than the length of a Broadway show.

Over the years, scores of individuals have been involved in these ambitious productions. Some of the most prolific writers in the past have been Walker S. Buel of the *Cleveland Plain Dealer*, Henry Suydam of the *Newark Evening News*, Arthur Krock of the *New York Times*, Phelps H. Adams of the *New York Sun*, Bernard Kilgore of the *Wall Street Journal*, Turner Catledge of the *New York Times*, Fletcher Knebel of the Cowles Publications, and Marshall McNeil of the Scripps-Howard Newspapers. But while there have always been outstanding contributors, a great many other members share in the writing.

A few of the club members have also been active in assisting Gridiron guest speakers in their preparations. Henry Suydam, for example, once wrote almost word for word a speech delivered by President Franklin D. Roosevelt. Fletcher Knebel helped President Kennedy on a couple of occasions, Walter Trohan helped Senator Robert A. Taft with his great speech of 1948, and some other members have helped out speakers of both parties. Non-Gridiron members have also been active in this respect, particularly Clark Clifford with Presidents Truman and Kennedy and various other Democrats. Even Bob Hope's gag writers have been asked to assist some speakers.

One thing typifies Gridiron skits, songs, and especially the speeches—they are always related to political issues and personalities of the time. Naturally, this brings together people of different parties, and sometimes even bitter political opponents. It is one of the great and certainly unique strong points about the American system, that such people can gather under one roof on these occasions to laugh at themselves and at each other. It exemplifies the fact that while politics in America is as intense as in any other country, most of the personalities of politics here have a sense of humor and generally don't let pomposity overwhelm them.

In no other country of the world does an institution similar in form and stature to the Girdiron Club exist, although there are groups of somewhat the same nature in Canberra, Australia, Albany, New York,* and a few of the other state capitals in this country.

On some occasions, Presidents and other guests have been annoyed by Girdiron skits, but for the most part, the club has nearly always used restraint. As a reminder of this, every dinner opens with a ritual. As soon as the President, or on the rare occasions of his absence, the principal guest, has arrived at the center of the head table, all lights are extinguished while the Gridiron chorus sings a verse of "Music in the Air."

Then the president of the club makes a brief speech while the room is still dark. Toward the end of it, as a huge gridiron is flashed on, he intones the traditional line, "The Gridiron glows, but it never burns."** In 1924, one Gridiron president, William Brigham, stated the Gridiron philosophy perhaps most cogently: "With malice toward none and humor for all."

While it is true that occasionally a bit of malice may have crept in, probably over the years these Gridiron dinners have had a substantial influence in easing the tensions of political life and making it more civilized in its controversies. At the same time, it is likely that the club has had considerable effect upon American life in general, by revealing a great deal of the wit, the thinking, the character, and sometimes even the previously unknown political plans of Presidents of the United States and other leading figures.

---

*The Legislative Correspondents' Association's annual dinner is notable.
**Some presidents have revised this to "The Gridiron singes, but it never burns."

In these situations especially, background information on the political issues and personalities of the time is vital to understand what took place on the Gridiron stage and at the podium. That information is interwoven throughout this book.

Here then are ninety years of American Presidents and other politicians on the Gridiron.

I

Both Sides of the Hot Gridiron

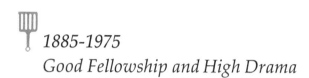

1885-1975

Good Fellowship and High Drama

Gridiron dinners are primarily designed for entertainment and good fellowship among leading figures in American political life and the Washington press, but they have also frequently had their dramatic announcements of administration policy and their revealing cross fires of debate between Presidents of the United States and other prominent people in government.

For example, Woodrow Wilson, nine months before he was elected to a second term in November 1916 on the Democratic party cry, "He kept us out of war," clearly forecast American entry into World War I when the timing was appropriate.

"Valor strikes only when it is right to strike," he said. "Valor withholds itself from all small implications and entanglements and waits for the great opportunity when the sword will flash as if it carried the light of heaven upon its blade."

After his reelection, he spoke in even stronger terms to the Gridiron Club on December 9, 1916, when he said that America's role in the future was to "see that the balance of power in the world is not disturbed; that aggression is held back; that selfishness is condemned; and that men regard each other upon the same footing as human beings."

In other words, the Germans must not be allowed to win.

The United States entered World War I four months later.

In more recent times, and particularly in the light of the actions of the Ninety-third and Ninety-fourth Congresses toward both President Nixon and President Ford, an off-the-record speech at a Gridiron dinner by Lyndon Johnson achieves new significance.

It was made when he was Senate majority leader during the Eisenhower administration. He described his philosophy of the Senate by saying he rejected "the jungle tactics which seek to tear down the President by tearing down the institution of the Presidency."

He noted that the government of the United States stands upon three great pillars—the executive, the judicial, and the legislative. He described the last as "a deliberative body and not a free-wheeling grand jury. . . . If one of these pillars wages guerrilla warfare against the others, our freedoms are weakened." The role of the opposition, he said, was "to fight on principle but to fight in a principled manner."

At a Gridiron dinner in 1945 President Truman discussed the decision he had made to drop the atomic bomb in Japan, a decision which he described as "the most terrible decision a man ever had to make."

"The Secretary of War, Mr. Stimson, and I weighed that decision most prayerfully," he said. "The President had to decide. It occurred to me that a quarter of a million of the flower of our young manhood [the estimate of the casualties that would have occurred had the United States tried to invade Japan] was worth a couple of Japanese cities, and I still think they were and are."

At a dinner in the spring of 1941, Franklin D. Roosevelt cited the loss of the spirit of good faith among nations and declared that "this war springs from the broken treaty, the ignored word, the violated faith." While he was speaking, a messenger from the *New York Times* brought Arthur Krock a dispatch that Hitler had invaded Yugoslavia and Greece—a dispatch which Krock handed to the President when he concluded his speech.

While hitherto unpublished statements of this nature have some historical importance and show something of the character and viewpoints of various Presidents, far more characteristic of Gridiron dinners is the direct good-natured, witty gibe at political opponents, well illustrated by a remark of President Ford when he was House minority leader, about Lyndon Johnson.

Johnson had referred to Ford's followers in the House as wooden soldiers, which led the Gridiron Club to put on an act in which Ford was drilling "the wooden soldiers that Lyndon praised so highly." Ford's impersonator sang:

Backward, wooden soldiers, to the *status quo*,
With old Ev [Dirksen] and Gerry, let no progress show.

In his speech, Ford referred to the song and commented that "what the President calls us in public—wooden soldiers—is nothing compared to what he calls us in private."

In another instance, Herbert Hoover, who during the years of his Presidency had been somewhat humorless, exhibited a mellowing gentleness at the May 1947 dinner, after the Republicans had won a majority in Congress. Referring to this, he commented to President Truman ever so softly, "But to elaborate would be an indelicate implication that I am seeking a recruit to my exclusive union of ex-Presidents."

Of all Presidents, John F. Kennedy was among the most adept with such sallies. In 1962 the Metropolitan Club in Washington was one of those from which several Kennedy administration people had resigned in protest because its membership included no blacks. Arthur Krock, one of its prominent members, had written a few pieces in the *New York Times* that were less than laudatory of some of President Kennedy's policies.

"Krock criticized me," said Kennedy, "for not letting President Tshombe of Katanga come here. So I told him we would work out a deal. I'll give Tshombe a visa, and Arthur can give him a dinner at the Metropolitan Club."

Kennedy was also skillful in disarming criticism by laughing at himself in his Gridiron speeches. When he was running for reelection to the Senate from Massachusetts and was much talked about as a candidate for President, the religious issue was getting considerable notice. He said he wasn't making any plans for the Presidency, but "should I be elected, I do hope that Methodist Bishop Bromley Oxnam will be my personal envoy to the Vatican—and he's instructed to open negotiations for the Trans-Atlantic tunnel immediately."

In Kennedy's Senate campaign, the extensive use of Kennedy money was an issue, and his speech that night followed a song containing the line, "For the bill belongs to Daddy," which led him to pull from his pocket a supposed telegram from Joseph P. Kennedy.

"Dear Jack: Don't buy a single vote more than is necessary—
I'll be damned if I'm going to pay for a landslide."

• • •

One of the most notable instances of a President and a Vice
President laughing at themselves before a Gridiron audience occurred in 1970. There was a great deal of public discussion at that
time about President Nixon's supposed "southern strategy," designed to win Republican support in a group of states that for 100
years had been predominantly Democratic.

The Club had finished its skits, the opposition speaker had
delivered his thrusts at the administration, the dessert had been
served in the Presidential Room of the Statler Hilton Hotel, and
Jack Steele, Washington editor of the Scripps-Howard Newspapers and president of the Gridiron Club, rose to his feet.

"Gentlemen, the Gridiron Club has but one toast: To the
President of the United States."

The members and guests rose, murmured "The President,"
drank their champagne and sat down, waiting for the President
to speak.

But President Nixon was not at the lectern. A murmur of
wonderment went around the room—where was he? A moment
later, the President walked up on the stage and said something
along the following lines.

"Instead of responding to your gracious toast from the lectern, as is the custom, I have asked your president tonight for
permission to respond to it from the stage."

He noted that there had been numerous skits making reference to alleged disagreements between himself and Vice President Spiro T. Agnew.

"Before all of you," he said, "I want to put this thesis to the
test, and I would appreciate it if the Vice President would join me
on the stage so that I may question him in detail."

Agnew came up on the stage.

"Mr. Vice President," Nixon went on, "they seem to imply
here that you don't go along with me on all phases of government
policy, and I would like to have your candid responses to a few
questions. First, what about this "southern strategy" we hear of
so often?"

Agnew clicked his heels, saluted and answered, in a deep
southern accent, "Yes suh, Mr, President, Ah agree with you
completely on yoah southern strategy."

There followed two or three similar questions, to which

Agnew replied in the same way, except for the accent. And then Nixon popped the key inquiry at him.

"And now, Mr. Vice President, I hear that you think you can play the piano better than I can."

The same heel clicking, the salute, and "Yes sir, Mr. President—no, no, no, I never said that, Mr. President. I never said I can play the piano better than you can."

"Well, now, to demonstrate that you're always in tune with me, I'm going to suggest we play the piano for the members of the Gridiron Club. Mr. Steele, may we have the pianos, please?"

The stage curtains opened revealing two pianos. Nixon walked over to one and said, "Gentlemen of the Gridiron Club, what I have determined to do tonight is to play those songs, some of them, that echo the memories at the dinners of this club, the favorite songs of some of the former Presidents who've been honored here in this room. If it happens that they are all songs that are favorites of Democratic Presidents, that proves that we are trying to bring the nation together.

"I will begin with what I understand was the favorite song of Franklin D. Roosevelt, "Home on the Range."

Both walked over to the pianos, and Nixon started playing. After a moment, Agnew came in on the other piano, pounding it and drowning out the President with "Dixie." They finished to much merriment.

Then President Nixon rose again and said, "Now we would like to play Harry Truman's favorite song, the "Missouri Waltz."

He started the gentle lilt of that well-known theme song of every Missouri politician. Again Agnew came in, drowning him out with "Dixie." By this time the place was in an uproar.

"Hold it, *hold* it!" said Nixon. "Not that." Now there've been some—you'll just follow me, Mr. Vice President, you'll learn. Now I want you to *follow* me. On this song, I give you one more chance, this one.

"This was a man who has received a few barbs tonight [Lyndon Johnson]. We're not on television, but I hope somebody will report to him that we played his song."

Nixon began "The Eyes of Texas Are Upon You," and again Agnew drowned him out with "Dixie."

By this time the laughter was so loud that one could hardly distinguish the music.

Then Nixon rose again and said to Agnew, "Sometime we're going to learn here. This is your last chance. This happens to be my favorite song, so let's be sure you follow it, you understand? I think this will work."

He went over to the piano and started playing "God Bless America." This time the Vice President played it straight, and the two of them together played in perfect unison, while the audience rose to its feet and sang it with them.

Thus ended the Gridiron dinner of March 1970, the first and only time a President of the United States has appeared on the Gridiron stage. Both President Nixon and Vice President Agnew remained for another hour or so at Richard L. Wilson's afterparty, and the talk about their "act" went on into the night. It was the high point of Nixon's joviality to newspapermen generally, and to the Gridiron Club in particular.

While many people in the audience probably anticipated the Nixon-Agnew reelection in 1972, it is doubtful if any imagined that it would occur by such a thumping majority of the electoral votes that it would be suggested, at the following dinner, that the Nixon administration should appoint ambassadors to Massachusetts and the District of Columbia. And certainly no one in the entire audience could have envisioned that just four years later both of the participants whom they cheered so loudly that night would be forced out of office before their terms expired.

• • •

Laughing at themselves and their own parties is not usually the public stance taken by political leaders seeking reelection to office, but at Gridiron dinners it has often been the broad highway to spectacular success.

At the December 1939 dinner, when President Roosevelt was still being very coy about his plans for a third term, there was a skit set on the sands of Egypt, where a mammoth Sphinx held in its mouth a long cigarette holder, almost a Roosevelt trademark. Following his reelection, there was another Gridiron skit set in the Roosevelt library at Hyde Park near the close of "President Roosevelt's ninth administration." Everyone wore long beards, and there was also a Sphinx with a long white beard.

Roosevelt loved it, and when he was introduced at its conclusion, his first words were, "Nine terms! Gentlemen, it is too much! There ought to be a law against it. At least there ought to be an American tradition against it. One of those absolutely sacred American traditions against more than eight terms."

It was also at a Gridiron dinner that President Eisenhower, in a whimsical way, first declared his support for Richard Nixon as his successor. Protocol seated him to the right of the president of the Gridiron Club, and Vice President Nixon was seated on the Gridiron president's left.

Eisenhower referred to the number in the audience who were ambitious to succeed him and commented, "Now it occurs to me, as we look at this table and its seating, that it would be far less bother just to move a man to this seat very easily and very simply by moving two chairs than making any big fuss around the table."

His closing line that night was, "Good night, and again, don't forget, just don't disturb the table too much."

Robert A. Taft made a Gridiron speech in April 1948, when it looked as though Truman had little chance of reelection, and there was widespread opposition to his renomination within his own Democratic party. Taft turned directly to the President, and proclaimed that he represented the loyal opposition, and that the Republicans were so loyal that "we alone today earnestly and unanimously desire to see you nominated, Mr. President."

That dinner, and the one following it in December after Truman's surprise victory over Thomas E. Dewey, provided a good opportunity for the Gridiron Club to laugh at itself. At the April dinner, before the election, they had sung to Truman, "Now Is the Hour When We Must Say Good-bye." At the December dinner it was redone by the Gridiron chorus, singing into microphones behind the curtain. Then the curtain opened, and a revised version was sung by the Gridiron chorus, dressed in top hats, white ties and tails, but no pants. This time they sang:

> Now is the hour
> When we must break the news,
> We who predicted
> Dewey could not lose.
> We saw the crowds,
> Heard Harry's every word;
> Then voters everywhere
> Gave us the bird!

Dewey opened his speech on a similar note, by recalling how his initial invitation to speak at a Gridiron dinner came just after he had been defeated in his first race for governor of New York, and how flattered and surprised he had been.

"Again, I am flattered," he said, "but, believe me, gentlemen, I shall never again be surprised by anything." Then he told how "there was no uncertainity about this campaign. For the election, you remember, was in the bag."

He insisted that neither he nor the newspapermen with him felt too badly about their unanimous error, because during the campaign he had met Truman just once, at the ceremonies for the opening of Idlewild Airport, and at the meeting, as the photographers were asking for "just one more," Dewey quoted Truman as saying to him, "in that homey way of his which is so attractive, 'You will have to get used to this when you are living in the White House.' So, gentlemen, it really was unanimous."

Continuing his friendly gibes at the President, he told him not to blame the pundits and the reporters too much, and also not to believe "anything you read, Mr. President, until you have digested the solemn analysis of why you lost, published in the *Panama Star Herald,* the Sunday after election, under the by-line of a well-known columnist and political expert, your old friend Harold L. Ickes."*

The good nature of other losers was also illustrated in their Gridiron speeches immediately following Presidential elections. Adlai Stevenson, for example, told his audience in 1952 that "the fact was, of course, that the General was so far ahead of me we never saw him, and I was happy to hear that I had even placed second."

Some of the other notable speeches by defeated Presidential candidates were those by Landon to Roosevelt in 1936, by Goldwater to Johnson after the 1964 election, and by Humphrey to Nixon after the 1968 election. All of them were witty and in the best of taste, and all elicited similar responses from the winning Presidents.

Landon, the first defeated candidate to confront his victor at a Gridiron dinner, referred to the President as "our good American personification of Santa Claus," and commented that "even if he didn't wear the traditional Santa Claus whiskers in the campaign, the people recognized him on November third."

He had come to the dinner, he said, because "I felt it the American way to show the world that in our democracy the principal contenders in a campaign can sit down together at the same table in the spirit of fun.

"Here, opponents break bread together, instead of breaking

---

*To facilitate distribution, some columnists have to write well in advance of publication. Obviously, Ickes' column had been written before the election occurred. It was killed in all papers except the *Panama Star Herald,* where somebody had evidently goofed.

each other's necks. A very different situation from what we see in so many foreign countries."

In 1957 Adlai Stevenson referred to himself "as a man who has twice been tempted, and twice suffered the consequences of his weakness.

"Just what made me think I could do better the second time escapes me now," he said.

As for the profound effect which the Middle Eastern war had had on the campaign, he commented that the Republicans hadn't counted on the Middle Eastern explosion just before the election, and "neither did I.

"Now I don't say that the administration planned it all; indeed I see no evidence of any planning in the Middle East. But in 1952 General Eisenhower at least had to say, 'I will go to Korea.' This time the Middle East came to him!

"After witnessing the magic, the alchemy, by which a foreign policy failure is converted into a political success, I have concluded that we poor Democrats have a lot to learn from you Republicans."

In March 1965, the first dinner after Goldwater had received his trouncing from President Johnson, he looked out over the white-tied audience and expressed his satisfaction at being "here in this foxhole in the war on poverty." Discussing his own bleak future, he said that he'd thought of getting a job but had to admit that was "a revolting thought after twelve years in the Senate.

"The President offered me a job," he said, "with one of his radio stations, and I hadn't even known he had one in the Baffinland."

In a serious vein, Goldwater called upon everyone, as individuals, to "eliminate hate and misunderstanding from our daily lives and replace them, instead, with love and understanding.

"And, lastly but certainly not least," he said, "we should hail our President when he is right and pray that he is right all the time—for he is *our* President and our help must be always his to ask."

In March 1969, after the Chicago convention riots, when the defeated Hubert Humphrey came to the first Nixon dinner, he told the audience that his involuntary transition from political to academic life had been easy, "especially since I had my riot training last fall."

The last time he had seen Nixon before this dinner, he said, was on Inauguration Day.

"He was taking his oath, and I was muttering a few of my own."

Turning directly to Nixon, who had been Vice President for eight years and then out of office for a similar length of time, he said, "Mr. President, your own life has inspired me. May I be so fortunate.

"I have been close enough to high office over these past twenty years to know the pressures and problems that our President and Vice President must bear, day after day—the splendid misery. Winning the peace is a lonely battle.

"Our hopes and prayers are with them. May good fortune smile upon them—until November 6, 1972."

In another speech on a later occasion, after the bombing of North Vietnam, he announced to the assembled Gridiron guests that he had received a late bulletin that "President Nixon has just ordered the bombing of Jack Anderson."

In few other countries in the world would such good-natured raillery occur between the victors and the vanquished. For example, as late as May 1975, Anthony Wedgwood Benn, one of the more leftist and controversial members of the Labor party cabinet in Great Britain, revealed that he had never spoken to Mrs. Margaret Thatcher, Conversative party leader. He was quoted in the *Wall Street Journal* as saying, "It's extremely difficult to have friendships across political lines."[1]

And as early as 1905, Charles Willis Thompson commented on "the hobnobbing" at the Gridiron dinner of Theodore Roosevelt and William Jennings Bryan, by saying that "the words, manners and actions of the two men manifested the fact that they entertain a genuine esteem and admiration for each other."[2]

Perhaps it was put most effectively by Phelps H. Adams of the *New York Sun* in 1948 when, as president of the Gridiron Club, he referred to the tough and bitter Presidential contest that had taken place just a month before between President Truman, Governor Thomas E. Dewey, and Governor J. Strom Thurmond.

"Yet tonight," he said, "all three of these men are here to join us in an evening of good fellowship and good humor—to laugh at each other, at us and at themselves. In any other land in this unhappy world, *that* would be a major miracle. Tonight, in America, it is simply another Gridiron dinner."

• • •

But not all of Gridiron dinner history is so good-natured. In the serious portion of their speeches, many Presidents and other important political figures, from Theodore Roosevelt to Lyndon Johnson, have expressed their views pointedly and have strongly criticized their opposition.

On three occasions, Theodore Roosevelt spoke with great forcefulness to his political opponents.

In March 1898, right after the sinking of the *Maine,* Assistant Secretary of the Navy Roosevelt shouted across a crowded room, "We will have this war for the freedom of Cuba, Senator [Mark] Hanna, in spite of the timidity of the commercial interests."

And later, as President, at another Gridiron dinner, he leaned over the table and shook his finger at three United States Senators, who were opposing the Panama Canal, among them again Mark Hanna, and he thundered at them, "The canal is going to be built. I am saying here, as I have said elsewhere, that all obstacles placed in the way will be removed."

The other occasion was his celebrated attack, first upon J. P. Morgan, H. H. Rogers of Standard Oil, and E. H. Harriman, the father of Averell Harriman, and then upon Senator Joseph Foraker of Ohio. The last he lambasted with such ferocity that it broke up the dinner after Foraker had been given a chance to reply, which he did with equal vigor. The details of this extraordinary encounter are related in the chapter on Theodore Roosevelt.

Years later, at the second Gridiron dinner after becoming President, Franklin D. Roosevelt also took the occasion to strike out at his critics, who by December 1933 had already become quite vocal. He started off with a bit of whimsicality about being reminded that the administration's honeymoon was over, and receiving reports that there were "a very large number of somewhat sore brides in this country.

"I cannot and do not expect," he went on, "that even in the stress of the needs and necessities of this period criticism will be lacking." Then he expressed contempt for dishonest and nonconstructive criticism by attacking those people in the jungle of depression who were sitting and criticizing the others who were trying to cut their way out.

"We are too busy clearing away the underbrush," he said, "in order that once more we can find the open road for us to bother our heads about the brethren who still sit complainingly on stumps."

On another occasion, Roosevelt took great glee in striking

back at the opposition speaker, who had been H. L. Mencken, by quoting from Mencken's own writings several of his most extreme and attention-getting opinions, among them an opinion once expressed of editors generally, a quotation which concluded with the words:

"It is this vast and militant ignorance, this widespread and fathomless prejudice against intelligence, that makes American journalism so pathetically feeble and vulgar, and so generally disreputable."

Three days afterward, Mencken wrote to Sara Mayfield:

"I got in a bout with a High Personage at the dinner and was put to death with great barbarity. Fortunately, I revived immediately and am still full of sin."[3]

One of Roosevelt's notable speeches was at the April dinner of 1936, when he gave an elaborate set of advice to those Republicans who aspired to be his November opponent. He began by suggesting to the eventual candidate that he get himself a group of editors and political writers of national importance, such as "Mr. Walter Lippmann, whose English is so limpid and so pure that the trigonometry of public affairs is made clear overnight to the kindergartens of America."

Or Mark Sullivan, the "incurable optimist," who "tells you that all is well with America. . . . His high collars of optimism are as high today as they were in the spring of 1929."

Or David Lawrence, who had made a reputation by correctly predicting, state by state, the close election of 1916, and whom Roosevelt assailed in the words, "Once in his quarter of a century of writing he was right."

Or Arthur Krock, "who will guarantee to give you, more clearly than anyone else, the point of view of the farmer, the laborer, and other members of what he would call the 'lower classes of America.' "

On another occasion, Franklin D. Roosevelt, demonstrating his extraordinary facility for cutting opponents, thundered, "If privately and publicly you exercise your constitutional right not to hitch your wagon to great ideals, don't cut the traces of your neighbor who is trying to hitch his wagon to a star."

But it was at the spring dinner in 1939, when his foreign policy was under criticism by some, that Roosevelt struck his strongest blow.

He pointed out that while American leadership was striving "to guide the destinies of our people through the mazes of this troubled world, . . . the government-controlled, censored press beyond the Atlantic and Pacific rings with the denunciations that certain gentlemen in the Congress and outside the Congress have seen fit to hurl at our national leadership. . . . If, at some far off future time, the United States of America is reduced to the category of a second-rate nation, if we are told how to run our internal affairs, if we are told with whom we may or may not trade, then you will find statues to these gentlemen to whom I refer in the public squares of Berlin and of Rome."

• • •

Gridiron dinners have also helped cultivate more civilized relationships among political opponents.

President Eisenhower was the first American President to have, during six of the eight years he was in office, a Congress controlled by the opposition party. Senate Majority Leader Lyndon Johnson closed a Gridiron speech during that time by pointing out that the people in both parties were men of good will, and the "burden of leadership falls on you [President Eisenhower].

"For we must have unity—the unity of free men. Mr. President, gentlemen, he concluded, "there is no greater problem before our nation tonight. Together we can solve it."

Eisenhower responded by referring to the last sentence of Senator Johnson's speech and by emphasizing the effect of the foreign situation on domestic problems.

"This is an American problem," said Eisenhower. "How does America meet it? By joining ranks together, joining hands.

"No one man, no one party could possibly do anything about it unless all were very definitely joined in this great effort. It is my faith, my conviction, that with the joining of hands that Senator Johnson mentioned, we cannot fail. The truth and decency of free government is bound to prevail over the lies and deceit of dictatorship in the long run."

It was also at a Gridiron dinner in 1966 that President Johnson described his own political philosophy by saying that "I am a free man first and an American second, public servant third and a Democrat fourth, in that order."

Then he paid tribute to the opposition by saying it had been a long time since he had dealt "with men who have thought in terms of party labels."

"These days," he said, "our problems are so serious, our trials are so exacting, that nearly every man I call on is a free man first, and for that I am deeply grateful, and because of that I have complete and absolute confidence in the ultimate outcome."

Presidents and other figures prominent in American political life have delivered witty, strong, and inspirational speeches before their Gridiron audiences since the club began, and practically all Presidents have struck back at the Gridiron Club and its membership. In the very first speech made by a President before the club, Benjamin Harrison said, referring to the press, that this was "the second time that I've been called upon this week to open a congress of American inventors."

Woodrow Wilson, in December 1916, told the Gridiron Club that nothing could get under his skin.

"I've been accustomed to reading fiction," he said.

• • •

Not all of the club's satire has been directed at Presidents. In 1975, when for two years Congress had been assuming a new aggressiveness, a Gridiron chorus, costumed as French revolutionaries and led by "Citizen Humphrey," sang to the tune of "Love Is Sweeping the Country":

We already run Congress
Now we're moving downtown;
Ford can't balk us—we'll rule by caucus—
We're turning things all upside down.
We are running the whole show,
Jerry's running behind;
We listen for applause while we're making laws,
Playing diplomats, bossing bureaucrats;
We are running the country,
Yes, running it out of its mind!

Many others over the years have felt that Gridiron "glow" or "singe," depending on their reactions. The Supreme Court has certainly come in for its share, and in all instances except that involving one justice, the Court has responded with laughter and good grace.

By 1935 President Roosevelt was indicating displeasure with the "nine old men" on the Court who had declared some of his actions unconstitutional. With reference to Supreme Court decisions always being announced beginning at twelve o'clock on Mondays, the Gridiron Club had the song:

It's time to take your places,
You'll hear the verdict soon.
Oh, it's better than the races,
On a Monday afternoon.

You'll hear what folks were thinking
In eighteen hundred ten,
And Latin words a-linking
What happens *now* with *then*.

And years later, after the Warren Court had thrown out some criminal convictions on the grounds that proper procedures had not been followed, a character in a Gridiron act sang:

The cops said I had made a confession,
But no lawyer was there at the time.
The Supreme Court decreed it illegal,
And so now I can go back to crime.

But the most biting comment came at the April 1940 dinner, just a few months after President Roosevelt had appointed former Governor Frank Murphy of Michigan as associate justice, a man with no conspicuous craving for anonymity. Murphy had taken his seat on the court and promptly gone on vacation for several weeks at New York and Miami Beach, where he had been photographed in the company of scantily dressed bathing beauties, much to the unconcealed disgust of Chief Justice Charles Evans Hughes. At that dinner, a hefty Gridiron character came on the stage daintily clad in a green bathing suit, carrying a green parasol, and sang several verses, ending:

Moon over Miami,
Hot spots in old New York.
That's where I go *quo warrento*,
For judicial work!

Moon over Miami,
Res ipsa loquitur,
A cozy nook—with a big law book,
On Miami shore!

Murphy never came to another Gridiron dinner. Generally, the satire in Gridiron skits is good-natured and does not burn, as it did in this case, but there have been a few other occasions when it did.

For example, while Harold Ickes was secretary of the interior in Roosevelt's cabinet, the club, under the presidency of Raymond Clapper, put on a Donald Duck skit, in which Donald was interviewed by a reporter and to all questions answered, "Quack! Quack! Quack!" But to the last one, "What do you think of Secretary Ickes?" he crowed like a rooster, strutted and patted himself on the chest.

This was one of the skits that was long remembered by Gridiron guests and also by Ickes, who never accepted another Gridiron invitation.

Franklin D. Roosevelt had reacted long ago to Gridiron satire noting that "a member of the club smiles and crows and chortles when he is holding the gridiron—but if somebody else gets hold of that gridiron and looks sternly in his direction, he runs like hell."

The most notable occasion on which a President felt so "burned" by Gridiron skits that he did not attend another dinner as President involved Harry Truman during his second term, when the Gridiron Club had a song to the tune of "Alexander's Ragtime Band."

> Come on and hear, come on and hear,
> Harry's rag, tag, bob-tail band!

Eventually Truman forgave the club, and later from his retirement in Independence Missouri, did come to a dinner. But satire which caused severe irritation has been the exception, and in the ninety-year history of Gridiron dinners the skits have been predominantly good-natured in their raillery and received by their targets with good grace. Over the years, numerous Presidents have paid high tribute to the club and to the function it performs in American life.

Franklin D. Roosevelt himself told a Gridiron audience that in December 1936, "the Gridiron Club is not regimented, and it brings to us all the saving graces of humor and perspective. It is good for me to be here. It is good, I think, for the chief justice to be here. It is good for Governor Landon to be here. It is good for Republicans and Democrats and Socialists and Communists to sit at these tables and laugh at themselves and at each other. The Gridiron Club offers twice a year the largest of mirrors for us all to look at ourselves in. As we think of those sections of the world in which fear, hatred and bitter political rivalries have great peoples within their grasp, who of us cannot feel a spirit of humble gratitude to Providence that our national destinies are emerging from the strains of recent times with our American tradition of tolerance and perspective unimpaired?"

One often wonders about the reactions of ambassadors of many countries, including the Soviet Union, who have regularly attended these dinners which would not be tolerated in their own countries. One also wonders what kind of reports Soviet ambassadors under Joseph Stalin sent back to Moscow.

In its ninety years, the Gridiron Club has become a national and even an international institution. Its singing, under the tutelage of the leader of the Marine Band, from John Philip Sousa down to the present, has been pretty good. Its acting, while not comparable to professional standards, has varied all the way from hairy-legged "females" doing ballet dancing to superb performances by Paul R. Leach as Donald Duck, and the club's most widely known teetotaler, Roscoe Drummond, as a drunken sailor.

The singing, acting, banter, and satire, both from Gridiron members to public officials and from public officials to each other and to themselves, typify the freedom of the press in America as well as the members' and guests' general good nature, good humor, and the ability to laugh at themselves and not take, for one night at least, the problems of the world too seriously.

Clark Clifford, eminent Washington lawyer and former secretary of defense, once characterized the dinner in a Gridiron speech. Referring to the annually repeated line, "The Gridiron glows, but it never burns," he said, "I don't believe it. I have heard that statement made many times. I still don't believe it. The gridiron glows, but it never burns—any member of the Gridiron Club.

"Year after year, I have seen more casualties carried out of this hotel in the spring than occurred during the Great Fire of London."

Then he went on to say that "you Gridiron men have discovered the golden formula."

"You have a big dinner each year; you get tickets for your respective bosses so they'll be seated with the bigwigs. Then you get all dressed up and appear before the throng as close intimates of the great and near great and, at the conclusion of the dinner, your efforts are warmly praised by the President of the United States. Boy, what an idea! How I have wished that we lawyers might have thought of it first."

II

Grover Cleveland and Benjamin Harrison

1885-1897
Earliest Gridiron Bedevilments

The Gridiron Club was the brainchild of two Washington corre-spondents, Major John M. Carson of the *Philadelphia Ledger*, and H. V. Boynton of the *Cincinnati Commercial Gazette*. It resulted from several abortive efforts to create an organization of news-papermen, all of which had failed because the correspondents did not want to take in local newspapermen, and the local news-papermen did not want to take in correspondents. This con-troversy was never really resolved until the formation of the Na-tional Press Club in 1908.

But Carson and Boynton thought there should be an organi-zation of the correspondents which would be social rather than professional, although high professional attainment would be a prerequisite for admission. The two were close friends, and talked the matter over frequently with other newspapermen, ac-cording to Gridiron records, until a committee was set up by all of them to prepare a plan. That committee reported on January 24, 1885, at a dinner meeting at Welcker's Hotel in Washington. This was during the administration of Chester A. Arthur and about six weeks before Grover Cleveland's inauguration as Pres-ident of the United States.

Approval in principle was given at this meeting, and the second one was called one week later, January 31, 1885, at which the plan was adopted and Major Carson's suggestion of "The Gridiron Club" as a name was unanimously accepted.

At that time Benjamin Perley Poore,* correspondent of the *Providence Journal* and other papers, was the most widely known Washington correspondent, and in order to launch the club with as much prestige as possible, he, who had participated in the meeting, was elected its first president. There were fourteen correspondents present at this meeting, although others were taken in promptly and the club lists thirty-two as charter members.

The first formal dinner was held on February 28, 1885, with eighteen members, Vice President-elect Thomas A. Hendricks and eleven other guests present. President-elect Cleveland did not attend.

A Twentieth Anniversary book published by the club in 1905 recounts that for the first year dinners were held monthly, except for the summer months. The chief amusement, after securing the acceptance of distinguished individuals, was "to carefully study up the most effective way of bedevilling such guests as were called up to speak." It also noted that "before the year was over Gridiron sentiment was growing strong against such barbaric methods, and before its second year ended they were a thing of the past, except where speakers exceeded the brief limits allowed to bores."[1]

It appears from the records that the first Gridiron president had made his office quite noted for some of his rather racy stories, and during the second year the club adopted an ironclad rule that "Ladies are always present, reporters are never present." This has been quite generally observed ever since, although, with a few exceptions in the early days, women were not invited guests at Gridiron dinners until the dinner of April 8, 1972.

The early dinners of the Gridiron Club were modest compared to today's. About half the club members attended, and the number of invited guests rarely exceeded a dozen. Restaurants and hotels demanded cash in advance, and on one occasion there were only seven members and three guests present.

However, its reputation grew, and by 1889 the *Washington*

---

*For over thirty years, he was the columnist widely known as "Perley"; he also signed himself and wrote a number of books bearing the name "Ben: Perley Poore."

Post, in commenting on a dinner, said that "the Gridiron Club has evidently come to stay and is today the best known of all the Washington clubs. It gives the most notable dinners in Washington and entertains the most notable guests."[2]

Furthermore, by that time the Gridiron had begun to develop its later custom of parodying songs. In 1888, members voted to admit a small number of limited members who did not need to be Washington correspondents. It was nearly a year later that the first two were elected, Hubbard T. Smith, author of "Swinging in the Grapevine Swing" and John Philip Sousa, director of the Marine Band.

Grover Cleveland's relations with newspapermen had never been exactly superb, and certainly not comparable with those of Franklin D. Roosevelt, Dwight D. Eisenhower, or John F. Kennedy. When Cleveland had been governor of New York, his relations with those who covered Albany were far from excellent. His campaign for the Presidency in 1884 had been a very bitter one, and many newspapers opposed to him had gone to lengths which even today would be regarded as extreme. Cleveland had few real friends among the correspondents, the Presidential press conference had not been invented, and a man named Daniel Lamont, later secretary of war, was set up by the president as a buffer between him and the newspapermen.

If people think today that Spiro Agnew's criticism of network television was extreme, they should have listened to Grover Cleveland at a Harvard banquet while he was President, in which he referred to "the silly, mean and cowardly lies that every day are found in the columns of certain newspapers, which violate every instinct of American manliness, and in ghoulish glee desecrate every sacred relation of private life."[3]

It was not until Cleveland's third year in office that the Gridiron Club had the audacity to invite him to a dinner. During his second term, after the intervening four years of President Harrison, Cleveland was invited on several occasions. These invitations were presented by a committee of the club headed by Major Carson, with whom Cleveland had closer relations than with any other member of the club. The committee was received each time with great courtesy, but the invitations were formally declined on a plea of the pressures of public business, and the fact that he did not like dinners anyway and avoided as much as possible all such public functions.

Major Carson later reported that the President had privately confided to him that he didn't think he would "fit in" and that he was "still of the opinion that Presidential dignity would be greatly ruffled by submitting to the 'fun you boys would have with me.'"[4]

But maybe it was just because he hated to leave even for an evening the young wife he had married during his first year in the White House.*

Perhaps Cleveland's attitude toward newspapermen and toward the Gridiron Club was also influenced by the way in which he had come to the Presidency. He never conformed to the current conception of the successful political leader: great articulateness, plenty of charisma, knowledge of how to handle successfully the media of communication—of which in those days the prime one was newspapers—and the hearty laughter of a good fellow.

His early life had been hard. His father died when he was sixteen, leaving him and his older brothers to support the family. He chose a law career and settled in Buffalo, New York.

Robert Lincoln O'Brien, who served as press secretary to President Cleveland in his second term, related in a speech on June 10, 1940, as reported in the *Washington Evening Star* the following day, that "Mr. Cleveland was an unknown lawyer leading a simple life in Buffalo when James Garfield was inaugurated" on March 4, 1881.

"Garfield didn't even know there was such a man at that time," Mr. O'Brien said. "Cleveland had never been to Washington and had been to Albany only once. This was just four years before he became President."[5†]

Buffalo, like many other cities, was suffering at the time from a corrupt city administration. In the summer of 1881, at the age of forty-four, Cleveland was nominated by the Democrats for mayor and won on a campaign of reform.

Cleveland vetoed city contract after city contract which had been padded in favor of political contractors and won wide fame as the "veto mayor"—so wide that less than one year after he

---

*In June 1886, Cleveland delighted the nation with his marriage to Frances Folsom. The twenty-one-year-old bride had been Cleveland's ward since her father died in 1875. He had been one of Cleveland's law partners. Never before had a President been married in the White House, and reporters pried into every detail with what Cleveland called "colossal impertinence."

†In contrast to the world travels of Presidents today, O'Brien stated years later, in an interview in the *Los Angeles Times* of October 27, 1949, that "Cleveland never in his life got farther west than Lincoln, Nebraska."

took office as mayor he was nominated by the Democrats for governor of New York and won in the election of 1882. He pursued the same policies in New York, not seeking to do what was popular but seeking to do what he thought was right.

Two years later the Republicans nominated James G. Blaine for President. Blaine had been involved in some financial maneuvering that looked questionable, and a considerable number of Republicans, who became known as "mugwumps," withdrew from the convention upon his nomination and announced that they would vote for any honest Democrat. The Democrats responded by selecting Grover Cleveland—just three short years after he had first emerged to public notice.

The campaign was a bitter one, but Cleveland won a close election.

As President his character did not change. He kept firm control over everything, delegated sparingly, often worked until 2:00 or 3:00 A.M., and sometimes even answered the White House telephone himself. But because his methods antagonized a good many people, and because of labor unrest and controversy over the tariff and over the coinage of silver at a ratio of sixteen parts of silver to one part of gold, Cleveland was defeated in 1888 by Benjamin Harrison. Then, four years later, he defeated Harrison to return for a second term.

So, with this background, it is not strange that he did not cultivate the Washington correspondents.

While there may have been in the speeches of club members, or in the interruptions of other speakers, some lampooning of the members of President Cleveland's cabinet and other individuals in his administration during his first term, little record of the details exists.

Certainly there were no songs poking fun at either the President or his administration because it is recorded in the Gridiron Club's history of its first twenty years that the first song was sung at the April 1889 dinner, just after the inauguration of Benjamin Harrison as President.*

However, during Cleveland's second term, starting in 1893, and after Benjamin Harrison had had an intervening four years in the Presidency and had attended several Gridiron dinners, the situation was different.

---

*It was a spoof on job applicants, entitled "I've Got My Papers on File." This dinner was also the first at which a large lighted gridiron was hung behind the head table.

At the beginning of President Cleveland's second term, the club gave a dinner to the members of his cabinet, and all but two of them accepted and came.

Then the club presumed to give the new cabinet members some advice. Frank Hatton, editor of the *Washington Post,* was president of the club, and as a former cabinet member himself, he assured the members of the cabinet that they would learn after a time how to conduct their offices. The general gist of his advice was to sign the papers brought to them by the messenger and not to ask any questions.

Some original verses were sung at this dinner in relation to President Cleveland and William C. Whitney, who had been Cleveland's manager at the Democratic National Convention and had successfully secured his nomination. The title was "Me and Whitney, or the ballad of the politician who was on the right side at Chicago." The words themselves have long disappeared into the limbo of the past.

Early in President Cleveland's second administration, he withdrew from the Senate a treaty which would have annexed the newborn Republic of Hawaii to the United States. He then sent James H. Blount of Georgia as "Paramount Commissioner to the Hawaiian Islands." Acting under instructions and using the naval power which was stationed in Honolulu, the commissioner dismantled the Republic and restored Queen Liliuokalani to the throne of her ancestors.

How soon President Cleveland may have known of the completion of this action is not clear. Hawaii was then a very isolated group of islands. The first the American people knew of it came from an Associated Press dispatch from Auckland, New Zealand. The Associated Press had learned of it when a slow steamer from Hawaii came into port at Auckland with persons on board who knew of the action.

When the Gridiron dinner of 1894 took place, the initiation skit, in which all new members are first presented to the Gridiron audience, consisted of a burlesque of this action. The initiate, Frank V. Bennett, was brought in on a wagon, dressed in royal robes and preceded by two members of the club made up as hula-hula girls. Another member represented the Paramount Commissioner made up as Uncle Sam, another was commander in chief of the armed forces, and two others were officers of the army and navy.

One of the guests at the dinner was Minister Lorin A.

Thurston, who had originally overthrown the monarchy in Hawaii. At the time, the deposed Queen Liliuokalani had declared that he must be beheaded. As the skit went on, when the "Queen" was restored to her ancient throne and then was about to be "annexed," President Hatton inquired, "Is there anything you would like to say before you are annexed?"

From the folds of her dress the "Queen" drew a huge papier-mâché ax and answered viciously, "Not to the Gridiron Club, but I would like to have a few minutes' conversation with Minister Thurston."

Several members of President Cleveland's cabinet were present at the dinner and regarded the skit as a rather harmless burlesque, but President Cleveland was deeply annoyed, and this undoubtedly precluded any possibility that he would attend a Gridiron dinner during the remainder of his term.

It was the first time that a President of the United States had been angered by a Gridiron skit, but by no means the last time.

One of the features of the Cleveland administration had been a long period of disagreement between the President and Senator David B. Hill of New York.

In 1892, when Cleveland was a candidate for renomination, Hill, who was at that time the undisputed boss of New York, persuaded that delegation to fight for his own nomination. W. Bourke Cockran, a congressman from New York, placed Hill in nomination and, in doing so, bitterly assailed Cleveland at the Chicago convention. Hill continued his opposition after the Cleveland election to a second term by fighting the Wilson Tariff Bill and by leading an attack on two of Cleveland's nominations for the Supreme Court, which resulted in their defeat in the Senate.

At the time of the Tenth Anniversary Dinner in January 1895, there was much discussion and gossip which had been created by a formal call made by Senator Hill on the President, and the acceptance by the senator of an invitation to attend a State dinner at the White House.

This was used as a vehicle for a skit to initiate four new members of the Gridiron Club.

There were half a dozen Gridiron members in the skit, but the four principals represented President Cleveland, Senator Hill, Secretary of War Daniel Scott Lamont, and Private Secretary Henry T. Thurber. It began with the two principals advancing slowly and finally shaking hands across a table decorated with a bottle of rye. Hill held a long knife behind his back and Cleveland, a large ax. After some innocuous comments, a quarrel developed between Lamont and Thurber, each claiming that he was responsible for bringing about the reconciliation. But Tammany Hall, represented by a man in a tiger skin, denounced them both and claimed he was responsible, because the tiger was getting awfully hungry while New York's two most illustrious Democrats were squabbling with each other.

The controversy was finally settled by revealing that the whole thing was spurious, and the make-ups of characters Cleveland, Hill, Lamont and Thurber were pulled off, and they were revealed as new members of the Gridiron Club.[6]

In the last year of his Presidency, Cleveland was displeased again. There was a dispute between the United States and England over the "Schomburgk line" between Venezuela and British Guiana, upon which Great Britain based a claim of a fairly large slice of Venezuela.

The United States was exercising the Monroe Doctrine, and President Cleveland sent a very strong message to Congress, which the British had characterized as a bluff.

In a skit, the president of the Gridiron Club was ordered to take charge of recruiting forces and prepare for action. Champagne bottles were opened and the corks popped.

The Earl of Dunraven had just challenged for the America's Cup, and an impersonator of Joseph Pulitzer, who was at the dinner, warned the Prince of Wales to beg the Earl, in case he bombarded New York, to aim to the right or left so as not to hit the great brass dome of the *New York World*.

A member impersonating the secretary of state recounted the problems of the Boundary Commission in the wilds of South America. They had captured, he said, the real subject of the dispute.

"What is it?" asked the president of the club.

"The Schomburgk line."

It was then brought in, around a large wheel, and proved to be about 100 yards of elastic, which was unraveled, cut up and distributed around the room.

Franklin H. Hosford of the *Detroit Free Press* finally ended the skit with a jingoistic speech in which he declared:

"Though New York be in sackcloth and Washington in ashes, though the Caribbean become a crimson sea of carnage and rivers of gore roll down into oceans of bloodier blood, the

Schomburgk line shall remain safe and forever in possession of the United States. . . Lay on, Macduff, and damned be he who doesn't stand by this bluff."

Again Mr. Cleveland wasn't pleased.

But Cleveland mellowed in his later years and after he ceased to be President did attend at least one Gridiron dinner, as did his immediate predecessor, Chester A. Arthur.[7]

• • •

Benjamin Harrison was as great a contrast to Grover Cleveland as John F. Kennedy was to Harry Truman. By nature somewhat austere, he was nevertheless very witty and had long been a favorite of Gridiron members before he was elected President in 1888.

He was the first President of the United States to attend the Gridiron dinner as President, although he had been a guest several times before he moved into the White House. He had been in office nearly three years before he came to his first dinner as President in January 1892, although he had accepted and planned to come the year before but was prevented from doing so by the death of a member of his cabinet a few days before the dinner.

His speeches before the club were among the most humorous to which it had ever listened, reported Gould Lincoln in the *Boston Transcript* on April 20, 1909.

"As a speaker, somewhat in contradiction to this solemn exterior, he was extremely versatile."

He enjoyed the gibes of the newspapermen instead of taking offense at them. He could laugh at himself, which is one of the greatest assets of a man in public life, and he could laugh at those who laughed at him.

It happened that the January 1892 dinner was held the same week as a convention in Washington of patent men and inventors. Harrison had addressed that gathering, and his opening line in his speech at the Gridiron dinner was, "This is the second time that I have been called upon this week to open a congress of American inventors."

Members of the Gridiron Club, quite competent in lampooning Presidents, have frequently been lampooned by them, notably Presidents Hoover, Roosevelt and Kennedy. All of them have played heavily on the inaccuracies of newspaper reporting, but Harrison was the first one to sound that note.

"I have been interested very often in reading accounts of cabinet meetings," he said. "The accuracy of these reports—once

in awhile—is marvelous. At other times, I have read that the
cabinet has under consideration a subject of great importance,
and yet that subject has not been mentioned."

But he went on to laugh at himself and his cabinet officers:

"I will say, however, that if the cabinet had for the most part
confined its deliberations to the subjects which the newspapers
say were considered instead of the trivial matters that were under
consideration, the cabinet officers and myself would have been
occupied to better purpose."

Frank Hosford, who was one of Harrison's strongest opponents in the Gridiron Club, sought out at the conclusion of the
dinner Perry S. Heath of the *Indianapolis Journal*, who was Harrison's greatest friend in the Gridiron Club.

"Perry," said Hosford, "your man Harrison is a wonder. I
didn't think it was in him."

"Oh, he's all right on his feet," replied Perry. "It's only when
he sits down that he falls down."[8]

This January 1892 dinner was a first not only because it was
the first time a President of the United States had been a guest,
but it was also the first dinner in which a music skit with costumes was undertaken. It was a pleasant skit entitled "The Country Band" and was based on Harrison's childhood life on his
grandfather's farm in North Bend, Indiana, during the years
when his father was in Congress.

Wearing various costume-uniforms, and playing some regular and some trick instruments, the band marched into the
dining hall, led by a drum major. Bringing up the rear, wearing a
big grandfather's hat of the vintage when his grandfather was
elected President in the "Tippecanoe campaign," and beating a
big bass drum, was the cartoon caricature of Harrison in the 1888
campaign. The band enthusiastically sang:

> In a little town out West,
>   Where I lived when but a boy,
> They had a silver cornet band
>   Which was my pride and joy;
> And many were the times
>   When I played hooky all the day,
> To follow up some street parade
>   And hear that old band play.
> The tuba was the butcher's boy,
>   The cymbals, Irish Dan;
> The alto was the village swell;
>   The snare drum our hired man;

The baker beat the big bass drum;
  And father used to say,
The cornet was a sporting man
  But, lordy! he could play!
Ta-ran—ta-rah, *Zing! Boom!*
Ta-ran—ta-rah, *Zing! Boom!*
And we knew the band was coming down the street.

Although 1892 was a Presidential election year, there was little reference to the upcoming election in the January dinner, quite in contrast to Gridiron dinners today in election years. The dinners at that time tended to concentrate more on the congressional situation, and this was especially true during the Harrison administration.

The election of 1888 had been a fairly uneventful one. President Cleveland felt it beneath the dignity of the President to campaign actively, and Harrison confined his activities to a "front porch" campaign from his home in Indiana.

The chief issue had been tariffs, with Harrison supporting high ones, and Cleveland low ones. Although Harrison trailed Cleveland in the total popular vote by 90,000, his support was so distributed that he carried states which had a handsome majority in the electoral college, where the vote was 233 to 168.

A broad legislative program was enacted, including the Sherman Antitrust, the McKinley Tariff Act, and a program to build a two-ocean navy. Government expenditures were rising, with the total approaching a billion dollars a year. The culmination of these things led to the loss of the House of Representatives to the Democrats in 1890 and the reduction of the Republican majority in the Senate to six.

Democratic tendencies for controversy among themselves erupted in a bitter contest between three House members for the Speakership—Charles F. Crisp, William L. Wilson and William D. Bynum. This was treated by the Gridiron Club in the 1891 annual dinner, with each of the three men portrayed as the Speaker.

Crisp, who eventually won, led off and was introduced by a song to the tune of "I Want To Be an Angel."

I want to be a Speaker and with Speakers stand,
  A book of rules before me, a gavel in my hand,
And when the caucus meets here, I am going for to try
  To be elected Speaker, or know the reason why.

When it was Wilson's turn to speak, he related how he had

asked one congressman to vote for him, and the congressman replied, "Tom Reed [the previous Speaker of the House] has been mighty hard on us, and we ought to get even. Let's give 'em the meanest man we've got. I'm for Bynum."

One other song during the Harrison administration referred to a famous filibuster which occurred against the so-called "Force Bill" in the final days of the administration.

This was the Lodge Election Bill of 1890, which had passed the House and was then before the Senate. Its purpose was to prevent discrimination against Negro voters in the southern states, and it was denounced in the South as an attempt to bring back the horrors of Reconstruction.

The Republicans were trying to pass the bill, but Senator Arthur P. Gorman of Maryland led a Democratic filibuster against it, which was successful, although the leadership of the Senate ran all-night sessions to wear out the filibuster. One of the constant problems was maintaining a quorum in order not to give the filibusterers a rest.

At the following Gridiron dinner there was a parody of the "Tit-Willow" song from *The Mikado*, as follows:

> Mr. Gorman, of Maryland, sat in his chair;
>   Saying, "Quorum, no quorum, no quorum;"
> So the roll of the Senate was called then and there
>   To make up a quorum, a quorum.
> Only twenty responded; "O where are the rest?"
>   "You'll find them," said Edmunds, "at home and undressed";
> So the Sergeant-at-Arms started out in his quest
>   To capture a quorum, a quorum.[9]

In the election of 1892 Harrison was renominated and chose Whitelaw Reid, editor of the *New York Herald Tribune*, as his running mate. The Democrats renominated Cleveland, along with Adlai E. Stevenson, grandfather of the Adlai Stevenson who ran twice against Eisenhower.

But there were many dissatisfactions rising in the country, particularly among the farmers, who had been subjected to falling farm prices, and a third party populist candidate subtracted a substantial percentage of the popular vote and twenty-two electoral votes from the Republican strength, resulting in the election of Cleveland for a second term, and the rise of William McKinley.

President Harrison had spoken once at a Gridiron dinner prior to his election to the Presidency, and he spoke on one further occasion in 1900 after he had retired from the Presidency.

The Gridiron records contain no reference to the content of these speeches, other than the fact that in the later one he touched, in a humorous way, upon the weak points of Washington journalism—apparently a favorite Gridiron theme of his. Comments of members who were contemporaries and heard the speeches praised his wit and said that both speeches were great successes.

III

William McKinley

1897-1901
*And Gridiron Club members from
"the tented field and barrooms of
New York"*

Except for one ten-month period, William McKinley served in the House of Representatives continuously from 1877 to 1891. The interruption came in 1884, when the House voted to unseat McKinley and to sustain the claim of Jonathan H. Wallace that he had defeated McKinley in the election of 1882.

The issue with which McKinley was most closely identified while he was in Congress was high tariffs to protect American industry from foreign competition, and in 1888 he was the sponsor of the McKinley Tariff Bill, which raised those levies to a new high level. But the Democratically controlled state legislature of Ohio took care of him by gerrymandering his district, so that he lost the congressional election of 1890. This was probably what indirectly made him President in 1897.

After losing his congressional seat, he ran for governor of Ohio, was elected and gave the state an administration which proved quite popular. It was his election as Governor that really brought him to the direct attention of Marcus A. ("Mark") Hanna, the Cleveland industrialist and politician, who in 1892 sponsored a McKinley-for-President campaign in the convention which resulted in his receiving 182 votes but losing, of course, to Benjamin Harrison.

Upon McKinley's reelection as governor in 1893, Hanna began to plan his campaign to nominate and elect him President in 1896. Hanna was so successful in developing support for the Ohio governor that McKinley was nominated on the first ballot.

That was the year that the thirty-six-year-old William Jennings Bryan delivered his famous "Cross of Gold" speech and stampeded the Democratic National Convention to win its nomination, on the issue of the free and unlimited coinage of silver at a ratio of sixteen parts of silver to one of gold. This placed the tariff issue in the background and made sound currency the big issue. McKinley won by a substantial electoral vote but a much narrower popular vote.

It was against this background that he attended his first Gridiron dinner as President of the United States in March 1897, although he had been a frequent guest while he was in the House of Representatives. It was also the first dinner attended by Mark Hanna, who was to become almost a national political boss and who had just been elected to the Senate. At this dinner he made his first speech in Washington.

His introduction followed a skit on the spoils system, which was very much in effect in those days, and since both Hanna and McKinley came from Ohio, much fun was made of how Ohioans were going to populate the new administration.

The caricature of the heavy-drinking newspaperman was also still prevalent at that time, and when Hanna was introduced he immediately made a hit with the audience by remarking that he knew many members of the Gridiron Club—that he had "met most of you on the tented field and in the barrooms of New York and Chicago."

Twelve years later, Gould Lincoln, writing in the *Boston Transcript*, commented that:

"When Mark Hanna came to Washington as the New Napoleon of Republican politics, there was some doubt as to how he, as a successful and somewhat arrogant man of business, would accept the ribbing which the club would be disposed to give him. He instantly fell in with the organization and until the day of his death practically never missed a Gridiron dinner."[1]

Incidentally, it was at this dinner of March 1897, that the Gridiron Club first printed a chart of the seating list with long tables running down from the head table in the form of a grid-iron.

• • •

The dinner of March 26, 1898, held after the sinking of the *Maine* and about a month before the opening of the war with Spain, was one of the notable early ones. Among the guests were Senator Hanna and Theodore Roosevelt, then assistant secretary of the navy.

War feeling was running high in the country, President McKinley didn't want to get into a war with Spain, and Senator Hanna was a strong opponent of it. In a not exactly impartial way, Gridiron Club President Hosford dwelt upon the prominence of Ohio in the councils of government and introduced Senator Hanna by turning directly toward him and saying, "Senator Hanna, can we have this war?"

Forsaking the role of witty rejoinder, Hanna made a serious speech against the war. At its conclusion, the president of the Gridiron Club introduced the next speaker by saying, "At least we have one man connected with this administration who is not afraid to fight—Theodore Roosevelt, assistant secretary of the navy. . . ."

It was a dramatic confrontation between the new, rising assistant secretary of the navy and the powerful political leader who had elected the man of his choice as President of the United States.

Roosevelt rose.

"We will have this war," he said, "for the freedom of Cuba, Senator Hanna, in spite of the timidity of the commerical interests."[2]

At another dinner in 1898, after the war had been concluded, victory was the principal theme.

This was the largest dinner ever given up to that time by the Gridiron Club. Two hundred and two people were present, including President McKinley, who did not speak, however, until the end of the dinner and only to express his pleasure at being there.

Early evidence of the Pan-Americanism that was to follow the Spanish-American War developed at this dinner. The guest list included not only the President and Vice President of the United States, but Lord Farrer Herschell of Great Britain; the president of Costa Rica; John Hay, the secretary of state; most of the members of the American cabinet; premiers from Canada and

Newfoundland; and practically all of the officers of the army and navy who had been active in the war.

In the atmosphere of solidarity between America and the countries of South America and the British Empire, the club sang "God Save the Queen" and introduced Lord Herschell, "whose admirable speech was heartily applauded," according to the *Washington Post* of December 4, 1898.

• • •

There was considerable delay in the Senate over ratification of the treaty with Spain, and by the time of the January 1899 dinner, which President McKinley attended, it was still unratified. The club went into "executive session of the Senate" and debated until a roll call was demanded.

It was a typical Gridiron debate. An impersonator of Senator George F. Hoar of Massachusetts, who opposed ratification, said he did not want the Constitution trampled upon "in order that a few American tradesmen may sell rum, calico and oleomargarine to the benighted pagans of the Eastern Archipelago."

An impersonator of Senator Lodge, also of Massachusetts, predicted that the treaty would be ratified and announced that he proposed to offer a resolution entrusting the Philippines to the care of a commission consisting of Richard Croker, leader of Tammany Hall, and Thomas C. Platt, U.S. senator from New York.

"Let the first new experience of a liberated people," he said, "be with the gentle despotism which has proved so great a boon to our other island possession—the city of New York.

"They will find conditions in Manhattan Island not so very different from their own. They are not in touch with American sentiment. Neither is New York. They are accustomed to a monarchical form of government. So is New York. They are not yet ripe for assimilation. We have been trying for two hundred years to assimilate New York without success. The full and dazzling light of liberty, too suddenly confronted, might blind their untried eyes. Let them approach it through familiar shadows and let Platt and Croker guide their faltering steps."[3]

Charles A. Boynton of the Associated Press, then president of the Gridiron Club, put the question of ratification to a vote, announced that the vote was unanimous, and impressed solemnly upon the club the importance of maintaining secrecy and not revealing what went on behind closed doors.

As he finished, there was a great turmoil at the doors, and

Crosby Noyes of the *Washington Star* came rushing in one door with a large bundle of extras under his arm, and Beriah Wilkins of the *Washington Post* came in another with an equally large bundle of *Posts*. Each was crying, "Extra! Extra! All about the ratification of the peace treaty in the executive session of the Senate!" Papers were distributed to the guests as a souvenir of the dinner.

At this dinner Senator Mark Hanna and Tammany Hall leader Richard Croker met each other for the first time. The reception committee had established the custom of asking all prominent guests to sign their names in a large Gridiron book. As Croker approached to do this, he found Mark Hanna just in the process of writing his name. Each looked at the other for a moment and Croker, who spoke first, said, "Your face seems familiar."

"I ought to know you," replied Hanna, "from your pictures."

They were introduced by a club member and Croker continued, "I knew your face, but I missed that suit with the dollar marks."

"And I'd have been sure it was you," replied Hanna, "if you'd worn that striped suit."[4]

This was one of the early manifestations of one of the important contributions of the Gridiron Club to American politics, in bringing together in a friendly and jocular way people who are often bitter political opponents.

It was at this dinner that the custom, since observed at all dinners, was initiated with the words of the Gridiron president, "Gentlemen, the Gridiron Club has but one toast: To the President of the United States."

• • •

By the time of the December 1899 dinner, the United States had been in serious trouble in the newly acquired Philippines because of an insurrection started by a Philippine native named Aguinaldo. He had just been captured, and the Gridiron utilized this event as the vehicle for the initiation of Rudolph Kauffmann, managing director of the *Washington Star* in 1899.

Turmoil and shouts in the wings! A scared man with hair erect and wearing a South Seas costume of grass and leaves burst into the dining room saying, "Save me! Save Me!" He ran to an improvised jungle, hotly pursued by United States generals, who hauled him out of the jungle. Each claimed to be the captor of

Aguinaldo, when General Otis, in command in the Philippines, arrived at the scene in dress uniform. He blue-penciled the reports of the other generals and dictated to Washington the dispatch, "The Army under my command has the honor to present to the nation Aguinaldo, the insurgent chief, as a Christmas present."

At this point Aguinaldo was paroled under the condition he would become a member of the Gridiron Club. Kauffmann removed part of his Aguinaldo disguise and declared this was his highest ambition.

This skit, when reported in the papers at the time, brought about considerable criticism of the Gridiron Club from the opponents of the Philippine acquisition. The Club was accused of treating humorously a matter which they regarded as very serious indeed.

• • •

As the political campaign of 1900 approached, the dinner held on January 27 that year was the first one at which William Jennings Bryan was a guest. He was already actively campaigning for renomination and still beating the drums for the free and unlimited coinage of silver at sixteen to one.

At this dinner twelve Gridiron minstrels were introduced, all wearing white hats bound with silver except one which was conspicuously gold. Henry Litchfield West of the *Washington Post*, president of the club, inquired as they came in, "Who may you be?"

"We are the Sixteen-to-One Minstrels," replied the interlocutor.

"There is no sixteen to one there," objected the president.

"There is no sixteen to one anywhere," was the reply.

Then they sang directly to Bryan:

Oh, where have you been Billy boy, Billy boy?
Oh, where have you been, Silver Billy?
I've been after delegates
And I've got most all the states;
Bet your life Silver Billy is a winner.[5]

During the campaign of 1896 Bryan had been strongly opposed by the leaders of the railroad industry, and as he rose to speak after this skit, he remarked that he saw more railroad executives sitting at this dinner than he'd seen in all the time since the campaign of 1896.

It was at this dinner that William Jennings Bryan and Mark Hanna met each other for the first time. Bryan, who sat next to the president of the club, remarked to West during the dinner that he had never met Hanna personally, so at its close West summoned Hanna and introduced them.

"I have frequently heard of you, Mr. Bryan," said Hanna.

"And your name is not altogether unfamiliar to me," was Bryan's laughing reply.[6]

The two chatted cordially for awhile about the campaign in which they had been such bitter opponents.

• • •

By April 1900 it was apparent that President McKinley would be renominated and that William Jennings Bryan would be his opponent. The dinner guests were resolved into a convention with many banners and signs, all satirical.

It was obvious by this time that Senator Mark Hanna was the unquestioned boss of the Republican party. A member impersonating Hanna declared that this would be a convention on the Philadelphia plan: "The delegates have nothing to do but furnish the enthusiasm."

As the vehicle for introducing the speakers, the club went through the roll call of states. Delaware yielded to New York, and Senator Chauncey M. Depew arose and made a very vigorous nominating speech for "the man who. . . ," "the man who. . . ," "the man who. . . ," who, in the end, proved to be himself. He closed by saying he was absolutely sure of election if nominated by the Gridiron Club.

In line with the influence in that period, before primaries, of party leaders in picking Presidential candidates, the selection of a ticket was referred to a committee by the Gridiron Club at the end of the speech, with Mark Hanna as chairman.

• • •

The election of 1900 was largely a rerun of that of 1896. Theodore Roosevelt was nominated as the Vice Presidential candidate with McKinley, and their slogan became prosperity and "four more years of the full dinner pail."

Bryan chose as his running mate Adlai E. Stevenson, who had been Vice President during the last term of Grover Cleveland. Their campaign was very largely for free silver and against "imperialism."

McKinley's victory was about two-to-one in the electoral college and about seven-to-six in the popular vote.

At the Gridiron dinner of December 8, after the election, the principal skit revolved around the creation of the "Gridiron Museum," to which various members of the club made contributions.

One was a stuffed elephant "marched to death in a sound money parade." Another was a sixteen-to-one jackass, "species almost extinct, name of contributor withheld by request."

Several relics from the campaign wardrobe of Mr. Bryan were suggested.

"This is the hat through which Mr. Bryan talked for sixty-four days," was the first one.

"This is the shoe with which Mr. Bryan kicked the octopus."

"I contribute the platform," said another member, "which was never used."

"Here," said another, "is a pair of trousers worn by Mr. Bryan when he straddled the sixteen-to-one issue."

"The collection will not be complete," suggested another, "without the crown of thorns and cross of gold."

With that, Gridiron Club President West brought the skit to an end by declaring, "This closes an epoch in American history."

And indeed it did, for with the assassination of McKinley a few months later, and the accession of Theodore Roosevelt to the Presidency, the old issues declined, even though Bryan did run once more.

It was also at this dinner that an impersonator of Richard Croker first uttered the line, later credited to Croker himself, "You can't harness the Tammany tiger to a wild jackass of the prairies."

At this dinner, former President Benjamin Harrison was a guest and a speaker. He recalled many experiences with the club, both as a senator and as President. He touched in a humorous way upon his favorite Gridiron subject, the weak points of Washington journalists, but was altogether complimentary and according to Gridiron records, made a great hit.

• • •

Skits relating to Presidents were fairly mild in the early years of the Gridiron Club, and this was certainly true of the January 1901 dinner following the reelection of McKinley with his new Vice President, Theodore Roosevelt, hero of San Juan Hill.

In fact, the inauguration of the president of the Gridiron Club was the vehicle of satire as McKinley began his second term. This was the year that Arthur Wallace Dunn, author of

Gridiron Nights, which is such a valuable source of early Gridiron history, was president of the club.

Complaint was made by the chairman of the inauguration committee that the president of the Gridiron Club had not been properly inaugurated. So he was asked to join the new ceremony. He was brought into the room, solemn and arms folded, sitting in a small vehicle drawn by four blacks labeled "Philippines," "Puerto Rico," "Hawaii," and "Guam," to represent the new world-wide influence of the post–Spanish War United States. The propellants for this inaugural carriage were driven by a man who walked along its side, and who was made up to look like Mark Hanna wielding a big whip.

On the other side of the carriage was a member dressed in a hunter's costume, carrying a rifle and made up to look like Theodore Roosevelt. He was followed by an aide carrying a mountain lion, since the new Vice President at the time of that dinner was in Colorado hunting mountain lions.[7]

Gridrion member Alfred J. Stofer, costumed and made up to resemble William Jennings Bryan, who had been defeated for the second time by McKinley, entered with banners reading "Nomination 1904, Nomination 1908, Nomination 1912." He waved all the rest aside and proclaimed, "Your candidate I cannot be. I would rather write than be President."[8]

It was less than eight months after this dinner that President McKinley was assassinated in Buffalo, New York.

At the close of the next dinner, Charles Emory Smith, the postmaster general, gave what the *Washington Post* described as "an eloquent and feeling tribute to the late President who was known personally to nearly everyone in the room." Herndon Morsell then sang "The Song That Reached My Heart."

This ended an era of relatively conservative thinking and brought to the Presidency the young and vigorous Theodore Roosevelt, with his highly activist and expansionist program. With this change, considerable transformation also occurred in the way the Gridiron Club handled Presidential policies.

IV

Theodore Roosevelt

1901-1909
TR Swings His Big Stick at a
Gridiron Dinner

The ascension of Theodore Roosevelt to the Presidency on September 6, 1901, brought with it a whole new series of issues for the Gridiron Club to satirize.

The forty-two-year-old President, the youngest in American history, proceeded after a period of relative quietness to unloose all his youthful vigor in trying to change some of the things that he thought needed change.

Although he had been a civil service commissioner in Washington and was assistant secretary to the navy at the time of the outbreak of the Spanish-American War, he attained his great national prominence as a leader of the Rough Riders in their assault upon San Juan Hill. This helped propel him to election as governor of New York in the fall of 1898, and to the Vice Presidency in the election of 1900.

Roosevelt's administration as President was noteworthy for his policy in foreign relations, expressed as "Speak softly and carry a big stick"; for his building of a large naval force; for the building of the Panama Canal, primarily so that the navy could move quickly from the Atlantic to the Pacific or vice versa; but above all, for his controversies with big business, which gave him the title of "trust buster."

The Northern Securities Company had been formed by J. P. Morgan, E. H. Harriman, and other business leaders to control railroads in the West. Roosevelt thought this constituted an unjustified use of economic power and in 1902 brought suit for the dissolution of the company. In 1904 the Supreme Court upheld the government and Northern Securities was dissolved.

His administration also brought suits against John D. Rockefeller's Standard Oil Company, which resulted eventually in its dissolution, and against the "tobacco trust," to dissolve that. In all, more than forty such antitrust suits were filed during Roosevelt's seven and a half years in the Presidency.

Roosevelt always insisted that he was not antibusiness, but merely wanted to regulate some of the major activities of business which involved the public interest. Nor did he confine his use of the "big stick" domestically to business; he applied it on occasion with equal force to labor. In 1902 when there was a bitter coal strike, he intervened and, with the help of J. P. Morgan, enforced a settlement through arbitration.

In 1903 the Elkins Act was passed, prohibiting railroads from making rebates to shippers. Later Roosevelt proposed new railroad rate legislation. These policies produced major controversies within Roosevelt's own party and led to serious conflicts in the Senate between the President and numerous Republican senators who disagreed with him. It also led to the most celebrated controversy ever to occur at a Gridiron dinner.

One of Roosevelt's principal Senate opponents in the railroad legislation was Joseph B. Foraker of Ohio, who had been a strong supporter during Roosevelt's first term. In fact, Mark Hanna had Presidential ambitions, Foraker had succeeded in causing the Ohio convention to declare for Roosevelt. But with the advent of the railroad rate legislation, Foraker became a bitter opponent of the President.

At the club's dinner of January 26, 1907, an "emperor skit" was produced. The Gridiron Club was careful not to depict Roosevelt directly in this role, referring in the skit to the empire ten years hence. Richard V. Oulahan, then of the *New York Sun*, who later as head of the *New York Times* bureau became one of Washington's most distinguished correspondents, played the role of the emperor.

Two members of the cast, identified as J. P. Morgan and H.

H. Rogers, vice president of Standard Oil Company, were costumed as tramps and were given jobs by the emperor.

The emperor asked who the last President of the United States had been, and when he was told that it was Theodore Roosevelt, the emperor asked, "Why didn't he become king?" And the answer was that he had said at a Gridiron dinner that he would not accept a third term, and the Supreme Court had held that his word was constitutional.

The club used this emperor vehicle for various digs at the President and at others, and following it, Clifford K. Berryman, cartoonist of the *Washington Star*, came on the stage and drew some cartoons.

"Draw a cartoon," he was asked, "of the man the Senate loves best."

There gradually emerged the features of Theodore Roosevelt.

"Draw a picture of the man the President loves best," was the next command.

And then the features of Senator Joseph Foraker appeared.

On August, 3, 1906, a small detachment of Negro soldiers from the Twenty-fifth U.S. Infantry, in retaliation for the treatment they had received from the citizens of Brownsville, Texas, went on a rampage into the town, which resulted in the killing of one citizen. They quickly returned to camp without any of them having been identified.

An investigation resulted, during which every one of the 167 men in the three Negro companies refused to identify any of the people involved, whereupon President Roosevelt discharged all without honor. He took the position that if no one admitted guilt, all would have to pay the penalty. This action created widespread controversy in the North, where the Negro vote was at that time pretty solidly Republican.

Senator Foraker, not averse to embarrassing the President, along with Senator Benjamin R. Tillman of South Carolina, initiated a Senate investigation of this affair and it became a much-discussed controversy. A large number of the Republican senators supported Foraker, while the majority of the Democrats supported the President.*

The club had a souvenir booklet of cartoons by Clifford K.

---

*This Brownsville controversy was finally settled sixty-six years later, when in 1972 the Nixon administration, through Assistant Secretary of Defense Robert F. Froehlke, announced that the concept of mass punishment was contrary to army policy, and ordered the discharges changed to honorable for all of the 167 men involved.

Berryman at the dinner with a little verse under each one, and under Foraker's they had a line from a popular song title of a few years earlier, "All Coons Look Alike to Me."

The cartoon of Foraker and the reference in the souvenir book infuriated Roosevelt—not really at the Gridiron Club but at Senator Foraker. The result was that the President attacked Foraker with great ferocity in his speech, and that Foraker came back at the President with a counterattack which broke up the dinner. Guests were never served anything beyond the terrapin, and no further acts in the show were put on the stage.

The Gridiron Club's rule about speeches being off-the-record could not survive this, and papers all over the country carried references to what the *Washington Post* called "a battle royal." Comparatively few direct quotes have been preserved, and some of those differ because the quotes that were printed in newspapers were obtained mostly secondhand from what those at the dinner could recollect, but the President was described in the *Post* as having delivered his attack "in a high, strident pitch, and sandwiched with gestures more than emphatic."[1]

Foraker went back at the President with a ringing speech to the effect that his conscience required him to do his duty as he saw it, and that he was going to do this no matter what the President of the United States thought.

The *New York Evening Post* said that Foraker "concluded in ringing tones, with a wave of the hand toward the President, in these words: 'You know, Mr. President, I love you so.' "[2]

But the most complete and accurate account of what happened did not emerge for another twenty-four years.

At a Gridiron dinner in 1931, Samuel G. Blythe, who was at that time an eminent writer for the *Saturday Evening Post,* and who had been Gridiron president on the dramatic night in 1907, gave in a hitherto unpublished speech the details of what had happened in the Roosevelt-Foraker controversy.

Blythe explained that the President was "not in good humor when he arrived," that he was "angry at the Senate" and "had had a hard week."

He also explained that there were ten or twelve "captains of finance" on the guest list, including J. P. Morgan, H. H. Rogers of Standard Oil, and E. H. Harriman, about all of whom President Roosevelt had made critical remarks in the past. He noted that these men, with other lesser industrial and financial people, were sitting pretty much together at one table.

Early in the dinner, reported Blythe, Roosevelt saw the little souvenir book of cartoons, with its references to the Brownsville case and Senator Foraker, which "incensed him" and caused him to make "several caustic comments about it to me and to others sitting near him."

"Then he began a close scrutiny of the guest list," said Blythe. "I was busy with the dinner, but once, when I looked around at him, I saw that his jaw had tightened, that he was more or less excited and showed signs of eruption. . . .

"The terrapin was just coming in when he leaned over to me and asked when he was scheduled to speak.

" 'At ten-thirty,' I told him.

" 'I would like to speak now,' he said, 'if it can be arranged.

" 'Certainly,' I told him, and arranged it."

Service was stopped and Blythe introduced the President.

"While the President did not confide to me his reason for getting thus early into action, I sensed it immediately. He was angry of the implications of the 'all coons' line, and he found facing him not only his principal antagonists on his Brownsville policy, but ten or twelve of the plutocratic gentlemen on whom he had regulatory designs. He was in a forum where he could say what he liked, without fear of publication, and he just couldn't wait. He was in a hurry to get at it.

"He began rather cordially, with the usual complimentary sentences about the Gridiron Club and then turned squarely toward the eminent financiers sitting not thirty feet from him. He became emphatic at once. With accusing finger he pointed at these astonished plutocrats and told them what he had in store for them. He was vigorous, almost violent. The captains of finance listened with strained attention and with stony faces. I remember Mr. Morgan, with a big cigar clenched in his teeth, glaring at him as he talked. The guests began to get excited and there was considerable applause as he went on.

"After he had finished removing the hides from these wealthy citizens, and he made a complete job of it, he picked up the little book of cartoons, which was open before him at the Foraker picture and read:

"J. B. Foraker sez, sez he,

" 'All coons look alike to me.' "

"He threw the book on the table, and almost shouted, with all the usual Rooseveltian dental and other emphasis, 'Well, all coons do *not* look alike to me.'

"Never taking his eyes from Senator Foraker, who sat directly in front of him at the far end of one of the long tables extending at right angles from the head table, he summarized his stand on the Brownsville matter with extreme vigor, and no mincing of words, and with particular and personal reference to the opposition of the senator from Ohio. By this time the diners, then greatly interested and excited, were standing in the back rows, and a lot of them had crowded into the well. The President had plenty of friends there, and they applauded him enthusiastically. After he had said all he wanted to say, and he talked for more than half an hour, he closed with a conciliatory sentence or two, and sat down amid much cheering.

"I had been watching Senator Foraker. When I was a boy, in the Blaine campaign, I rode twenty-nine miles in a springless wagon, over country roads, on a cold October day, to hear him make a speech. They called him Fire Alarm Foraker. He was sitting facing the President, and staring at him, nervously twisting a napkin in his hands.

"Senator Foraker was not on the program, but what was the program to a situation like that? Here was a chance for a debate such as we never had had before. Here was drama in the raw. Of course, I did not know whether Senator Foraker, who had no idea I would call on him, would get up and make a conciliatory speech, or whether he would lash out in defense of himself. So, phrasing my introduction to give him a chance to be either agreeable or aggressive, but determined to get him on his feet and see what would happen, I called him up. As I did so, I took a side look at the President. He was just as much astonished as Foraker.

"The senator rose hesitantly, and began to talk slowly, as if undecided how to meet the emergency into which I thrust him, but in two minutes he was in his stride. He shoved back his chair, stepped out so he could talk directly to the President, and announced he was a senator from the state of Ohio, in his own right, beholden to no person as to his opinions or actions on public questions save the people of his state, and not to be intimidated or coerced by any person whomsoever, not even the President of the United States. . . .

"Not for nothing did they call him Fire Alarm Foraker. He not only gave a three-sixes alarm, but he set the fire. Up to that time the President had had all the applause, but Senator Foraker had not been talking for five minutes before the anti-Roosevelt contingent, led vigorously by the occupants of Millionaires' Row, by most of the senators present, and joined by many of the guests who were on their feet, crowded to the front or standing on chairs cheering the defiances of Foraker, waving their napkins at him and otherwise urging him on. I have no doubt that was the first time J. Pierpont Morgan ever waved a napkin at any speaker, but he made a flag out of his that night. So did his plutocratic companions, and so did far more than half the guests. No sight like that was ever seen in this country before or since.

"Senator Foraker talked too long, as most orators do. In fact, after he had finished his speech, cheered on by the napkin wavers, and the hand clappers, he practically made it all over again, but his supporters loved it. They would have listened for an hour. Presently, with a final shout of defiance, he sat down amid a great burst of cheering.

"By that time the dinner, in the sense of being an occasion for eating and drinking, was a wreck. All waiters had been shooed out of the room, and no food had been served. I had abandoned the regular program. Many a Gridiron actor carries about with him to this day unspoken lines prepared for that night. The guests were milling around, and the excitement was great. Scores rushed over to congratulate Foraker. The comment was clamorous.

"President Roosevelt, astonished and angry at my temerity in calling on Senator Foraker, and highly incensed at Foraker, half rose once to interrupt. I told him he would have a chance for rebuttal after the senator had finished. A few minutes later he tried to interrupt again and I told him that while he was President of the United States, and as such I respected him, I was president of the Gridrion Club and that this was my dinner and not his. Therefore, he could not speak until Senator Foraker had finished.

"Then he rose, loudly cheered by the crowd, for it was a crowd then and not a dinner. After I got a semblance of order with my gavel and had told the guests and club members that the President had some further remarks, he began vehemently. In a short time he calmed down, and when he closed was neither bellicose nor belligerent. Not that he retracted anything he had said, but he wanted to ease the strain.

"However, this did not work, and I cast about for more expert emulsifiers. So I called up [Speaker of the House Joseph E.] Uncle Joe Cannon. He told us that all that had happened was unimportant and besought us to forget it. He said, 'If the floor of this great hall should suddenly cave in and all the people here be precipitated to the cellar, while it would be a calamity, it would not deter the progress of the United States.' Uncle Joe didn't get over so well. The hall was still buzzing. The guests were popeyed with excitement. President Roosevelt sat fiddling with a fork, and talking occasionally to people near him. I tried another emulsifier or two, but it was no use. The show had been too big for epilogues from minor characters in it to get attention.

"It was then nearly midnight, so I asked Herndon Morsell to sing, 'The Song that Reached My Heart,' made the customary announcements and adjourned. President Roosevelt left immediately. The diners, hungry but not thirsty, for this was in 1907, trooped out of the hall and all that night and all next day the city hummed with the story."[3]

Senator James E. Watson of Indiana, then a young congressman, was present at this dinner and also at the dinner in 1931 when Blythe reported the details to club members and guests of that day.

Watson, in his memoirs, *As I Knew Them*, published after his retirement from the Senate, confirmed Blythe's recollection of what had happened.

"His recollection and mine," said Watson in his book, "agreed in practically every detail."[4]

The confrontation between Roosevelt and Foraker—certainly the most sensational confrontation that ever occurred at a Gridiron dinner—was the subject of talk all over Washington and of stories all over the country for a considerable period of time. The Gridiron records contain pages and pages of clippings of newspaper accounts that were printed, including those of several papers which took sharp exception to the publication of details of the incident.

Arthur Krock, one of the most distinguished of Washington correspondents, recalled that Roy Vernon of the *Chicago Daily News* was on the waiting list of candidates for admission to the club and was present at this dinner as a guest.

"When the dinner ended," said Krock, "he went to his sponsors and informed them that it was his reportorial duty to send his paper a report of the row and he would do so, whatever adverse effect it might have on his candidacy. He did break the story, and soon afterward was elected to membership."

The club itself passed a resolution at a special meeting on

January 30, directing the executive committee "to endeavor to ascertain the origin of reports published in several newspapers purporting to give an account of the Roosevelt-Foraker incident," but publication had already gone so far that it apparently overwhelmed the efforts of the club to run down the sources of the leaks.

The split between Roosevelt and Foraker was never healed during Roosevelt's Presidency. When the senator next came up for reelection, William Randolph Hearst charged that Foraker had been receiving money from the Standard Oil Company while he was senator, in exchange for legislative activities in behalf of or against pending legislation. Roosevelt, according to Mark Sullivan's *Our Times,* inspired a newspaper dispatch in the *Cincinnati Times-Star* with a headline, "Roosevelt Believes To Support Foraker Is Party Treason."[5] Foraker failed at reelection and departed from the national scene.

This was not the only occasion on which President Roosevelt talked directly to some of the guests at a Gridiron dinner, but it was the only occasion on which any of them talked back.

• • •

After unsuccessful efforts to conclude a Panama Canal treaty with Columbia, a section of that country covering the proposed canal route revolted, whereupon President Roosevelt recognized the Republic of Panama with great haste, and soon concluded a treaty with that country ceding the Canal Zone to the United States. This provoked some discussion as to whether the United States had had a hand in fomenting the revolution.

At a Gridiron dinner soon after this, three new members were being initiated. They were undergoing questioning as to their professional qualifications.

"If you were looking for a tip," they were asked, "as to when a revolution would break out in Columbia, what would you do?"

"I would camp on the White House steps," one replied.

Some opposition was developing in the country to Roosevelt's plan to build a canal, and one of the open opponents of it was the powerful Senator Arthur P. Gorman of Maryland. Nelson W. Aldrich of Rhode Island and Hanna were also involved, but in a less conspicuous way.

At the dinner of January 30, 1904, President Roosevelt, after some preliminary remarks in a humorous vein, launched, as he frequently did on subsequent occasions, into a serious speech, this time on the canal about which he was very determined. He defended his course up to that time and then, leaning over the table and speaking directly to Senators Gorman, Aldrich and Hanna, who happened to be seated fairly close to each other, he thundered at them:

"The canal is going to be built. I will say here, as I have said elsewhere, that all obstacles placed in the way will be removed."[6]

"At all events, the impression was made," said Arthur Wallace Dunn, who was present at the dinner, "that the President was 'talking at' the Senators, and for a second time during the evening there passed down the spines of those around the tables that tingle of excitement which one feels when something seems about to happen which you hope will not happen, but which you would not miss for the world if it should happen. A few years later the Roosevelt-Foraker affair was just such an event."[7]

On another occasion a prominent businessman undertook to lecture the President at a dinner. It was E. H. Harriman, railroad magnate and father of Averell Harriman. When called upon to speak, he addressed the President directly and told him in very plain language how business felt. Using references in the skits to keep his comments witty and inoffensive, he nevertheless indicated to the President before a very substantial and impressive audience that he was far from happy with many of the Roosevelt policies.

But Roosevelt was quite capable of handling the situation, and by what persons who were present described as "numerous witty rejoinders" poking fun at Harriman, he succeeded in preventing these two speeches from developing into anything that might be called a confrontation.

There was a very brief skit alluding to the Roosevelt practice of occasionally calling in some of his subordinates and lecturing them rather severely. One of the victims of such a lecture had been Lt. Gen. Nelson A. Miles, who was somewhat of a military hero. On this occasion a man appeared in the room dressed in a general's uniform but with a bandage over his head, his arm in a sling, patches on his face, and every evidence of having been badly injured.

"Why, General, where have you been?" someone asked.

"I have been to call on the President—"

Curtain.[8]

Roosevelt shrieked and roared, and Miles, whose dressing down from the President had gotten into the newspapers, seemed to enjoy it equally.

Throughout his administration, Roosevelt was a very color-ful figure and seemed always in control of every situation except in the Foraker instance and one other. When Owen Wister was meeting with the President at the White House, Roosevelt's daughter Alice kept disrupting the conversation by running in and out of the room with questions to her father.

The story is told that Wister asked the President if there wasn't anything he could do to control Alice, and that the President replied, "I can do one of two things. I can be President of the United States or I can control Alice. I cannot possibly do both."[9]

With all his colorfulness and all his controversy, he remained a very approachable figure. Years later, in 1955, at a members-only Gridiron dinner in honor of James Hagerty, then press secretary to President Eisenhower, Gould Lincoln of the *Washington Star* related a characteristic event in the Theodore Roosevelt administration.

He said he had come to the White House to get some information about some unimportant matter from the secretary of the President. This was after Roosevelt had built the West Wing of the White House.

"As I arrived at the door," he said, "there was no guard. I went in. No one was inside. I kept walking, reached the secretary's office. No one there. Kept on walking until I came to a stairway leading up from the basement.

"Coming up the stairs was Teddy himself, eyeglasses, teeth, and all. He was clad in a sweater. He had been playing tennis on the White House court.

"President Roosevelt looked up at me and grinned, and said, 'What do you want?' I told him, and he suggested where I get the information.

"If I tried an operation like that today, the Secret Service, the Army, Navy and Marine Corps, and Jim Hagerty would have me drawn and quartered, in no time flat."

But in those days, as today, by no means was all the banter directed at the president or even the administration. At one of the Roosevelt dinners, after J. Pierpont Morgan had assisted the President in settling the coal strike, there was a song:

Pierpont Morgan played the organ,
　　John Mitchell played the drum;
The railroads played the same old game
　　And the price was twelve per ton.

In his speeches, President Roosevelt frequently referred to "money kings," "captains of industry," and had coined the phrase "malefactors of great wealth." Therefore, in this particular skit, it was announced that the Gridiron police "have rounded up and brought here money kings, captains of industry, monopolists, corporation cormorants, and malefactors of great wealth."

At this time perhaps the most celebrated lawyer in the United States was Chauncey M. Depew, then senator from New York and an almost permanent guest at Gridiron dinners because of his wit and his popularity. So, the skit continued:

"It is customary for the court, when persons are brought before it without means of employing counsel, to assign some young and briefless attorney to conduct the defense. I will thereupon appoint Chauncey M. Depew as counsel for the defendants during these proceedings."[10]

Elihu Root, who was secretary of state in Roosevelt's second administration, and who had the reputation of being a rather cold individual, figured in a preconvention skit in 1904, in which it was suggested that someone should open a fur store near the Convention Hall in Chicago, because "the delegages to the convention will have to have something to keep them warm while Elihu Root is talking."

At one of the dinners there was a song based on "Baby Mine," about Speaker Cannon and Controller of the Currency Charles G. Dawes, both of whom came from Illinois.

> From the land of Suckers many,
>   Illinois, Illinois,
> But of statesmen, few, if any,
>   Illinois, Illinois.
> For two years there'll be a pause,
> Then we'll have young Charles Dawes.

Sometimes the satire even turned to the newspapermen themselves. In an initiation skit, Henry Hall of the *Pittsburgh Chronicle-Telegraph* instructed the initiate candidates.

"Do not imagine that because you have been accredited as Washington correspondents you are at the pinnacle of your careers. You have much to learn. Your principal duty will be to write stories of the secret sessions of the Senate, secret cabinet meetings, and the innermost thoughts of the President. Of these secret meetings you will make bold statements of fact on what ought to have occurred. The senators and cabinet officers will be so pleased to see themselves credited with intelligent and timely observations that they will never deny the reports."[11]

At the January dinner in 1904, which was attended by Senator Mark Hanna although he was ill, there was a ventriloquist act which was the vehicle for considerable joshing of President Roosevelt and various others in his administration.

Hanna and Roosevelt were not getting on well, and an impersonator of William Howard Taft, then governor of the Philippines, announced that he was afraid he would catch cold sitting in the room occupied by Elihu Root. Senator Hanna's impersonator suggested that he should go to the White House. He would get warm enough seeing how glad the President was to greet Hanna.

Senator Nathan Bay Scott of West Virginia was a very vocal advocate of Hanna for the Presidential nomination that year instead of Roosevelt, and all through the act someone continued to shout at intervals, "Hurrah for Hanna!" The *Washington Star* reported that Hanna seemed to enjoy it immensely.

But this was the last dinner Hanna attended. About two weeks later he died.

• • •

After Roosevelt's election in 1904, there had been considerable complaint by some Democrats that he had stolen most of the planks of the Democratic platforms of 1896, 1900 and 1904.

At the Twentieth Anniversary Dinner on January 28, 1905, a little over two months after Theodore Roosevelt had been elected for a second term over Judge Alton B. Parker, the Club forecast directly that William Jennings Bryan would again be a candidate. This was done in a song:

> Parker butted in, he was licked like sin,
> Then a cry went up all o'er the land—
> "Bring back Billy Bryan, he's the only man
> That can lead the Democratic band."

It was suggested in the skit that President Roosevelt and Mr. Bryan, both of whom were present at the dinner, should put on a joint debate.

"What's the use," was the next line. "They are both on the same side."

At the conclusion of this song Bryan was introduced. He related how he had seen Roosevelt take plank after plank of his platform until he found very little left. He predicted that the remainder of the planks would be appropriated before very long, and Roosevelt, in his speech, made the retort that the good things in the Democratic platform were absolutely useless in Mr. Bryan's possession, "because he would never be in a position to put them in operation."[12]

"The most interesting sight of the dinner was the hobnobbing of the President and Mr. Bryan," wrote Charles Willis Thompson, "and if there were any present who had been under the impression that these two had been indulging in gallery plays at each other's expense, such persons must have been immensely enlightened. The words, manners and actions of the two men manifested the fact that they entertain a genuine esteem and admiration for each other; and here again was a result born of the freedom of the Gridiron, which could not have been so manifested anywhere else, because the freedom that was the cause of it would be lacking."[13]

A good example of the way the Gridiron Club lampooned Roosevelt occurred at that dinner in a song:

Don't you remember just three months ago
That we had an election day;
When Parker and Davis went down with a thud
Like a stone in the Chesapeake Bay.

Now let the men who are beating their wives
Beware of the flogging they'll get,
And warn all the railroads with ruinous rates,
To hustle in out of the wet;
Let England and Germany, and Russia and all,
Know that they can't monkey with us;
We'll have a strong navy to fight with, by gravy,
If we ever get into a fuss.

Chorus:
Roosevelt, Roosevelt, you are the man we praise,
Roosevelt, Roosevelt, strenuous all your days;
Roosevelt, Roosevelt, now let the eagle soar,
Over the land, with big stick in hand,
You are President four years more.

It was also at this dinner that there was the famous impeachment skit of Speaker Joseph G. Cannon. The club, some of its members forming themselves into a committee of the Senate, listened to the impeachment charges, among which were:

"That the said Joseph G. Cannon has, on numberless occasions, violated the cardinal principle of the American government that 'the majority must rule,' by making one and the Speaker a majority of 386.

"That notwithstanding the expressed views of many senators the said Joseph G. Cannon has openly insisted upon the floor of the House of Representatives that said House was a coordinate branch of the government, much to the mental anguish of many constructive statesmen, such as Henry Cabot Lodge, Philander C. Knox, Orville H. Platt, et al.

"That the said Joseph G. Cannon has not only refused, but persists in refusing, to take the oath of allegiance at the White House more than once a day.

"That the said Joseph G. Cannon has been guilty of pushing up too many chips on a 'bob-tail flush.' The ground of impeachment in this charge being that he was caught in the act.

"That the said Joseph G. Cannon rejected with scorn and much profanity the offer of the presidency of the Senate, thus thrusting upon the people Charles Warren Fairbanks."[14]

To an extent unlike other Presidents before or since, Theodore Roosevelt, at Gridiron dinners, often outlined policies and stated positions which later were made the basis of messages to Congress, public speeches, and State papers.

Although the income tax was not enacted until the administration of Woodrow Wilson, the first suggestion of it by a President was made by Roosevelt at a Gridiron dinner and later repeated publicly. His railroad rate regulation proposal in a message to Congress had been previously discussed at a Gridiron dinner, and frequently he indicated future executive actions in his speeches.

Such important information was conveyed in advance to the Gridiron Club and its guests at this Twentieth Anniversary Dinner, when Whitelaw Reid of the *New York Herald Tribune* was a speaker. Gridiron President Carson praised him as a distinguished newspaperman and a great friend of the Gridiron Club, and commented that there were current reports that he was to be honored by being appointed as ambassador to Great Britain.

"That is correct!" interjected President Roosevelt.[15]

Prior to the President's introduction, there had been a skit in which members of the club impersonating various prominent senators and other individuals each claimed to be "the original Roosevelt man." Major John M. Carson of the *New York Times* and *Philadelphia Public Ledger,* one of the founders of the Gridiron Club and one of its early presidents, had been given the honor of being reelected president for its Twentieth Anniversary. He rose to introduce the President. No doubt the guests had been edified by the skit, he said, but he had the pleasure of introducing to the company (and he turned and bowed to the President), "the original Roosevelt man."

The President received an ovation described as tremendous.

● ● ●

By 1906, President Roosevelt's deep commitment to the Panama Canal had become somewhat of a problem to him. Progress on the canal had been slow and had run into all sorts of red tape. So when President Roosevelt arrived at the assembly room for the January 27, 1906 dinner, he was met by the committee.

"At that moment a signal was given, a strain of martial music was heard and in from the corridors came a section of the Marine Band, the members dressed in the white duck uniform used in the tropics. . . . They marched through the room and into the banquet hall, playing the air 'When Johnny Comes Marching Home.' Behind them came twenty members of the club, attired in blouse and jumpers and carrying shovels and pickaxes. By prearrangement the guests fell in behind and the whole company marched into the banquet hall singing:

"We're going to dig the big canal,
      Hurrah! Hurrah!
We're going to dig the big canal,
      In Pan-a-ma!
In Panama we work tonight,
We'll do some diggin' before it's light,
And there'll be no more shenanigan when
      The dirt begins to fly.

"They say there's been extravagance
      In Pan-a-ma!
They say there's memories of France
      In Pan-a-ma!
But now that we are on the job
The bloomin' old plant will have to throb,
For there's goin' to be some diggin' done
      Here in Panama."[16]

The dinner played heavily on the canal. At one point, a member walked on the stage and distributed huge wads of stage money with great prodigality. He lighted a cigar with a $1,000 bill and scattered bits of money on the floor.

"What does this exhibition mean?" asked President Richard Lee Fern of the Gridiron Club.

"I am giving an imitation of the Panama Canal Committee," was the answer. Then there were other references to what was believed to be the prodigality of the project.

A Gridiron character standing in the plaza in Panama said, "So this is where they are going to dig that canal."

"Have they decided whether it will be lock or sea level?" someone asked.

"It is going to be unlock."

"Unlock what?"

"Unlock the treasury."

There was a scene representing this central plaza in Panama where the canal organization was shown at work. Nearly all of the people involved were chiefs or press agents, and no one was doing any constructive work. The chiefs were spending their time listening to every phony who came along with any crazy idea and giving him a hearing. Then a character impersonating President Roosevelt came on the stage, sent everyone else scurrying, and declared that he'd dig it himself if necessary. The chorus converged and to the tune of "Drill, Ye Tarriers, Drill" sang:

"For Congress," says he, "I don't give a fig;
There's a canal to be dug and I want ye to dig."
Then it's dig ye tarriers, dig;
   And it's work all day,
   In the good old way;
   With a pick and a shovel,
   And a horse and a dray;
Then it's dig, ye tarriers, dig.

In his speech that night the President referred directly to this skit, saying that he could appreciate the impatience of a great many people over the delays and that whatever might be the facts or how much the picture given here might be exaggerated, thereafter "as long as I am President the dirt will fly on the Canal Zone."

Shortly after this dinner, a prompt reorganization of the canal force was ordered by the President, and in effect, the idea was transmitted that Roosevelt expected to see some dirt fly. But even though he had made an inspection trip to Panama in his determination to get action, progress seemed slow to many people who did not understand the engineering difficulties. This caused the club to put on another Canal Zone skit in December, with a song to the tune of "He Walked Right In, Turned Around, and Walked Right Out Again."

> Our President to Panama sailed in a warship big,
> To see what progress had been made, and watch
>   the workmen dig.
> Shonts, Stevens, and the rest of them all got a
>   hustle on,
> But they dropped their shovels, spades and picks
>   the moment he was gone.
>
> He sailed right in and turned around,
>   then sailed right home again.
> His trip across the isthmus strip,
>   took him only hours ten.
> He asked his questions on the fly,
>   and scarcely stopped to say good-bye,
> He sailed right in and turned around,
>   then sailed right home again.

But the entire January dinner was not pitched toward the canal. President Roosevelt's love for big game hunting of both animals and corporations frequently came in for ribbing, as in this skit:

"What's this I hear about the President going to India to hunt big game?"

"Don't you believe it. He has good hunting for big game here for several years yet."

The tendency of those days to forecast on the part of the club was exemplified by a song "Billy Taft," to the tune of "Rosie Magee," the chorus of which was as follows:

> He is with us tonight and just spoiling
>   To prove his weight,
> The political pot's a-boiling
>   And the farmer pays the freight.
> Pushes railroads to lower the rate
>   Mixes senatorial stews
> Raises ruction in Ohio state
>   Waiting for Teddy's shoes.

But not always did the Gridiron Club lampoon Roosevelt. Sometimes they were almost idolatrous, as in their adaptation of George M. Cohan's song, "Yankee Doodle Dandy."

Mister Roosevelt, Mister Roosevelt,
>   You are ready to do and dare.
Mister Roosevelt, Mister Roosevelt,
>   You believe in a deal that's square.
So good luck to you and good health to you,
>   We all give you a welcome here,
With a loud huzza and a hip, hurrah,
>   Now all join in a rousing cheer.

• • •

It was at the January 1906 Gridiron Club dinner that President Roosevelt delivered his famous "muckraking" speech.

This was in the day of Lincoln Steffens, Ida M. Tarbell and others who were probably the first "investigative reporters." They had lashed out at the meat packers, the Standard Oil Company, and other, similar targets. It was their exposure of some of the conditions in meat packing plants that led to the passage of the Pure Food and Drug Act in 1906.

Most of the earlier attacks had been on people and corporations which were regarded as enemies of the President, but eventually articles appeared on such subjects as "The Treason of the Senate" and "The Shame of the States." In their attacks the muckrakers were frequently very unfair, and they made no attempt to give a balanced or objective picture of the situations about which they wrote.

This infuriated Roosevelt, and at this dinner he devoted his speech to an attack upon them. None of the Gridiron members were classified as muckrakers, and it is quite probable that most of them agreed with the President's viewpoint. After the dinner some of them urged the President to say publicly what he had said at the Gridiron dinner, and a little later, at the laying of the cornerstone of a new House office building, he delivered substantially the same speech publicly. Some of its memorable lines were:

"The men with the muckrakes are often indispensable to the well-being of society; but only if they know when to stop raking the muck, and to look upward to the celestial crown above them, to the crown of worthy endeavor. There are beautiful things above and round about them; and if they gradually grow to feel that the whole world is nothing but muck, their power of usefulness is gone."[17]

This speech led Charles Willis Thompson, in *Presidents I've Known*, to comment that the speech had "crushed the muckraking trade, necessitated a hasty revision of the year's editorial program in many a magazine office, brought about a saner and healthier mode of public thinking—and added a new word to the language."[18]

• • •

While not directly related to any man who ever attained Presidental office there was one notable speech at a Gridiron dinner on December 7, 1907, that might have put a man in the White House had he not died before his time came.

The record of it is found in a *New York Times* story written just shortly after the death of Governor John A. Johnson of Minnesota, who was the speaker involved. The *Times* was almost lyrical in its account of this speech.

"The Gridiron always introduces its speakers, not with a speech, but with a song, usually addressed to the prospective speaker, and gently derisive of him," said the *Times*. In this case they sang a song entitled "Poor John," the burden of which was that "poor John"—that is, Johnson—wanted the nomination, but couldn't have it, because Bryan wouldn't let him.

"The governor arose, and the first glimpse of him in the great dining hall of the Willard somehow dissipated every tenaciously held idea of the stolid Scandinavian."

" 'Poor John?' he said. 'I appreciate the honor; but don't you think, when you look back at 1896, at 1900, and at 1904, you ought to say 'Poor Bill'?' "

The writer of the *Times* article said that Governor Johnson "had the unusual experience of being the possessor of a Presidential boom that was started by a speech that was never reported."

"The effect of that unreported speech," he went on, "was greater than that of many more pretentious speeches that have been reported. It made Johnson the leading figure in the Democratic party, aside, of course, from Bryan, and led to a train of events that might have brought him to the White House in 1912—had he lived."

One of the remarks that the *Times* informant recalled was that in the midst of a keen, clever eulogy of Minnesota, Johnson enumerated the products in which she excelled every other state, and concluded, with a humorous glance at the somewhat forbidding Vice President Fairbanks:

" 'And her production of artificial ice exceeds even that of

Indiana,' a witticism which brought the Vice President, chuckling, to his feet, while everybody else roared and stamped. . . .

"As the governor finished and sat down there was such a scene as had seldom been witnessed in the Gridiron Club. Speaker Cannon began it. He leaped up from his place and darted around to Johnson's table to grasp his hand in both of his. Hardly a second behind him came Senator Foraker and then Secretary Root, and after them there piled up a mass of statesmen, business men, newspaper men, lawyers and judges, all excited and delighted, all falling over themselves to scramble for Johnson's hand."

Although the text of this speech was not quoted in any newspapers, various stories were printed, lauding Governor Johnson for his talk before the club.

"As a result of it," the *Times* said, "the anti-Bryan men fell in behind Johnson with real loyalty and enthusiasm where they had expected to give only a perfunctory support to the most 'available' men. . . . If there had been a real chance to nominate an anti-Bryan man [at the Denver Convention in 1908], it would have been Johnson. He was in training again for 1912, with an outlook for better luck, when he died."[19]

• • •

The January 1908 dinner, attended by President Roosevelt, was pitched heavily toward the forthcoming Presidential campaign. There had been intimations that President Roosevelt preferred his secretary of war, William Howard Taft, as his successor, but there were many other candidates eager to get the nomination. This inspired a *Gridiron Club Campaign Song Book*, containing sixteen songs to sixteen different potential candidates.

To symbolize the various Presidential booms, balloons were suspended from each table. During the evening a crystal ball was introduced on the stage and was consulted in a skit commenting on the potentialities of the various candidates. After satirizing many of the others, the oracle finally declared that William Jennings Bryan had declined the nomination, whereupon the crystal ball was acknowledged to be a fake and all of its previous disclosures were repudiated.

The postelection dinner, held on December 12, 1908, was notable in that the guests included not only the President and the Vice President but also President-elect Taft and Vice President-elect Sherman. The defeated candidate, William Jennings Bryan, declined the club's invitation. This was perhaps fortunate, since the Gridiron records show that when President-elect Taft was invited to the dinner he remarked that he was getting a little tired of being put up against Bryan, and that if that was to be the situation, he would rather not attend.

A feature of the dinner was a good-bye skit to President Roosevelt, who had announced that after his term ended in March he would take off for Africa on a wild game hunt.

"Good-bye, Roosevelt, good-bye, Roosevelt," sang the chorus,

> Good-bye, Roosevelt, you're going to leave us now.
> Merrily you'll roam away, roam away, roam away;
> Merrily you'll roam away, over to Africa.

Then followed an African hunt skit. The scene was a small tent before which stood a Zulu with a spear, an orderly in uniform and a man in khaki. Within the tent could be heard the clatter of typewriters and the sound of a man dictating (at a rate of a dollar a word, it was explained) messages which were addressed to *"Scribbler's Magazine"* and to the *"Lookout"* (the *Outlook* was a leading magazine at the time, to which Mr. Roosevelt was to become a contributor).

From time to time shouts would be heard, and the Zulu would dash into the jungle and return with some sort of an animal. These trophies were all photographed by the orderly and then two shots were fired.

"Bully, got them both," cried the hunter, and the Zulu rushed in with a toy donkey and a toy elephant. Then the hunter dictated:

"I have just secured two fine specimens. One is an Elephantus G-O-P-oribus. I have owned and managed the United States prototype for many years past. As a matter of scientific interest I note that the African Elephantus G-O-P-oribus has not the initials T. R. on its flank, indicating ownership, which I shall have corrected at once. The other specimen is the Assinorum democratimus, which we slaughter once every four years, regularly, in the United States."

In the ensuing celebration, the typewriters were smashed, and when the orderly announced that there were no more typewriters in Africa, the hunter declared it was time to go home.

The dinner closed with a farewell song to Roosevelt before introducing him for his speech.

If in a speech you want to preach
    To help the human race;
If on a tramp through waters damp,
    You lead a merry chase;
If far away you go to slay
    The lion in its lair;
What'er you do, we say to you
    You beat them everywhere.

There's not another Roosevelt in the world like you;
You paint the whole horizon a bright red hue;
There's not a stunt one thinks of you would not dare to do.
There's not another Roosevelt in the world like you.

• • •

The dinner on January 30, 1909, was principally a farewell to President Roosevelt and Vice President Fairbanks, since the chiefs of the new administration were not present. Each was presented with a large golden Gridiron.

In presenting Roosevelt his Gridiron, Henry Hall, president of the Gridiron Club, told him that it might be of use during a trip to Africa, to broil lion steaks or rhinoceros chops. He accepted it and announced that this would be his last Gridiron Dinner; "Washington is no place for ex-Presidents," he declared.

One of the features of this dinner was a group of "Gridiron proverbs," among them:

"The big stick is mightier than the Speaker's gavel."

"Be slow to anger, but don't let the other fellow hit first."

"A good name is better than riches, but good names for offending statesmen cannot always be mentioned in society."

A "political will" of President Roosevelt was read, in which the outgoing chief executive disposed of the White House, the Congress, "my policies," the big stick, his tennis cabinet, and other things, to various members of the incoming administration. The spirit of the dinner came out in a song which began, "Now listen and I will sing you a song of a man you know full well." The chorus revealed his name:

Roosevelt, Roosevelt!
    A very good Dutch name.
Roosevelt! Roosevelt!
    A name for the hall of fame.
Big stick! You know of it!
O, my! We say good-bye.
There never was a man named Roosevelt
That wasn't a damn fine President.

For this dinner there was published a *Gridiron Almanac for Statesmen, Journalists, Real Newspaper Men, Mollycoddles, Malefactors of Great Wealth, and General Family Use.* On one page it contained, under a spreading eagle, a list of Presidents of the United States, which consisted solely of the line "Theodore Roosevelt, etc."

It was at this dinner that President Roosevelt, whose capacity for enjoying a laugh at his own expense has been exceeded by few Presidents, became a bit annoyed. He had appointed a commission to go around the country and investigate and report upon the condition of the farmers and the people in general.

The scene for this skit was a country store with assorted farmers present, and the commission was depicted as city slickers, whose questions produced only scorn from the farmers.

Roosevelt, who believed in his commission, didn't mind the Gridiron Club laughing at him but didn't want his commission laughed at. However, his unhappiness about this was not so great as to offset the long period in which he had enjoyed Gridiron Club skits, even on those few occasions when they seemed to be directed straight at him.

After his death the Gridiron Club, on January 10, 1919, adopted a resolution saying that he filled "more pages in the annals of the Gridiron Club than any other half dozen men," that he was "acclaimed by the world as the greatest personality of his time," and that he was "particularly adapted to Gridiron exploitation."

"His resourcefulness, activity, exuberance and, more than all else, his good humor and appreciation, enabled the Gridiron Club to portray in wit and satire the chief events of seven crowded years. No other man in such exalted station ever lent himself so willingly and successfully to the needs of the club. It was a give-and-take game he played and he played it fair. He accepted with every evidence of pleasure the shafts and darts sent his way, and, like a true sportsman, replied in kind, blow for blow and jest for jest."[20]

V

William Howard Taft

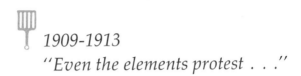

1909-1913
"Even the elements protest . . ."

While the emphasis in the January 30, 1909 dinner had been on the departing Roosevelt, there were some references to the incoming President Taft.

Mention has already been made of the *Gridiron Almanac* produced at that dinner. It was a curious calendar, consisting of the full months of January and February and only four days in March (inaugurations were then held on March 4). For the remainder of the month of March there was a statement, "After this there is no telling what will happen."

But for March 3, in what was perhaps the Gridiron Club's most accurate prediction in its history, the announcement read:

"Blizzard, TR preparing to leave the White House."

And for March 4:

"Taft day—Rain, sleet, snow, high winds, thunder and lightning."

Precisely this occurred.

On the night before, Roosevelt had invited the Tafts to spend the night with him at the White House. It was the night of the worst blizzard Washington had ever had. The winds were high and more than a foot of snow was dropped on the entire city, completely disrupting all transportation and inauguration plans. As Roosevelt and Taft were having breakfast in the White House, Taft looked out the window and commented, in reference to his succession to the Presidency, "Even the elements protest."[1]

Directed primarily at the convention which nominated him, the souvenir at the January dinner had been a bronze steam roller with the name Taft printed on the front and the Gridiron emblem on the rear. Encased in boxes, this souvenir, which was in the form of a paperweight, was at each plate. A song referred to it.

> Taft! Taft! Taft!
> Steam roller! Steam roller!
> Who-oo-oo-oo!

Taft was an enthusiastic golfer and immediately after his election relaxed for a few days playing golf. He had, at that early date, steadfastly refused to give any indication who he intended to invite into his cabinet.

The incoming President was introduced for his speech by a golfing skit, centered on a diminutive boy who carried a bag of golf clubs.

"At great trouble and expense," explained a member, "the Gridiron Club has brought from Hot Springs that caddie who accompanied Mr. Taft around the links. The caddie knows more administration secrets than anyone else on earth."

To find out who the new President's cabinet appointees would be, a song was sung to the caddie:

> When you were out walking, with Mister Taft talking,
>   Did he mention Will Loeb's name to you?
> Did he tell you some stories of Hitchcock and Vorys,
>   Or intimate Garfield would do?
> Did he chuckle with you as that broth of a boy,
>   Dickie Oulahan, came to his mind?
> Did he say there's a ban on our Uncle Joe Cannon
>   And a much better Speaker he'd find?

> Yip! my caddie, I say, I say;
> Yip! my caddie, I say!
> Who will be in the cabinet?
> Taft can tell, but he will not—just yet.
> Yip! my caddie, I say, I say;
> We're all of us golfers today;
> If we want to belong, we must sing him this song—
> Yip! my caddie! Hooray!

Taft had a hard time during his administration. He was

really much more inclined by nature to the judicial role, which he later resumed years after the Presidency when he became chief justice, than he was for the rough and tumble of politics. After a career which was chiefly judicial, he had resigned from the Sixth Circuit Court of Appeals to accept an appointment from President Roosevelt as governor of the Philippines.

It was, indirectly, the job he did there that made him President of the United States, for his administration was one of the best examples of colonial government in history. In 1904, when Elihu Root stepped out as secretary of war, Theodore Roosevelt appointed the highly popular Taft to fill the vacancy. After Roosevelt declined to seek reelection in 1908, he let it be known that Taft was his choice to succeed him. As secretary of war, Taft was nominated on the first ballot and easily defeated William Jennings Bryan's third attempt at the Presidency.

Taft was completely lacking in political ingenuity and gimmickry.

After he became President, he refused to support the liberals in their attempts to curb the powers of Speaker "Uncle Joe" Cannon. He got into a controversy with Gifford Pinchot, then chief forester in the Department of the Interior, and eventually fired him. He believed in the protective tariff law but thought some tariffs were too high. He asked Congress to pass a tariff reduction law, but when it arrived at his desk it had more increases than decreases. He signed it nevertheless.

All these things lost him the support of liberals, and when in 1910 Theodore Roosevelt returned from a prolonged African hunting trip, he began making speeches around the country, indicating that he was a candidate for renomination. Every school boy who ever had a course in American history knows how Roosevelt bolted the Republicans, organized the Progressive "Bull Moose" party, and ran as the third-party candidate in 1912, making the defeat of Taft and the election of Woodrow Wilson inevitable.

• • •

The first dinner at which Taft was present as President occurred on April 17, 1909, and the jolly chief executive was reported in the papers to have greatly enjoyed a song obviously referring to his extensive girth and a trip he had made to Georgia—a parody on "Marching Through Georgia."

Sound the good old dinner horn, we'll sing another song,
About the trip that Taft once made when with digestion strong,

He ate his share of everything that they would bring along,
As he went eating through Georgia.
We tackled the opposum that they took such care to bake,
We ate canned watermelon and a dish they called hoe cake,
We didn't even draw the line at alligator steak,
As we went eating through Georgia.

Hurrah, hurrah, we sound the jubilee;
Hurrah, hurrah, 'twas something fine to see,
We put away three meals a day,
And sometimes three times three,
As we went eating through Georgia.

Another song, symbolizing the kindlier attitude of the new administration, was entitled "Please Leave the Dear Old Trusts Alone; They're Seeing Things at Night."

Even this early in the Taft administration, premonitions appeared in the Gridiron skits of the change that would lead former President Roosevelt to run again in 1912 and split the Republican party. In this song the trusts informed Attorney General George Wickersham that they were tired and sleepy too, and appealed to him to put them in their little beds.

Come, Georgie, come,
Bid us good-night,
    And do not fill our hearts with dread.
We're tired now, and sleepy, too;
    Come put us in our little bed.

The *Boston Transcript* the morning after the dinner alluded to the fact that the Taft family always had a cow near at hand. "They kept," said the *Transcript*, "a specially imported cow on the grounds of the Malacanan Palace in Manila, where animals of that species are a great rarity. They now have on the White House grounds, where she may be seen by all beholders, a cow which furnishes at least a part of the domestic supply of milk for the White House—just a little personal peculiarity of the Tafts. . . . "

This cow inspired a skit in which a very clever imitation of a cow was introduced. She was led by a member of the club, and behind her came a dainty milkmaid in sun bonnet, carrying her milking stool and pail. Scott C. Bone, vice president of the club, who presided at this dinner, wanted to know what all this meant.

The keeper of the cow explained that there had been a lot of loose talk about the possum being the animal emblem of this administration, as the teddy bear had been of President

Roosevelt's. But that was all nonsense, he said. The emblem of this administration is the cow, and this is it.

"What are you going to do with her?" asked the vice president.

"Milk her. That is what all the politicians are trying to do to her owner," answered the keeper.

The spirit of the dinner was perhaps best expressed in a Gilbert and Sullivan parody from *The Mikado*, sung repeatedly throughout the evening.

> When a man ascends the ladder of distinction,
> And becomes a power throughout his native land,
> Oft his friends become a matter for extinction,
> And he scans them with an air intensely bland;
> Now the eyes of all are fixed upon a figure
> Who will guide the ship of state through storm and calm
> And we're wondering if friendship's days are over—
> Days which held a simple and delightful charm.
> Now that Taft is at the top,
> Must familiar days be dropped?
>
> Can't we call him Bill now that he's President?
> Can't we call him Bill now any more?
> As we see him riding by with his head held up so high,
> Can't we greet him as in days of yore?
> Can't we stroke his hand and say "Hello, Bill?"
> Will he turn us down and pass us o'er?
> Is he really quite intent on the "Mister President?"
> Tell us, can't we call him Bill any more?

And every time the song was sung, President Taft waved his hand and said, "Yes, yes."

The *Washington Star* the next morning reported his reactions.

"They had President Taft and the new cabinet on the grill last night at the annual spring dinner of the Gridiron Club, held at the New Willard Hotel. Mr. Taft has frequently taken a turn on the spit in his previous varied official capacities, but this was his first experience as a Presidential victim. He used to think it was lots of fun to see President Roosevelt and President McKinley over the coals, and last night he had a taste himself.

"Apparently he liked it, for the smile never came off once."

• • •

To many people, President Taft, calm and unspectacular, was quite a relief from the flamboyant and disturbing Roosevelt.

This was recognized by the Gridiron Club at its December 1909 dinner.

> Now Roosevelt once was President.
>   O yes, he was;
> But Mister Taft now runs the job,
>   O yes, he does;
> Roosevelt now has gone a-hunting,
>   Shooting with his might and main;
> So the politicians warble
>   This musical refrain:
>
> We love, we love, we love Roosevelt,
>   But oh you Taft!
> He's gone away to Af-ri-ca,
>   But oh you Taft.
> He said he would come back again,
>   And thereupon we laughed;
> We love, we love, we love Roosevelt,
>   But oh you Taft."

By December 1909 considerable effort was rising among the Republicans in the House to curtail the powers of Speaker Uncle Joe Cannon. In a skit in which a medium named Madam Paladino was consulted, "Uncle Joe" asked her, "What shall I say when the insurgents ask me to resign?"

Madam Paladino was much upset and refused to write an answer. Her manager exclaimed, "Madam Paladino is a lady and will not take down such shocking language as is suggested by your query!"

• • •

The tariff was still a hot issue during President Taft's administration, and at the February 1910 dinner, with a view that was perhaps not entirely unbiased, the Gridiron Club presented a skit in which the various trusts, lumber, whiskey, beef, coal, and tobacco, were depicted by gorgeous young ladies—at least as gorgeous as Gridiron men could portray. A bunch of gaunt consumers, proclaiming a cannibalistic purpose, attacked them. But they were frustrated by a portly dame labeled "Mrs. Tariff," who claimed that all these darling beauties were her own progeny and dared the ultimate consumers to touch a hair of their heads. She sang:

> I'm as happy as can be
> With my children at my knee,
> For I take care of them and they take care of me.

When others disagree,
There's peace and harmony
In the bosom of my family,
My family.

This was also the dinner at which there was a skit built around "The Back from Elba Club." To the music of "The Marseillaise," dressed in long capes, and wearing Napoleon hats with the emblem "TR" on the front, they marched onto the well in front of the stage.

The Grand Marshal, carrying a big stick, called the roll of members, among them Grand Marshal Henry Cabot Lodge, Field Marshal Gifford Pinchot, Major Nicholas Longworth, and Drummer Boy Alfred J. Beveridge.

The last name on the roll call was the "Only One," and the entire party answered, "Absent in Africa." The chorus then broke into a song.

When Teddy comes marching home again,
     hurrah, hurrah,
We'll give him a hearty welcome then,
     hurrah, hurrah!
The club will cheer, the boys will shout,
The malefactors will all go out
And we'll all get jobs when Teddy comes
     marching home.

The dissatisfaction of the Republican liberals with the new Taft administration was further emphasized in a song, to the tune of "I Wonder Who's Kissing Her Now," which was somewhat inverted in the parody:

In an African jungle a bold hunter sat
     On the skin of a slaughtered baboon;
Where the dig-dig and bongo were teasing the cat
     And the ostrich was singing a tune.
Said he: "Mollycoddles, so harmless and tame—
     These are all that I find as I roam;
It is really a shame, and I long for big game,
     The kind I am used to at home."

I wonder who's cussing them now;
I wonder who's busting the trusts;
Wonder whose feelings are deeply stirred
By the short and ugly word.
I wonder who's wielding the stick;

I wonder if Taft's learned the trick?
Malefactors of wealth who do business by stealth—
I wonder who's cussing them now.

Even the initiation skit for new members was utilized to get across a merry gag. George Edmund Miller, Washington correspondent of the *Detroit News* and one of the initiates, was being questioned. He said he supported James Beauchamp ("Champ") Clark for the Speakership but he was perfectly satisfied with Speaker Cannon, and then he admitted that while he had prayed for long life for Bryan, he did so because he wanted a Republican always in the White House.

The growing estrangement between Theodore Roosevelt and President Taft was the subject of a series of letters supposed to have passed between them, which were printed on an elaborate menu card. The first letters were signed "Bill" and "Theodore" and were quite cordial. Later ones became more formal, and finally they were signing their names "T. Roosevelt" and "W. H. Taft." Taft's last letter was returned to him from the post office at the Roosevelt home at Oyster Bay, marked "Not called for."

• • •

The congressional elections of 1910 resulted in the loss of the House of Representatives by the Republicans and, in general, defeats around the country.

The Clifford K. Berryman cartoon of acts in the December dinner published the next day in the *Washington Star,* effectively dramatized the triumphant arrival of Champ Clark, the new Speaker-to-be. His inaugural procession was made up of a vanquished and dispirited group, but the cartoon showed Clark in a Roman chariot, cracking the whip over the two donkeys which pulled it. Uncle Joe Cannon, Representative Sereno E. Payne (author of the Payne-Aldrich Tariff Act), and Representative John Dalzell of Pennsylvania (a power in tariff legislation) were chained behind the chariot. As it entered the hall, Cannon was shouting at Clark, "Dictator! Czar!" When they reached the center of the well, Clark, assuming an oratorical pose, said, "I am the Democratic resurrection. This is the greatest time since Andy Jackson climbed over the cotton bales into the White House."

Cannon asked plaintively, "What are you going to do with me?" And Clark replied,"I have something good for you—the chairmanship on Disposition of Useless Papers. That's the place for the Aldrich-Payne-Smoot tariff law."

The Mikado was used as the vehicle for the national skit of the evening, preceding the introduction of President Taft. Characters included Nanki Jo Cannon, Poo Bah Senator Cummins, Pish Tush Champ Clark, and Nicholas Ko Ko Longworth, the public executioner who sang a song declaring that he "had made a little list."

On this list was Uncle Joe Cannon, Speaker of the House, who was under heavy attack by liberals in the Republican party led by Representative George W. Norris (later a senator), and who was due to be deposed in March because of the change in majority in the House. His "Nanki Jo" song went:

> A wandering speaker I, a champion stand patter
> With parliamentary chatter
> In good old days gone by—
> But I've struck out and they've put up another batter
> My hopes they seek to shatter
> And all in vain I try
> To catch the speaker's eye.

Chorus: Speaker's eye.

As the executioner was about to perform his act on Uncle Joe, a portly Mikado, thinly disguised as the President, intervened and said, "Gentlemen, let us not behead this great and popular statesman. I have in mind a more cruel and lingering fate for him. He shall stay in Congress as a helpless minority and be chained to his seat during the debate on rules."

At the conclusion of the skit President Taft spoke.

He reminisced about his earlier career when he was a judge in Ohio and the then Governor Foraker and Judson Harmon were trying to have his term extended.

"How times change!" said Taft to the merriment of the crowd.[2] For at the time of this dinner, the retired Foraker was opposing Taft, and Harmon was a candidate for the Presidential nomination in 1912.

• • •

President Taft attended the February 18, 1911 dinner, as he had all dinners of the Gridiron Club during his Presidency. This dinner was presided over by Richard V. Oulahan of the *New York Times.*

The main skit relating to Taft was one called "The Tariff Whoop." It pictured the plight of a Kansas member of Congress who had been shrieking for tariff reduction.

Kicked up such a terrible din,
    That President Taft suggestively laughed,
To cut rates he started right in.
    He framed a Canadian treaty,
Put farm produce on the free list,
    But the Kansas insurgent held views so divergent,
And he begged his colleagues to desist.

Chorus:

Great guns,
Holy smoke,
Can't Bill Taft take a joke?

The main thrust of the dinner, however, was focused on secondary figures in the administration and on Congress, where President Taft now faced a Democratic House, to be presided over, beginning a few days later, by Champ Clark of Missouri.

One of the ironies of Champ Clark's accession to the Speakership was that he, as a leader of the Democrats, had cooperated with the insurgent Republicans in the House fight against "Cannonism." This had resulted in removing much of the power of the Speaker and turning a great deal of it over to the chairman of the Ways and Means Committee, who, in the new Congress, was Oscar W. Underwood.

Clark was brought on the stage with hands and feet tied with ropes. "I am Exhibit A," he said.

"Exhibit A of what?"

"Exhibit A of what a rules fight in one Congress can do to a perfectly good Speaker in the next."[3]

Half a dozen newly elected senators were guests of the club. They were assembled on stage and addressed by a club member as follows:

"In accordance with a benevolent custom, the Gridiron Club brings new senators around its festal board to be instructed as to their duties out of the boundless store of our knowledge of all public affairs.

"You are, or will soon become, members of that great and garrulous body, the United States Senate. Of course, you know that it is great, and you will soon know that it is garrulous. It is the national guardian of free and continuous speech. Lungs and language are the requisites to fame in the Senate. There may be limits to the domain of human thought, but so long as you can use the same words in so many different combinations to say the same thing, there are no limits to language.

"The Senate is a great body, and the best thing about it is that no state can have more than two senators. Some think we would be better off with none at all, but they are like Prohibitionists, who confuse and confound temperance with total abstinence. There seem to be none here. Representatives may increase and multiply themselves until there is standing room only in the House; but thank heaven, there must be new states before we can have more senators."

The admonition to the new senators was closed with this statement:

"The Senate is a great body. It is not decadent. It has numbered great men on its rolls; it numbers them now, it will continue to number them. The American people are not lacking in patriotism; they are not degenerate. They will never willfully elect weak or corrupt men to the Senate. Knowing that, we may roast you a little, but in our hearts we have faith in you, we trust you, and we bid you godspeed in the discharge of your onerous duties."

Considering that this was only three years before the beginning of World War I, it was interesting that the German ambassador was one of the guests, and to him, before his speech, was sung a parody of the "Schnitzelbaum" song. A large blackboard was on stage and the leader of the "Sängerbund," with a long pointer, indicated to the chorus, dressed in little German caps and wearing German wigs, various pictures which were lowered. They included President Taft, Kaiser Wilhelm, a suffragette, a steam roller, and a picture of former President Roosevelt labeled "Schnickle Fritz."

As evidence of the good relations that existed between the Gridiron Club and President Taft, on the twenty-fifth wedding anniversary of the President and Mrs. Taft the club sent them a handsome silver water pitcher and tray. Promptly thereafter, Gridiron president Richard V. Oulahan received the following letter from President Taft:

> My dear Mr. Oulahan:
> I write in behalf of Mrs. Taft and myself to express our very deep and heartfelt appreciation of the generous courtesy of the Gridiron Club in sending us the beautiful silver pitcher and platter. As long as I have posterity it will be handed down as an evidence of the cordial relations which I am proud to have maintained with a band of newspaper men, with whom I have agreed and disagreed as occasion has required but with

whom I have always been on terms of the pleasantest friendship and to whom I have been indebted for much gracious
hospitality.

Sincerely yours,

/s/ William H. Taft[4]

• • •

At the December 1911 dinner, the growth of the Progressives
was the major subject. The vehicle was a parody of *Faust*, in
which the principal characters were Progressive Faust (tenor
trustbusto), Miss Marguerite Democracy (collarandelbow so-
prano), and Stand-Pat Mephisto (bass campaignfundo).

Mephisto sang:

I'll gather you *all* in ere I have done;
For every party as it starts in life
Is led by a reformer, brave in strife;
And when his cause is won, he does his best
To bravely hold it safe 'gainst every test,
Defending each assault with all his powers.
We're all stand-patters—after we get ours.

In another skit, a song to the tune of "Alexander's Ragtime
Band" trumpeted the rise of LaFollette and his Progressives.

Come on along, Come on along,
Hear La Follette's own brass band;
Come on along, Come on along,
It's the loudest in the land;
It can make a bigger noise than you ever heard before,
Sounds like the boom of a Presidential war,
That's just the busy little band,
Yes it am.

They also had some fun with the Democratic perennial William Jennings Bryan. At one point it was announced by Gridiron
Vice President Louis Garthe, that William J. Bryan was waiting
outside. This caused great surprise because his name was not on
the dinner list and he was supposed to be outside the United
States at that time. He was brought in, however, and immediately started making a speech in his familiar oratorical style.

Turning to politics, he apologized for omitting Judson Harmon from his list of Presidential possibilities in 1912. "Harmon is
my man," he said. Next he had some kind words for Champ
Clark, then "the intrepid young statesman, Oscar Underwood,"
and finally he shocked his fellow Democrats by declaring for
William H. Taft.

"My admiration is for Harmon, my friendship is for Clark, my sympathy is for Underwood, but my vote will be for William Howard Taft," he said.

By this time the people were suspecting a hoax, and somebody questioned his identity. Then it was revealed that the man who made the speech was not Bryan at all, but an actor named Charles B. Hanford who resembled him strongly.

"Sir, are you a great actor?" asked the vice president of the Gridiron Club.

"I am," responded Hanford, "but so is William Jennings Bryan."[5]

At this dinner the Gridiron Club put out an eighty-page book, *Mother Goose in Gridiron Rhyme,* with cartoons by Clifford K. Berryman.

A sample:

Beat 'em up, beat 'em up, progressive man,
So we will, Bobby, as fast as we can;
We'll beat 'em and kick 'em and mark 'em N.G.,
Yours truly, T.R., Jimmy G. and Giff P.

And just to show that the high cost of living is nothing new as a political issue, here are a few verses on Old Mother Hubbard:

She went to the baker's
    To buy them some bread,
But wheat had gone up,
    Reciprocity was dead.

She went to the ale-house
    To buy them some beer,
But the cost of the drink
    Took away all the cheer.

The Dame made a curtsey,
    The Trusts made a bow;
The Dame said, "Your servant."
    The Trusts said "Kow-tow."

• • •

Since the progressive threat in the Republican party was growing, the principal attention of the February 1912 dinner was again directed toward this development.

"In behalf of W. J. Bryan," declaimed a member, "I demand to know what are the qualifications of your candidate."

"That he already has the job," was the terse reply.

The Progressives were represented by Robin Hood and a group of outlaws out among the tall trees (to which unsuccessful candidates would run in the end.) The characters included Will Scarlett Lafollowit, Friar Pinshow, representing Gifford Pinchot, the conservationist, and various other members of the LaFollette group.

Robin Hood sang a parody of an "Outlaw Chorus":

Cheerily, cheerily, all the day,
Merrily, merrily, on our way.
We are outlaws hearty,
Out among the trees,
Cut loose from our party,
Going as we please.

The three-cornered 1912 fight for the Presidency was forecast when LaFollowit sang, to the tune of "The Old Crossbow":

A statesman who dwelt on the Outlook's edge
    Was deft with his old big stick.
A dove of peace lit on his window ledge;
    He hit it an awful lick.
He stopped awhile, and to sigh began.
    They heard him both near and far:
"If you wait for the office to seek the man,
    The office says, 'Stay where you are.'"

At another point in the dialogue, a member asked, "Is Colonel Roosevelt saying anything about his candidacy?"

"Not more than a column a day."

Another feature of the dinner was a Presidential horserace, on which many bets were made. As the race was described by a man with binoculars: Champ Clark got off in the lead with Woodrow Wilson on the rail, William Jennings Bryan coming from behind, and Oscar W. Underwood swinging wide at the turn.

At the quarter, Woodrow Wilson was setting the pace and William Jennings Bryan was "plowing ahead."

At the half, Woodrow Wilson was leading by a neck over Champ Clark, and at the three-quarters, Champ was challenging Woodrow Wilson, while all jockeys began to whip their horses.

But the club did not forecast the victor. Just before the race ended, the betting ring was raided and everyone dispersed.

Later during the dinner, an impersonator of Theodore

Roosevelt entered on horseback, wearing a khaki uniform and the campaign hat of the Rough Riders. He reined up at the foot of the well facing the President.

"If a Progressive President is to be inaugurated, I am here," he said. Asked if he was a Progressive, he replied: "I am the original 'P.P'—Pinchot Progressive. These others are mere pikers."

"But you have said that you are not a candidate?"

"Maybe so, maybe so. But I have always found it convenient to have a string to every declaration."

At this point Bryan came in.

"I protest against that man," he said. "He stole all the planks in my platform."

"TR": That is real progress. Progressives take anything they can find. All we want is something to divert the people until we get the jobs.

• • •

The next dinner was held on December 7, 1912 a month after the election in which Taft had carried only Utah and Vermont, Roosevelt had carried states giving him eighty-eight electoral votes, and Woodrow Wilson had won because of the split in the Republican party, although he received a minority of the votes cast.

President Taft was present, but President-elect Woodrow Wilson, who was vacationing in Bermuda, was not, nor was Theodore Roosevelt.

Early in the dinner a Mexican in toreador costume announced that bull fights had become much too dull across the border and he was present to ask permission to take an American bull moose to Mexico. Gridiron president Louis Garthe leaned over, whispered to President Taft and then announced "I am assured by the President of the United States that you can have him, and welcome!"

A group of Mexicans came on the stage, headed by "Carmen" herself in swirling skirts. Another member of the cast wearing big bull moose antlers appeared, and Carmen called upon her matadors to do battle with this new beast. Don Champ Clarkio, in his brightest matador regalia, sang:

I know the way to get that Moose so grim,
Why don't they turn Bill Bryan loose on him?
If they did that I'd have a good excuse
For saying, "Go it Bill, go it Bull Moose!"

There was a call for "Don Taftio, the worthiest Matador of all." The cast was told that he was a good fighter and Carmen sang:

> Too good for any rough and tumble fray;
> Frank and forbearing and inclined to show
> A liberal mind to an ungenerous foe.

An impersonator of the chairman of the Republican National Committee said that he was at a disadvantage, because "Don Taftio makes me be too damn polite," and one of the toreadors shouted to everyone to "make way for Don Woodrow Wilson," who entered to strains of "The Toreador Song."

> Give three cheers for me,
> Give three times three,
> Senors, senors, you are all men of war.
> Bull Moose is feeling prime,
> Having a corking time
> In a fight, in a fight he takes great delight!
> Forth I will go, my skill to show;
> I'll bowl him over with classic lore;
> Lines of Euripides, phrases of Sophocles,
> Plato and Plutarch at him I'll bellow and roar!
> Oratory in all its glory, I'll hurl at him with might and main;
> He'll get no chance to tell the story;
> I will never let him explain.
> Come on, make ready,
> Toreador make ready;
> Now popular applause awaits thee
> Like a fascinating lady;
> Fame now awaits on thee.

Whereupon Don Woodrow turned upon the bull moose and stabbed him. The bull moose, falling, exclaimed, "He stabbed me with a Latin conjugation."

Don Woodrow then seized Carmen and led the party off the stage.

It was clear at this dinner that the sympathies of the club ran heavily with Taft. Although there was much satire of the President during his term, Taft was a popular fellow who never let it bother him, who laughed just as loudly at the skits directed at him as he did at those directed at his opponents, and who always made a witty speech at the end of the dinner. In a wave of nostalgic love and admiration, the club closed its show that night with a parody on "Moonlight Bay."

When the moonbeams shine
    On the O-hi-o
And electric lights on Vine Street
    Are all aglow;
Or if over the Rhine
    You should chance to be,
Won't you think of us in Washington, D.C.

We have met
    Where the broad Potomac flows.
With regret
    We will lose the friend that goes
When to Fountain Square you wander,
Won't you sometimes pause and ponder
On the friends so far off yonder,
    From the O-hi-o.

• • •

The dinner on February 1, 1913 was pitched almost entirely to the new administration, but at the end the club made its final farewell to Taft as President. To introduce Taft for his last speech as President, Gridiron President Rudolph Kauffmann rose and announced that the only formal toast of the club is the one to the President of the United States. At that point, before Taft was presented, Kauffmann recalled that Taft had attended every dinner of the Gridiron Club since 1905, and that although he was about to leave the Presidency, he would always be invited to any future Gridiron dinners. Kauffmann then presented him with a large golden Gridiron, inscribed "To William Howard Taft, President of the United States, as a token of friendship from the Gridiron Club of Washington, February 1, 1913."

Taft was perhaps the greatest devotee of the Gridiron Club among all Presidents. He attended his first dinner in February 1891, when he was solicitor general, and eighteen years before he became President. His Gridiron speeches were praised on many occasions by people who heard them: praised for their wit, for their clever response to skits, and for their comments about people on the political scene.

If he ever resented anything in the skits, he was careful not to show it, even in those cases where fun was poked at his overweight. For example, at the last dinner he attended as President, one of the initiates was introduced as "Mr. William of Cincinnati, who tips the scales at 360 pounds."

"Gracious, I protest against that," said J. Harry Cunningham, later to be secretary of the club for many years. "He'll break the back of the goat."

"Oh, no, he won't," was the reply. "He'll be careful. Ever since last November he's felt a great deal of sympathy for a goat."

But perhaps Taft did not always enjoy the dinners quite as much as, in his natural joviality and graciousness, he seemed to, for a year later he wrote of them:

> "They furnished a great deal of fun, some of it bright and excruciating and all of it of a popular flavor because it was at the expense of those of the guests who were in the public eye. After some training both as secretary of war and as President I was able to smile broadly at a caustic joke at my expense and seem to enjoy it with the consolatory thought that every other guest of any prominence had to suffer the same penalty for an evening's pleasure.
>
> "The surprise and embarrassment of foreign ambassadors at their first Gridiron dinner and their subsequent whole hearted appreciation of the spirit of these occasions, showed how unique a feature they were of Washington political life."[6]

However, in general, there was always a cordiality between Taft and newspapermen, whom he also delighted in ribbing. He once responded to a letter he received expressing concern over a newspaper story:

"Don't worry over what the newspapers say. I don't. Why should anyone else? I told the truth to the newspaper correspondents—but when you tell the truth to them they are at sea."[7]

Numerous other Presidents would have fared better at the hands of the members of the press, if they had been able to meet them with the equanimity and joviality of William Howard Taft.

VI

Woodrow Wilson

1913-1921
A vision of "the blue heaven,
signs of spring,
and the movement of free
clouds. . . ."

With the accession to the Presidency of Woodrow Wilson on March 4, 1913, vast changes began to occur in Washington among the newspapermen, in the Gridiron Club, and in the nation.

Eleven days after his inauguration, President Wilson held the first regular Presidential press conference.

Arthur Krock, later to become perhaps the most prestigious Washington correspondent of all time, was elected to the Gridiron Club, as he explained jocularly in a speech at a Gridiron dinner nearly forty years later, "to get somebody in it who was friendly to the new administration."

Far-reaching legislation spewed forth very much the same as it did during the first hundred days of the Franklin D. Roosevelt administration, but not as fast. In the first year the Federal Reserve System was established, and ratification of the constitutional amendment instituting the personal income tax was completed. In the second year the Clayton Antitrust Act was passed, and the Federal Trade Commission was created.

At the time, few people realized what vast changes in American society these actions, together with the forthcoming World War, would foment.

America was then a relatively calm and quiet country. When Woodrow Wilson took the oath of office, only about one million automobiles existed in the entire country. Skyscrapers were just beginning to rise in American cities; the Empire State Building would not be built for another twenty years. Prohibition and F. Scott Fitzgerald's jazz age were still several years in the future. Political campaigns were conducted in a relatively gentlemanlike manner, and in spite of the fact that he received only a minority of the popular vote, Woodrow Wilson was accepted and generally respected by the country.

• • •

President-elect Wilson did not attend the February 1, 1913 dinner which preceded his inauguration, but he was portrayed on the stage (a practice which has since been discontinued by the Gridiron Club so far as Presidents are concerned) holding his first cabinet meeting. Some of the typical gags ran as follows:

Wilson: Mr. Secretary of the Treasury, do you believe in the reform of the currency laws?
Secretary: No, not so much as in the currency of the reform laws.
Wilson: Precisely what do you mean by reform laws?
Secretary: Laws that make people do what I want them to do.

Wilson: Greetings, my Attorney General.
Attorney General: You mistake my title. I'm not the attorney general. I'm the residuary legatee.
Wilson: Residuary legatee?
Attorney General: Yes; Wickersham left me 400 uncompleted trust prosecutions. . .

Wilson: What is your trust policy?
Attroney General: To bust those we can't trust and trust those we can't bust.

Wilson: Under recent court decisions what happens when a trust is reorganized?
Attorney General: The small stockholders lose theirs quicker.

At the conclusion of the skit, each cabinet member was invited by the President-elect to give him a memorandum on what policies he should enunciate in his inaugural address. After filing by and presenting their memos, they went offstage.

Wilson: (Stands alone, looking them over for a moment, and concludes the act) This is odd. Each one of these memorandums makes the same suggestion. They all say: The thing to bear down on hard is one four-year term for the President of the United States.

To inaugurate Rudolph Kauffmann as president of the club and to satirize the coming inauguration of President-elect Wilson, the club put on an inaugural parade headed by a band. There were capped and gowned professors, Tammany rooters, the "Wanta-eata-pie" fraternity, and a group of suffragettes.

Woman suffrage was rising strongly as an issue in 1913, and the Gridiron Club staged a suffragette rally with a song that sounds similar to some of the cries heard today.

> We want pants, we want pants,
> So do our sister, cousins, aunts.
> Equal rights we want with man,
> Keep them from us if you can.
>   *Suffrage!*

In the 1912 campaign there had been much talk of reform by President-elect Wilson and his supporters. At one point in the dinner, a chorus of the disappointed converted the song about wanting a girl just like the girl who married dear old Dad into:

> I want a gang just like the gang
>   We had in days gone by.
> They never heard
> Folks who said a word
>   Of this uplift so high.
> We'd vote our heelers and repeat the list;
> For an argument you used your fist.
> I want a gang just like the gang
> We had in days gone by.

• • •

President Wilson and all his cabinet attended the first dinner after he had been inaugurated, which was held on April 12. The major skit at this dinner was an old-time melodrama, set in a lighthouse whose keeper was William Jennings Bryan, the new secretary of state.

It was a dark and snowy night, and there was a ship, the *T. Jefferson Platform,* offshore needing guidance. William G. McAdoo, Wilson's son-in-law-to-be, was a Coastguardsman, and many of the people in the new majority, such as Champ Clark, Oscar Underwood, and others constituted the group of individuals concerned for the safety of the ship.

The villain, of course, was a man named for two famous high tariff senators of the day—Boies Penrose and Reed Smoot. Penrose Smoot, King of the Wreckers, with long mustachios, a big black hat, and a dangerous and stealthy manner was this big desperado.

The ingenue, Miss Tariff of course, came on the scene, and Smoot promised her everything: "I'll dress you like Sheba's queen."

But Miss Tariff rebuffed him, as amid sounds of wind and thunder offstage, Oscar Underwood rescued her and Smoot slunk off.

"Bryan" manipulated the light and attempted to guide the ship past Dissension Rock. McAdoo asked him what the *T. Jefferson Platform* had aboard and a voice answered, "Fifteen thousand officeseekers."

"What shall we do?" asked many in unison.

And Bryan stepped to the front of the stage, extended his hands hopelessly and appealed directly to President Wilson across the room, "Mr. President, what shall we do?"

Whereupon Rudolph Kauffmann bent over as if to consult President Wilson at his side and answered, "President Wilson says take the ship to sea again and scuttle her."

The dinner closed with an elaborate Independence Bell, which was lowered down over the head of President Wilson while the chorus sang, to the music from the operetta *Chimes of Normandy:*

> In the days of old the leaders of the nation
>   Gathered 'round so bravely, each with pen in hand,
> Stanch and stalwart signers of the Declaration,
>   While the Independence Bell rang through the land.
>   Then its tones grew silent,
>   Vigilance was sleeping,
> As men chased the dollars wisely, but too well;
>   And around us gathered specters, grimly creeping,
> Till at last we found a man to ring that bell—
> Found a man to ring that Independence Bell. . . .
>
>   Here's for strength and courage that we need to ring it.
> We think we've found the man to ring that bell—
> Woodrow Wilson, you're the man to ring that bell!

President Wilson began his speech by saying this was his first night out since he had come to Washington, and that he "had profoundly enjoyed it. I have lived among good fellows all my life and I have found another bunch."

He noted that he had done some "unconventional things in this very conventional town," but that he got a singular impression from the newspapers that "whenever I do a perfectly natural thing, I am told I have done something unprecedented."

Wilson had delivered his first message to the new Congress in person and he said that since in the last month he had experienced "a certain sense of isolation," he wanted to go up to the Capitol "to see some of the fellows, and see what they looked like." He also noted that "there is no living being whose pride would not be hurt by having his message read by a reading clerk, particularly when most of the members during that reading were quite excusably in the cloakroom."

Having thus disposed of the congressmen, he turned his attention directly to those at the dinner.

"A singular thing about you newspapermen is that you are taking it for granted every day that it is incredible that there is not a fight on somewhere. You announced the interesting fact that when I met the Democratic members of the Finance Committee of the Senate, it was for the purpose of having them tell me where to get off. One of the papers said that. Now, I do not remember being told where to get off. I distinctly remember that the result of the conference was a general understanding as to how we were all to stay on.

"And every morning I pick up the paper and see that there are all sorts of friction, if not already in existence, just about to be created. I must be exquisitely lubricated," he said, raising his glass. "I do not feel any friction."

He said he didn't find much fun in standing up and making a speech when there was no business to be transacted, but it was lots of fun when one could "make particular remarks about particular individuals, named by name, Christian name and all," which "gives spice and directness to discourse which is not set down in the books of rhetoric, but which is exceedingly serviceable for accomplishing the end in view, which is the concentration of public opinion upon certain gentlemen who have not very handsome wares to exhibit.

"The function of public speakers," he continued, "now is largely the function of swinging the searchlight. And the great fun in swinging the searchlight is to see the fellows who dodge and to see the fellows who stand up and face the light."

Then Wilson went on to give his conception of the Presidency and how he would try to handle it.

"You have paid me a very deep compliment tonight, perhaps without being aware of it. You have interpreted, for I have gleaned that you understood, my conception of the part that I have to play.

"The Presidency of the United States, gentlemen, is a very great office. We hope and believe that it is an immortal office which may be lifted higher and higher for the guidance of a people and the guidance of free men throughout the world. But pray do not confound the man who occupies it with the office itself. The fundamental feeling that I have is that I am not identified with that office. I am the person for the time being allotted to administer it, and the only way in which I can administer it is by constantly feeling the grip of other men fastened upon my hand, not only to guide me, but to accompany me in the great task that is assigned me. . . .

"I am trying to get at the job by all the natural short cuts that I can think of, for the job is to understand and to be understood. It is not to stand off and imagine myself identified with the dignity and immortality of a great office, but to think myself identified with the men with whom I am trying to cooperate, so that we may think common thoughts.

"For if we do not, we cannot have common purposes. Surely that is the reason why some of the men present have honored me with a peculiar confidence. They have paid me the compliment of believing that I was not fool enough to think that I knew the whole thing. They have paid me the compliment of recognizing that I was going about trying to learn from others, not trying to instruct those who have been longer in the game than I have. . . .

"John Morley once said that anything will look black if you hold it up against the light that blazes in utopia. But you do not have to hold it up that way. You have to let the light shine upon its face, and then the gleam will be returned by the shining surface you expose to it. And when I see men doing what they are doing now, forgetting party prejudices, turning to one another with honest disagreements and honest differences of opinion, and trying to work out a common purpose by understanding each other, then I know that we are facing the light, and all we have to do is move forward together in order to fulfill the hopes of a great people that waits on us."[1]

The *Washington Herald* commented that although Gridiron dinner speeches are never public, Wilson's "was greatly enjoyed by all who had the good fortune to hear it. It was thoroughly in keeping with the spirit of the occasion and made a delightful impression.[2]

• • •

President Wilson had planned to attend the December 13 Gridiron dinner, but on the day of the dinner he was ill with a severe cold and sent the following message, which was read by President Kauffmann:

> I am deeply chagrined and greatly disappointed that a very severe cold still keeps me indoors and will prevent my attending the banquet of the club this evening. "Deeply chagrined" because I seldom misbehave myself in this way and am ashamed and disappointed because I was looking forward to the evening with keen anticipation of pleasure. I am sure that I will miss you much more than you will miss me, and I wish for you the jolliest and most rewarding evening.[3]

However, Vice President Marshall and all the members of the cabinet were present to see the actions of the new administration satirized.

The bill creating the Federal Reserve Board was about to be passed, and a meeting of the Federal Reserve Board was the vehicle for the initiation skit.

The chairman of the board was "General" Coxey, who in 1893 had led an army of unemployed in a march on Washington, and the members consisted of various other persons, including Harry K. Thaw, slayer of Stanford White; Jack Johnson, the boxer; Charles F. Murphy, leader of Tammany Hall; and William Sulzer, a maverick governor of New York, who had won in spite of Murphy's best efforts and was later impeached.

Coxey needed $100,000,000 immediately, and Thaw put it up, saying, "It cost me more than that to stay four weeks in Canada."

After various discussions of how the Federal Reserve Board was going to manage the currency, the initiates, who included Arthur Krock, then of the *Louisville Courier-Journal,* and J. Fred Essary of the *Baltimore Sun,* were brought in. They were asked to produce their initiation fees and dues. They said they couldn't pay, and when asked why not, one responded that "the administration's policy of pitiless publicity has been so secretive that we can't get any news, and we've lost our jobs."

However, it was determined that they had some negotiable

assets on which the Federal Reserve Board would loan money, because it had the power to "issue currency on first-class commercial paper, cotton bales, corn tassels and so forth."

Essary said he had Sulzer's scalp, and he asked Murphy how much he'd lend on that. Krock said he had Woodrow Wilson's letters asking if there was not some way to knock Bryan into a cocked hat. When asked if he'd found a way, he replied, "Yes; the President appointed him secretary of state."

Mexico was in turmoil. General Victoriano Huerta was the dictator, and Wilson sold arms to the revolutionaries against him. This suggested the vehicle for a dictator skit, in which it was announced that the United States had been Mexicanized and that a dictator had taken over the reins.

A detachment of the Mexican army raced on the stage, led by Senor Bryanna, who announced that he had seized the Presidency. "That's the only way you could get it," cried a voice.

But Senor Bryanna dispatched his army to find some of the revolutionaries: Champero Clarkista, Senor Marshallera, and various senators. Bryanna was overthrown, succeeded by the Clarkista dictatorship, which was in turn overthrown and William Alsorandolph Hearst was declared a dictator.

Last to seize the throne was Senor La Follettero, who had beguiled the army by convincing them that he was "the only honest man," he said so himself.

"I wanted the Progressive nomination for President. The Bull Yoose stole that from me. Now I am dictator, and, as such, I shall myself do a little larceny and murder."

The chorus had some advice for the administration:

> If Roosevelt yearns for the jungle,
> Let him go, let him go, let him go.
> If he could somehow get a hunch
> To invite old Huerta down to lunch,
> If Huerta would go for a visit
> Where the Amazon's waters flow,
> > Theodore might show
> > Huerta where to go.
> > Let him go, let him go, let him go.

But perhaps the most prescient skit of that evening was the Gridiron Club's "School for the Study of the Income Tax," authorized by constitutional amendment in 1913. Some of the dialogue went as follows:

"What, then, is taxation?"

"Taxation is the process whereby the people pay money to maintain in office men who pass laws taxing the people."

"Why are new forms of taxation necessary?"

"In order that the economies of a new administration may be carried out for the benefit of the people."

"What is economy?"

"Economy is the hope of the minority and the despair of the majority."

"When do minorities cease to be economical?"

"When they win an election."

"What is an income tax?"

"An income tax is 5,000 words of law and 500,000 words of explanations and interpretations."

"Was an income tax necessary?"

"It was, because the Democrats had to reduce the tariff and because they needed something to take the minds of the people off the high cost of living."

"Suppose the reduced tariff does not reduce the high cost of living, what will happen?"

"Then there will be another reduction: of the Democratic majority in Congress."

"How is net income described?"

"In four or five thousand words of solid nonpareil type."

"Then the income tax is a complicated law, is it?"

"There never will be but one law more complicated—the law that will be passed amending it and making it simpler in its operations."

Looking at it today, this dialogue seems to represent a somewhat better understanding of the income tax than that held by one of its proponents on the Senate floor, William E. Borah of Idaho, who declared in the Senate debate, "It is inconceivable that the rate would ever go as high as 10 percent!"

• • •

President Wilson accepted the invitation for the February 1914 dinner but withdrew because of a cold.

In view of the fact that World War I broke out less than six months later, it is noteworthy that the German ambassador and the Austro-Hungarian ambassador sat side by side at the head table.

This dinner, given on Valentine's Day, was characterized by the valentine spirit. The menu took the form of a large valentine, with color cartoons having a little verse under each. President Wilson's read:

Hail to the Chief, the Common People's friend!
May health and fortune's smile be ever thine;
May the whole nation's praise thy steps attend,
And 1916 bring a valentine.

"John D. Rockefeller, Jr." was emerging from Sleepy Hollow with the cry, "To arms, to arms, ye brave!"

"Charles S. Whitman," district attorney of New York and later to be governor, was shown eating a platter on which was the head of Charles F. Murphy, leader of Tammany Hall.

"Oscar W. Underwood" was made to say: "It's easy enough to sink a boat. The real job is to keep her afloat."

And "William Edgar Borah," standing with one foot on an elephant and the other on a moose, was described.

He rides 'em east, he rides 'em west,
He'll choose the one that rides the best;
Maybe the elephant, maybe the moose,
But one thing's sure—he's got to *choose!*

Even the German ambassador, Count J. H. von Bernstorff, who later became almost a cyclonic storm center, was pictured sawing wood and "making good."

The dinner was directed largely at lesser figures in the administration rather than the President. For example, "Charles F. Murphy," who was not exactly in the good graces of the administration, appeared in a cabinet skit, and was asked, "You know the President, don't you?"

"Sure," he answered, "but it ain't mutual."

Then, in a parody, he sang:

You made me what I am today,
I hope you're satisfied;
You drug and drug me down until
I've no safe place to hide;
You've shattered each and every hope,
You stung me from the start,
And though I feel blue, may God bless you,
That's the curse of an aching heart.

• • •

The first dinner given after World War I began, took place December 12, 1914. Neither von Bernstorff nor any of the ambassadors of the warring nations were present. The sole representative of the diplomatic corps was the Spanish ambassador. Nor was President Wilson there, although Vice President Marshall and Secretary of State Bryan attended.

The event was characterized by rather strict avoidance of the one subject too serious to be touched upon: the war. Consequently the humor was based heavily upon the 1914 congressional campaigns, in which the Democrats had lost sixty-one seats but still retained a narrow majority.

One major skit was "Old Homecoming Week," in which the Capitol was the old home, and several recent Republican absentees from the House of Representatives were returning, including Uncle Joe Cannon and Nicholas Longworth. All agreed that the old place had run down quite a bit and showed evident signs of grave mismanagement. "Nicholas Longworth," who had married Alice Roosevelt, daughter of the former President, and would later become a famous Speaker of the House, explained that he'd brought all his family back except his father-in-law, who at that time was remaining at Oyster Bay, "the lonesomest place on earth." Theodore Roosevelt's impersonator arrived and neatly converted "Mandalay" into "Oyster Bay."

> I'm on the way to Oyster Bay,
> Beneath my sheltering roof I've got to stay.
> > I sing a song
> > Of things gone wrong,
> On the last election day.
> I'm no longer trusted,
> They have got me flustered,
> And the big stick's busted.
> That's why I'm on my way to Oyster Bay,
> I've come to say good-bye.

President Wilson, in office a little over a year and a half by the time of this dinner, had already shown some disposition not to be too receptive to advice from other members of his party. Consequently, the club put on an act called the Common Counsel Club, which was described as "composed of officeholders who have accumulated a large fund of advice to give the President and are now waiting patiently to have the President ask them for it."

For example, Secretary of State Bryan was mentioned as being a candidate for the Nobel Peace Prize, and that he could probably get it by establishing permanent peace in Mexico.

"How would you advise the Administration to go about it?" asked Roy Vernon of the *Chicago Daily News*.

"Give everyone plenty of firearms and let nature take its course," was the reply of Louis Arthur Coolidge of the *New York Recorder*.

Even in those days, when World War I was in its early stages, when the government of the United States operated on a budget of a little over $1 billion, and when Woodrow Wilson had invented the phrase "New Freedom," the Gridiron Club members seemed to have an idea of what was coming.

"What is the New Freedom?" asked Roy Vernon.

"The New Freedom," was the answer, "is Universal Regulation."

The problems of the income tax were dealt with rather lightly by two members of the club, Vernon and Richard V. Oulahan.

Vernon remarked that [Secretary of the Treasury] McAdoo seems to be getting in worse and worse with this income tax muddle. He has issued several thousand circulars interpreting the law and now it is up to him to issue another circular interpreting the interpretations."

"I know how to handle the income tax," replied Oulahan. "Don't make any return at all. If you swear to anything whatever you're bound to commit perjury and that's a prison offense. If you don't make any return they can't do any more than fine you, and in that case the government has to do the figuring."

Navy Secretary Josephus Daniels, in his efforts to be strictly neutral, had forbidden the singing in the navy of the famous British marching song which became almost the song of World War I, "It's a Long Way to Tipperary." But the music committee parodied it into:

> It's a long way for Woodrow Wilson,
>   It's a long way to go;
> It's a long way for Woodrow Wilson,
>   For another term, you know;
> What will be the outcome remains to be seen;
>   It's a long, long way for Woodrow Wilson,
>   'Til nineteen sixteen.

In the absence of President Wilson, the closing speech was delivered by William Jennings Bryan.

• • •

On February 13, 1915, the Gridiron Club held its Thirtieth Anniversary Dinner. There was little reference to either President Wilson, who was not present, or the European war. The principal gibes were directed at the proposed Prohibition Amendment which was before Congress, to William Jennings Bryan, who was present and spoke; to Speaker Champ Clark; and to "statesmen" in general.

The latter was handled in a music skit patterned after *The Pirates of Penzance* and was called "The Pirates of Politics." The pirates included a prohibition pirate, a suffragette pirate, a progressive pirate, and so forth, and were announced by the pirate chief to be "as fine a band as ever bolted the convention or scuttled a political party."

"But we are not pirates," protested one, "we are reformers."

"Merely a distinction without a difference. Both pirates and reformers would like to sail the ship of state."

One of the pirates observed that "this town is full of statesmen," and then sang a parody of "A Policeman's Lot Is Not a Happy One."

> When the politician's not dispensing buncombe,
> —'spensing buncombe,
> Public documents and other simple joys,
> —simple joys,
> He can only wink and laugh and gently chuckle,
> —gently chuckle,
> At the way he puts it over on the boys,
> —on the boys.
> But the statesman gets the perquisites and places,
> —sites and places,
> He has nothing left to want for 'neath the sun,
> —'neath the sun,
> That's the reason why this town is full of statesmen,
> —full of statesmen,
> For the stateman's lot is sure a happy one,
> —happy one.

In the course of the inauguration of Edgar C. Snyder as president of the club, he was put through a literacy test. One of the questions was "Can you read?"

"I have read the *Omaha Bee* for thirty years."

"That's no test of literacy."

And another:

"Are you familiar with ancient history?"

"Well," drawled the president, "I remember when William J. Bryan first ran for President."

Then, in an indirect reference to Vice President Marshall:

"Have you read any Indiana author?"

"No, the Lord forbid!"

He was then declared qualified and inaugurated.

In the act initiating three new members, one of them was identified as the constitutional Prohibition Amendment.

"Congress won't adopt me, so I've come to the Gridiron Club," he said.

"Have you any friends in Congress?"

"I have plenty of friends on the floor but none in the cloak-rooms."

Not long before this dinner, President Wilson had remarked that the Republican party had not had a new idea in thirty years, and the Borah pomposity and verbosity was ridiculed when an actor representing him was asked, "What, in your opinion, constitutes an idea?"

"An idea, viewed in the light of a long line of constitutional precedents, and upheld in the Addison pipe-dream case, consists in the contemplation of methods pursued by men who, with far less natural equipment than myself, have succeeded, by hook or crook, in reaching the White House."

An impersonator of Speaker Clark was asked what his idea was of hard times.

"The Baltimore Convention," he replied [at which he had been defeated for the Democratic nomination by Woodrow Wilson].

"Well, Mr. Clark, what did you say recently about the Presidential nomination in 1916?"

"I said that if Wilson made good, he could have the nomination. And if he didn't make good, nobody would want it."

"Do you want it?"

"No."

• • •

By the time of the second 1915 dinner, held on December 11, President Wilson had declared a policy of preparedness and watchful waiting in the face of the German submarine warfare. This was designated as "The Preparedness Dinner," but in addition to patriotism, politics was also an integral part of it, because of the Presidential election eleven months hence.

At least ten of the individuals, whose names were under discussion for the Republican nomination in 1916 were present at the dinner—all, in fact, except the one who won the nomination, Charles Evans Hughes. To present them, President Snyder called each of them to the rostrum and, when they were assembled, said, "Gentlemen, I desire to present you to one of whom you'll hear a good deal in the year 1916—Woodrow Wilson."

This came as a surprise as much to the President as it did to the aspirants, and as they departed for their seats two men advanced from the dressing room, one in the black robe of Supreme Court justice and the beard that was unmistakably that of Mr. Justice Hughes.

"I tell you I won't stand for it," cried this interloper. "I will not allow my name to be placed on the ballot in Nebraska."

"But you might be elected," was the suggestion of the other.

"Do you realize," said the disguised one, with a gesture of despair, "what it means to be Nebraska's favorite son?" And with that he bolted from the stage.*

In 1915, neutrality was severely tested by the heavy loss of American life suffered when a German submarine sank the British passenger vessel *Lusitania*. Secretary of State William Jennings Bryan resigned, deeming Wilson's protest notes to Germany too strong.

So the Gridiron Club, satirizing the changed atmosphere, put on a skit called "The Saccharine Soldier," with fancy uniforms, big red and white candy canes such as are sold at Christmastime, and the cast, led by an impersonator of Bryan, waving the candy canes in the air and beating time to music, from Oscar Strauss's *Chocolate Soldier*.

There was a rather devastating satire on what was regarded as Mr. Bryan's idea of preparedness.

> We are nice little plaything soldier men,
>> We are just sweet and charming.
> We would not go to fighting, when
>> It would be most alarming.
> We are nice little sugary soldier men,
>> We ought to be in dresses.
> Wher'er we go, we meet the foe
>> With speeches and caresses.

And then:

> Why should we ask sufficient powder?
>> What do we want with dreadnaughts bold?
> Give them a dish of good clam chowder,
>> Serve them a cocktail, frapped, cold.
> We have no use for continentals;
>> We pay no heed to war's alarms,
> If we should see some regimentals,
>> We will embrace them in our arms.

---

*Nebraska was the home state of William Jennings Bryan.

The saccharine soldiers ran into difficulties. All their chewing gum had been captured by a girl's school. Two wagonloads of Chautauqua contracts had been destroyed. And when the news was brought to Bryan, he cried, "War certainly is hell!"

"Suppose," asked one of the actors, "some unfeeling foreigners should fire a forty-two-centimeter gun at us? What would we do?"

The answer: "Run away."

The skit ended with Bryan singing his version of "Good-bye Girls, I'm Through" to the Wilson administration.

> All this hullabaloo about a bigger navy
>> And talk of continental troops and such
>>> Is shocking to my sense of right,
>>> I'd rather talk a lot than fight,
>> This program nauseates me very much.
> You may recall that I was once a statesman,
>> And held a big position in this land;
> But when my chief assumed a firm position
>> I quit the job and joined the peaceful band.
>>> And so I said without a sigh
>>> To the chief as I went tripping by:
>
> Good-bye, chief, I'm through,
>> I'm leaving now, you bet;
> I say good-bye to you
>> With more or less regret;
> I go to save the nation
> With lecture and oration,
> So I bid you fond adieu,
> Good-bye, chief, God bless you,
>> I'm through.

But, with characteristic purpose in Gridiron shows of trying to forecast the action of the country, after Bryan said his good-bye a Gridiron actor commented "that fool talk sounds absurd to me," and announced that he was through with the "candy soldier" business and "this tommyrot of fighting an enemy with speeches." Then he sang a Gridiron rendition of "Stout-Hearted Men."

> Should enemies appear at hand,
> To threaten our beloved land,
> Shall we for lack of proper care
> Surrender all that we hold dear?
> The liberty our fathers bought,
> The splendid ideals that they taught—

Shall these be made a sacrifice
Through preaching peace at any price?
    No. No. *No!*
    No. No. *No!*
We'll be prepared for any foe,
We'll care not if he comes, or no;
We'll be prepared with shot and shell,
To blow him straightaway into—*well!*
And that's our answer to the world,
We'll keep the Stars and Stripes unfurled,
Don't let us hear you any more.
    No, not any more!*

The war spirit which was beginning to rise in America was amply reflected in this Gridiron dinner. Singing directly to the President at the close of the dinner, the chorus declared that:

We take our stand back of you, Mr. Wilson,
Strength to your arm we give;
    You're the leader of all,
    We respond to your call,
We will stand firm with you for the red, white and blue;
No party or faction divides us in twain.
We're just plain Americans, proud of the name;
    Let the world realize
    Naught can sever these ties,
We take our stand back of you.

President Wilson was introduced. "By this time," the *Washington Star* commented the next day, "the company had been lifted out of the spirit of fun and facetiousness, and when the President arose in his place the great banquet hall fairly trembled with the outburst of acclaim and patriotic enthusiasm."[4]

The President that night was deadly serious, as he explained some of his philosphy and his views related to the very difficult problems of foreign affairs and peace in December 1915.

He began by noting that underlying all the fun-making at Gridiron dinners there was "a very serious vein of thought and intention, and this evening that feeling has been stronger upon me than usual.

"There has been jest, there has been thrust, there has been sarcastic implication, but through it all there has run a serious

---

*In another skit, prepared but not presented at this dinner, a character representing Benjamin Franklin gave his comments on preparedness: "I am already on record. In my newspaper I stated that if you make yourself a sheep, the wolves will eat you."

idea which I take it is the idea of the present moment among the American people."

Referring to the speech that night of former Speaker "Uncle Joe" Cannon, the President talked of his tracing the development of America and the "flavor from the individual initiative which was necessary in that time.

"And then my thought came on to the present time," Wilson said, "when America has almost been made. Her bloods are not yet entirely mixed and united, but she has built, and built strong and solidly, from coast to coast, and there is no longer any centering of our thought upon merely domestic enterprises. We now stand to make or mar our character among the nations of the world. . . . I wonder if we realize the full responsibility that is upon us?

"I know what that last song meant. I happen to be President, but that song would have been sung no matter who was President. It means that America is now ready to follow responsible leaders of her own choosing and that it wishes to be led in some direction in particular and not to drift; and the responsibility that rests upon me is not so much, so far as I have the power, to choose the course which I individually might prefer as to do my best to interpret the spirit and purpose of the country for which for the time being I speak. I must listen and try to interpret; I must remember and try to reproduce. . . .

"I am quite sure of several traits that belong to us and that we wish to express and strengthen. One is that we are not afraid either of our own identity or of anything that anybody else can do to us. America is characterized by the spirit of self-confidence and, in the best sense of the word, self-sufficiency. But America is also characterized, though upon the surface it may not seem so, by an abhorrence of extremes. America does not like the extreme radical, and it cannot continue to grow if it submits to the extreme conservative. Reaction is out of the question. America can never turn back and never will turn back, but the pace at which she advances she wishes to be a well considered and moderate pace. She wants progress but she wants ordered progress; she wants well considered progress. She wants to drive down stakes that represent the point which her thought has reached and she will never pull those stakes up again."

Speaking of the Wilsonian policy of preparedness, he noted that this should be done "with all moderation" and with avoidance of extremes. America, he continued, would not want to be ruled by any class. This included the military class and the lawyer class.

"Legalism," he said, "is the enemy of progress, and militarism is the end of progress."

The avoidance of extremes was the principle under which the preparedness program had been conceived, he said. Whether it was adequate he conceded to be debatable, but the principle behind it was not debatable.

"We want a nation sufficient for self-defense," he said, "and yet we do not want a nation which submits to the military spirit. . . . Look at what we are witnessing in the world, gentlemen; look at the combination of parties and the disappearance of party lines in Great Britain and France and Germany and Italy, and because we happen not to be engaged in this terrible struggle shall we omit to do the same handsome thing and combine all counsels in order that the nation may be saved!

"Why, gentlemen, the equipoise of the world in a way depends upon us. It is one thing, and a comparatively easy thing, to combine parties to conduct a war, but it is a more difficult and a more handsome thing to combine parties in order to preserve and glorify peace. . . .

"My hope and ambition for America is that in the months immediately at hand she shall exhibit to the world an example of combined and amicable counsel for the best fortunes of America and of the world such as no other nation ever exhibited. I for my part can testify that in the things I have been permitted to propose I have no conscious partisan feeling whatever, and I challenge all men of all parties to come to the assistance of the nation with their unprejudiced counsel. For this is the thing, the only thing, which will make America what she boasts, that she has always been the leader of the world along the paths of liberty and of peace."

Then, coming to one of the more practical problems that existed at that time, President Wilson made an appeal to the press to exercise a great sense of responsibility.

"There is one thing that is particularly dangerous just now, gentlemen," he said, "and that is to publish conjectural versions of what is going on in the foreign relations of this country. Nothing could be more dangerous than that. We are at peace with all nations. I hope and believe that there is no pending question which need disturb that feeling, but there are many difficulties which may be thrown in the way by speculative accounts of what is being said and done and what is to be expected, and I should hope that the gentlemen of the press would seek to learn from the secretary of state, if they will be so gracious, what it is wisest for them to say and not to say.

"The secretary playfully outlined some of the things that you do after your interviews with him and I know from my own conferences with him that his feeling for the representatives of the press is my own, the feeling of the greatest cordiality and confidence, but you do some very dangerous things sometimes: in saying, for example, in a case such as he cited that a message has been received which has not been received, and the reasons the secretary did not say anything which were the reasons which you yourselves give. Those things are immediately transmitted to foreign nations and constitute part of the transaction thereafter, because they constitute part of the mental atmosphere in which the foreign mind acts and the foreign government responds.

"I am uttering this counsel and making this request with the greatest seriousness of purpose, because we can manage American affairs by common counsel but our common counsel will not determine what other nations are going to do. Whenever we make a move, the next move is not up to us but is up to some other government, and we ought to be very careful how we set the stage for what they are going to do. This is a concrete example, gentlemen, if I may say so, of the sort of spirit which should prevail in America. Things are not easy. If you could read the dispatches which I hourly read, you would see how infinitely complicated the threads of the foreign pattern are, how many influences are at work which do not appear on the surface, how many things there are which it is best not to talk about, how many things there are which bid us suspend judgment and wait until the next move is made; and I adjure every man who feels his responsibility as an American citizen to reflect upon these things and not make it more difficult than it inevitably is to keep the balance even in our transactions with foreign countries."

Then Wilson went on to analyze what patriotism meant: "a deeply grounded principle of action which bids every man subordinate his own interests to the interests of the common weal and to act upon that though it be to the point of utter sacrifice to himself and everything that is involved."

He compared patriotism to Christianity, which, he said, "makes a man forget himself and square everything he does with a great love and a great principle, and so does patriotism.

"I believe, and you believe," he concluded, "that the interests of America are coincident with the interests of the world and that if we can make America lead the way of example along the paths of peace and regeneration for herself, we shall enable her to lead the whole world along those paths of promise and of achievement. So, gentlemen, I believe that we should go away from here tonight feeling that we have renewed our pledge to each other to think of America before we think of ourselves and before we think of anything else. . . .

"Peace will come to the world when we love our fellowmen better than we love ourselves, and for my part the love of my fellowmen translates itself in action into my belief in the capacity of America to set the example of freedom and of liberty. I believe that individually we are of little efficacy but that united as Americans we may make conquest of the spirit of the world, and that that spirit, turning to us as in those first days of hope when the republic was set up, will see that there burns in the East as in the West a light that shines around the world, kindled at the hearths of American homes and burning in the imaginations of those who lead the American nation."[5]

• • •

The preconvention dinner of February 26, 1916 was notable for several events: for being the first occasion when Warren Harding, who was to succeed President Wilson four years later, was a speaker at a Gridiron dinner; for some rather mild and gentle kidding about the approaching conventions; for the continued reference to Theodore Roosevelt as a political figure; and most of all, for an outstandingly revealing speech by President Wilson.

The inauguration of a new president of the Gridiron Club, Louis W. Strayer of the *Pittsburgh Dispatch,* was utilized for the opening sallies, chiefly directed toward the Republicans. An elaborate inaugural parade was interrupted when the Progressive party objected to the inauguration of President Strayer until assurances had been received that he had the endorsement of former President Roosevelt, whereupon a number of reporters from Bermuda—where Roosevelt happened to be at the moment—came in with conflicting accounts of who the former President would accept. Charles Evans Hughes headed the list, along with such others as Philander C. Knox, secretary of state in the Taft cabinet, Elihu Root, Senator Borah and others.

But eventually the latest reports eliminated everybody except Justice Hughes and Mr. Strayer.

This was pretty good prognostication on the part of the Gridiron Club; Hughes later did in fact become the 1916 Republican Presidential candidate.

In other skits there were some references to the policy of preparedness and to the rising furor in America over Prohibition. One definition of preparedness advanced at the dinner was "drinking two cocktails before delivering a speech in Congress for Prohibition."

This was the first dinner at which a "guest skit" in the form in which it is performed at Gridiron dinners today was presented. The guests who were called to their feet included many leaders of business, but not many politicians.

Henry Ford, whose automobiles were ridiculed as "tin lizzies," was one of the guests called upon, and he was asked what he would do to help along industrial preparedness. He said, according to a Gridiron member standing beside him, that he would donate his peace ship as an auxiliary to the battleship fleet, and that he would sell his automobiles to the government at cost—$17.50!

But the most political of the skits was laid at the two gates of railroad trains: one destined for Chicago, where the Republican Convention was to be held, and the other for St. Louis, where the Democrats were to meet. The two gatemen questioned all ticket holders.

Former President Roosevelt was one of those who arrived at the Chicago gate, followed by William Barnes, Republican leader of New York. Barnes carried an ax which he described as an olive branch, and when asked upon whom he intended to use the ax, he looked at the former President and replied, "I'll give you two guesses."

It closed with Bryan trying to catch the Democratic train and presenting a ticket which was rejected by the Chicago gateman as a half-rate clergyman's ticket, but which the St. Louis gateman accepted on the grounds that "he's a half-rate clergyman." However, the trains had started and the St. Louis gateman opened the gate again to let Bryan run for it if he wanted.

"But you'll have to be some runner."

Bryan, dashing through, yelled back, "I am. I've been running for twenty years!"

Leading up to President Wilson's speech, the Gridiron Club,

with perhaps a little less skepticism than was shown months later in the very close election, to the tune of "Camptown Races," sang:

> All through the land they're talking,
>   Wilson, of you;
> Some say you'll win in walking
>   Race number two;
> Opponents fiercely brawling,
>   Threaten anew;
> And everywhere they are callin',
>   Calling for you.

All in all, the skits were fairly mild, and President Wilson took note of this: "I find I am seldom tempted to say anything nowadays unless somebody starts something, and tonight nobody has started anything."

The speech which followed had little humor in it but was an extremely revealing one concerning the character and thinking of Woodrow Wilson. And it did contain a few shafts aimed at Congress, politicians, and sundry other public characters. He mentioned that there had been a great deal of talk about candidacy for the Presidency and commented:

"It is not a new feeling on my part, but one which I entertain with a greater intensity than formerly, that a man who seeks the Presidency of the United States for anything that it will bring to him is an audacious fool. The responsibilities of the office ought to sober a man even before he approaches it."

He then went on into a documentation of his belief that "the point in national affairs, gentlemen, never lies along the lines of expediency. It always rests in the field of principle."

He also believed that the United States was not founded upon any principle of expediency but "was founded upon a profound principle of human liberty and of humanity," and that "whenever it bases its policy upon any other foundations than those, it builds on the sand."

Standing there before a dinner of distinguished Americans while Europe was engaged in a devastating war, Wilson combined a gibe at Congress with an eloquent call to high motives.

"It seems to me that the most enlightening thing a man can do is suggested by something which the Vice President said tonight. He complained that he found men who, when their attention was called to the signs of spring, did not see the blue heaven, did not see the movement of the free clouds, did not think of the great spaces of the quiet continent, but thought only of some immediate and pressing piece of business. It seems to me that if you do not think of the things that lie beyond and away from and disconnected from this scene in which we attempt to think and conclude, you will inevitably be led astray. I would a great deal rather know what they are talking about around quiet firesides all over this country than what they are talking about in the cloakrooms of Congress."

He referred quite graciously to Senator Harding and his speech in which he had said that we ought to try when we are a hundred million strong to act in the same simplicity of principle that our forefathers acted in when we were three million strong.

"I heard somebody say," said President Wilson, "that the present population of the United States is one hundred and three millions. If there are three million thinking the same things that the original three million thought, the hundred million will be saved for an illustrious future.

"They were ready to stake everything for an idea, and that idea was not expediency, but justice. And the infinite difficulty of public affairs, gentlemen, is not to discover the signs of the heavens and the directions of the wind, but to square the things you do by the not simple but complicated standards of justice."

Although in future months much was to be made by Wilson's supporters of the fact that "he kept us out of war"—and this was probably the major factor in the very close election victory he had over Charles Evans Hughes—Wilson nevertheless, in this Gridiron speech, indicated quite clearly that the inevitable future of America would be getting into the war.

"America ought to keep out of this war," he said.

"She ought to keep out of this war at the sacrifice of everything except this single thing upon which her character and history are founded, her sense of humanity and justice. If she sacrifices that, she has ceased to be America; she has ceased to entertain and to love the traditions which have made us proud to be Americans, and when we go about seeking safety at the expense of humanity, then I for one will believe that I have always been mistaken in what I have conceived to be the spirit of American history.

"There is no question what the roll of honor in America is. The roll of honor consists of the names of men who have squared their conduct by ideals of duty. There is no one else upon the roster; there is no one else whose name we care to remember when we measure things upon a national scale. And I wish that whenever an impulse to settle a thing some short way tempts us, we might close the door and take down some old stories of what American idealists and statesmen did in the past, and not let any counsel in that does not sound in the authentic voice of American tradition.

"Then we shall be certain what the lines of the future are, because we shall know we are steering by the lines of the past. We shall know that no temporary convenience, no temporary expediency, will lead us either to be rash or to be cowardly. I would be just as much ashamed to be rash as I would to be a coward. Valor is self-respecting. Valor is circumspect. Valor strikes only when it is right to strike. Valor withholds itself from all small implications and entanglements and waits for the great opportunity when the sword will flash as if it carried the light of heaven upon its blade."[6]

• • •

The election of 1916 was so close that many newspapers proclaimed the election of Charles Evans Hughes late that night, only to discover the next day, when final California returns were in, that California had gone for Wilson by 4,000 votes, giving him the victory.

Many of the editors of these papers were at the dinner held on December 9, which was also attended by President Wilson and the new secretary of state, Robert Lansing.

Since the Gridiron Club has never been particularly averse to chiding the members of its profession for their errors, all of the editors and publishers present who had made this mistake— about a dozen of them from various sections of the country— were asked to stand and were asked by the club, "Did you or did you not, on about the evening of November 7 and the morning of November 8, 1916, falsely print, publish and declare that one Charles Evans Hughes had been elected President of the United States?"

They pleaded guilty and the Gridiron members, with a gesture of disgust, trailed off the stage.

The skits that year centered largely around Prohibition and woman suffrage, both of which were becoming hotly debated issues.

William Jennings Bryan, since his resignation as secretary of state, had espoused the cause of Prohibition with great fervor, and the Gridiron Club had a character representing him sing:

They got the cross of gold from me;
The Nobel prize I've hoped to see,
Now, humbly bearing my cross, I come
To say "You shall not crucify the bum
Upon the cursed cross of *Rum.*"

The skit on the suffrage movement was based on the fact that a women's special train had toured the west in the last Presidential campaign in behalf of the vote for women. The Gridiron Club had the "Millinery Special" stopping at Kidderville, Kansas. The mayor prepared the audience by announcing that the special was going to stop in Kidderville for fifteen minutes.

"It's entirely a woman's party," he said. "These ladies come from Fifth Avenoo, Noo York City, and from Newport, which is a sort of down-East Chautauqua for the idle rich, near as I can make out. Last year they had a series of monkey dinners, and this year their diversion is politics and the higher thought. . .

"The only men aboard the train is the crew, and every one of them is older than Uncle Joe Cannon."

The train arrived and a lady by the name of Mrs. G. Mortimer de Scads, with something less than diplomatic understanding of the situation, addressed the crowd.

"Good people—especially good women: It has been so interesting to come into the west and meet the—ah—masses who really are so necessary to our—ah—civilization. We of the leisure clawses really feel it a duty in this critical period to enlighten you regarding vital issues about which you have little time for study."

The inflationary effects of the European war were already being felt in the United States, and in the "Gridiron Follies of 1916" a colloquy occurred between a Kansan and the chairman of the Republican National Committee, who asked, "What went wrong in Kansas?"

"I can tell you," replied the Kansan. "Two-dollar wheat, ten-dollar hogs, Ford machines, and player pianos."

"Do you think he kept us out of war?" asked the politician.

Whereupon the Kansan replied, "I dunno. But somebody got us out of debt."

Charles F. Murphy, leader of Tammany Hall, had not "delivered" for Wilson as expected, and an impersonator sang of his fate in the song whose first line title was so appropriate for him:

Forsaken, forsaken,
    Forsaken am I;
The Tammany Tiger
    Is turned out to die;
I go to the White House
    And find the door barred,
For Wilson still lives there
    And his heart is so hard.

Henry Ford and his peace ship to Europe, which had been widely ridiculed both there and in this country, were satirized in a parody of the song, "I Didn't Raise My Boy to Be a Soldier," which went:

He didn't raise his Ford to be a jitney,
He brought it up to be a real machine;
He didn't send his peace ship over yonder
All loaded down with fudge and choc'late cream;
He didn't carry Michigan for Wilson,
He didn't do a lot of things he tried;
    If Henry had his way
    There'd be no war today,
He'd have the soldiers busy making flivvers.

But while all laughed during the evening at the foibles of the campaign, the spirit of the dinner was represented in a boxing bout skit. Prominent political leaders were called from their tables to the stage. The national campaign chairman for each party and others took places in the ring as seconds for the bout which was about to occur. It was one of the first times that the club used the real people in a skit, instead of actors made up as the characters they represented.

When the two Gridiron prize fighters were brought on, they clasped hands, the gong sounded, and the manager cried, "Go to it!" But the principals only smiled at each other and continued their handclasp.

The manager, after consulting with the principals, announced, "I have made a mistake. These men tell me they do not want to fight; they are through fighting. All they wish to do tonight is to shake hands in this public way so the world may know that since the campaign ended Democrats and Republicans are standing shoulder to shoulder, their watchword 'America first.'"

The band played "America" and the Republican campaign manager, Mr. Willcox, and the Democratic, Mr. McCormick, marched from the stage arm in arm while the audience cheered and applauded. And thus the Gridiron Club proclaimed the solidarity of the country behind President Wilson as he faced the European crisis four months hence.

Both the Japanese ambassador and the President spoke at this dinner, but there is no available record of the ambassador's speech. The *Washington Herald,* however, reported the next day of the President that "his enjoyment of all that was said and done was manifest to all present."

President Wilson began his speech in a light mood, with references to the Gridiron dinner skits and to the campaign which had ended only a month before.

"I think the spirit of the occasion can never be mistaken at the Gridiron Club," he said. "There is a great deal of fun made of individuals, and sometimes of policies, but it never cuts very deep. Particularly does it not cut deep when you know the men who are making the fun. I know these men; I know their temper, and they could not ruffle mine.

"I am of that temperament not to be hurt except when something gets under my skin, and I want to say to the amiable gentlemen who conducted the recent campaign on the other side that nothing got under my skin. I have been accustomed to reading fiction all my life."

The campaign, he said, was "not interesting, because it was not a discussion of what we ought to do. It was only a discussion of who ought to do it." The Republican editors, he thought, had been "singularly lacking in inspiration as to any ideas." We were living, he said, "in a world which means business now if it never meant business before.

"Now, if never before, the motto is 'Put up or shut up,'" Wilson said. "If you have got nothing to suggest, the world will be impatient of the noise made by your vocal organs.

"And a great deal has to be suggested, a great deal that is of vital importance. In the charming and playful speech just made by the distinguished ambassador from Japan, he intimated that diplomatists would not be needed in the temple of peace. I am not sure that that is true. They will not be needed to accommodate differences, but they will be needed to interpret the spirit of nations to each other, for that is the foundation of peace. Nations are led into war with one another because they do not understand each other, or because the interest of their rulers is not consistent with their own interests in matters of national life and relation. And the thing that the world does need is interpretation, is the kind of vision which sees beneath the surface into the real needs and motives and sympathies of mankind.

"It is a fearful thing that is going on now, this contest of bloody force, but it is going to do one fine thing. It is going to strip human nature naked, and when it is over, men are going to stand face to face without any sort of disguise, without any sort of attempt to hoodwink one another, and say to one another, 'Men and brethren, what shall we do for the common cause of mankind?' And when that question is asked, what answer are we going to make and what contribution is America going to make to that answer?"

In its way, this speech of Wilson forecast the kind of appeal to the world he would make when, at the end of the war, he was to head the American delegation at the Paris Peace Conference.

We had not yet learned, he said in continuing his speech, "what the object is," but America's role in the future he saw, was "to see that the balance of power in the world is not disturbed; that aggression is held back; that selfishness is condemned; and that men regard each other upon the same footing as human beings.

"Gentlemen," Wilson declared, "there is only one meaning to democracy. Democracy means that the man who considers himself as belonging to a class with a separate set of interests from his fellowmen is an enemy of mankind. He does not belong to the family; he does not deserve to be taken into counsel; he is by temperament and point of view an antagonist of the great mass of mankind. That is the meaning of democracy. It is a deep spiritual meaning. . . .

"I am happy for one to live in a time when the great problems of statesmanship are no longer political problems at all, but problems of how to work out common rights, how to relieve common suffering, how to see that those who lack the ordinary equipment of mankind are assisted by the rest who have that equipment, and how all the levels are raised and all the needs served as at a common table. . . .

"The day of cold thinking, of fine-spun constitutional argument, is gone, thank God. We do not now discuss so much what the Constitution of the United States is as what the constitution of human nature is, what the essential constitution of human society is, and we know in our hearts that if we ever find a place or a time where the Constitution of the United States is contrary to the constitution of human nature and human society, we have got to change the Constitution of the United States. The Constitution, like the Sabbath, was made for man and not man for the Constitution. I have known of some judges who did not perceive that. I have known of some judges who seemed to think that the Constitution was a straitjacket into which the life of the nation must be forced, whether it could be with a true regard to the laws of life of not.

"But judges of that sort have now gently to be led to a back seat and, with all respect for their years and their lack of information, taken care of until they pass unnoticed from the stage."

It was twenty years later that this attitude toward the Supreme Court, first suggested by Woodrow Wilson, was to come to a crisis under Franklin D. Roosevelt. But Roosevelt eliminated the word "gently" from his thinking.

"And men must be put forward," said Wilson, "whose whole comprehension is that law is subservient to life and not life to law. The world must learn that lesson, the international world, the whole world of mankind.

"Now, that is not a party question. . . . There has been a very noticeable tendency of Republicans in the last four years to vote with the Democrats, not because one side were Republicans and the other Democrats, but because they were all alike Americans and interested in things that served America. I want to say here and now that I do not respect a Republican or a Democrat who does not put America before his party. Now the happy circumstances of the time is that we can forget about the campaign and remember the United States."[7]

• • •

The winter dinner of February 17, 1917, less than two months before America was to enter the first World War, due to the seriousness of the situation, was very mild on both foreign affairs and President Wilson, and was devoted primarily to domestic topics of little consequence today.

Both President Wilson and Vice President Marshall were present, and the dinner was notable in retrospect as being the first one at which a speech was made by Herbert Hoover, then listed on the seating chart as simply "Herbert C. Hoover, London, England."

The war spirit was running high in the country, and most

believed it was only a matter of time before America would have to join the Allies formally. Consequently, there was a strong patriotic emphasis in the dinner, which was perhaps best exemplified by the entrance into the hall of a platoon of uniformed navy men, led by a brisk young ensign. They marched in, to the center of the hall, presented arms to the President of the United States, and unfurled an American flag. Then the Gridiron Club quartet sang "The Star Spangled Banner."

The changes in the Senate and House as a result of the election were satirized in a song by Tudor Morsell, one of the famous Gridiron vocalists, impersonating James Martine, senator from New Jersey who had been retired in the election.

> Goody-bye, dear old Senate days,
> Farewell, all those Senate ways;
> Oh, the wonderful sights and all of the joys,
> The wonderful fights with all of the boys,
> I'm here to say adieu to you.
> You've been awf'ly good to me,
> I've seen all there was to see,
> But the enemy swept New Jersey clean,
> And threw the hooks into Jim Martine,
> So good-bye, my dear old Senate days.

A group of suffragettes had picketed the White House, and the Gridiron Club parodied "Camping Tonight on the Old Campgrounds" into "Camping Tonight on the White House Grounds."

The coming Prohibition received its notice too, primarily because the District of Columbia was about to go dry. They used the Negro spiritual "Old Black Joe" to comment on this.

> I hear their kill-joy voices calling, *"Booze Must Go."*
> I hear them, I hear them—though my head is aching so—
> I hear the voice of Sheppard calling, *"Booze Must Go."*

At the time of this dinner, the Germans had resumed unrestricted submarine warfare, and two weeks before the dinner, on February 3, President Wilson had broken off diplomatic relations with Germany.

A memorandum in Gridiron files by Ira Bennett, 1917 club president, reported that Wilson said to him, toward the end of the dinner, "Perhaps you had better not call upon me. Whatever I should say tonight might be misconstrued or given too much meaning."

Bennett urged him to speak, he reported, on the grounds that Congress might cooperate with him more effectively if they knew what was in his mind; also, that there would be surprise and apprehension if he didn't speak. Vice President Marshall also urged him to speak.[8]

Wilson accepted the advice and did speak, but very briefly—scarcely more than a hundred words. He expressed his appreciation for the "interesting entertainment," but said he was going to ask to be excused "from making the vain attempt to add to so delightful an evening.

"The things that I am constantly thinking about," he said, "are not at present things that are suitable to discuss, and I would not try to lead your thoughts away in a vain attempt to speak upon other topics."[9]

Six weeks later, on April 2, he went before a joint session of Congress to ask for a declaration of war. It was in this speech that he first used the phrase, "the world must be made safe for Democracy."

• • •

There was some question about holding a dinner in December 1917 because of the war. Ira Bennett and the executive committee had recommended that a dinner be held, and at a special meeting it was decided, by a vote of fourteen to five, to approve this recommendation and hold the dinner.

President Wilson was invited, accepted and came to this dinner of December 8, along with the Vice President and about a dozen ambassadors and ministers from Allied and neutral countries.

Herbert Hoover had been appointed food administrator and was also a guest at the dinner. Since this was a wheatless and meatless dinner, conforming to the Food Administration regime, at the outset Mr. Hoover was asked to approve the menu. He objected to the roasts.

"But," said Gridiron member William E. Brigham of the *Boston Transcript*, "there are no roasts."

"Then, Mr. Hoover, says, this can't be a Gridiron dinner."

"Oh, tell him to wait awhile," shot back Brigham.

Since laws had been passed making the District of Columbia dry, no alcoholic beverages were served at this dinner. This led to a skit in which the dinner was "raided" by the chief of police and several persons searched.

George Creel, who was chief of information for the government, was first and he was caught with the goods. By a bit of sleight of hand the police chief pulled a liquor bottle out of Creel's pocket, but announced, on examining it, "It has been deleted. Mr. Creel is up to his old tricks."

The president of Standard Oil Company, A. C. Bedford, was approached, and he announced that he refused to be searched. He had something valuable in his pocket. They searched him anyway, but produced only a single one dollar bill.

"What's valuable about that?" asked the chief.

Another policeman replied, "Mr. Bedford says you'd think it valuable if it was your salary from the government for a whole year."

Next was a member of the Board of Governors from the New York Stock Exchange.

"Let him go," said a club member. "Any man who buys stock these days needs liquor for medicinal purposes."

Whereupon the police chief said to President Bennett, "That seems to be about all, Sir. Go ahead with your dinner."

Bennett: I'm glad you give us a clean bill. You will always find that the Gridiron Club obeys the law.
Chief: The Gridiron Club! Is this the Gridiron Club?
Bennett: Certainly. What do you think it is?
Chief: Help! Help! I thought it was the Anti-Saloon League. Come on, men, we're in the wrong place.

There were also serious periods in the dinner. Frank A. Vanderlip of the War Savings Committee and Henry Ford were asked to come on stage along with Henry Hall of the Gridiron Club. After some preliminaries by Mr. Vanderlip, Hall asked for buyers of War Savings Stamps. He really put the bee on numerous guests by calling the names of some prominent persons and asking them how much they would subscribe. Blanks were then passed around among the diners, gathered up and presented to Treasury Secretary William G. McAdoo, who was a guest. Mr. McAdoo counted up the subscriptions and announced that a total of $131,930 had been subscribed.

The main thrust of the dinner had a strong patriotic, support-the-government, win-the-war angle—perhaps more so than at any other dinner in Gridiron history.

For example, in a skit on the new and onerous wartime taxation, they had an "interpreter" of the new tax law on stage, with taxpayers asking questions:

Question: What is net income?
Answer: Entirely a matter of conscience.

Question: Is the President subject to the tax?
Answer: The President is subject to all kinds of attacks.

Senator Robert M. LaFollette of Wisconsin was one of the few in Congress who were critical of the war.

Question: What is a foreign partnership?
Answer: Jeremiah O'Leary, Bob LaFollette and the Kaiser.

Question: What is a domestic partnership?
Answer: Woodrow Wilson and 100 million Americans.

There was a skit in which "Gridiron ingenuity has fallen down." They were mortified because they couldn't devise a skit "striking directly at the common enemy." It was explained that "the Gridiron 'secret service' gathered a mass of ludicrous documents for presentation here tonight, intrigue and propaganda designed to satirize German diplomacy."

Even as early as 1917, the State Department and other government agencies were keeping close covert watch on everything done by the enemy. Therefore, a member responded, "But the executive committee has just declared unanimously that the wildest fancies of Gridiron invention are not half so funny as the *real* stuff that has fallen into [Secretary of State] Lansing's hands."

Then they mildly satirized the snafus of a huge war bureaucracy. A Briton asked, "Tell me, old top, what is your procedure for expediting war supplies?"

"Oh, we have a perfect system," a Gridiron member replied. "The War Industries Board has absolute control, except when the War Trade Board intervenes, in which case the Food and Fuel Administration has power to appeal to the Priorities Board and the Council of National Defense; but the Shipping Board, through the Emergency Fleet Corporation, is free to act independently of the Interstate Commerce Commission, except in interstate transportation, in which case the Railroads War Board is called in to confer jointly with the Federal Mediation Board, the Federation of Labor, the Smithsonian Institution, and the WCTU."

"My word!" exclaimed the Briton. "How like our British system!"

But while they were satirizing the war bureaucracy, they

paid a very stirring tribute to American industry, which was creating the materials that, with the men, became the decisive factor in the war. In the guest skit they called the names of all the industrialists present one by one, asking them to stand, and then said:

"Captains of industry, generals of capital and labor, field marshals of private enterprise in times of peace; now donating their time, their energy, their brain to the service of their country. Gentlemen, you honor us by your presence tonight. May you be with us again in a happier hour, that we may honor you for your part in the realization of that hope with which you now help to inspire us."

One of the problems of December 1917 was providing the shipping to carry American soldiers, supplies and matériel to European battlefields. Thus, the full Gridiron chorus rendered a song of the day, "Sons of America," as follows:

Ships for America
Hurry on full steam,
Ships are our vital need
To defeat the submarine;
Ships for America
The seas must be free,
No Kaiser's hand shall crush
    the Land of Liberty.

But in the music skit and in the introduction of President Wilson, the patriotic spirit reached its highest point. They used the music skit as a vehicle for singing many of the war songs of the period.

Somewhere in France is the lily
Close by the English rose . . .

Come lead our France to victory
Joan of Arc they are calling you . . .

Keep the home fires burning
Till the boys come home . . .

Oh, Tommy, Tommy Atkins,
    you're a "good 'un" heart and hand
You're a credit to your calling
    and to all your native land . . .

It's a long way to Berlin but we'll get there
    Uncle Sam will show the way;

Over the line, then across the Rhine
  Shouting Hip, Hip, Hooray;
We'll sing Yankee Doodle Under the Linden,
  With some real live Yankee pep, Hep,
It's a long way to Berlin but we'll get there,
  And we're on our way, you bet.

And the skit closed with the "Battle Cry of Freedom."

Freedom Forever, Freedom for *all*,
Freedom Forever, Hear ye the call;
While we rally round the flag, boys,
Rally once again,
Shouting the Battle Cry of Freedom.

At the end of the dinner, instead of the usual toast to the President, he was introduced by a brief pageant. There was a military bugle call and three members came to the center of the hall carrying French, Belgian and Russian flags; a second call and three more, bearing the British, Italian and Japanese flags and marching to the tune of "Tipperary"; a third bugle call and three more members carrying the Cuban, Brazilian and American flags, to the music of "Yankee Doodle." They faced the chair and dipped colors. A soldier and a sailor in uniform took their places at each end of the massed colors, and Gridiron President Ira Bennett rose with a military salute and said:

"Mr. President, the united civilization of the world salutes you!"

At the end of Wilson's speech, of which no copy exists either in the Gridiron records or in the Wilson Library at Princeton, the orchestra played "The Star-Spangled Banner."

• • •

Because of the war, no dinners were held for two years. Before their resumption on December 13, 1919, the war had ended, and President Wilson had made his historic trip to Paris as head of the American delegation at the Versailles Peace Conference.

"If Wilson stepping off the boat," wrote William Bolitho in his book, *Twelve Against the Gods*, "had announced, in the tone he once possessed, world-disarmament, British fleet and German, French army, and Italian submarines, Gibraltar, Malta, Aden dismantled, and with that the abandonment of all the tariff barriers of the world—those of his own country first—as his unalterable terms, I am at perfect liberty to believe that he would have won. . . . The common people wherever he walked screamed for him to do it. . . .

"No one has ever had such cheers; I, who heard them in the streets of Paris, can never forget them in my life. I saw Foch pass, Clémenceau pass, Lloyd George, generals, returning troops, banners, but Wilson heard from his carriage, something different, inhuman—or superhuman. Oh, the immovably shining, smiling man."[10]

This was the high point of the Wilson career. He obtained the League of Nations he so much wanted as a part of the treaty, but had to make many compromises to do so. America was fast moving in an isolationist direction, and when in the fall of 1918 he asked for a Democratic Congress to endorse his proposals, the people gave him more Republicans than Democrats.

In the Senate, the League of Nations encountered vigorous opposition, primarily from Senators Henry Cabot Lodge, William E. Borah, and James A. Reed.

Wilson went back to Paris in March of 1919 and obtained some revisions, in an effort to make the treaty more acceptable to the Senate. He returned to the United States, and in the fall embarked upon a speaking tour to take his case to the American people. He collapsed on his train at Pueblo, Colorado, on September 25, 1919, and on October 3, suffered a paralytic stroke.

Consequently, at the December 13, 1919 dinner, he was not present, and Vice President Thomas R. Marshall substituted for him.

Because of the President's illness, there was no reference to him in the skits. One of the principal skits depicted representatives of the United States, Great Britain, France and Italy, and the head of the Secretariat at a meeting of the League of Nations, a meeting announced as being governed by the first of President Wilson's famous fourteen points, "Open covenants openly arrived at."

The head of the Secretariat explained that "a Secretariat is a great many people who would like to live in Geneva."

There was a move to provide that they be appointed by and with the consent of the United States Senate. This led the French member to ask what the Senate had to do with the League of Nations, and the American member replied, "The Senate of the United States *is* the League of Nations."

When discussion of the items on the agenda arose, the first question was a dispute over pasture lands between the Kurds and the Wheys. This was referred to the Committee on Dairy Products, and it was suggested that the committee ought to meet in some remote and neutral place. The island of Nankipoo was suggested and this was agreed upon.

Item number two on the agenda was a petition from Senator Gilbert Hitchcock and the Democratic members of the Foreign Relations Committee that President Wilson's favorite poem be set to music and adopted as the patriotic hymn of all nations. The American member said this poem was "Oh, for a Lodge in Some Vast Wilderness."

In view of the high hopes held by many for the League of Nations, the music skit was appropriately entitled "Utopia."

> This is the land of Utopia
> Here's where the pickings are fine,
> Here's where the grafter
> Would find a rich pasture,
> Here would the profiteer shine;
> Here there is no tax collector
> To lift a big slice from your roll,
> This is the land of Utopia,
> The land that the people control.

It was explained that Sir Thomas More didn't have a king in his utopia, but that "we've got one in ours, thereby improving on Sir Thomas and making ours a true democracy."

The king proved to be a coal king, who sang:

> Yes, my own idea of greatest fun
> Is high-priced coal and a short weight ton.

The skit closed with the king remarking that "It's the same old story. All hunting utopia where they can get the best of everyone else, where they can get something for nothing."

The chief reference to the Presidential situation in this dinner consisted of a song in which the principal aspirants, Secretary of the Treasury McAdoo, Attorney General Mitchell Palmer, Senator Atlee Pomerene, James M. Cox, Speaker Champ Clark, and Vice President Marshall, were all waiting to hear the word as to which one the President would pick.

> We have been waiting for you, Chief, to speak,
> Waiting for more than a year;
> For we have been anxious to know where we stand,
> Won't you give us the true steer?
> Oh, does your duty impel you to take another term?

Give us the dope that is true,
Oh, you may believe us, you'll greatly relieve us,
For we are waiting for you.

• • •

In 1920 the spring dinner, held on April 10, made no mention of the sick President Wilson. It was primarily based on the coming political conventions, on the defeat of the League of Nations, and on the old perennials of previous dinners: Prohibition, woman suffrage, and William Jennings Bryan.

The President was represented by Secretary of State Robert Lansing, who was the guest of honor but made no speech. A Senate group of "Bitter Enders" sang of their victory in defeating the Versailles Treaty on November 19, 1919, and stated their case in song.

We've a kingdom of our own
With Liberty upon the throne,
And every man is King, all right*
And every woman is a Queen by right;
In our own background we'll stay,
From foreign strife we'll keep away,
To our affairs we'll strictly 'tend,
On our resources we'll depend,
And we'll leave the world alone,
So *h-a-p-p-y* we'll be
In this country of our own.

The commander of the American Expeditionary Force, General John J. Pershing, was a guest at this dinner, and the club, in a rather touching song, spelled out the country's admiration of him:

Oh, we sent you over there to lick the Hun,
And you did the job with neatness and dispatch,
You put Bill Hohenzollern on the run,
For every trick he had, you'd one to match.
May your luck be never failing,
    may your love be ever true,
God bless you, Johnny Pershing,
    here's your country's love to you.

There was a song at this dinner to William Edgar Borah, the lordly senator from Idaho, whose majestic head of hair and voice that could always be heard throughout the Senate galleries were

---

*Preceding Huey Long's campaign cry of "Every man a king" by about fifteen years.

already making him a national figure. He looked like a senator should, and he had an arrogance that permitted him to criticize anyone. There were various verses in this song directed to different candidates in the Republican party, and each time the chorus, to the tune of "Roll, Jordan, Roll," rang out:

> Roar, Borah, roar,
> Roar, Borah, roar,
> The candidates all tremble in the knees
> When they hear Bill Borah roar.

There was also a skit entitled "The Three Mediums," in which the principals wore long black robes and a Ouija board was operated by Ashmun Brown. The Ouija board gave forth the usual type of Gridiron comment on the various candidates who were being talked about for the coming conventions.

But the high point of the evening proved to be a speech by Senator Henry Fountain Ashurst of Arizona, which turned out to be one of the great satires on professional politicians of all parties.

Ashurst was a tall and imposing individual who had been elected when Arizona was admitted to statehood in 1912. He was known as a flowery and flamboyant orator with a great command of language. He started off by addressing the Gridiron Club as if it were the convention of the Democratic party, and by describing the wonders of Arizona.

"A populous land before the Pyramids were built," inhabited by people who "smelted gold and silver, from Arizona's hills, into chieftains' and queens' girdles long before Caesar's shouting legions and laureled ensigns brought tribute back to Imperial Rome."

Then he proceeded to nominate the state's candidate for President:

"My candidate," he said, "has shared the common fate of all wise men—he has not escaped calumny. For example, whizzing javelins of slander are now being directed toward him because of his ingenuous statement that he would rather read Irvin S. Cobb than Spencer, Darwin or Huxley, and that he prefers Jimmie Montague's jingles to Ibsen's iambic pentameters."

Whether or not Ashurst knew the specific kind of verse which Ibsen used, it was immaterial to him, because he was the kind of orator who never allowed anything to interfere with the resounding phrase.

"Because my candidate can and frequently does, deliver a speech which is serenely detached from all information," continued Ashurst, "the envious have called him a word-milliner; a dealer in the plumage of phrase, but even envy itself confesses that he never commits syntactical errors.

"My candidate is a practical man and when sowing wild oats, used care to see that there was always a generous admixture of Rye therein. He knows that a Socialist is a Bolshevik who has been shaved. He knows that so long as America has her Senate she will be Master of the Air. . . .

"And only recently he has published a philosophical disquisition (which I commend to you younger delegates here who are seeking promotion in politics) entitled *To succeed in Politics you must cultivate a memory that easily forgets!*

"He is a man of courage, not of doleful sentiment or of lachrymal moisture, and as example of his doughty courage, I need but remind you that he became a champion of national Prohibition from the very moment it became obvious to him that national Prohibition was inevitable.

"Although a cynical and careless world has thus far failed to discover a trace of his greatness, I who know him best, take pride in assuring this convention that he is a composite of the contemporaneous great men of the day—the Honorable

Henry Fountain Ashurst from Arizona."[11]

This kind of laughing at oneself, which, so far as Gridiron files show, was initiated by Senator Ashurst, proved to be one of the most certain routes to the success of a Gridiron speech. It was later utilized most effectively by President Kennedy, Vice President Agnew, and to some extent by others.

• • •

After the 1920 election in which Senator Warren G. Harding won a decisive victory over the Democratic candidate James M. Cox, the December 11 dinner made scant reference to the still sick and retiring President Wilson, but was devoted mainly to the election, to Congress, to the perennial subject of Prohibition, and to the President-elect.

In opening the dinner, Gridiron Club President W. W. Jermane remarked that "post mortems, of the political variety, are frequently unfruitful; but there is no good reason why they should be uninteresting."

Announcing that they were going to hold such a post mortem that night, he stressed that "the light would be deflected to pass through Gridiron lenses" and then expressed the hope that this would only "increase its searching power."

"Not all of it, however, will illumine the past;" he said, "we shall hope, also, to reveal something as to the future. We shall want, in other words, to look forward as well as backward, thus proving again, if proof were necessary, that the world's tomorrows, after they have arrived, are found to be strangely like its yesterdays."

Then he read a telegram from President-elect Harding, expressing his regrets at his inability to be present, extending his "cordial greetings and good wishes to all members of the club," and expressing the hope that his regrets would be outweighed by "agreeable anticipations of meeting with you on future occasions."

In those days, the members of the preelection Congress convened the first week in January and had what was termed a "lame duck" session, lasting until Inauguration Day on March 4.

In one of the skits, an impersonator of Presidential Secretary Joseph P. Tumulty remarked, "Well, Congress is with us again."

"What's that?" sharply demanded the personage partially obscured behind the desk.

"I said, Congress is *with* us again," repeated the secretary.

"May I suggest, Tumulty," stated the personage, "that it would be better for you to say, 'Congress is in session again.'"

The refusal of the Senate to approve the covenant of the League of Nations was treated in a parody of Shakespeare's Marc Antony oration over the dead body of Julius Caesar, delivered by an impersonator of Senator Gilbert M. Hitchcock of Nebraska, an opponent of the League.

> Friends, Romans, countrymen, lend me your ears
>   (and hold your own tongues)
> I come to bury Covenant, not to praise him.
> The evil that leagues do lives after them;
> The good is oft interred with their bones;
> So let it be with Covenant. The noble Harding
> Hath told you Covenant was ambiguous.
> If it were so, it were a grievous fault,
> And grievously hath Covenant answered it
> But Harding says it was ambiguous,
> And Harding is an honorable man.
>
> If you have tears, prepare to shed them now.
> You all do know this mantle; I remember

The first time ever Covenant put it on.
'Twas on a Paris evening, in his tent,
That day he mustered up the Nervii
To circumvent Lloyd George and Clemenceau.
Look, in this place ran Cabot's dagger through;
See what a rent Philander Knox hath made;
Through this the well elected Harding stabbed.

Oh, what a fall was there, my countrymen!
Then I, and you, and all of us fell down
While Warren Harding flourished over us!

Farewell, O Covenant, lie low and sleep well;
Farewell the pomp of words and Article X,
Farewell the cloud-capped towers and gorgeous dreams,
Farewell the fourteen points and visions all—
While we, your weeping friends, stand by and say
Here was a Covenant! When comes such another?

Prohibition was treated in a duet to the tune of "Reuben and Rachel," a popular song of the time.

Rachel:
Reuben, Reuben, I've been thinking
What a dry world this will be,
When there's no illicit drinking,
Only ginger ale or tea.
Reuben:
Rachel, Rachel, you stop thinking,
For that time will never be,
While there's hootch there will be drinking,
You can take that tip from me.
Rachel:
Reuben, don't you think reformers
Are a very funny lot,
Trying to make earth a heaven,
Spoiling all the fun we've got?
Reuben:
Rachel, you have said a mouthful,
And to all the world I'll tell,
These reformers talk of heaven,
But they're always raising hell.

The initiation skit, in which Roy Roberts of the *Kansas City Star*, Clinton W. Gilbert of the *Philadelphia Evening Ledger*, and Stanley M. Reynolds of the *Baltimore Evening Sun* were initiated, poked fun at newspapermen. Each of the three initiates was called upon to explain his forecast on the Presidential election, as illustrated by this colloquy with Roberts:

Member: Did you give the solid South to Governor Cox?
Roberts: I believe I did.
Member: Did he get it?
Roberts: Not exactly.
Member: Did you criticize the political bosses for making blunders?
Roberts: You bet I did.
Member: Did you write about the sensation that was going to be sprung next week?
Roberts: Yes, indeed. I was always a week ahead of it.
Member: Did you fix up a prediction that would cover the result both ways?
Roberts: I admit that I bought an underhold on the result.
Member: Did you say that, while the country would certainly go Republican, on the other hand, in certain contingencies and provided certain things happened, it would go Democratic?
Roberts: Why, we all do that.

President-elect Harding had run a peculiar campaign, in that most of his important pronouncements were made to various groups that assembled before the front porch of his house in Marion, Ohio, as Benjamin Harrison had done in 1888. It was referred to as the "front porch campaign." Instead of traveling around the country, select groups came to him, and he outlined his policies and philosophies to them and, through the newspapers, to the country.

In the music skit one of Harding's associates, Harry Daugherty, played KoKo and sang the Gilbert and Sullivan song, "As Someday It May Happen, That a Victim Must be Found."

The victims included practically all of the major characters in the Wilson administration, and a typical stanza ran:

March fourth it sure will happen
That Joe Daniels will go out,
I've got him on the list,
I've got him on the list;
He's going home to Raleigh
Full of medals for the South,
And he never will be missed.

Continuing the Gilbert and Sullivan theme, an impersonator of Senator John W. Weeks of Massachusetts, who was later to be secretary of war, sang an adaptation of "When I Was a Lad."

> In the big campaign we are passing through
> I am captain of an efficient crew,
> I gather in the cash and garner in the votes,
> And even in a pinch I negotiate the notes.

Chorus: And even in a pinch he negotiates the notes.

> I garner in the votes so skillfully,
> I want to be the ruler of our big Na-vee.

Chorus: He garners in the votes so skillfully,
> He wants to be the ruler of our big Na-vee.

The two principal speakers of the dinner were Vice President Marshall, who was appearing for the last time at a Gridiron dinner as Vice President of the United States, and Senator Henry Cabot Lodge, Republican leader of the Senate, chairman of the Committee on Foreign Relations, and chief architect of the defeat of American adherence to the League of Nations.

In presenting Vice President Marshall, who responded to the toast to the President at the end of the dinner, President Jermane gave him a large gridirion as a souvenir, with the comment that "we like him, and we half suspect that he likes us sometimes, and we don't want anything that happened on November 2nd, or that is to happen at any other time, to mean that we are to see him no more at these dinners. If we can have our way about it, he will be present in the future just as regularly as in the past."

And then Jermane announced that a token similar to this one had been sent with the very best wishes of the club to the President of the United States, "who many times has been our guest of honor, but who, because of illness, has been prevented from attending our more recent dinners."

• • •

No chapter on Woodrow Wilson at the Gridiron Club should be closed without relating a story divulged more than twenty years later by Helen Essary, wife of J. Fred Essary of the *Baltimore Sun* and distinguished Gridiron member, in a column published in a Washington newspaper.

It was in the last year of President Wilson's administration and he lay desperately ill from a paralytic stroke, which had so affected him that he was unable to function as President. Joseph

P. Tumulty and the cabinet had been carrying on the best they could, but no one else knew at that time how serious the President's illness was. It had been carefully concealed as actions were taken in his name.

Some of the people around him began to wonder whether it was fair for him to continue, or whether he should be announced as incompetent and Vice President Marshall be permitted to succeed to the office.

It was decided, Mrs. Essary reported, that the Vice President must be approached for his ideas, but the situation was too delicate to be handled carelessly, because Mr. Marshall might insist on moving up to the higher office, and the effect of the public knowledge of the President's incompetence might also be devastating to the country.

"Somebody must go to Mr. Marshall," wrote Mrs. Essary. "Somebody who could be trusted competely with the facts of this hazardous moment. Mr. Marshall was even then unaware of the seriousness of his Chief's illness. The truth had been kept secret. . . .

"What man was there to take this message to the Vice President? The few close, loyal friends of Mr. Wilson debated the choice in troubled whispers. At last they came to a decision. There was a certain newspaperman, a much-respected Washington correspondent, who knew Vice President Marshall well and who had discretion, tact and loyalty.

"Out of the whole city of Washington, out of the whole country in fact, this man, whose profession it was to tell, was chosen to handle and keep secret the vital mission.

"He went to Mr. Marshall. Met him in a solemn conference, at which no one else was present, and laid the cards as he saw them on the table, gave him the honest story of Mr. Wilson's illness. He said to Mr. Marshall, in effect, you can be President of the United States if you wish. You know this. But do you think it would be good for the nation at this time? The decision is in your hands.

"The Vice President hesitated for a while. Chewed on one of his famous cigars. Talked and listened and then said, 'Well, Fred Essary, I believe we'll let things stay as they are. I don't believe it would be smart to upset the country any more right now.'

"The newspaperman went back to Woodrow Wilson's friends and gave Marshall's message. They were relieved of some of their anxiety. Woodrow Wilson continued nominally the President of the United States.

"Thomas Marshall kept faith. Woodrow Wilson's close friends kept his secret.

"And as for the newspaperman—he had a story that would have electrified the world. He never wrote it."[12]

VII

Warren Gamaliel Harding

1921-1923
Scandal on the Horizon

Warren Gamaliel Harding attended his first Gridiron dinner on November 16, 1914, just after he had been elected Senator from Ohio, and that night he was one of the Republican speakers. Although he was a frequent guest in the meantime, it was close to six and a half years later, on April 9, 1921, before he attended his first dinner as President of the United States

The intervening years had given little indication that this first-term senator would be the next President, and it was somewhat of an accident that he was. Harding was a very amiable man, who enjoyed friendships within the Senate, even among political opponents. His six-year term was rather undistinguished, but he made many friends and voted pretty much the straight Republican party line.

When the Republican National Convention opened in Chicago in 1920, most of the delegates were for either Governor Frank O. Lowden of Illinois; Major General Leonard Wood, former army chief of staff; or Senator Hiram W. Johnson of California. But behind the scenes, Harry H. Daugherty, a shrewd Ohio political strategist, was working hard for a compromise. After four inconclusive ballots, on which the supporters of none of the three candidates seemed willing to transfer their support to any of the others, the convention adjourned in deadlock.

That night at the Blackstone Hotel, in a smoke-filled room— not the first such, but the first to get the label—a meeting of the powerful political leaders in the Republican party agreed upon Senator Harding as the compromise candidate, and the next day he was nominated.

He had been a newspaper publisher in the small town of Marion, Ohio, and his small-town background remained with him throughout both his campaign and the Presidency.

The country had been through a horrendous experience: World War I, and then the bitter controversy over the League of Nations, which led to the breaking of President Wilson's health and the termination of his strong leadership. Harding sensed that the country was tired of war and controversy and made his principal campaign appeal for a return to "normalcy."

He was elected overwhelmingly, with 404 electoral votes against 127 for James M. Cox, the Democratic nominee, and by a popular vote plurality of over seven million. He made some extraordinarily good appointments—the respected and distinguished Charles Evans Hughes as secretary of state, Andrew W. Mellon as secretary of the treasury, Herbert Hoover as secretary of commerce, and former President Taft as chief justice. He also made some extraordinarily bad ones, based largely on personal and political friendships.

He promptly signed peace treaties which did not include the League of Nations covenant, reduced taxes, raised tariffs, and for the first time in the history of the country placed quotas on immigration. "Back to Normalcy" was in full swing.

But Harding's capacity for friendship, which was to lead to much trouble for him, was recognized and satirized at his first Gridiron Dinner as President. A character wandered on the stage, proclaiming that he was from Marion and that "me and Warren are old neighbors." He was asked if all the people in Marion expected government jobs and replied, "No, indeed; the chief of police, the city clerk, and the preachers will have to stay there, I reckon."

At another point, inquiry was made as to the identity of a very lonesome and despondent individual wandering around the hall.

"Yes, I am lonesome," he said. "I am the only surviving private citizen of Marion, Ohio."

The small-town character of the President's background was celebrated to the tune of "My Home Town Is a One Horse Town," as follows:

Out in Marion
Nearly everyone
Calls his neighbor Bill or Dan;
We have electric lights
And a lot of sights
To impress most any man.
You should see Main Street on Sat'day night
Then talk about your Broadway crowd;
It's some city, don't waste your pity,
Of our town we are proud.
My home town is a darned good town
And it's big enough for me;
The population are real and true,
You'll find they're the kind of folks like me and you,
Our town gave to the world a big event,
You came there to select a President,
My home town is a darned good town,
And it's big enough for me.

The idea was even carried to the inauguration of the president of the Gridiron Club, North O. Messenger of the *Washington Star*. There had been some open talk about the cost of the Harding inauguration, and after a simple ceremony in which Mr. Messenger was declared inaugurated, a Gridiron member asked:

"How much did that inauguration cost?"

Richard V. Oulahan of the inauguration committee responded "S-s-s-h-h-h! Thirty cents, but don't tell Senator Borah," whereupon Messenger commented, "I must say that for simplicity and economy this inauguration excels anything of its kind I have recently seen."

As the club continued to play on the factors that proved within a year or two to be President Harding's greatest weakness, the relationships of senators with their old colleague came in for a bit of spoofing in the verses of one of the songs.

Do senators now, with a manner that's bold
Address him as Warren, like they did of old?
Oh, no, they're quite formal, to please him they try,
For they are all hungry for patronage pie.

None of the Gridiron dinners of this period failed to lament that they were then, of necessity, nonalcoholic. This was done at

Harding's first Presidential dinner with a parody of "Let the Rest of the World Go By."

> With some one like you
> Who makes good home brew,
> I'd like to steal away for life,
> From all this strife;
> Some place that's known, to us alone,
> Where no Volstead agents come.
> We'll set up a still
> On some pretty hill,
> Out there beneath a kindly sky;
> We'll build a sweet little nest
> Somewhere in the west,
> And let the rest of the world go *dry*.

With the change of administrations, there came, of course, a big changeover in the executive branch of the government, and the demand for patronage by Republicans was the subject of considerable raillery. At one point, each of the new cabinet members was asked to stand while veteran Gridiron member Henry Hall gave them advice about how to handle this and other subjects. With memories of an austere predecessor, Elihu Root, he said to the dignified and somber Charles Evans Hughes, "In all friendliness, I urge you not to adopt the 'hail fellow, well met' style with us [newspapermen]. Don't slap us on the back and call us 'old man,' as did that genial fellow, Elihu Root."

It is perhaps significant that as far back as 1921 there was widespread complaint about the mail service, and the new postmaster general was asked if he thought he could improve the mail service.

"I don't see how I could make it any worse," he responded, "and I can improve the personnel."

The principal music skit was set on New Jersey Senator Joseph S. Frelinghuysen's yacht with the President aboard. The yacht was stuck in a mudbank. When the senatorial skipper was asked the whereabouts of the President, he replied that "he motored to the golf links. He'll have time to play eighteen holes in the twelve hours before high tide."

A Kentucky colonel aboard wanted to know who the President was going to appoint as commissioner of Internal Revenue, the service which was the bête noire of the operators of private stills. In a parody of "Down by the Old Mill Stream," the colonel sang:

How sad and still tonight,
By the old distillery;
     And how the cobwebs cob
     In its old machinery;
But in the mountain tops
Far from the eyes of cops,
Oh, how the moon shines on the moonshine,
     so merrily
How sad and merrily.

The yacht in mud skit was the vehicle for introducing a character representing Charles G. Dawes, later to be Vice President under Coolidge and already famous for his picturesque language. He entered with phrases with which he had been identified:

"What the hell. Damnation and tarnation. Hell and Maria."

"Charlie Dawes approaches quietly," someone noted.

"Yes," said the impersonator of Dawes, "I just left those blithering idiots who were investigating war expenditures. Told 'em where to head in. . . . I might have cussed a little but I held my temper. A man's got to cuss or cry, and I didn't cry."

But while less than five weeks after the beginning of the Harding administration the Gridiron Club seemed to have touched upon its weaknesses, it nevertheless characteristically closed the dinner with a song designed to warm the President's heart.

Mr. Harding, we have something to tell you,
And it's worthwhile listening to,
It's a little man-to-man talk,
We say it sincerely to you:
We like the way you've started working,
We like your manner and your style;
No task seems big enough to fright you,
We know it's true, you're a man, through and through;
You're solving great problems of the nation
Problems of vital application,
But without fear or trepidation;
And America stands back of you.

Those were the days of many speeches, and at this dinner they were made by Boies Penrose, Charles Evans Hughes, Dr. Charles Sawyer, Vice President Coolidge, and to close the dinner, President Harding.

It is unfortunate that none of Harding's Gridiron speeches survive, unless they are still locked in private files maintained under the jurisdiction of Harding associates and their successors. Harding's speeches were reported in Washington newspapers at the time to have been quite good and quite impressive, although the Gridiron rule against publication was carefully observed and not even the meagerest quotations from them are available.

• • •

The December 10, 1921 dinner, the second attended by Harding as President, attracted a large number of foreign guests. The Disarmament Conference had been on in Washington for about a month when the dinner was held, and many of the participants were present, including Lord Arthur Balfour, foreign minister of England, Jules Jusserand of France, and the ambassadors of many other countries.

Among other distinguished foreign guests were Lord Northcliffe, publisher, and H. Wickham Steed, editor of the *London Times*; Stephane Lausanne; and H. G. Wells.

While there was considerable raillery directed at President Harding and the "Good Ship Normalcy," the Disarmament Conference was treated with respect and deference, because it seemed at that time to be a momentous undertaking.

Toward the end of the program a member of the club came on the stage and addressed the diners as follows:

"Five great powers, meeting here in Washington, have achieved in a month's time more than all the world achieved for disarmament in a quarter of a century of aspiration and effort. To these five powers the Gridiron Club tonight pays homage. We feel that it is fitting for us to look upon five symbols which represent these powers, banded in common cause, whose work here is translating the great vision into fact. The symbols we shall show you are not those of war, but of peace. Tonight they stand together as closely bound by ties of brotherhood as they were in the day of a world tragedy. We ask you, gentlemen, to look upon them!"

Then, one by one, the silken banners of Japan, Italy, France, Great Britain and the United States were borne into the room, each by a bearer attired in the military uniform of the country represented and each heralded by the national anthem of that country, played by the Marine Band. Every flag was received with tumultuous applause, all present standing. When the five had been grouped, a member of the club announced that "to these five flags, united in the task that a barrier against war shall be built high and strong and imperishable, the Gridiron Club offers its salute."

To the music of "The Star Spangled Banner," the flags were marched off, and Lord Balfour was introduced to speak.

The other speakers that night also reflected the great public interest in the conference. They were Lord Northcliffe, Secretary of State Hughes, and former President Taft, in addition, of course, to the closing speech by President Harding.

With all the wars that occurred from the thirties to the seventies, it seems a little incongruous that there should have been so much hope for the Disarmament Conference as was reflected in this dinner.

The Gridiron Club did not attempt to put the "Good Ship Normalcy" on the Gridiron stage, but used a technique of receiving radio messages during the evening from the ship at sea.

They started off with the first information that the ship was "running on even keel. Band playing. Everybody singing. Not a care in the world."

A later one reported that it was "followed by a fleet of privateers. Correction: Make that last word read *profit*eers. Lookout Daugherty finding some stowaways and many barnacles."

Another: In deep water. No bars.

Another: Stokers and coal passers all want to be First Officers. It's a bitter night at sea. Just passed between two large icebergs. Now steering Northern Lights.

Then: Usual afternoon athletic events took place on hurricane deck for entertainment ship's company. Bob La Follette sparred four rounds with Boies Penrose and Bill Borah shadowboxed the compass.

And another: Ship rolling heavily. Cannot account for it as sea is calm.

Later: Mystery solved; Chief Engineer George Harvey is rocking the boat.

And the final message: Now in foreign waters. Pilot Hughes aboard. Skies fair and sea calm. Eight bells and the larboard watch. All's well.

In the nostalgic good fellowship that has so often characterized Gridiron dinners, they welcomed back former President Taft, now chief justice, with a parody of "Look for the Silver Lining."

He looks for a silver lining, when'er a cloud appears in the blue,
He knows that somewhere the sun is shining, and that the right
  thing to do
  Is make it shine for you.
His heart full of joy and gladness, He always banished trouble and
  laughed,
He always looked for the silver lining, our great Chief Justice
  William Howard Taft.

In view of the comparatively low taxes of that day, and the fact that this was the first year of Andrew Mellon's continuous yearly reduction of taxes for almost a decade, it also seems a little strange that they should have had a song called "The Taxpayer's Lament." Tudor Morsell, one of the club's outstanding limited members, sang:

Not a dollar that I earn will stay with me,
They are hard enough to get, take it from me.
But throughout the whole year around,
Taxes pull me to the ground,
I'd weep no more if some place could be found.
Some happy spot with no taxes to pay,
Let me take my pocketbook and leave me there to stay.

The perennial Prohibition gag consisted of a song to the tune of "I Dine Tomorrow with a Diplomat," in which a man insisted that he was a prohibitionist.

I insist I'm a prohibitionist
But I like a drink now and then.
I'm against the demon Rum
Cause it is not good for some;
And to set a good example
Licker red I never sample
When there is anyone around
Or the vile stuff can't be found.

The close of the dinner was friendly to the administration and optimistic. The chorus sang:

We jest sing and have our fling,
But never fears oppress us,
Hope springs eternal in our breasts,
And nothing can depress us.

So do not fret or stew,
There's work for all to do.

We've had hard times but there's
Good times coming in 1922.

• • •

Despite substantial majorities in both houses of Congress, President Harding found it difficult to get much accomplished. Congress seemed more concerned with patronage, speechmaking on old issues, and with internal bickering. There was an obvious lack of leadership in both houses.

Both dinners of April 22 and December 9, 1922 were attended by President Harding, and the congressional problem was the main theme of the April dinner.

In a leadership skit the Gridiron Club advertised for a leader for the Republican party in Congress and received and read numerous responses.

A discredited scientist replied, "I have proved that the earth is flat with a solid dome. So is the Republican party. Will take leadership."

"Henry Ford," whose cars in those days frequently developed rattles, responded, "The Republican party in Congress is suffering from political rattles. I am an expert on rattles."

"Charlie Chaplin," who often had pies thrown in his face in his early movies, answered, "The Republican party in Congress is demoralized from lack of pie. Make me leader and they'll get lots of it."

"Einstein" replied, "I have proven that time is non-existent. So has your Senate. Nevertheless, I would rather lecture to the French Academy without a net than take a chance on leading your Congress. Until I am sure that sound does not exist I must decline."

And the final one came from "Houdini": "The Republican party in Congress is in a hell of a box. I am the only one who can get it out." Then to the tune of "Oh Dear, What Can the Matter Be?" he belted out:

The people have voted with sober reflection,
Republicans now in a state of dejection,
    For Congress went slopping along.

We suffer a long oratorical revel
Of speeches that are on a very low level—
The people between the deep seas and the devil,
    While Congress goes slopping along.

By December, however, the club was beginning to look forward to the 1924 election. It was at this dinner, in a guest skit by Tom Brahany, Arthur Henning, W. W. Jermane, and William Brigham of the Gridiron Club, that they called to their feet a large number of business leaders. The first one was Girard Swope, president of the General Electric Company,

"What have you to say?" Asked Mr. Brigham.

Jermane replied, "Mr. Swope says he has nothing to say."

A similar reply was given in behalf of each of the others, whereupon Senator William E. Borah was quoted as commenting, "Gentlemen, you are running true to form. Your modesty is only exceeded by your discretion. You have the businessman's slant on Washington investigating committees: "Tell them nothing.'"

By the end of 1922, the Bull Moose party founded by Teddy Roosevelt in the 1912 election had largely fallen apart, but its supporters were still a distinct faction of the Republicans in the Senate. That night, under "the Gridiron's spreading chestnut tree," there was an elaborate parody of the witches' scene from *Macbeth,* in which Senators William E. Borah, Hiram Johnson, and Robert La Follette were the three witches.

The impersonator of Borah soliloquized on whether it was better to remain within the party and swat the administration, thereby affording the Democrats much glee, or to become a new party man in name as well as in deed.

To the tune of "Listen to the Mocking Bird," the club correctly identified the two leading figures in the famous 103-ballot deadlocked Democratic Convention of 1924.

The Democrats are happy, are happy, are happy,
They're feeling fine and snappy,
    For they think they'll win in 1924;
They're working like damnation, damnation, damnation,
In a hopeful expectation,
    And already there are candidates galore.

Listen to the McAdoo, listen to the McAdoo,
    He says that he is not a candidate;
Listen to the McAdoo, listen to the McAdoo,
    But you can bet he'll never hesitate.

New York is Democratic, Democratic, Democratic,
And the party is ecstatic,
    With a half a million margin not a myth;

They say they have a winner, a winner, a winner,
And they'll bet you a good dinner
   They can put across a man named Alfred Smith.

Listen to the Alfred Smith, listen to the Alfred Smith,
   As he whispers to his friends that he's all right;
Listen to the Alfred Smith, listen to the Alfred Smith,
   As he tells you there is no one else in sight.

Listen to the Underwood, listen to the Underwood,
   As he talks to you of tariffs that are low;
Listen to the Underwood, listen to the Underwood,
   "A better man," HE says, "I do not know."

And even the outcome was forecast at another point, when a member of the cast recited a limerick:

Democrats are *now filled* with cheer,
The election has lessened their fears;
But please to remember
The only November
They win in is in an off-year.

• • •

The February 10, 1923 dinner, Harding's last, was notable primarily for the restraint shown by the club on his developing problems. Largely, these were not public knowledge at that time, but there was widespread criticism of "the Ohio gang," chief of which was Attorney General Harry M. Daugherty. Most of them were old friends of Harding's, and he enjoyed them as both social and poker companions as well as members of his administration.

Three months later, Jesse W. Smith, a friend of Daugherty's was to commit suicide after it had been revealed that he was arranging settlements between the Department of Justice and alleged law violators. There were charges of misuse of funds in the Veterans' Bureau, which later resulted in the suicide of its legal adviser and the imprisonment of its director. And there was criticism of the Teapot Dome oil leases, later to be investigated by the Senate and to result in the conviction for bribery of Secretary of the Interior Albert B. Fall. While the main revelations came out later, there was already considerable gossip going about in Washington.

Depression in the farm states had led to the serious slippage of Republican congressional strength, and, in general, things were beginning to get rough for the administration. But the references in the Gridiron skits to these problems were sparse.

Mainly, the dinner consisted of good-natured joshing of individuals. Since it occurred four days before St. Valentine's Day,
there were valentines read to several of the prominent figures in
the cabinet, including Andrew Mellon and Herbert Hoover. The
one to Hoover is significant in that it showed the stature which
he was already developing despite the attacks that had been
made upon him by Democrat James A. Reed of Missouri.

> Oh Hoover, Herbert Hoover,
> You're our obstacle remover,
> Be it miners' strikes or storage dams,
>   or other damned things.
> You're our scientific prover,
> Our statistical Who's Whover,
> Our business world reprover:
> In fact, the whole three rings.
> You're our foremost vacuum sweeper,
> Our sower and our reaper;
> With meatless, wheatless, heatless days
>   you filled us long with dread;
> So it's strange you cannot fashion
> Some effective way to ration
> That incessant flow of language
>   Jim Reed pours on your head.

However, the main music skit was a Gridiron version of the
operetta *Robin Hood,* entitled "Robbing Good." The band of
wicked outlaws, led by the income tax collector, the landlord, the
coal man, the bootlegger, and various other public utilities men,
householders, plumbers, milkmen, icemen, and even janitors,
proclaimed:

> Finer outlaws were never seen,
> Robbers free as we know how to be,
> Robbing everyone that we can see.

A consumer complained, "I'm a consumer in a bad humor,"
the landlord proclaimed that he was raising the rent each year,
and the tax collector sang, to the tune "I Am the Sheriff of
Nottingham":

> Yes, pay! I would if I were you.
> You may gaily try but you never will descry
>   Such a wholesale robber as I!

Harding had announced that after Congress adjourned he
proposed to take a vacation in Florida, and therefore the Gridiron
version of "Old Folks at Home" was sung to him.

Way down upon the Indian River
In Florida,
Now all your thoughts are turning thither,
Where you can rest or play.
Soon you will leave on your vacation,
Gladly to roam.
You'll find the sweetest consolation
Far from the Statesmen at home.
Leave your troubles all behind you
Mid the palm trees deep;
Go where the lame ducks cannot find you
Where alligators creep.

Soon you'll be strolling on the beaches
Down Palm Beach way,
Far from intrigue and Senate speeches,
Far from the donkey's bray,
When you are playing golf or fishing,
Or sailing o'er the foam,
We know that you will not be wishing
For politics back home.

The President's speech that night was reported by the newspapers to have been a felicitous one, but it was obvious that he was deeply concerned with the developing problems.

Consequently, in June 1923, seeing the necessity of trying to revive confidence in his administration, Harding embarked upon a long speaking tour across the country, to Canada (he was the first President to visit Canada while in office), and on to Alaska.

On the way back, Harding, who was never accused of any lack of honesty himself, only too much misplaced trust in others, received a coded message from Washington about the Senate investigation of oil leases. He was reported by the papers to have appeared very tired anyway, and this message evidently depressed him. He fell ill in Seattle, and his trip was halted in San Francisco. After a few days he died, presumably of food poisoning and pneumonia, although no autopsy was ever performed.

VIII

Calvin Coolidge

1923-1929
"Silent Cal" maintains
his reputation

Calvin Coolidge, "Silent Cal" from New England, was now the thirtieth President of the United States. He had risen quite suddenly into national prominence in 1919, when as governor of Massachusetts he had called out the militia to end a police strike in Boston.

In spite of his reputation for solemnity, Coolidge was a devotee of Gridiron dinners. He attended his first dinner in December 1919 as governor, every dinner given during the two and a half years that he was Vice President, and all but two dinners during the five and a half years that he was President. Although he made his thorough enjoyment of these dinners obvious to all, he still managed to keep his reputation for silence reasonably well.

At his first dinner as President on December 8, 1923, he was not listed on the program to speak. He had evidently begged off to Arthur Sears Henning of the *Chicago Tribune*, then president of the club. But the club decided to make him think better of it on the spot, by closing the dinner with a song to Coolidge based on the tune "Three O'Clock in the Morning."

Now it is late in the evening,
    You are our honored guest,
Clock ticks give us a warning
    That you must seek your rest.
Gridiron lights o'er you flaring
    Soon will be dimmed for the night.
We hope and pray, Mr. Pres-i-dent
    That you will sleep tight.

Hear Mr. Coolidge our tune,
    You may sleep in the morn
Till the clock strikes noon.

Now approacheth the morning,
    We've dined the whole night through;
Dinner guests all are calling
    For a few words from you.
Oh, please sir, heed our entreaties,
    You may be sure if you do
We will all keep right on boosting
    Forever, Cal, for you.

Even "Silent Cal" couldn't resist that, and the *Washington Star* reported the following day that "to this, President Coolidge responded in a charming speech, which, under the rules of the club that 'no reporters are present,' cannot be quoted." Since this speech was off-the-cuff, no record of it exists.

A unique feature of this dinner was that all living sons of President Coolidge and former Presidents of the United States were invited to the dinner and were "stood up." Most of them attended, the most notable exception being Robert Todd Lincoln, secretary of war under President Garfield and from 1897 to 1911 president of the Pullman Company. He was living in Manchester, Vermont, was eighty years old, and regretted that the state of his health was such that it was impossible for him to come.

• • •

The Gridiron Club was so widely known by the third decade of the 1900's that a fellow by the name of Jules Howard Ford, using the alias Doc Waterbury, started selling club memberships at $100 or $200 apiece, or whatever he could collect. A surprising number of people, some quite prominent, who had heard of Gridiron dinners were taken in by this imposter, who was finally caught.

He was convicted, however, first on another charge arising out of a scheme he had to supply the libraries for the American army in France. After serving a term in Auburn prison, he was paroled and brought up again on a charge of grand larceny, arising out of the sale of Gridiron memberships. He pleaded guilty, but it was said on his behalf that he had been adequately punished for the crimes he had committed, and a letter was introduced from the warden of the prison expressing the belief that, if released, he would be a law-abiding citizen.

The judge suspended sentence. Ford's lawyer was Ferdinand Pecora, later famous as the relentless inquisitor of America's financial leaders in a stock market investigation of the depression era.

• • •

Substantial change had been made in the cabinet by President Coolidge prior to the December 1923 dinner. Some of the old members were gone.

Many of the vacancies had been filled with New Englanders. Consequently, the main skit at this dinner was entitled "The Landing of the Pilgrims in Pennsylvania Avenue." It was performed on a stage set with a background view of the Presidential yacht *Mayflower* riding at anchor.

Impersonators of John W. Weeks, secretary of war; Senator Henry Cabot Lodge, Senator George H. Moses of New Hampshire, Senator Frank B. Brandegee of Connecticut, and C. Bascom Slemp, principal aide to the President, all trooped in along with others.

"Now that we are here," said Weeks, "let's be a long time getting out."

Moses added, "We take possession of Pennsylvania Avenue in the name of Calvin Coolidge, New England, the Republican party, and four more years."

These Pilgrims, like the earlier ones that came on another *Mayflower,* were bothered by Indians too, the Indians this time being the Progressives, chiefly Senators William E. Borah, Hiram Johnson, and Robert M. La Follette.

"The waves of party insurgency," said the arch-Conservative Moses, "dash high on the rock-ribbed coast of our republicanism. Who will pour oil on the troubled waters?"

With Coolidge-like brevity, Henry Cabot Lodge replied "Slemp." Brandegee chimed in, "Remember, we don't mean Teapot Dome oil."

Johnson, La Follette and Borah, all costumed as Indian chiefs, were asked by Slemp if they were of the Third Party tribe.

Borah: Not yet. We not a bad Indian. We see good even in a Pilgrim. We handle these other Indians for you.
Slemp: On what terms?
Borah: Heap simple. Adopt my policies and make me president of the colony.

In the end, Slemp's question of who was going to lead the third party against this colony ended up with Borah, Johnson and La Follette each saying, "I will lead it." To this, Slemp replied, "Just as long as they're all chiefs, we're safe."

Actually, it was La Follette who led the third party in 1924, running as a Progressive, but he failed to make enough headway to win any electoral votes except those of his own state of Wisconsin, or to prevent Coolidge from being easily reelected with a majority of the total popular vote.

Other than the act of the three Indians, there was comparatively little reference to the approaching 1924 elections. There was a song referring to the chronic complaint, evident in practically every administration, of all the people who want to see the President personally but can't get in to do it, "You've Got To See Bascom Slemp Each Day or You Can't See Coolidge at All."

The dinner closed with a song adapted from "Cut Yourself a Piece of Cake."

> Election year is coming round, soon it will be here,
> The pot will soon be boiling when the candidates appear;
> The Democrats will make a fight to win with McAdoo;
> What do you think about it, boys, for it is up to you.
>
> The Grand Old Party has a man who's in the White House now,
> He's learned to run the government without a single row;
> He surely will be chosen, if Adams tells us true;
> What do you think about it, boys, for it is up to you.

Curiously, there was no mention in the dinner of Alfred E. Smith, the governor of New York, who had already become prominent as a contender for the Presidential nomination in 1920. Later, at the Democratic National Convention in 1924, he was to become deadlocked in a historical 103-ballot fight with William G. McAdoo, which would prevent the nomination of either.

Smith had been invited to this dinner, but declined.

• • •

Although the Harding administration scandals, particularly Teapot Dome, were attracting a great deal of public attention as the first 1924 Gridiron dinner was held on April 26, the references to them in the dinner skits were still infrequent and somewhat bland.

William E. Brigham, then president of the club, in the traditional speech in the dark, put forth at that dinner the Gridiron philosophy perhaps better than it has ever been explained by anyone else.

"We have our own opinions and we state them in our own way; with malice toward none and humor for all. It is not the Gridiron habit to assume more than the attitude of amused onlooker, to do more than extract what fun we may from the various situations which present themselves. If we appear critical, it is not in the spirit of the censorious; if we refuse to take seriously some men and things, it is not that we are lacking in respect.

"We have met tonight in a hectic and exciting period. While entertaining our friends to the limit of our ability, it is also part of our task to remind them that God reigns and the government at Washington still lives. We make no sport of tragedy, we assail the name of no man. Never shall the Gridiron flash upon discouragement or ill nature, on aught except the well-intentioned merriment of a few brief hours."

"With malice toward none and humor for all" most cogently summed up that Gridiron spirit which has always characterized the club, with very few exceptions. And the line, that it is part of the Gridiron members' task to remind their guests, who have always been for the most part politicians, that the government in Washington still lives, was certainly apt after the Teapot Dome scandals had erupted.

The opening song, to the tune of "My Little Nest of Heavenly Blue," alluded to it in these words:

> We do not intend to show a picture "done in oil,"
> We've turned that one to the wall;
> We'll display instead a good old portrait time can't spoil,
> One that smiles upon us all.
> Smiling still through all this stricture
> Is your Uncle Sammy's picture—
> It's a portrait scandal cannot soil.

The Senate, always a target for Gridiron fun, was characterized during this dinner by an impersonator of Dr. Sigmund Freud, who concluded that the Senate "suffers from Traumatic Fixation, Hysterical Amnesia, and Hallucinated Complexes," that "it has an ego freed of all ethical restraints," and that "it is suffering from a bad brand of external and internal stimuli" and "confounds the banality of its problems with the conspicuousness of their manifestations."

Senator George H. Moses, one of the better-known and more outspoken members of that body, and a strong administration supporter, participated directly in this skit by rising from the floor, unscheduled, and interrupting with the statement that no one could analyze the Senate except one who had lived in it six or eight years.

"This stuff he has just read," said Senator Moses, "is all bunk. In the Senate today some are under indictment, some under injunction—none under restraint. It is like a nursery where a new hobby-horse has been introduced. All want to ride it at once and fight to get on.

"Our aim is greatness, but we aim to be great not in the opinion of the wise, but in the opinion of tomorrow's newspapers. Each senator, after making a satisfactory agreement with his creator, goes on an oratorical jag. You would think to hear him talk that he has the welfare of the country at heart, but he is mainly concerned with the next vacant office. . . .

"There's mud on the cart and you can't blow it off. Most of the investigators want it to stay on so they can talk about it, and blame it on the Republicans. Well, the nearest thing to a Republican in disgrace is a Democrat in office. If you like the smell of sawdust, now that the bars are closed, get close to a statesman. Most of them are stuffed with it. . . . I guess that's enough psychoanalysis for tonight, and it isn't Freudian either."

Another crack at the Senate occurred in the little snapper (a very short skit with a snappy last line), in which it was stated that a new charge had been brought against Secretary Andrew Mellon, a charge of "reducing the human race."

"What do you mean by that? Has he killed somebody?"

"No. He tried to make a monkey out of a senator."

The 1924 Presidential campaign was coming up. Conventions were only two months away, and the main thrust of this dinner consisted of the club convening a "national political convention" in which it readily conceded the Republican nomination to Calvin Coolidge, with no significant objections.

The Democratic Convention, however, was quite a different situation. The club put on an inquisition act, in which an inquisitor-general, accompanied by an executioner, issued subpoenas for a number of distinguished persons. The first witnesses were "The Three Musketeers," impersonators of Charles F. Murphy of New York, Thomas Taggart of Indiana, and George E. Brennan of Chicago—all opponents of the McAdoo candidacy.

Identified as "expert political swordsmen," they were asked what they intended to do in the forthcoming political campaign and shouted out in a chorus, "McAdoo!" Under examination, however, they revealed that they had a candidate, but declined to name him because they wanted him to be nominated.

A cowboy who identified himself as McAdoo rushed in as soon as the Three Musketeers had departed. He announced that he was "William the Conqueror" and that he would be nominated on the first ballot "even if I have to claim residence in every state in the Union."

Although the club devoted much attention to the Democratic contest, the final music skit, based on *The Mikado*, summed it up.

> If you want to know who we are,
>   We are here now to nominate,
> In a manner most singular,
>   A President up-to-date.
> The wisest thing we have done,
> Is pledging ourselves to none,
> That is our idea of fun.

There was, perhaps, an inference of prediction in the Gridiron Club's selection of John W. Davis as the Democratic speaker.

At the conclusion of the dinner, President Calvin Coolidge spoke, this time without any public prodding from the floor. However, no record of this speech or any of the others that Coolidge made at Gridiron dinners exists in the Gridiron records or could be found elsewhere.

• • •

After a resounding Coolidge victory in 1924 over John W. Davis and Charles W. Bryan, a brother of William Jennings Bryan, the Gridiron dinner of December 13 opened with a resounding crash offstage, accompanied by yells and screams. The president of the Gridiron Club asked Harry J. Brown, correspondent of the *Portland Oregonian*, what all the racket was about.

"Don't be alarmed, Mr. President," Brown answered. "That is merely the silent vote going for Silent Cal."

After the three-week long, bitter, divisive convention in Madison Square Garden, the Democratic compromise candidates had obtained 136 electoral votes, mostly in the South, and Robert M. La Follette's performance had been dismal. Coolidge swept the rest of the nation, and in a skit the question was asked, "How many leaders does the Republican party have?"

"Fifty-one in the present Senate and 225 in the House, counting the Progressives,"answered Rudolph Kauffmann of the *Washington Star.* "And there will be more in both houses in the next Congress unless someone recognizes that somebody who got an eight million majority in the last election has earned the right to lead."

The dinner was heavily strewn with campaign references, including a political auction, in which the ineffectiveness of the Teapot Dome scandal on the willingness of the people to vote for Calvin Coolidge was treated. Various campaign relics were sold.

When a battered teapot was introduced, the auctioneer asked for bids on "the famous campaign teapot."

A chorus of dissent went up:

"Who wants that? It's no good."

A character representing John W. Davis shouted, "I tried my best to make that teapot work, but somehow it wouldn't draw."

La Follette commented that "John and I wanted to hold the election on Teapot Dome, but the people went to the Boston teaparty instead."

"Not a single bid?" wondered the auctioneer. "Very well, we'll just send this back to the Senate where it came from. No matter how battered the issue, the Senate can use it still."

Finally, he put up a copy of the Constitution for sale, announcing that "it can't be sold without paying royalties."

"To whom?"

"Calvin Coolidge," replied the auctioneer.

"Calvin Coolidge isn't the author of the Constitution."

"No, but he got the copyright on it for campaign purposes," flashed back the auctioneer.

The year 1924 was the first time that the national conventions were broadcast by radio. Individual radios were not too common, but during the conventions, all over the country, downtown stores put up loudspeakers on the street so that people could gather in groups to hear actual broadcasts, and the interminable 103 roll calls of the Democratic Convention. The public impression created by that convention no doubt had considerable influence in producing the easy and commanding Coolidge victory.

Thus, when the Gridiron auctioneer brought out a radio amplifier, everybody bid for it except the chairman of the Democratic National Committee, who said he didn't want it and commented, "They'll never broadcast another Democratic Convention if I can help it!"

But the auctioneer announced this was a very special amplifier, the one used by President Coolidge for all his campaign speeches. It was knocked down to the Republican chairman, who examined it and reproached the auctioneer by saying, "Why, this Coolidge instrument isn't an amplifier at all. It's a Maxim silencer!"

In the Madison Square Garden convention, Alabama had stood firm throughout and on every ballot cast twenty-four votes for its favorite son, Oscar Underwood. A package marked "24 Alabama" was offered for sale in the skit, and both Smith and McAdoo tried to buy it.

"Sold to Governor Smith," said the auctioneer, "who is going to teach the Southern Democrats to sing 'The Sidewalks of New York.'"

The Progressive platform was also put up, and a character impersonating the chairman of the Republican National Committee announced that the Progressive platform wouldn't elect La Follette.

"No," said the auctioneer, "but it elected Coolidge."

"Governor Smith" inquired if the auctioneer had a copy of the Democratic platform. "Yes," he replied, "why do you want it, Governor Smith?"

Smith: I'm going to rewrite it for 1928.
"McAdoo": The next Democratic convention won't go to New York.
Smith: No, but the nomination will.

Four years later it did, but the South refused to sing "The Sidewalks of New York," and Governor Smith's campaign was just as disastrous as Davis's had been.

While the Gridiron Club has never hesitated to lampoon anyone else, it has also, on some occasions, not spared its own members. At this dinner Richard V. Oulahan, correspondent for the *New York Times*, examined various eminent correspondents who had traveled the country appraising the political situation in each of the states they visited.

Carter Field, head of the Washington bureau of the *New York Herald Tribune,* was forced to admit he had written of California that "if the election were held today, there would be no telling what the result would be."

Charles G. Ross of the *St. Louis Post-Dispatch* admitted he had said that "while Davis was sure to carry Missouri today, a situation might arise tomorrow which would bring a large number of German votes to Coolidge — if the Germans failed to respond to La Follette's appeal." [Missouri went to Coolidge.]

J. Fred Essary of the *Baltimore Sun* admitted he had written that "the Maryland situation was very complex, but I said that the main question was whether Coolidge or La Follette would run second to Davis."

Oulahan: And what happened?
Essary: Through a sudden shift in sentiment, Mr. Coolidge was first and Mr. La Follette third.

Arthur Sears Henning of the *Chicago Tribune* proclaimed that his paper was the "greatest newspaper in the world," and confessed that he had temporized by saying that "Coolidge would carry the country unless there was a sudden change."

Robert Barry of the *Philadelphia Ledger* admitted he had written that "Coolidge would surely carry New York if Al Smith's vote was not heavy enough to pull Davis through, and that if Coolidge carried the State by a heavy majority and pulled Roosevelt [Theodore Roosevelt, Jr., Republican candidate for governor] through with him, it was certain that both Davis and Al Smith would lose New York."

Jay G. Hayden of the *Detroit News* said he had written of Michigan that "the situation was complex, but it was undeniable that after President Coolidge gave a sap bucket to Henry Ford . . ."

Oulahan: That'll do, Mr. Hayden.
Hayden: Hold on now, Mr. Oulahan. Let me ask what election predictions did *you* write in the *New York Times?*
Oulahan: As a Republican with progressive as well as reactionary tendencies, representing a leading Democratic newspaper of independent proclivities, which showed its independence by supporting Davis and forgetting all about Bryan, I followed the strictly impartial course.
Hayden: But what did you predict?

Oulahan: I predicted the election of Coolidge in the very first edition of my newspaper that went to press on election night.

In Prohibition days, the embassy parties in Washington were extremely popular, because the diplomats occupying "foreign soil" at their embassies were not subject to United States laws and consequently could import all the spirits they wished to and serve them freely at their parties.

Sir Esme Howard, the British ambassador, was a guest at this dinner, which was interrupted at one point by Robert Armstrong of the *Los Angeles Times* arriving on the stage in an overcoat and hat with a telegraph blank in his hand and asking if Sir Esme Howard was a guest at this dinner.

Brigham: Yes, why?
Armstrong: I have a radiogram for him.
Brigham: You may deliver it.
Armstrong (Reading): To Sir Esme Howard from the London Foreign Office: Your request is entirely in conformity with diplomatic immunity, and we have shipped the extra supply for Yuletide.

In the 1924 election, two women succeeded their husbands as governors: Mrs. Nellie Tayloe Ross of Wyoming and Mrs. Miriam A. Wallace ("Ma") Ferguson of Texas.

Impersonators sang to the tune of "Son of a Gambolier":

Two governors, two governors, two governors are we,
We are the niftiest pair of dames that ever you did see.
Our program is to work all day and then sit up all night,
To run an earthly paradise, with everything alright . . .

Two governors, two governors, two governors, we are,
But when we get into a scrape, just watch us run to pa.

Another duet reminiscent of the campaign was sung by the two Bryan brothers, "William J. and Charles W." After a long series of verses about their political activities, they sang a new version of "It Ain't Gonna Rain No Mo'."

We always worked together,
We thought that plan was best;
But I lost all the eastern states
And Charley lost the west.

Oh, we ain't gonna run no mo', no mo',
We ain't gonna run no mo';
Its no use tryin' to elect a Bryan,
So we ain't gonna run no mo'!

The music skit at the end of the dinner was by an "Electoral College Glee Club," which sang a succession of songs relating to the campaign and its participants.

John W. Davis had gone to Europe and was not present at the dinner, and a soloist sang an adaptation of "Bring Back My Bonnie to Me."

'Tis too late, when the campaign is over,
    To sail for a far distant shore;
So far as concerns the election,
    He'd better have gone there before.

La Follette, to the tune of "Forsaken," lamented:

Mistaken, mistaken, mistaken, was I,
I thought I could win with calamity cry.
I thought the disgruntled, the sick and the sore,
Would flock to the standard I gallantly bore.

Charles G. Dawes, who had fathered the so-called "Dawes Plan" for Europe and was elected Vice President in that campaign, was also known for his spectacular language on occasion. He was greeted with this verse, based appropriately on the song, "Meerschaum Pipe":

There'll be no language picturesque, picturesque,
When he is sitting at his desk,
    When he's vice president.
        Watch him perspire,
        Then he'll retire,
        Hell and Maria!

And the rather low-pitched, folksy campaign of President Coolidge was satirized to the "Boola Boola" song.

Mr. Coolidge went up to Vermont upon a sunny day,
The movies took his picture as he pitched the new-mown hay.
He passed the sap to Henry Ford and called him his old pal,
He made a speech by radio, yet they called him Silent Cal.

McAdoo, after his defeat for the nomination in the 1924 convention, was a political casualty and did not even come to the December dinner. But Alfred E. Smith made the Democratic speech, and President Coolidge closed the dinner with a talk described as "felicitous."

• • •

The Gridiron's Fortieth Anniversary Dinner on April 23, 1925, was presided over by J. Fred Essary, head of the *Baltimore Sun* bureau.

In his speech in the dark, which opened the dinner, he welcomed the guests "with wide open arms."

"We invite you to join in the spirit of our frolic. And as that frolic proceeds we hope that we may touch no tender spot. But I would remind you, in lines which come to me,"

"That this is a cannibal feast,
We broil with our fish, bird and beast
A guest with each course—without fear or remorse,
For the scorch does not scar in the least."

It was a distinguished dinner, attended not only by President Coolidge, the Vice President, members of the cabinet, and several foreign ambassadors, but also by Chief Justice Taft, former Vice President Marshall, and many others.

However, one of those absent was former United States Senator Chauncey M. Depew, who had attended the very first Gridiron dinner in 1885, and practically all of them after that. This dinner occurred on his ninety-first birthday, and he wrote a very interesting and perceptive letter of declination (on the stationery of the New York Central Railroad Company, Chauncey M. Depew, chairman), which was read at the time and which gave his impressions of the reactions of many former Presidents.

I remember with keenest interest that first gathering of your association which has accomplished so much and has become so famous, and it is one of the sad limitations of life that I should be the only surviving guest of that wonderful evening.

It has been my good fortune to have met at your festive board all the Presidents of your period, except Cleveland who would not come; all the cabinet ministers; most of the justices of the Supreme Court, and those who made themselves famous either permanently or temporarily on Capitol Hill.

Harrison, who became so unpopular because of his harsh mannerism, developed under your genial influence his rare talents and superior gifts. McKinley exhibited with you that wonderful good fellowship which was his greatest political asset. Roosevelt, child of nature never tamed, entered with the most infectious enthusiasm into your play and lost his temper because your skit revealed a weakness in his policy. His furious quarrel with Foraker made a memorable night, but it was outside Gridiron rules. Taft's geniality radiated many a night of glorious time under the Gridiron.

Wilson enjoyed immensely his evenings with you, but never gave an indication that he thoroughly understood the humor of the evening. I recall the havoc he created one night when he essayed the Wilson idea of humor. The dollar a year men who were famous in many departments of American enterprises were all present. I sat that night in a group of them. Turning to them the President said, "My troubles with the war are very slight compared with the difficulties of satisfying my distinguished dollar a year associates. Each of them thinks he ought to have all attention and is unhappy if any is given to others of his group. The result is that I am like an opera impressario, every member of whose troup wants to be recognized, honored and applauded as the prima donna." I said to the dollar a year statesmen who looked very gloomy, "To whom of you gentlemen does he refer?" They answered in an enthusiastic chorus, "Not me."

Harding, on Gridiron evenings, distributed joy, happiness and good fellowship, as was his nature. I am sure that everybody appreciates the wisdom when he speaks, and the personality when he does not, of that symbol of sense and sensibility, President Coolidge.

It was a revelation and all-embracing happiness to be with Mark Hanna on a Gridiron night. Among all events of that remarkably active and dominant life, none equalled his enjoyment of Gridiron nights. . . .

The Gridiron Club is a mirror, it reveals the statesman to himself as he is; it is the greatest, most benevolent and beneficial creation to reduce the abnormal swelling of the head and enlargement of the chest. It has done and is doing a great work in giving to its guests the best evenings to be found anywhere in the United States. It rescues a large number of statesmen who are so obsessed with the idea that they may become President, that they live in a rarefied atmosphere and can do no work.

The Gridiron dissipates the brainstorms and makes them useful senators. For many years *Punch* has restored sanity to English public life; the Gridiron Club has done and is doing the same patriotic work for the United States.

With all good wishes that the Gridiron Club may pursue
its successful mission perpetually,

Faithfully yours,

/s/ Chauncey M. Depew

The reading of the letter produced an ovation for former
Senator Depew, whose wit and facility as an after-dinner speaker
had been experienced often by Gridiron guests.

There was also a Gridiron Parade, covering many reminis-
cences about things on "Newspaper Row" in 1885 (a member
complained that "some of our newspapers want us to use those
new-fangled typewriting machines, but I'm darned if I'm going
to do it!").

The main skits of the dinner were a Coolidge Circus and The
Vermont Villagers. The three-ring circus, not surprisingly, consisted of the executive, the legislative, and the judicial branches.
And it was suggested that, in view of the emphasis on economy,
money could be saved by bringing it down to a two-ring show.

"What does the proprietor say to that?"

"He says we ought to economize," was the reply.

"Which ring would he eliminate?"

"That's confidential, Senator, but I might tell you that he
thinks pretty well of the executive and judicial."

Later it was asked what the proprietor thought of Borah's
lion-taming act. His spokesman said, "He thinks we ought to
economize." To all other suggestions about reducing the circus,
the proprietor always wanted to economize.

A barker yelled, "See the side show! Better than the big
show! We have Walsh, the wild man, goes wild on oil and
sugar."

At one point the chorus was reminded, "You just remember
this is Calvin Coolidge's show."

And an impersonator of Senator James Couzens of Michigan
replied, "Don't worry. If we forget it, he reminds us."

The act ended when it was reported that "the La Follette
crowd has crawled under the tent and set up that three-shell
game again," whereupon the circus broke up and everybody left.

There had been a controversy between Senator Couzens,
who as an original partner of Henry Ford had become very rich,
and the Internal Revenue Service over the amount of his taxes.

The Treasury contended that he owed $11 million more than he had paid.

So there was a Couzens-Mellon duet, based on "Here in My Arms," from the Rodgers and Hart musical, *Dearest Enemy*. After a lot of banter, in which "Couzens" had said he'd never speak to "Mellon" again, "Mellon" suggested a compromise.

Couzens:
> Well, now, the thought of compromise
>   it seems to me is nifty;
> But you will have to come half-way,
>   and make it fifty-fifty.
>   *(They shake hands.)*

Mellon:
> Here, Jimmy, is my heart and hand,
>   and here our fighting ends;

Couzens:
> For what's a million, Andy dear,
>   between two such good friends.

Both:
> So now we'll smoke the pipe of peace,
>   and banish all our cares;
> We'll sing with glee, in GOP—
>   Two happy millionaires.

Naval disarmament was becoming a subject of intense discussion. The Gridiron decided first to disarm the drummer in the Marine Band and finally agreed that it was almost time for conversations: "Then let us march to a quiet place where we can begin conversations to consider whether we shall begin conversations."

There was an Al Smith snapper in which one member asked another why Governor Smith wasn't there. "Governor Smith sends word he is busy writing a manuscript entitled 'Wild Legislatures I Have Tamed.' He thinks it may be of some use to President Coolidge."

But the music skit, done by The Vermont Villagers, was directed primarily to President Coolidge and his determination to have economy in government. To the tune of "Tammany," they sang:

> Once there was a great White Father,
> Bear Ribs was his name;
> He had faith in Massachusetts,

And it brought him fame.
When he took the war-path,
There was purpose in his eye.
As he rode the el-e-phant,
This was his battle cry:

Economy, economy;
If of wampum you must spend,
Bear Ribs will not be your friend.
Economy, economy,
Save the tin, you'll always win,
Economy.

The economy drive, however, didn't go to such extremes as
the banishment of the Presidential yacht *Mayflower*. The President enjoyed the yacht but never went much beyond the Potomac
River in it. So, to the tune of "By the Blue Alsatian Mountains," a
soloist sang:

On the blue Potomac River,
Sails a vessel frequently;
It is called the yacht *Mayflower*.
'Tis a quiet place to be,
'Tis a quiet place to be.
For it never sails the ocean,
Out upon the raging main;
See the President stand steady;
Hear him utter this refrain:

O me, O my, O me,
Don't go far out to sea;
Let us keep within the river,
Where we'll always quiet be.

So the Mayflower sails the river,
Never out of sight of land,
For the President won't venture
Where he cannot safely stand.

The music committee, to the tune of "The Lost Chord," bemoaned the prospects of the Democrats after their resounding
defeat in 1924 and came forward with a prophetic suggestion.

It may be that some bright leader,
Will bring us to peace again;
It may be we shall not find it,
'Til we raise up a brand-new man.
It may be that Franklin Roosevelt

Will bring us to our reward;
It may be that only hereafter
We will find that lost accord.

Vice President Dawes had been absent from the Senate at a time when the confirmation of Charles B. Warren for attorney general was defeated by an equal division of senators present. Had he been there, Dawes could have cast the deciding vote. This created quite a furor at the time and Dawes, as one of the speakers, was introduced by a parody of "Slumber On, My Little Gypsy Sweetheart."

The bells for the roll call are ringing for thee,
And the Senate Old Guard is lonely;
Curtis* is there and is tearing his hair,
While you are absent only.

Slumber on, the Old Guard vainly waiting,
Waiting for you in the chair.
Where were you, Charles Dawes?

Then, Essary rose and said, "Gentlemen: The Vice President of the United States."

It is not recorded just how Vice President Dawes responded to that introduction.

● ● ●

The December 12, 1925 dinner, attended by President Coolidge, Vice President Dawes, and the new Speaker of the House of Representatives, Nicholas Longworth, dwelt heavily on the new Congress and whether President Coolidge, three years later, would run for a third term. To the melody "Ole Uncle Moon," a quartet sang:

Give a moment to the future,
    Think of 1928.

You hear much of Hughes and Hoover,
    And of Smith and McAdoo;
But they're list'ning and they're waiting
    To be told what Cal will do.

The opening song of the dinner was a parody of "What Do I Care?"

If Cal is silent and Dawes is not,
What do we care, what do we care

---

*Charles Curtis, the Republican leader of the Senate.

Beneath the Gridiron's light.
If Cal keeps cool and Dawes gets hot
What do we care, what do we care.
The Gridiron's shining bright.

In another skit, a character was trying to build a fire on the stage, and when asked what he was doing that for, he said it was "to smoke Mr. Coolidge out on the 1928 nomination."

"That will do," he was told, "this isn't the place to do any smoking out. And what's more, the Senate hasn't been able yet to smoke the President out on anything."

At another point in the cabinet and Congress skit, two carpenters came on the stage carrying a chest of tools, which they said they were taking into the Executive Offices. Herbert Hoover, secretary of commerce, who had recently added the Patent Office and the Bureau of Mines to his department, was asked to rise. It was remarked that "some say he is reaching for the Shipping Board."

An actor in the skit turned to the carpenters and demanded their purpose. One of them declared that they had "decided to nail down the White House before he got that too!"

But in the major music skit the attention was turned primarily to the new Congress, which had taken over at the beginning of the year. A group of members representing them sang a song strongly resembling "I've Been Working on the Railroad."

Congressmen are speechifying,
    All the livelong day;
Making speeches and replying,
    We have lots to say.
Fill the air with sound and violence,
    Can't you hear our noise;
Let the White House rest in silence—
    Listen to us boys.

This was in the days before welfare and other social programs, and the principal efforts of congressmen in behalf of their own districts were to get appropriations to be spent there, generally for developmental work on rivers, harbors, dams, or other public construction. Each year, all such appropriations were usually incorporated in one bill, known colloquially in Congress as the "pork-barrel bill."

But economy-minded President Coolidge was not too cordial to this type of legislation, and a soloist, paraphrasing "That Big Bass Viol," sang:

> On every creek where the minnows are swimming,
>   Or a place with a cross-roads store,
> We are willing to spend a million of dollars,
>   And then reach out for more.
> We'll slash with Coolidge all other bills,
>   It's like cutting through cheese or chalk,
> But down our spine will run cold chills,
>   If you close up the barrel of pork.

The system of various members of Congress putting members of their families on their staff payrolls as secretaries and assistants was more frequent then than it is now, and the Gridiron Club parodied the *Pinafore* song, "I Am the Monarch of the Sea."

> Each one has his secretaree,
> A member of his own family,
> For it helps his salary to enhance,
> By the aid of his sisters
>   and his cousins and his aunts.

There was also some raillery at the twenty cents-a-mile travel allowance available to members of Congress.

> There are miles that make us happy,
> There are miles that make us gay;
> For the miles, they help pile up the mileage,
> And for every mile we draw our pay.
> We collect when going and when coming;
> Also when we stay in town awhile.
> O, the miles that fill our lives with sunshine
> Pay us twenty cents a mile.

Reflecting the growing rebelliousness in Congress, the act closed with a parody of the song, "In a Kingdom of Our Own," from *The Royal Vagabond.*

> In a Congress of our own,
> We'll circumvent the President;
> We will rout him, we will flout him,
> Let the White House moan and groan.
> And if we like we'll spend the last red cent,
> We won't be bossed by any President.

• • •

For the first time since entering the White House, President Coolidge failed to be present at the spring dinner of the Gridiron Club on April 10, 1926. He had originally accepted, but had to withdraw his acceptance because of the death of his father. Consequently, Vice President Dawes was the ranking guest and the closing speaker at the end of the dinner.

Since 1926 was the sesquicentennial anniversary of the Declaration of Independence, the Gridiron Club utilized four major figures from the early days of the Republic for its satire on the present.

To the tune of "I Want What I Want When I Want It," an impersonator of George Washington belted out:

I fought King George up at Valley Forge,
So that you might be happy and free;
But you're slaves once again to a body of men
Who declaim and denounce and decree.

An impersonator of Thomas Jefferson, the founder of the Democratic party, sang to an air from *Ruddigore:*

My eyes are fully open to an awful situation,
So I've come from Monticello to deliver an oration,
For the Democratic party seems to droop and pine
    and languish,
And the prospect of the future fills my soul
    with pain and anguish.

Introduced as "the great predecessor of Andrew Mellon," Alexander Hamilton's impersonator enthusiastically sang to the tune of "Solomon Levi":

My name is Alexander; I'm a genius at finance;
The income rates and schedules I decipher at a glance.
I understand you have a man who thinks he knows the game,
He comes from Pennsylvania and Mellon is his name.

I knew that I would always live secure in fame and rank,
Although my name was never carved above a Pittsburgh bank.
I know why Mr. Mellon now directs the ship of state;
They couple Mellon's name with mine and that's what makes him
    great.

And "John Marshall," first chief justice, sang a parody of "Humoresque."

In my day the Constitution
Was a sacred institution,
And I struggled to preserve it as the law;
But by you it has been shattered,
Knocked about and sadly battered,
'Til I hardly recognize it any more.

The use of a White House "spokesman," which had become so prevalent under Coolidge, was the vehicle for the inauguration of Clifford K. Berryman, cartoonist of the *Washington Star*, as president of the club. A group constituting the inauguration committee came on the stage and demanded an interview with the current president.

From his seat at the head of the table, Berryman said he was the President's spokesman, and then proved himself as adept at evasive reply as any White House spokesman.

"Are you in favor of relief for the American farmer?" he was asked.

"On that point," replied Berryman, "I favor relief from the American farmer, not for him. However, I believe that patriotism requires that farming shall continue."

After asking other similar questions and receiving similar answers, the inauguration committee became more direct.

"What is your attitude toward the Eighteenth Amendment?"

"That matter has not been brought to my attention," the "spokesman" declared. "See the Treasury about that."

"If Mussolini comes to America, will you greet him in a black shirt?"

"That's as simple as the multiplication table. The past five years have been like an earthquake. We are living in a commercial age. I think that answers your question."

At this point, the "spokesman" turned upon his tormentors. "I want to say right here," he began, "that there is too much partisanship in your questions. My administration intends to enforce patriotism, not partisanship. When you support me and my policies, that is patriotism. When you ask me embarrassing questions, that is partisanship."

In another act, Senator Charles Curtis of Kansas, the majority leader, was revealed talking on the telephone to the White House.

–Hello, Mr. President. This is Charley—no, Charley *Curtis,* not Charley *Dawes.*

–That's right, yes, yes. Ha ha. That's a good one. That's what I think of him too.

–But I'll say this for him. He hasn't missed a session since——

–Now, Mr. President, here is what I really wanted to take up with you. You know a number of the boys have to run for reelection this year. The Republican senators have been pretty loyal and supported your program. They wonder whether you might give out a statement asking for the election of a Republican senate——

–Hello, hello——

(Shakes receiver hook up and down)

–Hello, I was talking to the White House.

–Oh, I see, the party at the other end rang off.

The relationship of President Coolidge with Congress, and particularly the attitudes of two of its most outspoken members toward the President, were satirized in a Brutus and Cassius skit, with Senator Borah representing Brutus and Senator James A. Reed of Missouri, the most articulate Democratic critic of the administration, representing Cassius.

They both feared the people would "choose Calvin a third term."

A sample of the dialogue:

Borah:

We senators walk in his silent shadow
And no one sees or hears us any more.

Reed:

We at some times are masters of the vote.
The fault, dear Borah, is not in our noise.
It is his silence makes us underlings.

Borah:

Borah and Calvin; what should be in that Calvin?
Write them together, mine is as fair a name;
Sound them, it doth become the mouth as well.

Reed:

And Borah spends a dime as soon as Calvin.

Borah:

Now, in the name of all the GOP,
Upon what meat doth this our Calvin feed
That he is grown so great?

Reed:

Meat? You mean wheat cakes.
That's why I have this lean and hungry look.
I'm never asked to breakfast at the White House.

There was also a skit based on the alleged diary of Frank W. Stearns, an intimate of Coolidge at the White House. After many quips about the President had been read from the diary, it was put up for auction. Following some rather conventional bidding, a mysterious stranger rushed in and bid a million dollars. As the syndicate manager knocked down the diary to him, he asked, "What do you want it for?"

"I intend to suppress it."

"Who are you?"

"I am the White House spokesman."

In this skit, the White House spokesman was played by Theodore G. Joslin, who did become the White House spokesman in the Hoover administration.

The closing music skit was given over to a glorification of the want ad, from which many "advertisements" were read. For example,

"Wanted: Calvin Coolidge's job. Wm. G. McAdoo."

Another asked for nineteen additional assistants for the secretary of commerce, and to the tune of "Forty-Five Minutes from Broadway," they sang of Herbert Hoover:

> Every problem is asked for by Hoover;
> He will apply for each task:
> Though he must feel the strain,
> No one hears him complain,
> Nor additional pay does he ask.
> Whether it's shipping or static,
> Or merely making things pay,
> From rubber to bread,
> It is all in his head,
> And he's reaching for new ones each day.

The final ad was a "for lease" announcement on 1600 Pennsylvania Avenue. Everyone wanted to know who the new tenant would be, and the chorus closed the act by singing its version of "Will She Come from the East?"

> The White House soon will seek a tenant,
>   The little ad says it's so.
> The GOP has plans dependent,
>   It does not want to go.
> The Democrats would like to lease it
>   For the next four years or so.
> Where will the next tenant hail from?
>   We'd all like to know.

Vice President Dawes was introduced by a brief skit in which he appeared as "The American Chesterfield," and an impersonator announced that he hadn't dined at home since March 4, 1925, and that he had become the "professional guest of honor."

It was for this dinner that John Philip Sousa, for many years leader of the Marine Band and a limited member of the Gridiron Club, composed and first performed "The Gridiron Club March."

• • •

The 1926 election had been disastrous for the Republicans. Several of their prominent senators, including William M. Butler, the chairman of the Republican national committee, had been beaten, and party strength had seriously declined.

With President Coolidge back in his accustomed seat and Vice President Dawes also present, the December 11, 1926 dinner opened with a Dawes snapper, in which an alarm clock was brought forward as a gift for the Vice President.

Question: Don't you think that joke about the Vice President being asleep when the Senate defeated Charley Warren for attorney general is getting pretty old?

Answer: That isn't the point. The Republican majority will be so slim in the next Senate that the Vice President may have to be breaking a tie every few minutes.

The question arose as to who was presenting the alarm clock, and they dug out a card reading, "Yours hopefully, Calvin Coolidge."

The opening song referred to the President's love of fishing and the fact that he had taken a fishing vacation during the summer. To the tune of "On the Riviera," they sang:

If you would be a sport,
Of the real White House sort,
Then you must be an outdoor man
    like Calvin Coolidge.
With fishing rod in hand,
And bait that's sure to land,
Where trout—or votes—are waiting,
    you must stand.

So tonight we want to go a-fishing,
That's what all our Gridiron guests are wishing,
Fun is our bait, you men of State,
We'll promise to hook if you will wait.

Alfred H. Kirchhofer of the *Buffalo Evening News* and Mark Sullivan, historian and correspondent of the *New York Herald Tribune*, were initiated in a skit in which they came in costume disguises with tickets to the dinner, supposedly paid for in Kirchhofer's case by Samuel Insull of Chicago and in Sullivan's by the State of Pennsylvania. The initiates were stripped of their disguises, and the chairman of the initiation committee pretended he couldn't remember the name of the distinguished Mark Sullivan until he was prompted.

In a skit entitled "Desire Under the Slippery Elms of Vermont," a lot of farmhands were gathered together, played by impersonators of Dawes, Borah, Governor Lowden, Speaker Longworth, and Senator James Watson of Indiana. When party chairman Butler entered and asked where Calvin was, he was told he'd gone fishing.

Butler: Always fishin' but don't catch nothin'.
Longworth: He caught something November second.
Dawes: I hope they ain't taking pictures of him fishing.
Borah: Naw, Calvin won't let them picture fellers get within gunshot of him this year.
Longworth: What's come over him? Calvin used to pitch hay for the movies right smart.
Dawes: Yep, he couldn't have done that better if he had been a born movie actor.
Butler: Calvin's all right, best hand I've got. He's smart, he's saving, never does anything impetuous, and consults nobody but Maw Stearns and me.

Then the "Third Term Baby" was brought in and somebody asked what Calvin thought of it? Stearns replied, "You ought to see him shinin' up to it in his quiet way, when he thinks nobody is looking."

The skit ended with a reference to the sunset in the background, and Dawes said, "If we only knew, fellers, whether it's sunset for Calvin or sundown for us!"

President Coolidge had given a private interview to Bruce Barton (instead of one of the Washington correspondents), which was the occasion for an inquiry into why he did this, in a snapper.

"Bruce Barton," it was pointed out, "is a notable writer of fiction, isn't he?"

"Yes."

"It seems to me your question answers itself."

Charles Evans Hughes, who had retired as secretary of state

a year earlier, but had not yet been appointed chief justice of the United States, was a speaker, and was introduced by a parody, the refrain of which went:

> You're as welcome as the flowers in May,
> Do you think you will come back to stay?
> For the White House has not moved away—
> Do you think that you'll come back some day?

President Berryman presented him in these words:

"Our next speaker made a speech in New York for Jim Wadsworth and Ogden Mills. They lost. He made a speech for Senator William M. Butler in Massachusetts. Butler lost. We feel that we have absolutely nothing to lose, but everything to gain if the Honorable Charles Evans Hughes makes a speech for the Gridiron Club."

There was a Sherlock Holmes skit in which the eminent detective tried to discover who lost the November election. He discovered that the New York Progressives didn't lose it, because they defeated Senator James W. Wadsworth and Ogden Mills. His associate Watson discovered that the Democrats lost Congress, but Holmes said, "No, they won seven seats in the Senate."

There was considerable comment about the alibis of those who lost, when Watson inquired, "Didn't the President lose Massachusetts?"

And Holmes answered, "No, he won the House of Representatives and said it was a great victory."

Watson then asked, "Can it be possible that the President is a member of the Alibi Club?"

They both shushed each other and marched off the stage.

This was the first year that the club embarked upon a policy of having a separate Democratic skit and another Republican skit, the formula which persists to this day.

The primary thrust of the Democratic skit was an attempt to find the Democratic nominee for President in 1928. He was brought on battered and bandaged, tattered and disreputable-looking, and prolonged efforts were made to identify him. The only thing they could agree on in the beginning was that "of course, you can tell by looking at him that he's a Democrat."

They went over all the potential Democratic candidates but didn't positively identify him as any. Finally, they asked him who he was and he said, "What the hell difference does it make?"

In a White House chef skit the chef was applying for a pension and thought he ought to be entitled to it because "the pet raccoon at the White House thought I was a congressman and bit me."

Inquiry was made of some of his most effective recipes. For example:

"What do congressmen like best?"

"They like pork, without beans. Under this administration, they get beans without pork."

"What do you serve Democratic senators for dessert?"

"Ice."

"Why doesn't the President have more senators to breakfast?"

"There aren't any more."

"Why doesn't he invite more House members?"

"He's had all those who eat with a fork."

Vice President Charles G. Dawes, not noted for his delicacy of speech, had once shouted "Hell and Maria!" and thereafter he had been referred to with some frequency as "Hell and Maria Dawes." The Gridiron Club put on a duet with "two of the most famous personages on the political vaudeville stage—Helen and Maria," done by Arthur Pierce and Tudor Morsell costumed as children skipping rope but smoking Dawes' underslung pipes and bowing from the hips elaborately to each other.

Pierce:
Everywhere we get applause,
Helen.
Morsell:
Maria.
Pierce:
Cause we're friends of Charlie Dawes,
Helen.
Morsell:
Maria.
He couldn't do without us,
He needs us every day.
List'ning to sen-a-tors, why, what else
    could he say?
Pierce:
When that Warren vote occurred,
Helen.
Morsell:
Maria.

Pierce:
> We were napping, so you've heard,
> Helen.

Morsell:
> Maria.
> But we are not down-hearted;
> This comforts us, you see.
> If we had been awake, where would
> > John Sargent be?
> [Sargent was appointed attorney general after Warren was turned down.]

Morsell:
> If, to make a winning race,
> Helen,

Pierce:
> Maria.

Morsell:
> They should put us in first place,
> Helen,

Pierce:
> Maria.
> They'll hear, if they should open
> To us the White House door,
> Things in the White House that it never heard before!

There was a fishing skit located at Paul Smith's in the Adirondacks, where Coolidge had spent a vacation. After comments on Coolidge's fish and what he caught and didn't catch, an Indian arrived named Al Smith.

"What tribe?" somebody asked.

"Tammany," answered the Indian. "I own all the territory around this lake. Say, I know all about this man who was fishing up here last summer. He gave me a fish. I put it in a museum."

"Because it was so big?"

"Oh, no; because I was afraid to eat it," retorted the Indian.

Senator Oscar Underwood of Alabama, who had received twenty-four favorite-son votes on each of the 103 ballots at the Democratic National Convention in 1924, was the Democratic speaker. He was retiring from the Senate, and was introduced by a song to the tune of "Won't You Tell Me Why, Robin?"

> A Democrat you are, Oscar,
> > The only one we've known
> To step down from a job, Oscar,
> > When it was all his own.

> We wonder why you passed it up—
>   This Senate seat you hold—
> And so around the Gridiron Board,
>   We're waiting to be told.
> The honors that your State bestowed
>   You yield without a sigh.
> Won't you tell us why, Oscar,
>   Won't you tell us why?

The other major skit was directed chiefly to the Republicans and was on "The Harmonious Senate." This was the year in which William S. Vare, elected to the Senate from Pennsylvania, was denied his seat because he had spent too much money to get elected, and "Senator George Norris" of Nebraska, who was one of the principal opponents of Vare's seating, sang a song to the tune of "Show That Fellow the Door."

> There's a man named William;
>   Other name is Vare;
> He wants to be seated,
>   Senators, beware.
> Frank L. Smith's another,
>   Who spent lots of dough,
> If you take my judgment,
>   They both will have to go.

The witty and vitriolic tongue of "Senator Byron Patton ("Pat") Harrison," Democrat of Mississippi, closed the skit to the tune of the "Song of the Vagabonds."

> Come, all you fellers of Dixie land,
>   You northern gentry of Tammany,
>
> And all together we'll fight and stand
>   To save the Senate from harmony.
>
> We must try to win in '28
> And we can't afford to wait.
>
> Democrats together, we will ask you whether
>   You'll bow down to GOP?
> You will bow in sorrow if you vote tomorrow
>   With this Coolidge coterie.
>
> Forward, forward, vote against our foe.
> Onward, onward, the Democrats will go.
>
> Luck's been bad, let's break it;
> Here's our chance, let's take it,
>
> And to hell with harmony!

This particular dinner was focused more on the President than perhaps any other that had been given up to that time. While it all *seemed* good-natured kidding, the Gridiron Club made it plain to him that in fact this was also just the way they really meant it, in the closing song immediately before his introduction.

Someone's dreaming night and day,
  Wonder who?
Dreams of four more years to stay,
  Hope it's true.
He may find that happy fate
  When Miss 1928
Meets him at the White House gate,
  If he'll say:

Let me call you sweetheart,
  I'm in love with you;
Don't take someone else
  Who would not be as true.
For the Grand Old Party
  No one else would do—
Let me call you sweetheart,
  I'm in love with you.

• • •

The first 1927 dinner was held on February 26. In those days inauguration took place on March 4, and sessions of the old Congress ended automatically on March 3. Ashmun Brown of the *Providence Journal,* president of the club, in his opening speech in the dark described the dinner as a "farewell."

" . . . a going-away party, as it were, to the Sixty-ninth Congress, which in a few days is to pass into history, while some of its members pass into retirement. There is sorrow in some quarters at the passing of this Congress. In justice, it is to be said that such sorrow is not universal."

This introduced the opening song, a parody of "Lucky Day."

Goodbye, Congress—soon you're going home.
Welcome, silence, then, under the dome.
And when they hear at the White House
Congress is going away,
What will Mister Coolidge say?

When Congress leaves things never go wrong,
And life goes on just singing a song.
Oh, boy, I'm lucky, I'll say I'm lucky—
This is my lucky day.

The main thrust of the dinner, however, was international affairs. In addition to President Coolidge, the speakers were announced as President Machado of Cuba and Vincent Massey, newly appointed minister from Canada, who made his first public appearance in this country at the dinner. A larger number than usual of foreign ambassadors had been invited.

The international conference at Geneva was wallowing in complications. A satirical skit was presented representing three neighboring nations assembled in an international conference, on sea, land, and air defenses. Cuba was represented by a sugar planter, "who raises cane in the summer and helps American tourists to raise it in the winter"; Canada, by a Royal Mounted Policeman; and the United States by "Mr. Babbitt, who visits Canada when he is thirsty and Cuba when he is dry."

The credentials of all the delegates were quite in order—"they'd been rejected by the Senate." When it was asked whether the Senate would pass on any agreement that would be reached there, the audience was told, "We don't have to worry about that; it won't happen in our lifetime."

The 5-5-3 naval ratio which had evolved at Geneva was suggested by the United States as a proper proposal for the allocation of sugar production.

After deciding to refer the Cuban sugar question to the Utah beet industry, to deal with the Canadian wheat matter "in a direct and practical manner," and to view with sympathetic interest the national awakening in China, the delegates submitted the report "that this conference on land, sea and air has conformed to all modern precedent and has come to land where it began, after being at sea and in the air."

Owing to a sudden illness, General Machado was unable to attend the dinner, but his speech was read by the Cuban ambassador. (Machado, in a gesture of exculpation, later invited the entire Gridiron Club to come to Cuba as his guests. They did not go.)

The Cuban president alluded to the American help in the struggle for freedom in his country at the time of the Spanish-American War, and then to the efforts to aid Cuba afterward:

"Cuba will always remember that . . . when our country, totally devastated by a most destructive war, presented a sombre picture of want and sorrow . . . when all were prey to contagious and deadly diseases, such as yellow-fever . . . [America] came to the rescue of those unfortunates with all the necessary means . . . bringing back faith and hope to their souls.

"The history of that period is in our eyes one of the most beautiful pages of the history of the United States, which ought to serve as a lesson to all the countries of the world and especially to those of our continent."

He closed by saying that the miracle of development in Cuba over the years since the Spanish-American War could not have been possible without the unlimited capital and help offered by the American people, and, somewhat ironically, he pledged the "unchangeable friendship" of Cuba for America.

At about this time, Laurence Stalling's *What Price Glory* was a big hit on Broadway, and the Gridiron Club put on its own version of the play in "Over the Top with Kellogg."* The cast came marching on, led by "Sergeant-Major Kellogg" and singing:

> Tramp, tramp, tramp, the boys are marching.
> Forward Kellogg on the run,
> Although Sherman may be right,
> We are not too proud to fight,
> For the diplomat's the man behind the gun.

Marine diplomacy, it was decided, would help solve all the problems of the administration, and the chorus sang, to the tune of "Sailing (Sailing Over the Bounding Main)":

> Coolidge, Coolidge, this is the way to do—
> Just call the marines and they will get another term for you.

A character representing Senator Borah strode on the stage demanding the withdrawal of all marines at once. Kellogg ordered him put under guard, and it was announced that Congress had dictated long enough. It was decided that they should march up Capitol Hill and tell the congressmen where to get off, whereupon they sang a parody of a *Pirates of Penzance* song.

> We are the bold marines,
> Everywhere they need us,
> Everywhere they speed us,
> Statesmen can all resign,
> For here come the bold marines.

---

*Frank B. Kellogg, who had succeeded Charles Evans Hughes as secretary of state.

President Coolidge was introduced to the strains of the hymn, "The Old Rugged Cross."

Everyone's wondering whether he'll run,
But it seems that the answer is plain;
There is a place where his work has begun
And it's calling to Calvin again—

Just a big old White House,
With a leaky old roof—
But it's calling, calling again.

• • •

On August 2, President Coolidge, while vacationing in the Black Hills, had summoned newsmen to his office in the Rapid City High School and handed each one a slip of paper saying, "I do not choose to run for President in 1928."

Three months before that, Charles A. Lindbergh had startled the world by making the first solo flight across the Atlantic to Paris, and in the previous two years Navy Commander Richard Evelyn Byrd had been the first man to fly over the North Pole. Both were present at the December dinner.

With all the public attention these two air heroes had received, it was only logical that in its December 10, 1927 dinner, the Gridiron Club should depict the Democrats around an airplane, "*The Spirit of Discord*," arranging a record-breaking, non-stop flight to the White House. Into the group marched William G. McAdoo, announcing that there was something in the old plane that was his and he wanted to get it.

"What is it?" he was asked.

"A monkey wrench I threw in there in 1924."

President Coolidge was not at the dinner, and the administration was represented by Vice President Dawes, who responded to the toast to the President at the end.

The country was still debating just what President Coolidge meant by his rather ambiguous phrase "I do not choose to run." Some thought he meant he would not run, while others thought he preferred not to, in other words, did not choose to, but would if drafted.

So the December dinner opened with a song to the tune of "High, High, High Up In the Hills."

Politics is in doubt;
How is it coming out?
No one knows who will be the next in the White House.

Candidates in despair,
Everything's in the air;
Everyone's guessing and getting nowhere at all.
Oh, it is—

High, high, high up in the air,
Doing the campaign fling.
High, high, high up in the air,
Nobody knows a thing.

Ashmun Brown, president of the Gridiron Club, in his speech in the dark noted that the dinner occurred "on the eve of great political battle," and that many were there "who will be prominent in the fray.

"Some will," he said, "or rather may emerge with the distinguished service cross; we warn all to be cautious lest an entirely different type of cross be given you."

In a candidate skit the Gridiron Club's prognostication was precise in one respect at least. Charles Curtis of Kansas, Republican leader of the Senate, was awarded a Distinguished Service Cross for conspicuous bravery—he did not run to cover while others did, but instead went over the top and declared himself a candidate for President of the United States.

"Senator," Richard V. Oulahan said, as he presented the decoration, "the Gridiron Club indulges the hope that such heroism will be rewarded by nothing short of second place on the ticket."

The 1928 ticket turned out to be Hoover and Curtis.

All of the potential candidates who were present—about a dozen of them, including General John J. Pershing—were asked to stand. Jay G. Hayden asked: "Haven't you overlooked somebody up at the head table?

Oulahan: I know who you mean, but I won't call his name.
Hayden: Why not?
Oulahan: Because I don't care to have an underslung tobacco pipe
flung at my head!

They focused on the absence of President Coolidge with a "radio broadcast," in which a well-known commentator of the time, Graham McNamee, was supposed to be broadcasting the Gridiron dinner. The broadcast related how, in the absence of President Coolidge, when the band played "Hail to the Chief," Vice President Dawes marched in, and then commented, "And, folks, you should have seen Secretary Hoover's face. He looked like he had walked into another disaster and was in need of some relief himself."

The Democratic speaker was John W. Davis, who had led the party in 1924, and he was introduced with a new version of "Among my Souvenirs."

> So when, for twenty-eight,
> They seek a candidate
> To face a martyr's fate,
> I have this consolation—
> While others make the fight,
> I am at peace tonight—
> The nomination is among my souvenirs!

The major music skit presented by "The Gridiron Opera Company" was a version of *Julius Caesar*, entitled "Chooso Non Runnorum." It was announced that Julius Coolidge "hath put aside the crown." To the "Pilgrims' Chorus" from *Tannhäuser*, a soloist sang:

> Behold this crown, with no one to wear it,
> For Coolidge says he no longer can bear it.
> Let us choose now a man as our candidate.
> To lead us to vict'ry in twenty-eight.

After considerable discussion about possibilities, the chorus paraphrased "The Isle of Our Dreams."

> Oh, the Grand old Republican party
> Has a plenty of men of renown.
> But in trouble and care as we search here and there
> We wonder just which one to crown.
> And the Grand old Republican party
> For the first time is burdened by fear.
> We need someone like Cal
> Who can lick Governor Al
> Who can bring home the bacon next year?

• • •

President Coolidge, Vice President Dawes, Secretary of Commerce Hoover, Senate Majority Leader Curtis, and most of the other potential Republican candidates were present at the spring dinner on April 28, 1928.

Since the nominating conventions were only two months away, the dinner focused heavily upon them. Among the first skits was one about a man who would be available after March 4, 1929, and was seeking employment.

He was described as "industrious, thrifty, hard-working, always on the job, has no fads, doesn't play golf, knows how to wear a sombrero, ride a bronco, and pitch hay. He doesn't disturb his fellow workers by a lot of idle chatter, and he's an expert in minding his own business."

He had recommendations from Herbert Hoover, Charles G. Dawes, former Governor Frank O. Lowden of Illinois, and Charles Curtis.

"Why is he giving up his present job?"

"He got cold feet when he counted the number of Smith families."

The main Republican skit was entitled "The Twelfth of June [date of the Republican Convention], or What Have You," and was set in the telegraphic press section at the Republican National Convention. A Washington correspondent was writing the story of the proceedings and noted that at one point the following telegram was received from the White House and read to the convention:

Have a heart. There are plenty of great Republicans better able than I to stand four years more of Gridiron dinners.

Herbert Hoover was placed in nomination, the correspondent noted, and the customary parade of states was started in his behalf. It was at first thought to be led by Hiram Johnson, but instead, it developed that Johnson was walking out of the convention hall. He noted that it was very hot there "but the mercury dropped three degrees when Secretary Hoover walked past Vice President Dawes and former Governor Lowden."

Senator Borah was always a problem in the Republican party organization, and this was recognized in a song to the tune of "Old Man River."

Ol man Borah, dat ol man Borah,
He must say somethin', but don't know nothin',
He just keeps droolin', he just keeps droolin' along.
He don't like London, he hates Geneva,
He keeps the world in a constant fever,
This ol man Borah, who just keeps droolin' along.

The great political scandal of the 1920s was Teapot Dome. In January 1924, Albert B. Fall, secretary of the interior in Harding's cabinet, admitted receiving loans of $100,000 from Edward L.

Doheny, an oil tycoon, and of more than $200,000 from Harry F. Sinclair, head of the Sinclair Oil Company.

It had been in the spring of 1922 that Fall had leased the Teapot Dome field in Wyoming to Sinclair, and the Elk Hills field in California to Doheny. These facts later were brought out in a Senate investigation headed by Senator Thomas J. Walsh, Democrat of Montana. On the basis of these revelations, Fall, Doheny and Sinclair were indicted for conspiracy against the United States.

Fall beat the conspiracy charge but later was found guilty of accepting a bribe, fined $100,000 and sentenced to jail for a year. Sinclair and Doheny escaped conviction on both counts, although the former served a short sentence for contempt of the Senate committee.

The leases were canceled, and on April 7, 1924, Coolidge dismissed Harry M. Daugherty as attorney general and replaced him with Harlan F. Stone, later chief justice of the United States.

Doheny's attorney had been Frank Hogan, a well-known and highly popular Washington barrister, the Edward Bennett Williams of his day, who was reputed to have charged Doheny a million dollars for defending him. Later on, one night at a dinner given to Hogan by fellow lawyers, and at which numerous Gridiron members were present, there was considerable joshing of Hogan about the size of his fee in the Doheny case.

When he rose to reply, he referred to this and commented, "Only once in a lifetime does a lawyer get for a client a multimillionaire who is scared."

The Teapot Dome scandal had been very embarrassing to the Republican party, but since it had occurred entirely in the Harding administration it was of no particular embarrassment to Coolidge personally, who was not identified in any way with it.

In a skit at this dinner, Will H. Hays, who was having trouble as a fund raiser for his party, was impersonated by Arthur Sears Henning, who did a parody called "Hays' Elegy in a Campaign Churchyard":

> The oil-can tolls the knell of good old days,
> The low-browed herd suspects the GOP,
> The oil-men jailward plod their weary ways,
> And leave the world to darkness and to me.

> Beneath these rugged beams, this derrick's shade,
> Where heaves the turf o'er Teapot's mould'ring heap,

There in an oil-well's depths forever laid
My campaign deficit was buried deep.

The boast of Butler, Mellon's pomp of power
And all that Sinclair, all that wealth decreed
Await alike the inevitable hour—
The paths of glory lead to Walsh and Reed.

The forthcoming Democratic Convention in Houston, Texas, was burlesqued in a skit involving the Texas Rangers, led by Sam Houston, and the Tammany delegates, who were described as the toughest Indians in the world—Tammany braves, led by Governor Alfred E. Smith wearing a brown derby. They were "out to steal that mangy old Democratic mule." The braves reworded George M. Cohan's "Give My Regards to Broadway."

We are the boys from Broadway,
The Bowery and Union Square.
These are the duds we wear on Howston Street,
In honor of our Mayor.
This is the way we're learning
To mingle with the White House throng.
We get the tip from Boss Olvany
That we'll all be there ere long.

"We'll give you a better tip than Olvany gave you," said a Ranger. "When in Houston, Texas, don't mention Howston Street, New York."

"That may be true," said a Tammany brave, "but you haven't named anyone who can stop Al Smith on any street."

The campaign theme was set forth by the vitriolic and abrasive "Senator James A. Reed" of Missouri, to the music of "Dream Kisses."

Every day I hammer at the GOP.
While I roam about all by myself.
Ev'rything I read says Al an' Victory,
While my photographs are on the shelf.
I hope that Houston will not be so cold,
So I go on with purpose bold.

Keen speeches, mean speeches
From this sharp tongue of mine,
Should thrill 'em and fill 'em
With a doctrine of brine.

While it has been traditional at all dinners to satirize public figures, in their pretensions, their motives, their exaggerations, and their dissembling at times, the club has also not missed many opportunities to poke fun at newspaper foibles. At this particular dinner, when Frank Noyes, president of the Associated Press, was introduced, Arthur Sinnott of the *Newark Evening News* took up a position behind him and responded, "Mr. Noyes says the Associated Press never comments, interprets or thinks."

In another skit, Dame Rumor presented her 1928 style show in rumors, old and new. "And false and true," piped up a Gridiron member.

The rumor factory was described as "the one industry which never shuts down," and one of the best-known models was "Coolidge will run again." Another was that Smith "may spurn nomination," that "Kellogg will quit as Secretary of State," and that "the dry law will be modified."

Somebody wanted to know whether these rumors could be marketed and Dame Rumor said, "You can always sell them to the newspapers. They'll take anything. The newspapers are Dame Rumor's best friends."

The dinner closed with a song to President Coolidge, to the tune of "They Didn't Believe Me."

> Since you said you did not choose
> Every one has sought a ruse,
> And I've talked until I'm blue
> Telling people it was true.
>
> They never believed me,
> They never believed me,
> That to this third term chance you've answered, No!

• • •

Coming after the 1928 election in which Herbert Hoover had defeated Governor Smith by 444 to 87 electoral votes, and in which several Southern states had gone Republican for the first time, the Gridiron dinner held on December 8 was heavily slanted toward the results of the campaign.

President Coolidge was present and closed the dinner with a speech. The other speeches were by Senator Borah, the somewhat unstable Republican, and by Senator James A. Reed, the Missouri firebrand orator. Reed had opposed as ineffectual the Kellogg-Briand Pact outlawing war as an instrument of national policy, and in closing the Senate debate on ratification had de-

clared, "The armies of the world have trod down avenues car-
peted by treaties such as this."

President-elect Hoover, who had been on a goodwill tour of
Latin America, was returning to this country on the battleship
Maryland.

John J. Raskob, the Du Pont executive who had induced his
company to make a large investment in General Motors, and who
had been selected by Governor Smith as chairman of the Democratic National Committee, appeared as Hamlet, the "melancholy
magnate," and delivered "a soliloquy on the brown derby."
Later in the dinner he lamented his failure to elect his candidate
and sang:

> Swing low, sweet Cadillac,
> Coming for to carry me home.

In another song, a chorus garbed as Southern gentlemen and
Kentucky colonels did a Gridiron interpretation of Stephen Foster's "Massa's in de Cold Ground."

> Way down in Dixie,
>   Hear dat mournful sound,
> All the Democrats are weeping,
>   Smith lies on the cold, cold ground.

And Senator "Carter Glass" of Virginia, one of the Senate's
most distinguished Democrats, chimed in with:

> Gone are the days of Cox and W.J.,
> Gone are those votes from the cotton field away,
> Gone to the North, and the South is deep in woe,
> For Democrats are voting now with Old Black Joe.

Senators Pat Harrison of Mississippi, Harry Hawes of Missouri, Key Pittman of Nevada, and Mr. Jouett Shouse of Kansas
City, later chairman of the Democratic National Committee,
were offered to cartoonists as models for a drawing, "Napoleon's
Marshals at Waterloo."

Senator Borah was introduced as a speaker by a little snapper
in which he was asked to "tell us what is your present view of our
prospective President."

And Richard Oulahan, standing behind him replied,
"Senator Borah says he regards Mr. Hoover as a noble experiment who must be worked on constructively." (Hoover had described the Prohibition Act as a "social experiment noble in motive.")

The show then adjourned to the deck of the battleship *Maryland,* where a chorus of leading Republicans, headed by an actor representing Vice President-elect Curtis, were masquerading as sailors and singing:

Sailing, sailing,
Through the Culebra slip;
Sailors we, all full of glee
To be on Hoover's ship.
Sailing, sailing
While the canal does foam—
Many a gob will want a job
When Hoover gets back home.

The Republican respect for some of its irregulars was phrased in a song, the key lines of which ran:

We don't like bull-moosers
Except when they're losers—

The skit ended with all groups proclaiming that they were real, original Hoover men:

Tramp, tramp, tramp in step with Hoover
All the boys have ceased to roam.
    Some of them put up a fight
    But they're back in line tonight
Don't forget us, Herbie, when you come back home.

Since the dinner was occurring at the outset of the Christmas season, the club did a parody on what was described as Mr. Hoover's favorite theme, the American home.

'Twas the night before Christmas
    And all through the house
Not a creature was sleeping,
    Not even a mouse.
The glasses were set on the
    mantle with care
In hopes that the bootlegger
    Soon would be there.

And then, to St. Nick:

So take your cheap presents
    To Paris or Rome;
It's plain you don't know
    The American Home.
I'm sure you'll agree
    There's no need for St. Nick

With a person named Hoover
> To do us the trick.

But I heard him exclaim
> Ere he drove out of sight,
Happy Hokum to all
> And to all a goodnight!

The Democrats were pictured as gypsies in a skit in which the Al Smith defeat was charitably explained because "Andy Volstead, he gave us the blues." And then they sang:

Gee, but we'd give our jobs to see
> Our whole gang in line.

An impersonator of Vice President Dawes read "The Letter of a Self-made Has-been to His Successor," Vice President-elect Charles Curtis of Kansas, who had come under considerable criticism for using the phrase "too damned dumb" in the campaign.

" 'Hell and Maria' was my line, but 'too damned dumb' will get you just as far," said Dawes. Then he issued ten commandments for a Vice President, among which were:

Don't buck the President if you want to stay more than four years.
Don't waste time saving Europe; they don't vote.
And, above all, don't do your sleeping in the daytime.

President-elect Hoover was satirized in only one fairly brief skit purporting to be a Movietone news made by Mr. Hoover from the bridge of the U.S.S. *Maryland.*

He began by asking the guests at the Gridiron Club "not to applaud and eat into my 'raddio' time." He expressed his gratitude to President Coolidge, who had not been too active in the campaign, "for giving his entire autumn to actively campaigning for my election." He said that his "great predecessor's" annual message to Congress showed that under his administration every problem had been solved.

"Nothing is left for me to do," he said; "hence, I shall call a special session of Congress to do it."

He closed by looking forward to the time when he would be able to attend the Gridiron Dinner in person: "I shall enjoy your jests at my expense to the utmost, in accord with the example set by my predecessor. As he said to me once, slapping me on the back, 'Herb, those Gridiron dinners are what I enjoy most—next to cabinet meetings.' "

Since this was Coolidge's final dinner as President of the United States, the dinner was closed with a Coolidge farewell by the entire music committee, which began by singing to the melody of "Duna":

When you came as President
        In nineteen twenty three
You had us all a worryin'
        For your levity
But you took it like a good sport.

But now there comes a new man
        To sit there in your place
And to feel the Gridiron sting
        With smile upon his face.
You are weary of the White House
        And of the great white dome
The green hills of New England
        Call you home.

Then, inspired by George Washington's farewell address, Richard V. Oulahan delivered the group's good-bye to "our fellow citizen."

"The period for a new inauguration of a citizen to administer the executive government of the United States being not far distant, and the time actually arrived when our thoughts must be employed in making life miserable for the person who is to be next clothed with that important trust, it appears to us proper, especially as it may conduce to a more distinct impression of the Gridiron voice, that we should now apprise you of our sentiments toward you and advise you in the way you should go."

He was warned against the mischiefs of Wall Street partnerships, presidencies of life insurance companies and college presidencies. "It should be your true policy to steer clear of permanent commitment against a return to the political world."

Oulahan advised Coolidge that "toward all future candidacies for your high office, have friendship for all but entangling alliances with none. Then we shall feel that perhaps your future attendance with us here will be a prospect from which you do not choose to run."

Following this, the chorus reaffirmed the invitation to future dinners.

So now adieu!,
We say to you!

We shall always look for you
    beneath the Gridiron.

On this note, "Silent Cal" made his final Gridiron speech as President of the United States.

• • •

The Coolidge era was definitely closed with a special dinner of the Gridiron Club on March 2, 1929, at which Vice President Charles G. Dawes was the only guest. This was done in appreciation of his devotion to the club over many years. Sorrow was expressed that he was going back to Chicago, and then the "good-bye" began. An elaborate program booklet, entitled "Hell and Maria," was prepared and distributed. In the brogue of Mr. Dooley, the fictional character created by Peter Finley Dunne, this booklet contained a farewell to the General which began:

> "Niver fear f'r th' Ginr'l. He'll be right at home an' in his el'mint. Luk at th' jaw iv him. He'd go agin a batthry iv Marines iv he thought he was right. He's a two-fisted fightin' man. Befure he's home two months he'll be headin' a movemint t'amind th' rules iv gang warfare so that th' industry can function smoothly an' in accordince with th' best modern methods."

The major songs relating to General Dawes from previous Gridiron dinners were all sung again, with the notation that one song at the spring dinner in 1928 "indulged in some prophecy which proved to be a real gem." This song was about the upcoming Kansas City convention and the possibilities of a deadlock developing. It ended:

When the Hoover show no new supporter draws
And the Lowden forces grow cold to his cause,
    They will gather in a room
    And they'll start a night-club boom
And the lucky one, we hear, is Charlie Dawes.

And perhaps indeed, he was the lucky one, because it was Herbert Hoover who had to deal with America's greatest depression.

IX

Herbert Hoover

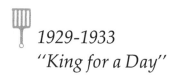

1929-1933
"King for a Day"

The first dinner attended by Herbert Hoover as President was held on April 13, 1929, five weeks after his inauguration. Roy Roberts of the *Kansas City Star* was president of the Gridiron Club that year, and very early in the dinner he was inaugurated in a skit in which he and President Hoover were indicted for conspiracy—Roberts had allegedly conspired to get the Republican Convention held at Kansas City and "by the use of insidious poison in a newspaper known as the *Kansas City Star,* permitted it to become known that the said Herbert Hoover should be nominated for President by the convention aforesaid."

Hoover, on the other hand, was indicted because "the said Herbert Hoover, out of gratitude, launched a surreptitious movement to procure the election of the said Roy A. Roberts as president of the Gridiron Club."

Immediately after the consummation of the plot, it was charged that Roberts went to Missouri and concealed his identity by becoming managing editor of the *Kansas City Star,* and that Herbert Hoover fled to South America disguised as a news photographer.

When asked what they said to the charge, Roberts replied, "Guilty as indicted, and proud of it." Then, leaning over to President Hoover, he announced, "President Hoover says he received the electoral votes of forty-one states, and I understand that my election was also unanimous. If that is a conspiracy, make the most of it."

Presidents of the United States have generally come from the professions, the law having contributed the most, but Hoover's election constituted the first time that an engineer had been in the White House, unless one could stretch the background of George Washington sufficiently to put him in that category.

Consequently, in this dinner there was considerable banter about the engineering methods that the new President would use. Hoover cabinet officers, when introduced, proved to be mere robots, all being mechanical men with Hoover faces. Recommendations by various cabinet members and senators were dropped into a large sausage grinder called "The Hoover Machine" and emerged in extremely altered form. The major members of the administration appeared on the stage dressed as mechanics and surveyors, but wearing top hats. One proclaimed that "at last the engineers have landed on Pennsylvania Avenue. This is the most important landing since the Pilgrims landed on Plymouth Rock, Corbett landed on John L. and Herbert Hoover landed in the GOP."

In other Gridiron highjinks, the actors all appeared as fishermen carrying rods and reels, and it was announced that this was a fishermen's administration and that "he fished for the nomination for eight years and he got it; he fished for the election for five months and he got it; give him two more months in the White House and you'll see him throw out a line baited for a fish called '1932'."

Then they sang, somewhat prophetically, to the tune of "The Isle of Our Dreams":

In the administration of Hoover
    It's a cinch in the cab'net, you know;
He's the spokesman, it's true, and the
        Colonel House, too,
    You others need only lie low.
For the path is not all lined with roses,
    And brickbats are part of the game.
When a target they hunt, he'll be there out in front—
Who but Hoover will get all the blame?

Hoover had his problems with Congress, for although he had a numerical majority in both Houses, there was quite a body of Republicans in the Senate, mostly from the Middle West and West, who voted about as frequently with the Democrats as they did with the Republicans on major issues.

President Hoover had called an extra session of Congress to meet the Monday morning after this Gridiron dinner, and the Gridiron Club put on its version of how that session would be operating in August. Here it was on the Gridiron stage, with the members using palm leaf fans and apparently exhausted by the heat, since this was before the days of air-conditioning.

An impersonator of Vice President Curtis called the Senate to order, advising them "to try not to be too damned dumb," and suggested that since it was so hot and they had so much to do, without objection the reading of the journal should be dispensed with. "James T. Heflin," an Alabama maverick not exactly universally respected for his intellectual capacity, immediately objected.

"James E. Watson" of Indiana protested and said he hoped the senator from Alabama would withdraw his objection because "President Hoover called us into session in April, and here it is August and we've done nothing."

Heflin: I'll withdraw my objection if senators will give unanimous consent for me to speak for four hours on why I am the most popular member of this body.
Watson: No spikka da English.

Curtis noted that unanimous consent was refused and asked the Senator from Alabama if he persisted in objecting.

Heflin: No, I'll withdraw it and object to something else later. I intended to make my speech at this time, but I notice there is no one in the press gallery.

At this point, Curtis's telephone rang, and it proved to be President Hoover wanting to know why something hadn't been done on tariff, farm relief, and other important matters. Curtis had to inform him that the Senate hadn't done anything on any of these things, but "we'll send you a nice bill regulating the size of catfish in Boulder Dam canyon.

"You say you don't give a Boulder Dam—what—what—

hello—" Watson rose and said, "Mr. President, Mr. President, I have just been informed a truckload of embassy liquor has been seized in front of the capitol. I move a recess of thirty minutes."

In response to this news, they all yelled "Aye!" and ran out.

Since Vice President Curtis was one-eighth Kaw Indian, there was an Indian music skit relating to him. He was depicted as the Emperor of the Tribe of Bunk and sang a parody of "How About Me?"

> For as a candidate,
> I seemed to captivate,
> But as Vice President,
> I fear I'm forgotten
> And maybe, the baby, I kissed to win a vote,
>> Now puts its arms around Hoover, but what about me?

One of the tribal chiefs addressed him as "Big Chief Charlie," and to the beat of "Ogalalla," intoned in song:

> Big Chief Charlie, hot tamale!
> For the Big Chief swore,
> That you ought to get more,
> At the White House door,
> If you are a Kaw.

The skit closed with a song based on "Arrah Wanna."

> If you wish to be a chieftain in the tribe of Bunk,
> Don't attempt to be a statesman full of noble junk,
> Find a cabin to be born in, or a farmhouse plain,
> You will find the good old hokum will go big in your campaign.

The speakers' list at this dinner was perhaps as impressive as it has ever been at any dinner. Besides the President, the other speakers were Chief Justice Taft and Franklin D. Roosevelt, who had just been elected governor of New York.

The introduction of the only man in history who had been both President and chief justice was a rather touching one, pointing out that in February 1891, when Taft was solicitor general, he had attended his first Gridiron dinner, that at a dinner as early as 1906 his election to the Presidency had been foreshadowed in a Gridiron song, and that in 1907 a Gridiron song had suggested he might also become chief justice.

Further along in the dinner, Roosevelt was introduced by a song to the tune of "Tommy Atkins." It also proved later on to be pretty good forecasting.

O, Franklin, Franklin Roosevelt,
Is there something in a name?
When you tire of being governor,
Will you look for bigger game?
Will you wish for something higher;
When at Albany you're through?
When weary of the State House,
Will the White House beckon you?

Because the new President came from California, the final skit was based on the Forty-Niners. Half the cast was costumed appropriately, while the other half was costumed as Twenty-Niners. To the tune of "On Wisconsin," they sang:

Forty-Niners! Forty-Niners!
    Glory to the name!
We have won the Pres-i-den-cy
    To add to our fame.
California! California!
Now will run the show.
Ho! Westward! Ho! Ho! Ho!
    Hell-roarin' go.

The dinner closed with a song to the President sung by Tudor Morsell to the popular refrain of the tune, "King for a Day."

Life is but a dream,
Make that dream supreme,
You're King for a day.
Don't forget that cabinets crumble,
Parties tumble,
Gather glory while you may,
Tolerant of all,
President of all,
You're king for a day.

This was just six months before the big stock market crash in 1929, and it is doubtful if anyone at that dinner realized that the "day" they sang about would not last much more than six months.

Hoover's first Gridiron speech as President made little reference to the skits in the dinner but was primarily a rather whimsical comment on the newspaper profession in Washington. He remarked that he had been coming to these dinners for over seventeen years and that from them he had received "much political education."

"As skeptical as some may be of the result," he said, "yet no one will impeach the ability and earnestness of my instruction.

"And I have found in all the representatives of the press at all times a desire to be helpful in most unexpected ways. For instance, they daily assist me beyond my greatest hopes by their suspicious research work in new implications for my most carefully formulated phrases. I discover by the time an idea of mine has filtered through the clear and crystal minds of one hundred different correspondents, that particular idea throbs with a sense of courage and public service, that it has sinister implications, that it is impractical, that it spells malevolence, that it is weak and vacillating, that it is filled with personal bias, that it bristles with idealism, sanity, and progress. When I take refuge in silence, the gentlemen of the press again assist me by the workings of their own speculative minds to the extent of column one, page one. And, always helpful, they promptly extend to me the privilege of denial. I do not wish to seem ungrateful for this cooperation, but I decided some time ago that I ought not to destroy the confidence of managing editors in their correspondents nor to dull the spirit of imaginative writing."

Hoover went on to say that as President he seemed to have two separate duties, "which occasionally in some degree seem to conflict." One was not to start anything that would occasion conflict and dissension, and the other was to provide the press daily with exciting news of something about to happen. "These are duties difficult at times to perform simultaneously," he said.

Noting that "ours is a government by opinion and the press is the most important part of that process," he proclaimed a desire to cooperate and to open "the book of the government to the public to the largest degree."

Then he referred to a fishermen skit and said that even fishing is news when the Chief Executive participates. And he explained his love of fishing. "Fishing," he said, "is the only labor or recreation open to a President in which both the press and the public are prepared to concede privacy."

Referring to his recent South American trip, Hoover paid the newspapermen tribute for the "effectiveness and devotion with which they, each of them, interpreted our countrymen to our neighbors."

He said that his profession as engineer "does not deal with magic. Its miracle is only the constant and everlasting building of brick on brick, stone on stone, by which, in the end, great institutions are created."

Then he appealed for everyone's cooperation, saying that "our form of government can succeed only by cooperation" with Congress, the press, business, and in social leadership.

"I have no feeling," Hoover said, "that my position is, as Mr. Morsell has just told me, 'A king for a day'. . . . It is just a job of bringing about such cooperation as I may between those who lead the forces which ebb and flow through a great people. . . .

"I am well aware of the difficulties of a program of close cooperation. It is much less heroic for the President to cooperate than to carry the banner of the people against the bastions of Congress. . . . The objects to be gained by cooperation within an administration between the administration and Congress, between the administration and the leaders of our economic and social forces, are not the pawns of politics; they are not the headlines of the newspapers. They are the prosperity, the contentedness, the moral and spiritual advancement of the American people."[1]

But the appeal for cooperation fell on rather deaf ears in the Congress, where a year and a half later the Democrats took control of both Houses.

• • •

By the end of 1929, President Hoover's commitment to economy in government was still intact, but the application of the principle was beginning to come under question.

During his incumbency as secretary of commerce, the plans had been made and most of the construction done on the new Commerce Department Building, then the plushest of the departmental buildings. It had cost $17.5 million, and when Hoover, as President, came to dedicate it, Genevieve Forbes Herrick of the *Chicago Tribune* wrote the unforgettable lead, "President Hoover today dedicated the new Commerce Building, which cost $2.5 million more than the Louisiana Purchase."

The December 14 dinner took place several weeks after the first bad breaks in the stock market. The subject was too serious for jesting. Gridiron President Roy Roberts referred to it lightly in his speech in the dark, pointing out that since they had last gathered under the Gridiron many grave problems had arisen: "Stock market liquidation and liquidation of Congressmen's baggage; tariff in low and politics in high; the Old Guard in a Blue Funk and the President in the Blue Ridge [Hoover personally owned a camp on the Rapidan which was a predecessor to Camp David]; the coalition declares a war in Washington but the

Dove of Peace coos in London [referring to the forthcoming London Naval Conference]."

He pointed out that everyone was bewildered, but that "the Gridiron proclaims the Prosperity of Laughter and the Business Revival of good humor. There will be depression tonight," he said, "only for those who take themselves too seriously."

The only other reference to the market crash of any consequence was in the guest skit, where a great many people were called to their feet with margin calls, and it developed that the account of Pennsylvania's conservative Republican leader, Senator Joseph R. Grundy, was "Short two senators, three representatives and a flock of press agents."

The skit ended with the suggestion that they should all go out and invest in the "Hoover Business Pulmotor."

Of all the liberal Republicans, Senator Smith W. Brookhart of Iowa was perhaps the most unpopular, largely because he was the most undiplomatic in his language.

A short time before this dinner, Senator Hiram Johnson of California had been the only member of the Senate Foreign Relations Committee not invited to the White House to dinner one night. This was later explained as a great "inadvertence."

At the outset of one of the skits, there was a crash at the curtain, and Charles G. Ross of the *St. Louis Post Dispatch* avowed that he'd "bet they are keeping Senator Hiram Johnson out of this dinner—by an inadvertence."

Dick Oulahan replied, "Not at all. They are keeping out Senator Brookhart—and it is *no* inadvertence!"

With the beginning of the depression, the power of the Senate began to rise dramatically. This was aided by the presence of a larger number than usual of able, articulate and ambitious men. The Democrats had hired Charles Michelson, until then head of the *New York World* Bureau and a Gridiron member, to lock himself up in a room, read the newspapers, think, and develop speech ideas for Democrats in Congress.

This action, taken at the early stages of the Hoover administration, was perhaps the most effective use of a comparatively small amount of money that any political party has ever made. For Michelson ground out with great profusion ideas designed to fasten the blame for the depression upon Herbert Hoover, and the Democrats, particularly in the Senate, seized upon them with great avidity.

Newspapermen at the Capitol day after day congregated at

the Senate as the biggest source of news in Washington, and consequently, these speeches, these investigations, and these attacks were regularly on the front pages.

Hence the dinner was heavily devoted to the Senate, and at one point a character sang, "Every day I wallop Hoover—that will do the trick, I guess."

In a P. T. Barnum act, an impersonator of the famous showman surveyed many acts of the Senate and mournfully exclaimed, "Yet, they called *me* the Prince of humbug!"

Senator Thaddeus Caraway of Arkansas had already begun to develop his penchant "to start investigations just to make big business weep." Parodying James Whitcomb Riley's "Little Orphan Annie," an actor threatened:

An' all the other Senators just has the mostest fun
While Thaddy pumps the witnesses and frightens everyone,
A-list'nin' to the witch-tales 'at Thaddy tells about,
An' Caraway will git you, ef you don't watch out!

The club put on a satire on the London Naval Conference about to take place. Other acts involved a song called Rip Van Coolidge, to the tune of "Lover Come Back to Me," in which they implored the former President to wake up and come back.

Our stocks are low, and margins high
It was not so, when you were nigh.
Around the ticker tape we're singing
Coolidge, come back to me.

The final music act of the dinner was also pitched on Congress, and its main feature was Joseph Grundy singing, "I Have a Little List." It was a long song, in which he named practically every Democrat and every Republican in the Senate who had failed to follow the Hoover party line. It ended with the chorus singing a *Mikado* parody:

He's got 'em on the list,
    He's got 'em on the list,
And they'll none of 'em be missed,
    They'll none of 'em be missed.

The skit closed with a parody of the song "Roll, Jordan, Roll," which in its Gridiron version was "Roar, Congress, Roar."

President Hoover, in his speech at the close of the dinner, addressed himself directly to the situation that was developing, as it had been expounded in the Gridiron skits. He mentioned that it was the fashion in the Middle Ages to wear hair shirts to remind oneself of trouble and sin.

"Many years ago," he said, "I concluded that a few hair shirts were part of the mental wardrobe of every man. The President differs only from other men in that he has a more extensive wardrobe. We have had tonight an indication of the great variety of persons and organizations who cheerfully and voluntarily insist on acting as hair shirts for the President. I am not complaining; I am only explaining one of the things that train his soul and his public conduct in urbanity. Incidentally, you could discover from these proceedings why Presidents seldom worry about anything. They have so many troubles in the closet or stowed away in the ice box that when one of them gets tiresome they can always send for another, and by great variety maintain interest and a high cheerfulness of spirit.

"You have from time to time during this meeting," Hoover continued, "heard mention of the Senate, and you listened to observations upon the relations of the Executive with this great coordinate arm of the government. I have for some time also been an interested observer of these relations. I have even searched through the intimate history of my predecessors since George Washington, endeavoring earnestly to discover remedies, antidotes, sedatives, irritants, stimulants, and experience. The important thing I have observed from an inspection of thirty administrations is that there is nothing new on this subject. Presidents have long since learned that one of the undisclosed articles in the Bill of Rights is that criticism and digging of political graves is reserved exclusively to members of the legislative arm. But Presidents have also learned that they have one privilege not extended to members of the legislative arm—they have the option on when to talk and when not to talk."

He pointed out that there is always a group in Congress trying to build "a Scylla and Charybdis for the President to navigate," or setting "those old traps known as the devil and the deep blue sea."

"At various points in every important debate," he said, "the opposition never fails to call vigorously upon the Executive to exert leadership, to give direction, to use the big stick. If he yields to these temptations, he is immediately discovered to be meddling in the responsibilities of the independent arm of the government. This is the oldest form of the devil-and-deep-blue-sea trap.

"The Republican party has no right to complain; it has been the preoccupation of the opposition with this sort of deep and subtle political strategy over many decades that wins us national elections for our party."

During the first year of his administration, President Hoover had appointed commissions to study many problems and make recommendations to him. There had been a short act in the dinner called "Commission of the Month Club," which had ridiculed these commissions.

"You have been misled," said the President, "into the impression that I shall soon appoint one [a commission] every day. That is wrong—I shall probably need to appoint two a day" because the problems had become so complex, he went on to say, that "it is necessary that we make the fullest use of the best brains and the best judgment and the best leadership in our country. . . ."

He then launched into an eloquent four or five minutes of appeal for reason rather than emotion. "The most dangerous animal in the United States is the man with an emotion and a desire to pass a new law. He is prolific with drama and the headlines. His is not the road to the fundamental advance of the liberty and the progress of the American people at this time in our history. . . . The greatest catastrophe that could come to our country is that administration policies or legislation or voluntary movements shall be encouraged or enacted upon the basis of emotion, not upon facts and reason."

He praised the nation's newspapers and newspapermen for their actions during the final days of the stock market crash. Fear, alarm and pessimism had swept through the country, he noted, and if it had not been for the restraints of the Washington correspondents and the press generally, and their wholehearted cooperation, he pointed out that widespread panic might have occurred.

"We shall feel aftereffects," Hoover said. "But the outstanding contribution of the press was the entire abandonment of the search for conflict."

Then he turned to the London Naval Conference, designed to bring an end to competitive naval building, and pleaded for a similar attitude here. He asked that the differences which developed in London should not be painted as fights, campaigns and combats, but rather as "an earnest effort to find the area of agreement.

"Never in our history," he said, "has the press played so large a part or incurred so great a responsibility in our foreign relations as at present. The seasoned public opinion and the example of the American people have become the most powerful influences for peace and orderly progress of the world."[2]

• • •

By April 1930, the cleavage between the new President and the Congress had become very clear. And with the 1930 congressional elections approaching in the fall, the club devoted attention to this subject in its April 26 dinner.

The opening crash was traditional in those years at Gridiron dinners. When President Charles S. Groves inquired what it was, Richard V. Oulahan responded, "That was the Senate, welcoming President Hoover's nominees for the Supreme Court." (The Senate was in process of rejecting Hoover's appointment of Judge John J. Parker of North Carolina to the Court, on the grounds mainly that he had once, as a circuit court judge, approved a so-called "yellow dog" labor contract.)

In those days when there was no air conditioning in government buildings, Congress adjourned fairly early in the year, frequently in June before the hottest summer weather hit Washington.

Two years ahead of time the Gridiron Club appropriated Franklin Roosevelt's 1932 theme song, "Happy Days Are Here Again," to sing:

Congress leaving, no deceiving,
We'll be rid of them at last!
Hoover worries, party flurries
May become a thing of the past.

For peaceful days are near again!
The atmosphere may clear again—
So we'll sing a song of cheer again
If the Congress will adjourn.

Because farm prices were low and the farmers were complaining, Hoover had wanted to restrain foreign competition by raising the tariff on some farm products, but in the process the tariff was raised on many other things as well in the Smoot-Hawley Bill, which Congress eventually passed and Hoover rather reluctantly signed.

This was treated in a musical version of *Treasure Island*, called "The Pirate's Progress, or Down in the Sugar Barrel with

Smoot," with the leading high tariff proponents, headed by "Captain Smoot," all costumed as pirates. Among those pirates was "Senator Hiram Bingham" of Connecticut, the handsome, statuesque New Englander who had discovered Machu Picchu, the lost Inca city in Peru, eighteen years before.

> Oh, glad is the life of a pirate at sea,
> Aboard of a pirate ship.
> And a Senator's life is as gay as can be,
> With politics and statesmanship.

In another pirate song, based on "Things Are Seldom What They Seem," vagaries of the voting by Senators Royal S. Copeland of New York, Simeon D. Fess of Ohio and others were satirized.

> Copeland has a doctor's skill,
> Swallows down a magic pill,
> He's a Democrat on Sunday,
> Votes with Smoot and Fess on Monday.

> Black sheep dwell in every fold,
> Borah left the Party cold,
> Though he wanders in September,
> He's for Hoover in November.

Captain Smoot's troubles in holding his followers in line led to a parody on the song, "In the Olden Days."

> It was not like that in the olden days,
> Which have passed beyond recall,
> In the dear old Platt and Penrose days,
> It was not like that at all.

Senator Smoot, a good Utah Mormon, couldn't do anything about literature in the tariff bill, but he had embarked on a crusade to prevent the publication of books that he considered unfit for reading. Questions had been raised in the Senate about his definition of "unfit," and one day, he announced that he would illustrate what he meant the next day by reading certain pages from *Lady Chatterley's Lover* in the Senate. To packed galleries, both public and press, he read some of the more lurid sections.

So, in the skit at one point a stowaway was discovered aboard, who announced that he was Lady Chatterley's lover and that "there is no place for me in the United States, except on a Senator's desk." To the tune of "There Ought To Be a Law Against That," the stowaway sang:

Elizabethan language will not do,
The customs experts have their eye on you.
For lit'rature henceforth must be polite.
At Harvard they are teaching Harold Bell Wright.

Continuing to play on the troubles in Congress, a singer representing Senator James E. Watson of Indiana, the majority leader, lamented that:

The record's full of speeches
And the Party's full or woe,

and,

It ain't no fault of mine
If they will be asinine.

Former President Coolidge was living in Northampton, Massachusetts, and was occasionally writing pieces for some of the magazines. His price was reputed to be one dollar a word, which was quite a lot in those days.

"At that price, this 'Silent Cal' stuff disappears," was a typical comment. And another was that "At that price, it took him three pages in *Cosmopolitan* magazine to describe a bed of pansies on the White House lawn."

But concerning the Hoover administration, Coolidge was keeping very quiet. About a year later, Arthur Sears Henning of the *Chicago Tribune* went up to Northampton to see Coolidge. The depression was so bad in 1931 that there was some doubt about Hoover's renomination. Henning asked Coolidge about this and received the private, off-the-record reply: "If the nomination in 1932 is worth anything, Herbert Hoover, as sitting President, can take it; if it isn't worth anything, he's got to take it."

Even in 1930 there was some desultory talk of running Coolidge again, and a Gridiron member sang:

By a tree in Northampton a gentleman sat,
Singing: "Morrow, tomorrow, tomorrow" . . .
And he thought of the conference gone on the rocks,
And he read in the news of the prices of stocks,
And he sighed, as he gazed at the run in his socks,
    "Tomorrow, tomorrow, tomorrow."

Reacting to the deteriorating situation with the press and Congress, a Gridiron member at one point raised the question whether there might not be, the next year, a Democratic Congress. "There might be," he was told, "in spite of the Democrats."

Prohibition, scarcely ever overlooked at any dinner during the "dry" years, came up again. Hoover had referred to prohibition as "an experiment noble in motive," so in a skit a small boy named A. Noble Experiment commented that he thought everybody knew him and then sang:

Little Boy Blue Nose,
Come blow your horn,
There's a still in the meadow
And a kick in the corn.

It was nearly midnight before President Hoover was introduced with a parody on "Sweet Mystery of Life," which expressed concisely the Gridiron spirit:

Yet in song and jest alone our theme is written;
    For there's fun and fun alone in what we say!
For with President as well as with the Gridiron,
    It is but mirth alone that saves our day!

The President chided the Gridiron Club for its verbosity and recalled that, when the committee of the club had called upon him to invite him, they had said they were going to make a strong effort to shorten the program.

"There was then silence," said the President. "Feeling that something was required to restore the conversation, and not being entirely insensible to such subtle approach, I responded with an assurance that I would do my part in taciturnity.

"Of course, my share of taciturnity is one of those unequal divisions of time somewhat comparable with that sausage made of half horse and half rabbit by mixing one rabbit and one horse."

The President commented that during the evening he had witnessed "a chamber of horrors," such as prohibition, tariff, unemployment, and Congress, through amplifying and distorting lenses.

He noted that the "microscopes of hyperbole, satire, ridicule—and occasionally some real humor—are bound to be applied." But he added that the minor flaws of public events are enormously magnified by these lenses, and small segments of great problems "lifted out of all proportion to their relative importance.

"One's taste for Roquefort cheese can be permanently destroyed by a miscroscope. And a cheese mite amplified a few thousand times is one of the most sensational and terrifying beasts exhibited to man. And so it is with the amplifications tonight."

Referring to the Gridiron show as "this playhouse of fantasy and imagination," Hoover observed that "the emotions and horrors of the night have a way of dissipating with the sunrise," and that under the initiative of our people some of the sombre problems "have a way of curing themselves . . . in far better fashion than either the government or the Gridiron Club solves them.

"Years ago," he commented, "the railways were so tainted with sin that they became national campaign cries," and that "to be against the railroads was a final test of morals in political life."

Then he recounted how the scientists had brought forth the automobile, the truck, and on the waterways the Diesel tug, all of which competed with the railroads to such an extent that the device which had been created in the Interstate Commerce Commission as a means of holding down rates had been "turned into a device for holding them up so the railways can live.

"They [the railroads] have become tainted with poverty," he said, "and therefore with respectability."[3]

It was at this dinner that an incident was recalled which had occurred in 1900 during the Boxer Rebellion, when Tientsin was beleaguered by fanatical and frenzied Boxers.

Robert Barry, a Gridiron member, related from the stage how President Hoover, then a young mining engineer, and Mrs. Hoover were among the so-called "foreign devils" whose lives were imperiled for several months. Finally, the Marines reached Tientsin and marched into the city, accompanied by a famous British regiment, the Royal Welch Fusileers.

Years later, when General Pershing and the advance guard of the American Expeditionary Force in World War I stepped ashore at Liverpool, the British escort of honor there to greet them was the Royal Welch Fusileers.

In recognition of this, John Philip Sousa, former leader of the Marine Band and music director of the Gridiron Club, had composed his march entitled "The Royal Welch Fusileers." Barry explained the background, called Sousa to the stage, and there, before the President and the British ambassador, had him direct the first public performance of the march.

This so impressed President Hoover that he included in his speech an even more detailed recollection of the Tientsin siege and of the great relief of the 1,200 soldiers, sailors and civilians, a quarter of whom were Americans, who had held out until the day when they could be relieved.

· · ·

In the congressional elections of 1930, the combination of the persistent attacks inspired and planned by Michelson and the effects of the deepening depression resulted in the loss of control by the Hoover administration of the House of Representatives, and in the Senate the count stood at forty-eight Republicans, forty-seven Democrats, and one Independent.

Quite naturally, this resulted in heavy emphasis in the December 13 dinner upon the Democratic ascendancy and the plight of the Republicans.

It began at the very start with the customary offstage crash. To the question about what it was, came the response, "That was the American voter vindicating Mr. Hoover at the polls November 4."

In true Gridiron spirit this was followed with a song ending:

Life's no gloomy place,
Light your solemn face,
Let's have some fun!

They proceeded to do it in two major skits: the coronation of the Emperor, Michelson, by the Democrats, and Waterloo for the Republicans. The coronation of "Emperor Michelson" was one of the very few Gridiron skits in which a club member was the central character.

Entering with fanfare of trumpets and a march by the Marine Band, the music committee installed the elaborately costumed Emperor, played by Jay G. Hayden of the *Detroit News,* and the Lord Chamberlain announced:

"Gentlemen, we are gathered here tonight in the midst of this Byzantine splendor, for the coronation of our sovereign, the Duke of Dreams, the Maharaja of Mimeograph, Lord High Custodian of the Nightmare, Imperial Stretcher of the Long Bow, Creator, Originator and Grand Devisor of the Synthetic Interview, The Chief Democratic Press Agent—the Emperor Charles Michelson the First, out of the *New York World* by General Motors."

Then the chorus sang an adaptation from *Ruddigore.*

O Machiavelli Charles, his paper and his pencils,
He ruthlessly employed in carving things on stencils,

With fear he'd make them quake,
He'd duck them in his lake,
He'd break their bones, with sticks and stones,
And burn them at the stake.

Three distinguished ambassadors from the past arrived to pay him tribute: Baron von Munchausen, Frederick A. Cook, who had claimed unconvincingly to be the discoverer of the North Pole, and the writer of fairy tales, Hans Christian Andersen.

The Baron sang that "When I write an interview, everything I write seems true," and the chorus sang, to the music of a popular song, "They Didn't Believe Me":

And when I tell them,
And I'm certainly going to tell them,
That in the White House Roosevelt soon will be,
They'll never believe me.

Cook stepped up and sang:

Dashing through the snow,
In a one-horse open sleigh,
I saw John Raskob go,
Laughing all the way,
He waved a tabloid rag,
He tipped a wicked wink,
And said: "How simple 'tis to win,
With a jar of printer's ink."

Followed by the chorus:

Jingle bells, jingle bells!
Jingle all the way,
Oh what fun it is to be,
A Democrat today.

The Emperor finally responded:

"Gentlemen, speaking as Senator Copeland of New York, I thank you. Speaking as Senator Glass, I am caustic and satirical. Speaking for the Monday morning papers—as Senator Walsh of Montana—I fold myself in the Constitution. Speaking as Senator Fletcher of Florida, I can be dull and stupid, though it pains me, and speaking as three Democratic candidates for President, I can even keep Jim Watson and the White House guessing. In the immortal words of Archimedes, give me a portable typewriter and I will move the world."

In the Waterloo skit, the Republican chairman, Simeon D. Fess, was Napoleon, while other Republicans were his marshals.

Fess wanted the Old Guard to charge, and while his marshals looked through the binoculars they reported that "your Majesty's troops are falling back at Massachusetts. Heavens, they are following the wrong Coolidge!" (Marcus A. Coolidge, a Democrat and not related to the former President, had been elected senator from Massachusetts.)

Fess asked about Ohio, and Marshal Moses of New Hampshire replied:

Oh, the moon's behind a cloud along the Wabash;
For the Democrats are making all the hay;
In the sycamores the GOP is hiding;
On the banks of the Wabash, hell's to pay.

And so it went, through the various states. But there were a few victories to report to Napoleon. Two of the leading Republican insurgents, Borah in Idaho and Norris in Nebraska, were winning. Finally, Fess was despondent. It was the end. It was destiny. "When New York elects a Democratic Roosevelt," he said, "and Massachusetts a Democratic Coolidge, there is nothing left for the Republican party but to sue for plagiarism, or commit suicide.

There were other references to the election and to the economic conditions of the country, symbolized best perhaps by a lame duck skit in which Miss Prosperity had developed a lisp. She ended the skit saying, "Yeth thir! Come on boyth, leth go down to the White Houth and theranade Mithter Hoover with that thweet thong, 'Thinging in the Rain.'"

But while the Gridiron Club was looking to the future in predicting Roosevelt's election in 1932 in the Emperor Michelson skit, they also had a skit on revolutionaries at that dinner, referring to several such in Latin America, India (Gandhi), and with a minor mention of a Bavarian named Adolph Hitler. Asked about the "German revolution," Walker S. Buel, of the *Cleveland Plain Dealer*, in something less than perfect German, answered: "Ich weiss nicht was soll es bedeuten."

And Edwin W. Gableman of the *Cincinnati Enquirer* announced, "Mr. Hitler says that if France can loan one billion dollars to England, Hindenburg and Mr. Mellon ought to be out picking daisies."

This was the only comment at that dinner about the man who was to upset the world nine years later.

The ever-present Prohibition skit, referring to the increasing difficulties the government was having in enforcing the Volstead Act, parodied Arthur Chapman's poem, "Out Where the West Begins."

> Out where the moonshine's a little brighter,
> Where the sugar of corn is a trifle whiter,
> Where the drys go home just a wee bit tighter,
>   That's where the wets begin.

President Hoover, in a somewhat muted way, sought to strike back at the Gridiron Club by speculating on what sort of government we would have if it were conducted in conformity with Gridiron ideas.

He thought official life might be confined to those things which furnish raw material for news, entertainment, wit, and combat, and commented that sometimes he felt his administration was not doing its duty to the Gridiron Club in not producing more of these raw materials.

If the Gridiron Club were to organize a party to push its views, he thought its platform would have to advocate domination of government by excitement, that all attacks on the administration should be given a position on the front page, column one, and that opportunity for denial should be given an inside page, "provided the denial is peppy enough to maintain the combat."

Dwelling particularly on the Michelson skit, the President said that he had been "interested in the high distinction paid to Democratic party publicity," but that he would not have been "so partisan as to have referred to it as a great factory of synthetic myth and legend."

President Hoover attributed that party's need for Michelson to the Democratic failure to find "that array of defects which normally feeds the fires of their campaigns" and therefore they had to resort to the large expense of hiring a superman. The party, he said, had a history of notable accomplishments in campaign strategy of this sort, and he commented that it seeemed to be "an admirable method of retaining their position in opposition."

There had been some talk of an extra session of Congress and a reference or two about it in the skits. This inspired President Hoover to shoot a well-directed shaft at his triumphant political opponents.

"It is an extraordinary thing," he said, "that the whole

nation should shudder with apprehension and fear at the possibility of an extra session of its great legislative body. Such a possibility seems to have brought forth not only the satire of the Gridiron Club but the protest of practically the entire press, the representatives of organized labor, organized agriculture, and organized business. I take it that the community must now be fearful of its handiwork in the supposed Democratic victory in this election."[4]

• • •

The April dinner in 1931, orginally scheduled for April 11, had to be postponed until April 27 because of the death of Speaker Nicholas Longworth of the House. His funeral was on April 11 in Cincinnati, and the President, the Vice President, and most of the head table guests attended it.

The depression was deepening. There was comparatively little reference to it in the Gridiron dinner, because most people did not regard it as a laughing matter. In the one skit devoted to the subject, the emphasis was more political than economic.

Walker S. Buel, impersonating Robert H. Lucas, executive director of the Republican National Committee, came to the stage as "special sales agent of the committee," saying he wanted to sell "the Hoover record." He had a clothing store dummy hung with a suit which was badly tattered. It represented the Hoover record.

Lifting off the coat, he said, "Isn't that a wonder? All it needs is a little mending. I admit there is a hole or two in it," but they could patch it up, he said, so it would look "better than new."

There were two other skits touching on the subject, one based on the farm relief plan of the Republican national platform in 1928, designed to show how muddled both the farmers and Secretary of Agriculture Arthur M. Hyde were, and a brief prosperity skit, in which a reference was made to Senator George Norris's statement that what the country needs most is another Roosevelt.

The real barbs were devoted to Prohibition, the new Presidential Press Secretary Theodore G. Joslin, the Gridiron Club itself, the Progressives, chain newspapers, and to former President Coolidge, who was awarded the "Nobel prize for literature" by the club. The chorus sang:

> Two and two are four,
>   Rain is often wet,
> Iron is made of ore,

Fish are caught in a net.
Spending is a sin,
Saving is a gift,
Look at me and see the soul of thrift.
Heathens feed on rats and rice,
Polar bears live on the ice,
Though this lesson sounds absurd,
I get two bucks a word!

Despite the general decline in prices, his rates must have gone up.

The scene for the Prohibition skit was a ship, the *Eighteenth Amendment*, which was battered by gales and rocked by a storm, but still trying to make harbor under the command of an impersonator of "the Ancient Mariner, Attorney General George W. Wickersham." The chorus sang to the tune of "Sailing (Sailing over the Bounding Main)":

Pro-hi-bi-tion, sailing the stormy spray.
She's floating yet, but getting wet
And wetter every day.

Wickersham moaned:

Water, water everywhere
    Yet how the dry votes shrink;
Water, water everywhere
    And only Scotch to drink.

Wickersham had appointed a commission to study the problem of Prohibition, and the actor playing this distinguished lawyer announced that he intended "to do exactly what my commission recommended—look both ways at once, trust in Herbert Hoover, hope for the best, and expect the worst."

When Senate minority leader "Joe Robinson" asked, "Who will join Senator Fess and me in sticking to the ship?", a stowaway, "Al Capone," was the only one to volunteer. He sang:

You made me what I am today,
I hope you're satisfied.
You built me up and up until
I stand here in my pride.
I make a billion every week,
I've done well from the start.
Don't dare to repeal,
Or you will feel
The curse of an aching heart.

Then the Gridiron Club directed a few gibes at newspaper publishers. One of the best was at Roy Howard, whose Scripps-Howard chain had just purchased the financially troubled *New York World*.

A city editor wisecracked, "He has overturned 400 years of geographical science. In 1491 Columbus cracked an egg, and behold the world was round. In 1931 Mr. Howard cracked the Pulitzer will, and behold the *World* is flat."

Gene Buck, president of the American Society of Composers, Authors, and Publishers, and a principal librettist for the Ziegfeld Follies, which were so famous in the twenties and thirties, was a guest at the dinner. In an article about it later he commented that "the Washington newspaper correspondents write the best satirical playlets produced in America."[5]

President Hoover, at the conclusion of the dinner, responded to the toast with a comment on the show that he wouldn't characterize the Gridiron Club as the gyroscope of the ship of state, "but it does serve to keep humility in the crew."

He remarked that he had risen in humility and that while much could possibly be said in refutation, he thought nevertheless "it is good to live a few hours in the land of illusions whether they be illusions of fairies, illusions of wit, or illusions of wisdom."

Most people thought that things were pretty bad in 1931. Sir Willmott Lewis, Washington correspondent of the *London Times*, had also realized that things were going to get much worse and wrote in one of his dispatches that Americans would look back upon 1931 as the year of prosperity.

President Hoover, in the serious part of his speech, launched into a discussion of the difficult economic problem. He noted that similar depressions had followed about a decade after the Napoleonic wars and after the Civil War. The roots, he said, were in the destruction of war and the dislocation of social and political institutions which flows from wars.

He closed with a statement of his basic philosophy in relation to the depression.

"If, by the grace of God, we have passed the worst of this storm, the future months will be easy. If we shall be called upon to endure more of this period, we must gird ourselves for even greater effort, for today we are writing the introduction to the future history of civilization in America. The question is whether that history shall be written in forms of individual responsibility, and the capacity of the nation for voluntary cooperative action, or whether it shall be written in terms of futile attempt to cure poverty by the enactment of law, instead of the maintained and protected initiative of our people.

"This is a period when the ideals and hopes which have made America the envy of the world are being tested. So far our people have responded with courage and steadfastness. If we can maintain this courage and resolution we shall have written this new chapter in national life in terms to which our whole idealism has aspired. May God grant to us the spirit and strength to carry through to the end."[6]

• • •

The opening song at the December 12, 1931 dinner proclaimed that "When we give our Gridiron dinners, we invite both saints and sinners," and Jay G. Hayden, the president, declared in his speech in the dark that we live tonight in a land of illusion.

"We propose that you deliver over to us all of the cares of state and we promise on our side to settle everything. . . . We will guide the hand of a beleaguered Congress and still the voice of all of its boll weevils. We will light the road for an harassed and heckled administration. And finally—oh greatest of boons—we will pick the candidates and show how both sides can be elected."

An impersonator of John N. Garner, Speaker of the House of Representatives, presided in a skit on the cotton pickers' jubilee. The jubilee spirit emerged because the South had taken over most of the committee chairmanships and five of them were Texans. Garner proclaimed that "the Lone Star State is now the All Star State," and that the cotton pickers could have the rest.

In the guest skit, one of the persons called to his feet was Judge James H. Wilkerson of Chicago, who was described as "the world-renowned discoverer of a permanent residence for Al Capone."

"Al Smith," from the top of the Empire State Building, looked down upon New York and sang a new version of "The Old Oaken Bucket."

> The buildings of Wall Street, the bright lights of Broadway,
> The cops and speakeasies and tenements tall;
> And center of everything, there is the Wigwam—
> Old Tammany's bucket collects from them all!

The old soak-'em bucket, the silver-bound bucket,
The old white-washed bucket collects from them all!

This was only a few months before Governor Franklin D. Roosevelt deposed James J. Walker, the charismatic darling of Tammany, as mayor of New York, and thereby removed from himself as a Presidential candidate the stigma of Tammany Hall.

"Roosevelt" proclaimed in the skit that "our party is not the party of millionaires," and "John J. Raskob," Democratic chairman, replied, "I wish it were."

Impersonators of the leading Republican progressives, who had been thorns in the side of Herbert Hoover for the last two years particularly, came on the stage to the strains of Hindu music as the Three Mahatma Gandhis—George Norris, Hiram Johnson and Smith Brookhart.

They announced to "Senator Simeon D. Fess," Republican chairman, that their party had bolted from them and "hence we intend to overthrow you and Mr. Hoover."

"Senator George H. Moses" of New Hampshire, the court jester, looked upon this "as more Hoover luck."

In a duet between Fess and Raskob to the tune of "When the Work is Done Next Fall," the former sang:

Oh, Mister Raskob listen—of "Hoover
    luck" you've heard;
And that will reelect him, I pledge
    my solemn word.

Raskob:
    But Hoover luck is bad luck, that's
    where we have the call.
    It will be worse than ever—when the
    work's all done next fall!
Fess:
    You count on the depression, it is an idle dream;
    Do you expect the country to rally to that theme?
Raskob:
    You say the dream is idle? Well, so are one and all;
    The GOP'll be idle—when the work's all done next fall!

In a *Mikado* skit, it was noted that American marines were in Nicaragua to save American lives and properties, that the United States had set up a "puppet" government in Haiti, and Japan had taken the matter to the League of Nations, with the suggestion that the Kellogg Pact should be invoked.

George R. Holmes, head of International News Service in Washington, as Pooh-bah Dawes, announced that the Kellogg Pact was one of the Mikado's proudest achievements.

It has been a club custom for many years not to impersonate the President of the United States on the Gridiron stage. But the club skirted very close to the ban that night when the Mikado appeared, made up to provide some resemblance to Herbert Hoover. He paraphrased in song "A More Humane Mikado Never."

> All prosy, dull, political persons,
> Who chatter and bleat and bore,
> Are sent by the dozens,
> To Copeland and Couzens,
> Who speak from ten to four.

> The Watson or Walsh who utters predictions
> In statements to the Press
> Is made to dwell in a private hell,
> And drink water with Senator Fess.

Chorus:
> His object all sublime,
> We will achieve in time
> To let the punishment fit the crime,
> The punishment fit the crime.

During every Presidency there has been some friction between the White House and the Washington correspondents. The differences from administration to administration are only in degree. This is because the newspapermen are naturally an adversary force, seeking to find out advance plans, current thinking or, in some cases, alleged skulduggery in an administration or among its supporters.

It was not unnatural, with the whole country looking for devils on which to blame the depression, that this adversary situation should be particularly strong in the Hoover administration.

At this dinner the club put on a Scotland Yard skit, in which five detectives, all dressed in the costume of Sherlock Holmes, tried to solve a great mystery. "The freedom of the press," complained one, "is a noble experiment, but somewhat feeble-minded in conception and damnably annoying in practice."

Consequently, "to further good fellowship and unity of action among us," he declared certain things; namely, that nothing be printed until announced by the Royal Keeper of the Hush-Hush, that anyone in the Royal Household found speaking audibly to an outsider be incarcerated in a commission, and that every newspaperman found gathering news be turned over to the Imperial Master of the Bloodhounds.

The detective announced that he expected every policeman to do his duty. One of the detectives announced that 238 men were running down that story printed yesterday. "What story?" asked another. The first replied, "It said one of the palace dogs barked at the moon."

Efforts were also made to find out "about that story that the royal coach exceeded the speed limit." Another story had reported that the royal household will eat turkey for Christmas dinner. The skit ended when one of the detectives said, "These outrages have gone far enough! The Yard will get its man! Come on boys!"

President Hoover began his speech by observing that this had been "a highly educational evening. We guests fully realize that this is the semiannual occasion when the representatives of the press make their contribution to lofty ideals, to unity and solidarity of national action in the presence of national danger by rubbing the salt of wit, the vinegar of hyperbole, and the iodine of satire into the raw wounds of politics."

He noted the Scotland Yard skit and replied good-naturedly that this was a thorny subject as old as the government.

"It involves a theory," he said, playing on an old theme, "that the principal job of Presidents is to make news for both morning and afternoon editions each day, and particularly that it shall have a mixed flavor of human-interest story and a dog fight that will please the village gossips. A revered President, long since dead, once told me that there was no solution to this relation of the White House to the press; that there never would be a President who could satisfy the press until he was twenty years dead."

Then he explained his own philosophy on White House news.

Long and patient endeavor on both domestic and foreign matters, he pointed out, was required to bring about the meeting of many minds before action could be finalized. It was a "critical essential" in all such negotiations "to avoid the rock of announced positions and the inflammation of public controversy by which measures affecting men and nations may be wrecked before a common understanding may be reached through the long and tedious process of give and take."

Obviously, he noted, it was to the interest of the correspondents to find out and reveal the things that went on in these negotiations. And when they were unable to obtain this information, "they must satisfy the managing editor somehow at least by a column damning the government for secrecy, with forebodings and a dark conspiracy against public interest with Wall Street, or Downing Street, or some other dark alley."

But he sought to ameliorate the impact of this criticism by pointing out that the access of the press to the President and all other officials in Washington (there were, at that time, two Presidential press conferences a week) "is without parallel in any nation." And he reached the conclusion that for the most part, reporters cover public matters "intelligently, objectively, with astounding accuracy and penetration."

Nor did he limit his philosophical banter to the press. He noted that the head of St. Elizabeth's Hospital for the Insane in Washington had discovered that there was a pathological type which is known as the exhibitionist, and that this type seemed to congregate in the national capital.

One form which this exhibitionism took was illustrated by those "who visit the White House to say a hurried few words to the President and on leaving hand out a long statement to the reporters at the door on subjects that have never been or are little discussed with the President."

He mentioned that there were also other varieties of exhibitionists, but since he made it a practice never to say anything that could not be forgiven, he wouldn't pursue that subject.

He advocated cooperation. Referring to the fact that the American government is based on political parties, each of which should accept its full responsibilities, he said that the Republican administration had the responsibility of developing a program. The program it had proposed, he said, was not bipartisan and favored no one except those in need.

"I am as confident of the actual cooperation of our Democratic colleagues in national service," he declared, "as I am confident of their patriotism, but I do not doubt that they will contribute to the anvil of debate.

"I need not remind you that these are difficult times. Never in peace time have the Executive and the Congress been confronted with greater responsibilities. They are times which require broad sympathies and great sacrifices. They are times which require stern and resolute action of government and it requires equally stern and resolute action by citizens.

"The whole situation requires unity of action in our nation. It demands cooperation. It demands courageous action by governments and by men. It demands that men rise above party and political advantage."[7]

• • •

By the time of the April 9, 1932 dinner, the depression had become severe.

In this situation, Walker S. Buel of the *Cleveland Plain Dealer*, president of the club, tried hard to find some distracting or alleviating features. He declared that all the world was looking to Uncle Sam as the man with the magic hat who could produce the bunnies.

"Congress produces taxes and more taxes; the reconstruction finance corporation produces loans and more loans; economy produces commissions and more commissions; Geneva produces resolutions and more resolutions; and the Noble Experiment produces handsprings and more somersaults.

"All at the same time, westward the tide of politics takes its way, as both parties, with singular appropriateness, choose for their deliberations the Windy City."

There was scant but accurate reference to the approaching Democratic contest between Franklin D. Roosevelt and Alfred E. Smith. In a skit entitled "The Claim Jumpers," located in the "Bucket of Blood Ice Cream Shoppe of Campaign Gulch," the bartender, Calamity Jane Democracy, was serving a strawberry sundae to Rollo Franklin Rosebud. He had his claim staked out but remarked that there were a lot of claim jumpers around, including his wicked uncle, Big Shot Al, who had a black eye, obtained when he was prospecting in New Hampshire.

"Smith" decided that Rollo was claiming everything in sight and "we've got to stop him." Rollo replied, "Stop me if you can. I defy you, Uncle Alfred, and all your claim-jumping friends."

In another skit, the forthcoming Hoover election campaign was treated in a song to the tune of "Casey Jones."

> Come all you voters, if you want to hear,
> The truth about a great engineer.
> Herbert Hoover was the engineer's name,
> And a'diggin' in the ground is how he won his fame.

He's diggin' now as he never dug before,
He's diggin' now at the White House door.

A sales tax proposal was before Congress, and two of the prime leaders for and against it, respectively, were Bertrand Snell, Republican leader of the House, and Republican Representative Fiorello LaGuardia, later to be mayor of New York. "Snell" sang a new version of "O Sole Mio."

O Fiorello, be a good fellow;
For we will need you, in thirty-two.
The party counts on me,
And we can't have insurgency.

To which "Fiorello" replied:

O Bertrand Snell-o, it's no good to bellow,
For we have got the itch, we're going to soak the rich.
Raise income tax rates, for we won't have lax rates,
O Bertrand Snell-o, it's no good to bellow.

The Chicago Convention skit was notable primarily for a hotel employee who took an order for three cases of ginger ale, six cases of seltzer water, and five tubs of ice for Room 810, and then announced, in response to a question about what was going on in Room 810, "They're writing the dry plank."

The skit ended with a song based on "Look for the Silver Lining":

A platform of song and laughter
Might help to end depression and strife;
So let the planks show a brighter lining,
And let's bring back the sunny side of life!

Franklin Roosevelt was approaching that idea with his campaign theme song, "Happy Days Are Here Again."

The real thrust of the dinner came in the closing skit, with Mother Goose gathering her children around her "to speak our little pieces and sing our little songs."

There was a poor voter and what do you think?
He lived upon nothing but victuals and drink,
Victuals and drink were the chief of his diet,
And now he has neither and cannot keep quiet . . .

Rockabye, Hoover, on the tree top,
When the wind blows, the market will drop.
When the boom breaks, the prices will fall,
Down will come Hoover, Curtis and all.

And another verse:

Little Boy Coolidge, come blow your horn,
There's woe in the meadow and slump in the corn,
Where is the man that looks after the sheep,
He's down in the White House, fast asleep.

And:

London sterling's falling down,
Falling down, falling down,
London sterling's falling down,
Poor old Mellon!

Build it up with canceled debts,
Canceled debts, canceled debts,
Build it up with canceled debts,
God help Mellon!

And the final song before Morther Goose shooed her children off to bed was:

The farmer's gone to hell,
The farmer's gone to hell,
Higho, the cheerio, the farmer's gone to hell.

President Hoover didn't think it was very funny. However, always the gentleman, he commented rather good-naturedly after watching this show,"that humorists are obviously getting scarcer and scarcer. . . .

"This slump in humor," he said, "may be part of the general slump, or due to the World War or bank failures, or the threatened reduction in federal salaries, or the Congress, but whatever it is, I acknowledge at once that I am again to blame."

He lamented the fact that "there is certainly a world-wide depression in good-natured wit, in happy facetiousness, in stimulating whimsicalities and especially in downright kindly jokes." He announced the need of a few stimulating nation-wide jokes in this crisis.

"It would lift the soul of man to a point where hoarders would bring back their money and perhaps bankers would even make a few loans to their old townsmen."

But it was apparent that what the Gridiron Club had done, particularly in the last skit, hurt. "Obviously," he said, "there is no shortage in the national supply of that stabbing satire, searing irony, crushing ridicule, or sardonic hyperbole which brings a momentary snicker at the discomfort of somebody."

Then he went on to say that he had often given consideration to the subject of trying to organize a type of humor that would help people to bear up in adversity instead of giving them a determination to beat up their neighbors. He had thought of asking the Senate to investigate the bear raids on the national spirit of mirth, but he decided the result would be "certainly an atmosphere of despair." He had also thought of a citizens' organization "to make one or two jokes in a tentative way," but his survey of the civic groups who might be asked to take on such a task did not seem to promise "much hope of creative work and constructive joy."

He couldn't see the bankers doing this, or organized agriculture, or the Anti-Saloon League, or the stockbrokers, or the "so-called intellectuals with their unbroken record of total abstinence from constructive joy over our whole national history."

Instead, he would turn hopefully to the people to find their own happy jokes.

"When you recollect the tragic days of the Great War," said Hoover, "it was not the Gridiron Club, nor the Congress, nor the administration, nor the General Staff who formed flashes of kindly humor which stirred the courage and caused men to grin amid the sufferings of the moment. It was the men in the trenches themselves who fired the star shells of helpful jokes across the night of human despair."

In closing, he rather optimistically did not join those who bemoaned the attack upon his administration by the opposition party.

"Our people," he said, "are at times discouraged by the apparent partisanship in time of national crisis. But we must again needs remember that . . . other democracies in the despair of these three years have sought to build coalition government, but if you search their results you will find that they have weakened the national vitality by vacillation, or the impotence of positive action from internal friction, or have degenerated to dictatorships.

"Worse still, if there be no alternative party in time of great strain there may be no answer except violent revolution. Political parties having been elected to majorities whether in the executive or in the Houses of Congress have a positive responsibility to leadership and to patriotic action which overrides partisanship. Constructive opposition is essential to the spirit of democracy itself. The anvil of debate can alone shape the tools of government. . .

"Six months have elapsed of even more trying times in the nation and the world than any man could have anticipated. That confidence has been broken by occasional diversion into politics and a morass of demagoguery which at times swept one house. But in the long run when we shall look at this period in retrospect it will shine in our history as again proof of that great thing which democracy has need to prove and prove again.

"That is that in time of national emergency the majority of our citizens and public men and of our political leaders will unite their intelligence and their patriotism swiftly enough to save the nation from the precipice. That program which we initiated at the opening of the session has marched with steady and patriotic progress. We have interruptions due to the anvil of debate, invasions of the demagogue, and at times a lack of a sense of humor, but it marches along."[8]

• • •

The dinner of December 10, 1932, coming just a month and two days after Franklin D. Roosevelt had swept the country and many long-term Republican senators and congressmen had been defeated, was devoted primarily to the sad state of the Republican party and to the troubles of the incoming administration, which would take over three months later.

The Republican vehicle was "The Retreat from Moscow," in which actors representing Generals Simeon D. Fess, Republican chairman, and Reed Smoot, senatorial conservative leader, appeared on the stage in tattered uniforms, accompanied by the torn flags and broken guns of a defeated army, to sing:

> Where do we go from here, boys,
> Where do we go from here?
> Anywhere from Kansas to another hemisphere.
> The GOP is off the track,
> We need an engineer,
> Oh boys, Oh boys, where do we go from here?

The sad band had been "driven from Massachusetts with 80,000 Republicans lost, from Michigan with 125,000 lost, from California with 400,000 lost because of the desertion of 'Trumpeter Hiram Johnson', to say nothing of Iowa, 'birthplace of our noble Emperor,' with 130,000 lost."

On top of it all, Field Marshal Jim Watson, Republican Senate leader, had "fought on the banks of the Wabash once too often and lost his shirt." "Watson" was attired in a uniform made of the most tattered remnants to be found in the four floors of

"Jonesey's" Baltimore costume shop, for generations costumer of the Gridiron Club. Echoing the sentiments of "Brother, Can You Spare a Dime," he belted out:

Seven-cent cotton, thirty-cent wheat,
How in the world can a poor man eat?

Seven-cent cotton,
A carload of tax,
The load's too heavy
For our poor backs.
We all worked hard,
As hard could be,
We couldn't save the GOP.
No use talkin'
Any man's beat,
With seven-cent cotton,
And thirty-cent wheat.

In the disheveled ranks was a straggler who "wouldn't fight with us and now he wants to tell us how to reorganize our armies."

He proved to be "Senator William E. Borah" and he sang:

Teasing, teasing, I was only teasing you.
Teasing, teasing, just to see what you would do.

The major skit on the incoming administration, comparatively few of whose important figures were present at the dinner, was set before an Indian wigwam, where the intrepid explorer, "Franklin van Roosevelt," was negotiating with "Chief Curry" of the Tammany Indians for what he could get.

Van Roosevelt had arrived at Manhattan in a Dutch ship named the *Half-and-Half* and explained that "the ship was named after an old Democratic custom. Half of us want to do one thing, and half another," to which a Tammany Indian replied, "Just like us Indians—half of us wanted Smith, and the other half didn't want Smith—and look what we got."

The ship's admiral, "James van Farley," and his commodore, "Bernard van Baruch," plus others like Able Seaman "Hiram van Johnson," listened to Curry's announcement that he represented the five tribes of the five boroughs.

"Oh, yes," said Farley, "the five tribes—the Mohawks, Onondagas, Oneidas, Cayugas, and Senecas."

"No," replied Curry, "—the Murphys, Olvanys, McCooeys, Currys and O'Briens."

Van Roosevelt offered "the finest line of campaign promises you ever saw, glass beads, little mirrors, brass checks and spangles, and a farm without a mortgage, a man without a note, a bank with a frozen asset, and a home without a worry" in trade for the island. One of his group sang an adaptation of "Oh, Promise Me."

We promise you the best of everything,
Prosperity and happy days we'll bring.
Forgotten men will be remembered now,
And that new deal will come to pass, somehow—
We'll bring the rainbow down for all to share
The pot of gold we think—perhaps—is there;
Oh, anything on earth you want to do,
We promise you, we promise you.

The Indians were impressed but not satisfied. Then van Roosevelt drew forth a bottle of firewater and promised repeal.

"The country is yours," Curry said.

The other skits, for the most part, were related to the outgoing administration, but bore none of the sting of the closing skit in the April dinner. The dinner followed to a certain degree the paragraph in President Buel's speech in the dark, in which he said:

"To the victors of November, to those who won, we offer our sincere sympathy; to those who lost, we extend our heartiest congratulations. . . .

"Beneath the kindly glow of the Gridiron we meet as friends. That emblem, shining for nearly half a century, summons us again tonight to be merry, remembering that a light heart lives long."

It was exactly twenty years before that President Hoover had first been a guest at a Gridiron dinner, and in recognition of his friendship for the Gridiron Club over the years, Mr. Buel pointed out that during the years he had been President, Hoover had never missed a dinner.

"Whether he regarded this attendance as an obligation, however hazardous, of his high office, or whether he thought it was just good fun, perhaps he will reveal himself."

He called to the head table the three persons besides himself who had been presidents of the Gridiron Club during Mr. Hoover's administration: Roy A. Roberts, then managing editor of the *Kansas City Star*, Charles S. Groves of the *Boston Globe*, and Jay G. Hayden of the *Detroit News*.

Speaking for the club, Mr. Groves presented the President with a golden Gridiron, "as evidence of our esteem and good will, and a permanent invitation to attend all future Gridiron dinners.

The music committee sang:

Here's a health unto the President!
Here's a health to him tomorrow,
Here's an end to strife and argument!
Let the Gridiron banish sorrow.
So gentlemen now let us stand
So let us take the glass in hand,
And drink to him who rules this land.
Here's a health unto the President.
Here's a health to him tomorrow.

Buel announced the Gridiron Club has but one toast: To the President of the United States. Then Mr. Hoover embarked upon his last speech to the club as President.

He recalled the years over which he had been a frequent Gridiron guest and said that he had been accorded "all the grades of honor from the end of the table in the far corner to this close approach to the throne.

"The seat at the end of the corner table," he said, "is the most comfortable one."

Then, commenting upon the "objectives" of the Gridiron Club, he noted that one of them appeared to be "pointed instructions to government officials and political leaders as to their errors and shortcomings.

"This instruction," he said, "is enforced by the threatening Gridiron which, like the traditional schoolroom switch, hangs here behind the teacher's desk. These educational facilities of the Gridiron Club thus include a regular and rigid enforcement by way of roasting."

He remarked that over the years "the Gridiron process has perhaps improved its subtlety. . . . But, speaking seriously, I am deeply indebted, as is every guest, for the many happy memories of these events and their manifold proof that life is not all serious."

He spoke of the election with wit and without rancor.

"Well, as nearly as I can learn, we did not have enough votes on our side. During the campaign I remarked that this administration had been fighting on a thousand fronts; I learned since the campaign that we were fighting on 21,000,000 fronts. We had a good fight, and when our opponents recover from the glow of victory and undertake to perform the sad rites of burying their dead promises, that will be another story. And the Republicans will, no doubt, take care of that."

Then, in a very moving passage and with deep seriousness, he bade farewell to the Presidency:

"I notice in the press a generous suggestion that my countrymen owe to me some debt. I have said in part elsewhere that, on the contrary, the obligation is mine. My country gave me, as it gives every boy and every girl, a chance. It gave me schooling, the precious freedom of equal opportunity for advancement in life, for service and honor.

"In no other land could a boy from a country village without inheritance or influential friends look forward with unbounded hope. It gave to me a certain measure of success in my profession. It conferred upon me the honor of administering the world's response to the appeal of hundreds of millions of afflicted people during and after the war. It gave me high place in the war councils of the nation. My country called upon me to represent it in the reconstruction of human and economic relations between former enemies on the continent of Europe after the armistice. It gave me an opportunity for service in the cabinets of two Presidents.

"It gave me the highest honor that comes to man—the Presidency of the United States. For this fullness of life, for the chance to serve in many emergencies, I am indebted to my country beyond any human power to repay.

"Only a few rare souls in a century, to whose class I make no pretension, count much in the great flow of this republic. The life stream of this nation is the generations of millions of human particles acting under impulses of advancing ideas and national ideals gathered from a thousand springs. These springs and rills have gathered into great streams which have nurtured and fertilized this great land over these centuries. Its dikes against dangerous floods are cemented with the blood of our fathers. Our children will strengthen these dikes, will create new channels, and the land will grow greater and richer with their lives.

"We are but transitory officials in government whose duty is to keep these channels clear and to strengthen and extend their dikes. What counts toward the honor of public officials is that they sustain the national ideals upon which are patterned the design of these channels of progress and the construction of these dikes of safety. What is said in this or in that political campaign counts no more than the sound of the cheerful ripples or the angry whirls of the stream. What matters is—that God help the man or the group who breaks down these dikes, who diverts these channels to selfish ends. These waters will drown him or them in a tragedy that will spread over a thousand years.

"If we lift our eyes beyond the scene of our recent battle, if we inspect the fate of other democracies under the pressures of the past three years, there is outstanding demonstration of a remark I made at a former meeting of the complete necessity in modern democracies of maintaining two strong political parties.

"Block government among several parties leads not only to negative policies, but to destruction of all responsibility which carries government always on the brink of chaos. Coalition government leads inevitably to danger and often to revolution, for it offers the people no alternative through which to explode their emotions.

"To carry on competent government there must be a strong and constructive opposition. The Republican party now has that duty to the American people. But opposition cannot function without political organization, constancy to principles, and loyalty of men to their party. Likewise, no party in power can serve the country unless the members show loyalty, courage, and a willingness to accept the responsibility of government.

"Nor does this preclude that cooperation which far transcends partisanship in the face of common danger. That great common danger is still in the economic field both at home and abroad. During the past two years we have been fighting to maintain the very foundations of our own stability. That front can be held if no mistakes are made.

"Today one of the visible evidences of our economic problem is the impassable bridge between the debtor and the creditor. Either prices must rise or debts be reduced. Not one but many economic forces have brought this about. To increase prices we must give consideration to the continuing effect of the foreign situation. The vicious spiral of economic and social instability has been continuing in the great majority of foreign countries. If we would make a full and secure recovery, if we would prevent future relapse, we must consider major action in cooperation with other nations. But that cooperation does not imply that it shall be accomplished at the expense of the American people. Others must bear their just burdens and open hope to the people of the United States.

"To fulfill these tasks we must maintain a solidarity in our nation. We must maintain that cooperation at home which, while it maintains party responsibility, yet rises above partisanship. The new administration has my good wishes; it has the good wishes of every American, for in its success lies the welfare of our country."[9]

And so departed from the active stage of American politics the "King for a day," with a graciousness that was a factor at least to some degree, during the long years of his life after he left the Presidency, in converting the bitterness of those days to the respect and dignity which the country accorded him in future years.

X

Franklin D. Roosevelt

1933-1934
FDR and H. L. Mencken
Face Each Other on the Gridiron

In the last three weeks before Franklin D. Roosevelt took office, the depression had brought heavy runs on the banks. By March 4, 1933, five thousand had closed their doors. It was after taking the oath of office from Chief Justice Charles Evans Hughes, that Roosevelt had uttered the memorable line, "The only thing we have to fear is fear itself." He then set out on a drastic reconstruction program.

The second day after his inauguration, Roosevelt closed all the banks in the United States until the Treasury Department could examine their books and allow those that were in sound condition to reopen. He immediately called a special session of Congress to meet on March 9. The primary purpose was banking legislation, but once the Congress was in session, the new Roosevelt administration poured through a series of recovery and reform laws, to put into effect what the President called "a New Deal for the American people."

The drafting of these laws was generally under the supervision of the so-called "Roosevelt Brain Trust," headed by a former university professor, Raymond Moley. The bills were presented to Congress with a demand for immediate action. The demand was met. Most of the bills were passed overwhelmingly, and some of them on such short notice that the members of Congress did not even have an opportunity to read them before voting. This period was labeled later by Turner Catledge of the *New York Times* as the "Hundred Days," since Congress was in session for precisely ninety-nine days and then adjourned.

• • •

Approximately half of this hundred days was over when the Gridiron dinner was held on April 29, and the spirit of the dinner was beautifully stated by Charles G. Ross of the *St. Louis Post-Dispatch*, Gridiron president, in his speech in the dark.

Noting that this was the forty-ninth Gridiron year, he commented, "And what a year! The New Deal is upon us, and from the hand of the dealer the cards fly with bewildering speed. The hand is quicker than the eye, gentlemen, but it is not quicker than the ayes when the roll is called in Congress.

"Wonderland is all around us, and we shall show it to you tonight—a wonderland with a King and a Kingfish [first reference in a Gridiron dinner to Huey Long], a Jack [Garner], and some Jokers, with senators turning into reporters and reporters turning into a Secretariat and everybody turning handsprings—a wonderland, my countrymen, from which the men who wear hair shirts have been expelled by the men in asbestos pants.

"What a land and what a year! . . . The stein, if not the dinner pail, is full. We don't know where we're going, but we're on our way."

The dinner had one of the most notable guest lists of any up to that time: the President, Vice President John Nance Garner, Chief Justice Hughes, ambassadors of Great Britian and Italy among others, all the members of the cabinet, several governors, about two dozen senators, Vincent Astor, Bernard Baruch, Pierre S. du Pont, practically all of the new White House ruling clique, the male members of the Roosevelt family, Joseph Pulitzer, and Richard Whitney, president of the New York Stock Exchange, later to run afoul of new Roosevelt securities laws and end up in jail.

After the conventional inauguration and initiation skits, in which I myself was one of the initiates, Arthur Krock announced that "we are privileged to see and hear tonight the fire chief in the deep South, where everything is very quiet and lazy, and the peons are lying around." One of the early acts of Congress in the

Hundred Days was the creation of the Tennessee Valley Authority, to take over the old World War I Muscle Shoals power plant and transform the Tennessee River into a series of wonderland dams.

The chief announced that the peons were hoping to find something to do, and all of a sudden the hero of the skit came in. His name was Franklin.

"Here are you all lying around with shoals of muscles," Franklin said. "Why, this place ought to be called Muscle Shoals." Then they lay down again. But the hero, Franklin, wouldn't let them off so easy. He put his fingers to his mouth, whistled shrilly, and in came hordes and hordes of Moley-cules—members of Congress, headed by a beautiful girl.

"I dub thee Pioneer Spirit," said Franklin, "and I command thee to put life into these Moley-cules."

Whereupon, since the land was all bare and brown, Franklin sent the Moley-cules after more green, which proved to be greenbacks from the Treasury to string on the transmission wires and make wreaths.

In the end the peons lay down again. Everything was like it was before it became wonderland.

The prominence of the brain trust in preparing the new legislation was satirized in a scene on the campus of the electoral college, showing "a conference of the Roosevelt Brain Trust, otherwise known as the Daisy Chain Gang." Most of the members of the brain trust had academic backgrounds.

Headed by "Raymond Moley" and "Rexford G. Tugwell," another professor, a group of scholars in caps and gowns came onstage. Moley turned to Tugwell and asked if any of them had an unproved theory or a rejected thesis. A big shout of yes went up and Moley responded, "Don't forget to let me have them. We're going to write them all into law and try them out on the country."

"Do you think the country will stand for it?" he was asked.

"Right now the country will stand for anything."

Then a plain old-fashioned Jeffersonian Democrat entered with a cap and gown and was told that this was no place for him because "this administration is not plain, but fancy; not old-fashioned, but newfangled; not Jeffersonian, but Harvardonian."

"When we get through the country will be different," shouted Tugwell triumphantly.

"I'll say it will," yelled the plain Democrat, "with the Democratic donkey waving a Harvard pennant and Tammany Hall singing 'The Sweetheart of Sigma Chi.' "

The act closed with the professors singing, to the tune of "Bye-Low, Baby":

Phi Beta Kappa!
Phi Beta Kappa!
Phi Beta Kappa!
Phi Beta Kappa!
    Amen!

President Roosevelt had appointed William H. Woodin as secretary of the Treasury, and in one act the chorus sang:

Little Wooden Willie,
People thought him silly,
'Cause he had a knot-hole
In the middle of his head.
So he put a hat on,
And since he has that on,
Folks who called him silly,
Think he's very wise instead.

An impersonator of Theodore Roosevelt, in Rough Rider costume, told the audience that Polonius was out of date and that "what the world wants to hear is my advice to my fifth cousin." A few of the items of advice he had to offer were:

"Beware of entrance to a quarrel, but being in, be sure that the opposed may beware of thee."

"Give every man thine ear but few thy voice."

"Tell them nothing, but even to Huey Long say, 'That's bully Kingfish'."*

Ogden Mills, secretary of the Treasury in the Hoover administration, was the Republican speaker, and he was introduced in a mirage act of two unhappy political prospectors, Mills and Hoover, wandering in the desert of Nevada. Mills remarked that after all the campaign speeches he made, he would "have to keep quiet for a long, long time."

"Your speeches didn't help much," said Hoover sourly.

"And every time you talked," came back Mills, "the Democrats claimed another state—and got it."

The scene for the major music skit, which immediately pre-

---

*Huey Long had become quite a figure on the senatorial stage. He had long been known in Louisiana, and was now known country-wide, as "the Kingfish," after a domineering character in a radio program.

The first president of the Gridiron Club in 1885, Ben: Perley Poore, poses with his family and pet dog.

An early Gridiron meeting
held at Pine Forest Inn,
Summerville, South Carolina
in 1900.

John Philip Sousa, leader of the U.S. Marine Band, and first music director of the Gridiron Club. The Marine Band traditionally plays at the club's annual dinners.

XXTH CENTURY
GRIDIRON PRIMER.

WHEREIN

**Are laid down, in Easy Characters, adapted to
the most senile Understanding, the**

PRINCIPLES OF PATRIOTIC POLITICS

**Specially arranged for Bosses (easy and other-
wise), Henchmen, Heelers, Trimmers,
Floppers, Grafters, Watchers, Workers,
Mixers, Handlers, Satellites and
Satraps.**

COPIOUSLY EMBELLISHED
BY

Elegant and Stimulating Cuts, designed to amuse and
instruct, no less than elevate and adorn, the Minds
of Public Men; rendering easy the Problem
of separating Vice from Virtue, or discovering the differential Value of
Push and Pull;

TO WHICH IS ADDED AN ELEMENTARY

TABLE OF GASTRONOMY
FOR ADVANCED BEGINNERS.

**Compiled with conscientious Care and con-
structed upon a Novel and Improved Recipe
by a Gentleman living upon the Business,
From which Table both Wise and Foolish may
choose with Discretion or defy
The Dictates of Politeness and Prudence;
the Whole followed by a**

SOCIAL AND POLITICAL CATECHISM

in which are set forth the Rudiments of Good Manners
as well as Good Politics, enabling the Diligent
Student thereof to become by the End
of the XXth Century

(but no sooner)

THE PERFECT FLOWER OF MAN.

Issued for the improvement of the Pupils of the
GRIDIRON ACADEMY.
And entered according to an Act of the G. C. in the
office of the Librarian A. D. 1901.

Left: A Gridiron Club
       "primer" distributed to
       guests at a dinner in
       1901.
Right: A sketch of a Gridiron
       dinner in 1899 which
       appeared in Harper's
       Weekly. The "news-
       boys," following a
       skit about a session of
       the Senate,
       immediately began
       distributing copies of
       newspapers to the
       guests describing
       what happened at the
       "secret" session.
Below: Photograph of an
       early Gridiron
       dinner.

A collection of Cliff Berryman's cartoons which appeared in The Washington (D.C.) Sunday Star over the years depicting various Gridiron acts.

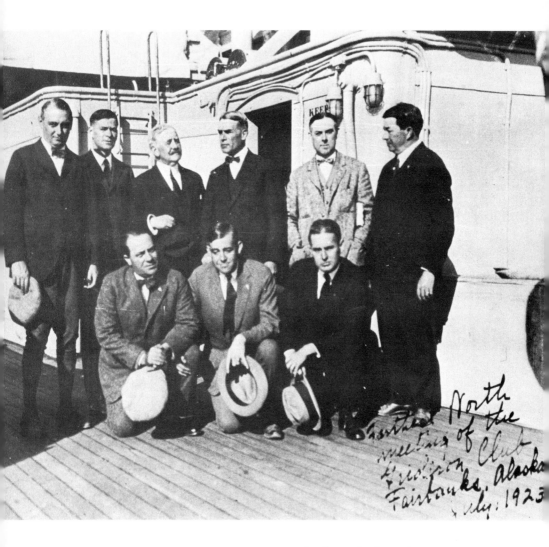

Farthest North
meeting of the
Gridiron Club
Fairbanks, Alaska
July 1923

In the early days, Gridiron Club
members traveled hither and yon
for sessions by boat, railroad car,
automobiles—and even camels—as
early Gridiron Club records show.

COMING OF THE GRIDIRONERS.

THE DINNER GIVEN THEM WILL BE A GREAT EVENT.

The Newspaper Men will be Accompanied by Distinguished Statesmen, Among whom will be Senators Depew and Carter and Congressmen Allen and Cousins—An Important Meeting of the General Committee Held Last Night.

With the Gridiron Club will come to Charleston:

Senator Chauncey Depew,
Senator Carter,
Private John Allen,
Congressman Bob Cousins and other distinguished national characters.

There was a very important meeting of the general committee for the festivities last night. The m[...] held at the Charleston Hotel an[...] that almost every member of t[...] [...]ee was present is confirmativ[...] that an abiding interest in the [...] is entertained by the people of [...] The enthusiasm of the members [...] mittee bore further testimony t[...] with which the workers have [...] of the arrangements. Capt Jam[...] ding, the secretary of the trea[...] the first chairman called on fo[...] and he gave one that caused g[...] fication to those who heard [...] Cap[...] Redding had finished th[...] tee went into the arrangement [...] tails of the entertainment.

Teh visitors will arrive in the [...] the Southern Railway Monday [...] The Gridironists will travel as [...] of the Southern under the specia[...] of General Passenger Agent Tu[...] one of the warmest friends [...] pushers have. Just as soon as [...] heard the boys were going to [...] Charleston he sent them an In[...] travel as the guests of the Sout[...] following extracts from a lett[...] by Secretary Richard Lee Fea[...] club, to Mr J. C. Hemphill, The News and Courier, tells c[...] ceptance of the Southern's invi[...]

"We have decided to travel by [...] ern Railway, which will run ou[...] a special schedule. I will advise[...] of the names of six or eight dis[...]

men who will accompany us on the [...]. Our party promises to number about forty. At a special meeting of the club, calle[...] to consider the invitation of the South-ern Railway, thirty-eight members were polled for the trip."

Mr R. M. Larner, of The News and Courier, wired Mr Hemphill last night:

"Gridiron boys enthusiastic over trip. We will come thirty-five members strong, with several Senators and Representatives of distinction—Depew, Carter, Private John Allen, Bob Cousins, sufficient to swell our party to about forty."

Among the visiting newspaper men will be the following:

David S. Barry, New York Sun.
Charles A. Boynton, the Associated Press.
L. White Busbey, Chicago Inter-Ocean.
Frank G. Carpenter, Carpenter's Syndi-

The Gridiron Club
of Washington, D. C.

SQUANTUM TRIP

THE GRIDIRON CLUB will leave for Squantum to attend the clam bake given by Senator Aldrich and Mr. Howland on

FRIDAY, JULY 22.

The Club leaves Washington in

Special Car Pennsylvania Railroad at

11 O'CLOCK A. M.

Leaves New York on Providence Boat, Pier 18, North River, foot of Murray Street, New York, at 6 P. M.

Transportation and staterooms provided for members who have notified Senator Aldrich and the Secretary of The Gridiron Club of their acceptance of invitation.

The following acceptances have been received:

Barry, Blythe, H. V. Boynton, Busbey, Carson, Clarke, Coolidge, DeGraw, Dunn, Fearn, Hall, Handy, Larner, Messenger, J. P. Miller, Randolph, Richardson, Rouzer, Seckendorff, Shriver, Snyder, Walker, West, Wynne, Young, Adams, Corwin, Dunnell, Bennett, Cunningham, Hay, Kaiser, Morsell, Nolan, Sousa, Xander.

Railroad transportation will be distributed by the Secretary, at Pennsylvania Railroad Station, Washington, just before departure of train. Staterooms will be given out on Steamer at New York.

John S. Shriver

Secretary.

Clifford K. Berryman's cartoon
depicting famous attendees of
Gridiron dinners during its first 50
years, which was distributed to all
guests at the 50th Anniversary
Dinner.

GRIDIRON PARADE · 1935

Above: Gridiron Club members pause for a formal photo during a dress rehearsal. At left, Phelps H. Adams in his regal getup as Charles de Gaulle at the 1964 dinner.

A SURPRISE ON THE MENU.

POLITICAL POTPIE

Above: A contemporary cartoon about the Teddy Roosevelt-Senator Foraker battle which broke up a Gridiron dinner in 1907. At right, a letter from the governor of Virginia denying responsibility for the leak that led to widespread publication of the incident. The story (below) appeared in the New York Evening Post.

ROOSEVELT IN TILT

Sharp Debate with Foraker at Gridiron Dinner.

HIS POLICIES THE ISSUE

"All Coons Alike" to President; "All Persons" to Senator.

Foraker, Who Was Not on Programme for Speech, Was Called on After President Had Defended His Course on Brownsville and Japanese Questions. Rights of Senators Vigorously Championed by Ohio Statesman.

New York, Jan. 27.—A special dispatch from Washington says that the discussion between President Roosevelt and Senator J. B. Foraker, at the Gridiron Club dinner on Saturday night, is being whisperingly rehearsed in Washington to-day. The Gridiron Club's dinners are not reported for publication, except officially—that is, an account of the jokes of the hosts at the expense of their distinguished guests is prepared, censored, and issued, and the guests themselves may, in a spirit of jocularity, utter all sorts of statements that would be surprising to the country at large and find no mention of these extravagances in the press.

Invariably, speeches made by public men are broadly humorous and obviously not intended for publication. Not in years has a serious debate occurred, and never before was the President of the United States unpleasantly involved in the evening's performance.

To add spice, the guests were unusually interesting. In addition to the President and Senator Foraker, there were present Vice President Fairbanks, Speaker Cannon, J. Pierpont Morgan, H. H. Rogers, ... and Wil-......, a ...., and ....

Deprecates Senate's Agitation.

The President, when called upon, launched into a defense of his administration. He justified his various so-called policies, especially in the Japanese and Brownsville matters. He declared that the Senate discussion of the Brownsville incident served no good purpose, could have no result, and was purely academic.

In this portion of his remarks he used the catch phrase of a popular negro song, "All coons look alike to me."

He discussed his attitude to the corporations, and said it was well to have them controlled "while the conservative forces are in power."

Most of the criticism of his administration was based on a desire to make political capital, he said.

The President was extremely strenuous in a vocal and gesticulatory way, and entirely serious.

Senator Foraker, not on the programme, was asked by the chairman of the dinner for his reply.

If the President was serious, Senator Foraker was more so. He spoke long and impressively. He said the President would discover that the Brownsville discussion was not purely academic; that it had a significance that would be realized, and a result that would be recorded. He (the Senator) intended to express his opinion on the floor of the Senate, ignoring dictation from whatever source. He had always expressed such opinion and would always continue to do so.

All Coons and All Persons.

"Not only all coons, but all persons look alike to me," said Senator Foraker. "The oath of a United States Senator is as sacred as the oath of the President, and as high a sense of duty may inspire a Senator as that inspiring the occupant of the White House."

The Senator denied that the motive of a critic of the administration was, of necessity, an unworthy motive.

Mr. Foraker's well-known eloquence of manner was effective, and when he concluded in ringing tones, with a wave of the hand, toward the President in these words: "You know, Mr. President, I love you so," the applause was loud.

Twice the President attempted to still the applause, evidently with the intention of making a running debate, but the hand-clapping continued to almost the point of embarrassment. When order finally was secured, the President got the floor, raised his glass, and proposed the health of the Ohio Senator.

The speech of the President and the reply of Mr. Foraker consumed so much time that the dinner was adjourned before four or five speakers on the programme could be heard.

Lyle C. Wilson, for many years head of the United Press in Washington.

Bernard Kilgore, head of the Washington bureau of The Wall Street Journal, later Chairman of Dow Jones & Co., Inc.

John Miller Carson, Philadelphia Public Ledger, one of the founders of the Gridiron Club.

Arthur Krock, Washington correspondent of The New York Times, taken when elected to the Gridiron Club.

Clifford K. Berryman, cartoonist of The
Washington Star.

Raymond Clapper, nationally-known
columnist killed in World War II.

Roy Roberts, Washington correspondent
and later editor and publisher of The
Kansas City Star.

Arthur Wallace Dunn, Washington
correspondent of The St. Paul Pioneer
Press and author of "Gridiron Nights."

Two Gridiron Club members as "Hula-Hula girls" in an 1894 skit about the annexation of Hawaii.

ceded the toast to the President, was set at Jefferson's Monticello at midnight, where Mr. Jefferson and his friends were about to have a nightcap before turning in. The chorus sang:

> The strife is o'er, the battle won,
> The Democrats have now begun,
> Their program thus to measure,
> Their faith in us to treasure.
> No more shall despot rule this land,
> No more shall king his will command,
> The Democrats will make us free,
> Perhaps in 1933!

A servant announced that a lot of men were coming up the mountain, "dressed in clothes like o' which I never done see before," whereupon in marched impersonators of Marshal Pilsudski of Poland, Mustafa Kemal Pasha of the Turkish Republic, Stalin, the Lord of all Russias, and Herr Adolph Hitler, Chancellor of the German Reich, who, with his retinue, threw over the tables and chairs and pushed everyone else aside.

"Was it for this," moaned Jefferson, "that I wrote the Virginia Statute of Religious Freedom?"

And finally, the Italian chief of state, Benito Mussolini.

"Enough, enough," cried Jefferson. "Was it for this I wrote the Declaration of Independence? Tell me, Marshal Pilsudski, the United States has not one of these?"

"Of course," Pilsudski answered. "You've got one and he's as good as the best of us."

"His name, his name!" pleaded Jefferson.

Pilsudski drew Jefferson to him and whispered, whereupon Jefferson exclaimed, "Well, I'll be damned!"

Mussolini sang:

> The Constitution's much too slow,
> We need a boss to tell the Congress where to go!
> For Mr. Roosevelt's here and showing us tricks,
> Shades of Seventeen Seventy-six!
> For history doesn't mean a thing,
> Since Mr. Roosevelt is King!

The act closed with an actor singing that "a dictator's lot is not a happy one."

• • •

The following Monday, the *Washington Times* related that Will Rogers had been in attendance, and quoted Rogers:

"Did you ever go to a dinner and have to stand up and not even get any dinner? Well, I did Saturday night, at the Gridiron dinner to President Roosevelt in Washington. It sure was worth it."[1]

A note in the Gridiron files by Ernest G. Walker, club historian at the time, explained the situation. Rogers had telephoned from New York on Saturday afternoon at three o'clock to say that he would like to attend the dinner, but was told that there was not a seat available at that late hour.

He came anyway by plane and in business clothes, and mingled with the cast in the dressing room. One of them offered Rogers his seat, but he declined it and was told that the next time he wanted to attend a dinner, if he'd make it known before three o'clock on the afternoon of the dinner date, efforts would be made to accommodate him. Rogers, however, did stand in the ballroom and saw the show, and the *Times* quoted him as commenting:

"Ogden Mills and the President both made good speeches. I think these things do a lot of good to help keep those big boys' feet on the ground. But, say, I would stand on my head to see another one."[2]

Roosevelt's speech at this dinner was not preserved. It is the only one missing from the dinners that he attended.

• • •

When the time arrived for the dinner on December 9, 1933, the New Deal was well under way, and a large number of new government agencies had been created and were operating.

"New men tread the stage," said President Ross, "new ideas have been incubated. The alphabet has come into its own, while the multiplication table has cracked under the strain."

The show opened with an alphabet parade: NRA (National Recovery Administration), AAA (Agricultural Adjustment Administration), RFC, HOLC, CCC, and so on down the list. Among the new alphabetical agencies appeared also such things as NERTS, WCTU, TAX, BVD, GYP, GIN, and at the end, IOU and SOS. While the procession of fifty Gridiron members was marching across the stage, the Marine Band played "Wintergreen for President."

To emphasize the universality of the Roosevelt influence, and to play upon his avowed purpose of doing something for "the forgotten man," there was a snapper on Garner, who had given up his powerful position as Speaker of the House of Representatives to become Vice President—a snapper in which "Garner" sang to the tune of "Forgotten":

> I have vanished to times prehistoric,
>> Where the cave man and dodo went;
> And I am forgotten, as they have been—
>> For I am the Vice President!

In a barroom skit celebrating the end of Prohibition, which ended with the chorus singing, "Oh, no, we'll never get drunk any more," there was a song in which the seldom-recognized, cultured language of Huey Long was satirized.

> Jack Garner works on the prairies,
> And on his coat lapel,
> Is the fragrance of the violet,
> The geranium as well.
> The Kingfish works in the washroom,
> And I make no complaint,
> But the prairies have a fragrance,
> That the lavatories *ain't!*

General Hugh Johnson, administrator of the NRA, had achieved a reputation for his hammer and tongs treatment of business, and his colorful language and strong temper. Even Roosevelt had had some difficulties with him, although he was an outstanding figure in the administration. General John J. Pershing was called to his feet at one point in the dinner, and was described as "the last man General Hugh Johnson took orders from."

The plight of the Republicans was heralded in a song from a darkened stage, paraphrasing "Where Oh Where Has My Little Dog Gone."

> Where, O where is the GOP?
>> We've asked since thirty-two. . . .
> It's hard to suppose, for nobody knows
>> Where elephants go to die.

The lights came on, revealing a stage set with a nudist colony fence, in front of which stood impersonators of Ogden Mills and Fiorello LaGuardia. The latter had been elected mayor of New York largely as a result of the prominence he received as the great attacker of the "villains" of the depression, the bankers of Wall Street.

To the tune of "Hallelujah, Bum Again," LaGuardia sang:

O why don't you dress
So people won't stare?

And a soloist behind the fence replied:

How the hell can we dress
When we've nothing to wear?

LaGuardia:

O when did you lose
Your clothing, and how?

Soloist behind the fence:

We were following Hoover
And look at us now!

Then, to the music of "Without a Song," the chorus sang:

Without a job, our party's at an end—
Without a job, the voters we can't bend;
It just plays hob, we haven't got a friend—
Without a job.

A character impersonating the defeated Jim Watson further delineated the Republican distress by singing:

O the moonlight's fair tonight along the Wabash;
But from this spot I find I cannot stray;
For my coat and pants and shirt were left a-hanging
On the banks of the Wabash, far away!

Immediately following this skit, Arthur H. Vandenberg of Michigan, a rising young senator at the time, was introduced as the Republican speaker and made the first of several outstanding speeches which he delivered at Gridiron dinners.

He paid tribute to President Roosevelt, "the chosen leader of our people (who are required under our system of discipline to stand by their bargain for three more years), the Captain-General of America's war on the depression (and America never yet has lost a war), a man of gallant heartfulness and high adventure— the courageous, colorful, and entirely too persuasive President of the United States."

He had, he said, enjoyed the last two Gridiron dinners more genuinely than those over the preceding four years, because "it is so much easier to be critical than to be correct. (Mr. Michelson, please copy.)"

He found it much more fun to throw the bricks, even if when he was formerly a newspaper publisher in Michigan an occasional libel suit did result. "I was once charged $4,000," he said, "by a Michigan jury for intimating that one of our Democrats proposed to 'organize a little Tammany.' But it was worth it to get a judicial determination of Tammany's status as gauged by midwestern morals, in pre-LaGuardia days. . . .

"The times move," he said, "and we move with them. . . . Congress passes an economy bill and then appropriates $11 billion. After reducing all government wages, we threaten to jail private industrialists who do not increase wages. We condemn sales taxes and then applaud them when disguised as processing taxes. We painfully balance our budget—and then blandly charge all unbalancing expenditures to a collateral budget which cheerfully ignores all limitations and maturities. We ask for confidence —and then break Uncle Sam's word to his bondholders [to pay in gold] for the first time in 140 years. We condemn and consolidate yesterday's commissions; and then multiply them beyond precedent tomorrow. . . . We close banks and open saloons. . . . 'Happy days' and 'happy warriors' are at war. We whirl in a pollyanna paradox. Even the compass has vertigo. But God knows we do 'move.'

"New problems bring new answers. Once we had just one 'noble experiment.' Now we have a litter. . . .

"These are all good-tempered observations, on the threshold of another desperately important Congress. But may I say with all sincerity that I hope the administration may be spectacularly successful in servicing the nation.

"I would uphold the President to the last possible degree. But there is need—even from his standpoint—for a wholesome patriotic minority at such a perilous hour to help scrutinize these programs for their own hazards, particularly when democracy wears chains all around the globe."[3]

Turning more directly to the new administration, the Gridiron Club followed this with a skit entitled "Alice in Blunderland," in which Henry Ford, the "Knave of Tin," was placed on trial under instructions from the Queen of Codes: "Verdict first, testimony afterwards!"

He was finally instructed, when his new dictator model would go on sale the following week, "to keep Herbert Hoover's picture off the windshield."

Prior to the introduction of President Roosevelt for the final speech of the dinner, the club did a gold skit built around King Midas, who represented an academic economist and "who almost starved to death because all that he touched turned to gold." King Midas, proclaiming that he was an expert, said:

> Give me a government to fool with!
> I would do things to people, to nations, to the world!
> I will turn the universe to paper!

Jesse H. Jones was head of the Reconstruction Finance Corporation at that time. An actor asked, "Who ever thought that when Jesse H. Jones built a wooden stadium to nominate Alfred E. Smith in 1928, he would become financial dictator of the universe under Franklin D. Roosevelt in 1933?"

He was followed by an actor impersonating Senator Elmer Thomas of Oklahoma, who announced that he learned the game of finance when he sold beads to the Indians, and the Indians sold him stock in an oil well. "Reciprocal deception is the life of trade," he said, and to the tune of "Not for All the Rice in China," he sang:

> Not for all the oil in Tulsa,
> Not for all the francs in France,
> Would I exchange the pleasure,
> That I get from every measure I advance.
> Not for all the loot in Wall Street,
> Not for all the bull in Spain,
> Would I give up inflation for the nation,
> Though I'm driving it insane . . .
> Not for all the trumps in contract,
> Not for all the queens in chess,
> Would I agree to hesitate, annihilate, or interrupt
> The printing press!

The skit closed with everybody on stage singing:

> We're in the money,
> In paper money,
> We've got a lot of what it takes to get along!
> We'll all have money,
> Although it's funny,
> Old man depression, you are through, you done us wrong!
> We never see a headline, 'bout a breadline today,
> And when we see the landlord,
> We can look that guy right in the eye,
> We're in the money,
> In paper money,
> Let's spend it, lend it, send it rolling along.

This put President Roosevelt on the spot, but with the resiliency for which he had always been noted, he rose to the occasion magnificently.

"I am a little puzzled," he began. "I had really expected that the satirists of the Gridiron Club would turn their wit and wisdom on some really live subject. Here I find that you are still talking about that old accomplished fact—the Recovery Program."

He went on to say that the one piece of news not yet discovered by the Washington correspondents and by "the erudite and orthodox politicians and economists, who still delight in the admirable philosophies of Louis XIV and George III—of Jay Gould and Mark Hanna," was that the Recovery Program was working.

Mentioning the opening parade of the alphabet, he characterized this as a "delightful prologue" and "part of our educational campaign."

Turning this satire upon himself, he said that he recognized he had used up most of the letters of the alphabet. "It will please you, I know," he went on, "to learn that I have this morning requested AAP, the Association of Administration Pedagogues, to dig me up a new alphabet. We need still more education in our soup, but it will be purely American soup."

Then Roosevelt gave a foretaste of the kind of vigorous debates that were to develop later, between himself and his critics.

"Every day or so now I am reminded by newspapers and magazines that the administration's honeymoon is over. I must be frank in telling you that I had not realized that I had been on a honeymoon. But at the same time reports come to me that there are a very large number of somewhat sore brides in this country. And the latest dope story is that some of them are getting sorer and sorer.

"I cannot and do not expect that even in the stress of the needs and necessities of this period criticism will be lacking. All of us in positions of responsibility today welcome and definitely seek honest and constructive criticism. When that kind of criticism comes it is worthwhile and does the country much good. But those two adjectives, 'honest' and 'constructive' describe certain qualities in him who does the criticizing. First of all that word 'honest' presupposes that the critic is without guile and is not seeking through his criticism some special gain or profit for himself, and also that his criticism is based on a cross section of the needs of the country as a whole, weighing every part of our national needs in their true relationship.

"The other adjective, 'constructive,' implies that the critic will offer some substitute method, some alternative for reaching the desired end—for the better building on a permanent basis.

"When one is in a jungle, he has to try to cut himself a path in order to get out. If the wrong direction is taken, the only thing to do is to go back and try another one. We have too many people in the jungle of depression who are sitting still on stumps, telling those of us who are wielding the brush hook and axe that we are headed in the wrong direction and that the best thing we can do is to come and sit down on the stump with them and complain about our hard luck.

"We are too busy clearing away the underbrush in order that once more we can find the open road for us to bother our heads about the brethren who still sit complainingly on stumps.

"To me the wonderful fact that will stand out all the days of my life, no matter what the future may bring forth, is that the overwhelming majority of the men and women of this country and the overwhelming part of the press of the country has been willing to work and work hard in the common cause, and it is just too bad about the few people who have seen goblins and screech owls behind every bush."

He launched into a discussion of the issue of freedom of the press, "one of these hobgoblins which might have the sole merit of being amusing to children if it were not so silly—a sort of Halloween hobgoblin produced out of a pumpkin's head."

He denied that his administration had ever thought of attempting to infringe upon the constitutional liberties of the press, which he defined as "the right of a newspaper publisher to serve up the news and serve up his own opinions or interpretations of the news in any shape, manner or form he may wish to use."

"This includes," Roosevelt said, "the right to demand of his reporters that they color their news stories to conform with the political or other objective of the editor. I am happy to say that most editors do not demand this of their reporters, but I am sorry to say that some editors do."

He described what freedom of the press did not include: obscenity, the right to employ small boys and keep them away from school, the right to run a newspaper office in violation of the sanitary code, and the right to employ anybody for rates of pay that do not conform to the accepted American standard.

"The best proof," he said a bit more abrasively, "that the

newspapers of the United States have an excellent understanding of the simple fact that no curtailment of the freedom of the press is contemplated is the fact that they have given front page space to news of other industries who are falling in line by well nigh unanimous accord in adopting the codes of self government in cooperation with the NRA and at the same time have relegated this trumped-up controversy over the newspaper code to the obscure spaces among the advertising columns."

December 1933, was a period of considerable monetary turbulence, and in closing, President Roosevelt addressed himself to this subject. He said that "one disturbing thought" that came to him day after day concerned the "fluctuations and the uncertainty of the currencies and the exchanges of other nations." He commented on the gyrations of the pound and the franc and pointed out that this was a problem for importers and exporters making contracts in foreign lands, in that "they cannot be sure what kind of money they will be paid in on the fulfillment of the contract." He expressed the hope that the other nations of the world would so stabilize themselves that "we can all be stable— they as well as ourselves."

It is not a question, he reminded his audience, "of whose baby has the measles," but rather of hope for the stability of world currency and for an increase in the exchange of goods between nations, "not with the thought of making one nation rich at the expense of another but of letting all nations participate in the profits of world trade."

Then, in closing, he said:

"We who are the guests of the distinguished members of the Gridiron Club know that in the quips, the skits and the satire there is much solid gold and that more than one true word has been spoken here tonight in jest. I am grateful to all of you for another happy evening—and may I say in bidding you goodnight that I hope the charming brides to whom I have referred will soon be feeling better."[4]

• • •

Problems developed in connection with the April 1934 dinner. It was scheduled for April 7. About ten days before this, President Roosevelt had gone fishing off the coast of Florida on Vincent Astor's yacht, *Nourmahal*. On April 1, Stephen T. Early, Roosevelt's press secretary, telephoned Gridiron President James L. Wright of the *Buffalo Evening News* that James Roosevelt, who was in Palm Beach, had called to say that his father had not been well since arriving, and that if he had to return to Washington for the Gridiron dinner Saturday night he felt the whole benefit of his vacation would be wiped out.

Early asked whether it would be possible to postpone the dinner for a week. Fortunately, the ballroom of the Willard Hotel, where the dinners were then held, was available for Saturday night, the 14th. All this is documented in a memorandum from Wright to Ernest G. Walker, setting forth for the club record the circumstances of the postponement.

Wright called a meeting of the executive committee and, in response to Early's request, insisted that nothing be said about the illness of the President, because that would alarm the country. All members of the committee except one favored postponement. Wright's account noted that "the President sent me a telegram of appreciation of our courtesy, and said he was looking forward to being with us a week from Saturday."

Later Wright went to the White House and had a frank talk with Early. "He told me," wrote Wright, "that for the first few days the President was aboard the yacht, he was confined to his bed, and was mentally depressed. You will recall that Congress had overridden him on his veto of the bill to restore cuts in veterans' compensation and Federal employees' salaries after he had left Washington for Florida.

"Early said it was not until Sunday night, the night before he telephoned me, that the President had shown any interest in anything connected with his yachting and fishing trip. He said that the family had decided that instead of his vacation being beneficial to him, it would be detrimental if he should have to return Friday to be at our dinner Saturday."[5]

• • •

The keynote for the April 14, 1934 dinner was set by Wright in his speech in the dark, when he said, "Tonight, in the New Deal, everything is wild. There are no "down cards." If there is a Joker in the pack, we hope it will be exposed. . . .

"A year ago, the fourth of last March, we heard these words: 'The country wants action—and action now.' We have had it."

The opening skit was a Salvation Army rally, in which the chief characters were impersonators of Secretary of Labor Frances Perkins and General Hugh Johnson, director of the National Recovery Administration.

Sister Perkins proclaimed that she had the New Deal religion "all over." General Johnson appealed to the crowd to "come up, friends, and get a dose of the New Deal religion. . . . If you don't the old Devil will crack down on you. . . . Come up to the mourners bench, you economic sinners. Oh, my rugged individual friends, do you want to be damned! Come up and be saved. . . . Come up and be saved, you profiteering bums. . . . "

And to shouts of "Glory, glory hallelujah!" General Johnson exhorted, "Now's the time to get a big shot of the New Deal religion, and those that hold back will be kicked into the outer darkness. . . . Come up to the mourners bench, you chiselers. . . . Get the New Deal religion or get hell."

Then the whole chorus, led by Frances Perkins, sang their version of "That Old Time Religion."

'Tis the New Deal religion,
And it's good enough for me.

It was good for Rexford Tugwell,
It was good for Raymond Moley,
It is good for Vincent Astor,
And it's good enough for me.

It's been sanctified by Congress,
It's been OK'd by Wallace,
It's been swallowed whole by Rainey,
And it's good enough for me.

Overriding the Roosevelt veto of the bill raising veterans' benefits was the first gesture of independence Congress had made since the Roosevelt administration had come into power. An impersonator of Vice President Garner, wearing a Roman toga and a top hat, came onstage and delivered a parody of Marc Antony's oration over the body of Caesar.

Congress, 'twas said, had sunk so low
None was so poor to do it reverence.
'Twas called great Caesar's rubber stamp,
His bond slave, chattel, fawning hound,
Which, when he oped his lips, dared not to bark.
Then came the Ides of March. The tarpon called
And Caesar, hasting seaward, left behind
A solemn mandate to the vassal branch.
Then up rose McKellar, Cutting, McCarran, Smith and Walsh;
They ripped that mandate into shreds and cast
Them to the breeze. See what a rent the envious
Copeland made! And this and this the faithful McAdoo.
Not that they loved our Caesar less but that
They feared the Legion more.

In a satire on the Roosevelt leadership, Arthur Krock announced from the stage that great figures of hope had roamed through the past and that "tonight we present them, in quest of their great leader."

Those great figures included impersonators of General Coxey, Coin Harvey, Sockless Jerry Simpson, Carrie Nation and others. They proclaimed what their leaders had done.

"Put all the poor in the banks, and all the bankers in the poorhouse."

"Our great leader, who has so gloriously made judges out of old women, and old women out of judges."

"Our great leader, who has crucified gold on a paper cross."

"Our great leader, who has made one bale of cotton grow where two would grow before."

"Bring us our leader," shouted Coin Harvey, "who has made criminals of all the millionaires, and millionaires of all the criminals."

"Where is our leader?" they all shouted.

Then a mammoth picture was flashed on the screen—of William Jennings Bryan!

Senator David A. Reed, an aristocratic, scholarly, Republican conservative, was depicted on the stage as lamenting the passing of his favorite frigate, *The Constitution*. To the tune of "America the Beautiful" he sang:

> Farewell, farewell, O shattered hulk
> And battered stern and prow;
> In youth you well protected us,
> We'll sing your requiem now.
> Look! Faltering there her threadbare sail
> Against the horizon shrunk;
> She founders in the New Deal gale!
> The Constitution's—sunk!

Wright introduced Senator Reed as the Republican speaker, labeling him "the weather-beaten skipper of this old craft."

No record of Senator Reed's speech can be found, but Martin Hayden, now editor of the *Detroit News*, who attended the dinner, wrote a memorandum about it, in which he noted that the senator had used statues as his speech gimmick:

"He developed the theme that the L'Enfant Plan for the capital provided a number of squares and circles, each to be graced with a statue or memorial to some famous personage. But, said the senator, we'd never developed enough famous men to fill them all. Therefore, he suggested, we should switch to statues for 'infamy' and he opined that the then-current Roosevelt administration abounded with possibilities.

"For instance, he suggested, we could have a statue to the man who dreamed up the idea of dollar devaluation which destroyed our credit at home; and another for the author of the gold devaluation which destroyed our credit abroad; and then there could be one for the genius who thought up the air mail contract cancellation and directed unprepared Army Air Corps flyers to kill themselves trying to carry the mails." There was more in the same vein. . . .

"FDR, who manifestly did not know in advance about the speech, got up [at the end of the dinner], seized upon the same gimmick theme and murdered the senator.

"In other days and before he was physically handicapped, he said, it was his habit to walk about Washington on a Sunday looking at the statues and refreshing his recollections of history. He said he recalled several which the senator seemingly had forgotten.

"There was, he said, the magnificent memorial to Abraham Lincoln, the first U. S. President to devalue the dollar. And not far away, he said, was the tall white obelisk in honor of George Washington, the man who said the hell with the Continental Congress and led the Continental Army the way he saw fit and created our nation.

"And, he continued, across from the White House was the statue of Andrew Jackson, sitting astride a reared-up horse just as Jackson would have had it. He, said Roosevelt, was the President who defied the constitutionalists, took control of the federal finances from the money lenders in Philadelphia and brought them to Washington where they belonged.

"There were other examples, but he concluded with the reference to the memorial to John Paul Jones. His comment: 'I want to particularly call that to the senator's attention because of the inscription it bears: "We've just begun to fight." ' "[6]

Following Senator Reed's speech, the club did a series of skits satirizing the New Deal and its leadership.

In a Noah's Ark skit (Public Works Project No.1), Republican National Committee Chairman Everett Sanders and former Secretary of the Treasury Ogden Mills received the pairs of representatives of the pre-Roosevelt era, who were now fugitives upon the face of the waters.

It was a curious bunch of pairs who were announced, covering the gamut of most of the political figures of that time; for example, Al Capone and Columbia University's president, Dr. Nicholas "Miraculous" Butler; the dapper and debonair "Jimmy" Walker and staunch birth-control advocate Margaret Sanger; the Hoover Attorney General George W. Wickersham and the prohibition zealot Bishop James Cannon; the conservative writer and historian Mark Sullivan (played by himself) and the sexy evangelist Aimee Semple McPherson; and J. Pierpont Morgan and the midget who had jumped upon his lap during an interval in the Pecora stock market investigation. The chorus sang to the strains of "Shenandoah":

> So listen to our tale of woe,
> There's one wide river to cross.
> God knows we have no place to go!
> There's one wide river to cross.

After all were aboard and considerable discussion of the situation had taken place, they sighted land and prepared to debark on Mount Ararat. The skit closed with the comment that as for Franklin D. Roosevelt, he reigns at the moment, "but the rainbow in the sky tells us that the time will come when he ain't goin' to reign no more."

> He ain't goin' to reign no more, no more,
> He ain't goin' to reign no more,
> Now how the Hell can Sanders tell,
> That he ain't goin' to reign no more!

The final music skit depicted "Anatole France" on Penguin Island, with all the penguins around him. They were existing through the sufferance of a benevolent penguin government and their great penguin ruler who, "guided by the light of reason alone," was able to direct himself to the stars.

The ruler was described by various penguins as having "the claws of a lion," "the wings of an eagle," and wearing "a football suit and calling himself Quarterback."

His main formula was that all penguins are entitled to jobs and that their wages must be 10 percent higher and their hours 10 percent lower.

Anatole France thought that a wonderful scheme, but the chorus sang "Did You Ever See That Scheme Working," and concluded at the end:

Well the scheme isn't working,
And the team isn't smirking,
And the dream, it may never come true!

One of the penguins then explained that "our great ruler's technique is to prove his existence through continual action. It leaves no time for thought." And another remarked, "Do not forget that if the penguin people fail to support our ruler, a new one will come upon our island more terrible than the first. Let's give three squawks for our great Quarterback!"
They squawked appropriately and the chorus sang:

In our Penquin bonnet,
With all the frills upon it,
We'll be the proudest Penguins in the Penguin parade.
We'll be all in clover,
The world will look us over,
We'll be the proudest Penguins that the New Deal has made.
On the Avenue, Penguin Avenue,
The photographers will snap us,
We'll all be for sure in the rotogravure.
Oh, we will rave about it,
We'll sing, and scream and shout it;
That we're the proudest Penguins in the New Deal parade.

In his speech that night, the President turned satirist. He said that while on his fishing and relaxing trip he had done some thinking about the forthcoming dinner and that the natural thing to do was to change places
"I asked myself," he said, " 'What would you do if you were a member of the Gridiron Club instead of the President of the United States?' "
He said he soliloquized that they would have to have a skit on the New Deal and on various individuals involved in it, from Harry Hopkins to Vice President Garner. The skit would be about an overridden Presidential veto, and would end by demanding that the head of the present administration answer the question, "Where do we go from here?"
He mentioned that he had just seen a new president of the Gridiron Club inaugurated, "who, I understand from confidential reports, is a club conservative." He went on to say that he understood that there were many groups and factions in the organization and that the club had no plans now for the fall dinner.

The skits then would depend on the trend of events. "And so do the policies of the administration," he said.

At the current dinner Roosevelt noted no sparseness in the club's efforts to bring about an examination of the officials and policies of the government and commented that "no process that tends to make us more sensible of our duties and more sure not only of our objects, but of the processes by which we seek to obtain those objects, is otherwise than welcome.

"I think that this principle should extend beyond the government," he continued; "to put it bluntly, I believe that the time has arrived when the Gridiron Club should put some questions to itself.

"You have brought together a brilliant galaxy of the wealth, influence and talent of the United States. . . . Do you think, for example, that you have been funny enough to make them feel that their journey hither was worthwhile? I put it to your honored president, who, if I understand your constitution, is supreme in these affairs, and who has neither a Congress to consult nor a Supreme Court to satisfy, whether he thinks that the Gridiron is living up to its reputation?

"Naturally, as a guest, I must reserve my own opinion on the subject. If I indulged in splendid commendation, I would be subject to the charge of fulsome adulation to my hosts. If I took the other extreme, I would be unmindful of the obligation imposed on every guest to appreciate the effort and to make no strictures on the performance.

"The Gridiron Club is the only body that can gracefully investigate your imposing organization. If reform is required, you alone can do the reforming. I am sensible, of course, of the controversies that must arise in a body composed of fifty eminent critics, each of whom is convinced of the infallibility of his judgment and his own special qualifications to say what is true in art and what is true in politics, what is true in finance, what is true in relativity.

"I know the danger of listening to gossip, and the greater danger of accepting such gossip as absolutely veracious. It is true, according to reports, that the Gridiron cloakrooms are seething with tales of discord that compel attention even though there may be doubt of the accuracy of such tales. It is rumored on the highest authority that the Gridiron musical committee, hereafter referred to as the GMC, and the committee responsible for the unlyrical or gag part of the entertainment, to which we will refer for the purposes of brevity as the GGC, have not the highest opinion of the productions of each other.

"If your investigation should determine that your show has not been up to standard, perhaps whatever is lacking may be attributed to these administration controversies. Forgive me if I also advert to another report, emanating, I may say, also from the highest Gridiron authorities, that there is criticism in your membership over the radicalism of your president. I am not stating it as a fact but simply repeating a report current all through the nation that your president has gone to the extreme left in determining that hereafter there shall only be one skit per year based on Alice in Wonderland. While I am about it, I may as well tell you the whole of the story. It runs to the effect that one of your ex-presidents is in open revolt because he is not allowed to take the part of Alice herself, or of the white queen, but always finds himself cast to the role of a white rabbit. . . ."

His conclusion was serious.

"I would leave you tonight," he said, "just a couple of thoughts about the responsibilities of the office I now hold. As I entered the last days of the campaign of 1932 it was increasingly apparent that, if I came into the Presidency of this country, my lot would not and could not be an easy one.

"I sensed that, as would anyone within sound of my voice in this unreported speech of mine this evening. The idea bore down upon me when I became President-elect, and again when I was inaugurated. As I went into office there were closed banks, others that must be closed, general unemployment, a feeling of anxiety throughout the country, and a milling around of men and women who had but little hope for tomorrow.

"What has happened so far all of you know. I have said and repeated in public statements and radio addresses that there must be a way out of this confusion. I also have said that this administration probably would make mistakes, but would undertake to correct such mistakes as soon as their fallacies became known.

"From the outset, the administration has sought constructive criticism, whether in the news columns, the editorial pages, the stage or a club which, for nearly fifty years, has held up the looking glass so that men in public life might glimpse themselves.

"We are going to carry on, I trust in a nonpartisan, nonpolitical way. The woods are clearing. I bespeak the cooperation of all

Americans, however they may feel about past or pending legislation in Congress, albeit I would not ask any member of the executive or legislative branches to sacrifice their own personal convictions if they regard such convictions as in the interest of the country.

"The more of these dinners I attend, the more grateful I am that there is a Gridiron Club, and let me assure you that I have full appreciation of your versatility and that I constantly marvel at your continued enthusiasm. And let me go further and tell you, in all sincerity, that however much fun you get out of the President of the United States, it isn't a tithe of the fun he gets out of you."[7]

• • •

At the December 8, 1934 dinner, as the New Deal was progressing further, Gridiron President Wright said in his opening speech, that the Washington monument had been washed down and the Republican party washed up.

"The Watchdog of the Treasury has been driven off by the Kitty of the New Deal," he said. "The donkey has been crossed with the pink zebra in the Northwest. The elephant, denied peanuts in Pennsylvania, has crashed 'The Jungle' in California. The tiger, housebroken in New York, is now a domestic pet, and the good old Blue Eagle has quit soaring in the sky, to sit on the nest where its fledgling is hatching.

"Only the Gridiron Club, venerable with the years, hidebound in the traditions of its founding fathers, clings to the past. It, too, may feel the urge to step in line, click its heels, march in the parade, lest failing to do so it shall be denied elbow room at the counters of the more abundant life."

Appropriately for the season, the opener consisted of a Santa Claus skit with a recitation of "Twas the Night Before Christmas," ending with the lines:

Every stocking was filled ere the saint turned to go,
And the manna had fallen as thick as the snow;
And they heard him exclaim, as he flew out of sight:
"Merry Christmas to all—and be sure you vote right!"

Then the chorus sang:

You better watch out, you better be good,
Better not pout, but vote as you should—
Santa Claus is comin' to town.

He's making a list and checking it twice,

Gonna find out who's treating him nice,
Santa Claus is comin' to town.

In a New Deal Hotel skit, it was revealed that General Hugh
Johnson was no longer its manager, but that Donald R. Richberg
had taken over and Madame Perkins was the telephone operator.
The faithful had gathered there to hear the election returns, and
"Richberg" predicted that "the time is coming when we'll pine
for the good old days, when we could blame everything on
Johnson."

The good news of the election returns poured in (a month
before, Roosevelt had greatly increased the Democratic representation in Congress), and "Louie Howe," the President's close
personal associate for many years, proclaimed, "One more election year like this, and we'll all have our jobs forever!"

"Moley" asked, "It would cost a lot of money, wouldn't it?"

"Howe" replied, "What do we care? It's worth it; we are
nearing our goal—the greatest national debt in history!"

Then one of the bellboys sang:

We're always chasing rainbows,
    Watching debts piling high;
Our schemes are just like all our dreams,
    Ending in the sky.

New dealers always see the sunshine,
    We never think about the rain;
Somebody must be paying sometime,
    We hope it will not cause a pain—
Aha! We're always chasing rainbows,
    Singing a happy little bluebird refrain!

This was an apt introduction for Henry L. Mencken, introduced as a critic of the New Deal, who explained the hot spot in
which he had been placed.

"I am put up here," said Mencken, "to speak a kindly word
for the solvent and the damned, or, as the more advanced thinkers say, for the Rotten Rich."

Then Mencken poured satire and sarcasm on President
Roosevelt. He said he must begin by confessing "that we millionaire newspaper reporters have all gone down the greased
chute like the rest of you.

"Run us through a meat chopper," he said, "and you
wouldn't recover enough negotiable assets to load a single car-
tridge of baloney. The only thing we have left is our liberty to

doubt whatever we are told. But even that isn't worth much any more, for how are you going to doubt the unintelligible!''

He noted, however, that there really wasn't much to complain of, because ''even if the current flow of so-called ideas is somewhat confusing, it must be admitted that the show going with it is really nifty.

''Every day in this great country is April Fool Day. Even its wars usually produce quite as many comedians as heroes. Where on earth will you find a match for Congress, now that John Ringling has retired? Or for the NRA, now that cannibalism is prohibited by law?''

Then he turned to the brain trust.

''There seems to be a high mortality in the brain trust,'' he said, ''but its brains apparently renew themselves like the lost claws of a Chesapeake crab. Their functions, also, are not altogether dissimilar. Nobody knows precisely where the brethren have landed us, and least of all the brethren themselves. Maybe we are out on a limb. Maybe we are up in the stratosphere that Jim Wright was just talking about, and can't get down. Maybe we are down in Dr. Beebe's diving-bell, surrounded by sharks, swordfish, chiselfish, stuffed-shirtfish, dolefish, brainfish, and other such monsters. As for me, I am willing to believe anything once—so long as the professors deny it.''

And then, in a typically Menckenian manner, he told about having had the pleasure of showing his pastor around Washington some time previously, while Congress was still in session. He quoted the pastor as saying:

''My boy, you cherish a chimera if you ever hope to turn out the smart fellows who now own and operate this government. They have enlisted for all eternity, and they'll still be on deck after eternity is past and forgotten. They have night and day keys to the White House, they carry Congress in their vest-pocket, and even the Supreme Court is far too dignified to menace the seats of their pantaloons. Long after you are dead and gone back to your primordial manganese, hydrogen, ptomaines, rat-poison, beer-foam and printers' ink—long after you pass out they'll still be running this great country, and this great country will be liking it. When you tackle such wizards, you are trying to derail the solar system.''

Bearing in mind that this was after the repeal of Prohibition, Mencken said that he should add, for the sake of the record, that ''the good man got off his speech in the middle of Pennsylvania

Avenue in the early part of 1932. He was not speaking of the brain trust, but of the Anti-Saloon League."[8]

For hours the Gridiron Club touched with satire and ridicule upon every issue which had been debated in the congressional campaign. In the 1934 congressional election, many well-known Republicans of long-standing in both Senate and House had been retired by the people and replaced by New Dealers. The sad state of the Republican party was touched upon in a Gridiron version of *Faust*, with "Henry Fletcher," chairman of the Republican National Committee, cast as the professor who, after juggling vials, fooling with vapors, wearing rabbits' feet and lighting tapers in the cellar in which he had taken refuge, finally sold his soul to Mephistopheles.

It was easy to guess who was Mephistopheles in this skit when he sang to Fletcher:

> For now, thy troubles to dispel,
> I come, a squire of high degree,
> In scarlet coat, with Russian trimming,
> A cloak with new ideas a-swimming,
>   An old-age pension in my hat,
> And (*slapping wallet*) with each vote,
>   a six-room flat!
> A long sharp sword to turn the switch,
> I fool the poor and damn the rich.

There was much moaning among the chorus about the lost characters, typified by Walker S. Buel's lines:

> And in a thousand drawing-rooms the hearts do bleed,
> For the bright wit and brilliant brain of David Aiken Reed.

But the hero who can through was "Vera Vandenberg," who had won in Michigan.

> Sometimes she's sharp,
>   sometimes she's flat,
> But she won an election for all of that.

Someone pointed out that although their methods now appeared passé, Aldrich, Root and Penrose were "darned good in their day," and the "Soldier's Chorus" was paraphrased:

> Glory and love to the men of old,
> Fletch-er should copy their methods bold,
> Courage in heart and the cash in hand,
> Already to fight, already to die,
>   Those jobs to demand.

There was a long, rollicking duet to the tune of "The Man on the Flying Trapeze," between impersonators of former Secretaries of the Treasury Andrew Mellon and Ogden Mills. The first stanza referred to the President's attitude early in his administration that "the banks must be good, and all money changers must take to the wood." Later verses reflected his changing attitudes toward bankers over the preceding year and a half.

When the bankers' convention assembled in town,
He threw both his arms round their necks—
OH!
He flies back and forth with the greatest of ease
Just like a man on a flying trapeze.

The dollar has been well devalued;
It's now fifty-nine-point-oh-six;
And business gets dizzy while trying to watch
The dollar performing its tricks—
OH!
It flies up and down with the greatest of ease
Just like a man on the flying trapeze.

There's just one thing left, we Old Dealers know—
If you can't lick 'em, you must join the show;
Elections have recently told us so,
And that's what we'll all have to do.
So we all must learn acrobatics
And to turn somersaults at our ease;
For in spite of our money, the voters all vote
For the man on the flying trapeze—
OH!
We'll turn many flip-flops while trying to please
The man on the flying trapeze!

The American Liberty League had been formed, and three of its most prominent figures were two former chairmen of the Democratic National Committee, John J. Raskob and Jouett Shouse, along with Pierre S. du Pont. It was not exactly an organization to promote the New Deal, and it was satirized at the dinner with these three coming on in top hats, raising money in great quantities to save the Constitution, and deciding to save not only the Constitution, but the Preamble and all the amendments—except the eighteenth!

But the outstanding skit of the dinner, and one which is still remembered by those that were present, was one in which the progress of prosperity, under the leadership of President

Roosevelt, was handled in a travesty enacted in the interior of a Pullman car on the Prosperity Limited.

An elaborate set had been devised, showing three sections of a Pullman car, with berths made up, the center one labeled "Section 7A," a reference to the controversial Section 7A of the National Recovery Act.

As the lights went up, a porter in blackface, played by Arthur Pierce, came in with the old-fashioned ladder. A passenger in one of the sections stuck his head out and inquired, "When does this Prosperity Limited start, George?" The porter replied, "De Prosperity Limited ain't got no regular time for starting. It starts jest as soon as de New Deal special gits offen de tracks. It's in a wreck up de line."

Then two passengers arrived, "Henry Ford" and "William Green," president of the American Federation of Labor. Both had tickets for Section 7A and both demanded that section and no other.

They brandished the tickets and the porter examined them.

"Gemmen, I shore is sorry," exclaimed the porter. "As chairman of the Board of Conciliation, it seems ter me that some bonehead in de main ticket office done made a mistake. Lordy! Lordy! Here's sumpin. Youse both of you got Section 7A."

As Green and Ford scuffled to get into the lower berth and Green accused Ford of "trying to cheat the poor down-pressed laboring man out of his lower berth," Green turned to the porter and asked where the train went.

"De Prosperity Limited don't go no regular place, gemmen," the porter answered. "It jest roams around, like. Sometimes it goes to de left, and sometimes it goes to de right, and sometimes it jest backs up, according to de way de engineer makes up his mind. But mostly it don't go no place, and don't git nowhere. De engineer of this train certainly is indefinite."

After more scrapping and complaining by passengers in the other two berths, the conductor came along and told the two disputants to stop their racket because the Prosperity Limited was about to start.

The porter asked the conductor, "Where is we going this time, Boss, jest up on one of the sidings, like we done the last time? Where's the engineer taking us this trip?"

The conductor responded that the engineer would take them "where I tell him to take us. Get me? I'm the guy that owns this railroad. Get that? The engineer works for me."

Then, turning to Ford and Green, he shouted, "Get in your bunks, you two troublemakers, and don't let me hear any more of your yap, or I'll throw both of you off the train."

He reached up and pulled the bell cord. A locomotive bell rang, a locomotive whistle blew, and there was the sound of wheels grinding as the conductor shouted, "All aboard! This train is going to Prosperityville."

Quietly the porter muttered, "I certainly has heard a lot about that town, but I ain't never been there yet."

"All aboard," the conductor yelled again. Then he turned to Green and Ford. "You men ought to be glad you ain't sleeping on the floor. Get in your berths. This train's headed for Prosperityville. Shut your traps, or get off."

Ford and Green conversed briefly and Green said, "That's a bully idea, Henry."

As the noise of the moving train increased, they threw their clothes into the upper berth and crawled together into lower 7A, with their bags.

"Next stop, Prosperityville!" shouted the conductor.

As he exited, swinging a lantern, he was followed by the porter, who shook his head dubiously and said,

"Better get there quick, 'cause somethin' tells me those gemmen ain't goin' t' stay in the same bed long."

• • •

President Roosevelt devoted his speech that night primarily to H. L. Mencken and the Gridiron Club skits. He started off by saying that even in the Gridiron Club, "the old order changeth."

For years when, as assistant secretary of the navy and governor of New York, he had attended dinners, he recalled that they always opened with a terrible crash, that the president of the Gridiron Club would say, "What was that terrible crash?" and that Mr. Blank would go to the platform and, in impressive tones, announce something like this:

"Why that was Jim Farley trying to explain how the Democrats lost Vermont."

Or perhaps he would say, "Why, that was Senator David Reed trying to get out of the tornado in Pennsylvania."

Then he referred to the alphabetical parade which had opened the dinner the preceding year instead of the crash and noted that the crash was probably a thing of the past, because that night the proceedings were opened with a Santa Claus parade.

"If this continues," he said, "you will soon have what the distinguished Chief Justice of the United States might call a precedent."

Turning to Mencken, upon whom he was very easy in the beginning, he felicitated him upon "the temperateness of his remarks and criticisms.

"I had really expected more fireworks, in the inimitable Mencken style. When he deals so gently with the achievements and misachievements of the present administration I opine that we must be pretty good, after all.

"But why," he went on, "is Mr. Mencken here tonight as the 'opposition speaker'? My understanding of Gridiron dinners has been that there are only two unreported speakers—one a spokesman for the administration temporarily in power, the other a critic thereof. Thus, through the years, the Gridiron Club has heard Republicans and Democrats and there has been much mirth as the oratorical rapiers flashed.

"Has the Republican party reached such a paucity of talent that no one branded GOP could be conscripted tonight to do his stuff? How is Mr. Mencken branded? I never regarded him as either a Democrat or a Republican. After following his writings I'd rather listed him as a follower of that famous old Irishman who landed on our shores some years ago and announced, as he got off the boat, 'I don't know what sort of government you've got over here, but whatever it is I'm agin it.'"

The President noted that at times some of Mencken's "pungent strictures" were "irritating," but, he said, "my appetite is invariably whetted for more and his writings give me a chuckle after a hard day at the office." Then he compared "the constructive character of his utterances this evening with the super-constructive character of his past writings."

Speaking further of the Gridiron Club, he said he had never taken away from a Gridiron dinner "a feeling of pique or resentment," and that the country needs a club like this "to keep satirical check upon administrations and public men as they come and go."

"But before I come to a more serious vein in my own remarks, a protest or so should be registered. Wasn't it rather unkind that the Gridiron Club had to have a skit on 'Vera Vandenberg'? My good friend, Senator Vandenberg, has been celebrating the November elections all by himself. He is one of the few employed Republicans. . . . Nevertheless, the club was considerate of 'Vera Vandenberg' when he was not cast along with Messrs. Andrew W. Mellon and Ogden L. Mills in the 'Man on the Flying Trapeze' skit."

He thought further that they should have a "word of sympathy, rather than a sizzling on the Gridiron" for Henry P. Fletcher, chairman of the Republican National Committee. "There appears to be a demand in certain quarters," he said, "not related to my own political party, that he be deposed. I'm not in favor of that. Let's have at least two more years of Fletcher."

And his final comment about the show was on that Section 7A Pullman car skit.

"I liked that skit tonight wherein William Green and Henry Ford were starting off on a trip together, whatever may have been their differences over the proprietorship of a Pullman car berth. When you can get these two gentlemen in the same sleeping car with Mr. Harriman and Mr. Hecht I feel assured that we will get to 'Prosperityville' ahead of schedule."

Then he was really ready for Mencken, "my old friend, Henry Mencken." Knowing him, the President had anticipated his probable line of attack and had set his aides to work to find the most absurd and contradictory quotations he could from Mencken's writings. These he proceeded to read with high glee to the audience. There were several of them, but the most notable was Mencken's comment on editors, taken verbatim from Mencken's book, *Prejudices: Sixth Series.*

"There are managing editors in the United States," he quoted, "and scores of them, who have never heard of Kant or Johannes Muller and never read the Constitution of the United States; there are city editors who do not know what a symphony is or a streptococcus, or the Statute of Frauds; there are reporters by the thousands who could not pass the entrance examination for Harvard and Tuskegee, or even Yale. It is this vast and militant ignorance, this widespread and fathomless prejudice against intelligence, that makes American journalism so pathetically feeble and vulgar, and so generally disreputable."[9]

After having thus handled Mencken with a smiling barbarity which would have done credit to Genghis Khan, he spent a couple of minutes describing the achievements of the administration and expressing the "conviction that at last this country has weathered the economic storm and we can see the mountain peaks of better times."

He predicted the new Congress convening in January would

"swing along in a spirit of cooperation that has existed between the executive and legislative branches of the government in all periods of national emergency.

"We have now reached that point in our program when, guided by the experiences of the past, we can retain its good features and eliminate the impracticable ones. In this endeavor, whether or not it be satirized as the program of a Santa Claus, I seek the continued cooperation of the Congress, your own organization of news writers, and the American people, regardless of political faiths."[10]

XI

Franklin D. Roosevelt

🍴 *1935-1936*
FDR squares off against
his opposition in business
and the press

The Gridiron dinner of April 13, 1935, was its Fiftieth Anniversary Dinner, and to celebrate the occasion with a new first, President Roosevelt participated from the head table in several lines of a skit, the first time this had been done by a President.

There was an air of nostalgia about the dinner, along with some fairly biting satire of the New Deal and of those, such as Senator Huey Long, Dr. Townsend and numerous others, who were to the left of the New Deal.

An elaborate souvenir for each person attending the dinner was drawn by Clifford K. Berryman, cartoonist of the *Washington Star* and a club member, with remarkably good facial likenesses of 142 of the most famous guests who had attended Gridiron dinners over its first half century.

Ulric Bell of the *Louisville Courier-Journal*, president of the club, set the tone when he noted that the Gridiron Club had begun half a century ago "to bestow its wisdom upon the leaders of this land."

"It has given its counsel freely throughout the years. Sometimes this advice has been heeded, sometimes ignored. Either way, the results have always been the same.

"From the time of Cleveland to the time of Roosevelt, through all the intervening regimes, chaos always has been just around the corner. But somehow the country has survived not only these various national administrations but one hundred and twenty-seven Gridiron dinners.

"You are taking your own chances on this one—we mean this Gridiron dinner. . . . If the Gridiron singes slightly, there will be the balm of melody and jest and goodwill to soothe. So let it flame."

The dinner opened with a historical procession: five groups corresponding to five decades of Gridiron Club history, all in costumes appropriate to the period, starting off with the "Cleveland Marching Club," featuring such characters as Richard Croker, the Tammany Tiger, Coxey's Army, and Buffalo Bill. For each decade, characters representing the principal figures marched across the stage and around the hall, ending with Father Time. Every one of the fifty active members of the Gridiron Club, and all of the associate and limited members who were present, participated in this and finally massed upon the stage to inaugurate Mr. Bell.

There was a skit set in Welcker's Restaurant on an evening in 1885, satirizing the meeting at which the Gridiron Club was formed. This provided an opportunity for the chorus to sing several songs intimately connected with the Gridiron Club, "Swinging in the Grapevine Swing," "De Watermilion Hangin' on De Vine," and "Sweet Genevieve." It ended with the chorus singing:

> Come, landlord, fill the flowing bowl!
> Until it doth run over,
> Come, landlord, fill the flowing bowl,
> Tomorrow we'll be sober.

James Roosevelt and five other sons of former Presidents of the United States, going back to Richard Folsom Cleveland, who had accepted invitations to the dinner, were called to their feet and given an ovation.

And in commemoration of the event, Captain Taylor Branson of the Marine Band composed the "Gridiron Golden Jubilee March," which was played to an audience for the first time by the Marine Band orchestra, with Captain Branson wielding the baton.

In the political part of the dinner, some of the better-known members of the Roosevelt administration were presented in an act in which the principal character depicted P. T. Barnum, "the historic predecessor of Franklin D. Roosevelt." Barnum presented "the most amazing group of oddities ever brought together under one administration":

> The fat philatelist, patron of the mails, known around the world for her generous nature. Fatima Farley.
> The living skeleton. He plows under pigs and plants platitudes. Señor Enrico Wallace.
> The world's most accomplished word swallower. He can swallow anything from a nutmeg to a Farley appointee, from a China egg to a Chief Justice. Pasha Homer Cummings.
> The midget of the midwest. This little freak, left over from the Chicago Fair, was brought here tonight at a cost of $4,800,000,000. General Tom Thumb Ickes.

It was just at the point where Barnum was describing them all as "just one happy family" that "Ickes" socked "Farley" on the head with an inflated bladder.

"Ouch!" said Farley. "If that little shrimp of a Tom Thumb Ickes doesn't mind his own business, he's got to go back to the Republican party."

Agriculture Secretary Wallace's proposals to restrict farm production and kill a lot of little pigs were ridiculed by Farley, who sang:

> Henry Wallace told the farmer
> Kill the pig he must,
> Not to grow another thing
> And let the plowshare rust.
> So all that Henry's raised this year,
> Is another cloud of dust.

The act ended with Barnum announcing that this conglomeration was only the beginning. Then he brought on Jumbo, "the world's thinnest living elephant," who was asked whether he thought we'd ever elect another Republican President. Jumbo wagged his head "Yes" and jumped up and down, while Barnum shouted, "By gosh, folks, I think I was wrong. Jumbo's got me beat. He thinks *two* suckers are born every minute!"

A lobbyist skit designed to give some clues to the Caraway Senate Committee, which was investigating lobbyists, ridiculed the accomplishments of the gentlemen under scrutiny.

It was set in the office of an unnamed lobbyist, who had been chased out of Representative Sam Rayburn's office and had just returned to dictate his report to Mr. Adam Sap, chairman of the board, American Umbrella Menders Association.

He directed his stenographer to call Senator Norris's office and tell him that Mr. Kiddem A. Long wished to speak to the senator. There were loud noises through the telephone and the stenographer said, "The senator says to tell you he intends to break your neck the next time he sees you."

He went on with the letter in phrases which were taken almost verbatim from a colloquy that had occurred between Senator Vandenberg and a witness before the Caraway Committee.

"You will be pleased to know that Senator Norris is getting warm and I can look for action there the next time I see him. Senator Borah and I had lunch today."

Stenographer: You didn't have lunch with Senator Borah.
Lobbyist: Senator Borah had lunch, didn't he?
Stenographer: I suppose so.
Lobbyist: I had lunch, didn't I?
Stenographer: I'm sure you did.
Lobbyist: Well, then, Senator Borah and I had lunch today. *(Goes ahead with the dictation)* But nothing conclusive to report. *(Continuing further)* I saw the President today.
Stenographer: Oh, did you really?
Lobbyist: Well, I saw him at the ball park, but it isn't necessary to put that in. *(Resumes dictating)* I saw the President today, and he seemed quite pleased, and in a cheerful mood.

Now, in closing, I say that we should arouse the umbrella menders to save the Constitution, and incidentally to increase the appropriation for this bureau.

That's all. Just write it out, sign my name, and run along.

Ho hum. Well, that's another day. Now if I can only get Congress to investigate me, I'll have my name plastered all over the newspapers, and I'll be solid with the big business moguls for the rest of my life. What boobs they are!

At this dinner for the second time since World War I, a Soviet ambassador was at the head table. So were the ambassadors of Germany, Great Britain, and several other European countries. In a foreign skit, "Sir John Simon," British foreign secretary, was at an airport on the continent awaiting the arrival of his conferees.

An attendant explained that the reason they were late was that "there is a thick fog over Europe. It is hard for statesmen to find their direction."

But soon they began to arrive: impersonators of Premier Pierre Laval of France, Mussolini, Hitler, and Maxim Litvinoff, commissar of foreign affairs of the Union of Socialist Soviet Republics.

They all wished to associate themselves with some noble sentiments expressed by Sir John, and then proceeded to order further armaments.

"Soviet Russia," said Litvinoff, "does not hesitate to do its part for the welfare of the proletariat. I shall order 10,000 tanks from Great Britain and the United States to exhibit our high regard for capitalism. The world must be saved from chaos even if the Communists have to do the job."

He was followed by Hitler, who announced that "the German government, ever faithful to its obligations, hereby declares that all treaties, unilateral, bilateral and multilateral, are at an end."

Coming back to the American scene, the Gridiron quartet presented a medley which included some comments on the New Deal.

> O we come to the end of a perfect plan
> Approved by the old brain trust;
> We thought it would help the forgotten man
> Till it turned out a perfect bust.

The act closed with these verses:

> Good night, New Deal;
> Good night, New Deal;
> Good night, New Deal;
> We're going to leave you now.
> Merrily we roll along, roll along, roll along;
> Merrily we roll along—
> Into—the deep blue sea!

The skit in which President Roosevelt participated was set in front of a wigwam in an Indian encampment, and it was revealed that various opponents of Presidential policies had been adopted into Indian tribes because "the Indians are the only ones who get anything out of the New Deal—they have nothing to lose."

Several characters depicted were Donald Richberg, chief counsel of the NRA; Secretary Perkins; Hugh Johnson, head of the NRA; Senator Borah; Senator Patrick A. McCarran; and a chorus of Indians.

Richberg arrived with a message from the "Great White Father," relating how the quarterback had carried the ball successfully from the four-yard line to the three-yard line.

"In fact, our progress has been such," the message said, "that we are now convinced only one thing remains to be done to complete our program of restoring to America its true inheritance.

"I propose to give the country back to the Indians."

The startled Indians went into a huddle and came up with their answer:

No!

No! No! A thousand times No!
You cannot give us this mess.
No! No! A thousand times No!
We'd rather die than say Yes.

Then Richberg said to President Roosevelt, at the head table, "I regret to report, Sir, the Indians won't take the country back."

President: I really don't blame them.
Richberg: The Republicans might be willing to take it.
President: Well, they can't have it.
Richberg: Then what shall we do about these Indians?
President: If you can't lick 'em, join 'em.
  Madame Perkins thought that was a good idea: We'll join 'em and kid 'em along.
President: And Mr. Richberg, will you please tell them all about next year?
Richberg: You mean about the election?
President: No, no, about the trees we're going to plant.
Richberg: But will you keep the country after all, Mr. President?
President: Why do you think I'm planting all those trees, Mr. Richberg? (This was a reference to a large tree-planting program which President Roosevelt had initiated out on the great prairies to prevent depletion of the soil by dust storms.)

Everybody shook hands, the Indians gave a massive war whoop, and the skit closed with a song to the tune of "Indians and Trees."

> According to *Who's Who*,
> Columbus and his crew,
> They landed here that well-known year
> Of fourteen ninety-two;
> Four hundred years had vanished
> And another forty more
> When Franklin D. came o'er the sea
> And stepped upon the shore.
> Now how to rule this land he'd found
> Columbus couldn't say—
> And Franklin is no better off,
> For no one knows today!
>
> Indians and trees,
> Indians and trees,
> That was what Columbus found,
> Just a happy hunting ground.
> Indians and trees,
> Indians and trees,
> Congress wasn't there to fret
> And there was no public debt.
> Look what's happened, just look around today,
> Look what's happened, since we got NRA!
> That's why we're planting trees again,
> To go back if we please—
> Go back and live again among
> The Indians and trees!

The President's reaction to all this was described the following Monday in a nationwide radio broadcast by Edwin C. Hill, who was the David Brinkley of his day.

"Nobody enjoyed the fun more than the President himself as he sat at ease, smoking a cigarette stuck in a long, white holder. Not one person among the five hundred guests failed to note with the utmost satisfaction that the President, obviously, had never been in better health in his life. Sitting quite near me, watching the play of emotions on his expressive face, studying this most interesting of human beings, this speaker was struck by the fact that there seemed to be hardly a line of care in his face. Cheeks and eyes glowed with the brightness of sound health. I don't believe there is a man of his age in America today who can reckon on a finer constitution, on sounder physical excellence which must go with tremendous mental work, than this same Franklin Delano Roosevelt. Even when they stepped on his toes just a little, he wore the smile that could not come off. He laughed outright when they sang this one:

"Washington founded this nation,
Jefferson gave it a name,
Hamilton helped its creation,
Adamses helped it to fame.

"Jackson and Cleveland and Wilson
Did much to help it survive, somehow
In spite of the Hardings and Hoovers—
But, heavens, just look at it now!"[1]

President Roosevelt, in the spirit of this Fiftieth Anniversay Dinner, responded to the "Indians and Trees" skit with a speech that was both witty and gracious.

"In 1885," he began, "when the Machiavellian idea occurred to a group of Washington newspapermen to found this club, I was an infant of not quite three. Little did the parents of that innocent child realize that he had been brought into the world to become, for a time, the semiannual victim of the most publicized private dinner in the world. It is an ironic circumstance that on these occasions the hosts place their target against a background of roses. Food and drink are put before him to act as sedatives to his sensibilities. If good digestion wait on appetite there are times when a few eupeptic tablets would be much appreciated.

"Fellow-guests, you have enjoyed tonight an entertainment that was the result of weeks of artful preparation and careful rehearsal. It represents the distillation of a peculiar mixture of chemical elements existing nowhere but in the brains of Washington correspondents.

"Their most unpremeditated works are the regular articles that appear under their names in what are referred to as great metropolitan journals of opinion and instruction. Sometimes one of our hosts provides a half-hour's recitation of events on the radio, or goes profound and contributes to one of the fifty-cent magazines. But their more solemn judgments, their *real* views of this American political scene, are reserved for Gridiron evenings.

"And what appears to us tonight as so excruciating, so absurd, so meriting our jocose tolerance, will tomorrow form the basis of dispatches for which the authors will hope to receive Pulitzer prizes and degrees of Doctor of Literature.

"In response to their well-planned wit, the President of the United States, at the conclusion of the proceedings, is invited to burst into spontaneous merriment. Like Cyrano de Bergerac, he is expected to compose a *ballade* while he wields his rapier and thrusts home. One of us, who was both silent and subtle, retorted with a series of spontaneous statistics from the *World Almanac.*"

Then he went on in nostalgic reminiscence about his predecessors during the period of Gridiron history.

"I have just had the unique honor of raising my glass in a toast to ten of the eleven Presidents of the United States who have occupied the White House since the foundation of The Gridiron Club"—the adjectives Roosevelt used were interesting—"the gracious Arthur, the incorruptible Cleveland, the gallant Harrison, the tragic McKinley, the assertive Roosevelt, the genial Taft, the lonesome Wilson, the gregarious Harding, the frugal Coolidge and the patient Hoover.

"Each of these men had his problems to meet; each of them met those problems in the light of his own philosophies, his own experience, his own capabilities and his own conscience.

"I shall not attempt to describe the feeling I had as I drank that series of toasts, except to pause for a moment—still, I fear, in the role of an amateur de Bergerac—to examine the life of one President who happened *never* to have been a guest at a Gridiron dinner—Grover Cleveland.

"He was elected governor of New York with the aid of many thousands of Republican votes. He found Albany a vestibule to the White House. Some of his Cabinet appointments received violent denunciation from the Republican press. He vetoed a general pension bill, based on the principle of allowing relief to veterans not because of wounds incurred in service, but upon the ground of service and present disabilities alone. The persons interested in such legislation turned upon him as an enemy to old soldiers and many of them running for office promised friendship as a bait for soldier votes.

"He often answered White House telephone calls. Out of the Treasury came the problem of a shrinking balance that threatened even to disappear. The opposition charged him with running the government on borrowed money in time of peace. He negotiated a general arbitration pact which the Senate mutilated until it was no longer useful. He went on record against inflation. He enjoyed his family, his fishing trips and his summer home. Of him Oscar S. Straus once wrote:

> 'The actor, Joseph Jefferson, with whom he fished and near whom he lived in his summer place "Gray Gables" on Buzzard's Bay, testified that he was a mimic of high order, told a good story, and might have been a great actor.'

"Gentlemen of the Gridiron Club, I share your regret that Grover Cleveland never attended one of your dinners. He would have made a superb target for your jests. Being 'a mimic of high order and a great actor,' he would have given thrust for thrust in a manner of which his present successor is incapable.

"The guest lists of this club since 1885 show the names of a United States Civil Service Commissioner [Theodore Roosevelt], a Representative in Congress [McKinley], a United States Senator [Harding], a Secretary of War [Taft], a Secretary of Commerce [Hoover], and an Assistant Secretary of the Navy [Franklin D. Roosevelt himself]. All of them later sat in the chair in which one of them has been sitting tonight. I have therefore been examining tonight's guest list with some degree of speculative interest.

"During all that time since 1885 the Gridiron Club has pursued its entertaining existence. It has been free from all responsibility. It has suffered from nothing worse than those semiannual attacks of exhibitionism that take hold at the vernal and winter equinox, and which provide delightful evenings for those invited to dine with the patient.

"Tonight we saw at the opening of this dinner a procession of American phenomena—Richard Croker; 'General' Coxey; 'Buffalo Bill'; Mark Hanna; the 'full dinner pail'; William Jennings Bryan; 'Uncle' Joe Cannon; Carrie Nation; the first airplane flight of the Wright brothers; the Winton automobile; Andrew Carnegie; the discoverers (real and otherwise) of the North Pole; the novel 'Three Weeks'; the 'New Freedom'; the League of Nations; the 'Ohio Gang'; 'Keep Cool with Coolidge'; the Brown Derby; the 'Great Engineer'; and the 'the Forgotten Man'.

"I am the latest exhibit, and I shall not be the last, in that procession. There should be some philosophic comfort in the reflection that there is a kind of slow rise and fall in the social, economic and political life of the United States, as of other countries; that what is new tonight is old tomorrow, that what was old in 1895 becomes new in 1935; that what shocks us at one moment amuses us at another; that the radicals of one period are the conservatives of the next; that some conservatives become sages and some radicals saints; and that the forward march of science and truth will continue their irresistible progress in spite of the obstruction of individuals and the detours of circumstance.

"I noticed at the end of your parade the figure of Father Time, and it brought to mind the lines of Austin Dobson chiselled on Lorado Taft's great fountain at Chicago:

'Time flies you say? Ah, no!
'Alas, Time stays, *we* go.'

"Gentlemen, in behalf of my ten predecessors in the White House since 1885, and in my own behalf, I give you—on its fiftieth birthday—

''Good Health and Long Life to The Gridiron Club.''"
. . .

By the time of the 1935 winter dinner, held on December 14, the controversy between President Roosevelt and business forces was quite sharp. Business people, who in general had supported the Roosevelt moves during the first hundred days in 1933, had found that many of the programs, at least by their standards, were not working very well, and that the vast number of new regulations by the federal government were onerous.

One subject of great criticism was the vast sums of money which President Roosevelt was spending. They were small by comparison with today's expenditures, but they were huge in comparison with those in the Hoover administration, whose largest national budget had been three billion dollars.

President Roosevelt had already applied the phrase, "economic royalists," to his opposition, and within less than a year's time was to declare, in a speech at Madison Square Garden closing his 1936 campaign for reelection:

"I should like to have it said of my first administration that in it the forces of selfishness and lust for power met their match. I should like to have it said of my second administration that in it they met their master."[3]

In view of this developing situation and the spending of the administration, the opening chorus sang:

As he rides along the avenue
With a great big bunch of dough,
Which to everyone he'll throw,
There's one thing we'd like to know—
Whether 1936 will see

The end of the gorgeous spending spree
Of the man who broke the bank at Monte Carlo!

The President had written to some clergymen a letter which
had boomeranged. In a skit between "Stephen Early," press secretary to the President, and "Marvin McIntyre," who served as a
sort of political secretary, they started asking how the word "secretariat" originated. McIntyre had an explanation.

"You remember that letter the President put out to the
preachers? Well, the President found out later that Henry Fletcher
[chairman of the Republican National Committee] had slipped
that letter onto your desk. And he says, 'When Fletcher was
sneaking around the White House, where was my Secretary
at?' "

Toward the end of the skit, McIntyre decided that the newspapermen had thought up the word "secretariat"; "I know how it
is, Steve. I used to be a newspaperman myself."

This threw Early into fits of laughter.

"I don't see what's so funny about that," McIntyre insisted,
"So did some members of the Gridiron Club!"

This dinner was replete with skits satirizing the New Deal.
As a result of what many people regarded as useless work being
created by Harry L. Hopkins' Federal Relief Administration, the
word "boondoggle" had come into use, and for a couple of years
the *New York Sun* had run a daily example of the boondoggle
from its Washington bureau.

The club put on "A Midwinter Night's Dream," in which
"Harry the Hop," as Roosevelt used to call him in jest, imagined
a gay boondogglers' roundup on the moon.

"What a dream," said Hopkins. "First I dreamed in millions,
then I got to billions, now I'm dreaming in trillions. Won't the
President be proud when I tell him a way to spend trillions!" A
soloist impersonator sang:

I'm headin' for the boondogglers roundup,
With gadgets and tools and a screw loose I ride;
To the man in the moon to help him run the tide.
I'm headin' for the boondogglers roundup.

The fact that the country was still in the depression wasn't
allowed to escape the notice of the club's distinguished guest. In
a scene at Fort Knox, where "Secretary of the Treasury Morgenthau" arrived with a bag of $2 billion in gold, the sentries ques-
tioned him, and after he told them he just wanted to put in

another $2 billion in gold to make it $10 billion altogether, the first sentry said, "Ten billion—that's a powerful lot. Mister, could you spare a little old thin dime that a fellow could use, could you, Suh?"

Morgenthau countered, "What's a thin dime to a country with ten billion in gold?"

"What's ten billion in gold to a country without a thin dime? That's what I wants to know," shot back the sentry.

But in spite of all their satire, the Gridiron dinners have always had also a touch of love and respect for many of the great characters of American life. At this particular dinner, Gridiron President Bell noted the presence of a famous American who was there again at a Gridiron dinner. "We ask him to stand for a moment when his name is called—General John J. Pershing, General of the Armies of the United States." The ovation was terrific.

A satire on the large number of loafers who had worked their way onto relief rolls while refusing to work was dovetailed into a skit on William Randolph Hearst, just back from his "worldwide tour searching for a land where I can live without supporting the government." The great tax rebellion involved such characters as J. P. Morgan, Aimee Semple McPherson, Charles Chaplin, Robert R. McCormick (then publisher of the *Chicago Tribune*), William Powell, James Cagney, and others.

At the other end of the square was a fellow in squalid attire whose name was "Jones or Smith or Brown—it doesn't matter much." He belonged to the tax-exempt class. He sang:

Oh, I got plenty o' nuttin',
An' nuttin's plenty fo' me.
I get my check,
What the heck!
I's loafin' de whole day long,
(No use complainin')
Got no job,
Want no job,
I belong!

But perhaps the dreamers reached heights even beyond that of the boondogglers on the moon when at the end of the skit Bill Raymond, as Aimee Semple McPherson, sang a new version of "In the Sweet Bye and Bye."

There's a land that is fairer than day,
And by faith we can see it afar.

Where there are no more taxes to pay,
And our bonds are forever at par.

We shall sing on that beautiful shore,
The melodious songs of the blest,
And we'll pay income taxes no more,
With our check-book forever at rest.

During the mid-thirties there was considerable emphasis upon neutrality, which led to the passage of the Neutrality Act. "Secretary of State Cordell Hull" and his assistant were examining various materials under microscopes to determine whether their exportation would be dangerous. One of them was cotton. An assistant told the secretary that cotton seemed like a harmless substance and he didn't regard it as a munition of war, whereupon Hull responded, "It's useful to put in one's ears so you can't hear Ickes talking about oil. Suppose we call it 'conditional contraband.'"

There was also a rollicking duet between "Attorney General Cummings" and "Secretary of Commerce Roper," to the tune of the popular song "Frankie and Johnnie," Johnnie being General Hugh S. Johnson, the boss of the NRA. Cummings sang:

Franklin and Johnson were buddies,
Lordy, what a friend was Hugh.

Swore he'd be true to Franklin
As long as the skies were blue—
He was our pal, but he done us wrong.

Franklin gave Johnson money
Gathered for PWA.

Roper:
Johnson took Franklin's money
And spent it on NRA—
He was our pal, but he done us wrong.
Cummings:
Perkins and Richberg watched Johnson
Gettin' too big for his suit.
Roper:
They waited for him at the White House
And the guns went rooty-toot-toot—
He was our pal, but he done us wrong.
Roper:
Johnson grabbed up his pencil,
Wrote himself out a roast,

Cummings:
> And sent it to Scripps-Howard
> And the *Saturday Evening Post*—
> He was our pal, but he done us wrong.

Roper:
> So bring on a rubber-tired taxi
> And bring on a rubber-tired hack;

Cummings:
> For Johnson's gone on a one-way ride
> And they ain't gonna bring him back.
> He was our pal, but he done us wrong.

There were two unscheduled events at this dinner: First, Norman Thomas, perennial Socialist candidate for President, who was to be the opposition speaker, failed to show because of a transportation foul-up and did not speak; and second, the Gridiron dinner was put to a new use which resulted in considerable tightening up after that in Secret Service security.

Several plaintiffs in suits against oilman Henry L. Doherty had been unable to get to him to serve the necessary papers. But lawyers, upon reading that Doherty was going to be a guest at the Gridiron dinner, conceived a brilliant idea. Handsome young Gerald W. Sickler, a former George Washington University law student dressed up in rented white tie and tails, strolled nonchalantly into the dining hall, picked up a seating list, and walked over to the table where Mr. Doherty was seated. He introduced himself, gave Doherty the Sigma Chi grip, and then served the stack of fourteen subpoenas.

According to an Associated Press story, "the ruse failed, however, because a court later held the process server was improperly appointed."[4]

But it did make the papers all over the country, and the Secret Service was chagrined that a thing like this could have happened, because they realized, that after having been in all the papers, it might suggest an idea to a Presidential assassin at some future dinner.

Republican prospects in the upcoming Presidential campaign eleven months later were depicted around a campfire in a mountain scene in the "remote hiding-places of the survivors of that classic melodrama, 'The GOP Follies.' " They were cooking a form of Roosevelt chowder, made from a piece of pork that wasn't raised, an ear of corn that was plowed under, a potato that didn't grow, and one of Agriculture Secretary Henry Wallace's speeches.

Impersonators of all the potential Republican candidates were on the scene: Borah, Vandenberg, Alf Landon, Frank Knox, plus some dark horses. Enthusiasm had begun to run high when it was announced they'd won elections in Norwich, Tonawanda, New Rochelle, Oneonta, Newburgh, Poughkeepsie, Seagirt, and Worcester, Massachusetts.

They proposed to stage a revival of "The GOP Follies" in Washington, but the question arose, "Where will we stay? The cast of 'The New Deal Vanities' has bought up all the houses, mansions, apartments and hotels." (One of the most noteworthy of these was the fifty-room mansion on the Potomac, with gold fixtures in the bathrooms, where Joseph P. Kennedy lived, in "true Rooseveltian frugality," while he was chairman of the SEC.

They started down the mountain to initiate their great revival, and the skit ended with a song.

> We'll be comin' down the mountain when we come,
> *When* we come.
> We will have a man of fame, though we do not
>   know his name,
> We'll be comin' down the mountain when we come.
> Will it be with Governor Landon when we come?
> *When* we come.
> Will we find our chances best, with the
>   Coolidge of the west?
> Will it be with Governor Landon when we come?

The tension between President Roosevelt and the Supreme Court had been building up, because of the Court's refusal to approve the constitutionality of some of the Roosevelt measures. Already New Dealers were referring disparagingly to the members of the Court as "the nine old men." This was to culminate three years later in President Roosevelt's attempt to "pack" the Supreme Court by seeking legislation to give him the right to appoint six additional justices.

Thus, as a prelude to the toast to the President and to his speech, Chief Justice Charles Evans Hughes and five other members of the Court who were at the dinner were presented and asked to stand. Then, onto a stage set with four white Greek columns, described as a magnificent marble temple of the Acropolis, came nine characters dressed as Roman or Greek soldiers. In the skit that followed, written by Henry Suydam, correspondent of the *Newark Evening News,* they were presented as "the wisest men in the entire world." Furthermore, it was announced that once a week "revelation is given by these nine wise men." A soloist sang an adaptation of "On a Sunday Afternoon."

> It's time to take your places,
> You'll hear the verdict soon.
> Oh, it's better than the races,
> On a Monday afternoon.
> You'll hear what folks were thinking
> In eighteen hundred ten.
> And Latin words a-linking
> What happens now with then.
>
> You see them scowl,
> And you hear them growl,
> You watch them prowl,
> In a sable gown, it's the talk of the town.
> Now you can hunt for omens,
> Beneath the harvest moon,
> Give *me* those thrilling moments,
> On a Monday afternoon.

The nine wise men were later identified, not as Supreme Court Justices but as the most bitter opponents of the New Deal: John W. Davis, former Senator David A. Reed, Frank J. Hogan, George W. Wickersham, Jouett Shouse, and others.

After a considerable bit of banter, the skit ended with a song.

> It ain't necessarily so,
> It ain't necessarily so,
> They say that they're wiser,
> Than Khalif or Kaiser
> But 'taint necessarily so.
> Methus'lah lived nine hundred years,
> But who calls that livin'
> For people to give in
> To nine men what's nine hundred years.
> I'm preachin' this sermon to show
> It ain't nessa, ain't nessa, ain't nessa,
>   ain't nessa,
> Ain't necessarily so!

President Roosevelt's speech at this dinner was built entirely around the anticipated opposition speaker, Norman Thomas.

Beginning on a light note, he referred to the "semiannual flagellation which falls to the lot of Presidents" at Gridiron dinners.

"I suppose I should be in a mood," he said, "of appropriate humility and contrition for all the sins I have committed and all the wisecrack statesmanship which I have failed to display. I do not feel depressed, however, because, sitting here in 'buggy-drivers' row,' it is obvious to me that as long as the Gridiron Club is in general supervision of our government, there is a final appeal to that Gridiron court of sublime judgment, to which all of us can resort."

He referred to a brief satirical motion picture which had been shown during the show, entitled *A Newer Deal*.

"I suppose," he continued, "that picture was meant to suggest that the inauguration of my good friend Norman Thomas as President of the United States would mean a turn to the right, a movement in the direction of conservative principles of government, as compared with policies in effect under the present administration. Alas! I am afraid that few guests at this dinner realize the inroads that so-called Socialistic principles have been making on American government for a long time past."

Recounting how he had gone back over the Socialist and Socialist Labor party platforms of years past, he summarized all the things they had advocated which had since been enacted into law under various administrations: reductions in the hours of labor; a progressive income tax; inheritance taxes; pensions for aged workers; relief for the unemployed through the building of public works; forbidding of child labor; compulsory insurance against unemployment, illness, accident, invalidism, and old age; equal suffrage for men and women; minimum wage scales; publicly-owned power; the outlawing of war; independence for the Philippines; increased federal subsidies for many things; and numerous others.

"I could go on," he declared, "with further citations of the inroads that ultraconservative Socialist principles such as these have made on American life, at least from the time of the administration of President Andrew Johnson in 1865. Congress and Presidents have often succumbed to them. Even such radicals as Ulysses S. Grant, Grover Cleveland and Calvin Coolidge were unable to resist them.

"Therefore, if the present administration is to be charged with turning to the right and with following the false gods of Tory Socialism, how could mere theorists, such as we, be expected to detect fallacies that such practical, hard-headed men as Theodore Roosevelt, Taft and Hoover, fail to resist, and who even went so far, and with such outstanding success, to urge upon the Congress their Tory principles?

"Gentlemen, I feel very strongly that the inauguration of Norman Thomas as President of the United States in 1937 would be a terrific anticlimax. Of course, I must admit that you will find some of the Socialist planks that I have read in the Democratic and even in the Republican platforms of the period. We all realize that certain, broad, fundamental social, humanitarian and economic objectives are not the exclusive possession of a single political group, and that with the development of a more tolerant and more enlightened public thought on these subjects it is possible in ever greater degree to put them into effect."

Then, in conformity with the satirical nature of what he had recounted, he went on to expound his own philosophies and, at the end, to turn it back again on his presumed opposition speaker.

"If some of the measures that the present administration has sponsored for the relief of agriculture, for the social protection of the infirm and the aged, for the protection of bank deposits and investments, be considered Socialistic, then all I can say is that some of the Republican gentlemen gathered at this board are going to suffer a profound shock when they read the Republican platform for 1936.

"Let us not deceive ourselves with tags, titles and labels. Let us not attempt to argue with epithets. Public opinion, political candidates and platforms will differ from time to time on the degree to which the broad principles of human betterment can be translated into practical application. But I do not believe that even the most conservative person present would desire to have most of the legislation which I have described, common to all parties and going back to the period of our rebirth as a nation in the sixties, stricken from the statute books. These principles are part of American life, most of them accepted as commonplaces of government.

"I am not one of those who fears for the survival of our political institutions, or of the broad structure of our national economic life. I believe that part of the genius of our form of government is its adaptiveness to the needs of changing times. The wise and sound general principles upon which our government rests, and from which our peace and happiness are derived, were not intended to become rigid formulae, inflexible, resistant to the stresses and strains, to the greater interchange of opposing forces and different tensions, out of which true progress arises.

"If you wish proof of that statement you have but to compare the present conditions of life in the United States with those existing in some other parts of the world. Let me read you a brief quotation from a recent book:

" 'By and large Americans have had great liberty of speech and press. But the apologist for either Communism or Fascism who cites certain notable and shameful abridgments of liberty in America as proof of the utter hypocrisy of our Democracy and the complete similarity of conditions here and'—I will omit the names of the countries—'talks nonsense. The very meetings at which he makes his statement, if conditions were reversed, would, as a matter of course, be suppressed in these countries.'

"The author of that statement is Norman Thomas. . . .

"I cannot tell you who will be inaugurated President of the United States at that first midwinter inauguration in 1937. But of course I have some ideas on that subject, and even a certain preference. Whoever the man turns out to be, of one thing I am certain—that the United States will continue in the future, as it ever has in the past, to solve its own problems in accordance with its own democratic traditions, and that so long as that tradition controls and guides our destinies, the progress of the American people will be irresistible."[5]

• • •

The attention of the country was strongly concentrated on two things at the time of the April 18, 1936 dinner: the problems of the New Deal and those created by the New Deal, and the national conventions and who would be the Republican nominee. Since President Roosevelt's renomination was taken for granted, the dinner was devoted primarily to these two subjects.

Edwin W. Gableman, correspondent of the *Cincinnati Enquirer* and president of the club that year, welcomed the guests in his speech in the dark "to a preview of a political year which begins in confusion and will end—in November."

"The national colors," he said, "wave over a Treasury in the red, candidates in virtuous white, and taxpayers very, very blue.

"We march toward conventions and campaigns. Republicans are trying to decide how far to go along with the New Deal, and the New Deal itself is trying to decide the same thing."

The stage skits were opened with an announcer calling attention to the fact that this was the 160th anniversary of Paul Revere's ride and that "the patriots once more are in arms! Here comes Paul Revere Hearst with his valiant editors!"

The Gridiron chorus, dressed as Continental soldiers, came charging on the stage, and an impersonator of their leader, William Randolph Hearst, sang to the strains of "Yankee Doodle":

These New Dealers all are reds,
      and I am going to chase them;
Just follow me, my valiant men,
      and quickly we'll efface them!

The country's going to the dogs
      with all these professorials,
The only way to save it is
      to read my editorials.

The constitution is attached,
      I shall be its salvation.
I'll save the freedom of the press
      and Hearstize all the nation!

William Randolph, ha ha ha!
William Randolph's handy.
He will slay them with his pen,
O isn't he a dandy!

The issue of the Supreme Court, headed by Chief Justice Charles Evans Hughes, which was to emerge two years later in the Roosevelt court-packing bill, was still simmering, though not yet to a boil. This was touched upon in two skits, the first a Tobacco Road fantasy, with Jeeter Lester telling his wife what he'd do if he were president.

Jeeter: Well, I certainly would crack down on everybody that didn't agree with me including the Supreme Court.
Ma Lester: Well, suppose the people showed they was strong for the Supreme Court?
Jeeter: Why I'd shut up mighty quick—till after the election.

The internal problems of both parties were emphasized in skits in which actors playing the Townsendites, the Coughlinites, the General Coxeyites, and Upton Sinclair on the Democratic side, and the American Liberty League on the republican side were all debating whether they should join the bandwagon.

On the Republican side, the emphasis was on Kansas Governor Alfred M. Landon, who had been most ably promoted by a Gridiron member, then editor of the *Kansas City Star*, Roy A. Roberts. The scene was the room of an humble prairie home with "Pa Landon" in overalls and "Ma Landon" in a gingham wrapper and sunbonnet.

Several calls came from newspapers, and Ma Landon in each case answered and said that "the Governor is devoting his entire attention to the affairs of the State of Kansas. He cannot discuss national politics."

Finally a call came and she repeated the statement down to the line, "He cannot discuss—" but then said, "What newspaper did you say this was?"

She dropped her provincial twang. "Oh, it's so nice to hear your voice." To Alf she said, "It's Roy Roberts of the *Kansas City Star.*"

"Give me the phone," ordered Pa. "How are things going? Oh, is that so? Of course I'll take your judgment on this." He barked aside to Ma, "Take this: 'Governor Landon tonight issued the following statement: The way to balance the budget is to balance it.' "

And then he told Roberts that in view of the importance of this issue he was going to swing into action and hold a press conference.

Ma Landon put on a sunbonnet, grabbed a harp and started playing "Columbia, the Gem of the Ocean," while Pa Landon shouted, "Open the doors! Bring in the reporters! Start the mimeograph! Pass out the pictures! I'm going to make a statement and the *Kansas City Star* has scored a world beat!"

The scene for the Democratic skit was "Mutiny on the Bounty." An impersonator of Harry Hopkins explained their problems. "Whenever our New Deal craft gets going good in a fair wind and a following sea, we run into an uncharted constitutional reef and it takes us three months to get started again."

"Harold Ickes" explained that "the New Deal Relief Ship is a most peculiar floating object. For one thing, it has no Captain, or rather, it has nine Captains," all of whom were secreted up aloft and once a week their orders were sent down.

"It's no wonder we can't tell where we're going," explained Hopkins. "Sometimes six of the Captains think we ought to go in one direction, and three of them think we ought to go in another." The chorus sang:

> Nine old men on a White House chest,
> Yo-ho-ho and a bottle of rum!
> Flicking bits of fluff from their coat and their vest!
> Yo-ho-ho and a bottle of rum!

Led by "Henry Wallace," the crew decided to put six of the nine old men overboard "in an open boat with a ham sandwich made from a hog we didn't grow, and a bound volume of the speeches of Thomas Jefferson."

"Hereafter," yelled Wallace, "Hopkins and Ickes and I will run this Relief Ship! Let's give a cheer, boys, for the New Deal C's, the most wonderful C's in all the world! The SEC, the NEC, the RFC, the HOLC and all the rest." To the tune "We Saw the Sea," they sang

> We joined the New Deal to see the world
> And what did we see? The CCC.
> Right from the Pacific to the Atlantic
> C's are gigantic, C's make us frantic.
> There's the RFC, the SEC and D.C.
> There's the NEC to fix HOLC.
> There's more than that, that ends on a C.
> We never get seasick sailing the ocean,
> We don't object to feeling the motion,
> We're never seasick, but we are awfully sick of C's.

But the high points of the dinner were two skillful, satirical speeches, one by President Roosevelt and the other by one of his most vitriolic critics, Frank R. Kent, political columnist of the *Baltimore Sun.*

"I rise to address you," said Mr. Kent, "as that dreadful thing—a destructive critic, and therefore, of course, destitute of honor and devoid of shame. Or, to speak in the Michelsonian manner, a masked agent of Republican reaction, a tool of the predatory rich, a Tory, a Bourbon, a creature of entrenched greed—a man who believes that human rights and property rights coincide rather than conflict—in other words, an anti-New Deal Democrat—and one whose claim to Democracy rests upon the slender and ridiculous ground that up to now he never has voted anything save the straight Democratic ticket."

He said he did not know "how many of us there are in the country," but that he believed the number was large.

"Conceding, as I do," he said, "the great personal charm and high character of the President, still, we do not like his New Deal.

Nor do we like very many of his New Dealers. There is between us and them nothing in common save that apparently we all belong to the human race. To some extent, of course, we are in accord with the New Deal objectives—such as health, happiness, sunshine and a laborless life among the angels. . . . But from the New Deal methods, agencies, principles, policies, philosophy, finance and general trend we strongly dissent. These grieve our gentle Democratic hearts, baffle and confuse our simple and un-tutored minds. We have a vast distaste for what they are doing and the way they are doing it."

Then he shifted to the Republicans, where he said that "we find no comfort at all when we turn to that utterly dreary, unin-spiring, unimaginative, unenlightened aggregation known as the Republican party. . . . Nor do we contemplate that marvel of political ineptitude, the American Liberty League, with any de-gree of enthusiasm or pleasure. . . . The truth is that our dislike is wide, deep, all embracing. . . . We dislike every political agency in sight and with what seem to me sound and sufficient reasons. But what we are going to do about it no one knows. It has been suggested by a certain not entirely obscure Democrat [Alfred E. Smith] that we might take a walk. But, walk where and with whom?"

Then, saying that this was not a speech he was making but a confession, Kent explained his own "embarrassment."

"For example, when I accepted this invitation, which seemed so high an honor that I did not have the strength to decline, I was told that if I made a sissy speech the members of this Club would never forgive me. At the same time I was warned that if I spoke from the heart I probably would be torn to tatters by the President, whose large and bloodthirsty research staff has been going over my life and works, who has the last word on this occasion and an enormous advantage in that he cannot be an-swered. It was further delicately intimated that, once revealed in my true colors, my telegrams would be seized, my letters steamed open, my telephone tapped, my income tax returns ex-amined with a cold, unfriendly eye, and Mr. Michelson would hotly pursue me with his stink pots and poisoned gas. That's all a lot of nonsense. The boys, I think, were joking me. Nothing like that will happen.

"For one thing, no one can convince me that Mr. Farley, that great political idealist and gifted exponent of the Merit system, for one moment would tolerate any tampering with the mails. If the higher, ethical reasons did not deter him, he certainly would be by thought of the inevitable loss of business and its effect upon those jolly Post Office surpluses of which he is so oddly proud."

Kent turned then to Charles Michelson.

"As to Mr. Michelson, he seems to heave and pant under a heavy strain. Only the other day he excitedly discovered that the Republican National Committee was trying to popularize the articles of Mr. Mark Sullivan, Mr. David Lawrence and myself—an obviously hopeless task—but that seemed to him to make criminals of us and devils of them. I have known Mr. Michelson a long time. Few of his friends can look upon him today without sorrow. Once he was a newspaper man. His first downward step was taken when he became a political press agent; his next was when he developed as a ghost writer on a grand scale; and now, infected and inflamed with his own virus, I am told he considers himself a party leader. It is the bottom. He can no further go."

But he closed on a friendly and gentlemanly note, following his serious statement that he believed the forthcoming election was a vital one because it would determine the direction in which the country was to go.

"Yet I should like to say to the President, if he will permit, that while, in this campaign, I may be unable to wish him luck politically, that personally, and with deep sincerity, I do wish him continued good health and every possible personal good fortune and happiness."[6]

Harold L. Ickes, in his *Secret Diary*, noted that Kent's was "the most outspoken attack I have listened to yet in the presence of the President."

"He was," said Ickes, "like a little bantam cock fighting a big rooster. He said he knew that the President's extensive research staff had looked up everything which he had ever said or done and intimated that he was prepared for the worst. He plainly thought that he was offering himself as a martyr to a cause. . . .

"I kept wondering how the President would answer Kent because to have answered him would have been to descend to personalities. Shortly after he began to speak, I came to the conclusion that he wasn't even going to mention Kent or refer to what he had said. About halfway through, the President began to pay sarcastic respects to certain columnists and Washington correspondents and then I wondered whether he would include Kent. However, he did not. There was no slightest intimation that he had ever heard of Kent or that Kent had made a speech preceding his own. It must have been a sore trial to Kent to mount the funeral pyre, prepared bravely to suffer martyrdom, and then find that his posturing had escaped the attention of the man who was to apply the match to the faggots."[7]

Instead of replying to Kent, Roosevelt gave some amusing advice to his possible Republican opponents, nearly all of whom were in the audience. He noted that the vernal spirit of spring was in the air and with it, "wit renewed from the old sap blossoms forth anew.

"The thoughts of all of us," he began, "are thus directed toward the summer of promise that lies ahead—many promises. I will not inject a sour note by suggesting to some who are here that autumn, with its falling leaves, will follow, and that winter with its heavy frosts is equally inevitable."

"With the aid of high-powered glasses" he said that he noticed a number of gentlemen seated around the room who were "not satisfied to let well enough alone, or perhaps I should say better enough. These gentlemen aspire to become President of the United States. I admire their qualities of ambition and of self-sacrifice.

"One of them is a publisher," he said with gentle satire, "who has translated himself slowly westward from city to city until he has perched in the windiest of our great mid-western cities [Frank Knox, then publisher of the *Chicago Daily News*]. One of them, from Ohio, has perhaps the thought that if there have been two Adamses and two Harrisons and two Roosevelts, there might very well be two Tafts. And as a good friend of his distinguished father, I do not think it would be a bad idea at all—some day. Another is a western governor [Landon], who like all his neighbor governors has balanced his budget as called for in their state constitutions. Another, now a resident of the Capitol, presided over the destinies of a newspaper in a city famous for its imitations of Queen Anne and Louis Quatorze furniture—My goodness, Arthur [Vandenberg], what a royal background you have. Another senator, not with us, however, is that Demosthenes from the Rockies [Borah], our greatest protagonist of peace, except when it comes to peace within his own party. And still another, not present, is a citizen of California [Hiram Johnson], who, from past experience in Washington, should know better.

"And in order to be fair about it, your attention is also invited to your speaker—whom I leave to you to charactertize according to your own ideas on the subject."

Then Roosevelt pointed out that he had "one great advantage," in that he had learned lessons about running for the Presidency, and that he did not think it fair to hold that knowledge secret.

"The day would be incomplete if I did not, as usual, break some time-honored precedent," he declared. "I am going, therefore, to initiate these other candidates in some of the requirements of a successful campaign—to tell them how to act and how not to act; what to do and what not to do.
"Rule Number One:

"Get yourself a group of editors and political writers of national importance—men who will submit daily advice on what your policies should be, and how they should be put into effect. I have such a group and I am willing to turn over some of the most assiduous and untiring and consistent of these editorial advisors, of whom I have more than enough—turn them over to you other candidates and let you take your pick.

"For example, there is Mr. Walter Lippmann, whose English is so limpid and so pure that the trigonometry of public affairs is made clear overnight to the kindergartens of America.

"And I can offer a Gridiron member, my old buddy, Mr. Mark Sullivan. But I warn you before you take him that he is an incurable optimist. I should be compelled to cling to him if in these three long years there had only been one single expression of pessimism in anything that he has written. When he tells you that all is well with America; that there is not a cloud on the horizon of America, please discount him just a little bit. His high collars of optimism are as high today as they were in the spring of 1929.

"And then there is my friend, David Lawrence. There is a nag to take a long shot on. Once in his quarter of a century of writing he was right. He guessed the election of 1916.* It is just

---

*Roosevelt was apparently unaware of how it happened that Lawrence listed every state correctly in his 1916 election forecast for the *New York Evening Post*—quite a feat anytime, but especially so in so close an election as that of 1916. Lawrence told me years later that he had first written the story electing Hughes by a modest margin, but that Oswald Garrison Villard, then editor of the *Post*, made him rewrite it, saying that "we are supporting Wilson and you may be right, but we are not going to give up until the votes have been counted. We've got to elect Wilson even if it's only by a hair." Whereupon Lawrence pondered over it further, finally giving California to Wilson, and ending up right on every state.

within the bounds of possibility that he might guess right once more before he dies.

"And there is another Gridiron member, Mr. Arthur Krock, who will guarantee to give you, more clearly than anyone else, the point of view of the farmer, the laborer, and other members of what he would call the 'lower classes of America.'

"In addition to these gentlemen I could give you the names of columnists, news letter writers, inside dopesters, free lances and slaves. Their judgment and untiring vigilance is at the disposal of you, my fellow candidates. Whichever of you is nominated can obtain the benefit of their guidance. You can reach them—or perhaps it would be more polite to say—their addresses can be found by calling up the Republican National Headquarters.

"Rule Number Two:

"Finances are, of course, necessary to your campaign. Efficient machinery awaits you the day you are nominated, but during the following five months there will come times when a few extra million will come in very handy for you. For instance, I see by tonight's paper that in addition to purchasing a brain trust of their own, the Republican National Committee has gone in heavily for detectives. Yes, your expenses will be not only high but unusual. But I want again to help you. When you need that extra million or two, send a telegram addressed just to Wilmington, Delaware, and checks will come by return mail."

Rule Number Three was to be sure to dress for the part. Roosevelt recalled that at a recent Gridiron dinner, when Arthur Vandenberg was the Republican speaker, he had expressed doubt as to whether he had the proper clothes.

"I told him on that occasion," said the President, "That the entire White House wardrobe was his for the asking—shirts, collars, socks, underdrawers and, in particular, that long, black cutaway coat that I reserve for funerals. Tonight I extend that offer, not only to him but to all of you candidates."

He went on with Rule Number Four:

"This is for the Republican convention, not for all candidates. You must be sure to choose, as your standard bearer, somebody with a good radio voice, a pleasing smile, and, above all, a 'fireside' manner. There is great advantage in these qualities. If the public reaction to the candidate's speech is unfavorable, the blame can be placed on the unwisdom of the platform, but if the reaction is favorable, it can be credited to the radio voice and the 'fireside' manner.

"Rule Number Five:

"Be sure to have a platform of at least 25,000 words. That enables you to pick out any combination to suit the occasion— you can damn Wall Street in the West; you can damn the farmers in the great cities of the East.

"Rule Number Six:

"Select a campaign manager whom you do not know—one who has had no previous contact with the somewhat mundane compulsions of the American political method. Someone with no experience of practical politics, someone, let us say, in the great amateur tradition of Mark Hanna or Boies Penrose or John J. Raskob. Such a selection will embarrass the administration and, most important of all, provide material for a Gridiron skit at some future dinner."

His last rule, Number Seven, was that in financing the campaign a few large contributions are preferable to an infinite number of small ones.

"In your search for large contributions," he said, "make your unit an even dozen. Twelve millionaires are better than one, and this method has the further advantage that it avoids raising the issue of class consciousness. . . . And, my fellow candidates, when November comes I wonder if you will feel that the dollar has been further devalued or not.

"I hope that you will adopt these few simple rules," he concluded. "If you do you might win Vermont and Maine. If you don't, there may not be a single doubtful state."

Then, like Kent, he paid his personal respects to those whose campaigns he had been satirizing. But first, in a serious moment, he pointed out that the issues would be outstanding because "there is not a man, woman or child who has not a vital interest at stake in the solution of the great social and economic questions that confront us."

He added that most of the gentlemen he had mentioned were personal friends of his and he hoped they always would be. "The views and the principles of these gentlemen," he said, "are not mine, but I know them to be men of achievement and of character; men whose service—each in his own field—is bound to command our respect and whose patriotic desire for what is best for our people is above reproach.

"Should I have the good fortune to be the Democratic

nominee, I shall welcome one of these gentlemen to the battle that lies before us, confident that it will be a real campaign—a campaign, the issues of which can be clarified to, and understood by, the 45,000,000 voters of the land."

An interesting little sidelight on Roosevelt and the Gridiron Club appeared in relation to this speech in the Roosevelt Gridiron file in the library at Hyde Park. Under the date of April 14, 1936, four days before the dinner, William D. Hassett, an assistant to the President, wrote a memorandum saying that Henry Suydam, an associate Gridiron member, then special executive assistant to the attorney-general, had telephoned that he had a draft of suggestions for the President's speech at the Gridiron Club. The draft was attached and, with a very few minor changes, the President used it almost word for word for his advice to the Republican candidates.

• • •

The December 1936 dinner was held about six weeks after President Roosevelt had achieved a triumphal reelection by the largest electoral majority ever attained by a President of the United States since the second election of James Monroe in 1820. He carried every state except Maine and Vermont, as he had indicated he might in his April speech, and thereby added to the reputation for political sagacity of James A. Farley, who before the voting had publicly predicted precisely that outcome. He also increased his already heavy majorities in both houses of Congress. In the interval between the election and the dinner, the President had made a goodwill tour of South America.

The dinner took place on Monday, December 21. Both President Roosevelt and his defeated opponent, Governor Landon of Kansas, attended and gave speeches. Chief Justice Hughes was also present, as were the two other Presidential candidates, Norman Thomas, the Socialist, and Earl Browder, the Communist.

The stage for the skits and speeches was set by Gridiron President Edwin W. Gableman in his speech in the dark, which immediately followed the traditional opening of the dinner, a rendition of "Music in the Air."

"With the harmonious strains of that appropriate melody," he began, "we welcome you to an era of calm after the storm, of peace after the conflict, and a serenity of national spirit inspired by an irresistible ratio of forty-six to two. Yes, there is music in the air.

"So let us be friends. Let friendly feeling pervade the holiday season and usher in another year. Yes, let us be friends for the brief time permitted us—for in another two weeks Congress will meet again.

"Then, indeed, we shall learn who has met his match, and who has met his master.

"With that feeling upon us, we extend to the vanquished in the recent great encounter, our sincere congratulations, and to the victors, our profound sympathy.

"Since last we met, we have crossed the Rubicon and the Equator—and some of us have caught some fish.

"We turn our eyes toward the future, striving to pierce the veil to determine which fish were caught."

Following Gableman's speech, the show opened with a huge chariot drawn by Roman slaves, preceded by trumpeters, and followed by centurions, Roman senators and soldiers bearing banners inscribed "FDR Imp." The procession made its triumphal way around the hall to martial music by the Marine Band orchestra.

The timing of the dinner made it logical to have another Santa Claus skit, this time forecasting again the difficulties that were to develop two years later.

There was a Chief Santa Claus and eight other Santa Clauses, plus a little boy on the stage. It was announced: "Oyez! Oyez! Oyez! The Honorable, the Chief Santa Claus and the Associate Santa Clauses of the United States."

The Chief Santa Claus intoned: "We have before us the case of Johnnie Jones. The Petitioner's brief recites: 'Dere Santy Claus: I want a pair of roller skates and a bicycle and a book and a train that runs when you wind it up. I have been a good boy.'"

Four of the Santa Clauses immediately voted "No!" and four others voted "Yes!" The Chief Santa Claus asked each side to elaborate its opinions.

The no's said that it was contrary to due process under the Fourteenth Amendment, and that "this assault upon capital is but the beginning. It will be but the stepping stone to others, larger and more sweeping, until Christmas will become the war of the poor against the rich; a war constantly growing in intensity and bitterness. It is Un–

2nd Santa Claus: Con–
3rd Santa Claus: Sti–
4th Santa Claus: Tutional!

"And besides," their spokesman said, "the Petitioner has spelled Dear d-e-r-e." And again in sequence they repeated that it was "Un–Con–Sti–Tutional."

The fifth Santa Claus, speaking for those who had voted yes, argued that this case was clearly covered by the general welfare clause of the Constitution.

"Who are we to say," he asked, "that Johnnie Jones' general welfare will not be furthered by a pair of roller skates—"

6th Santa Claus: And a bicycle—
7th Santa Claus: And a book—
8th Santa Claus: And a train that runs when you wind it up.

"It is my opinion," he continued, "that the essence of the Petitioner's case is found in the paragraph which states un-equivocally that he has been a good boy. I know of no precedent by which we can refuse to give him a pair of roller skates—"
6th Santa Claus: And a bicycle—
7th Santa Claus: And a book—
8th Santa Claus: And a train that runs when you wind it up.

The Chief Santa Claus then announced that "we are con-fronted by a most unfortunate situation. We are divided four to four."

The first Santa Claus responded that it would appear to rest upon the Honorable Chief Santa Claus, to cast the deciding vote.

Chief Santa Claus: But, gentlemen, there lies the difficulty.
     I feel that under the long established practice of this body I am debarred from taking part in the decision. You see, I cannot have a disinterested opinion. I once was a boy myself!
Chorus of four on right: No decision.
Chorus of four on left: No decision.
Chief Santa Claus: No decision.

Although the Gridiron Club was a little rough on the Su-preme Court in this skit, and in some others during the period of Roosevelt's controversy with it, with one exception there never was any indication that any of the members of the Court, most of whom attended every dinner, bore any resentment—and certainly not Chief Justice Hughes.

Nineteen thirty-six was the year of the celebrated *Literary Digest* poll which initiated the development of that American phenomenon, the pollsters, predicting unqualifiedly that Governor Landon would win the election. That, and the more accurate prediction without a poll of Postmaster General Farley (also chairman of the Democratic National Committee), led to a skit in which the prophet Isaiah conferred with a group of other prophets.

Balaam prophesied that in his second term President Roosevelt would organize the government along the lines of economy, and Isaiah dismissed him immediately with the others, saying, "You're a bum prophet."

Various others made forecasts, and "Senator George Moses" announced to the group that since he had prophesied that Frank Knox would win the Republican nomination, and that he [Moses] would win the New Hampshire senatorship, he had quit the prophecy business.

They were about to elect Isaiah president of the Prophets Union when an editor arrived on the scene and said he claimed it.

"I'm the editor of the *Literary Digest*," he declared, but Moses responded, "You're not a prophet. You're the other Republican!"

Then a character representing Jim Farley came on the stage and announced that he was the only major prophet from then on.

"All of the rest of you," he said, "can go back to the minor league."

"Oh yeah?" retorted Isaiah. "So you think you're a prophet! Well you can't even qualify for this union. You didn't do any prophesying—all you did was count the names on the payroll!"

The Republican skit—one of Walker Buel's greatest—was based on the theme of the Gridiron hillbillies. Two of the principal characters were William Allen White, editor of the *Emporia Gazette* in Kansas, and Henry Allen of Wichita, both of whom had been strong supporters of Governor Landon.

To the tune of "Red River Valley," White sang:

From my home, far, too far I have wandered;
Now in Salt River Valley's my fate.
O I wish I'd remained in Emporia,
In a typical prairie state!

I got lost in the bright lights of Broadway,
In a fog over Pittsburgh I've been;
I saw all the wrong people in Jersey,
And I thought that our Alfred would win!

Take me back to my home on the prairie;
That's the country that I know the best.
O what is the matter with Kansas?
It's gone plumb to hell with the rest!

"John Hamilton," chairman of the Republican National Committee, commented, "If William Allen White's going back to Emporia and Henry Allen back to Wichita, who's going to furnish the wrong advice in the next campaign?"

"Gifford Pinchot" wanted the Republican party to get rid of its concentrated wealth. White said they had already done it—"Haven't you heard about the deficit?" Then he capered about singing to the tune of "The Farmer in the Dell":

The party's in the red, the party's in the red;
Go and tell the du Ponts, the party's in the red!

Two Senators, "Wallace H. White, Jr." of Maine and "Warren Austin" of Vermont, arrived and Austin sang, to the "Stein Song":

Give a cheer for dear old Maine,
Shout for Vermont as well,
They are GOP once again—
Republicans stand up and yell!

"Senator White" told "Governor Landon" that they had everything arranged for the comeback of the Republican party, and that he must immediately "move up where his real, truest and most loyal friends cast the heaviest vote for him!"

Landon: You mean I must move to Maine or Vermont?
Senator White: No, to Dutchess County, New York! [Roosevelt's home county, which had gone to Landon.]
Hamilton: We'll plant Dutchess County with sunflowers and wait for 1940!

And then, in a warm and touching tribute to Governor Landon, who was loved by all the newspapermen who had been on his train—although many of them probably voted for Roosevelt—the Gridiron chorus, led by George Myers, sang a new version of "Secrets" directly to the governor at the head table.

A sunflower climbed to your window,
And summoned you forth one day;
A sunflower blossomed in Kansas
And it called you far away.
So we all wore the badge of the sunflow'r,
With its content of gold not depressed;
And we followed from ocean to ocean,
'Till the sun set in the west—
O sunflower, we will remember!
O Suzanna will still be a tune!
For the sunflow'r which fades in November—
May bloom in another June!

In introducing the governor, President Gableman said that it "certainly must make us all swell with pride to know that here in the United States, if no where else in the world, the victor and vanquished of a national campaign accept without question the verdict of their fellow-countrymen, and once the battle is over, join hands in a common effort to carry the country forward to better things. . . .

"The appearance here tonight of the Governor of Kansas to bare his breast as does the President of the United States to the darts of the Gridiron Club, is outstanding evidence of the good sportsmanship that prevails throughout America."

Landon's response was equally as warm and gracious, beginning with his opening line, "The kindly welcome you have given me tonight has warmed my heart as Maine and Vermont did."

"Today, at lunch, Jim Wright asked now how the fishing was in Florida. I told him that it wasn't bad, but the fish were like the votes, I didn't get enough of them.

"I am delighted to be with you. At first, I was a bit surprised that you picked Christmas week for a famed Gridiron dinner.

"Then, I realized that this is the season we devote to the honoring of Santa Claus. So, it occurred to me, that perhaps you were honoring Santa Claus in our good American personification of Santa Claus, our chief distinguished guest.

"Now, I'm going to say it before he does, even if he didn't wear the traditional Santa Claus whiskers in the campaign, the people recognized him on November third.

"When I told a friend back home I was going to the Gridiron dinner, he replied, 'You certainly are a glutton for punishment.'

"I must confess, I'm disappointed up to the present. Your skits and songs thus far have been brilliant and clever, but the burning doesn't compare to the last four months.

"I came tonight, first to renew many of the fine friendships I made during the campaign. But, in perfect frankness, I came for another reason too. I felt it the American way to show the world that in our Democracy the principal contenders in a campaign can sit down together at the same table in the spirit of fun.

"Here, opponents break bread together, instead of breaking each other's neck. A very different situation from what we see in so many foreign countries."

He paid tribute to the Gridiron Club and said that the country gained by its activities, "and a more friendly rivalry develops when we meet those with whose opinions we differ."

The club had been reviewing the campaign a bit in its skits, Landon said, and he wanted to do some reviewing himself. If he weren't hampered by a devotion to the principle that a campaign pledge is sacred, he would propose right now a constitutional amendment, he said, that would turn over the running of the government to the Gridiron Club.

"What a cockeyed administration that would be. And I wonder if our critics would be quite so free and easy with their typewriters if they had the responsibility."

He said that a friend of his had written him recently that he doubted if his political experience had prepared him for the result of this election, and that he replied that his friend "didn't know us Jayhawkers. If there is one state that prepares a man for anything, it is Kansas.

"The Kansas tornado is an old story. But let me tell you of one.

"It swept away first the barn, then the out buildings. Then it picked up the dwelling and scattered it all over the landscape. As the funnel-shaped cloud went twisting its way out of sight, leaving nothing but splinters behind, the wife came to, to find her husband laughing. She angrily asked him, 'What are you laughing at, you darned old fool?' And the husband replied, 'The completeness of it.'

"The completeness of this election must bring to the administration a sobering responsibility. That should be true also of the opposition party. Just as competition is the life blood of business, so intelligent and constructive opposition is the heart beat of democracy. There should be no place for sniping, for mere captious criticism, but without opposition there cannot be true democracy.

"The opposition should guard against unreasoning criticism or dishonesty in attack. To serve democracy's end, and I might say also its own end, it should be fearless, plain spoken and intelligent, and insist on an accurate accounting of public funds. It should bring about a realistic understanding of an administration's proposals.

"While, of course, not the sole keeper of national liberties, it should always be on guard against any weakening of the foundation of representative government. In power, even with the best of intentions, it is easy, too easy, to move away from the landmarks of safety. Without making a fetish of tradition, democracy must be more careful than a monarchy. It is always the opposition's duty to fight to preserve the basic principles, the importance of which have been proved by the experience of all democracy.

"We cannot build either prosperity or government except on the basis of confidence and self-respect as a people.

"I came out of the campaign with many experiences and friendships that I shall always treasure. I see in this room, gentlemen of the press whom I really didn't know before, whose friendship and regard I hope I shall have to my dying day. I wish I had the time and the words to express how much our association in the past months has meant to me.

"Among all of these associations with newspaper men, one stands out. One publisher was outstanding. He was most unjustly criticized, but he was a great comfort to me, as well as to many others. That was the publisher of the dear old *Literary Digest*.

"The way the administration dodged on its future policies, just what the election decided, no one can be sure. But it did settle one thing. It is still necessary to check the *Literary Digest* polls."

"Mr. President," Landon said to Roosevelt, "I am delighted to see you back from your trip of peace to South America in such splendid health. Before taking my seat, I want you to know that there is one thing on which I think we can agree. We know the American people want peace.

"And no matter how much we may differ on policies, I believe in the old American tradition that politics ends at the water's edge. And to you, Sir, I pledge the utmost unity and cooperation in the difficult foreign situations confronting your administration. In all efforts to preserve peace in the world, there will be no party lines."[9]

A year later, Governor Landon and the White House released copies of two telegrams that had passed between them, in which the governor reminded President Roosevelt that a year before at the Gridiron dinner he had pledged "cooperation and support in the difficult foreign situations confronting your administration."

"That is a grand principle," his telegram continued, "and we must evidence our good faith in it. It means there must be no demagogic playing of politics at the expense of the country's unity in dangerous situations such as now confront us.

"Therefore, I want to renew my pledge, especially in view of the fact that so many members of Congress, of both parties, seem to have forgotten this basic principle of American politics and by their actions help create the impression on foreign nations that they do not trust your administration of foreign affairs. They would hamstring your conduct of extremely delicate foreign situations.

"These members are pursuing the same dangerous course followed by those members of the British Parliament who early in 1914 gave the impression that England either would not or could not fight under any circumstances.

"I congratulate you on your firm 'No' to the proposed legislation that would take away the power of Congress to declare war. You and I both know the American people want peace, but they want a peace that will enable us to maintain the respect of the other nations of the world."

Roosevelt's reply consisted of thanking Governor Landon "for the generous spirit of your telegram," which, he said, helped him "to meet the problems which confront our country in the field of foreign relations during these troublous times."

"The pledge," he wrote, "which you gave at the Gridiron dinner a year ago carried force because of the patriotic motive which prompted it. The renewal of that pledge not only strengthens the hand of government, but gives all of our citizens a good example."[10]

Two major music skits were focused directly on Roosevelt and the Democrats. The first was based on Richard Wagner's *Götterdämmerung* ("Twilight of the Gods"). The "gods" who were in twilight included Wotan Shouse, Brunnhilde Alice Roosevelt

Longworth, Siegfried Alfred E. Smith, Mime John J. Raskob, and assorted others, such as newsmen Mark Sullivan, Walter Lippmann, David Lawrence and Frank R. Kent. "Siegfried Smith" sang:

> He toined the tables on me,
> And now I'm washed up and through,
> He toined the tables on me—
> I can't believe that it's true.

"John W. Davis," 1924 Democratic Presidential candidate, reminded the group that "what has happened can happen again. Defeat comes to all men. The message I give Franklin is: 'What has happened to me can happen to him.'"

Of all the people who opposed President Roosevelt and his policies, one of the most irritating to him was Alice Roosevelt Longworth. Not only was she his cousin, but she had a capacity for coining phrases that was equally as good as his own. In this act she did not sing but was sung to by the chorus:

> She is more to be pitied than censured,
> She is more to be helped than despised,
> She is only a lassie who ventured,
> To write for the press, ill-advised,
> Do not scorn her with words fierce and bitter,
> Do not laugh at her shame and downfall,
> For a moment just stop and consider,
> That her cousin was the cause of it all!

The climax of the skit came when Raskob announced that "the man who tries to reach a third term with us around is going to have to pass through the *Magic Fire*."

"Fellow Jeffersonians, let's give him our theme song for 1940."

Then the chorus sang to music from *The Valkyries*:

> There'll be no third term
> There'll be no third term
> There'll be no third term—(repeated fourteen times!)

The Valkyries dashed on the stage and announced, "What cowards men are! Jump behind us on these horses and let's ride into the clouds of a brilliant political future for the enemies of Franklin D. Roosevelt. Perhaps it'll be in the next world, but let's go!"

The skit closed with the entire group singing a parody of "The Sidewalks of New York."

The closing skit immediately preceding President Roosevelt's speech was a musical extravaganza entitled "The Greater Ziegfeld or The World's Greatest Showman."

It was announced that the Gridiron Midnight Follies was a work of the Federal Theatre Project and that the author of the libretto was none other than Franklin D. Roosevelt. It consisted of little but a series of songs, the first of which was "My Man" sung by "Fannie Perkins Brice":

> He's cost us a lot, but there's
>   one thing that we've got—
> It's our Man!
> He's our Man!
> Cold and wet, deep in debt,
>   but all that we'll soon forget,
> With our Man!
> With our Man!
> He's there with the looks,
>   he's a hero out of books—
> Is our Man!
> Is our Man!

During the campaign, Roosevelt had declared, "I hate war." There was a "We Hate War" song; another one, which was a parody of "Look for the Silver Lining"; and several others, including "My Rambler Roosevelt."

> We call him Our Rambler Roosevelt,
> But where he's rambling to,
> Nobody knows!

The skit ended on a gracious and joyous note:

> From fair Niagara's fountains,
> To the far Rocky Mountains,
> They're winging, swingin' away.
> From the Swanee River to the home of the flivver,
> They're swingin' swingin' away.
> So everybody's happy,
> And everybody's O-kay,
> 'Cause you can't be blue,
> 'Cause you can't be blue,
> When the campaign's through,
> And you're swingin' the jinx away.

Since President Roosevelt had just returned from South America and there were numerous ambassadors of South American countries present at the dinner, he began responding to the toast with a paragraph in Spanish, in which he said he had made the great discovery that the overpowering influence of the Gridiron had not yet extended to the Southern Hemisphere.

"Our friends in our Sister Republics are handicapped by being limited to the reading of nothing but actual news. They lack the North American habit of interpreting news. Perhaps in the days to come you can offer your services."

Then, in English, he noted that this comment (which was perhaps not comprehensible to the non-Spanish-speaking members and guests) deserved everyone's serious consideration, "especially on an occasion like this which brings us together just before Christmas with larger grace and a more pervading spirit of good will than—shall we say—at the spring dinner when the Congress is in session."

At this point he turned to Governor Landon.

"I am delighted," he said, "that a fellow guest tonight is Governor Landon of Kansas. I felt it an honor to have him as an opponent. This morning we had a delightful talk about all kinds of things—international affairs, domestic problems and sport— fishing and shooting and the big outdoors. And may I say to him that his sense of sportsmanship is not confined to fishing and hunting, and that I appreciate his sportsmanship in the larger field."

Turning then to the skits, he professed to have "enjoyed every minute" of them, and then reverting to the newspapers, most of whom had opposed his reelection, he declared that "a number of us have found the various skits more factual than the writings of their journalistic authors during the recent campaign."

It was all done in good humor and with a smile, but nevertheless, Roosevelt was stating in jest a real complaint which he was never reluctant to reveal at Gridiron dinners.

He said from June to November he had become a more omnivorous reader of the papers than previously.

"In a great serial," he continued, "which ran for several months in the papers, one of the characters bore the name of Franklin D. Roosevelt. Whether this character was to be a hero or a villain I could not at first make out. But as that magnificent work of imagination developed, I decided that this character Roosevelt was a villain. He combined the worst features of Ivan the Terrible, Machiavelli, Judas Iscariot, Henry VIII, Charlotte Corday and Jesse James.

"He was engaged in a plot to wreck the American Constitution, to poison the Supreme Court, to demolish capitalism, to destroy old age security, to get us into war, and to assassinate all the men in the United States who had red hair or as newspaper publishers claimed the rank of Colonel*—in short, to blot from the face of the earth the United States as we have known it.

"I began to believe it myself. Didn't I read it in the columns of our great papers? These papers had been awarded prizes for their artistic makeup and sometimes even for their enterprise in ferreting out facts. Moreover, if the slightest doubt remained in the reader's mind, the most penetrating, permeating editorial intellect assured him that it was so.

"Yes, I began to believe it myself. One morning, about the middle of October, I became curious about this man Roosevelt and I went to a beautiful, old mirror of the early Federal period and took a careful look at him in the glass. He smiled. I remembered that one of the most damning indictments that had been brought against him was that selfsame smile. I smiled back. And after a careful examination I decided that all that this villain looked like to me was a man who wanted to be reelected President of the United States.

"He was reelected and the great 1936 campaign serial turned out to have a most surprising ending. On the morning of November fourth the editors decided that this villain was, after all, a reasonable person. He was deluged with editorial advice—suave advice, friendly advice, advice based on the apparent assumption that this man was really a reincarnation of a cross between Little Eva and Simple Simon.

"May I recommend this habit of standing in front of a mirror? It is a good habit. It restores perspective. It brings out all the blemishes one ought to know about.

"There was one other aspect of the campaign which was personally deflating to me—the newspaper poll. When I first entered politics there were no polls—we had only the prognostication of the political chairmen. Sometimes they were as right as Jim Farley and sometimes they were as wrong as John Hamilton. And by the way, here is a simple problem in mental arithmetic. If John Hamilton gets $25,000 a year for carrying Maine and Vermont, what should Jim Farley's salary be? . . .

"Yet as far as the American press is concerned, no one could admire it more than I. Its freedom, its technical facilities, its

---

*A reference to Col. Robert R. McCormick, publisher of the *Chicago Tribune*.

network of communications, its speed, its alertness and the plentitude of its coverage are unequaled in the world.

"Yet some people—mostly with indigestion or bad consciences—speak of the danger of the regimentation of our press. Let us analyze. Suppose the government of the United States were a dictatorship. Suppose the government required newspapers to purchase and print some of the canned editorial features dealing with national affairs that now fill our press! The outcries of editors present here tonight would be heard round the world! Gentlemen, it needs no government dictatorship to regiment the American press. Any regimenting of the American press which is present today or looms in the offing comes from the regimenting of it by the press itself.

"But the Gridiron Club is not regimented, and it brings to us all the saving graces of humor and perspective. It is good for me to be here. It is good, I think, for the Chief Justice to be here. It is good for Governor Landon to be here. It is good for Republicans and Democrats and Socialists and Communists to sit at these tables and laugh at themselves and at each other. The Gridiron Club offers twice a year the largest of mirrors for us all to look at ourselves in. As we think of those sections of the world in which fear, hatred and bitter political rivalries have great peoples within their grasp, who of us cannot feel a spirit of humble gratitude to Providence that our national destinies are emerging from the strains of recent times with our American tradition of tolerance and perspective unimpaired?"

XII

Franklin D. Roosevelt

1937-1938
The Supreme Court packing fight,
and white ties and tails

By early 1937 the controversy between President Roosevelt and the Supreme Court had reached a crisis. The Supreme Court, under Chief Justice Hughes, consisted of nine men, most of whom were over 70 years of age. The Court had declared unconstitutional several New Deal programs: the National Industrial Recovery Act, known as the NRA, the Agricultural Adjustment Act, the Railroad Retirement Act, and some lesser Administration measures.

President Roosevelt, after his overwhelming reelection to a second term, feeling that the Court might eventually nullify most of his programs, asked Congress to approve legislation which would have enabled him to appoint an additional six members to the Court, raising the number of justices to a maximum of fifteen.

This threw conservatives in Congress and around the country into consternation, and the President's opponents immediately denounced the proposal as a "Supreme Court–packing" bill. This bill became the most controversial proposal in Roosevelt's second term, and eventually led to a humiliating defeat for him.

It was against this background that the spring dinner of the

Gridiron Club was held on April 10, with both President Roosevelt and Chief Justice Hughes as guests.

It is hardly likely that this was one of the dinners which the President enjoyed most. Although the beginning of World War II was two years away, Adolph Hitler was already dancing his jig of triumph on the prostrate bodies of the leaders of several European states. And protocol, or some other arcane Washington thinking, required that Hitler's ambassador be seated at the President's right. Furthermore, the Japanese ambassador was seated next to Vice President Garner.

G. Gould Lincoln, chief political analyst of the *Washington Star*, not one of the President's favorite newspapers, was president of the Gridiron Club. To make matters still worse, the dinner was held on the night before Chief Justice Hughes' seventy-fifth birthday. At one point in the dinner the Gridiron chorus, joined by nearly everybody present, sang "Happy Birthday" to the Chief Justice, and the entire aggregation of people rose in a prolonged standing ovation, which could hardly have been interpreted by the President as anything other than a tribute to the Court which he was trying to reorganize.

Finally, the opposition speaker was Myron Taylor, chairman of the board of U.S. Steel, and the most important music skit of the dinner, presented immediately before the President himself was called upon to speak, was a Supreme Court skit, which was not complimentary to Roosevelt's "court-packing" plans.

President Roosevelt used the "fireside chat" by radio to the American people as a major tool of Presidential leadership, and a very effective tool it was. So the Gridiron Club put on a scene in the "modest suburban home of a Prince of Privilege," where the neighboring Economic Royalists were gathering for a cozy family evening by the fireplace, to listen to a fireside chat by the President of the United States.

The guests arrived: Mr. and Mrs. Bank President, Mr. and Mrs. Chamber of Commerce, Mr. and Mrs. Railroad Executive, Mr. and Mrs. Bar Association, and Mr. and Mrs. Wall Street.

"Lock the doors," said the butler, "and get out the liquor. They're all here." Whereupon the host announced that he had a "glorious surprise—listening to the President!" A soloist crooned:

Beside an open fireplace,
    We sit and wait for you.

We'd like to hear Paul Whiteman's band,
  And Major Bowes, and Sally Rand.
We really hate to miss the Gumps,
  But what else can we do;
There's nothing on the air tonight,
  But fireside chat—and you!

Then the host announced that everybody should be quiet and the radio would be turned on so that "we may not miss those first two words, 'My Friends.'"

The radio poured forth a broadcast of incomprehensible gibberish, but afterward host and guests alike commented on the "lovely, lovely voice." Then the skit closed with a soloist singing, to the tune of "My Heart at Thy Sweet Voice":

Oh why should people care
What platforms may declare?
Repeal the platform pledges,
O forget all that stuff,
Thy sweet voice is enough!

President Roosevelt had appointed Joseph E. Davies as ambassador to the Soviet Union, and the Gridiron Club put on a Russian ballet and pantomime on the life and works of Joseph E. Davies. With all in ballerina costumes, they danced about the stage, and the skit ended in a revel in Red Square.

The reaction of some of the Democratic leaders to the constant flow of legislative proposals from the White House was satirized in a duet to the tune of "I'd Like To Be in Texas," between Senator "Tom Connally" and Representative "Sam Rayburn" both of Texas, one verse of which ran:

Since the President informed us
What is in the White House bill,
I'd rather be in Texas
Than be here upon the Hill.

Although the personal relationships between Myron C. Taylor and President Roosevelt were friendly and gracious, Taylor, the opposition speaker nevertheless represented American business, which was a constant target and whipping boy of the Roosevelt administration.

When Taylor was introduced, he spoke of the honor of "being asked to speak at a Gridiron dinner in the presence of so distinguished a company. I must say," he declared, "I hesitated a few days before deciding to put myself at the mercy of the press, but I concluded that I had tried nearly all the thrills in life and I would add one more great experience."

Remarking that he couldn't "turn this only appearance of mine altogether to the lighter aspect of things," he then launched into a brief but serious speech, in which he wondered whether some of the standards which had made America great were not being undermined. He noted that there is "hardly a movement that one can make today in life in this country that is not in some respect affected or controlled by law."

This had been a cumulative growth through the years, he said, and told how as a young lawyer, somewhat confused by the immense number of laws and decisions, he had asked a great judge, "What is the law anyway?" and the judge replied, "Don't be disturbed, my son. The law is the last guess of the court of appeals!"

Proclaiming that it was "not to the permanent advantage of business to deceive anyone," and that no company which tried to could long prosper, he said that "today no man can honestly manage a business, be it large or small, without the fear that he is violating at least technically some law." And advice of counsel didn't help too much, he went on, because so many of the laws could be interpreted in any one of several ways.

Nor did coming to Washington help, because "one hardly knows where in Washington to find an officer of the government who will advise one in advance whether proposed action is permissible.

"Industry is a most potent instrument in human or industrial relations. It operates as a great factor for social progress in the degree that it serves the nation by providing and transporting an adequate supply of needed commodities at a price within the range of the purchasing power of the consumers, and at the same time seeks to pay adequate returns both to those who own the plants and their equipment and to those who work and make use of those facilities. There is, therefore, no real conflict in interest between these parties. A conflict can, of course, be created, but when that happens everybody loses. . . .

"Probably as long as human nature remains unchanged, no one is going to be wholly satisfied with the value put upon his services by somebody else. And so in keeping with this general formula, if we are to grow in happiness and in general well-being in the community, there must be established a more understanding and tolerant and sympathetic relationship between all classes of men and women."

This kind of comment seemed to be aimed directly at the President, who had not hesitated to accept the political advantage of espousing the cause of workers and "the forgotten men" against business and "the economic royalists."

"The weakest link," Taylor went on, "in the chain of human events through the centuries has generally been the defects of human nature itself. The defects in human nature based on greed and anger and vanity have leveled to the very dust most of our great civilizations of the past. Through the years of my own experience, I have achieved the greatest results, small though they be, and have attained the greatest happiness, and great it has been, from considering the point of view of others and from fairly reconciling my own with theirs. Rarely have I found a man who had not some, and often many, good reasons for his own point of view, even though in the beginning to me it appeared wrong."

Then he pleaded for better understanding of one another's problems and, in essence, without using Lincoln's phrase, for charity toward all.

While thus expressing his rather dim view of some of the attitudes of the Roosevelt administration, Taylor nevertheless closed on a gracious note to the President.

"In a world that in many quarters is confused, angry and militant, the most outstanding contribution to peace and to understanding between nations in recent years has been that extraordinary visit of our great President and his distinguished secretary of state to the republics of South America a few months ago. That illustrates, as nothing else has done in recent times, what I have been trying to say about the importance of direct understanding, of direct negotiation. . . .

"For the permanent peaceful solution of all great problems, there must be a meeting of minds and an honest attempt to try to understand the objectives of the other side. Only by this frank method of approach can our problems be solved on a national scale, free of class distinction.

"There is in this room a cross section that is representative of the power, influence and responsibility in American affairs as nowhere else in the world today. What then will we do with this power, and, more important still, with this responsibility?

"Mr. President, I am sure we here are all men of good will as you are, and by working together we can solve our difficulties so far as human hands and the will to do so can solve the problems of the moving world in which we live. We feel our and your very great responsibility, and we are prepared to serve."[1]

The mid-thirties was the period of sit-down strikes, and other skits at that dinner parodied the Republican party capturing the government by a sit-down strike and John L. Lewis taking over the Presidency, but the major skit of the evening, and the most biting one, was the Supreme Court act.

The stage was set with a long, elevated Supreme Court bench, behind which the chief justice and fourteen other justices stood, all made up to resemble Casper Milquetoast. The announcer declared that the Gridiron Club was taking its guests a few years into the future and giving them "a glimpse of what the Supreme Court may be *(long pause)*, and maybe not!"

One justice commented that "this Court is far too crowded," and another answered, "What do you expect in a packed Court—a private room and bath?"

The chief justice announced that the Court was required "to open its proceedings with choral obeisance to the White House. Let us salute!" And they sang in chorus the Gridiron version of "Nobody Knows the Trouble I've Seen."

> Nobody knows the opinions I sign,
> Nobody knows but Franklin,
> Nobody knows the opinions I sign,
> Glory, Hallelujah!
> Sometimes I take them all on trust,
> Oh, Yes, Lord!
> 'Cause mostly they are all marked *"MUST,"*
> Oh, Yes, Lord!
> If you should sign before I do,
> Oh, Yes, Lord!
> Just leave a place—
> I'll sign them too,
> Oh, Yes, Lord!
>
> Oh, nobody knows the opinions I sign,
> Nobody knows but Franklin,
> Nobody knows but that pen of mine,
> Glory, Mr. Roosevelt!

The "Court" then went through the procedure of admitting lawyers to practice, and it developed that all those contributing $1,000 or more to the last Democratic campaign could hand up their credentials and be admitted, while those contributing less could take their cases to the Circuit Court of Appeals.

Then they went into session, and at first declared unconstitutional a law passed by Congress that "flowers that used to bloom in the spring shall hereafter bloom in the winter." An impersonator of Attorney General Cummings protested, "But you don't understand. This bill is on the President's *must* list."

"Oh," said the "chief justice," "that's different! Why didn't you say so in the first place? All in favor of holding this act constitutional say 'Aye.'"

And the entire Court yelled "Aye!"

Notified that a Presidential message had just come to Congress on the subject of the Court, a justice soloist, to the tune of "It's De-Lovely," sang:

> The Court is young, its docket clear,
> But if you want our opinion, here,
> It's delib'rate, it's deceptive, it's de-lousy!
> I understand the reason why—
> You're all against it, 'cause so am I,
> It's delib'rate, it's deceptive, it's de-lousy!
> You can tell at a glance,
> What this Court will decide in advance,
> You can hear dear Brother Franklin murmuring low—
> "Let yourself go!"
> So if we're pressed to state our view,
> We hold our noses and say to you—
> It's delib'rate, it's deceptive,
> It's deplorable, it's delirious,
> It's *de novo*, it's delimit,
> It's debunk, it's de-lousy!

The "Court session" ended with the chief justice ordering all the other justices to get out the rubber stamps, and while they sat on the bench stamping papers, a justice soloist sang:

> One, two, better get through,
> Put on our coat and hat,
> We do the job like that,
> When we're working for you.
> Three, four, car's at the door,
> Hurry, for Heaven's sake,
> We know what stand to take,
> When we're working for you.
> Five, six, the law does tricks,
> When it harkens to your charms.
> Seven, eight, without debate,
> As we toss them to your arms.
> Nine, ten, stamp 'em again.

Gee, but we get a thrill,
In our judicial mill,
When we're working for you.

The President, in his speech immediately following this skit, made no reference to it, and in general made probably his most whimsical and conciliatory Gridiron speech. However, he did use the Myron Taylor speech to lead him into a discussion of culture, play and recreation.

"When I learned," President Roosevelt said, "that my old friend Myron Taylor was to speak at the Gridiron dinner tonight, I realized, in the first place, that because he and I agree on so many factors and fundamentals in our Governmental, social and economic problems he had not been invited in the usual sense, that he was to speak for the opposition, and I for the Government. He was invited, I assumed, and since hearing him I know, to speak as a representative, successful, educated and thoughtful American. And I am grateful to him for his fine statement of American ideals.

"But in thinking about him I said to myself, 'What is the first thing that comes into my head?' It is not Myron Taylor, the distinguished lawyer of New York; it is not Myron Taylor, the chairman of the board of the United States Steel Corporation; it is the Myron Taylor that I know best—the Myron Taylor who says to me, whenever he sees me, 'I am just waiting for the chance to take my holiday, to go back to Florence; I am just waiting for the chance to spend more time on my avocations and less time on my vocations.' And that is the kind of thing that I wish we did more of in the United States."

Pointing out that in the early days there was little opportunity for culture, recreation or the arts because of the rigors of breaking the wilderness and creating a country, Roosevelt traced the development of such activities. With the formation of the nation, he said, more attention was given to these things. He told how Jefferson had designed Monticello and the University of Virginia, how Franklin had delved into philosophy and science, and how Andrew Jackson, "when not unduly occupied by the Bank of the United States and the Supreme Court, turned his hand to horseracing." In a like manner he continued, going down through the years to "Mr. Mellon's great National Gallery of Art, the museums, the libraries, the universities, and indeed the whole range of the culture of today."

In other countries, he noted, the same cultural avocations

were widespread and not limited to those in high places or with large private means. People collect all sorts of things, "some even postage stamps," he commented, being himself a major collector in that field.

This led Roosevelt to a discussion of avocations and an opportunity for a gibe at his political opponents. "For example," he said, "at small cost and no great expenditure of effort, one might be active in Republican politics. That would be an avocation!"

"I understand that members of the Gridiron Club, when not rehearsing, find *their* avocation in writing occasional articles for the newspapers.

"There are college chemists who like to appear as witnesses before judiciary committees. There was a recent Vice President of the United States who composed music for the violin and fiddled it, and there is a current Vice President whose avocation—rare in politics—is to make no speeches. There is a member of the Supreme Court whose avocation is making speeches at fraternity banquets.

"For myself, I still hope to find time to read the *Washington Evening Star,* to which the chairman of this dinner is a distinguished contributor. God knows, reading the *Star* would have to be an avocation; it would almost be a life work—on a par with delving into the Mayan civilization, becoming a good chess player, or translating *Plutarch's Lives.* I have always wondered what one would find on page 148 of the *Star,* but I never got further than the editorial page, where its reckless expressions of opinion incite and inflame the populace. [The *Star* at that time—not so today—was the butt of many jokes in Washington about the blandness of its editorials, one being that it never took a really strong position on any subject other than "Save the Dogwood."]

"I fear that with this background Dictator Gould Lincoln will find it hard to restrain his iron impulses in directing the affairs of the Gridiron Club. Members, guard well your liberties against executive usurpation. Do not hitch your Gridiron horse and buggy to the *Star.*

"I am glad to see that the Gridiron Club is becoming more and more modern in its treatment of public questions. At one of your recent dinners, there was a skit about Noah's Ark. Tonight we have progressed as far as the Pharaohs and even presented the Imperial Russian ballet. You have caught up to within twenty years of today.

"The Gridiron Club, I think, needs more of the spirit of youth. You must catch your hobbies earlier. We have been shown very strikingly tonight that it takes hard work to start out at—well, forty-five—and hope to be a ballerina as a side issue to writing for the *New York Times*. [This was a reference to Lewis Wood, who had been the leading ballerina in the Russian ballet skit.] Some of our hosts have 'lovely, lovely voices.' We knew they could sing, we knew they could talk—now we know they can dance. Art for Art's sake is all very well, but future Gridiron audiences are going to suggest that the members of the ballet visit the barber before any future performance.

"And so I say to you of the Gridiron Club, razor or no razor, more power to you, to your voices and your legs.

"I announce as a fundamental policy of this administration that we seek more leisure, leisure for the press, leisure for the government—avocations for the Congress and for the judiciary—more time for the President to fish. In the times of our leisure when work-a-day cares are banished, we can perhaps smile a little more and find a greater refreshment for our souls. With the wise philosopher let us seek that little leisure in which we may not only grow in the sun, but also grow more ripe and mellow in the shade time of our lives."[2]

• • •

Whatever economic euphoria had developed as a result of the widespread legislation of President Roosevelt's first term had disappeared by December 1937, and the country was sinking back into a marked recession from conditions that had existed the year before.

President Roosevelt had been unable to get his court-packing bill through Congress, but he had had his first chance to appoint a Supreme Court justice. He chose Senator Hugo L. Black of Alabama. Black was promptly confirmed because of senatorial courtesy, even though his judicial experience consisted solely of a brief period as a young man on an Alabama municipal court, and investigative reporters had dug up the fact that he had once been a member of the Ku Klux Klan.

Fiorello LaGuardia, a Republican, had been reelected mayor of New York on a fusion ticket, and in Congress, despite President Roosevelt's tremendous majority of a year before and his increased Democratic majorities in both Houses, there was considerable grumbling. The first term honeymoon was over.

In this atmosphere, Gould Lincoln opened the December

eleventh dinner with the announcement that "our watchword tonight is cooperation—even if it must be compulsory."

"Out of a welter of discordant notes," he said, "arises the voice of business, chanting a recessional, 'Give us back, Oh Lord, our profits to keep.'

"On Capitol Hill the quality of congressional courtesy has become strained—although senatorial courtesy has been unrestrained.

"Even among the lowly GOP all has been topsy turvy. These old friends seem inclined to fall between those twins of political perdition, fusion and confusion."

But he noted that underlying conditions were not really that unstable.

"There is that warm feeling which exists," he said, "between William Green and John L. Lewis—very warm at times. . . . There is the cordial regard which Mr. Gay, president of the Stock Exchange, has for Mr. Douglas, chairman of the Securities and Exchange Commission. And finally we come to the splendid manner in which the economic royalists continue to absorb some of our best minds—the last of a long line, Charlie Michelson, and do I hear a bid, Jim Farley. We wonder whether economic royalists invariably swallow their invaders."

The dinner opened with a song about the merry-go-round breaking down.

> Why do all New Dealers feel so very blue,
> Talk of cutting taxes to pull business through?
> A merry-go-round was theirs
> And business paid the fares,
> We all went 'round and 'round and 'round
> When hark! A sound!!!
>
> O the merry-go-round broke down,
>
> The New Deal hit the ground;
> And business men went broke again.
>
> The budget's upward bound,
> And Franklin said, "Is my face red?"
> While the merry-go-round went um-pah-pah, um-pah-pah,
> Um-pah, um-pah, um-pah-pah!
> *The merry-go-round broke down!*

Following its custom of satirizing itself and its profession, the Club put on a skit entitled "The Seven Pillars of Wisdom." The "Pillars" were Heywood Broun, Walter Lippmann, General

Hugh Johnson, Westbrook Pegler, David Lawrence, Mark Sullivan (played by himself), and Dorothy Thompson.

As the actors depicting each proclaimed their devotion to various ideas and individuals, Pegler announced that he didn't like whatever his colleagues did like, and gave a Bronx cheer.

After Miss Thompson: "I don't like women."

After Lippmann: "I don't like war."

And then, when Lippmann pointed out that Democracy itself was not solely a product of peace, Pegler shouted, "I don't like peace."

Without mentioning Justice Black's name, the Gridiron Club had a lot of fun by announcing that "at this time we transport our guests to the center of the Southern nightshirt trade. A famous fraternal organization is having a special meeting. One of its most distinguished members is returning from the North to report on what's going on there. So all aboard for Birmingham, Alabama!

> When the midnight choo-choo leaves for Alabam',
> I'll be right there,
> I've got my fare.
> When I see those hooded heroes of the Klan,
> I'll grab them by the collar,
> And I'll holler:
> "Alabam'! Alabam'!"
> That's where you stop the train,
> That brings me back again
> Down home where I gained fame,
> Back where Birmingham, am,
> I will be right there with bells,
> When that old Klanductor yells,
> "All aboard! All aboard! All aboard for Alabam'!"

The Imperial Wizard and all the Kleagles, dressed in Ku Klux robes and hoods, went on to conduct their "Klavern," until finally the Wizard announced that "as we all know, since becoming famous our friend dropped the Klan. He has had nothing whatever to do with it since that time. He abandoned it. He completely discontinued any association with the organization. He has never resumed it and never expects to do so."

But a member yelled, "Here he comes now!" And all present shouted the words which open every session of the Supreme Court: "Oyez, oyez, oyez!"

Then the Klansman responded, "I never have considered

and I do not now consider the unsolicited card given me as a membership of any kind in the Ku Klux Klan. I never used it. I did not even keep it. If I ever had it, I don't know where it is. If I know where it is, I won't tell. The fact is I buried it—down near the Lincoln Memorial. My passport's in the cold, cold ground."

The skit ended with a new version of 'K - K - K - Katy."

> K-K-K-Klansman,
> Beautiful Klansman,
> You're the same old K-K-K-Klux I knew before,
> When the m-m-m-moon shines,
> Over the White House,
> We'll be watching at the K-K-K-Kourthouse door!

Roosevelt definitely didn't like this skit, but he restrained himself at the dinner and let his dislike be known through Steve Early.[3]

The Duke of Windsor, who was in the United States at the time, had been invited to this dinner but had declined. Nevertheless, the club, in what it described as a "Flight of Fancy," had a skit taking a swipe at the President, in which the well-known comedian "Stepin Fetchit" welcomed to his mountain cabin an unidentified duke, who arrived with a bag covered with hotel stickers, mostly from Monte Carlo. "You've been to all de countries, ah guess," said Stepin Fetchit, to which the Duke responded, "All but England—and Baltimore."

Fetchit: What you-all doin' up heah, man?

Duke: I am studying housing conditions and wages and hours. What's the condition of your wages, my good man?

Fetchit: Ah don' git no wages, no mo'.

Duke: What! No wages?

Fetchit: No, sah. Ah's been promoted, ah has. Ah gits an allowance from de gov'ment.

Duke: My word! I must make a note. And how about your hours of labor?

Fetchit: Labor! Ha, ha, man, you is behin' de times. Ah doan work no hours, no mo', no time—no sah! I'se on de no-hour day and de no-day week now.

Duke: My word!

Fetchit: Yes, sah, dat's one of de President's latest inventions. De President he issues a procumation and he 'bolish all unemployment by 'stablishing de no-hour day.

The Republican skit was cast on a desert island, where "the long-lost crew of the good ship GOP, which foundered in the New Deal hurricane had been discovered." The crew was satirized in a parody on "Sailing":

> Drifting, drifting, over the open sea,
> We went aground when people found
> We had no policy.
> Shipwrecked, shipwrecked, on a desert isle are we;
> O who will take us home
> And save the GOP?

To the tune of "Harbor Lights," characters representing Herbert Hoover and Alfred M. Landon, sang:

> Where are the harbor lights
> Which used to guide the Grand Old Party?
> Which on election nights
> Shone on to victory.

> But now election nights
> Are filled with sorrow and disaster;
> Where are the harbor lights
> To guide the GOP?

In another duet to the tune of "Why Do I Dream Those Dreams," impersonators of Mayor LaGuardia and Thomas E. Dewey both dreamed of the White House. LaGuardia sang:

> I see the White House just at eight,
> The table where they dine in state,
> Spaghetti on the White House plate—
>   Why do I dream these dreams?

And Dewey:

> I see the White House just at eight,
> I see a large-sized company;
> I see them shaking hands with me—
>   Why do I dream those dreams?

And in another stanza, Dewey, who had first come to national notice as the crime-busting district attorney of New York City sang:

> To others, Sir, my thanks all go,
> The folks who pulled me through, you know,
> Were "Lucky Lu" and "Cokey Flo"—
>   Why do I dream those dreams?

The Republican speaker was introduced by Gould Lincoln as "a political paradox—New Dealer, Socialist, Laborite and Republican all in one—Mayor F. H. LaGuardia of New York City."

No record of his speech exists in Gridiron files, but Harold Ickes, in his *Secret Diary*,[4] gave this account of it:

"Mayor LaGuardia, who was the other guest speaker in addition to the President, was the highlight of the evening. If he hadn't done particularly well in New York, he more than made up for it last night before the Gridiron Club. He spoke without notes but he was sparkling and witty. He kept everyone laughing. And yet back of his wit were many barbs. He kidded the President and he especially kidded Jim Farley and Senator Wagner in connection with the New York mayoralty fight. He addressed President Roosevelt at the outset as 'Comrade Roosevelt.' He spoke of the election as of a football game. Jim Farley, he said, was calling the signals for the Tammany team. This team was in desperate straits and he decided to try a forward pass. Jim hurled the ball straight down the field and it fell into the arms of Harold Ickes 'who was playing on my team' and 'Harold made a touchdown.' He made one good hit at the expense of the President when he said that he had the best 'necking voice' in the world. All the President had to do was to sit down by his fireside and neck over the radio. He remarked that he knew what necking meant and how anxious, after a session of necking, a man frequently was for a month or so until he was sure that nothing had happened. Then he related how, toward the end of the game when things were going badly with the Tammany team, Farley, in desperation, made an appeal to the President to get into the game and save it. Roosevelt told him just to get together and play the game and if Jim's team won he, Roosevelt, would lead the cheering.

"It really was a good speech, done in such good temper that no one could possibly be offended."

A "Lost Horizon" was the setting for another satire, this time on Roosevelt, who had recently been reported in the press to have had a toothache. The Grand Llama was seated on his throne in Tibet, when a priest informed him that there was a traveler desiring an audience and bearing a sacred relic, "the tooth of one of the great rulers of his country."

"He claims for it magic powers beyond belief," said the priest. "He says this sacred tooth is feared by all the unsanctified merchants of his own land. Many of them still bear its marks."

As long as he had the tooth, explained the traveler, Mr. Big smote his enemies until they were beaten and cowed. Then the sacred tooth was taken from him and at once he changed. He smiled upon his enemies, he invited them to his palace, he promised them a break.

"When Mr. Big had this tooth, he didn't spare the merchants. And could he bite! Now, no tooth, no bite."

The Grand Llama asked why this tooth was brought to him, and the traveler said, "I was afraid he might get it back and regain his magic powers."

In introducing another skit, a "Dialogue on Olympus," Walker S. Buel, the announcer, asked James Roosevelt to rise, and then he said, "We present a dialogue on Olympus between Jupiter and his little son, Mercury."

Jupiter asked what the state of affairs was on earth, and Mercury replied, "Nothing unusual; just wars, famines, revolutions, strikes, robberies, kidnappings, swindles, murders, mayhem, senators, floods, droughts, depressions—"

"Oh, yes," interrupted Jupiter, "those depressions—how do they stop them?"

Mercury: Every time they have a depression they get a New Deal. They soak the rich and give their money to the poor. That ends the depression.
Jupiter: Then, of course, the New Deal becomes permanent.
Mercury: No, the New Deal ends when the money gives out.

Told by Mercury that some Guild wanted to see him, Jupiter asked, "Is it the Newspaper Guild?" and Mercury responded, "What's a newspaper?"

Jupiter: Oh, I forgot, Mercury. The newspaper hasn't been created yet. I'm saving that up as a special torment for mortal rulers when the other torments give out.

The skit closed with Mercury reporting some fighting outside and Jupiter asked what it was all about.

Mercury: Well, some of the second-string gods think you shouldn't have a third term on Olympus.
Jupiter: Ho, ho, ho! They'd like to be up here themselves, wouldn't they?

Mercury: What are you going to do about it, Pop?
Jupiter: Son, you'll be surprised. Ho! Ho! Ho! Ho! Ho!

Cordell Hull was secretary of state, and the situation in
Europe was getting murkier as World War II approached. At a
time when Secretary Hull was having to meet renewing crises,
the principal song in one skit was a Gridiron version of "Mad
Dogs and Englishmen":

> Mad dogs and Cordell Hull go out in the midday sun;
> The Japanese don't care to,
> The Chinese wouldn't dare to,
> The Swedes and the Eskimos retire at the sound of a gun,
> They put their Scotch or Rye down, and lie down.
> In the Philippines there are peaceful scenes,
> When McNutt and Quezon snooze,
> In the Balkan States, all the Kings have dates,
> And the soldiers drink their booze;
> At twelve noon the Spaniards swoon,
> And no further fighting is done;
> But mad dogs and Cordell Hull go out in the midday sun!

Ignoring the Klan skit and taking his cue from the one on the
sacred tooth, President Roosevelt replied in his speech in the
spirit of the evening.

"Many of you who are here tonight have visualized the
mild-mannered old gentleman who now addresses you as the
fanged wolf to whom little red riding hood said, 'What big teeth
you have.' They forget, I think, the other moral of that childhood
tale: that if little red riding hood had not been an innocent little
idiot she would not have gotten into trouble with the wolf—for
the wolf was not a wolf at all, but only a kind police dog who was
trying to protect his master's house. And be it remembered that
the house did not belong either to little red riding hood or to the
police dog.

"This police dog did not go South to learn about teeth from
barracudas and sharks. But he obtained special training for the
Gridiron dinner by observing the sharp pointed sword which
decorates the nose of the sailfish. I, therefore, feel completely at
home tonight.

"The skit which we have seen which was called 'The Lost
Horizon' might have been called 'The Lost Tooth.' Nothing
arouses greater mirth on the part of the spectator than a
toothache, provided it is not his toothache. The immense satis-

faction with which columnists, cartoonists and editorial writers greeted a recent toothache—not their's, understand—was not without interest and even instruction for the victim. It made me think of what a member of the staff once said when he heard that Charles Chapin, the famous City Editor of the *Evening World* was ill—'Nothing trivial, I hope.'

"Even the Gridiron Club, proud of its subtle wit, has changed from gentle humor to dental humor. It was a good skit—but it was also a good toothache."

Then, turning to a nudist foreign affairs skit, Roosevelt remarked to the club that if some of its members had assumed "the privilege in your interpretative writings of calling every Progressive and every liberal Democrat a 'communist,' it is completely fair for me to announce to the world that the Gridiron Club of Washington, D.C., has gone for 'nudism.' You have exhibited the secretary of state without his pants. You have shown the British foreign minister without his pants. I can only assure you that neither of them would be in their respective cabinets if their legs looked like Gridiron Club legs."

Then he continued, "International affairs, Lord only knows, are bad enough—an 'ism' here and another 'ism' there—without you people having to drag 'nudism' into the picture. The only palliative to the nudist movement in international relations is that it is perhaps less dangerous than being all dressed up and no place to go."

There had been a song in the foreign affairs skit, a parody on "The Big Apple," to which the President referred in his speech by saying the Gridiron Club was on dangerous ground again when it used "the simile of the apple which Adam gave to Eve [*sic*], the apple of discord. There is too much apple-eating going on in the world anyway—not fine luscious, ripe Dutchess County apples, but applesauce made from apples with worms in them, and from unripe apples guaranteed to produce stomachaches. The world is getting more of this diet—breakfast, lunch and supper—than it ever had to swallow before. It would be ungracious of me to name the dieticians who serve it."

He observed that this diet of applesauce in some nations and "among small elements in our own nation," was producing "alarming symptoms." But he also said the overwhelming majority of people had become accustomed to declining it and filling their mental and physical needs with food of their own choosing.

"That was proven to be the case in November 1936," he said,

and he noted that he didn't think the health of the American family had declined much, if any, since that date.

Roosevelt then proceeded to pay a tribute to Governor Landon, who was present at the dinner, but in doing so he inserted a few gibes about the Republican party.

"And speaking of what up to November 1936 was known as the Republican party, I was very glad yesterday to welcome Governor Landon to the White House. He is a delightful gentleman and is much to be envied. He told me he was currying his own horse out in Kansas and I told him that I would honestly like to swap places with him—but that if he substituted for me in the White House he would have to take the toothache with it.

"Honestly, though, I am worried about the Republican party. Except for the dinner last spring, the Gridiron Club has been unable to produce a Republican politician speaker for three years.* Once they went to the Socialist party. Once they turned to the *Baltimore Sun*—a great metropolitan journal which belongs to its own party. Again they turned to the *Baltimore Sun*.

"And tonight, my fellow speaker has been my old friend, Major and Mayor LaGuardia. Surely you did not select him as a Republican speaker. Like the overwhelming majority of Democrats in this Congress and in this administration, he has been honored by being called a 'communist' and a 'red.' Like the overwhelming majority of Democrats in this Congress and in this administration, he has fought for the rights of the average citizen.

"The Mayor has been charged with being a friend of the New Deal. If that charge had not been made he would not have been elected.

"But, to return to the Republican party. One of the few remaining Republican governors officially asks that every present or former Republican leader be retired. Frankly, I should hate to see that happen. I believe in good will and I believe in good humor and the Republican leadership today is the greatest possible factor in maintaining good humor in the American people.

"And I should hate to see Arthur Vandenberg retired. Four years ago, I put that second cutaway suit—the one I wear to funerals—into mothballs for him. But I serve warning on him now that if he does not claim it on January 20, 1940, I am going to give it to the president of the Gridiron Club.

---

*Roosevelt was in error here; Landon had spoken in December 1936.

"And since the Gridiron Club has apparently given up the regular practice of having Republican speakers—for reasons into which we need inquire no further—I am hoping that you will go even more Democratic. I hope that at your next dinner and at intervals thereafter, I shall be invited as a guest who can sit here and have a corking good time without the menace of a speech hanging over me at the end of the evening. If the Gridiron Club will give me the pleasure of a night out, if it will accept me as a guest who does not have to speak (and I know those are two big 'ifs'), I shall make one other request—that as an old-fashioned hick Democrat from Dutchess County who is trying to make his dress suit last for another three years, I be permitted to come in a black tie and soft shirt instead of this traditional 'soup and nuts.'

"I have had a wonderful evening—I want to have other evenings even more wonderful.

"It could not be done in any other nation in the world, but it is wholly within the bounds of American propriety to take American public servants and American ideals for 'a ride' within these sacred walls. That is as it should be.

"Nevertheless, there are public ideals outside these walls where satire and ridicule and fun end. We have progressed far since the days when the favorite toast was 'My country, right or wrong.' Fair criticism of government, criticism of party, criticism of individuals—all are legitimate. That is as it should be. But ridicule of certain ideals at home and abroad is not legitimate.

"Somebody asked me the other day if I had any real hates and I told them that I had three. First, against the writer or the speaker who sneers at the objective of a more abundant life for the citizens of our land. Second, against the man who sneers at *all* who need and want jobs and tells them they could *find* work if they would only look for it. And third, against the man who pokes fun at or raises false bogies against the American efforts to encourage and seek peace among nations of the world.

"If privately and publicly, you exercise your constitutional right not to hitch your wagon to great ideals, don't cut the traces of your neighbor who is trying to hitch his wagon to a star. At the long last those who seek most highly gain most greatly. The people of the United States will see to that.[5]

This speech was characteristic of President Roosevelt, who struck back at Gridiron skits more strongly and skillfully than any other President has done, but who also praised the club perhaps more than any other President.

• • •

By the time of the April dinner in 1938, which was attended by both President Roosevelt and Vice President Garner, the rise of Hitler in Europe was becoming more and more menacing. He had unilaterally canceled the military clauses of the Versailles Treaty in 1935, and by the following year had militarized the Rhineland. His second overtly aggressive move, the *Anschluss* with Austria, occurred in March 1938, just a few weeks before this Gridiron dinner.

The situation was sufficiently tense that the German ambassador was not invited this time, and the ambassador of Japan, who was seated next to the President, was the only foreign ambassador present.

President Roosevelt arrived in his usual white tie, although he was continuing his efforts to get the dinner converted to black tie. Early in January, Byron Price, the president of the Gridiron Club, had been transferred to New York as executive news editor by the Associated Press. He resigned as president on January 8, and George R. Holmes, head of what was then the International News Service, was elected in his place.

Holmes was a strong Roosevelt supporter and one of the President's favorites in the press corps. Roosevelt wrote Holmes a letter on January 13, telling him that he was "thrilled that you have been elected president of the Gridiron Club, and if you start to get dignified with me, I will 'pull off' a personal skit on you!"

Then he took up the black tie issue.

"Your presidency will go down in history as the era when the President of the United States undertook to wear a black tie and dinner coat to a Gridiron Dinner—and got away with it."

Holmes's reply to the President was a classic:

> Thank you sincerely for your note. Regarding the tie, I should hate to see the new administration inaugurated on any such somber note as black suggests.
>
> To paraphrase very slightly a recent and memorable state paper: "I do not propose to let the people down."
>
> I am sure the President of the United States will not let the people down.
> Sincerely,
> George R. Holmes[6]

In the Gridiron file there is a "Memo for S.T.E. [Stephen T. Early]" initialed F.D.R. and dated January 17.

"Tell George that I loved his letter but it is the first time I have ever heard it suggested that 'the people' are dependent on 'white ties, top hats and tails.'"[7]

The April 9 dinner was opened with a parody on "Roll Along, Covered Wagon," by the Gridiron chorus:

Roll along, crazy world, roll along!
Upside down, dizzy planet, all gone wrong!
While the music of the spheres
Thunders, crashes in our ears
And the world joins the chorus of the song!
There's confusion that runs from pole to pole,
For the map's changing daily as we roll;
They are loony oversea,
But no loonier than we—
Roll along, crazy world, roll along!

In a slight change of order, President Holmes was inaugurated in a skit set in Vienna in the springtime, with a man and a girl sipping champagne in a restuarant. The Nazis came in with their "Heil, Hitlers," and announced that the "Furore" has taken Austria into the new Reich, and "you will now be permitted to vote on it."

Holmes interrupted with a demand to stop this travesty on popular government and was told by the Nazis that he misunderstood.

"This is a Gridiron Club election in the modern manner. Teller, what is the tally?"

The tally was reported, and the Nazi informed Holmes that he had been elected president of the Gridiron Club, whereupon all shouted, "Heil, Holmes." This was the prelude to Holmes's speech.

Taking the theme of the opening song, Holmes announced that it was indeed a dizzy world. "Cannon to the right," he said, "cannon to the left—and exploding congressmen everywhere. . . .

"The map of Europe has been changed, and still is changing—but no faster than the map of Congress. . . .

"Dictatorships have bloomed and blossomed abroad. There has even been some slight mention of dictatorship in this country. For details consult the *Congressional Record*, the *New York Herald-Tribune*, the nearest Republican—or perhaps your broker. For contradictory testimony consult Harold Ickes."

Paul McNutt, "tall, tanned and terrific," had just returned to Washington from a post as high commissioner to the Philippines. He had made several dynamic speeches on the way across the country and was being talked about as a possible successor to President Roosevelt in 1940.

An impersonator of McNutt dashed into a group of Grid-ironers on the stage and announced that he had to report to the President right away. He stepped to the front of the stage and speaking directly to the President, he said, "I report to you, Sir, there's a war in China."

Whereupon FDR, from his place at the head table, answered, "Yes, Paul, and had you heard that Dewey had sunk the Spanish fleet at Manila?"

Prior to the dinner, Ferdinand Lundberg had written a rather scurrilous book on America's sixty families, the wealthy who he claimed ruled the country. An act was set on Canton Island in the Pacific, which had recently been claimed by President Roosevelt along with Enderbury Island for the United States.

In the skit the sixty families had been banished to this island by the President, and as they arrived to take possession "in the names of the sixty ruling families of America—and Franklin D. Roosevelt," they sang, to the tune of "Are You from Dixie?":

> We are the sixty
> Oh we're the sixty,
> We're the families who had all the dough;
> Won't it be funny,
> Without our money
> For their taxes, where will they go?
> If you're a Rockefeller, Vanderbilt or—
>   just a Gould,
> Stay away from any place by Franklin ruled.

A character representing Pierre S. du Pont told "J. P. Morgan" that they shouldn't allow any Roosevelt on these islands. "In their native state, they're depressing enough."

The skit closed with du Pont announcing that "The joke certainly is on the country. It's got nothing left but Franklin," and Morgan chimed in that "we are saying goodbye to him, without even waiting for 1940. We've got plenty to remember him by!" Then the orchestra struck up "Thanks for the Memory."

> Thanks for the memory
> Of many a fiscal thrill
> "Horse and buggy" bill,
> "Dear Alben" and the other funny things
>   upon the Hill—
> How lovely it was!

Thanks for the memory
And "off the record," too,
Franklin, how are you,
And how are all the little dreams that
    never did come true?
How lovely it was!

So, thanks for the memory,
Of "Tugwelltown" of yore,
Santa Claus, and more—
You may have been a headache,
    but you never were a bore!
Awf'ly glad we met you, Cheer-ri-oo and
Toodle-oo,
And thank you so much!

The Republican skit was built around former President Hoover and Glenn Frank, a former president of the University of Wisconsin, who had recently been named chairman of a Republican committee to develop a program for the future, and who was the opposition speaker at the dinner.

"Frank" proclaimed his aim to form a coalition of Democrats with the Republicans, and "Hoover" asked him, "Did you ever hear of a canary swallowing a cat?

This was followed by the guest skit, put on by J. Fred Essary and Walker Buel, in which a large number of Republicans and Democrats were asked to stand, one after the other, and a quip was made about each.

It was noted that there was not "a candidate in a carload." Then Essary called to his feet "Mr. Franklin D. Roosevelt—Junior," and Buel shouted, "Mr. Hoover says, 'My God, are there two of them?' "

Considerable controversy had developed over one of Roosevelt's favorite projects, the Tennessee Valley Authority, and the Gridiron Club handled this in a memorable skit, in which Turner Catledge as "Maw," a mountain woman, discovered in a cabin in eastern Tennessee with numerous mountain boys and girls. "Maw" shouted to the children to gather 'round and sang:

Gather round me children and I'll tell a story,
of a feud back in the hills not far away,
When two factions got disputin' 'til they nearly came to shootin',
On just how the hell to run the TVA.

Oh, the TVA directors, they were split in different sectors,
And they took to New Deal feudin' when they'd meet.
They'd accuse each other quicker than it took your eye to flicker.
They would call each other, "liar! Crook! and Cheat!"

All their fightin' started one cold winter mornin',
When old Arthur Morgan, filled with honesty,
And suspicion, got to thinkin' that there sure was somethin'
    stinkin'
Near two other engineers in Tennessee.

TVA's administrators, they were mean and fearful haters,
But old Grandpa Morgan beat 'em to the draw,
And five thousand words of libel, in New England's monthly bible
Was the first thing that them other fellers saw.

When Paw Franklin heard the shootin' down the mountain,
He retched up and took his flintlock off the wall,
Grabbed his licker off the dresser,
And he said, "That derned perfesser's
Went and took another shot at Lilienthal."

Pappy aimed his double-barreled, cross the wood pile,
An he hollered, "Arthur put that gun away."
Tell me all about this shootin' and explain this yere disputin,
Or I'll blast some one right out of TVA."

In introducing Dr. Glenn Frank, Holmes referred to the ribbing
the club had previously received from President Roosevelt on not
being able to find a Republican to speak for the opposition. He
said that the club, "always alert to be helpful in matters of politics
and government, determined to find a Republican. After a long
and arduous search we were successful. He is here tonight. . . . It
is a pleasure at this time to present the chairman of the Republican Committee on Program, Dr. Glenn Frank."

No record of Frank's speech is available, but the recollections
of many who were present at the dinner agree that it was a
somewhat dull and ponderous exposition of party politics, fairly
devoid of wit. All comments in the Gridiron record about it emphasize that it was not very successful, and President Roosevelt,
when his turn came, won the debate with ease.

The principal Roosevelt skit pictured a captain aboard the
ship of state, which was described as "the old tub," on which
was about to occur "a dramatic incident on its cruise to
nowhere."

The crew was questioning the captain, who was smiling suavely and smoking a cigarette in a long holder, about "where we are today."

Captain: Well, it doesn't matter. It's where we're heading that counts.
Helmsman: Where are we heading, sir?
Captain: Oh, I've got lots of objectives.
Helmsman: Which do we reach first, sir?
Captain: Don't be old fashioned. We plan to reach them all simultaneously.

Before the toast to the President, the dinner closed with a wacky skit, which ended, however, on a patriotic note with the chorus singing:

Marching along, together,
Sharing ev'ry smile and tear;
Marching along, together,
Waiting for the skies to clear!

Riding the Roosevelt highway
Maybe we've lost our way;
But if you're doubtful of things at home,
Just look across the sea!
Our own dictator's an old pertater,
Name of Franklin D.!

Marching along, God's country—
Let's stay home in the U.S.A.!

"Like the Gridiron Club," said President Roosevelt as he rose to respond, "I hesitate to be serious. But let's stay home in the U.S.A."

Then he proceeded to try to take apart some of his detractors. The first of these was Jouett Shouse, former chairman of the Democratic National Committee, but in 1938 head of the American Liberty League, and whose name he noted, "with alarm and grave disappointment," was disappearing from the front pages of the newspapers.

"Mr. Shouse was unique in his field," he said; "he could dictate right to the mimeograph operator. The use of the mimeograph has been cited as a radical technique of this administration. As the words of Mr. Shouse cut into the stencil . . . a bulletin from the Department of the Interior, describing the progress of construction on the Grand Coulee Dam, underwent a mimeographic metamorphosis into propaganda and poison. In the end, however, the Supreme Court of the United States disagreed with Mr. Shouse, but it did not disagree with the Columbia River. Thus the front page became void of 'Shouse on the Constitution,' and breakfast lost its savor."

Turning then to Glenn Frank, Roosevelt told how at a dinner in the White House with an old friend ["John"], "we happened somehow to get on the subject of politics," discussing campaigns—how to win them and how to lose them. The unidentified friend had asked the President if he had unlimited power to do so, what kind of a political organization he would set up.

"I told him," said the President, "you know that I believe in brains. In fact, I have been criticized for bringing brains into the government. 'Brain Truster' became a Republican taunt of opprobrium. But I still believe in brains, so to beat this theoretical and ideal political organization I would look around for a college professor, or even the former president of some great university. I would reach right into academic life, and that man—if I could find him—that former college president, I would make chairman.

"Having made him chairman, I would tell him to enunciate a program, to find out, if possible, what his party stood for. After all, as has been well said, there are moments in life when we all have to truckle to principle. But even a 'Brain Truster' needs occasional advice and encouragement, so I'd give this former college president the title of chairman of the Committee on Program, and I'd give him lots of assistance. I'd invite all the best minds and the former best minds and, of course, the heaviest prospective contributors to think up a program. In fact, 221 advisers [the exact number on the Frank Committee] wouldn't be too many. And, by the way, there would have been 222, but, unfortunately, the last man called to serve with this mighty band of archangels, my good friend Landon of Kansas, gave them the once over and would not serve."

Then, with that Roosevelt facility for destroying an opponent while bestowing upon him the most ingratiating smile, the President proceeded:

"When I had picked the 221, I'd coordinate them," he said. "And how I'd coordinate them! Of course, coordination is a difficult job. As soon as you even mention the need for coordination, someone jumps up and denounces you as a totalitarian. I'd make this chairman on program, this great coordinator, an absolute dictator; I'd give him the works. And the name of this dictator would be, not Franklin D., but just plain Frank.

"What I said [to my friend John] that night in the White House all came true. I think John must have been a Republican, although his last name was not Hamilton. Dictator Frank is in command; he is searching for a program with his 221 collaborators; he is attempting to coordinate Herbert Hoover with Joseph S. Frelinghuysen, 'Charlie' Dawes with Roscoe Pound, and that great liberal, Charles Francis Adams, with Fiorello La Guardia.

"I'm going to reveal a Republican secret. Dictator Frank has a program for 1940. He's written it all out himself, but he keeps it locked up in his safe so that the 221 won't know about it. With the assistance of a dozen G-men, I managed to obtain a copy of this secret document. And I think I'd be doing the Republicans a real service to make public their program now, in 1938, rather than to keep an expectant world waiting until 1940. So here it is:

"Article One: The GOP can do no wrong—except to the GOP.

"Article Two: In order that the sacred principles of the American Liberty League shall not die, the following members of the American Liberty League have, among others, been appointed to the Program Committee of the Republican National Committee."

Then Roosevelt listed a group of Liberty Leaguers and ended the list with the comment, "O Shouse, where is thy sting!"

"Article Three: The Republican Committee on Program must rethink, restate and reinterpret to the nation the principles to which it adheres. In these changing times, the Republican position will change, too. Changes will be announced for morning release not less than twice a week. The 221 members of the Committee on Program are advised to remain alert in order to learn what changes Dictator Frank has decided upon for that particular week. Government by hunch must end. Government by opportunism must replace it.

"Let no one think that when I refer to Dictator Frank that Franklin is doing Frank an injustice. As long ago as December 1931, in the middle of President Hoover's term, Frank—not Franklin—was thinking in terms of dictatorship. In the *Nation* of December 23, 1931, Frank wrote an article on the then depression. Its title was 'If I Were Dictator.' He wrote, in part:

"The machine economy has brought us to the threshold of a social millenium, but we have lacked the wit to unlock the door. And my contention is that, instead of planning to adjust ourselves to the half-hearted and insecure existence that marks the current economic order, with its alternate swings between panic and plenty, we should be searching for the key that will unlock the door into this social millenium of prosperity, leisure and security, which science and the machine age have made possible. I think we know what the key is . . . The key is a wider annual distribution of the national income.

"But that wasn't all that Dictator Frank wrote. He said that first he should 'decree' the creation of an integrated national organization in each distinctive field of economic enterprise, with the elaboration of the machinery and methods of responsible self-government as the goal of these organizations. If that failed to work, Dictator Frank had an alternative."

Roosevelt then proceeded to read another quote from the past writings of Glenn Frank, in which the Republican speaker had advocated the imposition of "An unprecedentedly high tax rate" upon business, not because the government needed the money, but as a club to force businesses to distribute larger amounts of money, through higher wages, shorter hours and lower prices.

"It will be interesting," the President said, "to see whether Frank—not Franklin—now that he *is* a real Dictator will recommend his scheme of taxation to the next Republican National Convention. Dr. Frank once said of himself: 'After all, I'm only a journalist on parole.' As one journalist to another, I salute him. He's got the stuff! But a word of advice—a parolee is under constant observation. If his foot slips, back he goes into the hoosegow."

A typical Roosevelt assault.

Before closing, the President had about a page of copy which was serious, and he introduced it by noting that the Gridiron dinner had ended "on a note of somewhat disillusioned patriotism."

"We have our own troubles, it is true," he said, "but compared to what is happening elsewhere in the world, our fate is an enviable one. At least the map of the United States is not changing, our geographies are not printed on the loose-leaf system, our boundaries remain fixed, and our neighbors are inclined to mind their own business. So without arrogance or self-righteousness we can agree that this is indeed 'God's Country'—even though you'd never suspect it from the headlines in most of our newspapers. But we cannot afford to assume a superior pose with respect to nations and peoples whose situation is less fortunate than our own, and least of all can we afford to ridicule, or to regard with cynical condescension, the efforts of other governments, or the deep desire of other peoples, to maintain peace. We know now, if we never knew it before, that peace is not static; in a disordered world it is no longer one of the assumptions that underlies domestic life or international intercourse; it submits itself to no formula, nor is it shaped according to our prejudices and our preconceptions. Therefore, let us recognize the difficulties and the discouragements of those who are attempting to nurture peace and to maintain it, for the world needs good will and none of us, even as individuals, can afford to withhold it."

But he closed on a note of satire about the Gridiron Club itself.

"As for our own domestic welfare, as long as the Gridiron Club gives its dinners, as long as it puts the President of the United States in his place, as long as it tells government how government should be run, we need not lie awake nights with the specter of totalitarianism perched at the foot of the bed. If we fail to take the Gridiron Club's advice on how our jobs should be run, it will be our own—and the people's —loss.

"Long experience leads me to the unalterable opinion that no group in the United States—neither the Frank group nor the Franklin group—know how to run the United States. Our beloved nation's present and future can be made safe only in the hands of the members of the Gridiron Club. I salute you!"[8]

Gene Buck, president of the American Society of Composers, Authors and Publishers, was a perennial guest at Gridiron dinners during this period and after each one wrote for the Gridiron Club a critique of the show. He commented about this speech of President Roosevelt:

"I thought the President made the best speech of all since he has attended the Gridirons. He had poise, good humor, good ideas and was in the mood of the evening and, after all that is the big job. . . . He did kick around Glenn Frank but I thought Frank left an opening by being a little too heavy on that particular occasion."[9]

And Harlan Miller, a columnist for the *Washington Post* and other papers, commented, "I have never heard Franklin

Roosevelt deliver a wittier or more brilliant gridiron than his last Gridiron speech."[10]

• • •

Prior to the December 17, 1938 dinner, Adolph Hitler had already taken over a part of Czechoslovakia and was threatening Poland. Consequently, at this dinner the Gridiron Club placed the Polish ambassador in the seat of honor for diplomats— between President Roosevelt and Chief Justice Hughes.

Not only were things getting ominous in Europe as the triumphant Hitler was proceeding from conquest to conquest and threatening everyone, but in the United States there had also been a dramatic turn.

During the 1938 congressional elections, President Roosevelt had embarked upon his ill-fated "purge" campaign, to bring about the defeat in primaries of Democrats whose performance in Congress had been too conservative to please him, particularly on the court-packing issue. One of them was Senator Millard Tydings of Maryland. The President had spent an entire day touring the state of Maryland and making speeches against Tydings, which led to one of the most effective political slogans of all time on the part of the Tydings people—"Keep the Free State Free."

Tydings won handily and so did all of the other senators and congressmen against whom the President had campaigned, except one—Representative John O'Connor of New York, chairman of the House Rules Committee.

As a result of the purge campaign, the court-packing issue, and various other internal and economic dissatisfactions, the Republicans had made substantial gains in both houses of congress (seventy-five in the House, seven seats in the Senate), just a little over a month before President Roosevelt appeared at the dinner.

In typical Gridiron fashion, President Holmes opened the dinner in his speech in the dark by noting that "this wretched orb knows not the taste of rest: A maniac world, homeless and sobbing, through the deep she goes."

"The world is no longer simply strange," he said. "It is now completely cock-eyed. . . . Old standbys fail us. We used to believe in good old Munich beer. But we see now what happens when Munich beer is mixed with sake, Chianti—and *Anschluss*. . . . Even here at home we cannot be sure that democracy is safe, for you know what happened on November 8 when a lot of strange looking things crawled out of the woodwork.

"To celebrate that great Republican triumph, Alf Landon has gone to Peru to peer at the bones of Pizzaro. Czechoslovakia has been liquidated—but Wisconsin has been put back on the map. The Supreme Court has once more followed the election returns."

Then the Gridiron chorus trooped on stage and, with a re-wording of "Santa Claus Is Comin' to Town," sang of the election results.

> We used to have fun, used to be gay,
> Now we are sad the live-long day—
>
> Santa Claus has been voted down!
>
> Oh! You better watch out, Franklin D.
> Find a Brand-new Christmas tree—
>
> Santa Claus has been voted down!

Although not present at the dinner, Governor Landon was a character in an early skit in which, when asked who sent him to Peru, he replied, "I have a friend in the White House—I helped put him there."

It had been during October of this year that Orson Welles, a young man of twenty-four at the time, had put on his famous radio fantasy of the landing of the Martians in New Jersey. It was a fantasy which thoroughly frightened millions of people who had taken it for real.

The landing of the Martians was used as the vehicle for a satire on the Republicans, but the skit was notable primarily for an incident which it created, concerning this man who had scared so many. Since they based a skit on the Welles radio performance, the club gave him the courtesy of an invitation to the dinner, which he accepted. Gene Buck, in his letter to the club after the dinner, related in graphic detail what happened.

"You fellows," he said, "invited him down to the dinner, forgot to tell him what it was all about and that the President would be in attendance, so he grabbed a dinner coat, hopped a plane, flew to Washington, came over to the dinner at seven-thirty all alone, saw all the white ties and tails, got a peek at your program, at who was going to be there and proceeded to get real stage fright. He got so scared that he sneaked out of the reception room, grabbed an elevator, hopped a cab, went back to the Mayflower, packed a bag and was all ready to fly back to New York when Harry Butcher, who had come over to the table to inquire where he was as he was seated next to me, called Welles at his room, found he was embarrassed by the dinner coat, told him to attend anyway, and after the sketch was over Welles slid into his seat alongside of me, embarrassed and scared to death."[11]

The Martian skit was set in the year 6038 A.D. and the Republicans were portrayed as still suffering from the blight of "Old Guardism" and still searching for a leader.

One of the principal skits in the dinner was based on the purge campaign. Impersonators of all the conservative Democrats whose opponents President Roosevelt had supported in the primaries, headed by Cotton Ed Smith, senator from South Carolina, were on the stage, and as a chorus they sang a Gridiron version of "Sleepy Time Down South."

> When it's purgin' time down south,
> Franklin's on the rampage, a-comin', a-goin',
> Travelin' the time away.
> Ickes and Hopkins the dollars a-throwin',
> From now till judgment day.

Turning briefly in this skit from the purge itself, a character representing Postmaster General James A. Farley, chairman of the Democratic National Committee, was asked by "Senator Harrison" what he had to say to the President about a third term, and Farley responded by singing:

> Look down, look down that lonesome road
> Before you travel on.

The key song of the skit gave President Roosevelt the advice of the Southerners:

> Franklin, go west with your gold
> Go pension the old
> With all they can hold,
>   But in
> Famine, in flood or in drouth,
>   God bless you
> Franklin, stay out of the South!

The skit ended with a duet between Senators Tydings of Maryland and George of Georgia to "Old Cotton Ed, who wouldn't go where they told him to go." To the tune of "Uncle Ned," they sang:

> He fretted and he growled, he grunted and he stormed,
>   A fust class lynching was his urge,

But he 'woke one morning in time to be informed
    He was slated for the celebrated purge.

Keep out your fiddle and your bow, o, o, o,
    Heave on the shovel and the hoe,
We'll have one round for Old Cotton Ed,
    Wouldn't go where they told him to go.

Hang up your fiddle and your bow, o, o, o,
    Lay down your shovel and your hoe,
Gangway there, for Old Man Cotton Ed,
    He'll tell the New Deal where it can go!

Whereupon Turner Catledge impersonated Cotton Ed addressing an audience in South Carolina on the purge, his walkout from the Democratic National Convention in 1936, and white supremacy. For many years following this dinner, by general demand, Catledge repeated the alleged Cotton Ed speech at Gridiron after-parties in the suite of Richard L. Wilson.

There were no implications intended, but immediately after Catledge's hilarious recital of Cotton Ed on the stump, Thomas E. Dewey was introduced as the Republican speaker. He was then district attorney of New York County and had failed to make the grade against Herbert Lehman for governor of New York in the 1938 elections.

"His ability as a prosecutor," said George Holmes in introducing him, "has been conspicuously recognized by the people of New York who have *twice* declared they want him to be a prosecuting attorney."

It was Dewey's first appearance at the Gridiron Club in the course of his meteoric rise, which began with his election as prosecuting attorney in 1937 and culminated in his nomination for President seven years later. Unfortunately, no record of his speech exists.

The spectacle of people acting with a great degree of authority in the name of the President is not new in American politics. In the Roosevelt days it existed, with Tommy Corcoran, Harry Hopkins, Ben Cohen, Sam Rosenman, and many others making all kinds of calls to Capitol Hill and assertedly speaking for the President.

The Gridiron Club put on a skit about this between "Corcoran" and "Cohen." In his office, Corcoran was telling telephone operators to get various Senate and House leaders on the phone, one after another—Ambassador Joe Kennedy in London, Solicitor General Jackson, Senator O'Mahoney, who was conducting the monopoly investigation, and so on, almost ad infinitum. Operating with half a dozen phones, he had a message for each one which began, "This is Tommy Corcoran speaking from the White House." Cohen sat idly by.

The conversation with Ambassador Joseph P. Kennedy was perhaps representative.

"How about that telephone call to Joe Kennedy in London? Oh, he's at tea with the Archbishop of Canterbury, is he, and cawn't be disturbed? Wait until the Irish in South Boston hear about that! You tell him that this is Tommy Corcoran—speaking from the White House."

Then, when his conversations were drawing to a close, all the telephones began ringing at once. Corcoran picked one up:

"Tommy Corcoran, speaking from the White House." His voice dropped to awe, "Oh, Mr. President. Yes, Mr. President. No, Mr. President. All right, Mr. President."

He hung up.

Cohen asked, "Was he—er—speaking from the White House?"

Secretary of the Interior Ickes, never a favorite among the newsmen, had his leg pulled in a Ferdinand the Bull song, one verse of which went:

Harold Ickes, Harold Ickes, the man with the delicate ego;
Harold Ickes, Harold Ickes, there's nobody you call amigo.
Harold Ickes, Harold Ickes, at name-calling you are a bimbo—
Though you won't take the jackpot, you silly old crack-pot,
You're wonderful throwing the bull!

This was followed by the introduction of Postmaster General James A. Farley, then and long since a Gridiron favorite who had attended practically every dinner for more than forty years before his death in 1976. He was presented in a rather whimsical way.

"Speaking of bull," Holmes began, "the Gridiron Club is breaking with the tradition of having some outstanding politician speak on what is going on. The man I am about to present has only an academic interest in politics. He is a famous literary figure. He is, in fact, the author of a current best seller in the book marts. It is a pleasure at this time to present the Honorable James A. Farley."

Unfortunately, Farley kept no copy of this speech.

With the world getting more and more jittery about the rise of Hitler and the bellicose antics of Mussolini, the club closed the dinner with a skit set at No. 10 Downing Street in the Cabinet

Room of Prime Minister Chamberlain, who had returned from Munich triumphantly proclaiming that he had brought "peace in our time."

But now the prime minister, who had "lost his voice in a conversation with Herr Hitler," was conferring with British Foreign Minister Lord Halifax and other members of his cabinet. "Lady Astor," whose Clivedon set was suspected by some of having pro-Nazi sympathies, arrived on the scene and sang:

> Carry me back to old Virginny,
> That's where the coronets and tall tiaras grow,
> That's where the birds warble sweet in the Springtime,
> That's where meself and His Lordship long to go.
> That's where I labored so hard for the masses,
> Day after day 'til this ermine robe was torn;
> No place on earth do I love—at a distance—
> More than Virginny, the state where I was born.

"Lord Halifax" finally came to the conclusion that if the worst came to the worst because of President Roosevelt's complicity in the negotiations, and things were bad, they could blame it on the President.

"The prime minister," he said, "wishes to thank him for a perfect alibi." Then "Chamberlain" sang:

> You're a sweetheart, if there ever was one,
> If there ever was one, it's you.
> Munich without you was an incomplete dream,
> You made Hitler's pipe dream come true.
> Our search was such a blind one,
> And I was all at sea.
> I never thought I'd find one,
> Quite so perfect for me.
> You're a sweetheart,
> You're another Wilson.
> If there ever was one,
> It's *you!*

But the situation was really too serious to try to be funny about it. The skit ended with Lord Halifax noting that "the hour grows late," and saying that "soon it will be Christmas, and what a sad time for the world . . . what a sad time . . . "

The Gridiron quartet stepped forward and closed the show by singing without parody:

> Away in a manger,
> No crib for his bed,

The little Lord Jesus,
Lay down His sweet head;
The stars in the sky,
Looked down where He lay,
The little Lord Jesus,
Asleep in the hay.

President Roosevelt, who had embarked upon a policy of one Gridiron speech a year, nevertheless responded to the toast with a few pleasant and gracious words, without serious comment and without reference to the skits.

It is worthy of mention that a businessman, then little known, came to his first Gridiron dinner on this occasion. He attracted little attention, and his name was not mentioned in any skit. It was the man who two years later was to challenge Roosevelt for the Presidency, Wendell L. Willkie.

XIII

Franklin D. Roosevelt

1939-1945
The Sphinx Speaks:
"Nine terms! Gentlemen,
it is too much!"

In the spring of 1939 the menace of Adolph Hitler was apparent to all, and Gridiron President Raymond Clapper, one of the most distinguished correspondents of that time, remarked in his opening speech at the dinner of April 15 that "Rand McNally have to publish their maps in five-star daily editions like a tabloid."

"But things are not as bad as they seem. They couldn't be. Be not afraid. All we need is confidence—or even better, an occasional dividend."

The Republicans, he said, were going to carry the country in 1940 "if Tom Dewey [still district attorney of New York] has to put every Democrat in jail."

Referring to the administration, he commented that "there are no more rabbits in the hat. It is as empty as the pot that didn't have a chicken in it."

The show opened with a skit, "Hell's A-Poppin'," written by Bernard Kilgore, later to be publisher of the *Wall Street Journal.* Kilgore also composed some original music elsewhere in the 1939 show—the first time that any Gridiron member had done that.

Hell's a-pop-pin' ev-ry-where,
Hell's a-pop-pin' here,
Keep your seats
While the Gridiron heats,
For all we fear is fear.

Hell's a-pop-pin' on the Hill—
Cong-ress out of gear—
New Deal crew
Is a-bout all through,
But all we fear is fear.

Hell's a-pop-pin' ov-er-seas,
Hit-ler makes it clear:
Dou-ble check
On the Mun-ich wreck,
But all we fear is fear.

Hell's a-pop-pin' in the East,
China's on her ear,
War-like Japs
Draw their own new maps
But all we fear is fear.

Nazi bunds and com-mun-ists,
Schem-ers, plots and spies,
They're a-fraid of ev-ry-one
Cept-ing Mar-tin Dies.

Hell's a-pop-pin' ev-ry-where
What an at-mos-phere,
'Round the head
Of the guy who said
That all we fear is fear.

At this dinner President Roosevelt again took part directly from the head table in a skit. It was the inauguration of President Clapper. The scene was the district traffic court, where the "Presidential defendant," a back-seat driver, was accused of turning left when a traffic signal plainly directed him to turn to the right. The judge asked if anyone wished to be heard "before we find this defendant guilty," and a voice in the dark from the head table, President Roosevelt, said, "I do."

The spotlight turned on the President, and he continued. "I think I'm entitled to say something because both the defense and the prosecution describe only one remarkable type of person. I recognize the description. Is there nothing to be said for a man who does what he can every day in every way for the welfare of the world?"

The judge tried to interrupt him, but Roosevelt kept right on.

"Is there nothing to be said for a man who is willing to take the burden of the world on his shoulders? Is there nothing to be said for a man who daily shares the wisdom of the ages with all men? Can a man help it if he is omniscient? Is it fair to pillory such a man merely because he is—*a newspaper columnist?*"

The spotlight turned to Clapper, and the judge sentenced him to a year of hard labor as president of the Gridiron Club.

In a scene with King Arthur and his "knights and wizards of the round table," there was a grave emergency because "their pet dragon, named Business, after providing them with six years of rare sport is about to expire." The dragon was in very bad shape, and a discussion ensued on whether to try to cure him or let him die.

King Arthur settled this dispute by telling the advocates of letting him die, "But I'm not sure. Even I can't fool some of the people all the time. If this dragon isn't in shape to run in 1940, it won't make much difference whether I run or not."

The skit ended with a song, "You Don't Give Us Anything But Fear, Baby."

The isolationists in Congress were pictured on the island of Guam, where "the war-like gestures of the Roosevelt administration had driven them for a last stand."

In April 1939 it appeared that the two principal contenders for the Republican nomination the following year would be Thomas E. Dewey and Senator Robert A. Taft. Wendell L. Willkie had not yet appeared on the scene as an active candidate. The Gridiron Club, fortunately for its reputation as a seer, did not predict which one would win.

> A tisket, a tasket,
> We'll put 'em in a basket,
> We're going to bury the New Deal
> And win in 1940.
> We are truckin' on down the avenue,
> A-lookin' for that White House view.
> We are dig, dig, diggin' all around
> For our leader must be found.

The problems were pointed up in another song, "A Good Man (Nowadays) Is Hard To Find."

All the principal potential 1940 candidates were present at

the dinner: President Roosevelt, Vice President Garner, Senator Robert A. Taft, Senator Arthur Vandenberg, and Thomas E. Dewey.

Hamlet's gravediggers dug up a skull, and the impersonator of Dewey commented, "That's the trouble with our party. It has too many skulls." Then a ghost came in and announced that he was Dr. Townsend, who wanted to give everybody over 60 years old fifty dollars every Thursday,* and, in a song to the tune of "Oh, Promise Me," the GOP agreed he might be a pretty good candidate.

> We'll promise them the best of everything,
> With promises we'll make the echoes ring.

> The New Deal is a piker, we will show,
> We'll make security to thrive and grow.
> Hearing the message of the GOP
> The voters will, as in a vision, see,
> A life made perfect as a diadem,
> We'll promise them, we'll promise them!

"Thirty years ago," said President Clapper in introducing as the Republican speaker Senator Robert A. Taft, who had been elected the previous November, "a Roosevelt moved out of the White House and a Taft moved in. The Gridiron Club would like to know whether this is about to become an old American custom."

But Senator Taft's speech on that occasion, quite in contrast to one that he made at a later Gridiron dinner, was not a success. Harlan Miller, a Washington columnist of the time, wrote a few days later that "after hearing Senator Taft talk at the Gridiron dinner, an eminent publisher congratulated Tom Dewey on the speech."[1]

It was not yet evident in 1939 either that Roosevelt would run for a third term or that he would replace Garner with Henry Wallace, but Garner, while he was very discreet about it, was apparently losing some confidence in the New Deal approach to the economy.

There was a skit between several of the more conservative Democrats, including Senator Harrison of Mississippi and Senator Byrnes of South Carolina, and there was talk of Garner for President. A song continued that speculation.

---

*Dr. Francis E. Townsend was a California political figure who had in fact proposed that $50 in government money be given to everybody over sixty every Thursday.

Ol' Man Garner,
That Ol' man Garner
He don't say nothin'
But he must know somethin'
He just keeps runnin'
He keeps on runnin' along.
He don't make speeches
On wheat and cotton
And them that makes 'em
Am soon forgotten
But Ol' man Garner
He just keeps runnin' along.

This was the closing song of the dinner, after which the traditional toast to the President was drunk, and he responded.

With little reference to the skits, Roosevelt chose to razz the newspapermen. "President Clapper, members of the American Society of Inventors," he began, borrowing an old line from Benjamin Harrison, "and fellow guests.

"It is a great privilege for us laymen to be here tonight with this society, which, through the daily perpetration of inventions, is carrying on a noble American tradition."

He reminisced about the old days, "half a century ago, before that stimulating virus 'imagination' had infected the inventive genius of the press."

News was dull then, he said. "Nobody knew who wrote the news, there were no by-lines, no personalities, no commentators, no interpreters, no columnists. Few people knew or cared who owned the newspapers, and when they did know it was because the individual paper was the personal vehicle of an individual like William Cullen Bryant or Horace Greeley, who had made their marks chiefly in other fields; or it was a James Gordon Bennett, who sent Stanleys to Africa to discover Livingstones,* or conducted his newspaper from the deck of a yacht in the Mediterranean.

"Inventors in those days were puny souls who invented cotton gins and sewing machines and reapers and electric lights, all of them rare luxuries which took affluence and riches to use. How you, the members of this society, have improved on that, for your inventions go morning, noon and night into the homes of over one hundred million people, rich and poor alike.

---

*I have corrected President Roosevelt here. His text spelled it "Livingstons." This isn't the first time I ever attempted to correct him, but it's the first time I succeeded.

"When I was a small boy I learned in Sunday school that it was useless to hide your head under the covers at night; there was One way off there in the sky somewhere, who knew what you were thinking. In Washington I have learned all over again that it is no use trying to keep your thoughts to yourself. Omniscient gentlemen of the press sit behind their Remingtons or Underwoods in their well-stocked offices, putting down on paper everything you think and everything you are going to think and everything that you ought to think, but don't."

Roosevelt said he often wondered who that "person close to the White House" was, "who sees all, knows all, and tells all." He thought maybe it was Pete the peanut man, who in those days ran a peanut stand just outside the White House gates. But, if so, he commented, "your true newspaperman protects his news source. Pete—if it is Pete—is safe."

Then the President turned to Senator Taft, saying that "you inventors are not the only people who have improved on things." Recalling that the Washington of 1933, when he landed there, was very different from the administration of Grover Cleveland, he offered to give a little advice "to my young friend Bob Taft.

"In all friendship," he said, "I call his attention to the fact that the Washington of 1939 is by no means the Washington of 1909.

"But that older Washington, that prewar Washington, that happier Washington, that simpler Washington, was not without its charm. President Taft was, I believe, the first President to use an automobile. The members of the cabinet considered themselves fortunate to have a brougham and pair placed at their disposal, with an old Negro coachman, in a well-vaselined top hat, to drive them in their unhurried progress from one occasion to another. Secretaries of state were able to rusticate in salubrious northern climates during the feverish Washington summer, and if an infrequent cablegram arrived from one of our missions abroad, there was a great to-do in the department to open the safe and find the code-book.

"James Bryce used to walk in the cool of the evening on upper Connecticut Avenue, near Du Pont Circle. Friends used to fall in with him and discuss 'the American Commonwealth' or ask him if he thought the English were treating the Irish right. People picnicked on Massachusetts Avenue, where an imposing row of embassies now stands. A stagecoach line, the renowned Herdic, transported passengers from U and Sixteenth Streets downtown. An overland trip to Mount Vernon was an all-day job, with the wheels often up to the hubcaps in mud. On the south side of Pennsylvania Avenue, where great government buildings spread their chromium elegance from square to square, stood public markets. Negro women with their pushcarts and their barrows offered a well-plucked fowl, a jar of home-made pickles or the all-curative herbs, sassafras for spring tonic, catnip tea for teething babies, white oak and red oak bark for chills.

"That was a Washington that we shall never see again. You will never see it, Bob, nor shall I. It is gone."

Roosevelt spoke of that world as being without fear, without hatred, and without the fierce clash of impetuous ambitions.

"No," he said, "the Washington of 1939 is not the Washington of 1909, and still less the Washington of the first administration of Grover Cleveland. And now that Bob Taft has come back to us after these many long years, I fear it will take him well past 1940 before he becomes eligible for membership in the new order of things.

"Just as the democracy of 1886 could not be the model for the democracy of 1933, so the Republicanism of 1909 cannot be the model of the Republicanism of 1940. Yet I am going away from here tonight fairly bursting with the importance of knowing who the next Republican candidate for President will be. I thought when I came here that I already had the secret. Here beneath the roses the American Society of Inventors and I both have made the great discovery. You my fellow guests keep it dark. It may be a full year and a quarter before the excited public is given the name of Doctor Townsend.

"This announcement will not be made until the Republican managers have polled all the successful Republican candidates of the 1938 off-year election and have got the unanimous reply: 'It was Doc Townsend who pulled us through.' What has happened once can happen again. Republics are sometimes ungrateful, but Republicans never! The Republican promise of sweeping economies in government will disappear in 1940 under the sun of Doctor Townsend's smile."

Then, as he frequently did in his Gridiron speeches, Roosevelt closed on a serious note. He said that 1940 was still in the impenetrable future and the world was moving fast.

"The United States is conscious of its strength and patient in the assurance that this strength gives us. But mere patience is not enough. With patience must go knowledge, information, a facing of the facts.

"The facts and conditions of the years of 1914 to 1918 are not to be slavishly copied any more than the facts and conditions of 1909 or 1886.

"It is just as stupid, just as mendacious for orators to assume that we would send another army to France in the 1917 style as it would be to make orations against sending an army into Canada in the 1812 style.

"American leadership is striving, according to such wisdom as is vouchsafed to it, to guide the destinies of our people through the mazes of this troubled world, the world of 1939. All currents of opinion have a right to be heard, and are being heard. But out of discussion will arise, let us hope, a unified national sentiment, for here, if ever, partisanship should cease.

"The government-controlled, censored press beyond the Atlantic and Pacific rings with the denunciations that certain gentlemen in the Congress and outside the Congress have seen fit to hurl at our national leadership.

"It has been well said that the grave responsibility imposed in the conduct of foreign relations sobers those who bear it. It is a pity that those who are not immediately concerned with that responsibility some times show a lack of sobriety. I wish that this sobering sense could come to that minority of Americans who today have made themselves the heroes of a censored foreign press. I need name no names.* But it will not take inventive genius on the part of this society or of its guests to fill in the names. I refer to those Americans in and out of official life who enjoy an amazing popularity with certain governments overseas.

"If, at some far off future time, the United States of America is reduced to the category of a second-rate nation, if we are told how to run our internal affairs, if we are told with whom we may or may not trade, then you will find statues to these gentlemen to whom I refer in the public squares of Berlin and of Rome.

"Personally, I would rather see statues in American cities to all leaders of other nations who have striven successfully for the maintenance of world peace and the continued existence of democratic government.

"Gentlemen, let us have peace. Let us have peace at home; then shall we be in a position to put forward the unified strength of our hearts, our minds, our most fervent and humble hopes for the maintenance of peace abroad."[2]

---

*But he was obviously referring to a few members of the Senate, of which the most notable was Senator Gerald Nye of North Dakota.

Roosevelt received a standing ovation at the end of his speech; earlier in the evening a similar one had been given to Hjalmar Procopé, the Minister of Finland, whose country was then under attack by the Soviet Union.

• • •

World War II had been in progress for over three months at the time of the dinner of December 9, 1939, but the fighting was so desultory that it was being referred to as the "phony war."

Since one can hardly laugh about war, that dinner made scant reference to it, and President Roosevelt had by that time adopted a policy of speaking at only the spring Gridiron dinner each year. Two speeches a year of this nature he thought placed too much burden upon him. But he did attend the dinner and responded briefly and graciously to the toast to the President at its conclusion.

During the years since 1933, President Roosevelt, in spite of all his new policies, had been unable to eradicate the unemployment problem, but as America began to prepare for its own defense and the war orders poured in from England and France, the economy began to show substantial improvement. Clapper, in his speech in the dark, commented that Wall Street was making money again, although "the Republicans didn't plan it that way.

"New Dealers don't like it either," he said, "because ham and eggs are going to the wrong people."

Clapper continued, "In 1916 the Democratic slogan was, 'He kept us out of war.' In 1939, the Republican slogan is, 'We kept *him* out of war.'"

President Roosevelt was being very coy about whether he would run for a third term in 1940 and refused to make any public statement of his intentions. This inspired Clapper to comment, "We don't know what begins in '40 because our Wizard of Oz won't tell us anything except that he hopes the weather will be good on the next Inauguration Day.

"Nevertheless, we confidently expect that our friends, the Democrats, will fall for anything the people will stand for and that our friends, the Republicans, will stand for anything the people will fall for."

The opening skit was the only real reference to the war, and it paraphrased a war song of the time:

> British soldiers sing they'll hang their washing to dry
> Out on the Siegfried line.
> Here's a U.S. version of this song for you and me,
> Here's the song that *we* will sing.

For neutrality—
We're gonna hang out the washing on the Three Mile Line.

There were the usual political skits, in one of which an impersonator of Secretary of Labor Frances Perkins sang "My Heart Belongs to Frankie," and another, a Rip van du Pont skit, in which the modern Rip van Winkle wakes up to find that "that man is still here." However, after some persuasion from impersonators of Winthrop Aldrich, John J. Raskob and Tom Girdler, he decided he'd enter upon the "cash and carry policy and go to see our chief." The characters all exited to "Happy Days Are Here Again."

But in spite of the difficulties of putting on a dinner under these circumstances, this particular one had two notable skits and at least one notable speech.

Secretary of the Interior Ickes, never too popular with the newspapermen because he disliked them heartily and spoke his mind with great candor, was depicted in a Donald Duck skit, which was written by Bernard Kilgore and was superbly performed by Paul R. Leach of the *Chicago Daily News* and Kilgore.

The announcer said that one of the most distinguished New Deal members of the cabinet had kindly consented to come to the stage and give his views on some of the outstanding issues of the day. "He will answer questions propounded by one of our own members, disguised as a reporter. Mr. President, may I introduce that outspoken defender of the right to speak freely, usually referred to as Honest Harold."

Leach entered in an elaborate costume as Donald Duck, and the conversation began with the reporter saying, "Our readers would like to have your view."

Donald Duck turned upon him with, "Who the hell are you?"

Answer: I'm a reporter—
Duck: Qu-a-a-ck
Reporter: And I wanted to ask what you think of the Republican prospects for 1940?
Duck: (With obvious disdain) Quack, quack, quack.
Reporter: Would you mind telling us what you think of newspaper publishers?
Duck: (In high dudgeon) Qu-a-ack! Quack! Qu-a-ack!
Reporter: I see. What do you think about columnists?
Duck: Quack! Quack! Quack!
Reporter: Do you favor a third term for President Roosevelt?

Duck: (Affirmatively and softly) Quack.
Reporter: But what about that tradition against a third term?
Duck: (Takes off reporter's derby and replaces it with a dunce cap)
    Quack. Quack. Quack.
Reporter: On that subject I suppose you know what General
    Hugh Johnson said.
Duck: Quack! Quack! Quack!
Reporter: Now remember, Mr. Secretary, there are laws against
    libel.
Duck: Qu-a-ack! Quack-quack. *(Sounding like* "go to hell").
Reporter: O.K. O.K: Now one final question. What do you think
    of Secretary Ickes?

Whereupon Leach, whose costume was most ungainly and
top-heavy, crowed like a rooster, strutted and patted himself on
the chest so vigorously that he fell flat on his back and lay there
crowing vigorously while he tried unsuccessfully to get up. Ickes,
not realizing that this was an accident, was even more offended
by the ludicrous spectacle the duck presented.

President Roosevelt roared uproariously at this skit, but Secretary Ickes' laughter was forced. In his *Secret Diary* he wrote:

"Here was the revenge of a newspaper crowd employed by
Republican publishers, most of whose papers I have severely
criticized. . . . I think that this was just an attempt to hurt and I
haven't the slightest doubt that a lot of people present were
pleased."

Then he listed some conservative guests that he thought
"must have been overjoyed" and commented:

"It was some consolation to me that this stunt was pulled off
by a stuffed shirt organization that had such guests as these, to
say nothing of Tom Girdler and others who might be named. . . .
I had already resolved that I wouldn't attend the next dinner in
April and I think that probably the dinner last night is the last
that I shall attend."[3]

It was the last dinner to which he ever came.

The other notable skit was built around President
Roosevelt's taciturnity about a third term. The scene was in the
Sahara Desert, where an eight-foot-high Sphinx in the image of
Roosevelt, with a long cigarette holder projecting at a jaunty
angle from its mouth, had been constructed by James Preston.*

*Superintendent of the Senate press gallery for many years, and a limited Gridiron
member.

Roosevelt was so pleased with this skit that he asked the Gridiron Club if he might have the Sphinx, and it may be seen today on exhibition in the Roosevelt Library at Hyde Park. After the dedication of the Roosevelt Library, *Life* magazine used the Sphinx as the picture of the week in its issue of July 4, 1941.

The skit was introduced by Lewis Wood of the *New York Times,* chairman of the music committee, who said that the club "takes you now to a far away place in the world where a group of Democrats in near desperation have journeyed in search of the answer to the most perplexing question of all time. The scene is the Sahara Desert. The time is now. The Sphinx is—you guess who!"

Impersonators of Thomas G. Corcoran and Benjamin V. Cohen, two of the brain trust advisers of President Roosevelt, opened the skit and Cohen sang:

I'll turn, Boss, to thee,
My shrine thou shalt be,
Till the sands of the desert grow cold.

Corcoran announced to the group of prominent Democrats who had come in, "If your hearts are right, oh you evil ones, you may find the answer, whether you like it or not. I am Thomas G. Corcoran, the Great Tommy the Cork, High Priest, Major Domo and General Factotum of the Sphinx."

An impersonator of James A. Farley sang:

We've come a long way together,
Since we met back in old New York State,
We've weathered all kinds of weather,
Just to keep him the head of the slate,
But now we have come to the question,
And the answer we've just got to know,
We've come a long way together,
And we may have a long way to go.

John L. Lewis had once referred to Vice President Garner as a "poker-playing, whiskey-drinking, evil old man." After a reference to such a person being among the group, the impersonator of Garner stripped off his Arab robe, revealing a cowboy suit, two six-shooters, a bottle of whiskey in his belt, and a royal flush stuck in his hatband. He announced that he was getting tired of running around with a bunch "that don't know where they're goin' and are depending for decisions on a Sphinx. As for me, I'm headin' for the roundup." He sang:

I'm headin' for the White House,
Try and stop me if you can.
Listen to my Texas song!
How it beckons and I reckon
That the White House longs to be,
To be free again, just to see again
A Democrat like me!

Then an impersonator of Paul McNutt of Indiana, who spoke for the Democratic party at the dinner, and who was already widely talked about as a strong aspirant for the Democratic nomination if President Roosevelt did not run for a third term, stepped forth and sang:

I'm the Sheik of Terre Haute,
My skin was tanned, you'll note,
Out in the Philippines,
My "it" outshines Marlene's,
I've character and strength
And when I win, at length,
I'll tell them just what's what,
The Sheik of Terre Hutt.

The skit ended with a parody on "One Alone," written by Phelps Adams and sung directly to President Roosevelt.

Here before the Sphinx we stand
But he's silent as the sand,
Keeping locked the secret
In his heart of stone.
He who knows all things the best
Answers not our burning quest,
So we turn to you, now
You and you alone!
One alone
Can make it known
You alone
What is your decision?
Will you run?
Or are you done?
Must all our plans undergo revision?
Will you be
Eternally
The one to hold our party's nomination?
We've come to you
The way we always do

It rests with
You alone.

Those who were present recall that Paul McNutt made a very favorable impression with his speech and distinctly aided his ambitions for the Presidency if Roosevelt did not run, and the Vice Presidency if he did, but no record of it exists in the Gridiron files.

McNutt's ambitions were subsequently considerably dampened, when word leaked out that he was under income tax investigation by the Internal Revenue Service—which eventually found nothing wrong. There was much suspicion about who initiated the inquiry.

A really notable speech was made that night by a young man of thirty-two who had burst over the Republican political scene like a star shell on the Fourth of July, Harold Stassen, the Republican governor of Minnesota. He had stood up successfully to the labor unions in his state, and despite Minnesota's long liberal and Democratic tendencies, he was so popular that the polls showed 80 percent of the people of Minnesota thinking he had done a good job.

He himself was not eligible for the Presidency in 1940 because he was too young, but just a few months after this dinner he joined the meteoric campaign of Wendell Willkie, was Willkie's convention floor manager in Philadelphia, and by astute leadership was a big factor in bringing the Republican nomination to Willkie.

He was introduced by Clapper as "a man whose majority went up after his election instead of down."

"This sizzling Gridiron of our nation's capitol," Stassen began, "bears at least one resemblance to the football gridiron with which we in Minnesota are more familiar. It is plenty rough. As a mere sophomore in the school of government, now that the ball has been snapped to me, I am frankly uncertain whether to pass, punt, or run with the ball.

"However, I recognize that I have one distinct advantage tonight. I am perhaps the only man at this head table who is willing to say unequivocally, 'I will not run for President in 1940.' "

Paying his respects to the Washington press gallery, he remarked that it was "through their eyes that we in the Middle West observe national affairs.

"In addition to their reporting of events," he said, "we have also found that they always predict correctly what is going to happen. That is, among them they always predict every possibility and all we readers a thousand miles away have to do is to discover which one is right."

Then shifting quickly to President Roosevelt, he continued that "if the reports that you bring us are in any respect lacking . . . we can always obtain a crystal clear picture of our national government presented objectively, dispassionately and impartially by tuning in on a fireside chat.

"The metaphors used by the President have been very helpful. His reference to the quarterback technique in his administration gave us a better understanding of those headlines we read so frequently—'New Deal Shifts to Right,' and 'New Deal Shifts to Left.'

"We could sympathize with the quarterback when Ray Moley came out of the huddle and headed for the wrong goal, then again, when Henry Wallace turned up out of bounds in California. There have been times when the fumbles of the team have been alarming, and they've been slow on the 'recovery.' Sometimes it seemed to us that the quarterback was the only member of the team who knew all the signals. We did get right up on the edge of our seats when every man in the backfield bobbed up with the ball, and we rose right up for a good look at the razzle, dazzle when Garner and Farley galloped around right end; Ickes skirted the left; Wallace bucked the line; and the quarterback threw a delayed pass to McNutt, all on the same play."

Out in Minnesota, he noted, they had been among the first to make many of the real advances in social welfare. But, he said, "we have learned by the hard and expensive way that the royal economists of the New Deal can be just as mistaken as the economic royalists. . . . Happily, we have been among the first to correct these mistakes, and generously, we hope the nation will not be too far behind."

Then Stassen set forth a Republican program which was largely to be adopted as the basis of the Willkie campaign the following year.

"Labor relations should be improved—not by cracking down on business and not by crushing labor, but by extending a helping hand to both."

Elaborating, he called for mandatory cooling-off periods before either a strike or a lockout, labor conciliators and labor courts, and a moderate code of unfair practices as to both capital and labor.

He urged parity subsidies for the farmers, aggressive marketing of surpluses at home and abroad, and an agricultural program "controlled more by workers in the field and less by field workers from Washington."

He called for research and invention and discovery as a means of developing new industrial enterprises to "bring work to men standing idle in the streets, and to capital lying idle in the banks. It must be encouraged by relieving it of many of the burdens that established industry can and must bear. . . . Courageous capital willing to venture out into new fields can be let out of the doghouse without being led into the White House."

He called for a sounder financial base for the government, simplification of administration, and government employees who "are servants of the people instead of corporals in a political army."

"I am convinced," he said, "that this revolution would be worth the price even if it involved abandoning the Jackson Day dinners."

He sounded a call against the domination of government by business and also the domination of business by government.

"In the separation of the two," he said, "we see the safeguarding of individual rights and a defense against special privilege, either economic or political."

"Government, in our view, must supply a cushion against the harsher features of a free economic system, but it cannot successfully furnish a bed on which society can go to sleep."

He advocated "more missionary work for democracy with a breadbasket than with a bayonet."

"History has shown that the rights of the individual citizen have been wrested from rulers," he said, "by the people within a country and not by those from without. Dictators and totalitarian states and the loss of liberties have occurred when economic difficulties either formed the background for the iron hand to fall or caused the people to voluntarily exchange their liberties and a known lack of food for a hope of better nourishment. It is rather our destiny to demonstrate the success of free individual enterprise under a democratic government on this continent, and to so utilize the great productive capacities of this country, that we help to bring about a world environment of abundance in which dictators cannot thrive."

These Stassen described as the landmarks which "we of the Midwest seek to establish."

"We note," he continued, "that Noah seems to have been the inspiration for one persistent practice of successive national administrations. They present their blessings, two by two. We vividly recall—'Two chickens in every pot,' 'Two cars in every garage,' and 'Two blades of grass where one grew before.' And this administration has given us two unions in every shop, two secretaries in the Department of War, two days of Thanksgiving, two secretaries of state, the one that works late at his office and the one that is Early at the White House. Some say two cabinets, the one with Murphy and Farley, and the one with Cohen and Corcoran. There are times when we are inclined to advocate the extension of this principle so that we have two Presidents, one to take care of domestic affairs, and one to watch for and report submarines off the Coast.

"Gentlemen of the Gridiron—May I express to you my appreciation for this invitation. I salute you on your great traditions. Mr. President, may I say to you that I realize the heavy burdens and extreme responsibilities of your position. Even though I disagree with the sum total of the New Deal, I respect your judgment and the integrity of your motives. May I assure you that my remarks tonight have been given in the 'spirit of the evening.' "[4]

This speech was in the top Gridiron tradition: partly serious, partly witty, with the wit directed both at his Gridiron hosts and at the opposite party and its leadership, and all delivered in a gracious, friendly spirit. It did much to make Stassen a figure of national stature.

Immediately after he finished, the Gridiron Club put on a Stassen snapper. Ulric Bell walked out on the stage in an apparent interruption of the program.

"Who are the gentlemen with you?" President Clapper asked. "I do not recognize them as members of the Gridiron Club."

"They are not," answered James L. Wright. And then they were announced: Former Governor Alf M. Landon of Kansas, Colonel Frank Knox of Chicago, John Hamilton, chairman of the Republican National Committee, Charles D. Hilles and Henry P. Fletcher.

All were on the stage in person. Bell announced to Clapper that "after hearing that brilliant oration, these Republican kingmakers decided to simplify party strategy. They have concluded not merely to delay their 1940 convention, but to dispense with it altogether and draft Governor Stassen at once as the party nominee."

"This is very embarrassing to me," Clapper replied. "In introducing Governor Stassen I omitted to say that a few little items like the Constitution of the United States and the calendar stand in his way. He will be only 33 years old and therefore ineligible to be elected President in 1940."

There was consultation on the stage. The participants held a brief whispered conference, shook their heads, and closed the skit with Bell announcing, "I have just consulted Governor Landon and he makes this suggestion: If the President of the United States feels now as he did about Thanksgiving Day, maybe he will oblige the Republicans by changing the date of Governor Stassen's birth." [That year President Roosevelt had proclaimed Thanksgiving Day as the third Thursday in November instead of the fourth.]

• • •

By April 13, 1940, the "phony war" had heated up. The fall of France was two months away. Norway and Denmark had been invaded by Hitler, but the seriousness of the conflict did not seem to really come home to the American people, as it would upon the fall of France.

Nor had President Roosevelt yet indicated whether he would seek a third term.

Consequently, the Gridiron dinner of that evening was heavily aligned toward the President and the upcoming election. In one skit he was referred to as "Public Enigma Number One," and Gridiron President Mark Foote of the Booth Newspapers, in opening the dinner, noted that "now everybody is in the dark—especially about the plans of a certain person."

Roosevelt was present and was scheduled to speak, so Foote said, "Maybe the Sphinx will speak tonight, if he isn't still in the dark himself."

In the opener, the chorus, costumed as owls on a darkened stage, hooted "Who? Who?" and sang:

Whom will they nominate?
Whom will they elevate?
Roosevelt, Garner, Farley, McNutt?
Vandenberg, Taft, Dewey? Tut, Tut!
Who in this room tonight,

Who has the answer right?
Who? Well, you ought to know who . . .

Curiously enough, the Gridiron Club, which had been quite prophetic in 1928, 1932 and 1936, did not mention in this skit the name of Wendell L. Willkie, president of the Commonwealth and Southern, who two months later was nominated as the Republican standard-bearer. Nor was he mentioned in any other respect, except for being asked to stand in the guest skit and hear himself identified as "an electric dark horse who may discover politics is just one big futility system."

In fact, it had been only two nights before the dinner, and too late to rewrite any skits, that Willkie had had his celebrated debate over the third term with Harold Ickes before the annual dinner of the American Society of Newspaper Editors. This was the debate which electrified his audience and sent back home scores of newspaper editors across the country convinced that Willkie's was the one Republican voice which correctly reflected the thought of the American people. This reaction had substantial effect in leading to his eventual nomination.

Word of the Sphinx skit of the year before had gotten around so widely that Roosevelt was being frequently referred to as "the Sphinx." Even in the traditional inauguration skit, in which the President participated directly from the head table by tugging at Foote's arm and whispering to him immediately after he was presented with the gavel, the big question was alluded to. Foote replied to the tug at his arm, "That's a good idea, Mr. President. I won't say anything now about not taking another term."

There was a brief skit about other Democratic possibilities, laid in a lamasery in the Himalayan Mountains, where the Tibetan Democratic National Committee, searching for a new Grand Lama, received a report from Confucius. Confucius said, in turn, that it might be Paul McNutt, who appeared wearing a Roosevelt mask; that it might be Cactus Jack or "Sunny" Jim and two or three other lesser lights, all wearing Roosevelt masks. The chorus sang:

Confucius say one thing is true today,
Ev'ry Democrat
Looks just like that!
Remember what Confucius say!

Sumner Welles had come upon the scene as a Roosevelt ambassadorial representative abroad, and this was no more pleasing

to Cordell Hull and his associates in the State Department than
Henry Kissinger's role in more recent years was to the Nixon
State Department prior to the time he became its secretary. The
situation was epitomized by a Welles solo:

> When I ambass,
> I just ambass for Franklin,
> President of U.S.A.
> And when I write,
> I only write to Franklin,
> A picture postcard every day.
> When I report,
> I just report to Franklin,
> That is how I get this way.
> And when I talk,
> I only talk to Franklin,
> Cause he tells me what to say!

The Republican skit focused upon those presidential aspirants who seemed at the time most likely to receive the nomination, but omitted the one who did eventually get in. An impersonator of Senator Taft sang his version of "I Want a Girl Just Like
the Girl That Married Dear Old Dad."

> After a Roosevelt you need a Taft,
> Close the window on the third term draft.
> I want a job, just like the job
> They gave to dear old dad.

Then a character representing Thomas E. Dewey, costumed
as Little Lord Fauntleroy, chimed in to the tune of "The Little Red
Fox":

> N'yah, n'ya, n'ya, I'm the wonder boy,
> N'ya, n'ya, you can't catch me,
> N'ya, n'ya, n'ya, I'm the glamour boy—
> Infant pro-di-gee
> On each fine speech I work for weeks,
> Casting a binding spell;
> I want a chance to wear long pants
> And give the New Deal hell.

Then "Vandenberg" sang to the tune of "The Man on the
Flying Trapeze":

> Oh, I'm no New Dealer, but still it's a fact
> I treat the New Dealers with infinite tact;
> It's just that I don't feel like being exact—

While the office is seeking the man.
   That's me. *(Spoken)*

Chorus:

Oh—He flies thru the air with the greatest of ease.
The Michigan man on the flying trapeze.
He's doing his best all the voters to please.
While the office is seeking the man.
Vandenberg again *(solo spoken):* "That's *me!*"

The emphasis was understandably on Vandenberg here, since he was to be the Republican speaker, and the act closed with some references to two major Republican contributors, Joseph N. Pew and Pierre S. du Pont, who lived in the vicinity of Philadelphia, where the Republican Convention was to be held:

Phil-a-del-phia here we come
Where we get the money from.
A platform, a ticket;
On with the wind.
The New Deal, we'll lick it;
We know just the place to kick it.
Phil-a-del-phia here we come
Eight long years are almost done.
Give us back ten million votes,
Phil-a-del-phia here we come.

Senator Arthur H. Vandenberg, whose earlier appearance at the Gridiron Club in 1933 had not been an overwhelming success, referred to that occasion when he said he was "bidden to this rostrum by the Gridiron Club to express the humbled greetings of an all but extinct minority to their smiling and far too persuasive conqueror."

"We had met," he said, "not only our match but our master—to borrow a later bare-fanged presidential idiom at Madison Square Garden. That speech seven years ago was a difficult and somber assignment. But time marches on!"

"Then," he said, "it was 'Hail to The Chief!'" Tonight, it is 'Good-Bye, Mr. Chips.'"

While Vandenberg may not have won any sweepstakes on that prediction, it nevertheless was a delightfully witty farewell which he paid to President Roosevelt.

"In this eighth and final year of Fireside Chats, of Vitamin I, and of annual promises to balance the budget, I am permitted the exquisite pleasure of speeding this departing administration upon its skidding way. I do so gladly and with great cheer. By the time we meet again at these harrowing but hospitable Gridiron boards, America will have convalesced.

"Of course, I do not overlook the cruel fact that this may be *my* 'Farewell' too—and I want to say it first before the distinguished chief speaker of the evening gets a chance which he would never overlook. . . .

"But I feel there are some other acknowledgments that should be made upon the occasion of such an historic 'last supper.' It is always charged that Republicans are ungrateful. Let not that be said of us in 1940. We owe infinitely much to these eight years. We have learned so much about what never, *never* to do again! Indeed, if we profit by the experience, it will *almost* be worth the 65 billions it has cost us!"

Then Vandenberg stopped his raillery to pay a very touching personal, "as distinguished from my political," compliment to the "departing President."

"However much we may quarrel over policy, there is one point at which I can join his loudest psalm-singers. Speaking of the man himself, I do not hesitate to say that I never knew a more gallant soul who has laughed triumphantly at the handicaps of life and given his country a superb example of personal courage and a personal challenge to 'carry on' to victory, no matter what the burden, no matter what the odds. His example to us in this regard has never been equaled and it will never be excelled."

Noting that he was in a "mellow mood tonight," he said that without exploring the dubious details too closely, "I do not hesitate to assert that history will accord him credit for making America social-minded."

"Of course, history will have some other things to say which I charitably pass in the spirit of the moment."

Continuing the raillery to the President, to whom he addressed his remarks directly much of the time, he noted that these great things about Mr. Roosevelt were "adequate achievements for any man."

"A third term might spoil it all—because we have yet to make these visions work. Indeed it will be the final tribute of his intermittent wisdom when the President decides, at last, to let the Republicans 'take the rap' for the next four years.

"Anyway, no further tenure is necessary to make an imperishable dent upon posterity. No indeed; they'll not forget because they will still be paying for this administration in 2000

A.D. Our children's children will find new meaning in the alphabet when they look back to see what cost so much in the pell-mell prodigality of halcyon Hyde Park days when a billion was just pocket change and when a battleship was just a fishing smack. They will learn their higher mathematics, as well as their astronomy, from a study of their inherited national debt. In that distant day they will say: 'How wise the New Deal was to create a National Youth Administration so as to encourage the development of new generations to pay its bills. . . .

"There will be yet other things to immortalize this errant and erratic era. The maxims—ah, the maxims that will be handed down! Sound maxims—maxims whose brilliant truth is hammered home by what happened when their authors departed from them!"

Then Vandenberg quoted a couple of "for examples" from Roosevelt's earlier speeches and writings: one about the family living within its income and that being equally true of the nation; the other, about the "master minds" back in the Hoover administration who thought they were "almost God-like" in their ability to manage and regulate.

"I pursue the maxims no farther lest they break your hearts."

"I have said this fabulous era needs no further time in which to leave its epitaphs. We shall remember it for thirty years whenever we glance up and down the bench of the Supreme Court and read its new decisions. We shall remember it in gold and silver when like Midas, we sit amid this sterile hoard and pine for more teeth to fill. We shall remember it for $100 dinners and $250 autographs, memorials to these mad moments when money was no object—or was it? We shall remember it in the travail that shall try men's souls ere we can disfranchise Santa Claus again—and restore Thanksgiving to its traditional date and justification. We shall remember it in the cemeteries of private enterprise where the victims of the New Deal are entombed. We shall remember it for Henry Wallace—and his little pigs; and for Harold Ickes—and his little puns. We shall remember it for rare Jim Farley—State Chairman, National Chairman, and itinerant Postmaster General—who thus, like all Gaul, is divided in three parts. We shall remember it for inimitable 'Cactus Jack' whom John L. Lewis enshrined in the hearts of his countrymen. But most of all we shall remember it for the amazing personality of its dominating genius who so captured the imagination of the people that they even forgot they were still unemployed.

"And now comes the great accounting in November. It is shrouded in apparent mystery because no one seems to know whether the examples of Washington and Jefferson are to be repealed. But much of this uncertainty is needless. I am greatly surprised that the journalistic members of the Gridiron Club missed the tip-off on this third term business. It came the day the President asked Congress for $2,500 for a Hoover portrait to hang in the White House. He never intends to look at that for four more years."

Noting that some newspaper writers had predicted that the 1940 campaign would degenerate into harsh and muddy personalities, Vandenberg said he trusted that "the wish is not father of the thought."

"I know," he admitted, "that no national campaign can be a kid-glove affair," and he had no objection to bare knuckles. "But even bare knuckles need not hit below the belt."

Speaking against any "relighting of the hateful fires of religious or class prejudice," he turned serious and said, "What happens to any of us politically is of no moment to the country; but what happens to our country is of vital concern to us all. America stands at the cross roads of destiny. It is a common destiny in which we shall all finally stand or fall together. Though we contest with utter vigor for the prevalence of whatever attitudes and policies may possess our souls, may we ever remember that we finally must be all for one and one for all against the vicissitudes of fortune—and perhaps against the world! . . .

"Mr. President, in great good spirit, I present to you my compliments; and I wish you every good thing in life—except votes. And please don't offer me that funeral suit of yours again. It's too late. The funeral is all over.

"Guests of the Gridiron Club: I bid you be of good cheer. The future is bright with hope. The Republicans are just around the corner. And anyway, if America could survive the last seven years, it can survive anything."[5]

Not very good political prognostication, but great satire. And even President Roosevelt seemed to like it.

In the Democratic skit, before President Roosevelt's speech, the scene was set in the Roosevelt Library at Hyde Park. The time was near the close of President Roosevelt's ninth administration.

Everybody wore long beards and there was also a sphinx with a long white beard. The skit opened with Stephen T. Early, press secretary to Roosevelt, being asked how the boss was feeling today and replying that "he's still worrying about not being able to get out of this job of being President."

Another Roosevelt aide, Pa Watson, said: "If he only had quit away back there in 1940. Everybody wanted him to quit."

"Everybody but him," retorted Early.

A Congressional committee arrived on the scene and "Senator Harry Byrd" of Virginia commented about a fine portrait of the President, to which "Senator Pat Harrison" of Mississippi replied that "you don't have to look at that likeness to know he's still President. All you have to do is look at the Treasury's books."

This was followed by a song sung by a bearded Treasury Secretary Morgenthau.

> Though your hair has turned to silver,
> Nothing else has changed its hue.
> For the Budget's still unbalanced
> And the Democrats are, too.
> Through the years with you we wander,
> In a rosy cloud we're led—
> You are still the same old Franklin,
> And we still are in the red!

Senator Byrd noted that the Sphinx was first introduced at the Gridiron dinner in 1939 and asked if it had been silent all this time.

"Yes," said Harrison, "he gave one little hiccup that night and hasn't said a word since."

Then, the chorus sang:

> Springtime brings mem'ries of the long, long ago,
> When this old Sphinx had a voice.
> We learned to listen on the old radio
> When we had no other choice.
> Though candidates say they will tell all in May,
> Your voice is silent, we know,
> Oh Franklin!
> Dust off the larynx, let us hear that old voice—
> Have courage, my boy, to say "No"!

It was noted that there were no more precedents to break— "he's broken them all."

"No more money to spend—he's spent it all."

"No more appointments to make—everybody's working for the government."

"And no more Republicans to oppose—they've all been deported to Little America, and elected Dick Byrd as president and a wicked old penguin as vice president."

President Roosevelt's latest appointment to the Supreme Court had been Frank Murphy, former governor of Michigan and, immediately preceding his appointment, President Roosevelt's attorney general.

Murphy had taken his seat on the Supreme Court at the session which opened in the beginning of October. After a few days in Washington he had decided he needed a vacation and had gone to Miami for an extended stay. Chief Justice Hughes was not happy about this, because the work load of Supreme Court justices was heavy, and Murphy wasn't around to write opinions or participate in cases. Furthermore, while he was down in Miami, pictures had appeared in the newspapers of Murphy on the beach surrounded by a group of chorus girls in rather abbreviated bathing suits. This was too much for what Chief Justice Hughes thought was the dignity of the Court.

On private occasions around Washington, Hughes had made no effort to conceal his opinions about the new justice. The skit touched upon this by noting that the President didn't have Supreme Court trouble any more because of the numerous appointments he had had up to that time, whereupon Harrison remarked that "there are only eight justices anyway."

"What happened to the ninth?" asked Senator Byrd.

"Associate Justice Frank Murphy will tell you about that," replied Senator Harrison.

At this point, "Murphy" came on the stage dressed in a green bathing suit and carrying a green beach parasol and sang:

Moon over Miami
Hot spots in old New York.
That's where I go, *quo warrento,*
For judicial work!

Moon over Miami,
Pro bono publico.
A place to do a case or two
When the tide is low!

Moon over Miami,
Res ipsa loquitur,
A cozy nook—with a big law book.
On Miami shore!

Murphy did not record his opinions of this skit in a diary as Harold Ickes had, but he never came to a Gridiron dinner again.

The skit closed with a parody on "Serenade" from *The Student Prince*, in which the bearded men pleaded with the President to close the story after thirty-six years in office.

> Overhead the stars are shining,
> As they shone in days gone by.
> Let us bring back days of long, long ago
> Let us wake without repining.
> From this dream of greater glory;
> Only you can tell us how, O Franklin!
> Break your silence, close the story—
> Let us awaken—now!

The President loved it.

"Nine terms! Gentlemen, it is too much!" were Roosevelt's opening words. "There ought to be a law against it. At least there ought to be an American tradition against it. One of those absolutely sacred American traditions against more than eight terms.

"While I agree with that galaxy of willing Barkises who insist that no man is big enough to refuse the Presidency at least in the first instance, nevertheless, I do not think any man should be compelled to accept it as many as nine times.

"I know people, many of them in this room, who do not think that any man ought to serve even a second term. I strongly suspect that there are men in this room who want to whittle even that down, so far as certain other gentlemen, also present, are concerned. In respect to the other fellows, they are fierce and vocal believers in the 'no-term tradition.' Let that chip fall where it may.

"But nine terms—that is, indeed, a terrible prospect to face. I hope you will give generous applause when I express the wish that all of you who are here tonight will give me your aid and support in limiting the American tradition hereafter to eight terms.

"And the panorama is only partly alleviated by the knowledge that one of the rewards is the privilege of having a ringside seat at these Gridiron dinners.

"But, after all, it is possible to pay *too much* for your supper.

"However, speaking just for background and not 'off the record,' I do enjoy these dinners and I always will.

"I enjoy seeing all the old familiar faces, beaming as they do tonight with the bright spirit of goodwill and friendship for this administration.

"Yes, I enjoy all the old familiar gags—the changeless humor of the horse and buggy variety that I have come to love. I enjoy the haunting melodies of the old tunes of my childhood, the lusty, gusty, hairy choruses—and the Marines—and I miss old Taylor Branson tonight, always keeping the situation well in hand.

"All the old familiar faces. It is a never ending source of wonderment and mystery to me—the wealth and the power that you manage to crowd into this one room.

"Standing here I couldn't toss a bouquet or a biscuit out into this sea of hard-boiled, smiling faces without hitting a man qualified, on the one account or the other, to be an American senator or an American diplomat.

"I am sorry I did not think of that before I ate my biscuit. But perhaps it is just as well, for if I had hit somebody with said biscuit I would have been accused of tossing the mantle of Elijah on the new Elisha.

"Yon bearded sphinx glowering at me is a bit disconcerting to humor or an attempt at it. But I must pay tribute to the Gridiron Club by saying that most of its members really have a sense of humor. That does not apply to the minority of them who are columnists, and interpreters, and commentators—in their case they have a very highly developed sense of rumor.

"And after seven long years here I note another characteristic of our hosts of tonight. A member of the Club smiles and crows and chortles when he is holding the Gridiron—but if somebody else gets hold of that Gridiron and looks sternly in his direction, he runs like hell."

Roosevelt referred to a skit in which a character said that he had refused to tell whether or not he had a mortgage on the little old house on Pennsylvania Avenue. The President said he didn't have one, but that in one of the closets there was that suit which he had once promised to Arthur Vandenberg seven years ago, to wear at his inauguration. It was getting a little out of style, he said, and Arthur hadn't called for it yet, and "frankly, I am wondering if he ever will."

"We keep it in moth balls and it will still be good enough for next January, but I am afraid that is the last chance for Arthur—and I will have to give it away to the old-clothes man, because the trousers are much too big in every dimension for either Bobby

Taft or Tommy Dewey—and I don't think they will grow enough to be able to wear them until 1944 or later."

This was not the speech of a man who didn't plan to run.

Then Roosevelt referred to "John etcetera Hamilton" and a lot more of his "Republican friends" who had been keeping their thumbs in the dike because they feared a domestic flood—whereas for seven years everybody had known "that there has not been any danger of drowning."

"But, nevertheless," he continued, "I take my hat off to them for their charming simplicity and their childlike faith in keeping their thumbs in the dike.

"And Arthur, though perhaps he does not know it, got off, in one of his rare radio speeches, a line that will find its place among famous quotations. He said, 'A state of mind is the hardest thing possible to defeat.'

"Nothing could be truer, even from the standpoint of a man on a flying trapeze. You cannot defeat a state of mind by sticking your thumb in the dike or by sticking your tongue in your cheek—or, as a lot of people are coming to realize, by sticking your neck into a primary."

What goes on "in a certain other political party" was none of the business of "us Democrats," he said, and then drew a comparison with circuses.

"That trapeze act is good and the rest of the circus that has come to town is good," he commented, and then proceeded to reminisce about the circus coming to Dutchess County when he was a boy, and how the "very immature of all ages" ran up and down the streets to follow the circus parade.

Dr. Glenn Frank, who was present at the dinner, Roosevelt said, was "ballyhooing one of the smaller circuses—a 17 million circus following in the footsteps of a 28 million circus" (a reference to the 1936 Presidential vote). The President said that his circus had "almost all of the attractive features of the bigger show."

But their posters, he continued, "seem to agree that their circus this year embodies a change of heart. They say, 'If we can't lick 'em, let's jine 'em.' I say, let them come in but not on their own terms. Their proposal is not merely to join the New Deal but to take over the management. And looking around me again, I don't think any of them have quite grown up to that. And my old nurse Jim Farley says they'll be big enough in 1960. And Jim knows babies."

Then, turning serious, he said that the Gridiron dinner was "a good deal of relief for all of us—because for an hour or two it takes our minds off of what we know to be the more serious happenings of today and the more serious threats of tomorrow."

The news, he said, was making everyone realize that we "will be affected for good or for evil, whether we like it or not, by the wars that rage on other continents."

Without identifying anyone, Roosevelt referred to the suggestion "by one who seeks the highest public office" that the United States should keep out of the wars in Europe and Asia. "He is right in that—but also that the United States has no interest and will never have any interest in the restoration of peace in the world."

"That suggestion is contrary to the highest ideals of the American people; it is contrary to the policy of the American government; it is contrary to the American wish that we do everything possible by peaceful means to help day in and day out to bring lasting peace among the nations of the world; it is contrary to American ideals based on the simplest teachings of Christianity—American ideals that look to the security of the American people, not just by building up our army and our navy, but also by encouraging all nations, with us, to reduce armaments and to widen greatly and fairly the commercial and cultural relations among all nations.

"All people in this room are ready to give lip service to the proposition that domestic politics stop at the sea shore. It is a pity, therefore, that any aspirants for public office should honor that precept in the breach by seeking to expand domestic politics into the foreign field.

"In our attitude toward wars abroad, we can afford to be at one among ourselves. In our attitude toward staying out of those wars, we can equally afford to be at one among ourselves. And in our desire to further the cause of peace and speak out boldly against the cause of aggression, we can afford to be at one among ourselves—mere vote seekers to the contrary notwithstanding."

Then he read to the Gridiron Club the announcement he had released for the next morning's newspapers on the Nazi invasion of Denmark and Norway. That statement ended with the comment that if civilization is to survive, "the rights of the smaller nations to independence, to their territorial integrity, and to the unimpeded opportunity for self-government must be respected by their more powerful neighbors.

"That needs no elaboration or elucidation," he said. "It speaks, I hope, I think, I deeply believe, the thought of the people of the United States of America."[6]

• • •

France had fallen six months before the December 1940 dinner, and the Battle of Britain was reaching high intensity. America was supplying arms and aircraft to England and was building up its own massive arsenal and military forces.

The situation was just too grim for any Gridiron laughter. But on the unity of America and the world waiting for the sunrise and happy days to come once more, the Gridiron show could unite.

Just a month earlier, President Roosevelt had been reelected to a third term. With this, with Wendell Willkie, with Henry Wallace, and with the Democrats and the Republicans, the Gridiron Club could have a lot of fun.

Vice President Garner had been retired by President Roosevelt, and consequently, the big controversy at the Democratic Convention in Chicago had been over his new running mate. The President had told the Democratic leaders that he wanted Henry Wallace, then secretary of agriculture, nominated, but the Convention obviously preferred Paul McNutt and might conceivably have nominated him had he not withdrawn his name.

The President's demand for Wallace produced considerable revolt among political leaders of the party, who did not appreciate Wallace's midwestern populism.

There were still many signs of dissent, among them a small, satirical boom for journalist Bascom N. Timmons, a 6'3" member of the Gridiron Club from Texas. He was a familiar figure around the nation's capital, where he and his organization were correspondent for nearly thirty southwestern newspapers.

Timmons's Gridiron colleagues and their friends staged an amusing "parade of delegates" down Michigan Avenue on his behalf. The pictures made all the papers and Timmons's name was placed in formal nomination. On the roll call he received one vote—his nominator's.

However, in spite of all the griping and ridicule, there had been nothing for the Democratic Convention to do but to follow the wishes of its leader. It could not nominate him for a third term and repudiate his choice for a Vice President.

Later, Timmons, who had known Wallace for many years,

encountered him and in a most solemn fashion commented, "Mr. Secretary, after you defeated me for Vice President my first inclination was to be angry. But now I have become philosophical about it and bear no malice, because I realize that although you won, we were really not very far apart after all—I had one guy for me and you had one guy for you."

For the Gridiron dinner of December 14, 1940, the club hoped to stage a repeat of the Roosevelt-Landon exchange in 1936, and invited Willkie to be the opposition speaker. Willkie accepted, but President Roosevelt, for the first time since he had become President, declined the Gridiron invitation and arranged to go vacationing in the Caribbean on the cruiser *Tuscaloosa*.

This caused considerable criticism of Roosevelt, on the ground that since the vanquished candidate was willing to come and speak, he should have agreed to be there also. The White House felt the sting of criticism enough that it released publicly its letter of declination to the Gridiron dinner and insisted that no snub to Willkie was intended.

This situation provided the cue for President Mark Foote's opening remarks:

"Tonight the Gridiron Club makes its contribution to the cause of national unity. During the late unpleasantness, by a series of strange coincidences it happened that the paths of the President of the United States and the Republican candidate did not cross. By a series of strange coincidences, they do not cross tonight. The Great Inspector and the Great Crusader are still more than twelve hours apart."

And then, referring to the election results, he pointed out that President Roosevelt did not get a chance to "realize his 'ambition' to retire."

"But Vice President Garner got his. The two-term tradition still stands—for Vice Presidents."

The dinner opened with the Gridiron Club satirizing itself in a skit entitled "Uncle Franklin's Dog House," in which the announcer said that "the Gridiron Club always correctly predicts election results." There followed then a repetition of numerous songs from previous dinners which had proved to be something less than accurate in their forecasts, among them: "There'll Be No Third Term," "The Merry-Go-Round Broke Down," "Thanks for the Memory," "There's a Hole in the Old Hickory Bucket," and "Roll out the New Deal."

It closed with a new song—a version of "Farmer in the Dell."

Oh, we knew it all the time,
We knew it all the time,
The Champ is still the Champion,
We knew it all the time!

During the campaign, President Roosevelt had made a speech in which he referred sarcastically to three Republican congressmen, Martin, Barton and Fish—Republican House Leader Joseph Martin, Congressman Bruce Barton, and Congressman Hamilton Fish. This was celebrated in verse by impersonators of the three gentlemen the President had excoriated.

Oh we turned out to win an election,
It didn't turn out to our wish.
But we still are the pink of perfection—
Oh–
Martin
     and Barton
          and Fish!

Oh we searched for political knowledge,
A diploma for Wendell to swish.
But we flunked the electoral college—
Oh–
Martin
     and Barton
          and Fish!

Oh we managed to spend a few millions,
As a huge vote we tried to unleash,
But the other guy did it with billions—
Oh—
Martin
     and Barton
          and Fish!

The Republican skit was set in front of a Union League Club and was based on the dissatisfaction of the more traditional Republicans, such as Vandenberg, Dewey and Taft, with Willkie, whom they regarded as having improperly snatched the nomination from the party, or from these three, at its convention.

To the tune of "Abdul Abulbul Amir," they sang:

The Hoosier crusader was somewhat a bust
But sturdy and bravely he stands,
And the Oregon prune [Willkie's running mate, McNary]
     doesn't lie in the dust

Right back in the Senate he lands.
Time was when the Hoosier crusader rode high
And the chances for vict'ry looked good,
When the GOP thought that this team might get by,
And was rather afraid that it would.

A group of editors who had supported Willkie's nomination, headed by "Roy Howard," gave their impressions of the election results, and Howard sang:

I'll never smile again
Because I bet on him.
He'll never yacht again.
Next time he can swim.
The tears that fill my eyes
Are 'cause I realize
That our romance is through.
I'll climb no limb again
And get it sawed in two.
I'll never thrill again
To somebody new.
Within my heart I know I will never start
A boom again,
This time—honest—I'm through.

Then an impersonator of Willkie entered, turned to the audience, threw out his arms and said, "Join me, join me—because only the productive can be strong and only the strong can be a loyal opposition." He had made so many speeches during the campaign that his voice on several occasions had forsaken him, and at this point in the skit a page hurried forward and sprayed his throat. Then Willkie sang to the strains of "Invictus":

Out of the fight that smothered me,
Blacker it was than Gallup's poll,
I bring what's left of GOP,
But someone else must dig the hole.

I thought I'd take F.D. in camp,
You must admit I drew a crowd,
Beneath the left hooks of the champ,
My jaw is battered but still loud.

Dewey and Taft just get this straight,
Vandenberg, Hoover, the Old Guard's corps,
I still am master of your fate,
I'll be the boss in forty-four.

The skit ended with Vandenberg singing:

Hail to the scholar, hail to the scribe,
Hail, statesman, too—
We all want Willkie—the hail we do.

This served as the introduction to Willkie's speech, and he was presented by President Foote with references to the "verbal blitzkrieg" which he gave the country, and "to the valiant fight" he made.

"To lose with 22,000,000 votes is a real accomplishment," said Foote, "and magnanimously to toast the man who vanquished him is better."

No record of the Willkie speech exists in the Gridiron files or in the records of the Willkie family, but ASCAP President Gene Buck, in his after-dinner letter to the club, said this:

"He [Willkie] was very smart, in the first half of his speech, being satirical in the mood of the evening and in the second half put on his crusading clothes and I thought he made good. He is an extraordinary guy. . . . My God, where does he get that energy!"[7]

The scene for the Democratic skit was the electoral college, where the faithful had gathered to pay their respects "to the four horsemen of Kelly, Nash, Hague and Crump," the four big Democratic bosses, and "the greatest Quarterback of all time." Their cheerleader, adapting a phrase of Harry Hopkins, led the cheers.

Tax, tax, tax,
Spend, spend, spend,
Elect, elect, elect,
R-a-a-a-y!

But in spite of barbed references to the campaign, the club sang a "Sweetheart of Sigma Chi" parody.

The charm of his smile and the lilt of his voice
Are a blend of new-mown hay.
And that White House key stays with Franklin D.,
He's the sweetheart of U.S.A.

The dinner closed with what the Gridiron Club characterized as the post-election spirit of the nation, in a revue entitled "Reunion in America." Noting that politics makes strange bedfellows, impersonators of various pairs of people who didn't like each other very well were announced with fanfare as they entered together:

Secretary Ickes and Boss Kelly of Chicago!

Senator Norris and Boss Hague of Joisey!

William Allen White and Senator Hiram Johnson!

John L. Lewis and Tom Girdler!

Mayor LaGuardia and Boss Flynn!

Al Smith and Herbert Hoover!

They sang:
> Comrades, comrades,
> After election day;
> Politics made us playmates
> Happy and blithe and gay.
> Now that election is over
> Faithful whate'er may be betide,
> When danger threatens, old foes and old friends
> Will be there, side by side!

Characters representing big business and little business sang:

> The world, the world, is waiting for the sunrise,
> Franklin D., we'll face it with you.
> The past, the past, we'll put away behind us,
> Yes, we will—there's nothing else to do!

In another song, the Democrats and the "loyal opposition" proclaimed that they were for "just one more term for the sunshine of his smile!" And the skit closed with a song of unity at home, a version of "Sing a Song of Harvest," led by Edwin C. Steffe.

> Let us sing a song for happy days to come once more;
> Time is short, "It's later than you think,"
> But we'll do a job to make the nations blink,
> Heaven's blessings from above shower on the land we love—
> Sing a song of unity at home!

• • •

In the spring of 1941, the German air attack on England was beginning to wane, as the RAF, aided by American lend-lease, and inspired by the leadership of Winston Churchill, was shooting down more and more of the German planes attacking London. Nevertheless, there was great fear throughout America that Hitler might win the war. There was no second front at this time, since Germany did not attack the Soviet Union until June 22. But the United States, through lend-lease and direct sale to Britain, was giving strong industrial support to the "Allies," which then consisted of little more than heroic Britain.

In this atmosphere of tension, while events in Europe were moving swiftly, the Gridiron dinner took place on April 5, 1941. As if to underscore that tension, early in the dinner a messenger from the *New York Times* came and gave a Secret Service man, for delivery to Arthur Krock, a *Times* dispatch saying that the Soviet Union and Yugoslavia had signed a non-aggression pact. Krock promptly passed this message along to Secretary of State Hull and President Roosevelt, who was in attendance at this dinner.

The new vice president, Henry Wallace, was also there. Wallace had been under some criticism because he had been away at lunch when the administration lost a tie vote in the Senate, which he could have broken if he had been present.

But now, under the circumstances of the times, it was natural that the dinner would have a minimum of political disparagement and an emphasis on unity. I was president of the Gridiron Club that year, and in my opening speech in the dark, I sought to set this tone.

"Here in America the lights are still lit," I said, as the huge Gridiron behind the head table flashed on; "here we help to carry the torch; here the Gridiron shines; here democracy lives."

"On my right sits the man who came to dinner—and we welcome him warmly.

"On my left sits the man who went to lunch—and that just about ties it.

"Gentlemen, it is a pleasure to welcome you here in this last major capital of the world where we may gather together around the bowl and the table and laugh with and at each other. As long as the Gridiron shines, let no one tell you that there is not freedom of speech and freedom of the press in America. As long as the Gridiron shines let no one deny that the basic liberty of Americans lives.

"And so let us celebrate it tonight. Long life to it. Thumbs up. There'll always be an England. There'll always be democracy in America because we know how to use our liberty in unity."

There was considerable labor difficulty in the country, which was causing much annoyance to William S. Knudsen, former president of General Motors who had taken over the Office of Production Management. Early in the dinner, to the tune of "Oh

Susanna," impersonators of Knudsen and Sidney Hillman sang a duet. A couple of verses were:

Knudsen:
>I think there should be cooling off
>>Before a strike is called.
>It's hard to make the engine run
>>When all the wheels are stalled.

Hillman:
>Oh when the talk of cooling off
>>Is heard around the board,
>That's just the time for me to take
>>A crack at Henry Ford!

It ended with them agreeing to take their troubles to Bernard Baruch "and save democracy."

Even the Republican skit by Walker Buel was "a farewell to the two-party system," as the chorus sang:

>All the boys look to the White House
>Waiting for the OK sign.
>That lend-lease bill has busted up
>That old gang of mine.

One of the characters sang of President Roosevelt:

>O when I hear you speak
>So eloquently,
>I don't hear a speech at all
>I hear a rhapsody!
>And when at Hitler you
>May thundering be,
>Then loud through the star-lit blue
>I hear a rhapsody!

Then a character representing Willkie sang to the tune of "It All Comes Back to Me Now":

>Millions barred me from the White House
>But now its doors open wide.
>When Franklin calls, What a rapture!
>I get a hearty welcome inside!

At the end they decided that "if we can take what we've had for the past eight years, I guess we're ready for any future!" And the skit closed with a parody on "Memories."

>'Round us at twilight come stealing
>Shadows of days that are gone;

Dreams of campaigns and elections,
Dreams of debates pro and con—

Memories, Memories, dreams both bright and blue;
O'er the sea of memory we're drifting back to you;
GOP, democracy, draw the curtains, please;
You're gone for a while,
But still we can smile
At our wonderful memories!

Much effort was being made by the Roosevelt administration to develop good pro-American, pro-British relations with the Latin American republics. This led to a "Pan American Musical" written by Phelps Adams and Walter Karig. The scene was set in a Mexican village outside an adobe shack with a swinging sign that displayed a glass of beer and the proprietor's name, "Herman."

"There used to be a phrase known as Yankee imperialism," said the announcer, "but now to give you a very rough idea of the great change that is taking place south of the Rio Grande, we take you to the plaza in a small Latin American village where the *alcalde* and his aides are impatiently awaiting the arrival of two distinguished traveling salesmen from the United States."

The traveling salesmen proved to be impersonators of Vice President Wallace and James A. Farley, who had retired from the administration and had become the chairman of Coca-Cola International. When the *alcalde* announced that the two distinguished salesmen were about to arrive, the orchestra started to play "Begin the Beguine," and the chorus of Latin Americans sang:

Let us begin to begin,
Whatever it is Jim Farley is selling
We're eager to buy, desire is welling,
We want to begin right now to begin.

If all this seems strange you're out of date,
You don't understand the new economics,
Your old world ideas belong in the comics,
So watch us begin to begin.

We used to distrust all Yankee endeavor,
And we used to think they had no heart,
Now here we are swearing to love forever,
And promising never—never to part.

Yes, the Yankees are aw-ful-ly happy to lend it,
And as good neighbors we must do our best to spend it,
That's Democracy and may God help us to defend it.

It's really a sin
The clover we're in,
So come let's begin to begin,
So come let's begin—to begin.

A diplomat insisted that Farley couldn't sell anything Yankee down there, and his impersonator replied, "Go on, I can sell anything. Didn't I sell Roosevelt?"

"Vice President Wallace," who prided himself on his ability to speak Spanish, sang, to the tune of "Orchids in the Moonlight":

We love to speak Español!
Please do not listen to Adolf,
Benit's mucho bad guy—
We love your fiestas
Likewise your siestas
And our love will never die.
Here's salud and pesetas
Here's a long life to you
And the pesos we lend you can hurry to spend
Never mind IOU.

Jim Farley started passing out Coca Cola, and Herman started trying to sell his beer. "Ach Gott," said Herman, "first they lease it, then they lend it, and now they giff it!" Then Herman gave up and sang his version of "The Carioca."

Here I got Pilsner und mit it I give free cheese,
But what is Pilsner against these wealthy Yan-kees?
And as for Münchner they say, "Oh no, if you please
I think that I'll
Have some Coca-Cola, ja, and make it tall.
I'll have some Coca-Cola." Ach, no beer at all.
Und den dey smile!

I guess I can't beat Coca-Cola,
They stuff it right up my schnozola,
I guess I got to take my steins down and
    my signs down und I'm through.
Up in the states their buried gold rots,
But Hitler's currency is er-satz,

And so what else is there that I, Herman,
  a poor German, can do?

Wallace was about to loan them $6 million, or "in round numbers, $10 million." The diplomatic aide said, however, they must call Secretary of Commerce Jesse Jones first. It should be noted that Jones was the final arbiter of such foreign loans, and that frequently he wasn't as liberal as the Roosevelt administration would have liked him to be. When it was revealed, in answer to the diplomatic aide, that this was Jesse Jones's birthday and that he was at the Gridiron dinner, they decided to phone him.

By prearrangement Jones was to participate in the skit and say, when they asked him about borrowing $10 million, "That's OK. This is my birthday, and if it's for my friends the Latin Americans, give 'em fifty millions."

But Jones didn't follow the script. When they asked him from the stage about borrowing $10 million, he cupped his hand to his ear and said, "What did you say?" They said, "How about borrowing $50 million'?" and Jones said, "When people ask for money like that I don't hear very well. What did you say?"

The skit ended with a version of "South American Way."

Aide:
  Hi yi, hi yi.
  Now our friendship certainly fattens
  In that international
  Quite irrational
  Pan American way.
Wallace:
  You spend, we pay
  For we surely do love the Latins
  In that highly lyrical
  Hemispherical
  Pan American way.
Duet:
  There's nothing else to do
  We're in the same canoe
  So here's my hand to you
  For weal or woe!
  Now let us give a cheer
  For our own hemisphere
  And none of us need fear
  A foreign foe.

Herman:

> Ja-ja, ja-ja.
> Und I might yoost mention in passing
> Dot some naval bases
> In every place is
> Der Pan American way! I'm licked.

Mussolini, who had bravely declared war on France just before France fell to Germany, was depicted in another skit as the Wizard of Oz. Dorothy, the Woodman, the Bear, the Scarecrow, and Anzac ended up discovering that the wonderful Wizard was just a humbug, a fake, and a phony. At that point the Scarecrow snapped his fingers in disgust, "Oh, the—*deuce!*"

> We've been to see the Wizard, the Wonderful Wizard of Oz.
> We've been to see the Wizard, and a hell of a Wiz he was!

Senator Henry Cabot Lodge, Jr. of Massachusetts was the Republican speaker. He began in the best Gridiron style. He wondered why he had been chosen to speak for the opposition.

"One explanation, of course," he said, "is that the Gridiron Club desired to present a horrible example of what happens to newspapermen who go into politics. [For six years, Lodge had been in the *Herald-Tribune* bureau in Washington.]

"Another explanation," he continued, "is that in these days when national unity is the watchword, it is well to have as a speaker a Republican whose entire service has been under Democratic Chief Executives, ranging all the way from James M. Curley to Franklin D. Roosevelt. He thus gets into the habit of following Democratic leadership."

And then, a sly dig at Wendell Willkie: "I have recently noticed that this is not only a trait of Republican legislators. It is shared by Republican presidential candidates."

His third explanation was that "there was one man who said to me that I had been selected because in these days when foreign policy is paramount it was considered advisable to have a speaker who belongs to a family which so strongly favored the League of Nations—with reservations."

Turning to Lend-Lease, Lodge said that "these are considered great days for us League of Nations men.

"It is said," he declared, "that we have returned to the ideal of twenty years ago and that in passing the Lend-Lease Bill we turned our back on the isolationist days of the post war twenties and thirties. Once again, so we are told, we have embraced internationalism.

"I wonder if they are right. It seems to me that we lost the League of Nations because of the assertion that under the League covenant Great Britain had eight votes to our one. In the present situation, however, President Roosevelt has all the votes and Great Britain hasn't any."

Gently ribbing President Roosevelt, he noted that "we may not have followed TR to the point of adhering to the maxim of 'speak softly and carry a big stick.' For quite a while we threatened and lectured the world when our defenses were deplorably weak. We are now beginning to get a big stick but we are not yet speaking softly. At any rate we have stopped rattling the olive branch."

Coming to the question of national unity, he said that some people think this means that both sides to an argument will make some concessions so that all in the end will unite.

"Some of my colleagues of the majority, however, seem to think that national unity means that no amendments, however reasonable, are to be accepted unless you are absolutely forced to do so at the point of a gun. The kind of close fellowship which Jonah had with the whale is not our idea of national unity.

"You can probably get national unity if you make no concessions, but can you get it if you tell no one where you are going or how you propose to get there? That has been the problem facing some of us dull-witted Republicans."

Then Lodge became serious and said that the Republicans approved many of the sentiments being uttered by the "Late New Deal."

"Our trouble was," he explained, "that we liked the sentiments for a longer time than their authors did. We liked the idea of eliminating unemployment—not simply providing a stop-gap relief. We made studies. We devised plans. We assembled facts. But when we raised our heads from our labors we found that the caravan had moved on, that unemployment was no longer of interest to the leaders and that we should stop our efforts and concentrate on the new things—on how old the Supreme Court justices were, on how bad the monopolies and financial houses were, or on how important it was to switch the Civil Aeronautics Authority to the Commerce Department—everything, in short, except the elimination of unemployment—I might add everything except national defense.

"I have figured out that there have been eighty legally declared emergencies during the past seven years but none of the problems seemed to have been solved. . . .

"There has been the cry of emergency, then the hurried appropriation of money by Congress, then a few Executive fireworks, and then, presto! we go on to something else.

"The performance of course is thrilling. It makes us *think* that something has been done. Is this after all the essence of modern government—to make people *think* the problem has been solved regardless of the facts? To create thoughts, rather than to get results? Is this what the slow-witted literal-minded Republicans have been unable to see? I keep thinking of that lone ninety millimeter anti-aircraft gun which was photographed so often in the campaign. It was the only one of its kind in the United States. It was photographed so often, however, that we thought we had thousands of them and we felt correspondingly strong."

Then he enumerated some of the leading issues—the question of British victory, providing a proper national defense, and avoiding actual involvement in the war. On the first, there were various positions, but on the last two, he said, there was indeed unity. And he closed with a tribute to President Roosevelt:

"National unity," he said, "also depends upon a man. We have the man. His popularity is greater than ever before. Even the Groton and Harvard boys support him. Up my way the chief opponents of the post New Deal era are Democrats—and they have nowhere else to go.

"We have a President who can get a lot of national unity and a lot of Republican support even if he concedes very little and even if he follows policies with which many disagree. He can do this because of the confidence which so many have that he was in earnest when he said that he would labor for peace all the days of his life. He can do this because people believe in his ability; they do not think that anyone will make a sucker out of him. Nobody has yet.

"If the ability which he has shown, the personal courage which he embodies and the idealism which he so well expresses are applied to plotting America's course, you will see the Republicans in the front line of the big parade."[8]

It had been traditional in the Gridiron Club for many years never to depict the President of the United States as a character on the Gridiron stage, although on some occasions characters under other names have shown a resemblance. People on the stage talk about him, but he never appears. At this dinner the club found a way to observe the tradition technically but to get around it for all practical purposes.

The scene was a cabinet meeting, with the members of the cabinet around the table facing a big high-backed chair with its back to the audience. As the cabinet discussed various things, smoke puffs came out at appropriate moments from a long cigarette holder attached to the big chair, protruding upwards and visible to the audience.

Six of the cabinet members each requested $7 billion for a particular project: the State Department to establish schools for career men, the Treasury for a promotion campaign to sell Baby Bonds, and the Agriculture Department to hire seven million more county agents "who'll teach the farmers how to dig up the crops we taught them to plow under—those farm states that voted for Willkie last year can use a lot of learning."

Each time a puff of smoke came from the cigarette and each secretary said, "Thank you Sir, I knew you'd approve my plans."

Finally, before they were about to break up, "Secretary Ickes" interrupted, "Sir, you might think the Interior Department has nothing to do with national defense. But I have. I could spend seven billion dollars educating newspaper publishers—the kept press you know."

Three or four smoke puffs.

"Oh thank you Sir, I knew I could count on you."

Because of lend-lease, the Washington of April 1941 was swarming with British officials, and Turner Catledge, later executive editor of the *New York Times*, conceived a skit to close the dinner based on the relationships between Roosevelt, Churchill and the British.

An old couple reminisced on the stage beside a spinning wheel and sang:

There's an old spinning wheel in the parlor,
Spinning dreams of the long, long ago,
When the red coats and blue coats were fighting,
And there was no such land as we know.
My Grandmother spun by the fireplace,
Your Grandfather marched far away,
Now the red coats and blue coats are fighting,
But they fight on the same side today.

Catledge, costumed as Paul Revere, entered carrying a lantern which he held aloft. " 'Tis I—Paul Revere—the British are not coming! They're here."

As they marched in, the band struck up "Here Come the British," and Catledge sang:

> Paul Revere he took a ride,
> Just to look around the countryside,
> All at once his horse got skittish,
> Here come the British, bang, bang.
> Washington at Valley Forge,
> Tried to cross the river, look out George!
> All at once his boat got skittish,
> Here come the British, bang, bang, *Oh!*

Paul Revere announced that "the Yanks will be coming along," and as they did, a duet occurred between the Blue Coat chorus and the Red Coat chorus:

Blue Coats:
> Yankee Doodle says thumbs up,
> And may we please remind you,
> We hope you'll beat the enemy,
> We're heart and soul behind you.

Red Coats:
> Yankee Doodle, thank you, but,
> We're in a tough position,
> We've got the heart, we've got the men,
> But we need ammunition.

Blue Coats:
> Yankee Doodle goes to town,
> To help his British Cousins,
> He'll send 'em ships and guns and shells
> And bombers by the dozens.

Red Coats:
> Yankee Doodle, step it up,
> We think you're doing dandy,
> But we need somewhat more than that,
> To do the job up handy.

Blue Coats:
> Yankee Doodle says okay,
> More work and less oration,
> We'll give you all we can produce,
> To give the foe damnation.

Together:
> Yankee Doodle, here we go,

That's all we need to beat 'em
Our fact'ries, our R.A.F.,
Together we'll defeat them.

The skit, which consisted mostly of songs, ended in a rousing chorus:

Your fate and our fate, are the world's fate today,
Take heart as we start, sending guns on the way,
Our two lands forever, when war and hatred are gone, So!
Glory, Glory Hallelujah, we'll sing as we go marching on.

And immediately, the toast to the President was proposed.

Just as the Gridiron Club, in the world tensions of 1941, had pretty much abandoned its traditional satire (except for the Pan American skit), so President Roosevelt, in his response, offered little banter and talked to the audience quite seriously.

At the beginning however, he did take a gentle gibe at the Gridiron Club by recalling that he was in Washington during the period of World War I, from July 1914 to April 1917—"nearly three years of a life of unreality."

Alluding to the Gridiron habit of "playful cartooning of domestic political parties and candidates and Presidents and ex-Presidents," he said it was even then the tradition at the close of the dinners that the President should rise and "return blow for blow in a duel of wits, which would excite the mirth of your guests, and, at the same time, soothe and flatter the Gridiron Club, which even then was a serious organization—an organization which always regarded itself as a vehicle for laughter, but never as a subject for laughter."

Then he told of attending a dinner in July 1918 in the Elizabethan banquet hall of Gray's Inn, a dinner at which Churchill spoke, and Balfour, Smuts, and Laurier. He told how he sat next to the Lord Chief Justice of England, and after the macaroni had been served, huge pepper grinders were passed around the table, filled with vintage pepper 100 years old. The chief justice, he said, had told him that it was a great tradition at Gray's Inn to cover the macaroni a half-inch thick with black pepper. But then he related that the chief justice said, "but perhaps I should not urge you to throw your restraint to the winds, for new days have come, and the winning of the war against those who would destroy democracies is perhaps more important than the tradition of vintage pepper."

Concerning the atmosphere of 1941, the President said, "we are still fortunate that these dinners continue to serve to us the vintage pepper of Washington.

"Speaking of atmosphere," he said, "nevertheless when the very existence of our grandchildren trembles in the balance—when for a while we must postpone the renewal of the happy days of the historic 'give and take' of these dinners—we know there are some things in life which ought to be stressed in any gathering—and other things which we are compelled to put into camphor until the ways of peace come back again."

Roosevelt emphasized that he was not asking the club to lay aside its sense of humor and told how he had turned down a man just recently for appointment to a high federal office, "solely because he has no sense of humor, either in bad times or in good.

"I myself *think* I have a sense of humor, though some of you people, hardened by the misfortune of having to live in Washington under administration after administration, insist that I am not nearly so funny when you have to write a serious column.

"You and I have seen piping times of international peace when the lampooning of friendly foreign statesmen made very little difference to the affairs of the world, times when partisan appeals could be made ridiculous by limericks, when we could think in terms of winning elections in counties, or cities or states by viewing with local pride and damning with local alarm.

"But in days like these a new atmosphere makes the hallowed caricature a little less humorous—makes the subject of the legitimate peace-time abdominal operation a little less intriguing on the front page than it is when the patient may really go under the knife of life or death.

"By way of example, national unity was unquestionably a skit subject in 1932 or in 1936. But because of this thing, which I call 'atmosphere,' national unity takes on a tinge of sacredness in 1941.

"In a world of surprise, of sudden decision, of shock, of sacrifice, none of us can live with our emotions alone—our minds and our bodies stretched to tension point—not at least without an interlude of relaxation. The atmosphere of these spring days of 1941 allow for that relaxation.

"Let us look forward not to memories, as in tonight's song, but to the day when the restraints and restrictions that bind us now are swept away and all of us can come back to Gridiron.

"And we are happy at least in the knowledge that the Gridiron Club affords us a reminder that free speech is still in its possession and ours."

He also noted that free speech was "still in the possession of the President of the United States," and that so far as he was concerned it would always remain with all of us, "for that is where it belongs."

Then, revealing his own strong feelings about the war, Roosevelt became deadly serious and gave evidence in his closing remarks that he deeply believed the war must be brought to an end as a victory for the free nations.

"Some day, perhaps in the next century, a definitive historian will name this war. I hope he will call it 'the war for the restoration and preservation of faith.'

"I say this because this war was conceived in the breaking of faith. There are some of little faith who would go back to mistakes of policy or errors of judgment that were based on the occurrences that followed on the ending of the first World War—mistakes and errors which, nevertheless, were based on good intent.

"There are those among us, men of little faith, who laugh at the League of Nations—at the efforts to make peace among nations more secure; there are some who laugh at those who in 1921 under Secretary Hughes sought in good faith for a reduction in the naval armaments of the world; there are some who laugh at the sincerity of an American secretary of state, Mr. Kellogg, who initiated a pact among many nations for the peaceful settlement of problems between nations; there are some who would not stand behind another secretary of state, Mr. Stimson, who proposed not to overlook the flagrant violation of solemn treaties in 1931.

"And since that date, 1931, the sacredness of the pledged word, the sanctity of the spirit of good faith, has gone from bad to worse. I repeat that this war springs from the broken treaty, the ignored word, the violated faith.

"Yet, good faith, in spirit and in truth, has not perished. It has not perished in Great Britain; it has not perished in China; it has not perished in Greece; it has not perished in Yugoslavia. It has not perished in this hemisphere. It has not died in the United States.

"It has not fled from the hearts of millions of people on the continent of Europe or the continent of Asia—peoples whose

voices for a while are still, whose bodies for a while are in bond-
age, but whose faith in good faith lives on deathless.

"We eat, we drink, we are merry. But in our hearts we do not
laugh at faith—good faith. We keep our humor, but we know that
unless we restore the good faith of this nation and of all the other
nations upon earth, good faith will take flight beyond recall, and
the keeping of our humor will stand us then in little stead.

"So for the salvation of our good humor, let us bring back the
good faith of the world."[9]

Much earlier in the dinner, someone from the *New York
Times* had come with a dispatch saying that the Soviet Union and
Yugoslavia had signed a non-aggression pact. Now while
Roosevelt was still speaking, another *Times* messenger arrived,
bringing Arthur Krock a new dispatch that Hitler had invaded
Yugoslavia and Greece. Mr. Krock gave it to the President after
he concluded his speech.[10]

This was the last Gridiron dinner held while Roosevelt was
President. One was scheduled for December 13, 1941, which he
had promised to attend and address. But the attack on Pearl Harbor on Sunday, December 7, resulted in the cancellation of this
dinner on the following Monday morning.

• • •

In the preparations for the December 1941 dinner, there
arose a situation in which the Gridiron Club became one of the
few organizations ever to outmaneuver Franklin Roosevelt. A
year or so prior to this time, he had taken the position that while
he would attend two dinners a year, he would speak at only the
April dinner. Then he failed to attend the December 1940 dinner.
This was the dinner at which Wendell Willkie, his defeated opponent, spoke. It brought about a considerable degree of criticism of the President for apparently being unwilling to be
gracious to Willkie.

As preparations developed for the December dinner,
Roosevelt readily accepted the invitation to attend, but begged
off speaking. We asked him whom he would like to have speak
for the administration. He first suggested Secretary of State Cordell Hull, but Secretary Hull regretfully declined in August, saying that he was afraid the Japanese negotiations would be too
critical about the time of our dinner* and that he could not under-

---

*I was too naive at the time to recognize the significance of what he was saying.

take to prepare a Gridiron speech.

Then we conceived an idea of putting the President in a position where he would have to make the speech after all, by inviting Wendell Willkie to be the Republican speaker again. Willkie readily accepted, and we informed the President of this and asked him if he wouldn't reconsider his decision not to speak and make at least a brief speech at the conclusion of the dinner.

Seeing this as an opportunity to correct the impressions which had been spread about almost a year before, he said he'd think it over and then notified us that he would speak. But because of Pearl Harbor, the Willkie-Roosevelt encounter never occurred.

In the interval between December 1941 and December 1945, when the first postwar dinner was held, the Gridiron Club remained quietly active. Lewis Wood of the *New York Times,* who was president in 1942, proposed a private Gridiron dinner for members only, and the date chosen for this was February 28, the fifty-seventh anniversary of the formation of the Gridiron Club. Numerous skits were put on and several of the songs which had been prepared for the December dinner were sung.

But the most interesting one, and one which related directly to President Roosevelt, was a "Big Four" skit, with characters representing Roosevelt, Churchill, Chiang Kai-shek, and Stalin.

"Right this way," said the announcer, "to the River Nile and the Sphinx's inscrutable smile!" Then impersonators of Roosevelt, Churchill, and Chiang entered with the Gridiron chorus. Each sang his own verse, Roosevelt leading off with:

> In distant lands on Egypt's sands,
> A glorious autumn day,
> I sat upon a pyramid,
> And puffed my cares away.
> And as the perfumed smoke arose,
> Like incense burning yet,
> I saw a Fourth Term in the haze
> And smoked my cigarette!

Churchill sang:
> With Roosevelt and Chiang too
> I went to lands afar.
> I sat upon a pyramid
> And smoked my big cigar.
> And thought, as smoke like incense rose
> To all the gods there are—

There'll always be a Roosevelt while
I smoke my big cigar!

Chiang's verse went:
Where Roosevelt and Churchill were
That's where I too would be,
I sat upon a pyramid and sipped a cup of tea.
And as the perfumed steam arose
Like incense o'er the sand,
I thought of how Confucius say
"A Fourth Term would be grand."

"Joe Stalin" entered, asked what was going on, and was told by Roosevelt that "we are having a conference."

"Having a conference—without *me?*" laughed Stalin. "Haw, haw, haw!" And then he sang:

No matter where the cigarette
And big cigar may be—
No matter where Chiang may sit
To sip his cup of tea.
No matter how you boys may roam,
No matter where you go—
You can't get that Fourth Term until
You smoke a pipe with Joe!

Roosevelt stepped forward and dropped his cigarette holder in a box on the floor. Churchill and Chiang did the same, and all the chorus produced with flourishes their pipes like the one used by Stalin, and sang to "Farmer in the Dell":

We'll smoke a pipe with Joe,
We'll smoke a pipe with Joe;
The Fourth Term is our pipe-dream,
So—we'll smoke a pipe with Joe!

The major part of the rest of the show was the Gridiron laughing at itself—laughing at how it produces skits, its white-tie rule, its methods of selecting new members, its guest skits and its singing. For example, a birthday ballad contained the lines:

Henle and Clapper and R. P. Brandt
Some of them sing; all of them can't.

And there was even an act in which Henry Suydam was asked to write a skit in the manner of Walker S. Buel. This ended with a duet between Arthur Krock and Mark Sullivan, to the tune of "It Ain't Gonna Rain No Mo'."

Krock:
> When I sit down to topple,
> The White House from its place,
> How can I chide the Pres-i-dent,
> If He ain't goin' to make the race?

Sullivan:
> How can I brag of Theodore,
> Bring red to Franklin's face,
> In a column or two on what Hoover would do,
> If he ain't goin' to make the race?

Chorus:
> If he ain't goin' to run no more, no more,
> If he ain't goin' to run no more,
> It'll ring no bell to give him Hell,
> If he ain't goin' to run no more!

A skit on the selection of new members culminated in a limerick, again pointed at Arthur Krock:

> There was an old Krock named Arthur
> Who said: Why does the Gridiron Club barthur
> To elect to the club
> Any jerkwater dub
> When we can do worse by going no farthur.

This dinner set the pattern for the intervening years to December 1945. Several private dinners for members only were held during the period, some with fairly elaborate skits, and some only with a few songs, both new and old.

It was during this period that Commander Walter Karig wrote a letter to Charlie Ross, in which he said that his speech nominating Lyle Wilson for president of the club in 1945 "reminded us of the funereal meetings of the entertainment and music committees, at which few ideas were produced and those few downright terrifying to contemplate; it reminded us of arthritic caperings and hoarse bellowings of the chorus at early rehearsals, of the midnight sessions during which—with the dinner a week distant—the ultimate song hit was synthesized by filling Turner Catledge with whiskey and running his brain through a typewriter."

But the club continued throughout these years, in spite of

war pressures and restraints.

• • •

In the Spring of 1945, with the war in Europe obviously coming to an end, the Gridiron Club planned a dinner on April 14.

But President Roosevelt was not scheduled to be present. Lyle Wilson, president of the club, had written to him on March 14, hoping that he would come. In his letter, Wilson told Roosevelt that due to wartime circumstances the dinner would be different from any of the others, that it would be black tie (Roosevelt had won at last), that the guest list would be limited, that there would be no diplomatic or other foreign guests, and that there would be no publicity either before or after the dinner.

Wilson hoped he could come but said that "if your plans are such that you still will be in Warm Springs in mid-April, we shall lift our glasses as usual to the President of the United States to wish you well and wish you were here."

On April 9, three days before his death, President Roosevelt wrote Wilson:

> From my hideout in Georgia, I just want to say hello to you and all friends in the Gridiron Club. I wish I could be with you but unfortunately I shall not be back in Washington until sometime next week—when the stiff shirt season is over. I write this line with mixed emotions. What's this I read on my card about "black tie"? Has Gridiron conservatism surrendered to the spirit of modernism or is it that those mossy green tailcoats have finally fallen apart?
> The best of luck to all and a merry evening, too.
> Franklin D. Roosevelt

Vice President Truman was to speak for the President at the dinner, and other speeches were to be made by Gridiron members impersonating Thomas E. Dewey and Secretary of Commerce Henry A. Wallace.

Lewis Wood of the *New York Times*, during whose presidency no dinner with guests had ever been held because of the war, was given the honor of making the speech in the dark, and he was to proclaim "as the sun of victory rises, the Gridiron gleams again."

The dinner was never held because of President Roosevelt's death on April 12, 1945. However, there are a few things about it that deserve recording.

The skits that were prepared were heavy on the patriotic side, but there were three memorable songs, all written by Phelps Adams.

President Roosevelt had drawn a rather wide definition of the Western Hemisphere, and in a Greenland skit the quartet was to sing:

> From Greenland's Icy Mountains
> To Dakar's Stormy strands
> Guiana's crystal fountains
> Roll down the bauxite sands.
> From many an ancient river
> To many a plain held dear,
> You'll find F.D. has called it all
> The Western Hemisphere!

And, in another spot, an impersonator of Patrick Henry, pointing to the Statue of Liberty, was to sing:

> Because God made thee mine, today I'm free
> To shape the course of my own destiny,
> And guard these sacred rights I hold divine
> Because you made them mine.
> The right upon the seven seas to cruise,
> The right to publish my most cherished views,
> The right to win from life, and not to lose,
> And praise God as I choose.
> But since God made thee mine, I am not free
> To spurn the call of men in slavery,
> I still must serve eternally thy shrine
> Because God's made *me* Thine!

And then, toward the close, they planned to use the song that had been scheduled for the December 1941 dinner, canceled because of Pearl Harbor:

> Tonight we live once again
> Within the hearts of brave men.
> This night our spirit rides on
> And floods with hope each flaming dawn.
> The blood that crusted the snow
> At Valley Forge long ago
> Today is coursing fiercely through the veins
> Of valiant men who'll never wear chains,
> So tonight we live again.

And the final song of the dinner was to have been:

The world, the world, is waiting for the sunrise,
    When the darkness it may forget;
With Victory, the skies will shine in glory
    When the "Rising Sun" has set!

And so closed the Roosevelt era in the Gridiron Club—one of the great periods of both Gridiron and American history.

• • •

The Roosevelt era should not be passed over without some explanation of one of its unique features, the little Gridiron-like dinners given by Eleanor Roosevelt in the East Room of the White house. Her dinners were for the wives of prominent members of the administration whose husbands were at the Gridiron dinner, the wives of Gridiron members, and the newspaperwomen who regularly covered Mrs. Roosevelt.

They had begun in 1933, with a dinner in honor of Secretary of Labor Perkins, who was a woman, and therefore ineligible for an invitation to the Gridiron Club under the "males only" rules that existed at that time. The first one was quite informal; in fact, the principal items on the menu were hot dogs and potato salad, and there was no special program.

But as time went on, the party became known as the "Gridiron Widows Party," and at the second dinner some modest skits were presented, with Mrs. Roosevelt acting as mistress of ceremonies.

By December 1935, her parties had become almost full-fledged dinners on their own. The cabinet wives put on a "Victorian skit" and the "widows" put on a couple of skits satirizing the New Deal, the most amusing of which was called "A Royal Press Conference" and was a satire chiefly on Mrs. Roosevelt.

It began with a king of noble demeanor in ermine robe, accompanied by his queen, receiving the press together. The prime minister said that he was requested to announce that it would irritate the king to be questioned on matters of pending legislation. But "nothing," he said, "will irritate the queen."

The last of the innocuous and routine questions to the king was "What does your majesty think of the latest fashions for women?" whereupon the queen snatched the prime minister's written reply from the hands of the king, adjusted the microphone and took off with a speech that sounded very much like Mrs. Roosevelt's frequent radio appearances.

Mrs. Roosevelt, whose energy was unbounded and frequently took her to strange places, closed "the interview" enthusiastically explaining "On Thursday I am riding a bicycle down to Windsor and on Saturday morning I have an engagement with the Lord Mayor of Dover to swim the Channel to Calais for luncheon."

Mrs. Roosevelt wrote a widely syndicated column called "My Day," and at her 1937 dinner there was a skit satirizing her widespread travels, the author of which, it was insinuated, was "Eleanor St. Vitus My Day." It included this song:

Hi, diddle, diddle,
The cat and the fiddle,
The cow jumped over the moon.
The moon laughed and laughed and said,
    "You're too late—
Eleanor passed here at noon."

Little Boy Blue come blow your horn,
The sheep's in the meadow, the cow's in the corn,
But thinking of fences, and speaking of sheep,
When, if ever, does Eleanor sleep?

Another skit satirized the weekly meeting of the Senate ladies, and a parody on the "Stein Song" proclaimed:

It's always fair weather
    When Senate Ladies get together,
With food on the table
    And scandal in the air.

The following year, when the Supreme Court packing controversy was at its height, Mrs. Roosevelt put on a skit herself, in which she played a newly appointed Supreme Court justice. An impersonator of Justice James Clark McReynolds, one of the arch conservatives on the Court, gave up in disgust and said, "I quit," whereupon she said, "I will call up Franklin right away and tell him we have a nice new vacancy."

And in December 1939, while the Gridiron members were putting on the Sphinx act, the Gridiron "widows" correctly forecast a third term. In their act, the impersonators of the wives of the various Presidential possibilities for the following year each sang songs, and the one sung by the impersonator of Mrs. Roosevelt was:

I'm waiting for the '40 roundup.
Gonna saddle old Frank for the last time.
So long, old gals, I'll ride in on My Day,

I'm heading for the '40 roundup.
Git along, little Frankie, git along, git along.

The act closed with a grand finale, with Mrs. Jay Hayden, impersonator of Mrs. Roosevelt, singing:

Oh, give me my home,
Where the New Dealers roam,
And the Congressmen vote as they may.
Where never is heard an encouraging word,
And the press keeps on printing My Day.

The following year at the last of Mrs. Roosevelt's "Widows Parties" the highlight was a Santa Claus skit, in which Santa distributed amusing gifts to many of those present, and to Mrs. Roosevelt, a halo and a pair of wings.[12]

She evidently enjoyed these parties as much as the cabinet wives, Gridiron wives, and newswomen did. She had the supreme political asset of being able to laugh at herself.

XIV

Harry S. Truman

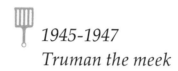

1945-1947
Truman the meek

One of the most notable of Gridiron dinners was held on December 15, 1945. President Truman had made his historic decision to drop the atom bomb on Japan and the war had ended.

The capitulation had been signed on the battleship *Missouri*, chosen in deference to President Truman. Many of the other major leaders of the World War II period were gone. Adolph Hitler had committed suicide in his bunker in Berlin, the dead Mussolini had been strung up by his feet for public gaze in Milan, Roosevelt had died, and the British had replaced Churchill with Clement Atlee. Of the major World War II leaders, only Stalin remained.

President Truman, at this stage, was being modest, taking the stance that he was trying to do his best, and he had widespread support throughout the country.

Lyle C. Wilson, head of the United Press Service and one of the most respected of all Washington correspondents, was president of the Gridiron Club.

Both President Truman and Governor Dewey of New York,

who had been Roosevelt's fourth term opponent, were present and spoke at the dinner. So many Missouri politicians had been pouring into the administration that the Gridiron Club stated "the right of every Missouri man to a job—full employment here we come!"

The opening skit was based on this idea. The entire Gridiron music committee, costumed as artillery men of World War I (Truman had been the captain of Artillery Battery D in the first World War), came on the stage and sang to the tune of "The Caisson Song."

Over hill, over dale,
    We're the boys who never fail,
While our Harry goes rolling along!
Hurry up, don't be late,
    Open wide that White House gate,
While our Harry goes rolling along!
For it's Hi, Hi, Hee,
    The boys of Battery D,
Missouri is marching, wide and strong!
    We're the White House mob
    And we'll fill up every job—
While our Harry goes rolling along!

The first major music skit was set before a torii gate such as that commonly built at the approach to Shinto temples. This gate however, was labeled "Supreme Allied Headquarters." The "Mikado" arrived to call on "General MacArthur," in order to find out how to make Japan democratic. One of Truman's major Presidential policies had been to bring the soldiers home from overseas as speedily as possible. But a chorus of GI's guarding the headquarters lamented to the tune of "The Flowers that Bloom in the Spring":

The Gen'rals and Admirals fight, snafu,
To see which will run the whole show.
Whether Army and Navy unite, snafu,
Our chances remain very slight, snafu,
Of a summer back home in the states.

MacArthur was not present at this dinner, but Admiral Chester Nimitz, navy commander in the Pacific, was there and the Mikado sang:

On a throne in a temple I once used to sit
Singing Nimitz, tit-Nimitz, tit-Nimitz,

Till MacArthur said: "Emperor, come off of it"
Singing Nimitz, tit-Nimitz, tit-Nimitz.
"Am I finished as Emp'ror, oh, Douglas?" I cried,
"Or may I with some other title preside?"
With a shake of his gold-crusted head he replied:
"Oh, Nimitz, tit-Nimitz, tit-Nimitz."

Then "General MacArthur" arrived as the sentries and soldiers were called to attention, and one announced, "Make way
for the Lord High Supreme Allied Commander in Chief of the
Allied Armies and Navies and Everything!"

MacArthur's impersonator strode on the stage wearing riding breeches, boots, a khaki shirt with his collar unbuttoned, and
a magnificent hat that had five big gold stars with little electric
lights in them that flashed on each time he pushed a button in his
hand. He sang a parody of a Gilbert and Sullivan lyric:

I am the very model of a modern five-star general,
I've information economic, social and ephemeral.
I know my diplomatic stuff, the sacred rules of protocol,
And know the way to make the head of toothy Mr. Moto roll.
At writing fiery, deathless prose, there is no man superior,
My skill at putting gold on hats cannot be called inferior,
I fashion triumphs night and day in manner not empirical,
I might have been the President if God had wrought a miracle.

I yield to no one in the art of putting out publicity,
Communiques that I indite are models of felicity,
I supervise my battles from a silver-hued B-29,
I watch my men advance below. Results are always plenty fine.
I've fought in Europe and the East, my medals are plethorical,
All doubts as to my skill at war can be at most rhetorical.
Although my contact with U.S. has largely been non-resident
If God so wills there's still a chance they'll draft me to be President.

One of the most remembered songs of all Gridiron dinners
came in a skit laid before "Happy Harry's Pie Counter." By December 1945 many of the old Roosevelt brain trust and administration appointees had either departed or been replaced by President Truman's choices, which came largely from the traditional
Democratic organization. Attorney General "Tom Clark" remarked that "there ain't nothing of the New Deal left in this
cabinet except a couple of old crusts." And former Secretary of
State "Edward Stettinius" explained that the New Deal survivors
"just go wherever Harry sends us—far, far away."

Then an impersonator of Frances Perkins, Roosevelt's secretary of labor, stepped to the front of the chorus and sang a parody on the "Whiffenpoof Song" written by Walker S. Buel.

> To the old Blue Eagle's feathers,
>> To the horse and buggy days—
> To the Felix and the Cork we loved so well,
>> Sing the old New Deal survivors
> Who are scattered far and wide
>> Since the magic of our music lost its spell.
> Yes, the alphabet of magic,
>> And the tricks we did so well—
> NRA and Triple A among the best;
>> Oh we had our day of glory,
> Although it could not last—
>> So we'll pass—and be forgotten with the rest!
>
> We're little New Dealers who've lost our way—
>> Baa! Baa! Baa!
> We're little New Dealers who've gone astray—
>> Baa! Baa! Baa!
> Little New Dealers, after the spree,
>> Damned from Kansas to Kankakee,

The whole chorus then dropped to its knees and with uplifted arms sang:

> Lord have mercy on such as we—
>> Baa! Baa! Baa!

While the next-to-last line may have shocked grammarians from places other than Yale, it was in tune with the thinking of most of the new Truman appointees, whose regard for the old Roosevelt brain trust was less than idolatrous.

This was followed by a song by an impersonator of Edward J. Flynn, Democratic leader of the Bronx and a close Roosevelt associate.

> I'm just wild about Harry—But
>> Is Harry wild about me?
> Flynn and O'Dwyer
>> May go higher
> Fighting the GOP.
>> Bob Hannegan's fine and dandy,
> Clark just as fine as he can be;
>> But I'm just wild about Harry—
> Is he just wild about—can he do without—
>> Is he wild about me?

It was pointed out that only one man could answer the question Flynn had raised. "We address it directly to the President of the United States," said an impersonator of Attorney General Clark, and as the spotlight turned upon President Truman at the head table, Clark added, "What about it, Sir?"

"It is the policy of this administration," replied President Truman, "to give a full and frank answer to any question. You say these pie-hungry Democrats are just wild about me. You ask whether I am wild about them. My answer is—Yes, I am just wild!"

The Republican skit was centered on Governor Dewey, whose impersonator was dressed in a Little Lord Fauntleroy suit. He was begging the barker at the big Republican circus to let him inside the tent, because he was "the smallest giant in the world."

The big barker looked at the diminutive Dewey and said, "Hm-m-m-m-m, giant, huh? Tell you what I'm gonna do, Tommy. When those other characters aren't looking, I'll sneak you under the tent and mebbe—mebbe if the donkey doesn't throw you next year—you can ride the elephant again!"

That was the introduction to Dewey's speech.

Dewey began by noting that this was the second time he had been invited to speak for the party of the opposition at a Gridiron dinner, and that he thought he'd discovered the formula for getting invited.

"In 1938," he began, "when a number of distinguished Republicans were elected to office in a resurgence of our party, I was defeated for governor of New York. So they gave me the consolation prize by inviting me to speak at the Gridiron dinner. Once again I have won the consolation prize.

"This time, however, it is a little different. I can speak wholly without inhibition or worry as to misinterpretation of my remarks. I am a member of a very small and exclusive club, having been elected by the people a year ago last November, to the position of elder statesman. The serenity of this position is copper-riveted by the fact that in selecting nominees for President, my party has an unbroken tradition of never having made the same mistake twice in a row.

"So as I view the passing scene with an entirely unjaundiced eye, it seems that it would be unfair for me tonight to comment too harshly on the gyrations of the present administration as it wobbles each day from left to right. As he walked over to the

White House each morning [President Truman was then living in Blair House while the White House was being repaired and refurbished], our distinguished guest started out by tossing one rose to the left and one rose to the right. The left received its favors as a matter of obligation and was not grateful. The right was profoundly grateful because they hadn't had any roses in twelve long years.

"But paradise in politics lasts such a short time. The left finds only the thorns on the roses it received. The right finds its roses were in truth intended to be not bouquets, but funeral wreaths."

He noted that everybody had been feeling sorry for the president, "but I refuse to extend any sympathy to Mr. Truman tonight. I assure him of my complete support in every act he may propose which is in the interest of the American people—but no sympathy. After all, I did everything within my power last year to spare him from these burdens.

"He asked for them and he has them with my enthusiastic blessing."

Dewey then spoke about some of the problems that "my distinguished friend has," and listed among them the 15 million returning veterans "looking for the paradise so skillfully promised them from the GI Bill of Rights." He noted that they also had a Veterans Law in the state of New York, but that there was a difference. "We have in New York," he said, "a surplus of something over $400 million dollars. For the information of the Democrats present, a surplus is an excess of receipts over expenditures."

He said he had discovered that the administration had a "new formula" in industrial relations which he described:

"First you have the President announce that the lid is off on wage increases, provided you do that without increasing any prices. Then you get yourself a nice big crop of strikes. Then you trot out that businessman's idol, the secretary of commerce, Henry Wallace. He announces that after a most careful survey, industry can increase wages by any large percentage that his crystal ball indicates, without increasing prices.

"Then you get a few more strikes. Next you have the price administrator fix prices on new products, giving not an increase, but a decrease. That helps a little more. Then you have the attorney general announce that he is going to prosecute business for violation of the Anti-Trust Act. This cheers everybody up on both sides. So, then you cap the climax by telling all the boys to go back to work, saying 'Papa will fix it all up.' So they compromise and stay on strike."

Dewey closed seriously with a strong plea for worldwide freedom of information so that people would have "the light of day" to help them "make an informed and intelligent judgment as a people and so that the hope of peace and of justice and of decency may have one more chance of survival in a world in which there is no peace."

And he noted that it had been four years since there had been a Gridiron dinner and that the Gridiron Club was "the symbol of all we believe in by way of free information all over the world."

"May we never again go through four years when the lights of the Gridiron dinner are dimmed. May its lights go on and on in all the years to come."[1]

One unrehearsed event occurred during this dinner. There was a reluctant bride skit inspired by the row over unification of the armed forces, in which Richard L. Wilson portrayed a tall, goofy-looking hillbilly kid with a toy airplane, representing the United States Air Force. Paul R. Leach of the *Chicago Daily News* represented the United States Army, and Roscoe Drummond of the *Christian Science Monitor*, dressed in a bridal costume, represented the United States Navy.

All were appearing before a marriage license clerk, the boy having come "to Mammy and Pappy's wedding." Congress was represented by a man in the traditional caricature costume, but he was carrying a big shotgun and he announced that "we durn near lost a war because of the squabbling in this family. From here on out these two here are going to live together peaceable and happy with their little boy."

The Marine Band struck up Mendelssohn's wedding march, and the congressman shouted, "March, you two, we're agoin' to the preacher."

As the skit ended, General Eisenhower and Admiral Nimitz both rose spontaneously from their seats at the head table, walked toward each other, and threw their arms around each other, while the audience stood and cheered.

The final skit was on the bridge of a showboat, "the Showboat of American foreign policy—blithe, carefree and gay—now drifting happily down the Missouri towards an unknown ultimate destination."

Secretary of State James F. Byrnes, Undersecretary of State Dean Acheson and Assistant Secretary William L. Clayton of Texas were all important figures in foreign policy.

"Full speed ahead," yelled "Skipper Byrnes," as he jangled the bell. "Full speed astern *(more bell)*. Full speed amidships *(helluva lot of bell)*. We're off!"

"Well, where are we going this time?" a sailor asked anxiously.

"Whadda you mean where is we going? Where is we been?" replied a more experienced deckhand.

Then a soloist stepped to the center of the stage and sang a song written by Arthur Krock, a parody of "On the Atchison, Topeka and the Santa Fe."

> Do you hear that whistle go woo-hoo,
> It's the State Department showboat that's a comin' through,
> You can always tell by her twists and turns
> She's the Acheson, the Clayton and the Jim-my Byrnes.
> See the same ol' smoke-screen 'round the bend,
> I reckon that the blackout's never gonna end,
> But the folks 'round these parts quickly learns
> She's the Acheson, the Clayton and the Jim-my Byrnes.
> Here she comes . . .
> Ooh, ooh, ooh,
> Hey, Jim, don't ever let her crash,
> Ooh, ooh, ooh,
> Cause she's got a list of passengers she shouldn't smash,
> And they're all bound for the Treasuree,
> For all of them was told that this here trip was free,
> And that loans *ain't* subject to returns
> On the Acheson, the Clayton and the Jim-my Byrnes.

Thirteen years later, this song was repeated at a private December Gridiron dinner for members only. Arthur Krock introduced it saying, "Acheson had yet to learn that if you drew on the map of the world a perimeter of our national security [as he did in a National Press Club speech—leaving out Korea], the Communists would believe you.

"He found out."

But by the time of this December 1945 dinner, Secretary of State Byrnes had already been to London for a conference with various governments. In a narrative song, his impersonator encountered "that great big Soviet bear." He shinnied up a tree and prayed:

Now Lordy, if you can't help me,
For goodness sake doan you help dat bear.

"Prime Minister Clement Atlee" of England and "Foreign Minister V. M. Molotov" were there, and the "Captain," arrived from his "PT-54, The Sacred Scow," and sang to the tune of "Alice Blue Gown":

If we don't hide the atom away
There may be big trouble some day.
Far safer 'twill be
Just to leave it to three
The atom—and Atlee—and me.

In his speech, President Truman did not refer to the skits in any detail, except to say that he had enjoyed the evening and that he always enjoyed himself at the Gridiron Club—a subject on which a few years later he was to change his mind.

He complimented Governor Dewey on his speech, saying that he had met Dewey for the first time on the main deck of the battleship *Missouri* on October 27, 1945, and that the governor "took my breath away by announcing publicly that I had made a good speech in Central Park on foreign affairs and he wholeheartedly approved it. He disagreed with Mr. Luce and *Time* on that subject. I am returning the compliment [about the speech] to Mr. Dewey."

Then he discussed his own position in the Presidency.

"I wonder if I could cry on your shoulder a bit about public service in reconversion and what happens to a Vice President when he suddenly falls heir to a great President and two wars' ends all in one fell swoop. You know in wartime men and women are patriotic—they'll stand hardship, sacrifice, abuse, bullets, foxholes, columnists, editorials and whatnot for their country's welfare. But let the war suddenly cease. These patriots become free men working in a free enterprise struggle and they begin to dip for the gravy. Their skins again become thin, and abuse and muck makes them timid. I found as a chairman of an investigating committee that even in wartime some of our greatest industrial and labor leaders could dish out criticism, but when they landed on the taking end, they just couldn't take it. A man in public life has to take it. Now I find none of the big boys want to take positions where the gossip columnists and the know-it-all editors can pick flaws in their public actions. I spend a third of my time begging good men to stay in public service or to come into it.

"When the great President passed on, everyone felt sorry for me—big business, little business, the press, the radio, labor, the Congress. Nearly everybody in the United States either came to see me, wrote me, or phoned me that he'd do anything in the world to help, and I'm sure all of you meant it.

"Then Germany folded up and Mr. Atomic Energy came along and folded up Japan and scared the rest of the world to death and then the exodus started and the Red Sea parted.

"I believe I've made a record—Walter Lippmann has said I'm great and a damn fool, Dorothy Thompson prayerfully wishes Roosevelt were back, and so do I. Frank Kent yells 'Savior' one day and 'wolf' the next. I've reached the topnotch in popularity according to Dr. Gallup. Now labor is mad at management, and they are both mad at me. I have made labor mad trying to give them a little public responsibility. Management says I'm worse than Roosevelt—a compliment maybe. Congress is off the reservation so far as I'm concerned. The navy is mad at the army, and they're both mad at me. Phil Murray is mad at Sewell Avery, and they'd both like to carry me out. Pat Hurley says he's for my foreign policy, and that I haven't any. Molotov is mad at Bevin, and they're both mad at me. And so are the Arabs, the Jews and the DARs.

"If the Gridiron Club would like to give me something for Christmas, I would suggest they send me Dale Carnegie's book, or I may have to start a new war.

"But actually, it is a great responsibility and I'm not shirking it. It has fallen to my lot to assume the greatest burden any man ever had, and I'm giving it all I have—it may not be enough, but I can't help that. You know that the most terrible decision a man ever had to make was made by me at Potsdam—it had nothing to do with Russia, or Britain or Germany. It was a decision to loose the most terrible of all destructive forces for the wholesale slaughter of human beings. The Secretary of War, Mr. Stimson, and I weighed that decision most prayerfully. The President had to decide. It occurred to me that a quarter of a million of the flower of our young manhood was worth a couple of Japanese cities, and I still think they were and are. But I couldn't help but think of the necessity of blotting out women, children and noncombatants. We picked a couple of cities where war work was the principle industry, and dropped the bombs. Russia hurried in and that war ended.

"Now we are faced with other equally momentous decisions. On them rest either peace and the greatest age in history or another armament race and total destruction of civilization as we know it. Men, friends, it is a time for prayer and solemn thought. Sherman was *wrong*. I'm telling you I find 'peace is hell'—and repeat."[2]

The Gridiron files contain the copy from which he read that night, signed:

"In fear and trembling
12-15-45 Harry Truman"

• • •

The nature of the President's speech at this dinner and the "in fear and trembling" signature on his copy were very characteristic of his attitudes and approaches during his early months in the White House, but as time went on his confidence rose, and after the spirit-lifting surprise of his re-election in 1948, it could only be described as becoming positively buoyant.

Many old Truman friends from Missouri held positions of various importance in the government by the time of the April 13, 1946 dinner, and Raymond P. Brandt of the *St. Louis Post-Dispatch*, president of the Gridiron Club, announced in his speech in the dark that "our most honored guest has served a year and a day of an indeterminate sentence; by good behavior between now and 1948 he may add four years more to that term."

He noted that the dinner was held on the anniversary of the birthday of Thomas Jefferson, of whom President Truman "is an ardent follower—with a difference."

"He is resolved," said Mr. Brandt, himself a Missourian, "that government of Missourians, for Missourians and by Missourians shall *not* be banished from Washington."

President Truman was having his troubles with Congress, and there was a skit in which a big wastebasket was loaded with bills that Congress had not passed.

A Gridiron soloist sang of the President:

He's got a lot of paper dolls that he has called his own,
    And they are bills that Congress will not pass.
For while the members are his friends,
There's a point where friendship ends;
    For votes and friends are different things, alas.

The skit ended with an impersonator of General Harry Vaughan, Truman's chief aide, singing:

And when the going's hard
Our Harry's still a card
On that you can rely,
No matter what the future brings
As time goes by.

One of the major music acts was centered on the upcoming 1946 congressional campaign. The atmosphere of that campaign was indicated in a parody of "It's a Grand Night for Singing."

It's a grand year for running,
And hopes are flying high.
As both parties' candidates want to be heard,
While throwing the bull at the sky!
It's a grand year for running,
For Democrats—and then
It's easy to see that the old GOP
Is trying to come back again!
Trying—trying again!

Harold Stassen was again the Republican speaker, but by 1946 he was no longer barred by youth from running for President, and a Gridiron soloist portraying Stassen sang:

Waitin' for my train to come in,
Waitin' for to find me some friends.
I've looked on every railroad of the USA,
Somehow those Republicans just ride away.
I see them go with Dewey and Taft,
Bricker seems to have quite a raft.
I come from Minnesota by the railroad track—
Now I'm afraid that choo-choo train will take me back.
I'm waitin' for my boom to begin—
Waitin' for my train to come in!

The skit closed with the chorus singing:

We are the candidates,
Bold, dashing candidates . . .
God save the United States!

Prior to the dinner, Secretary of Commerce Henry A. Wallace had delivered a speech in New York. A day or two before making the speech, Wallace had brought a copy of it over to the President and handed it to him. President Truman had thumbed through it briefly but did not really read it.

In his speech, Wallace praised the Russians at one point and evoked a big ovation from an audience which was obviously sympathetic to them. Since the "Cold War" was beginning to develop, and Wallace told newsmen that his speech had been cleared by Truman, the speech proved embarrassing to the President, who immediately asked Wallace for his resignation as secretary of commerce.

Former Governor Stassen used this for an oblique dig at the President in his Gridiron speech.

"When the president of the Gridiron Club invited me to speak on this occasion, I was tempted to respond that I would speak if, in accordance with the best of recent Anglo-Missourian diplomatic practice, the President of the United States would introduce me, and inferentially endorse, without looking at, my speech. But, on second thought, it seemed clear that this request would not be granted, as certainly, even a Missourian does not need to be shown twice."

Then, laughing a bit at the Republicans, he remarked that he did express some surprise to Brandt at being invited, because he thought "it was rather contrary to a well-established tradition of recent years, as it was my understanding that Republicans were not invited to speak until after they had been defeated."

He quoted Brandt as replying that the tradition was correct, but he was nevertheless eligible, for although he [Stassen] had not been aware of it, "the Gridiron Club knew that Colonel McCormick of the *Chicago Tribune* and his friends already had me stopped, and in the parlance of the press a stop counts for a defeat."

Then, turning his satire upon himself, he said that when he asked Brandt what he should talk about, he had responded, "you will be introduced as the speaker of the opposition, so use your own judgment," and had concluded by suggesting that he confine himself to "giving friendly advice.

"So friendly advice it will be," he remarked. "One of my congressional friends said, 'that'll be more appropriate anyhow because from what we hear in the Republican cloakrooms, you do not belong in the opposition.'

"The best advice," Stassen continued, "is usually the briefest. As I understand it, the President's primary complaint is that he did not ask for his present position, and his greatest desire is to be relieved of it. If this is correct, then the best advice that I could give is for him to keep right on the way he is going. It will all work out all right within the next two and a half years and the desire will be fulfilled.

"But the difficulty with this brief advice is that it's rather hard on the people of the country for the next two years.

Therefore I will proceed to give specific advice on [some] of the major questions with which the President and the country are concerned.

"First, I understand that the President is a little worried about the amount of confusion his administration has caused. The people of the country are also concerned about it. In fact, confusion is the only thing in which the administration has a high production record since VJ Day. I suggest that one way to reduce the amount of confusion would be to give Chester Bowles the authority to fix the price of confusion, and if it works out like the rest of his price fixing, I am certain there would be much less of it produced."

Referring to President Truman's occasional offhand remarks to the press, he said that while he would be the last one to suggest the desirability of "clearing it with Sidney," he did think it would be a good slogan to follow to "clear it with somebody." It will be recalled that President Roosevelt, before asking the 1944 convention to nominate Senator Truman as his running mate, had asked that it be cleared with labor leader Sidney Hillman.

Stassen's third suggestion was for a "labor jurisdictional air conditioner," because if he read the signs right, "the heat that will soon be generated by the friction between unions will make all previous labor management heat seem like a cool breeze on one of our beautiful Minnesota lakes."

Governor Stassen also pointed out that the "stoppage" of the President's program by the Democratic majority in both houses of Congress indicated that he needed advice on his relations with his Democratic party. "After very careful thought," he said, "the best thing to do here is for the President to simply conclude that the Democratic party is hopeless and proceed to form a third party. He could count on the assistance of Henry Wallace, Lee Pressman, and other lifelong Democrats. Of course it might well be pointed out that attempting to build a program requires some cohesion in the materials. It is possible that too many of the CIO planks have been getting mixed in, in place of the Democratic planks, and it is doubtful if anyone can erect a building with a mixture of prefabricated CIO planks jammed in against rough logs of seasoned southern white pine. In fact, it's pretty obvious that the Democratic senators and congressmen are about as reluctant to handle CIO planks as the AFL building tradesmen are to handle CIO prefabricated houses.

"If it's any comfort, it might be added, after the last meeting of the Republican National Committee, that the Democratic party isn't the only party that has a solid South. But seriously I do wish the President would keep the Democrats in line and keep them voting with his administration. We are having a difficult enough time liberalizing the Republican party without the Democrats invading our party and reenforcing the conservative side."

He closed by addressing President Truman directly and saying that his replies had been made "in the spirit of the evening.

"I express to you my best wishes for your next two years as President of the United States and assure you that you will have my support on basic questions which transcend party lines in the same manner that I gave it to your predecessor, the Honorable Franklin D. Roosevelt, a great personality, whom I sincerely miss at this Gridiron session tonight."[3]

Because the previous Donald Duck skit had been such a huge success, the Gridiron Club, in true theatrical tradition, put on another one, with Paul R. Leach playing the part of Secretary Ickes arriving at the Pearly Gates and being interviewed by St. Peter and the Archangel Gabriel. Wearing a neon halo, "Ickes" objected to the gate because it didn't have a union label on it, and finding other things also wrong, he began quacking until St. Peter laid a calming hand on his shoulder, saying to Gabriel that he'd straighten him out.

Ickes: What's that? Preposterous! Nobody can straighten me out.
Peter: Then why did you come here?
Ickes: To see what kind of a deal I could make.
Peter: What have you in mind? Another cabinet post?

Ickes replied that in Washington he was famous for his loyalty and turned on his neon halo. St. Peter phoned "the front office" for instructions and announced, "Mr. Ickes, by popular request of the angels, you are about to get a position you have deserved for a long time—*you* have been made Secretary of the Exterior."

The neon halo flashed furiously, and Ickes went into a prolonged and incoherent quacking as the scene was blacked out.

Ickes was not present to see this second Donald Duck skit.

The closing act, before President Truman's speech, was a scene on the moon, where "the weary pilgrims of the United Nations Organization [which had been created in 1945 at San Francisco] were searching desperately for a place to light."

It was pointed out that the citizens of Greenwich, Connecticut, "armed only with Clare Boothe Luce," had been successful in repelling an invasion planned by the UNO. "Through the magic of radar," said Richard L. Wilson, the announcer, "we take you now to Greenwich-on-the-Moon."

The cast included impersonators of Foreign Minister Bevin of England, Andrei Gromyko of Russia, Secretary of State James F. Byrnes, Senator Arthur H. Vandenberg, Joseph Stalin, and such miscellaneous characters as General Franco, Juan Peron, and a man in the moon.

Vandenberg sang to the tune of "No Can Do":

It's Johnny Bull and Uncle Sam and Uncle Joe
We have to find a place where we can set things right,
For if we can't agree we might begin to fight
And if we have another war 'twill be—Goodnight!
And so, U–N–O, U–N–O,
We must have peace—a piece of land, or there'll be no
U–N–O, U–N–O,
A place where we can settle down with U–N–O.

Stalin boasted that "in Russia we have real democracy. Nobody tells anybody. So everybody is equal." He announced that it was easy to find a place to "settle down."

"I have settled in so-o-o many places (checks off on fingers)—Germany, Poland, Hungary, Finland, Austria, Rumania, Bulgaria, Yugoslavia, Persia, Turkey—no, no, excuse me, not yet."

Franco sang a few snatches based on "Me and My Shadow":

Me and Peron and Stalin
Put Democracy on the run,
We've driven them loony as you can plainly see,
We dictators have all the fun!

The desire for peace was expressed by "Joe Doaks, the guy who digs the iron, plows the fields, bucks the rivets, pays the taxes." Private First Class Doaks, who said he wanted to tell them all something, sang, to the tune of "It Might As Well Be Spring":

I would rather see the White Way in its splendor
Than to see a burning city blaze and glow
I'd rather see a steamer full of tourists
Than a bomber diving low.
But I fear it's fight if we do not all unite
Behind the U–N–O.

The act ended with all lining up and singing, to the "Pilgrim's Chorus" from *Tannhäuser*:

Rejoice, oh, world, at peace we behold thee,
Let all mankind with good-will now enfold thee,
Now must we lay our weapons aside
In God's good way, in peace abide.
A bloody war our penance sore,
And greed and lust lie in the dust,
Be our remorse with blessing crowned,
Let grainfields hide the shell-torn ground,
With peace make all the world abound.

If erring man for peace would labor,
All others treat not as foe but as neighbor,
The hell of war would disappear,
We'd live and grow devoid of fear.
Hallelujah, hallelujah,
Eternally, eternally.

President Truman responded extemporaneously to the toast at the end of the dinner, and no record of his remarks is available.

• • •

In the 1946 congressional elections the Truman administration had fallen upon a disaster. Instead of having 56 Senate Democrats to 38 Republicans and 242 House Democrats to 190 Republicans, as in the Seventy-ninth Congress, the Eightieth consisted of 51 Republicans and 45 Democrats in the Senate, and of 245 Republicans and 188 Democrats in the House.

President Brandt, in his speech in the dark at the December 14, 1946 dinner, which incidentally had among its guests the Duke of Windsor,* announced that for many years Gridiron dinners had opened with a crash but tonight this wasn't necessary.

"That thundering noise you hear," he said, "is the echo from the November landslide. . . .

"In 1928 the Democratic party was regarded as hopeless. Only the Solid South and not much of that remained. In 1936, the Republicans looked equally defunct. Only Maine and Vermont stuck by the Grand Old Party. Who knows, maybe the Democrats can come back again.

"Politics are getting back to normal. There is an opposition party in the Congress. Or is it in the White House?

"The opposition is not confined to Congress. Somewhere in this room is the next President of the United States."

---

*Both the Duke and Duchess of Windsor attended the Sunday reception the following day.

Few in the room realized then that he was already sitting at the head table in the place of honor.

The show opened with a "Republican" chorus singing:

Hallelujah. Here we are!
Landslide, like a hay ride, it's a gay ride.

And then followed a parody on Vincent Youmans' "Great Day."

We've been down and out,
Now that we're in let's shout—
There's gonna be a Great Day!
We'll chase bureaucrats
Out with the Democrats—
There's gonna be a Great Day!

Next, in acknowledgment of Republican high hopes, the chorus followed with:

Roll out the New Deal,
We'll have a barrel of fun,
Roll in the Old Deal,
Democrats all on the run.
We'll take the White House—
Forty-eight vict'ry will see.
Now's the time to ride the wagon—
Here's the GOP!

Finally changing its stance swiftly, the chorus ended the act with:

God save America from GOP—
God save America from GOP!

With the strong emphasis on domestic affairs as a result of the election upset, the foreign affairs skit was relegated from closing skit of the dinner to the first music skit and was pitched heavily on the United Nations. To the tune of "On Wisconsin," an impersonator of British Foreign Minister Bevin sang:

On Britannia, on Britannia!
Our flag's never furled.
Leagues of nations come and go
But John Bull tops the world.

And the chorus of all the multinational participants sang to the tune of "Far Above Cayuga's Waters":

Far behind the Iron Curtain
Shutting out the view,
There sits Uncle Joey Stalin,
Tells us what to do!

He's for union of all nations
Russia shakes no fist.
If we're truly democratic
And turn Communist.

The act ended on a note of positive support for the United Nations, with the chorus singing:

That's the only choice before you, destruction or fraternity!
You're a team, or a mob, it's a question of chaos or harmony;
Must unite, or we fight, and you have to decide which one it shall be.
You're a team, or a mob, the choice is as simple as A, B, C.
One for all, all for one, or pick out your lot in the ce-me-ter-y.

The Republican congressional victory was satirized by the Gridiron Club in a scene in front of "the old GOP Livery Stable, from which the Republicans will set forth under the slogan, 'Forward to the Horse and Buggy Days!'"

"My, my," commented the stable man, "wasn't the country surprised by the way us Republicans got elected last month. Wasn't the Democrats surprised. And man Oh man, wasn't us *Republicans* surprised!"

He led the chorus in singing:

Put on your old gray bonnet
With the Hoover button on it,
And we'll hitch old Dobbin to the shay.
When the New Deal's over,
We'll be back in clover—
On inauguration day!

The Speaker-to-be, "Joe Martin," avowed that "it's the good old Republican doctrine that saves the country when the patent medicine fails, isn't it, Senator Taft?"

"Taft" responded that "it's the old time religion," and the chorus sang:

It's the old time religion, it's the old time religion, it's the old time religion—
And it's good enough for me!

It was good for old Mark Hanna, it was good for old Joe Cannon, it
    was good for Quay and Penrose—
And it's good enough for me!

It was good for old Joe Grundy, it was good for Grant and Harding,
    it was good for Smoot and Hawley—
And it's good enough for me!

It was good for Herbert Hoover, it was good for Alf M. Landon, it
    was good for Governor Dewey—
And it's good enough for me!

A character representing Governor Landon sang:

Forgotten me? You've not forgotten
The votes of Vermont and Maine.
The days that we sang, "Oh Susanna,"
And rode on the "Sunflower" train.
Now all of the things that I told you
Are coming at last to be—
And like birds winging home in the evening,
All the people have come back to me!

An impersonator of Senator John W. Bricker of Ohio, who
was the Republican speaker, sang a parody of "Doin' What
Comes Natur'lly," from *Annie, Get Your Gun*.

Some folks from Maine to Texas
Can't even write their name.
They sign their checks with "x's"
But they all vote just the same!
Folks ain't dumb where I come from
They ain't had any learnin'.
They just vote for GOP
Doin' what comes natur'lly!

No copy of the Bricker speech exists in the Gridiron records
or was otherwise obtainable, but it is recalled by those who were
present at the dinner as not being one of the more successful
Gridiron speeches. In fact, two weeks after the dinner, Harold
Ickes, in a column published in the *Washington Star*, commented
that "before his speech at the Gridiron Club dinner in Washington Senator-elect Bricker thought that he was running for the
Republican nomination for President. Now he is not only walking, he is limping."

The departed Secretary of Commerce Wallace, who was to

run as an independent against Truman two years later, was saluted in a "Retreat *to* Moscow" skit, in which "Wallace" was dressed in a Napoleon costume and his principal marshals were Senator "Claude Pepper" of Florida and "Elliott Roosevelt."

"Wallace" spoke in highly enthusiastic gibberish, such as, "We are perambulating for the greelsprail jarbanks of the heminfrax in the United States. Under our leadership we have bronwayed and ferticled the duven sprat in every walk of life."

Pepper announced at the end, "Boys, he's really making sense tonight."

Wallace replied, "And President Truman has seen this speech and approved every word!"

The Democratic skit was set in a tent, where the announcer said that the Democratic circus was packing up to leave town. "It was the greatest show on earth while it lasted," he claimed. A clown sang:

> Laugh and remember,
> The fifth day of November,
> Laugh for the sorrow
> That is eating our hearts.

While the Gridiron Club makes a business out of laughing at everybody, it is rarely mean. One exception came in a part of this skit, which involved Senator Joseph F. Guffey of Pennsylvania, who had been defeated. He was far from a favorite of newspapermen, so the club let him have it.

A character representing Senator John J. Sparkman of Alabama asked who that character was over there on the stage, and "Robert Hannegan" of Missouri, Democratic National Committee Chairman, replied, "That's our snake charmer, Joe Guffey. He lost his shirt, too."

*Sparkman:*Where's his snake.
*Hannegan:*Oh, the snake quit.
*Sparkman:*Labor trouble, eh?
*Hannegan:*No; it was a matter of personal pride with the snake.

The circus bareback rider lamented Senator Alben Barkley's demotion from majority leader to minority leader, to the tune of "A Nightingale Sang in Berkeley Square."

> That fateful night, November fifth,
> We had customers packed in for fair;

And the show was going simply swell
'Till the elephant got in Barkley's hair.

Wallace was another character in this skit and, when asked what he was grinning about, he said he had fallen on his head. "House Speaker Rayburn," also deposed in the election to a minority position, asked him how he got here anyway. "The last time I saw you," he said, "you were retreating to Moscow."

Then Wallace sang an adaptation of "The Man on the Flying Trapeze."

Once I was happy, but now I'm forlorn,
Out of the cabinet, back to the corn.
Haunted by piggies plowed under when born,
My body is blistered by Byrnes. *Jim Byrnes.*

Now this charmer who plotted my downfall and pain,
Said the Kremlin we never should please.
But I'll still save the world and the universe, too,
As I swing on my Russian trapeze—

Chorus:
Oh, he floats through the air
With his milk and his cheese,
The hottentots thrill at his Russian trapeze,
CIO banners he flies in the breeze,
He'll be back for the forty-eight show. *Oh No.*

The show ended with a song about the President, who not long before had been photographed playing the piano while leggy Lauren Bacall sat on the edge of it. One of the Gridiron singers, Bill Raymond, costumed as an acrobat, sang to the strains of the "Missouri Waltz":

Off in a corner, away from the show,
Someone is playing an old piano.
Thoughtfully, wistfully, so the notes fall—
Just for the love of the music, that's all.

What is he playing there, all the day long?
Thoughts of elections which didn't go wrong;
Dreams of Missouri which roll down the years.
Winning and losing, with laughter and tears.
Soulfully, hopefully, playing an old piano.

Upstage a piano played the final bars of the waltz, and the soloist continued:

Playing his own tune, familiar refrains.

Facing the music—at least that remains!

This was followed by the circus bandmaster singing a parody of "Blues in the Night."

> Our friends they done tole us
> Way back in September;
> Our friends they done tole us—sure!
> You don't have to worry
> And please don't send Harry—
> But then the landslide began.
> A voter's a two-face,
> A worrisome thing
> Who'll leave you to sing
> The blues in the night.

It closed with the whole chorus rousing the diners with their rewording of "Of Thee I Sing."

> Of us we sing, Harry.
> Courage is the greatest thing, Harry.
> Taft will shout and thunder,
> Fulbright raise a fuss.
> We've a right to wonder
> What becomes of us.

> Of us we sing, Harry,
> You will need that certain thing, Harry.
> Make the word "cooperation"
> Worthy of a mighty nation.
> To thee we sing.

The toast to the President was given and Truman rose to reply, extemporaneously. Hence, no text of his speech is preserved.

• • •

By the May 10, 1947 Gridiron dinner, the Republican Congress was in an effective blocking position against New Dealish measures, and Gridiron President Harold M. Talburt, cartoonist of the Scripps-Howard newspapers, reminded his audience in his speech in the dark, that "the only New Dealing being done around here now is with a deck of cards."

The opening act set the tone for the dinner. A chorus of pickets appeared, carrying all kinds of placards and singing three songs. To the tune of "Tammany" they complained:

> Prosperity, prosperity,

That's what Truman says we've got;
    what we've got is *not* so hot.
Prosperity, prosperity,
Lots of cash gone in a flash,
Prosperity!

Even in 1947 inflation was a problem. The opening chorus also sang:

We got plenty of nothing';
Jobs are easy to land,
This sounds funny,
But what good's money,
With prices in the air,
Up there, up there, up there.

And the third song, a parody on "Ain't We Got Fun":

Every time they pass a statute,
Ain't we got fun.
Every time that Harry gets cute,
Ain't we got fun.
Our tax is growing; we can't buy a car.
Our pants are glowing, they shine from afar.
Landlord's mad and getting madder
Ain't we got fun.
Times are bad and getting badder,
Still we have fun.
There's nothing surer; the rich get poor and the poor get poorer,
In this nation,
It's inflation,
Ain't *he* got fun.

The skit inaugurating the new Gridiron president was based on stand-ups of nine leading American cartoonists and again provided an opportunity for Gridiron members to laugh at themselves. They talked about cartoonists who can't draw, cartoonists who can't spell, and cartoonists whose work was "for readers who can't read." Then Talburt was described as "the cartoonist who hasn't done a day's work for Roy Howard since he was elected Gridiron president this year," and he was formally presented with the gavel.

The foreign skit satirizing the Truman Doctrine was set in a cannibal kingdom in Africa, and in a new version of "The Riff Song," the chorus of cannibals boasted:

All we need's a Communist or so

And we'll roll in Uncle Samuel's dough.
How can Truman save us from the foe
Till we find some pinks to overthrow
So let the Red Shadow come
We'll all cash in on it chum,
Come on, let's go.

And later:

I hear that Truman message plainly: "Hold back Joe!"
He's comin', he's comin', and he's bringing lots of dough;
Yes, Uncle Sam will save us all from Old Red Joe.

Then a character representing Stalin came on the stage and sang:

Ah-mer-ee-kahn-ski pay
To keep aus away.
You take dough—I stay,
Eet's the best Raw-shun way!

"General George Marshall" was next and he sang:

Any price you can pay, I can go higher,
I can top any bid offered by you.

"Henry Wallace" entered at this point announcing that he was the real representative of the American people, and that "even President Truman once approved a speech of mine."

"The Truman Doctrine," he said, "is all wrong. We must all be brothers. We must all be free."

"Free?" yelled the incredulous cannibal chief. "You mean we doesn't get paid? That's treason. Throw that robber in the stew pot."

As they are about to do it, the cannibal chief was told that "dat pot's cracked," and another member of the cast, representing Treasury Secretary John Snyder remarked, "A cracked pot, eh? What a coincidence!"

Wallace, from inside the kettle, sang:

I do all my pallin' with Uncle Joey Stalin
For with me, he is Number One,
And I think getting frisky
With Stalin's might risky
For you can't win the peace with a gun.

Fortunately perhaps, Wallace himself was not present at this dinner.

At the close of the foreign affairs skit, former President Hoover was presented, to speak at a Gridiron dinner for the first time since December, 1932, immediately after his defeat by Roosevelt. He received a very enthusiastic reception and recalled that he had attended his first Gridiron dinner more than thirty years before, when he was seated "at the far end of the corner table."

He had recently returned from a mission to Europe for President Truman and commented that he was "glad in this last skit to have been able to find some humor in foreign affairs."

He said he had hoped on this European mission, among other things, to investigate whether there was any humor left in European statesmen, because if there was "it would make our international relations more endurable.

"I hope," he said, "that we might at least get for the American taxpayer a few refreshing jokes as repayment for Lend-Lease and subsequent loans."

Then he told how a British food minister had been "moaning" to him over the hardships of their monotonous diet. To introduce a little lightness, he suggested that they could greatly improve matters "by reforming that institution of British self-castigation—the eternal boiled potato." He suggested employing a few French or Belgian chefs to teach them how to cook a potato, at least for official banquets. The food minister's response, he said, was "that we should discuss only matters of importance to the laboring classes."

Hoover then related how he had persisted in his quest for humor, but found no tangible results until he came to "the most tragic city of all the world—Vienna."

There he found an official who really wanted to help, and to illustrate the problem from which his country was suffering, he described a meeting of Bevin, Byrnes and Molotov. Secretary Byrnes, his informant told him, had taken out a plain silver cigarette case, and Bevin, noticing that it carried an inscription, read aloud: "To James Byrnes, from his devoted friends in the South Carolina Legislature."

Then Bevin remarked that he'd also received such a gift and produced a plain silver case inscribed: "To Ernest Bevin, from his devoted friends in the British Labor Party."

Molotov accepted a cigarette from both of them, and a little later on took out his own solid gold and bejeweled case, whereupon they noted that the inscription on his case read: "To Prince

Esterhazy, from his devoted friends of the Jockey Club of Vienna."

Hoover then turned to the dinner itself and noted with satisfaction that he was "not on your operating table tonight.

"But I can sympathize with Mr. Truman's difficulties," he went on, "in this matter as can no other man. I am fully aware of the skill and earnestness with which you cut up his ideology, his domestic and foreign policies. I can tell him, from long experience, not to look forward to much use of anesthetics."

The former President referred to the last time he had spoken at a Gridiron dinner, after the Republican defeat of 1932, and remarked that on that occasion "your speakers referred to the outgoing administration in those appreciative tones which politeness and tradition require for the dead.

"You may need," he said, "to search your barrel of sermons for that one again. Also at that time, I sought to comfort my colleagues by emphasizing the high importance in the democratic process of their forthcoming position as the opposition party. But to elaborate these themes would be an indelicate implication that I am seeking a recruit to my exclusive union of ex-Presidents." [Hoover was the only living ex-President at that time].

He recalled that in 1932 he had spoken of "the aid and comfort a President received from an opposition Congress," and continued, "Mr. Truman no doubt has realized during the past six months that they put more emphasis on the advice end of their constitutional relations than upon the consent end. Here again I can sympathize with Mr. Truman more deeply than any other living person. However, he has not yet probed the depths of their capacities in these directions."

Then he pointed out that the United States was most fortunate "in that partisanship does not reach such depths of hate and bitterness among responsible men as those which now infect much of this distracted world."

And, at a time when few people were saying nice things about President Truman, he paid the sitting President a touching tribute.

"I am glad to have this opportunity to say to you," he declared, "that President Truman has given high service to our country in repairing our broken dikes of safety which must guard our national ideals. Moreover, amid the thousand crises which sweep upon us from abroad, he has stood firm with his feet rooted in the American soil. He has brought to the White House new impulses of good will toward men."

He closed by saying to the Gridiron Club that he had, with time, "at least profited by your special prejudice against long speeches. That lesson has been rubbed in because in the past year I have listened to more long speeches in more languages than anyone not in the United Nations." [4]

This speech was a fine example of the mellowed Hoover, who, as he grew older and more detached from world affairs, grew also in respect among the American people.

As the Gridiron show continued, it turned its attention to a feud going on between Kenneth McKellar, Democratic senator of Tennessee, and David Lilienthal, chairman of the TVA. Turner Catledge had written a long song of fourteen verses about it, and he himself took the solo part. To the tune of "Turkey in the Straw," the song began:

> Gather 'round me children and I'll tell a story
> Of a feud that's killed relations of us all,
> Twixt old Tennessee McKellar and a vicious little feller
> From the mountains known as David Lilienthal

The vehicle for the Republican skit was a wayward bus load of impersonators of Republicans—Dewey, Taft, Bricker, Warren, Vandenberg, Stassen, and several others. Disaffected "Senator Wayne Morse" of Oregon explained what was happening.

"It has turned down Economy Avenue, backed up Budget Boulevard, skirted Lilienthal Lane, gone around Taxation Drive, and now it's come to a full stop in front of a Greek restaurant run by a guy named Truman, selling Turkish coffee."

The bus was described as a "wonderful definition of a straight-forward Republican program," and one of the occupants announced that its destination was the White House. "We don't care what roads we travel—just so we get there in 1948!"

Those portraying the various candidates sang revealing, although not always prophetic songs. "Dewey" led off with a paraphrasing of "Some Sunday Morning."

> Some summer morning, there's going to be
> One more convention for someone like me,
> Bands will be playing an old melody—
> Playing for someone like me.
> Banners and flags will flutter,
> Delegates marching, and then,

Say, can't you hear them utter:
"Now we've got Dewey again!"

Senators "Taft" and "Bricker," both from Ohio and both willing to be nominated but quite far apart in political philosophies, got together for a duet. Bricker sang to Taft:

Don't throw bouquets at me,
Don't praise my votes too much.
Don't tell other folks too much—
People will say we're in love!

And Taft sang back:

Don't throw your states to me,
Don't give me delegates.
Don't tell other candidates—
People will say we're in love!

"Stassen, the only real wayward bus driver," wanted the convention to be in Philadelphia because that was where Joseph N. Pew lived. Pew was a power in Republican Pennsylvania politics and one of the major contributors to Republican Presidential campaigns. He sang, to the tune of "Sioux City Sue":

Joe Sunoil Pew, Joe Sunoil Pew!
His oil is rich and so is he,
He'll spend it all on GOP
Joe Sunoil Pew, Joe Sunoil Pew—
There ain't no pal as true
As our own Joe Sun Oil Pew!

"Governor Warren" of California, who said that in 1944 "you wanted me to ride along as the mechanic," announced there would be no such thing this time; now "it's got to be in the driver's seat." He explained in song, to the tune of "I Tipped My Hat," that at the Chicago convention in 1944 he had "tipped his hat and slowly rode away," but now things were different.

But in forty-eight there'll be another day;
Maybe something else will come along my way.
If the job is Number One.
On both tickets I can run.
I'll hang up my hat and settle down to stay!

And "Senator Vandenberg," another potential candidate, sang a parody of "Songs of Songs."

In forty-eight, do not tempt your fate,

Once more an ancient tale unfolding.
Oh don't live a dream that fades with the dawn—
Sing some new song—
Don't wait too long.

This was the signal for the introduction of Governor Earl Warren as the Republican speaker.

Warren confessed at the outset that in this skit the Republican bus "did look rather wayward," and that there was a lot of "confusion about the schedule." But he said that when he was a youngster he had worked on a railroad, and he learned that "when a train or bus shuttles back and forth on side trips, or waits on sidings, it's not so much the fault of the crew as it is the dispatching.

"Here we have a perfectly good example of it. A Republican crew is trying to do its job on a system that still hires Democratic dispatchers.

"But it could even be worse. Suppose we had a Henry Wallace working on the bus—jimmying the brakes and sawing away at the steering gear. Wouldn't that be something? I know, because Henry came out and tried to direct the Democratic bus in California a year ago. He piled it up on a Primary Highway, and they're still picking up the parts."

Referring to the extensive past migrations into California, particularly by Oklahomans and Iowans, he remarked that "even Missourians were hitting the trail for Sunny California in large numbers until they suddenly heard about the big doings on the Potomac.

"But we don't mind the defection," he said. "We realize the Missourians got themselves into the union under the first Missouri compromise, and into Washington under the second. We don't mind them taking the country over for a while, because we know they will be coming back our way again right after 1948 . . . and we will welcome them with open arms."

Then, turning directly to the President and addressing him personally, Warren said he realized that without the good-natured sense of proportion which was so evident at Gridiron dinners, "your job, with all its vexations, would be unbearable. As a matter of fact," he continued, "I have often thought during the past two years—and it must have occurred to you—how much trouble a fellow can get into just by running for Vice President."

Recalling that they had had some tough football coach prob-

lems at the University of California, he said he could "fully sympathize with you, as head coach of the Democratic administration. I know how hard it is for a new coach to try to rebuild a
team when he is having so much trouble with the alumni association, particularly the unruly boys who remember being kicked
off the squad. With those fellows barnstorming on and off the
campus any coach would be a bit worried—with his contract
running out next year.

"Mr. President, we don't even mind your team using some
of our plays. The only thing we do ask is that you don't declare
our team 'off side'—while you are borrowing some of our players
to use in your own backfield."

However, the problems of the world, Warren noted in closing, "can be fairly regarded as a political football only in the
sense that when one party fumbles, it is up to the other to dive
for the ball.

"From these skits this evening it would appear that there
will be plenty of diving, and some nose dives, but when the
whistle blows after the final pile-up of 1948, I believe you will
find Republicans swarming all over the wayward ball—that is,
unless you Democrats have got the ball so inflated by that time
that *no one* can get hold of it."[5]

The Democratic skit was based on the party's missteps and
goofs, many of which involved Gael Sullivan, executive director
of the Democratic National Committee. He had written some
letters that backfired. "Sullivan" lamented that he had received
"two stripes across my back—from the President." James A. Farley at that time was president of Coca-Cola International. When
his impersonator was asked what he thought about the present
Democratic leadership, he replied, "It's the pause that re-
freshes."

Then the character impersonating Farley put his hand on
Sullivan's shoulder and sang:

> There's a rainbow round his shoulder
> And a millstone round his neck . . .
>
> Why a simple note to Carroll Reece
> Nearly put an end to aid for Greece,
> And his playful poke at Pepper
> Did nothing for Peace . . .
>
> No rainbow round his shoulder,
> That's a technicolor crutch,

Just a few words penned
To foe or friend,
And Gael's in Dutch!

Another character in the skit, Clark Clifford, one of President Truman's closest associates and advisers, was announced as "the White House Edgar Bergen." He told Sullivan that "President Truman wants to see you again—in the woodshed." Sullivan lamented, "Why, oh why, did I ever leave Chicago?" and sang to the strains of "Wyoming":

Oh give me back that city where the citizens are tame,
Where the voting's automatic and the counting is the same,
Where our boys tally double for all Democratic hopes,
But just give large round zeroes to Republicans—the dopes.

"Robert Hannegan" of Missouri, chairman of the Democratic National Committee, took a slightly different view, but even he was not optimistic as the 1948 election approached. The final verse of his song was:

Night and day we keep our fingers crossed,
There's an oh, such an ap-pre-hension, that forty-eight is lost,
Saving Turkey's good for Turks,
But the GOP at home may give us the works—
Day and night, night and day!

Another song gave some premonition of the Truman 1948 "give 'em hell" campaign. As an impersonator of Secretary of the Treasury Snyder put it:

Now Harry said, "In Forty-six
They muzzled me on politics,
I didn't fret, I didn't squawk,
But now I am big enough to talk."

That's what Uncle Harry said,
That's what Uncle Harry said.

The song went on about what Uncle Harry said, and it ended with the stanza:

When people tried to speculate
If Harry'd be a candidate,
He acted shy and murmered low,
"I'm just a guy who cain't say no!"

The skit closed with George Myers coming back to the old

"Rainbow 'Round My Shoulder" idea, with a parody of "How Are Things in Glocca Morra?"

> How are things in old Mis-sou-ra?
> Does that rainbow shine with hope and joy?
> Can they see the light in I-o-way,
> In Michigan and down in Illinois?
> How are things in Pennsyl-vanya?
> Is Rhode Island still New England's pride?
> Does that rainbow cast the slightest glow
> In O-hi-o?
> And does it shine at all on Dakota,
> Or Minnesota,
> All I ask is does that rainbow really stretch across the way,
> Or is it just a hopeful, gleaming ray,
> How are things in old Mis-sou-ra, this fine day?

President Truman, in responding, made some very generous remarks to both former President Hoover and Governor Earl Warren. He said he had received a lot of "helpful hints" and wanted to reciprocate; since at the last dinner he'd given some advice on how to get oneself elected to the Presidency, this time he wanted to go on from there and give another lesson "from the Truman primer."

There were various methods, and all of them, he said, were being tried. Then, with an obvious gibe at Governor Dewey, he announced that one of the methods of attaining the Presidency was getting elected governor of New York.

"That has been tried in the past and has succeeded. It is still a good formula. I'd like to add this further suggestion from the old copy books—If at first you don't succeed, try, try again. Platform and policies need cause no mental effort whatsoever. Just adopt the program of the Democratic party and say that you can execute it better."

Another approach which Truman described, with apparent application to General Eisenhower, was not to be a candidate at all; instead "be aloof, say that you wouldn't touch the idea of being a candidate with a ten-foot pole."

A third was what he described as "the senatorial approach." Here he was obviously talking about Senator Taft.

"Get yourself elected from the state of Ohio—mother of Presidents. In this approach, as currently employed, it behooves the candidate to ingratiate himself with labor. He should see to it that no legislation is proposed which is not approved by the great labor leaders of the country. You have noticed in the public prints how effectively this approach is being used and how it has won plaudits of organized labor. Maybe this is the sure-fire way to get into the White House."

A fourth method was to go abroad and consult with and interview foreign heads of states. "Obviously, one should consult with Generalissmo Stalin and publicize his views. I seem to have detected signs of this particular method being used." [Wallace had made a visit to Russia and talked with Stalin.]

Turning next directly to Governor Warren, he thanked him for having been so kind as "to say some rather complimentary things about me.

"One good turn deserves another. Now let me tell you how you ought to go about taking over this job of mine. You have already used the method successfully in California where you got yourself nominated on both tickets. I suggest to you, Governor Warren, that you give a national application to that formula and become a nominee of both the Democratic and Republican parties."

Becoming serious as he closed, Truman said that whichever of these methods he had described succeeds, "this country of ours will go right along.

"Our system is fundamentally sound," he told his audience. "This is the greatest governmental system in the world. Our press has helped to make it so. As I have said before, our press has done a particularly fine job in making clear to the people the full meaning of our policy of aid to Greece and Turkey. Our press can take some share of the credit for the resounding majority which the Greek and Turkish aid bill has just won in the House of Representatives.

"I am not here just to butter up the press. I don't think it is perfect. But, it is the best press in the world and it is doing a fine job. It is an integral part of our democracy.

"This year there was issued a memorial stamp honoring the memory of a great publisher [Pulitzer]—an immigrant, incidentally. One of his sayings is printed on that stamp. I am glad it is there so it will be read by everyone in our country. It expresses a profound truth: 'Our Republic and its press will rise or fall together.'

"Gentlemen, again I thank you for an extremely pleasant and profitable evening, and I hope that you will invite me back to your next dinner."[6]

This was a speech which Truman was apparently quite eager to deliver. His mother was seriously ill at the time in Grandview, Missouri, and there had been some doubt about whether the President would even come to the dinner. However, he did, and after the dinner took off at 3:00 A.M. by plane for Grandview.

• • •

President Truman's difficulties with the Republican Congress had been growing, and by the time the December 13, 1947 dinner took place, the President's own popularity had sunk lower than that measured for any other President since polling began.

Gridiron President Harold M. Talburt, in his speech in the dark, told the guests of the Gridiron that "we greet you in the spirit of laughter" and said that anyone creating a laugh in these times deserved the thanks of the nation.

"So we thank President Truman," he said, "for bringing Congress back into special session."

Noting they were on the threshold of another Presidential campaign, he remarked that "all the Republicans are running for President, all the Democrats for Vice President, and all the voters are running for help."

And then, in a direct forecast of the kind of campaign that would win President Truman an unexpected reelection, Talburt declared, "Democratic leaders reply that a Democrat's best friend is a Republican Congress and the White House prays for Senator Taft."

Talburt suggested that nothing be taken too seriously, "especially ourselves," and the writers of the foreign affairs skit took him at his word.

The skit was set at the North Pole in front of a large igloo, with a mailbox marked "S. Claus, RFD #1, North Pole," and a sign resting against it, "Moved—Forward all mail to Washington, D.C." At the left of the igloo was a totem pole with a Truman face grinning broadly and a sign, "Got enough? If not, see General Marshall."

The characters included Stalin and the principal Russians, Molotov, Gromyko, Vishinsky, General Marshall, then secretary of state, and various other Americans and Europeans.

It was 1952, five years in the future. Before the arrival of the Russians, Secretary Marshall and the chorus sang to the beat of "My Man":

Oh, there never was a plan just like my plan,
It's a plan that even I don't understan',

But the European nations made it pay OK.
What's the difference if we have no clothes or heat,
And we've all forgotten how it feels to eat.
For whatever my plan is, it's a whiz,
  for-ev-er-more.

The skit wasn't complimentary to the Russians. When they entered, led by Stalin, Molotov read the sign on the igloo and told him that Santa Claus lives there.

"A capitalist creation of small imperialistic minds," shouted Vishinsky, "an enemy of the proletariat—shoot him, too."

Peering cautiously into the igloo, Molotov observed, "I can see the whites of his eyes."

"Don't shoot!" yelped Vishinski. "Wait till he turns his back.

Then Gromyko sang:

Let me call you sweetheart,
And the world will be,
Cut up into portions,
Just for you and me.

I will take the land part
and give you the sea,
Let me call you sweetheart,
I'll be true to me.

In the guest stand-ups that followed, the club zeroed in on President Truman. Adolph Menjou was one of the guests, and as he was called to his feet by Walker Buel, Richard L. Wilson commented, "The 'State of the Union' is the title of President Truman's message to congress and Mr. Menjou's newest movie. The movie is good."

The Republican skit, described as a "preconvention preview of 1948," was set in a western ghost town, where characters representing all the potential candidates, Vandenberg, Taft, Dewey, Stassen, Eisenhower, Speaker Joseph W. Martin, Jr., and quite a number of ghosts, were looking for "gold in the hills and delegates on the plains."

"The Forty-Niners are gone," proclaimed a ghost, "Here come the Forty-Eighters!"

As the chorus poured in noisily, "Carroll Reece," chairman of the Republican National Committee, announced he was about to issue a statement on party unity. Everyone in the chorus shouted, "No, no," and Reece said, "Wonderful, wonderful. This will demonstrate to the country that the Republican party is united as never before. Senator Vandenberg, will you speak to us on party harmony?" In response, Vandenberg sang:

Feudin' and fussin' and a-fightin',
Always the GOP's excitin',
Candidates neighborly people, peaceful and sweet,
All except when they happen to meet.
Stassen, Taft and Dewey,
Of each other they say, "Phooey."

Let's get a liberal leader like *me*, and then
We'll go feudin' and fightin' again!

To the tune of "When You Were Sweet Sixteen," Taft sang:

I'm running as I never ran before,
Since first I strolled upon the White House scene.
Since nine-teen-eight put Dad's name on the door,
I've wanted to return there,
Since I was just—since I was just nineteen!

Governor Dewey announced that nobody was going to hear anything from him but a whisper until next year and sang:

Whisper and wait, there's no use tempting fate,
For talking won't win the nomination—
Talking just leads to tribulation.
Whisper and you can sweep the nation,
Whispering for forty-eight!

Stassen dreamed that he saw five stars, "and that face—it's everywhere." Then he sang:

Night and day and every hour,
All that I see is Eisenhower,
Always!

General Eisenhower entered from the wings, and to all questions about whether he was going to run and whether he was going to run as a Republican, he answered, "Just call me Ike." And George Myers, who played the Eisenhower part, sang to the tune of "Kiss Me Again":

Sweet GOP, whispers to me
Asking me what I will do.
Dewey and Taft
Feeling a draft,
Kansas is calling me too.

Democrats fear, what they will hear,
Hoping it will be in vain.
But it's too soon,
Sometime next June
Ask me, ask me again!

The act ended with Speaker Martin singing:

The papers are advising
Truman is finding his gait.
Beyond the blue horizon—what of forty-eight?

This was the cue for the introduction of the real House Speaker Joseph Martin, the Martin of Roosevelt's 1938 campaign cry against "Martin, Barton and Fish," who thanked the Gridiron Club for the privilege of speaking on the same program with the President of the United States.

"But I doubt," he said, "if ever, in the long history of the Gridiron Club, any other man has had the opportunity to address so many *next* Presidents.

"We seem to have some degree of inflation in the political as well as in the economic field," he continued. "That, however, is one phase of inflation which, we know, will be corrected with the passage of a few months. That is as certain as it is that Congress will pass a tax reduction bill in 1948."

Then in the best Gridiron tradition, turning to President Truman, Martin said, "You understand, of course, Mr. President, that this tax bill is really a fine gesture of cooperation. We heard over the grapevine that you and Mrs. Truman were having difficulties with your family budget and we seek to relieve the strain.

"Of course, we also have in mind 49 million other tax-payers."

With good-natured but cutting remarks, Speaker Martin alluded to the "sincere affection which we all have for Mr. Truman," and went on to say that possibly some of those in the audience are not entirely familiar with "my efforts to serve the interests of the President."

He told how he had personally introduced a joint resolution calling for a constitutional amendment which would make all past Presidents members of the Senate for life. "At that time," he said, "the Democrats had a majority in Congress so, of course, there was no action on the resolution.

"A few minutes ago," he said, "we saw some ghosts on the

stage and I am sure we all derived considerable amusement and some education from their antics. Politicians usually have a weakness for ghosts. They make useful and harmless issues. I have heard of them being used as candidates and I have been told that there are places where they vote in large numbers and with remarkable unanimity."

He said that over all the world for the past few years "we have been chasing a ghost named international peace," and that "we have used every conceivable method to induce that ghost to materialize into reality.

"We must recognize," he continued, "that our efforts have been unsuccessful thus far because there is a mighty power of evil at large in this world—a power that does not want peace. It does not want man to be free. It seeks to enslave and degrade him.

"This power has spread over much of Europe and more of Asia. . .

"We must halt the spread of this power abroad if possible and at any cost we must exterminate it in America.

"May I say in all seriousness I am delighted that the administration in recent months has shown signs of coming around to the position which the Republicans have occupied on this issue for years. Even those who come at the eleventh hour are welcome. But that does not mean that the most recent convert is entitled to lead the choir."

At this point, Martin became less serious and turned his satire directly to President Truman and inferentially to his predecessor, by pointing out that when we talk about charting the course of the ship of state, "it is quite natural to talk about the captain and the officers who will do the navigating.

"Up in New England," he said, "which has a considerable seafaring tradition, we have a quaint preference for captains or navigators who can chart a course to their destination and then stay on that course.

"I must admit that the voyage we have been on nationally for the past fifteen years has been exciting but, looking back at it, I get the impression that we have traveled about as far sideways as we did forward. . .

"And during all those years there was seldom a time when the captain was not shouting from the bridge that we were going on the rocks immediately unless the board of directors met and voted him more money to hire a larger crew. We are not actually on the rocks yet but it is my impression that the owners of the ship and the passengers have come to the conclusion that it might be a good idea to sign up a navigator who could locate some open water once in a while instead of combing the seven seas for rocks.

"Just now the rocks which seem to be exciting the navigators are the rocks of inflation. There is no doubt we are near them— we ought to be, we have been steering for them for fifteen years."

In his conclusion, however, Martin promised that despite the differences of opinion the country would stand together behind its President once decisions were made.

"We have our differences, yet we can, and do, have genuine respect for each other—just as I do for the kindly, distinguished President of the United States, for whom I have deep personal affection.

"We will battle over our complicated domestic problems; we will differ over the details of foreign policies, but once a decision is made we stand as one people—all united with the firm purpose of building a stronger and better America."[7]

This speech was a gentle and gracious rapier, but it was done in such good taste that when Martin concluded, President Truman rose, walked over and shook hands with him, while the guests at the dinner stood and applauded vigorously.

The Democratic skit, before the President's speech, was set in "Dr. Truman's Clinic." The announcer said that the Democrats were going crazy because "they know it's their turn to lose, and some of them are taking the treatment now in Doctor Harry's Clinic," whose chief medical practitioner was Senator J. Howard McGrath of Rhode Island—"Dr. Harry's first assistant, if you don't count Clark Clifford."

There was one chorus of interns and nurses and another of people who wanted to be Vice President. The second chorus sang, to "Twenty-nine Palms":

We are twenty-nine hopeful gents
Making like Vice Presidents.
We got twenty-nine plans and schemes,
Twenty-nine visions and dreams,
But it would be awful risky
To shout or to rejoice
'Till Dr. Harry announces his choice.

At this point, "Henry Wallace," who was to run as an independent Progressive the following year against President Truman, entered and announced that he was "Yogi Henry Wallace," that this was a lousy clinic, and that he was thinking of starting one of his own that would put this place out of business. Then Wallace sang:

> I wonder who's hissing me now,
> Wonder who just showed them how,
> It's surely not Stalin—he loves me
> Tee-hee-hee
> Yesss-ssir-ree.

> I know I can trust Molotov,
> I couldn't suspect Litvinov,
> Bet you can guess—it is just the U.S.
> No wonder they're hissing me now.

"Attorney General Tom Clark" followed and was told by "Dr. McGrath" that "some of our Democrats are having nightmares about you. Where were you last night?"

Clark replied, "I was out on a suing spree. I was anti-trusting them Republicans for Dr. Harry. Just listen."

> I'll sue them in my dreams,
> Jail them with my schemes.
> Railroads, bankers—what do I care?
> They just get in Democrats' hair.

Next came the "Literary Branch," Democrats in the Truman administration or the previous one who were now writing for the magazines, one of whom was "Henry Morgenthau," who sang, to "Smoke Gets in Your Eyes":

> They asked me how I knew,
> What I wrote was true.
> I, of course, replied
> Secrets from inside
> Cannot be denied.

> Speaking frankly, grudges must be settled,
> If only with a pen,
> And today they envy me the way
> The cash is rolling in.

He was followed by "Senator Claude Pepper" of Florida, clad in a red straitjacket, who announced that he was working both sides of the street, including the middle. He sang a parody of "Sun in the Mornin' and the Moon at Night," from *Annie, Get Your Gun*.

Tell me, New Deal, where is thy sting?
We're for the poor in the morning
   and the rich at night . . .

Harry, this is our winning plan—
Fat cats, also the working man . . .

Got no bank book, got no roll,
But Dillon, Reed still has a soul.
And with the poor in the morning
   and the rich in the evening,
We're all right.

"McGrath" then announced that although they'd worked this trick before, "it's the only trick we've got," and that nobody was crazy any more because "old Dr. Harry's treatments got results."

The skit closed with the announcement that the election was a year off, "but old Dr. Harry looks mighty pretty sittin' up there tonight—now don't he?"

And then the entire cast sang their version of "The Way You Look Tonight."

You're just our Harry,
With the smile so warm,
With the jobs to give,
We have got no other—so we love you.
That's the way we feel tonight.

The Gridiron Club then offered its advice on how Truman should conduct his campaign the following year:

Every time Reece opens his trap,
Gallup will boost your score.
Your campaign will be just a snap,
If he will talk some more.

Harry, never, never change;
Keep the voters charmed.
Or, if necessary,
Keep them frightened—
Just the way they are tonight.

Lean right,
Lean left.

Sit tight,
Be deft—

Just the way you are tonight.

Taking his cue perhaps from Speaker Joseph Martin, Truman in his speech said he liked "Joe" very much, that he appreciated his sentiments, and that he knew they were sincere. He continued with equally good humor, stabbing good-naturedly at the Republican Congress on high prices, at disagreements within the party, and at the party "surplus of candidates."

Since there was no Vice President at that time, Speaker Martin was next in succession for the Presidency. Therefore, Truman joked at length about his own health and, looking straight at Martin, assured the Republicans that he was hale and vigorous.

He closed on a note very similar to Speaker Martin's, that is, acknowledging their genuine respect for each other and the two parties, and that while they differed over details, they were all united in the goal of achieving a better America.[8]

A few days later, in a letter to his good friend Duke Shoop, Washington correspondent of the *Kansas City Star*, President Truman said that "I don't think I have ever enjoyed [a Gridiron dinner] any more in my life than I did the last one. The only difficulty with me," he said, "is, I have to sit on the 'Gridiron' until the last minute before I can really begin to enjoy things."

Then he added a strictly Trumanesque comment:

"My pretty daughter [Margaret] has been shoving me off the front page and I am glad of it."

He said she'd made quite a hit in Kansas City and added, "Tell Roy [Roy Roberts, editor of the *Kansas City Star*] that I appreciate most highly his kindness to her. I don't care a lot what you and Roy say about me but I am a little touchy about my family."[9]

• • •

The tone of the spring dinner of 1948, held on April 10, was set by Gridiron President Phelps H. Adams, as he welcomed the guests "in the dizzy spirit of spring—the season when the Presidential bee stings all the candidates; and all the candidates get set to sting the voters."

As for the Republicans, he commented that spring was circus time and that this was "the first time in history that an elephant has ever tried to run in four different directions at once—on a tightrope."

Then Adams pointed out that President Truman wanted Hawaii admitted as a brand new state. "Heaven knows why," said Adams. "We thought he was having enough trouble with the old ones."

The 1948 election was on the mind of every politically oriented person, and it was already apparent that President Truman was in deep trouble as a candidate for reelection.

The entire Gridiron chorus marched on the stage in the opener written by Marshall McNeil, carrying Republican, Democratic and third party banners and sang a medley from *Carousel*, beginning with:

> June is bustin' out all over
> All over the White House and the Hill.
> Ev'ry candidate is yearnin'
> And his hopeful eyes are turnin'
> To Convention Hall where he will fill the bill.

The Republican group sang:

> We got plenty ammunition,
> Lots of men with high ambition.
> We Republicans once more are White House bound.

The Democrats answered:

> Democrats this year are wishin'
> We could stop the party fission;
> As it is, we face November with regret.

The fired Henry Wallace was already indicating that he would be a third party candidate, in an attempt to split the Democratic vote with President Truman.

"Henry's bustin' out all over," sang the third party contingent, while the Republicans, in a reference to his trip to the Soviet Union, interrupted with, "All over with red, you mean," and the Democrats with, "Yeah, you got a first class phoney."

The turbulent foreign situation was dramatized in a firehouse skit, in which the fire chief was an impersonator of Secretary of State George Marshall. Fires were breaking out all over, and a character representing Marshal Tito of Yugoslavia, clutching a large box of matches and lighting a sparkler, sang:

> I don't want to set the world on fire,
> I just want Trieste to feather my nest.
> In my heart I have but one desire,
> Let me live in peace, But first give me Greece.
>
> I don't want to set the world on Fire!
> I just want to sew up Europe for Joe.

A little later, the "Grand Mufti of Jerusalem" was brought in because he had been caught "pulling fireboxes from one end of Mediterranean Avenue to the other." Presented as "just a big false alarm," he sang:

> I'm the Sneak of Araby
> I've pulled two plugs or three.
> At night when you're asleep,
> Through alleys dark I creep.
> I watch the engines roar,
> And then I pull some more.
> I am the Grand Mufti,
> The Sneak of Araby.

The Republican skit was set in Chinatown, where Republican leaders were searching for a candidate in the conviction that the GOP could win "even if we nominate a Chinaman." A Chinese laundryman was revealed as Herbert Hoover. He sang:

> Whom shall we nominate?
> Who will take every state?
> Taft, MacArthur, Dewey or Van,
> Martin, Stassen—we've got the man!

"Hoo Flung Dewey" entered and sang:

> You'll be loving me, always,
> I will love me, too, always.
> In Convention Hall,
> Then again next fall,
> I will lead them all, always, always.
> I'm a different guy, don't fear;
> I've got that new look this year.
> In the North or South,
> In the East or West,
> Dewey is the best—but always.

The problems of unity in the Republican party were satirized with "Senator Wayne Morse" of Oregon and some associates who were routed out of an opium den. They announced that they'd been "having the nicest dreams—about Republicans always agreeing with us." They were sent "back to your pipe dreams," as an impersonator of General Douglas MacArthur entered, dressed in mandarin robes and tended by lackeys who fanned him as he walked. He announced that he shouldn't be called "General" any more, he should be called "Available MacArthur," and sang:

When I grow too old to dream,
I'll remember Wisconsin.*
When my five stars cease to gleam,
That mem'ry will not depart.
So I shall return.
So let voting start.
And when I grow too old to dream,
I'll still have votes in my heart!

"Senator Robert Taft," when asked if he'd made up his mind, sang:

I take Harry's gospel whenever it's pos'ble.
But with a grain of salt!
The New Deal has lived fifteen years,
The New Deal has lived fifteen years.
All of those taxes
They've laid on our backses
Made it seem like nine hundred years.
I'm makin' this campaign to show—
They say if selected I won't be elected—
It Ain't Necessarily So!

At this point "General Eisenhower" entered and was asked by a delegate, "How about running for President?"

"So solly, please, he replied, "plevious engagement," and sang to the beat of "Civilization (Bongo, Bongo)":

Each morning the politicans
Figure out a new design.
They tell the dizzy population
How organization is fine.
And their educated orators
Holler out with plenty power,
That running the nation
Is the job for Eisenhower.

But—
Bongo, bongo, bongo,
Do not coax me any longer,
Oh, no, no, no, no, no.
Hope you will excuse it,
Nomination, I refuse it,
But I thank you so!

---

*Where he had won a Presidential endorsement.

They tell me White House might be
    just a dog-house,
That's what I fear.
So Columbia can have me,
That's my career!
You can offer me what you like,
But I'll still be Professor Ike.
So nominations, take them away!
Both of them!

The end of this skit was the signal for the introduction of
Senator Taft, who, in one of the great Gridiron speeches, took the
occasion to proclaim the loyalty of the "loyal opposition" to President Truman. He recalled that some people had thought, when
the Republicans won control of Congress in 1946, that the government had been turned over to his party—a notion which he
said was "premature."

The Republicans didn't have any real power to do anything,
he noted, "unless we get at least half the Democrats in the Senate
to go along with us," an event that happened "about once a
year."

Then, turning directly to President Truman, he said that in
spite of "our somewhat overrated victory in 1946, we remain the
loyal opposition.

"In fact, Mr. President," he went on, "the only loyalty that
remains around here exists right in that loyal opposition. We
alone stand by, and stand with and sometimes over the President. We alone today earnestly and unanimously desire to see
you nominated, Mr. President."

The audience loved it—uproariously—and even Truman
grinned happily at such a deft sally.

"After that, of course," continued Taft, "we leave you on
your own. . . . Loyalty would appear to be a forgotten quality on
the Democratic side. Certainly there is not much loyalty left
about Henry Wallace—although a great deal of left. Henry Wallace, who was once such a tower of strength that his nomination
as Vice President was deemed essential to the welfare of the
Democratic Party. He was a great man in the heyday of the New
Deal. He was secretary of agriculture. He was Vice President. He
ran the Foreign Economic Administration, which took over the
State Department. He was the secretary of commerce directing
economic policies during the early days of your administration.
He told us how he could raise wages without raising prices. Of

course it didn't work, but you tried it. His loyalty ran out at Madison Square Garden with the speech that you approved, Mr. President, without consulting your other secretary of state or your loyal opposition, and Henry is still running.

"And where are those loyal Southern Democrats, loyal even when attempts were made to purge them, loyal even when your predecessor said he wanted the poll tax abolished. We are told some of your closest advisers said you could stand firm and count on southern friends in the Senate and the House to handle everything at the proper time. They have handled it all right. They are part of the opposition now, but not quite as loyal opposition as we Republicans.

"What about Ed Flynn, Ed Crump, Jake Arvey, Jim Curley and the other city bosses? Are they still loyal? In 1936 Alfred E. Smith took a walk into the night. Today the city pavements seem to be crowded with stargazers.

"But perhaps Claude Pepper is still loyal. We've been trying to figure out whether he was a Southern Democrat or a Wallace Democrat or a New Deal labor Democrat. He might qualify as any of the three, but since he has been very careful not to say just where he is, perhaps he is still one of those scarce creatures, rarer even than the floogie bird, a loyal Democrat.

"Mr. President, as I said, we will do everything we can to see that you are nominated. . . .

"It is nice to have a man in the White House with whom we are on terms of first-name friendship—like Tom, or Dick, or Harry, or even Bob. Like every American I have the greatest respect for the White House and for the Presidency. This was instilled in me in my youth, perhaps to a greater degree than in most of my fellow countrymen because my address was once 1600 Pennsylvania Avenue. I like the old homestead.

"Also, seriously like every American, I have profound respect for the chief occupant of the White House. This is especially true in your case, Mr. President, although we are of different political faiths, because we were colleagues in the Senate, where I learned to like Harry S. Truman, the man.

"And so my approach tonight is in the kindliest spirit. But you puzzle your loyal opposition. We don't always know just how to be loyal and keep on your side. Most of us went along with your policy on the partition of Palestine, and then suddenly found you had left us for that seductive siren, a United Nations trusteeship.

"In order to be loyal, we ratified the Italian Treaty with an international Trieste, but now we find loyalty compels us to give Trieste back to Italy. We joined enthusiastically in your abolition of meat controls and all price controls during the election of 1946. You beat us to that one before we could get back to Washington. Then we suddenly are faced with the demand we eat all our words, properly rationed, of course, and swallow the whole mess again—red points and blue points and gas coupons, well seasoned with allocations and wage controls.

"No, Mr. President, you don't make it an easy job for us to remain a constantly loyal opposition. We rush in to help you abolish the greedy grain speculators 'trafficking in human misery,' and then we find you lose all your enthusiasm when we discover members of the official family right up to their ears in corn, in the middle of your administration.

"We embrace and acclaim the Truman doctrine in Greece, and rush on shouting into China, only to find that for some mysterious reason your secretary of state thinks Chinese communists are different from Greek communists.

"You make it a hard job, Mr. President, but seriously you really do have our loyal support. The nation faces a crisis which threatens our freedom and our way of life. We are prepared to stand with you to oppose the advance of communism on every front, foreign and domestic. We believe that the unchecked spread of communism would destroy the principles of liberty and equality and justice upon which this nation was founded. We join with you in your determination to make the armed forces of this country more than adequate to protect the safety and peace of our people.

"We like the way you begin a lot of programs, even if we can't always follow you to the end. We even like your taste in art and in German paintings. We are no judges of the artistic in architecture, but we like the looks of the $18,000 porch on the south side of the White House. Of course, we like the White House better."[10]

The speech was in the best Gridiron style and was a terrific success.

The Democratic skit was a masquerade to dedicate President Truman's new White House porch, where a love scene was staged between "Balonio and Trumanette," but it was Balonio and Trumanette with music, and the first song revealed the Democrats looking all over for a four-leaf clover:

No need complaining,
He's still remaining—
That man at the white house door!
We'll look all over
For four-leaf clover
As we never looked before!

President Truman's troubles with the Southern Democrats, both in Senate and House, were satirized to the melody of "Without a Song."

Without the South, our party's at an end;
Without the South, our troubles will not mend.
And Democrats are left without a friend,
Without the South! . . .
We'll never know what changed that southern drawl,
We'll never know where votes will go next fall—
We only know you-all will miss us-all,
Without the South!

James A. Farley, the most successful chairman the Democratic National Committee ever had, had broken with Roosevelt over the third term issue and retired from active party participation to become president of Coca-Cola International. He was welcomed back again by the party faithful, who commented that "the next time he takes a pause to refresh, I hope it won't last eight years."

To the tune of "I'll Take You Home Again, Kathleen," they sang:

We welcome you again, dear Jim,
Across the years both wild and wide.
To where your heart has always been,
Where Democratic friends abide.

Then they put a light in the window to try to get Henry Wallace back home again—a red light—and sang:

Won't you come home, Oh Henry,
Won't you come home?
Bring back Glen Taylor, too.*
We need his cowboy singing.
Your crystal ball.
You know you done us wrong.
'Member that stormy day that we drove you out

---

*Taylor became Wallace's running mate in 1948.

With nothing but a fine tooth comb?
You know you're to blame,
Well, ain't that a shame?
But Henry, won't you please come home?

But one of the characters objected and told Wallace that "we wouldn't take you back if you paid your own way home from Moscow."

A character who identified himself as Attorney General Tom Clark summarized the conclusions of the group by singing to the tune of "Chloe":

Har-ry!
Har-ry!
Hear us callin', we can't wait,
You must be our candidate . . .
Through the black of night
We got to go where you are.
If it's wrong or right
We got to go where you are.

"Party chairman McGrath" introduced four Harrys: Harry S. Jefferson, Harry S. Jackson, Harry S. Wilson—all wearing Truman masks, and Harry S. Roosevelt, wearing a T.R. mask. The last was a gibe at the occasion in a Jefferson-Jackson Day speech by Truman when he had misspoken himself and referred to former President Roosevelt as Theodore Roosevelt. Together they and the chorus all sang:

Now is the hour
When we must say goodbye.
Off for campaigning.
Travel far and nigh.
While we're away,
November will draw near.
When we return, we wonder
Who'll be here?

President Truman closed the dinner but had no script and his remarks are not in the Gridiron files. But Gene Buck, in his letter to the club after the dinner, commented that he liked "his human, natural, friendly talks without a script."

"He seems perfectly at home at Gridiron affairs and manages to generate a genuine love of fun, music and people—and to do that at a Gridiron affair with your type of guests, in his spot, is something I deeply admire. I am ever conscious that it is difficult for any President to really be himself in public."

XV

Harry S. Truman

(1948-1952)
Truman the Feisty

The dinner of December 11, 1948 was held just a little more than a month after President Truman had been reelected in the greatest surprise of any election in American history. The betting odds right down to the wire had been fifteen to one on Governor Dewey to win, and all the indications prior to the election, including the polls, supported those odds.

But Truman, the underdog, went to the country, campaigning not against his opponent but against the "do nothing" Eightieth Congress. He spoke with such fervor that in his later meetings there were roars from every crowd of "Give 'em hell, Harry!"

His own party was badly split, with Henry Wallace running against him independently on the left, and J. Strom Thurmond of South Carolina running against him independently on the right.

But when the votes were counted on election night, the middle western farm states, which had been projected as surely Republican, dropped in numerous instances into the Democratic column. Thurmond carried only four states in the South, and President Truman found himself reelected with 303 electoral votes to 189 for Dewey, 39 for Thurmond, and none for Wallace.

The three major contenders, Truman, Dewey and Thurmond, were all present at the Gridiron dinner and Dewey made a truly remarkable speech.

The election had had a profound effect upon President Truman. He was no longer the modest man of his first term, succeeding to a job that he had never anticipated and feeling a keen sense of his responsibilities. Now he was the triumphant and feisty victor, displaying with great pride the headline from an election night early edition of the *Chicago Tribune,* proclaiming that Dewey was elected.

The change was aptly demonstrated by remarks he had made at the dinner in April and again in December to Gridiron President Phelps H. Adams, as he sat down beside him at the head table. In April, Truman turned to Adams and said, "You know, I sometimes think the country might have been better off if I had turned out to be a pianist in a whorehouse." The astonished Adams replied, "I don't know about the country, Mr. President, but you sure would have had a lot more fun."

And later, Adams commented that in April "throughout the evening he gave me the impression at least that he had a rather overdeveloped picture of his own shortcomings."

In contrast, at the December dinner, Adams got the impression that Truman was quite bitter at all those who had opposed him, particularly the Southerners.

"In fact, his first remark," said Adams, "after the usual exchange of pleasantries, was [in reference to the Southerners], 'They're no better than Fascists—no better than Fascists.'"[1]

Adams opened the dinner in his speech in the dark with a reference to "the immortal spirit of Christmas—the spirit of sleigh bells . . . and reindeer . . . and good old Saint Harry."

Little children, he said, were writing their letters to Santa Claus at the North Pole, but Democrats "just write direct to Washington."

"This, indeed," he said, "is an age of miracles. Why, it's getting so you can expect one every 1948 years . . .

"No one can deny that with Harry Truman in the White House for four more years, the people face a promising future. They should. He promised them everything in the catalog. Why he even said he'd give Big Business the works. . .

"The big surprise, of course, was Iowa. It just goes to show that you can't fool those Iowa farmers. They know corn when they hear it. And speaking of corn, there was Hybrid Henry

[Wallace, a reference to the fact that his family had first developed hybrid corn], the greatest false alarm of the country. Why, he didn't even get two yokels to the acre."

Adams asked the Gridiron guests not to belabor the past but to look to the future and the spirit of unity. "But, gentlemen, there is something more precious than unity. It is America's most prized possession—good sportmanship. Only a month ago President Truman, Governor Dewey and Governor Thurmond divided the nation's electoral vote among them in a tough and bitter Presidential contest. Yet tonight all three of these men are here to join us in an evening of good fellowship and good humor—to laugh at each other, at us and at themselves.

"In any other land in this unhappy world, *that* would be a major miracle. Tonight, in America, it is simply another Gridiron dinner.

"So in the warm and friendly light of the Gridiron, let us for a while, relax and enjoy ourselves, secure in the knowledge that there is nothing seriously wrong with a nation which can produce such good losers and—what is equally rare—such a good winner."

Practically all the members of the Washington press corps had expected Governor Dewey to be elected, and the Gridiron Club used that fact for laughing at itself in the opener.

Marshall McNeil, music chairman, announced, "Mr. President, we concluded the spring dinner of the Gridiron Club, on the night of April 10, this year, with a beautiful, and what we then thought was a prophetic song . . . ."

From behind the curtain, the chorus resang:

Now is the hour
When we must say goodbye . . . .

Then the announcer came back.

"And so, Mr. President, in the interest of continuity we present a slightly different version of the same song, sung by the Gridiron chorus, in top hats, white ties and tails."

The curtains parted slowly, revealing the chorus dressed as described—but with no pants! They sang the December 1948 version:

Now is the hour
When we must break the news,
We who predicted
Dewey could not lose.

We saw the crowds,
Heard Harry's every word;
Then voters everywhere
Gave us the bird!

The act closed with a presentation to Governor Dewey of a Gridiron scroll inviting him to all future dinners of the Gridiron Club. This was a practice which up to that time had been reserved for Presidents of the United States upon leaving office. McNeil explained that this scroll had been prepared the previous June for someone else, but they now had decided to present it to "Ex-President Thomas E. Dewey."

The unification of the armed services had finally been effected, the Berlin blockade was on, and President Truman had ordered the airlift to Berlin. These events were treated in two skits. In the first, the audience was taken to the Pentagon, "that vine-covered cottage of harmony," where the generals and admirals were plotting against each other until "James Forrestal," secretary of defense, commanded their presence. They all saluted and ran off.

The Berlin blockade skit was set in a radio station in the Russian sector of Berlin. It ended with the arrival of the U.S. Air Force singing:

Off we go into the wild blue yonder,
Flying high into Berlin.
Valiant men tear the blockade asunder,
At 'em boys! And we will win!
Here we come bearing a rich new cargo,
Here we come bearing our gift,
In echelon we carry on,
Nothing'll stop the Allied air lift.

At this time the House Un-American Activities Committee was very active, and Whittaker Chambers had come up with "the pumpkin papers." This skit was the first one in which a character represented Richard Nixon, a young congressman on the committee. They were fishing for red herring but all the fish got away.

One other event deserves mention. In the guest skit, among those who were asked to stand was the new senator-elect from Texas, Lyndon B. Johnson, "who won by eighty-seven votes and is known as Landslide Lyndon." That nickname stuck.

Also in this guest skit was a little verse about General

MacArthur, not renowned for his skill in the art of self-effacement, and later to be fired by President Truman.

> Here's to the land of the Nippo,
> Which once was imperial sod,
> Till MacArthur arrived with his halo,
> And the Japanese learned about God.

The Republican skit was set in Fort Tomato, a Dutch-Indian settlement at Albany, where various characters had gathered "to examine the future of the Republican party's past." The first target was Dr. George Gallup and other pollsters. "Gallup" was an Indian medicine man who mournfully described himself as "low man on totem poll," and when "Senator Taft'" asked him if he could explain what had happened, he replied, "No, I'm selling new contracts for a poll to find out." Then he sang:

> Ah, sweet mystery of life, we have not found thee,
> Ah, we do not know the secret of it all.
> All the canvasses, projections and percentage—
> The ouija board, the magic wand and crystal ball.
> Oh, from poll to poll to poll we have been seeking,
> Elmo Roper, Crossley, I, all made it pay—
> But the answer put an end to all our striving—
> The votes were counted on election day!

It was possible that the pollsters were really right, but one of the problems that they had not counted on was the widespread overconfidence among the Republicans. This had led many Dewey supporters to go on with business as usual, be away on vacations, or for various other reasons fail to vote. (There were approximately 400 such known cases in the Du Pont headquarters organization in Wilmington, Delaware alone.)

This led a character representing Charles Halleck, Republican leader of the House, to comment that the trouble was that the Dewey train was too big. "If everybody riding it had got off and voted, we'd have won."

The reference to the train recalled that at a whistle-stop during the campaign, Dewey had come out on the back platform of the observation car and had started to speak to the crowd that pressed closely around the back of the train, when to everybody's horror the train started to back up right into the crowd. A tragedy was narrowly averted when the train stopped just in time. Dewey, pale-faced and obviously scared, turned and said audibly to all, "That engineer must be a lunatic." Democrats spread the quote in labor circles without explaining the circumstances, in an attempt to make it appear that Dewey was antilabor.

This led to a "lunatic engineer" character played by Ned Brooks, radio commentator, who also wrote the song and who announced that he was the man who could tell what had really happened. He sang:

> I'm a rambling wreck, but what the heck,
> I'm a lunatic engineer,
> A lunatic lunatic lunatic lunatic lunatic engineer.
> Like all good jolly fellows,
> I like my signals clear,
> I'm a rambling wreck, but, what the heck—
> I'm a lunatic engineer!

Campaign manager Herbert Brownell, played by Marshall McNeil, was asked to explain and he sang:

> Remember, November
> And all those precious votes,
>   they stayed at home.

And Gene Archer, playing Rip Van Hoover, commented that twenty years ago I stood in the golden sunshine, but now "I wake up in the lunar indigo—blue moon to you!" And he sang:

> Blue Moon, you saw me standing there free,
> Without a dream in my heart.
> No leader right except me!
> Blue Moon, you knew just what I was there for,
> You heard me saying a pray'r for
> Someone I really could care for!
> And then there suddenly appeared before me
> The only one the party said would please.
> I heard somebody whisper "Don't ignore me,"
> And when I looked, the moon had turned to cheese!
> Blue Moon, once more I'm standing here free,
> Without a dream in my heart,
> Nobody in step—but me!

"Governor Dewey" was asked why his campaign went flat when he pitched it on such a lofty note, and he replied "that always happens to a baritone who tries to hit high C." Then he sang:

> I sang them songs of Albany
> And tales of my great team.
> On unity that lovely word,

I really let off steam.
With nice platitudes I tried to make
Sweet White House visions rise—
But all my speeches seemed to wake
Was wonder in their eyes.

Then Arthur Pierce entered as "the Chinaman the Republicans should have nominated" and closed the skit by singing:

There's a great day coming tomorrow,
If tomorrow ever comes!

At the close of this skit, Gridiron President Phelps H. Adams introduced Governor Dewey. He did this by reading the text on the scroll already presented to Dewey in the opener. Noting that it had always been the custom of the Gridiron Club to present such a scroll to ex-Presidents of the United States, Adams said to Dewey, "We elected you President even if the people didn't. So as far as we are concerned, you are an ex-President."

Dewey, responding, noted that he had accepted the invitation to speak at the dinner on behalf of the Republican party some months previously.

"I was all set then—along with the rest of you—to attend the political funeral of my distinguished friend over at the center of this table. A number of courteous things had already occurred to me to say which I thought would be agreeable both to this festive occasion and to the spirit of its politically deceased guest of honor.

"Instead, I discover that he is very much alive, and I am the corpse.

"You know, except for what they said in print, everybody has been very considerate of my feelings during these past few weeks. I was in Arizona and did not read what was printed and practically nobody has asked me what everybody wanted to ask—how I felt on November 3.

"Well, I'll be glad to tell you confidentially. You remember the case when in the course of a very successful wake, one of the mourners, who had succeeded in drowning his sorrows, passed out cold. The other mourners were feeling no pain and they removed the departed to another room, placing their paralyzed friend in the coffin. They gently folded his hands across his chest, around the stem of a fragrant lily. And there he remained, sleeping it off, long after everybody had gone home. In the cold light of the dawn—about the time I got the bad news from Ohio and

Illinois—he came to. He smelled the lily. He observed the tufted white satin of the coffin. Rallying his faculties, he coldly analyzed his predicament: 'If I am alive,' he said to himself, 'what am I doing in this coffin? If I am dead, why do I have to go to the bathroom?'

"The basic facts of life are sometimes not pretty, but sometimes they can be very reassuring. After a careful study of the facts of the election, let me assure you, gentlemen, that the Republican party and its standard bearer are very much alive."

Dewey went on to tell how he had first been invited to speak at a Gridiron dinner just after he had been defeated for governor of New York and how flattered and surprised he was at that time.

"Again, I am flattered but, believe me, gentlemen, I shall never again be surprised by anything."

He reminded his audience that almost every member of the Gridiron Club had been through some part of the campaign with him at one time or another, and that they'd all had a good time during those pleasant months which preceded November 2.

"I think we all agreed, and a great many of you wrote that, out of all campaigns, this one was the best. Everything was smooth. The train was in the hands of experienced experts. For the first time in my life my speeches were out well in advance. We knew where we were going and we were always on schedule.

"There was no uncertainty about this campaign. For the election, you remember, was in the bag."

Then Dewey went on to discuss their "unanimous error" and told how he and President Truman had met once during the campaign at Idlewild Airport and how, as the photographers were snapping them, Truman had told him that he would have to get used to this when he was living in the White House.

"So, gentlemen, it really was unanimous. So don't blame the pundits too much, Mr. President. And don't blame the reporters too much. Because you know instead of interviewing the many Republican leaders in forming their opinions, they inquired of the Democratic leaders from Coast to Coast and from Arvey to Hague. Newspapermen and columnists are the only group who, like doctors, can bury their mistakes. And don't believe anything you read, Mr. President, until you have digested the solemn analysis of why you lost, published in the *Panama Star Herald*, the Sunday after election, under the by-line of a well-known columnist and political expert, your old friend Harold L. Ickes.

"There have been some who tried to find comfort in the fact

that a switch of 29,000 votes in three States would have reversed the results of the election. I have almost been tempted myself to ask for a recount, but on a second thought, as I read the somber news in the press, I don't think I will. To tell you the truth, I am getting just a little nervous for fear Mr. Truman may ask for a recount.

"One simple thing stands out in this election, as in all elections. The American people have had their way. So far as I am concerned, the people of our country are always right and I will support their decisions with all my heart.

"If there had been that difference of a few votes in the right places, or even if Governor Warren and I had a million votes more in the country and won by a clear majority, what we did not know was that in any event the Congress was not going to be Republican. We would have had a divided government in a time of crisis.

"So I bid you take heart. It is well that the Presidency went with the Congress. Under our political system, the American people, after a Presidential election, are entitled to have a united and responsible party government. I believe in party government and party responsibility. You, Mr. President, know what it is to have a Congress of your own party, as you had until 1947, and since then a Congress in the hands of the opposition. You now have a Democratic Congress, and I wish you luck. It's all yours. I hope you have better luck with it than you had with your last Democratic Congress."

Then, becoming serious, Governor Dewey reminded the Democratic party that it had a big job in carrying out all those campaign promises, and the Republican party that it had a big job in leading the opposition. He said that his party had stood for something in the election and that they meant it.

"For any mistakes of strategy I accept full responsibility," he declared, "but we will never be embarrassed by the things we said. We have nothing to take back and we charted a course for a free nation of which I shall always be proud."

He then called upon Republicans for the double task of supporting the principles of their platform, "regardless of who sponsors the bills and who gets the credit," and of cooperating "in every sound proposal for meeting the very grave problems that threaten us and the peace of the world." He said that this would call for good will from both parties, and he was confident that it would exist.

"I noticed the other day, Mr. President," Dewey said in closing, "that in response to a question, you characterized me as your greatest asset in the winning of the election.

"You won and you ought to know. Previously I had understood that this group or that group or another group was wholly responsible for your election and had already presented due bills for their achievement.

"But if you will insist that I am entitled to the credit, then I want to put your mind at ease at once. I don't want a single thing. Here and now I release you of any and all obligations. You are a free man. Unlike any other President in history, you now go into office without a single obligation to a living person. You have a chance to be a great President. I sincerely hope you will be. My heartiest congratulations and God bless you."[2]

The Democratic skit was preceded by a satire on Congress, in which a kindergarten teacher had all of the principal committee chairmen in the two Houses ("not one of whom was over eighty-six") as her pupils, and they were playing the Congress game.

"Senator Theodore Green" of Rhode Island, pouting because he wanted to be a chairman too, was told he wasn't old enough; he was only eighty-one and would have to wait a few years.

They went through the game, one group chanting "What do we do when labor comes?" and the other group replying, "We give them what they tell us to."

"What do we do when the farmer comes?"

"We give them what they tell us to."

With the next question, "What do we do when the National Association of Manufacturers comes?" the teacher pressed for an answer from "Congressman Adolph Sabath," who had a reputation for being extremely hard on business. He responded, "Teacher, my mommy washes out my mouth with soap when I say those words!"

The major Truman skit was set inside an Iowa barn at a cornhusking, and the chief characters, Speaker-to-be Sam Rayburn, Vice President-elect Barkley, and various other administration and congressional figures, were dressed in costumes that resembled those used in *Tobacco Road*. In fact, the character representing Barkley was addressed as "Jeeter Barkley," and he sang:

Oh, Dixie land am now forgotten,

We raise corn, we don't plant cotton,
Ioway, Ioway, Ioway Democrats.

Farm subsidies are paid in money,
Some folks say the money's funny,
Ioway, Ioway, Ioway Democrats.

Now we won't go back to Dixie,
Hooray, hooray!
In Ioway we've come to stay until in 1950
Away, away, we'll all go back to Dixie,
Away, away, away down south in Dixie.

Gene Archer, playing J. Howard McGrath, the chairman of the Democratic National Committee, explained their victory in a parody of "It's Magic."

He had no golden voice or mystic charms,
Just Wall Street "gluttony and greed" were his alarms.
He cast his winning spell
By merely giving Congress hell.
It's magic.
How else did he attain
Success in his one-man campaign?
It's magic.
Let me explain it now,
Those things that puzzled all the GOP.
They soon must realize our magic's name
    is just Hare-ree!

The Southern Democrats were represented by "Strom Thurmond" and "Miss Dixiecrat," who had "a little bundle in her arms." One of the characters sang to the tune of "You Are My Sunshine":

Do not drive us all out of the party,
We all sinned but we won't sin no more;
And we Democrats want to eat hearty,
Forgive and Oh please don't be sore.

A group came on the stage representing the various city bosses, among them Frank Hague of Jersey City, Mayor William O'Dwyer of New York, Jacob M. Arvey of Chicago, and Hubert Humphrey, newly elected to the U.S. Senate, after having served several years as the mayor of Minneapolis. Several of these had tried to persuade General Dwight D. Eisenhower to challenge Truman for the Democratic nomination, but he had declined.

Speaking for them, Arvey sang a parody of "Open the Door, Richard!"

> We picked Ike last summer,
> Felt sure he could win.
> Learned our lesson later,
> No means No to him.
>
> We ditched Harry Truman,
> Voters to him flock'd,
> White House door ain't open,
> Guess we'd better knock.
>
> Open the door, Harry,
> Open the door and let us in.

The problems of the group were summed up in a song to the tune of "Buttons and Bows."

> We promised much of cash and such,
> But our trouble always grows,
> Turks and Greeks and Eastern sheiks
> All count on us for a suit o'clothes,
> But all we got is worries and woes.

Then they decided at the end that their miracle man was going to have to pass some more miracles, and the act closed with an impersonator of Senator Millard Tydings singing to the melody of "All the Things You Are":

> Time and again we longed for a wizard,
> Someone to make our hearts beat the faster,
> What did we long for? We never really knew,
> Winning with Harry was our adventure,
> Seeing him fight, our hearts beat the faster,
> All that we got in all of this world is you.
>
> You are the man who gave the pledges
> That may make our next four years seem long;
> You are the man who told the nation
> That to depend on the GOP was wrong.
> You are the miracle that must repeat,
> If we're to go ahead you can't retreat.
> Some day there may be peace and plenty,
> And some day the world won't be askew—
> If all the things you said come true.

President Truman was then introduced. Like most of his other speeches, this one was off-the-cuff, and neither the Gridiron files nor the Truman Library contain any record of it, but a later press report said that "speaking extemporaneously, President Truman matched the humor and the sportsmanship displayed by the candidate he had defeated."[3]

It was plain that the President greatly relished the opportunity for speaking that this dinner provided, for in the Truman Library there is a letter which he wrote a couple of weeks before the dinner to Ralph McGill, editor of the *Atlanta Constitution*. At the end of the letter, in the President's own handwriting, he said, "Hope you'll be at the Gridiron. It will be in reverse this time!"[4]

• • •

The spring dinner of 1949 was held on May 21. In spite of Truman's victory, he was still faced with troubles with Congress, where the Republicans and the southern Democrats, under the leadership of Senator Harry Byrd of Virginia, managed to hold together a coalition of control on national issues.

Gridiron president Richard L. Wilson, head of the Cowles Publications Bureau in Washington, dwelt heavily on these problems in his speech in the dark.

"We celebrate tonight the birth of the welfare state," he said, "or, as some phrase it, the state of farewell. In the welfare state everybody gets something—the Navy gets the axe, Rita Hayworth gets Ali Khan, and President Truman gets the Byrd."

He noted the coming of the supersonic age. We had broken through the sound barrier—"except in the United States Senate."

He remarked how quickly the presidential political campaign had been forgotten. "Republicans act as if they had won it," he said, "and are getting the blame again. Democrats get no blame—and no action. The country remains safe from both parties."

Back in 1949 there was no particular inflation problem; it was to rise with the coming of the Korean War a year later. Consequently Mr. Wilson remarked that a dollar "goes farther than before."

"It was a great feat," he said, "when Washington threw one across the Potomac. Now we toss them across the Atlantic."

Immediately after the speech in the dark at every Gridiron dinner, the Marine Band, costumed in all its scarlet grandeur, marches on to the stage and plays two or three numbers. As soon as it had marched off at this dinner, Marshall McNeil, chairman of the music committee, came on stage and said that this band was out of date and was non-political. It had hailed every chief with the same song, "Hail to the Chief."

"That band has no ideology," he said. "But we have a band that plays the party tune. The Gridiron Club presents the Band of the Year!" The new band then marched on and played and the chorus sang, to the tune of "The New Ashmoleon Band":

> Here we are with November's vote behind us,
> Here we are with our Congress—so we say,
> And we hope that by June they will be voting
> What they sat on in March, what they turned down in May.

"We're the new non-partisan welfare society and fair-deal-we-got-the-mandate band," sang the chorus. "We're the new Jacksonian welfare society and Truman anti-lynching band."

> Though we march only slightly out of tempo,
> Though we play just a trifle out of tune,
> From the cradle until you're just a dodo
> We'll see to it that you receive a boon.

Then the chorus sang that they were "the new free enterprise welfare society without-a-reactionary band."

> If you're analytical, practical or critical
> You'll like us more the farther back you stand,
> But for us it's bully, it satisfies us fully,
> Our utopia's really close at hand,
> We're the new Non-Partisan Welfare Society
>   and Fair-Deal-We-Rule-by-Crony Band.

The opening skit was laid at King Neptune's Court at the bottom of the sea. The North Atlantic Pact seemed to include all the oceans, according to the Gridiron Club, so it looked like a good idea to get King Neptune lined up as one of the signatories. In this act, the guests were given "an eel's eye view of international diplomacy."

The navy had wanted another aircraft carrier built, but this had been blocked in Congress, and "Admiral Louis E. Denfeld," chief of Naval Operations, sang a variation of "My Bonnie Lies over the Ocean."

> My carrier's under the ocean,
> No atom bomb scuttled our pride,
> One obsolete cannon—named Clarence
> Just blasted her open—but wide.

Bring back, bring back,
Bring back my Navy to me, to me.
Bring back, bring back
Our Navy from under the sea.

Among the characters depicted were Foreign Minister
Robert Schuman of France, other signatories of the North Atlantic Pact, and Senator Arthur Vandenberg. King Neptune complained about the pact and wanted to know about "the rest of my
oceans," and "Senator Vandenberg" sang a parody written by
Phelps Adams:

Far-away places, with strange sounding names,
Are all quite familiar to me,
For all of these places with the strange sounding names
Now border the very same sea.
The ocean that beats on the rough Arctic shore
And laps on the sands at Capri,
Is just the same ocean that lies right at our door
Since I changed our whole ge-og-ra-phy.
The old North Atlantic has spread quite a lot
To I-Tal-y from Maine,
There'll soon be no country that touches it not
With the single exception of Spain.
They call me a schemer, well maybe I am,
But today I can follow the shore,
Of our North Atlantic all the way to Siam,
There's no other ocean no more.

The North Atlantic Pact constituted a very loose federation
and was a somewhat ambiguous document, so that it was frequently charged that it meant one thing in the United States and
another thing in Europe. A singer representing Foreign Minister
Bevin of England satirized this condition:

Though it's really quite emphatic,
It's not wholly automatic,
It's a very, very voluntary pact.
Yes, it is.
And it's my firm impression
That it leaves complete discretion
To each nation as to how it's going to act.
Yes, it does.
While there is in language floral
Quite an obligation moral
To go right to war when neighbors are attacked,

Still
It's a triumph diplomatic
About which we're all ecstatic,
It's a very, very voluntary—
　　Oh, it's *such* a voluntary—
　　Very, very voluntary pact.

Toward the end of the skit an impersonator of Stalin, who had been completely frustrated in his blockade of West Berlin by Truman determination and American B-29's in the airlift, became a mournful figure who lamented his fate. He sang:

It's a cruel, cruel world,
Yes, I am the sap who blockaded Berlin,
At B-twenty-nines I should lead with my chin,
Why sometimes I think I'd just better give in,
It's a cruel, cruel world.

In spite of the rather biting satire, this act, like all of them in that period, ended on a cheerful and hopeful note that acknowledged President Truman's efforts to bring about diplomatic solutions to the problems of the world. The chorus sang:

A dream come true; there are such things,
A faith that's new—a hope, that clings.
So let us bravely dream our dreams
　　and hitch them to a star,
And we'll go far because there are such things.

The congressional situation faced by Truman was satirized by a "Coalition Minstrels" act, in which an impersonator of Senator Taft sang to the tune of "Cruising down the River":

Voting in the Senate on a summer afternoon,
And saying no like Gro-my-ko
In a Russian croon.
The roll-call bells are ringing,
Though slightly out of tune—
Voting in the Senate on a summer afternoon!
On every tax we swing the ax,
The same on each reform;
Our windy speeches make a screech
Just like a summer storm.
We all vote "No" together,
We'll wreck each other soon—
Voting in the Senate on a summer, a bright summer, on a summer
　　afternoon!

And carrying on the idea in another song, Arthur Pierce, representing Senator Richard B. Russell of Georgia, a leader of the Southern Democrats, and Dwight Rorer, representing Senator Kenneth Wherry, Republican of Nebraska, put on a duet which Wherry began by singing: an adaptation of "Clancy Lowered the Boom."

> Up in the Senate Democrats thought everything was fair;
> They had a dozen extra votes and maybe more to spare;
> They said, "Let's change the Senate rules and give the program
>   room";
> They asked for a poll and called for the roll—
> Then we lowered the boom.

Russell:

> The labor bosses told us that Taft-Hartley act must go;
> We heard the same from AFL and from the CIO.
> They want the Wagner Act revived and brought out from the tomb;
> We heard the appeal that we must repeal—
> Then we lowered the boom.

At the end of the act an impersonator of Senator Eugene D. Millikin of Colorado set forth the "hope springs eternal" persistence of the Republican party in trying to burrow out from repeated Democratic victories.

> Some day we are hoping to find him,
> Some one, to restore GOP.
> Some one, with defeats all behind him,
> Who can lead us and call us
> To new victory.
> Some day, when the Fair Deal is over,
> Some day, when we sing jubilee,
> We hope to discover
> The man who can recover
> The world for the old GOP!

Three years later, the GOP was to find its man in Dwight D. Eisenhower.

This song was the signal for the introduction of Senator Millikin, who spoke for the Republicans. He was presented by Gridiron President Wilson who said that "the state he represents is rent by the Great Divide. That divide is no greater than the chasm within the Republican party." No text of his speech could be found.

The dinner closed with a very pointed Democratic skit set at

"Whistle Stop Junction," where the people were gathered awaiting the arrival of "a distinguished traveling salesman." Train whistles sounded and the crowd shouted, "He's a-comin'." But it wasn't "him," it was Vice President Alben W. Barkley, described as "the track-walker." He was looking for something, something that had been lost six months before, and he sang to the melody of "This Is the Story of a Starry Night":

> I'm huntin' for our lost mandate,
> We had it in our hands only six months ago,
> Where it's gone—or just how it went—
>   I do not know.
> I'm huntin' for our lost mandate.

Senator "J. Howard McGrath," still waiting for the train to come in, paid his respects to the President in language partly complimentary and partly not so complimentary:

> Once in love with Harry,
> But now we're stuck with Harry,
> Four years for sure now, fascinated by him,
> We must put up with him—till then.

> Once you plunge with Harry,
> Throw in the sponge, it's Harry,
> Ply him with billions, civil rights and power,
> Crises by the hour—so grin.

> You might be quite an independent voter,
> So care-free and game,
> But if you picked our Harry, think it over,
> You share the blame.

> So, now in love with Harry,
> Four years in love with Harry—
> Ever and ever, 'till fifty-two or later—
> Trouble is the answer may be
> That Harry wants to stay past fifty-three.

The crowd was still waiting for the "traveling salesman," when "Chief Justice Fred M. Vinson," in the role of Fire Chief Vinson of the Democratic Bucket Brigade, arrived. To the tune of "I've Got my Love to Keep Me Warm," he reported that:

> His bills are failing,
> The party's ailing,
> The GOP wants to rule—
> This is no time for him to be cruel,
> He's got Ole Fred to keep him cool . . .

Don't call no hard names now,
Coo like a dove;
We need no cuss words now,
We'll win 'em with love.

At this point a telegram arrived for Sam Rayburn, Speaker of the House, and "Rayburn" announced that it was a message from "him," reporting that he had hoped "to be out with you at Whistle Stop Junction. But," it concluded, "in view of the labor-bill battle in the house, I must remain in Washington to help celebrate our great *Victorious defeat!*"

As it dawned on the crowd that "he ain't a-comin'," Speaker Rayburn announced that he was sending a special substitute, the majority leader of the House, "Happy Hooligan John McCormack." "He's bringing music," said Rayburn, "to help sell our great welfare cause to Welfare-Society-and-Fair-Deal-We-Got-The-Mandate-Mr. Truman's-Rag-Tag-Band!"

Hooligan led the band on the stage and shouted, "Come on, voters! The good Lord himself would have set up the world as a welfare state in the beginning of time—only he couldn't afford it. *But Harry can–Harry can afford it*! Come on along!"

And then, accompanied by his band, he closed the dinner by singing to the tune of "Alexander's Ragtime Band":

Mr. Voter, Mr. Voter,
Better hurry and get some welfare.
Ain't you agein', ain't you ailin',
Here's the man to see; get it all for free.
Common people, common people,
Won't you listen to Harry Truman's
Rag, tag, brass band? Ain't you comin' along?

Com on along, come on and join
Mr. Truman's Welfare State.
Come on along, come on and join,
Harry's waiting at the gate.
He will greet a new born child with a pass that's good for life.
When it can vote he will get that child a wife.
That is the Welfare Plan what am,
Voter man.
Come on along, come on and join,
Let me take you by the hand.
Up to the man, the welfare man,
Who's the leader of this band.
And if you care to hear our economics
Played in jag-time,

Come on and hear, come on and hear,
Harry's rag, tag, bob-tail band!

President Truman laughed at the skit, as Presidents are supposed to do, but his laugh seemed a little forced. Never one to be shy about expressing his viewpoints, he later made it clear that he didn't like the song. He based his stated objections on loyalty to his associates in the government—they were no rag, tag, bobtail band—but it is also quite probable that he was equally annoyed by the lines about the welfare state and the general implication that the whole thing was being done with an eye to impressing the voters.

There is no available record of his extemporaneous response.

• • •

The situation in Washington had not changed much by the time the winter dinner was held on December 10, 1949. President Truman was still running the government pretty much as he wanted to, in spite of the failure to get some things approved by the Republican Conservative–Southern Democratic coalition. However, his situation was so strong that Gridiron President Wilson, in his speech in the dark, remarked that we were in the closing days of the first half of the twentieth century and commented that "in the next fifty years, the Democrats will have to serve only twelve more terms.

"At this mid-century milestone, President Truman is winning his fight to make life easier for the working man. Coal miners now only have to work three days a week. And Admiral Denfeld doesn't have to work at all."

He told the guests that the Democrats were really holding their own: "They lost Jimmy Byrnes—but they got back Glen Taylor."

"Republicans are still trying to land Wayne Morse. Some of them are afraid that if they aren't careful, they may do it."

By the end of 1949, there was considerable furor in the country about the Russians stealing atomic secrets, and the Truman administration had come forth with a new farm plan, identified with the secretary of agriculture as "the Brannan plan."

These two things were coupled together in a quip of Mr. Wilson's: "Russia has gotten a lot of our secrets. But the big one is still safe. Stalin has not yet been able to find out how we are going to make the Brannan plan work."

The cast for the opener consisted of two groups, one dressed in top hats, white tie and tails, representing the old Republican establishment, and the other, labor, dressed in caps and overalls. After each had expressed his respective belief in profits and dividends on the one side, pensions and strikes on the other, the two joined together and sang to the strains of "Winter Wonderland":

> In the White House we can count on Truman,
> Though he bawls us out in each campaign.
> He intends to see that every human
> Votes for him in fifty-two again.

> Later on, we'll arrange it
> So that they'll never change it,
> Fair Deal's here to stay
> Call it what you may.

> We'll live and die in Welfare Wonderland.

The initiation skit was used as a vehicle for one of those tributes that the Gridiron Club frequently pays to beloved members. In this case it was Robert Lincoln O'Brien, press secretary to Grover Cleveland, Washington correspondent, chairman of the U.S. Tariff Commission under Herbert Hoover and for a time under Franklin Roosevelt. For several years O'Brien had been publisher of the *Boston Herald* and was also one of Washington's most famous raconteurs.

The announcer asked O'Brien to stand while he related how fifty years ago the previous night, on December 9, 1899, O'Brien had become a member of the Gridiron Club and was admitted at the last dinner of the nineteenth century. He said that O'Brien had been charged at that time with finding "a model member of the Gridiron Club," described as "a man with flair, a man with the right look, a newspaperman whose perception is quick, a man who can register on the public mind. We want a man with the voice of a Tribune of the people. We need a star."

It had taken him fifty years, the audience was told, and now O'Brien was called upon to report that he had found the man. This served as the introduction of the initiate.

The bringing together of the army, navy and air force under the Department of Defense was being accomplished with some confusion, reluctance, and sabotage. It was not as easy as it had seemed when, at the December 1945 dinner, General Eisenhower and Admiral Nimitz had walked behind the President at the head table and thrown their arms around each other.

The Club had a skit entitled "Mutiny for the Bounty," in which Pentagon problems were satirized. A navy commander sang:

> I campaigned with Old Bull Halsey
> From Midway to far Nip-pon,
> And those fights were tough, but not as rough
> As War in the Pentagon.

"General Hoyt Vandenberg," head of the Air Corps, came back with a song based on "Riders in the Sky":

> There's only one blue yonder,
> Which we don't intend to share.
> We're gonna keep the Russians and
> The Navy out of there.
> We're pretty rough, we rarely bluff,
> We've a mortgage on the skies.

"Louis Johnson," secretary of defense, who was receiving a great deal of publicity in his efforts to cool the controversies, and who wasn't noted for his modesty, sang to the music of Rogers and Hammerstein's "I'm in Love with a Wonderful Guy," from *South Pacific*:

> They won't need a convention in fifty-two,
> Harry S. Truman can be my VP.
> Modesty stops me from claiming I'm tops,
> But I'm the most wonderful guy.
> I can sink a whole fleet without leaving my seat,
> And I don't mean canoes.
> I'm dynamic and tough as a bull, sure enough,
> If you don't share my views.
> Louis Denfeld is just an example.
> Sherman, take warning and Collins look spry,
> If you'll obey and say "yes" ev'ry day,
> I can be the most wonderful guy.

All of this led up to a representative of the American tax-payer coming on the stage and announcing that he was getting pretty tired of all this and had some advice to give.

> I'd like to wash the brass right out of my hair,
> I mean Admirals, Gen'rals, ground force and air,
> Symington, Johnson, Matthews, back to your chair!
> You got to earn your pay.
> I wish these guys would get right down to their work,
> Wipe out the Navy's grouch and the Air Force's smirk.

Let some sunshine in the Pentagon's murk,
If I could have my way.
Why don't you hurry up, straighten up, patch it up,
Stop the row, here and now,
Put your hand to the plow,
Or on election day—the voters—
Are gonna give those pol-it-ic-ians the air,
And gonna wash that brass right out of their hair,
What the fuss is about they don't know and don't care,
Get to work for U.S.A.

The scene for the Republican skit was at "Fishwheel Alaska," where the modern Forty-niners, who had seen their claim peter out, gathered to revive their hopes for a real strike. Their plight was explained by "Republican Finance Chairman Sinclair Weeks" in a solo to the tune of "Blue Shadows on the Trail."

Dollars are not dropping
In the Grand Old Party's bank,
And the checks we're getting,
     they are mostly blank!

But the rest of them decided that there were other things that they didn't have besides money. Various leading Republican characters sang couplets of a parody of "There Is Nothing Like a Dame."

We got Dewey, Stassen, too,
We got Warren, we got Taft,

We got candidates galore who
Are entirely free from graft.

We got disaffected Adm'rals
Quite unhappy with their boats.

What ain't we got?
We ain't got votes.

We got Hoover, Landon, too,
We got Saltonstall and Lodge.

We're loaded down with candidates
That we simply cannot dodge.

They're O such lovely characters,
And in many ways they're swell.

What ain't we got?
You know damn well.

We got nothing we can all go out and root for,
What we need is what there ain't no substitute for.

There is nothing like a vote,
Nothing in the world;
There is nothing you can quote
That is anything like a vote.

We had Gallup, Roper, too,
We had du Pont, we had Pew.

We had Girdler, we had Fairless,
And Joe Grundy saw us through.

We had everything we needed
For a wonderful campaign.

What did we get?
Vermont and Maine.

Lots of things in life are beautiful, but brother,
There is one particular thing that is nothing
        whatsoever, in any way, shape or form
        like any other.

There is nothing like a vote,
Nothing in the world.
There is not a thing afloat
That is anything like a vote.

Oh, some votes may not be clean
Or entirely free from sin,
But it's very nice to have them
If it's what it takes to win.
It's a waste of time to worry
Over what a vote is not.

Be thankful for
The votes you've got.

One of the Republicans thought that they might rely upon a "rallying moose call from our new chairman, Guy G. Gabrielson." An impersonator of Senator Wherry of Nebraska sang:

Blow, Gabrielson, blow,
Go on and blow, Gabrielson, blow!
We've been a-losin' in every fight,
But now we're lookin' to you for light,
So blow, Gabrielson, blow!
We been low, Gabrielson, low,
Mighty low, Gabrielson, low,

Oh we have had an awful fright,
With cloud by day and with fire by night,
So blow, Gabrielson, blow!
Go on and blow, Gabrielson, blow!
Make us again a happy band—
Take GOP to the promised land,
So blow, Gabrielson, blow!

In the final song of the skit, the Gridiron Club correctly forecast that in 1952 the Republicans would turn to General
Eisenhower, then president of Columbia University and at that
time a reluctant man who was not encouraging a draft. But the
club was wrong in assuming that Gabrielson would call on
Eisenhower; in 1952, Gabrielson supported Senator Taft.

However, in this skit Gabrielson blew his fish horn, the
lights dimmed, and the distant sound of approaching hoofbeats
was heard, until offstage a voice cried, "Whoa, whoa, Columbia."

"Eisenhower" entered and said, "I have heard your call of
distress. I have come to rescue you—I think. I still have a certain
academic doubt about it."

Then Gene Archer, as Eisenhower, sang a parody written by
Walker S. Buel:

Some enchanted evening,
You may see a stranger,
You may see a stranger
Across a smoke-filled room;
And somehow you know,
You know even then
That often you'll see him again
     and again.
Some enchanted evening
I will pick a party,
You may hear me speaking
Across a smoke-filled room.
And night after night,
     as strange as it seems,
The sound of my speaking will
     answer your dreams.

None can explain it in the GOP,
They give strange reasons why you may want me—

Some enchanted evening,
If you find no other,

If I hear you call me
Across a smoke-filled room,
I'll fly to your side
And make you my own,
Or all through your life,
    you may vote all alone!
Once you have found me,
    hour after hour,
Say to the nation,
"Vote for Eisenhower!"

Henry Ford II, the Republican speaker, noted with some whimsicality, that the honor of speaking at a Gridiron dinner was something "you customarily reserve for somebody more important than a young fellow from Detroit trying to make and sell cars."

Explaining that he had something he particularly wanted to say to "America's favorite bridegroom," Vice President Alben Barkley, who had presented his bride with an Oldsmobile. Ford addressed Barkley directly.

"Mr. Veep! Why—why an Oldsmobile? The President's wife rides in a Lincoln." He offered to drive the vice president home that night and give him a ride in a new Ford.

"And I can tell you right now that I'm prepared to make you a reasonable trade-in allowance on your old car. Nothing fancy, of course! I know you're only looking for a fair deal!"

He referred to "the people—the 150,000,000 of them who keep you and me in these white ties," but, he said, "tonight the people have taken the evening off. The boss is out [referring to the absence from the dinner of President Truman, who was vacationing in Key West] and we have the house to ourselves."

He noted that those who were there at the dinner were part of "the people," but he said, "to me you all look like customers. Handsome, well-heeled customers, every one of you.

"If it weren't for that fact, I might like to take a shot at what those of us who bellyache about taxes call the 'welfare state.' But to be perfectly honest, I would rather not send any of you home mad. . .

"At the same time, it wouldn't be very smart for me to strike out at business tonight. You know, that's the way one gets a reputation as a 'liberal.' It's an easy way out when you've got no better answer for some of our economic ills. You simply confess the sins of business, lambaste the hardshelled reactionaries, purge yourself of all sin, and walk hand in hand with the CIO toward a brave new world."

Nor did Ford want to antagonize the union men. "As far as you union men are concerned, we have a hard enough time as it is to keep from giving away the old homestead to Walter Reuther every year. I'd hate to make it worse for us by ruffling any of your tail feathers tonight."

So, he declared, he'd just like to talk about the people, "rich and poor, black and white, right and left," and he added, "I should like to include among 'the people' my own baffled minority group, the Republicans.

"About all I'm prepared to do," he said, "is say something about the way things look to me from a bleacher seat in Dearborn. Right-field bleachers, that is.

"From where I sit, the people seem to be firmly in the driver's seat, with a heavy foot on the accelerator. The rest of us have become back-seat drivers—and that can be a pretty jittery spot—especially when the driver gets talked into hugging the left side of the road.

"I might say that it has always been all right with me if the British want to drive to the left. That's their business. But, personally, I much prefer American traffic rules."

Ford noted that people had been encouraged to believe that Santa Claus "is going to stagger up on every doorstep sometime soon with all the goodies anyone could possibly wish for.

"Now don't blame all this on us businessmen and merchandisers. Political candidates have spent plenty of time thinking of ever better things to promise the people in order to get elected or stay in office. Union leadership isn't bashful, either, about exciting the minds of the people with pie-in-the-sky notions of one kind or another.

"But, my point is that the world we live in, with all its problems, is a world we have ourselves created, whether we like it or not. We can't blame it on each other or on anybody else.

"There's comfort in that thought, however. If we made today's world, we can make tomorrow's, too.

"All we have to do is to agree on the kind of world we want. Maybe what I'm suggesting is unification of objectives, but I guess unification is sort of a risky thing to talk about around here. Besides, I was once in the navy, myself."

Then, speaking seriously, Ford said, "If we can agree that what we want is a peaceful and prosperous world, then there are a few things we have to keep in mind.

"The first is that we will produce and deliver only to the extent that there is somebody on hand to pay the bill. Eventually, the check has to be picked up by the people—and that includes you and me.

"And I, for one, would much rather be a customer with money in my pocket free to buy what I want than the citizen of a state where someone gives me a ration book and tells me what I can have.

"The government isn't Santa Claus any more than the corporation, or the labor union, for that matter. The customer is Santa Claus.

"It also seems to me that we have probably kidded ourselves and the people long enough into believing that just around the corner is an Easy Street where there are no distracting problems.

"The plain fact is that we have a lot of problems, we've always had a lot of problems—we're always going to have a lot of problems. All we have a right to expect is progress—keeping on moving along—licking one difficulty after another—most of them difficulties we create ourselves in one way or another. In the process of licking them, we make exactly the kind of world we live in. If we want it any different, all we've got to do is to make it different.

"So long as we can keep free to solve our problems and keep on trying, we haven't any real cause for worry."[5]

The Democratic skit was built around a meeting of club members who were stymied trying to write a dinner skit.

"The Democrats," said the announcer, "have produced nothing new in long, long years. Club members have grown gray writing about the same old familiar faces and figures—who in turn have grown gray in the same old grand army of the Potomac payroll. In desperation, we present a last-minute meeting of the Gridiron music committee, working feverishly against the heaviest odds in American political history."

All sorts of suggestions were made by various individuals on the committee. Someone suggested a song about Vice President Barkley and sang a new version of "That Lucky Old Sun."

Oh boss, oh boss, I'm tired an' achin' with pain;
Please, boss; please, boss, forgive me if I complain,
Fussin' with Russell, scrappin' with Byrd,

Fight till I'm weary and gray,
But that lucky old Veep got nothin' to do
But laff at the Senate all day.

But to everything, the music committee chairman said, "No,
it won't do."

Another member suggested a song about General Harry
Vaughan, head of Truman's White House staff, who had been in
some trouble because of accepting gifts, such as a deep freeze.
The song suggested for him was:

It ain't so much a question of who gets 5 percent,
I ain't a man who looks for dividends.
My door is always open, you can see the President,
I really do attract the darndest friends!
I know it's something I should not admit,
But when they ask for favors, I fergit!

I'm just a guy who cain't say no,
I never learned to say "nix";
I always give them my ok
When I can put on the fix.
If a deep freeze you should yearn to own,
Why don't you give my telephone a ring?
I can get you loads of French perfume,
Or fix you up a date with Cyrus Ching.
Big-hearted Harry Vaughan am I,
I'm influential and quaint,
Never a single complaint,
Why should I be what I ain't?
I cain't say *no*!

A further suggestion was for a parody of "My Buddy."

Frank Costello's one of our band
Whose virtues we can all understand,
Our Buddy, our Buddy,
No Buddy quite so true.

Jackson once stood for the masses,
On common people he bet,
We ask you as Jackson's descendants,
How common can Democrats get?

Joe Adonis, sure he's our boy,
A chap whose company you'd enjoy,
Our Buddy, our Buddy,
In each election fight.

The committee members decided at this point that "we just don't have a skit, but we still have the Democrats and as long as they have Harry Truman and his Missouri Mule Train . . ." At that point, the chairman jumped up and said, "Mule Train! Now we've got something. The Democratic Mule Train! Here we go—Westward Ho! *Mule Train!*"

> Cryin' our wares to people near and far,
> Coppin' all the votes there are.
>
> There's a wage-boost for the miners on vacation at Miami,
> But for A&P 'n' Du Pont all we got's the double whammy,
> Though a headache we may be, we give aspirin for free,
>   Git a-long mu-le, git along.
>
> There's a loan for Henry Kaiser; there's a telly-phone that's rural,
> We got housing for the wiser folks who do their votin' plural,
> We got pensions for the old; and Fort Knox is full of gold,
>   Git a-long mu-le, git along.
>
> There's an irray-gation project that will give the farmers water,
> Then by subsee-dizin' prices we'll support the farmer's daughter,
> 'N' if that don't git us votes; we'll start givin' out mink coats,
>   Git a-long mu-le, git along.

The act closed with the idea that a natural climax would be a few lines of "Wagon Wheels," Vice President Alben Barkley's favorite song, and that somebody should impersonate him. But the chairman asked, "Why impersonate him, when he's right here in person? Mr. Vice President, Sir, won't you stand up at that microphone and join us in a chorus of your own favorite song, "Wagon Wheels?"

Vice President Barkley replied from the head table, "Of course, I'll be glad to." Then he himself led the singing of the final chorus.

> Wagon wheels; wagon wheels,
> Let's grease those band wagon wheels,
> On our way,
> Hap-py day,
> Wagon wheels rollin' along,
>   Band Wag-on,
> Wagon wheels rollin' a-long!

Since President Truman was in Key West, Vice President Barkley responded for him, but no text of his speech is available.

However, Martin Hayden, editor of the *Detroit News*, recalls that Barkley referred to the "nice idea" that Mr. Ford had had about the exchange of a new Ford for the Oldsmobile, but said the word "Lincoln" had always intrigued him.

Hayden relates, as a sequel to this exchange, how a couple of days after the dinner, in New York, Ford remarked to Earl Newsom, his public relations counsel at the time, that he was going to give Vice President Barkley a Lincoln.

Newsom, always a gentleman, but made of steel when it came to advising his clients, said, "No you're not. You should not give any automobile to the Vice President of the United States. It would just get both you and him in all kinds of trouble."

Henry Ford listened to his counsel and didn't do it. But on January 20, 1953, Inauguration Day, when Dwight Eisenhower became President and Barkley's term as vice president ended with the swearing in of his successor, and he was again a private citizen, upon his arrival home from the inauguration ceremonies he found a Ford representative waiting to present him with a new 1953 Lincoln.

• • •

The congressional campaign was warming up at the time of the May 13, 1950 dinner.

"The club in its sixty-fifth year," said Gridiron President Thomas L. Stokes of the Scripps-Howard Newspapers in his speech in the dark, "has lived through thirty-three years of Democratic Presidents and thirty-two years of Republican Presidents. So has the country. God loves America.

"Tastes in political programs change periodically—at least they used to. We wonder what an old-fashioned Republican President would look like—or any Republican President—or even an old-fashioned Democrat.

"We have been proud hosts to seven Republican Presidents and only four Democrats. But when a Democrat gets the job, he raises the pay, remodels the White House, and settles down for a long period of rent-control."

The Republicans, he said, were celebrating their first victory since 1946.

"They won the Democratic primary in Florida and a temporary Republican Congressman in Texas. All they need now is to cross the Mason-Dixon Line, going north, and invade the United States."

The opener consisted of a chorus divided into two sections: one of Democratic candidates carrying large pictures of Truman, flags, and a donkey insignia, and the other of Republicans with elephant insignia, flags, and signs labeled "Lincoln," "Hoover," and "McKinley.

The Democrats sang:

> We're off to fool the voters,
> The wonderful voters back home.
> We'll tell 'em we tried to save their dough,
> And cut down their taxes some.
> We'll show 'em them Reds are the worst there wuz,
> And we'll promise to save 'em becuz, becuz, becuz,
> becuz, becuz, becuz,
> Becuz of the wonderful guys we wuz.
> We're off to fool the voters,
> The wonderful voters back home.

The Republicans sang right back:

> We're off to fool the voters,
> The wonderful voters we need.
> We'll save 'em from strikes and poverty,
> And pay 'em those subsidies.
> We're for the Fair Deal and against it, too,
> Nothing at all that we cannot do becuz, becuz,
> becuz, becuz, becuz, becuz,
> Becuz of the wonderful guys we wuz.
> We're off to fool the voters,
> The wonderful voters we love.

In the Republican skit, an announcer said that the Republicans were off on a secret mission to the arid plains of New Mexico.

"Thirsty for votes as they face the 1950 campaign, they are studying the mysteries of rainmaking. They want to know: If scientists can make rain by shooting dry ice into the clouds, why can't Republicans make votes by shooting dry speeches into the air?"

The Republicans noted that their party "faced a barren waste without a taste of water," and one of them sang, to "Chairman Gabrielson":

> They won't give us anything but love, Gaby;
> Dough is what they say they've nothing of, Gaby—
> Democrats are fat cats,
> We are behind;
> Yet I'll bet we could get
> Victories we have pined for—

Big shots once our party chest would fill, Gaby,
There was always money in the till, Gaby;
Now they'll only risk a dollar bill, Gaby,
They won't give us anything but love!

An impersonator of General Eisenhower, still president of Columbia University, wearing a mortarboard hat, told the Republican gathering not to use that word "temptation" and sang:

You won't let me alone, I've always known
You are Temptation!
You keep calling to me, for GOP.
You are Temptation!
There in my college, handing down knowledge,
That is the place to be,
Believe me;
I don't know
All of the tricks of politics,
You are Temptation and I'm *not* yours,
At least not yet—
Please go away, but don't forget,
One thing I like, I'm always Ike
To you, Temptation!

"Governor Dewey," defeated less than two years before in the surprise victory of President Truman, sang:

There's no tomorrow, once you are through;
Now is forever—not 'fifty-two.

"Senator Wayne Morse," the maverick Republican who later turned Democrat, found the GOP in a dither, its leaders in a haze, and sang that:

They'd jinx their trouble and banish their jinx
If they knew what to say.

In looking for the real answer, they put the question to the new publicity director of the Republican National Committee and a fellow Gridiron member, William H. Mylander. Playing himself, Mylander said that he would like to have Senator Owen Brewster of Maine act on the slogan of Chairman Gabrielson, "Not tomorrow—today!"

The act closed with "Senator Brewster" and the chorus singing a parody of "Song of Love":

This is your time of times,
May be now or never;

> Bring out the magic rhymes,
> This may be forever.
> You need Congress in nineteen-fifty,
> And the White House in 'fifty-two,
> If from the Democrats you'd be free—
> This is your time of times,
> *Watch your step, GOP!*

Senator Morse was then introduced as the Republican speaker.

"What I gathered from the thrilling scene we witnessed a moment ago," he said, "is that after eighteen long years, It Ain't Gonna Rain No Mo'. It's going to snow."

Just a paper snowstorm, he said, a forecast of the day in November "when we expect to bury our Democratic friends under a blizzard of Republican ballots."

Morse, who faced a Republican primary contest in Oregon six days after the dinner, and who was never known for his self-effacing characteristics, said that he was "flattered to know that in my shy, modest self the Gridiron Club recognizes the natural and proper spokesman of the Republican party.

"The club's extraordinary discernment," he continued, "is deserving of tribute, which so far as I am concerned can be most appropriately paid by the Republican voters of my own state on May 19.

"In fact, my appearance here is, I think, sufficient answer to the suggestion I've heard whispered—whispered, that is, on the radio and in the press—a thousand times this week out in Oregon, that I am not a *real* Republican but a Democrat in disguise. Of course, any such statement really answers itself, because it's absolutely impossible to disguise a Democrat. They're so easily spotted, especially here in Washington, because ad nauseam they're plugging the idea that government can and should undertake to solve all problems for all people at all times. But as the founder of my great party once said, you can't fool all the people all the time."

Referring to President Truman's absence from the dinner (he was on a "nonpolitical" speaking tour around the country), Senator Morse expressed his sorrow that "the President is out making his nonpolitical quest for votes this evening," because he had a few things he wanted to say to him.

"But at least I'm glad he can keep one train running in America these days. Also I'm glad to see here speaking in his place the senior senator from Virginia. A lot of us Republicans wish he were speaking for the Democrats all the time—some of us for one reason, and some for another.

"I want you to know that I love Harry Byrd. I love him so much that I would be tempted to throw him a kiss if it were not for the fact that I am afraid that if I did some people here, who don't know me, might think that I worked in the State Department rather than the Senate of the United States."

He said that Truman "may have decided that this trip was necessary, to show that even though his party can't agree on civil rights, the Fair Deal or almost anything else, he still agrees with himself."

He had the impression from the speeches from the President's special train that the Democrats were united "and only mossback Republicans are out of step."

Then, referring to the Republicans, he said that they had a great team—"or am I understating myself?

"You should see our reserve of quarterback strength. We don't play the two-platoon system. Why, in the Senate alone we have at least twenty signal-callers. (And I don't mind calling a few myself.)"

For the fighting team spirit among the Republicans, Morse said, "the Democrats have only themselves to blame.

"Look what has happened. The Democrats repealed the oleo tax—and most dairy farmers are Republicans. Ask [Senator] Wiley. They cut down the subsidy on potatoes—and most potato growers are Republicans. Ask [Senator] Brewster. They transferred the subsidy money to the peanut growers—and who grows peanuts? The Democrats. Do you call that bipartisanship?

"The Republicans are united on at least one thing. The Elephant is fed up with being kicked by the hybrid, fractious Donkey. I believe it will not be revealing any party secrets if I tell you not to expect any cooperation in the form of speeches from [Senator] Jenner, extolling the merits of the President; or from [Senator] Wherry, nominating Acheson for the Hall of Fame."[6]

The Democratic skit was entitled "Happy Harry's Carnival," and the scene was a side show. It opened with the chorus singing to the tune of "Powder Your Face with Sunshine":

Happy are we with Harry,
Look at his great big smile,

Keeping the voters happy,
He wants to keep on living in his
    White House style.
Whistle stop for campaigning,
Traveling many a mile,
The nation's paying while Harry's playing,
Smile, smile, smile.

Ned Brooks, as a Kansas City Kid, sang:

We got it figgered out in Kansas City,
From Pendergast we learned a thing or two,
Of diff'runt ways there is for votin' double,
As pistol-packin' Democrats can do.
We settle all the arguments with our forty-fives,
Never have to worry nor to chafe;
'Taint no trick at all to control the City Hall
If you know the combination to the safe.

Everything's up to date in Kansas City,
We've gone about as fur as we can go;
They never seem to dope it out, even the F.B.I.
How Democrats are takin' in all the dough.
Everything's going swell in Kansas City,
Republicans will never have a show;
We got a nifty system there whenever the people vote,
A special way of countin', but it ain't the way you wrote;
We're careful to apologize before we cut your throat,
We've gone about as fur as we can go.

An impersonator of Vice President Barkley thanked him for the song and said, "It's nice to know things are going so well in Happy Harry's Home Town."

A messenger arrived with a telegram for Barkley, a singing telegram "from Happy Harry himself," and Barkley's impersonator warbled a parody of "They Didn't Believe Me."

And when I tell them how wonderful I am,
They'd better believe me . . .

And I'm cert'n'ly going to tell them,
Out at the whistle stops I'll sound the key.
They'd better believe me,
They'll have to believe me.
You'll never send me back to Missouri.

The act closed with "Senator Harry Byrd" singing:

You can pass the word that Massa Harry Byrd
Sho-nuff ain't givin' in;
Save your Confederate money, boys,
The South shall rise again.

Just as the Gridiron Club had chosen a maverick Republican to speak for them, so they chose a dissident Democrat to speak for that party, and the real Senator Harry F. Byrd was introduced at this point.

Senator Byrd began by saying that he wanted to mention "a well-known piano player." (This was after President Truman had been photographed playing the piano while Lauren Bacall was sitting on top of it.) "Lest you misunderstand," he hastened to add, "he is the Pianist Emeritus of the Gridiron, holder of the record for length of membership, for he was elected to this club nearly fifty-nine years ago." He then asked Henry Xander to rise and take a bow.

Byrd said that he was gratified that the Gridiron Club recognized and appreciated his services to his party, "even though some others may not."

"This assignment completely refutes the infamous charge that I am not 'still' a Democrat, even though candor compels me to say that at times I am quite 'still'. . .

"Statisticians here in Washington . . . have given an analysis of my votes and allege that I have voted 66 percent with the Republicans and 34 percent with the Democrats. I answer the charge simply and plainly. My name begins with B. I vote first and the Republicans vote with me.

"For twelve years, prior to 1932, the Democratic party wandered and fasted in the wilderness. Then, we won the Presidency and majorities in both branches of Congress. We ushered in the New Deal, as promised by our standard bearer. We pledged ourselves, in specific terms, to the New Deal in our national platform, and of all the New Dealers in the Democratic party, I was the most enthusiastic. I still am. I assert that I am the most loyal New Dealer remaining in the Democratic party, and I quote from that platform of 1932 to prove it."

He then summarized various planks in that platform:

Immediate and drastic reduction of governmental expenditures.

Consolidation of government departments and bureaus and eliminating extravagance.

Maintenance of the national credit by a Federal budget annually balanced and a sound currency to be preserved at all hazards.

Removal of the government from all fields of private enterprise.

No interference in the internal affairs of other nations.

"Our great New Deal leaders," he said, "have brilliantly interpreted this to mean that it refers entirely to the Socialist Government of Great Britain."

Contending that the leaders of the Democratic party ever since 1932 had "conspired to destroy the New Deal," Byrd said that that was the reason why "I, a leader of the original New Deal Democratic party, often cannot get more than five Democratic senators to stand with me . . . .

"I am stronger for the New Deal platform of 1932 than I ever was. We need it more," he said.

Turning then to the "Fair Deal Party," he commented that the dollar had been "renovated and reconstructed so attractively that everybody desires one or more," and made so flexible "that anybody can obtain one by the simple expedient of going on the government dole or working a few minutes under prevailing minimum wage laws."

Unemployment, he said, was almost a rarity.

"Citizens who are not employed by the government are free to seek engagements elsewhere. Nobody need want for work, unless his unemployment compensation expires before his social security payments begin."

Relations between labor and management could hardly be improved, he said, and "all this has been accomplished without seriously intimidating labor leaders."

Housing was rapidly being provided, he said, for those "who may desire to live indoors," and achievements in international relations "are even more astounding.

"Policies," Byrd said, "have been established of such admirable scope and effectiveness that our opponents desire them proclaimed as 'Bipartisan Policies.'

"Cooperation among nations has been promoted so successfully that disagreement, long before it occurs, can be discerned and foretold unerringly. Countries of mischievous inclination, as promptly as they are identified, are safely incarcerated behind an iron curtain, whence they may be released only by the unanimous vote in the councils of the United Nations.

"In short, gentlemen, we in the United States of America are living in a virtual utopia.

"And so, as the leader of the New Dealers of 1932, and apparently of the Fair Dealers of 1950—for, were I not, you would not have asked me to be their spokesman tonight—to this record I point with pride.

"And view with alarm!"[7]

In a barber shop skit, an announcer said that the Ides of March had passed but weren't forgotten, "because all that we had or hope to have we owe to the Bureau of Internal Revenue."

That organization he described as "Washington's most famous clip joint, Secretary Snyder's taxorial parlor."

The curtain opened on a barber shop front, with such signs as "Bare Deal Barber College," "Singeing a Specialty," "Bears and Bulls Sheared," "Incomes Trimmed," and "Boots Licked."

Various customers appeared and were properly singed sheared and trimmed.

The closing skit was on foreign affairs. The announcer referred to 1950 as the year of the flying saucer and said that "weird and whizzing objects are up in the air, and so is our foreign policy."

The scene was set at the National Airport in Washington, where a group of American statesmen were about to board a stratoliner, so they could "keep foreign policy debate on a very high plane."

In May 1950 there was much debate in the country over China, and Congressman Walter Judd, Republican of Minnesota, who had spent many years of his life in China, was advocating policies quite different from those followed by Secretary of State Dean Acheson. His impersonator sang to "Music, Music, Music":

Understanding Acheson
Puts my brain into a spin;
Double talk is all I hear,
It's just like flying saucers.
I'd give anything to see
Truman's foreign policy
Not revolve and disappear
Like saucers, flying saucers.
Saucers, I'm seeing saucers,
It's only Secretary Acheson
He's looking where he thinks he's been.

The plan must be to vex and fret
And confuse the Sov-i-et
And to win the cold war yet
With Truman's flying saucers.

Next came "Senator Joseph McCarthy" of Wisconsin who sang to the tune of "Somebody Lied":

In Washington, so I was told,
The reds are riding high;
My agents many tales unfold
About a Russian spy.
Officials have denied it all,
And say there's not a red,
None in the State Department,
And none beneath the bed.

There was more noise of flying saucers, and a group of Martians came on the stage "to establish universal peace."

The Martians told the assembled officials that they had come to start peace and get a $100 billion Marshall Plan loan, but all they had gotten was double talk, so they realized that they were on a "wild goose chase."

We came seeking a world at peace,
Where men are brothers and discords cease;
Seeking money with which to pay
To build a bridge across the Milky Way!

We came here on a wild goose chase,
And we'll fly now back to outer space.
Earth men, crazy men, on the loose,
You're just as wild as the old wild goose!

But they all decided at the end to let Secretary Acheson have the last word, and his impersonator ended the skit on an inspirational note.

When you walk through a world
    torn by storm and strife,
You won't be afraid of the gale,
If you're strong to defend
    your own way of life,
You'll find friends whose support
    will not fail.

Walk on through the cold,
Walk on through the storm,

Tho' the world is tossed and blown;
Walk on, walk on, with strength in your soul
And you'll never walk alone—
You'll never walk alone!

The dinner was closed with a speech by Chief Justice of the Supreme Court Fred M. Vinson.

"The President," he said, "is unavoidably detained with official business. Be it remembered, however, that there are dams out West as well as damns in the East. The western dams may be in need of inspection."

He spoke of his own difficult position, how he couldn't speak "about issues involving the cold war abroad or the hot war here at home. I concluded that my theme should be the motif of the evening—love and unity.

"In a recent campaign, there was considerable conversation about love and unity. So I conclude that if one speaks to such subjects he is staying aloof from politics."

Turning to the previous speakers for the two parties, he professed true fondness for each of them.

"Senator Wayne Morse," remarked Vinson, "is a brilliant technician and rhetorician on the governmental gridiron. He is fast on his feet; he can pass that ball like nobody's business— sometimes spectacular lateral passes. He is a skilled broken-field runner. He meets a foeman worthy of his steel.

"Senator Byrd of Virginia, suh, is a line smasher—a driving full back—at times a blocking back. The referee must not reply in kind. He must use self-restraint, which in these jittery hours might well be prescribed in moderate doses. But, in listening to these gentlemen tonight, I could not refrain from thinking—'Two souls with but a single thought; two hearts that beat as one.' "

He congratulated the Gridiron Club on its conception of "the jousting bout" between these two. "It is Don Quixote at his best," he observed.

Listening to them tonight, Vinson said, he had the same feeling he had experienced in being flat on his back with the flu and running a high temperature, while listening to the Rose Bowl Game in 1929. He heard the excited announcement that Riegels, captain of the University of California team, was burning up the chalk marks on the gridiron in the wrong direction. He had concluded then that he was delirious.

"Tonight, listening to the inspired spokesmen, with the

high temperature preceding my appearance before this celebrated Gridiron Club and their distinguished guests, I felt I must be delirious. I pinched myself and was happy to find that it was only a unique portion of a very fine Gridiron party. Friends, such a performance could only happen here.

"Your foreign affairs skit," he continued, "impressed me deeply. Remember the motif. Seriously, it is unity that will enable our country to preserve our institutions and our liberties. It is unity that will prevent the snuffing out of the lights of civilization. Love of country produces the unity that we have always had when the chips were down. In crisis, we will close ranks and walk together—and we will not walk alone. So long as we are alert, strong and united, we will have the pleasures and benefits that flow from argument and debate. That is the American way."[8]

• • •

The 1950 dinner was distinguished by one other event, a recording by President Truman, which arrived so late that it could not be played that evening. It was made seven days before the dinner occurred, a day in which Mr. Truman had made fourteen speeches, starting at Pocatello, Idaho, at 6:00 A.M., and ending at Pasco, Washington at 9:20 P.M.

The idea was that of Charles G. Ross, a former president of the Gridiron Club who was President Truman's press secretary. The recording was made by President Truman and those members of the Gridiron Club who were on his train.

In the recording, Arthur Sylvester of the *Newark News* asked President Truman if this nonpolitical trip means that "you will run again in 1952?" And Truman replied, "What do you think, Arthur?"

Robert L. Riggs of the *Louisville Courier-Journal* asked him if he displayed any difference "as between those two sterling Democrats of Idaho, Glen Taylor and D. Worth Clark?"

Truman: I shook hands with both.
Riggs: Of course you used the left hand with Taylor?
Truman: Don't you know I'm ambidextrous, Bob?

Numerous other exchanges of this sort occurred, and the president was very pleased with the recording when it was played back. It was flown to New York by Charles Collingwood of CBS, who offered it to Gridiron President Stokes, but by this time it was too late to set up the necessary amplification system and work it into the dinner schedule.

When Collingwood notified the four Gridiron members on the presidential train, they sent a joint telegram to the club, protesting, but it was too late to do anything about it, so the Gridiron guests never heard it.

Because of the start of the Korean War in late June 1950, no public dinner was held in December, only a private one for Gridiron members. This was also the case during 1951.

At the private dinner held that year Arthur Krock made a notable speech, in which he directed considerable gentle satire at both himself and the club.

He began by explaining that while other reasons were assigned, he knew that the real reason he had been asked to speak was because he was the senior active member, having been elected on May 10, 1913.

"There is," he said, "one path to distinction: to have been born before other people."

Then he "explained" how he came to be elected. He told how "an extraordinary thing" had happened in the November previous to his election; how Wilson, a Democrat of southern birth, had been elected president; and how two men, Arthur Wallace Dunn and Arthur Dodge, were the "rulers" of the Gridiron Club at that time.

"The revolutionary proposal was made to Dunn and Dodge," he said, "that the Gridiron Club bend to this deplorable situation by electing to membership in May a Southern Democrat, so that one of these odd specimens would surely be initiated in the sight of the Southern Democratic President at the December dinner.

"Not without basis was the Gridiron Club of those days charged with a pro-Republican bias in the choice of its members and those public men whom it lampooned. The new President of the United States was known to believe in the validity of the charge. So the revolutionary proposal was adopted.

"The high command comforted the horrified Old Guard by pointing out an obvious fact. This fact was that the addition of one, or even two, Southern Democrats would not establish a subversive influence because the northern Republican majority would remain overwhelming and the risky experiment need never be repeated. . . .

"If you should ask another relic of 1913 how much truth there is in this account of the elections in that year he may give you a dusty answer. He may say that seniority, based on the dates of nomination, accounts entirely for what happened; that in 1913, so unlike these days, the Machine always had its way and on schedule. But I urge you not to make such an inquiry, if only in remembrance of a colloquy between the young *London Telegraph* man and Sir Willmott Lewis [distinguished Washington correspondent of the *London Times* for many years]. 'As a former *Telegraph* man,' remarked Sir Willmott, 'may I ask why not a little more verification?' 'Ah,' was the reply, '*good* stories are apt to be ruined by over-verification.'"

• • •

The Gridiron Club resumed its regular dinners on May 10, 1952. Paul Leach of the *Chicago Daily News* welcomed the guests in the traditional speech in the dark.

"We welcome you again after two years," said Leach, "which saw never a dull moment. . . . Here at home order has been restored out of chaos . . . or vice versa. Confusion is better organized."

The White House had been done over completely, he noted, and was expecting new tenants, "but the politicians haven't learned a thing."

Then, in reference to scandals that had occurred in the Truman administration, he announced that "Democratic 10 percenters are trying to decide whether to pack up or dig in for undiscovered pots of gold. . . . Republican 5 percenters are waiting for the sunrise . . . so they can raise the ante. . . .

"Congress fiddles and investigates everything but itself while the President dictates his memoirs . . . and burns."

The opener was based on the "Wintergreen for President" song from *Of Thee I Sing*! A parade of Gridiron club members carrying various placards marched across the stage singing:

We'll all run for president,
We'll all run for president.
Every man a candidate,
Come along, it's not too late!

There was a further reference to the peccadillos of various people involved with the Truman administration, when in a pirate skit a soloist sang:

Ole man ribber,
We just keep stealin' along.

Then he said, "Lessee now—de deep freezes go on de upper deck—de twelve-pound hams go on de quarter deck—dey's for de two-bit pirates—de Form 1040-A's with de built-in exemptions—dey go—ah—dey go . . ."

But the pirate chorus got a sudden chill when they were joined on their moonlight excursion by an impersonator of Senator John J. Williams of Delaware, who thought he saw "something very fishy about this vessel" and announced that he was going to find out what it was. "There'll be no whoopee with Honest John Williams around!"

And then "Williams" sang:

Another deal, another fix, another case of politics,
Why can't we chop them, why can't we stop them
From makin' whoopee.
A lot of dough, a lot of loot,
They'll leave us hardly our birthday suit,
It's really killing to see 'em swilling
And makin' whoopee.

Although Truman had replaced J. Howard McGrath as attorney general, McGrath maintained his loyalty to the administration. His impersonator stepped out from among the pirates and sang:

Away back in forty-eight,
Harry, you thought I was great,
Now you've given me the gate
And said "good day";
But I'm always true to you Harry,
In my fashion.
Yes, I'm always true to you Harry,
In my way.

Though some people think I'm sore,
Cause you showed me to the door,
I'm not angry any more,
It's all okay.
I am always true to you Harry,
In my fashion,
Yes, I'm always true to you Harry,
In my way.

In an unexpected revision of this skit, the real McGrath left his seat at the dinner during this song, came up on the stage and stood beside the singer. As he finished, McGrath seized the microphone and said, "That's the truth, dammit, dammit, that's the truth!"

The Republican skit was set in the Donner Pass, where the "GOP Victory Special" was stranded in the snow, "motionless and lost in the High Sierras."

Republican Chairman "Gabrielson" came on the stage shouting for Bill Mylander, his chief assistant, and complaining that "things have come to a pretty pass." Mylander, again playing himself, reminded him that "Mr. Hoover certainly was right—for twenty years the Republican party has been just around the corner."

A Gridiron member representing conservative Senator Styles Bridges of New Hampshire tried to give the passengers some cheer. To the tune of "I'm on My Way," he sang:

> Pack your bag and pack your kit,
>   no time now to be slow!
> We know where we're goin' and,
>   by golly, here we go!
> Eisenhower, Bob Taft too; also
>   MacArthur, that's for certain.
> California's Warren's on his way—
> When will we get there? Fifty-two!
> What will we do there? We ain't certain—
> All we know is, we are on our way!

The songs of the various candidates began with one about the man least likely to get the nomination, Harold Stassen.

> I wonder what's become of Stassen,
>   that old pal of mine?

About Eisenhower:

> Our heads are up, we're on a hike,
> Our arms are swinging for we like Ike—
> We think in Nineteen-Fifty-Two
> Ike's the only one will do—
> *Sound off!*

Chorus:
> *Eisenhower!*

Soloist:
> *Sound Off!*

Chorus:
> *Eisenhower!*

Soloist:
> *We like Ike!*

Chorus:
> *We all like Ike!*

Soloist:
> We're not so certain what he's for,
> Or where he stands, or what's the score,
> But one thing's certain as can be—
> He says he's for the GOP!
> One other thing we know is true,
> And we're glad to enlighten you—
> This secret can no longer wait,
> We're certain he's a candidate!

The Taft song was a parody on "Dance Me Loose," and the chorus sang:

> The music plays and plays and plays,
>> we dance around the floor,
> The voters stay and stay and stay,
>> to hear me say once more:
> "I warm so easy, so dance me loose,
>> dance me loose, dance me loose,
> I warm so easy, so dance me loose,
>> it makes like victory!
> A victory for me,
> And for the GOP!"

The skit ended with "Chairman Gabrielson" saying that to achieve a Republican victory in November, "we must get more votes than the Democrats, and to do that we must ask the voters to love us again." Then the chorus sang the Gridiron adaptation of "If I Loved You":

> Our GOP won't be afraid or shy,
> We'd let no golden chances pass us by!
> Please invite us, in we would go—
>> like the good old days,
> Ever, ever you'd know—
> If you loved us—
> *How we love you!*

Former President Herbert Hoover, again the Republican speaker, whimsically reviewed the fishing habits of various presidents. He noted that three presidents, Cleveland, Theodore

Roosevelt and himself, had fished from boyhood, but that in modern times all presidents quickly began to fish soon after election. He recalled that Coolidge had begun his trout-fishing career with worms, and that "ten million fly fishermen at once evidenced disturbed minds.

"Then Mr. Coolidge took to a fly," he said. "He gave the Secret Service guards great excitement in dodging his back-cast and rescuing flies from trees. There were many photographs. Soon after that he declared that he did not choose to run again. . . .

"President Truman, prior to his 1948 election, appeared once in a photograph somewhere in a boat gingerly holding a common fish in his arms. An unkind reporter wrote that someone else had caught it. I can find no trace of the letter he must have received."

Presidents, he said, had long since learned that the American people respect privacy on two occasions, fishing and prayer, and that some presidents had taken to fishing.

"Two years ago," Hoover recalled, "my friend, General Eisenhower, burst into photographs from all angles, gingerly holding three very common fish. The augury was positive. A month ago General Ike stated that he was coming home to go fishing. Governors Warren and Stassen have not been in press photos with a fish! The augury swells up from 12,000,000 licensed fishermen that they are not likely to be nominated."

Recalling that he had first attended a Gridiron dinner forty years earlier, two years before the outbreak of World War I, he commented that at that time "confidence and boundless hope dominated the world." In the succeeding years, Americans had undertaken two gigantic military crusades "to impose freedom on mankind.

"But they brought not more freedom to the world or to America itself, but less freedom. Even human slavery has come again upon the earth."

However, Hoover said that he was no pessimist.

"I am too much of a student of the thousands of years struggle of mankind toward the light to lose my confidence in the regeneration of free men.

"The genius of our countrymen for productivity can even yet restore our economy from lost political statesmanship.

"Liberty has survived great confusions before. And men have recovered their safety and freedoms. But how? Because some men stood solid. They stood not because they knew the solutions to all these confusions, not even because they had the power to find solutions. They held firm as they held up the lamp of true liberty. They held until these furies passed because they clung to certain principles of life, of morals, of spiritual values and free men."[10]

Prior to this dinner, President Truman had been involved in what was, even for him, an unusual controversy with business. On April 8, Truman had ordered Secretary of Commerce Charles Sawyer to seize the steel industry and operate its nearly 100 plants in order to prevent a strike by about 650,000 members of the United Steelworkers of America. One of the major public issues behind this order was the importance of steel to national defense.

However, three weeks after Truman had given this order, and the mills were seized, Judge David A. Pine of the United States District Court for the District of Columbia declared the seizures unconstitutional and issued his own order restoring the industry to its private owners. Then, by the time of this May 10 Gridiron dinner, a United States Court of Appeals had temporarily stayed Judge Pine's order, and turned it over to the Supreme Court, which was scheduled to open its review of the case just two days after the dinner. (It turned out, that the Court's ruling against Truman's take-over did not come until the early part of June.)

It was with all this in mind that an announcer at the dinner sonorously intoned that this administration was all for business. "Of course," he continued, "it hasn't given everybody the business yet, but the battle has just begun. We take you now to a sandbagged command post behind the Federal Court Building, where the valiant Lieutenant General Charles Sawyer [Secretary of Commerce] is directing his Army of the Potomac."

The curtains parted and "Acting Defense Mobilizer John Steelman" and other administration figures began firing mortars (the noise of the firing was provided by the Marine Band). One of the mortarmen noted that they had the railroads, that they'd shelled big steel, and that they were about to move against Western Union and the oil companies.

"That ain't enough," yelled the character representing Sawyer, "let's get going!"

So they fired one on coal, and a man with binoculars announced a direct hit, with "nothing left standing but John L. Lewis."

Sawyer shouted again, "Fire one on Wilmington! I wanna get me a du Pont!"

They pulled the lanyard and the binocular man announced another direct hit.

"Not a du Pont left, sir."

They fired on Detroit, on the American League, the National League, the Union League.

"More, more, more," yelled Sawyer, until an explosion occurred on the stage and it was reported that "Judge Pine is firing back at us—just when the war was won."

They called the Commander-in-Chief on the telephone and told him that the courts were threatening to outflank them.

"What should we do?"

The skit ended with the man on the telephone saying that all the Commander-in-Chief wanted to know was, "How many divisions has the Supreme Court got?"

The Democratic skit was set in a frowzy, pioneer, frontier-type town. The announcer introduced it by saying, "If our guests have tears, let them prepare to shed them now. The Gridiron Club takes us to a wagon yard at Independence, Missouri, where a certain political party is in trouble as it seeks a pathfinder to lead it."

The storekeeper wouldn't give the Democrats any more credit, because "the Old Man" had deserted them in not being available for another term.

"Poor little lost Democrats," he said, "deserted by your Old Man. Well, speaking for all American businessmen, free enterprisers and the National Association of Manufacturers, you really touch my heart." Then he sang:

> May the good Lord bless and keep you,
> No, not here, but far away!
> You must find yourself another golden goose; hurray!
> May your taxes all be big ones,
> Just like those you made us pay.
> May the good Lord bless and keep you—
> Keep you far away!

Somebody wanted to nominate Hubert Humphrey, and "go lynch some businessmen," but he didn't prevail. They decided to "save all that lynching until after the election."

To the tune of "I'm in the Mood for Love," a character representing Averell Harriman proclaimed:

I'm in the mood to run!
Only New York is for me,
Funny, though few are for me,
I am a fav'rite son. . . .

I spend with ease and fervor
When Congress gives the dough,
I could be his successor;
Never forget—I told you so!

My race is well begun,
Ninety-four votes pledged to me,
Ninety-four votes—and Harry.
I'm in the mood to run.

"Senator Estes Kefauver" of Tennessee announced that he was available for anything, even "for getting my name in the papers," and he sang:

Pardon me, boys;
They call me Chattanooga Estes,
Primary whizz,
'Cause I gave Truman the biz . . .

There's gonna be
A certain votin' in November;
Gonna elect—
Little ole me, I suspect.

Another Democratic potential, although not a very strong contender, Senator Richard B. Russell of Georgia, wished that he was a President-to-be and analyzed his situation in song:

I wish I wuz part Northern Democrat,
I hate them rebels from morn till night,
But they got votes *plus* civil rights;
I wish I wuz part Northern Democrat . . .

I wish I wuz old Harry's choice this year,
I fight old Harry and all his crew,
But, think what a word from him would do!
I wish I wuz old Harry's choice this year.

A Gridiron member costumed as "Miss Democracy" who was claimed by both Kefauver and "Senator Paul Douglas" of Illinois, decided, however, that:

Oh, you can't ditch old Barkley,
He wins, don't forget;

Says he's a front runner
You'll never forget.

A-runnin's a pleasure,
Retirin's a grief;
He wants to march in once
To "Hail to the Chief."

He's got issues a-plenty;
If not, he'll tell jokes,
Be they old ones or new ones,
They'll panic the folks.

Now, don't worry, Alben;
Let 'em scheme, let 'em plot.
For if they ditch Barkley,
The Gridiron will not.

At this point the skit ended with a song written by Marshall McNeil and sung by him and the chorus.

Go back,
We must go back
Across the rolling river.

Oh, Democrats, pack up, get goin'
Back across the wide Missouri,
We've had our fun, we've got their money.

Go back,
Go back out West
Across the wide Missouri.

Dick cannot win and Adlai wouldn't,
Alben won't and Estes shouldn't.
Dear Harriman's a big bond clipper,
And Kerr—he can't go fur—
Across the wide Missouri.

The line that "Adlai wouldn't win" in this song was the only reference at the Gridiron dinner that spring to the man who was nominated two months later.

Vice President Barkley responded to the toast, but the text of his speech seems to have vanished from the scene as completely as many of the Democrats did from Washington after the November election.

• • •

By the time the December 13, 1952 dinner took place, General Dwight D. Eisenhower had been elected president in an overwhelming victory of 442 electoral votes (including, for the first time in Republican history, four of the southern states) to 89 for Adlai E. Stevenson. Eisenhower had been elected with Richard M. Nixon as his running mate. At first, Nixon's position on the ticket had been challenged because of a political fund raised for him in California, but he finally won both public and Eisenhower support with his famous "Checkers" speech.

The Eisenhower ticket just barely carried the Congress, with 48 to 47 and 1 independent in the Senate, and 221 to 211 and 1 independent in the House. It was the last time that a Republican president had his own party in the majority in Congress. But President Eisenhower was destined to get along quite well with his slim majority, partly because he had a fairly understanding and cooperative Democratic leadership. "Landslide" Lyndon Johnson, still serving his first term in the Senate after his victory in Texas in 1948, had become minority leader, and Sam Rayburn was minority leader of the House.

Neither President Truman nor President-elect Eisenhower was present at the December 1952 dinner, and the two speakers were Vice President-elect Nixon and the defeated Democratic candidate, Adlai Stevenson. President Eisenhower was in Korea, trying to end the war after his campaign pledge, "I will go to Korea."

Gridiron President Leach, in his speech opening the dinner, noted that the voters had called for a change and that "they got it. Now every campaign pledge is a mandate and every mandate is a headache."

The Stevenson campaign had ended up with a half-million dollar deficit, but the federal budget deficit was $10 billion. Leach remarked that "General Eisenhower and Governor Stevenson have at least one thing in common—the deficit. But the Governor's is only half a million. . . . The General's is ten billion."

Referring to the Congress, he said that "soon the Greatest Show on Earth opens under the big dome. The elephant will be walking a tight rope, as the donkey watchfully waits for him to slip. . . .

"So, to the Democrats it is rest you, Merry Gentlemen. To the Republicans, good luck and watch your step."

For the opener, the members of the Gridiron chorus were costumed as crusaders, carrying swords, pikes, and a large banner labeled "The Crusade." Each one had a small concealed Confederate flag, which he whipped out and waved wildly when the orchestra struck up "Dixie." They sang:

> Away down south in the land of cotton
> Harry Truman's done forgotten,
> Look away, look away, look away,
> Dixie land!

> In Dixie land where Ike was born
> Early on one frosty morn,
> Look away, look away, look away,
> Dixie land!

Eisenhower's cabinet had been announced by this time, and there was a skit, led off by an impersonator of George Humphrey, named as secretary of the treasury. To the tune of "There'll Be Some Changes Made," he sang:

> There'll be a change in your taxes
> 'Cause we said we would,
> So that you'll shout you never had it so good.
> Your bills will be smaller, your debts and your rents,
> We'll give you dollars worth two hundred cents.

The scene of the skit was the electoral college, and Herbert Brownell, named as attorney general, was announced as the new coach of the electoral college football team. His impersonator presented the new backfield: "Charles E. Wilson," secretary of defense; "Arthur Summerfield," postmaster general; and "Douglas McKay," secretary of the interior. All of them had had previous identification with General Motors. Summerfield sang for the group:

> We are the wheels of our Ike's No Deals
> In his gas tank we're the gas . . .

> In our merry Oldsmobile,
> Come away with our No Deal.
> Down the road of life we'll flee,
> Traveling hydromatically.
> We'll go Buick, if you say,
> Or perhaps by Chevrolet,
> You can go as far as you like with Ike
> In our merry Oldsmobile.

This was followed by a duet to the tune of "Friendship," between characters representing the outgoing Secretary of State

Dean Acheson, and John Foster Dulles, the incoming one.

Acheson:
>If you're ever up a tree, call on me.
>If you're ever in a mess, SOS
>If you ever lose your patience with Uncle Joe,
>Let me know.

Dulles:
>If you ever need a dime, any time.
>If you ever want a lift, it's a gift.
>If you ever feel so thirsty you want some tea,
>Call on me.

Both:
>It's friendship, friendship, what a perfect blendship.

"Sinclair Weeks," the new secretary of commerce-to-be, sang:

>There's no business like big business
>To run this U.S.A.

Chorus:
>There's no business like big business,
>If big business can stay,
>Stocks that we have cornered will rise in a boom,
>(Let you in—if there is room).
>You can make your money when the markets zoom,
>Let's give business its day.

The background for the Republican skit was a village in the Catskills, where Rip Van Winkle had just awakened from his twenty-year sleep. He was in front of a building which had a sign, "Harry's Tavern," with the "Harry's" crossed out and "Ike's" written in above it. "Thomas E. Dewey" was the proprietor, and Rip wanted to know what was going on. A character representing Speaker-elect Joseph W. Martin told him in song:

>Roll out the barrel,
>Roll in the No Deal today;
>Roll out the Fair Deal,
>Democrats all on the way!
>We are not certain
>Just what the answers will be—
>Hold your hats, we're off again
>With the GOP!

"Mrs. Oveta Culp Hobby," former commander of the WACs,

who in April 1953 became secretary of health, education and welfare, told about the part that women had played in the election:

> What the women say
> Rules the roost today,
> Voting as we never did before.
> For one we like
> And we *love* Ike!
> Rich man, poor man, thief,
> Doctor, lawyer, chief,
> Get our order that now is the hour;
> We play our part
> Right from the heart
> And from the heart we vote—
>   "Eisenhower!"

"Senator Robert A. Taft" remarked that "quite a number of Republicans say that they don't want jobs in the new Administration," and Rip commented, "I'll say times have changed." Then the chorus sang to the melody of "The World Is Waiting for the Sunrise":

> At last, the GOP can see the sunrise,
> Everyone thinks gravy is due.
> And every voice for its reward is calling,
> Ike, each voice is calling you!

"Senator Wayne Morse" of Oregon, who in a first step toward changing from the Republican to the Democratic party had declared himself an Independent in 1952, gave some advice to Republicans in song, to the strains of "Goodnight, Irene."

> So let me just whisper to others,
> If bolting a party is sin,
> And you're thinking of taking a walk-out,
> Don't leave when it's just going to win!

At this point Rip Van Winkle pulled off his whiskers, announced that he remembered who he was, and proclaimed, "I am Herbert Hoover!" Then, as the skit ended, he proceeded, as an elder statesman, to give some advice to President-elect Eisenhower:

> This ain't the army, Mister Ike!
> You have been doing as you like,
> You've had your own way in things before,

But you won't have it now, any more!

This ain't the army, Mister Ike!
Senate and House are just alike,
You may have thought they are just a bore,
But they won't bore you now, any more!

No longer bugles command,
This ain't the army, and this ain't its band!
This ain't the army, Mister Ike!
Politicians on the hike.
You may have kept them outside your door,
But you won't keep them out any more–more–more–
No, you won't keep them out any more!

Vice President Nixon was not introduced immediately after this skit, as is customary, but rather after one which followed, a "Doghouse" skit involving Lassie, Rin-tin-tin, President Roosevelt's Fala, the Hound of the Baskervilles, and Nixon's Checkers—all in the "Canine Hall of Fame."

Fala announced that the Canine Hall of Fame was convened as a special court of inquiry to hear charges against Checkers, "who wants to be vice president." The charges were: (1) chasing a red herring, (2) unmitigated modesty, and (3) public bankruptcy, to all of which Checkers pleaded "not guilty."

The Hound of the Baskervilles, with an English accent, decided as to Checkers that "his master has pleaded a lack of resources requiring a certain—er-ah—political fund," and that he was "jolly well guilty."

Lassie sympathized with him because he belonged to "a family that has nothing but a cloth coat—my deah!"

Asked by Rin-tin-tin if he had a suitable kennel, Checkers replied, "I've got a cloth-lined kennel with a fur-lined mortgage."

Fala pronounced the verdict, "I'll tell you, Checkers. Your story doesn't add up. But it makes the doggondest television program you ever saw. We find you clean—clean as a man's tooth."

No copy of Vice President Nixon's speech was obtained at the time by the Gridiron Club, and whatever text exists is in the Nixon pre-Presidential papers deposited at a National Archives facility at Laguna Niguel, California, and not open to inspection at the time this book was written.

The Democratic skit, "Mutiny Against the Bounty," was set

on a remote island in the Pacific, where the survivors had gathered "after 100 days at sea . . . following the wreck of the Democratic war sloop, The *Bounty*." The chief character was Captain Adlai Bly, costumed to resemble Charles Laughton in the same part. Senator Estes Kefauver was portrayed in a badly tattered Daniel Boone outfit, carrying a rifle bent into a right angle. One of the shipwrecked crew announced, "We won. We are safe at last. We don't have to clean up the mess."

But Captain Bly thought that "the mess cleaned us up." "Averell Harriman" predicted "stormy weather from now on," and Bly asked him to sing his thoughts, to which Harriman replied, "I'm going to sing it just like you would."

> Don't know why—there's no sun up in the sky,
> Stormy weather!
> Since those votes and I ain't together,
> I didn't have enough.

> Harry took my side—the blues walked in and met me,
> Stayed right by my side—ole Gen'ral Ike he whupped me,
> All I did was pray that Harry soon would let me
> Run my campaign by myself.

"Jake Arvey," Democratic boss of Chicago, told Bly that "the CIO, the AF of L, the UMW, the ADA and the SPCA—they all say you belong to them." Then Arvey sang his version of "You Belong to Me."

> In the East we didn't do too well,
> Even Curley couldn't ring the bell,
> Listen, Adlai, to the truth I tell,
> You belong to me.

> Way out West we didn't take a state,
> Though the Treasury was used as bait,
> Just remember, Adlai, that it's fate,
> You belong to me. ·

A member of the cast announced that far off in the distance he saw a man walking, just walking, and outgoing "Vice President Barkley" described him in song, as the skit closed with a pleasant farewell to Truman:

> It looks like Harry, walkin', walkin',
> Walkin' to Missouri,
> Got a twinkle in his eye.

> He says he's happy his job is done,

Got time now to have some fun,
From here on his worries will be few,
I guess his favorite sport will be,
To check on the GOP,
To see what those snollygosters do.

Could be his pockets are stuffed with plans,
For journeys to far off lands,
If things get so dull it really hurts,
And he's got plenty of souvenirs,
To cheer him for years and years,
Including ten dozen Key West shirts.

Perhaps a teacher of history,
Is what Harry'd like to be,
He smiles when he hears that classroom bell.
Before each lesson got under way,
Some student, I'm sure, would say:
"Good morning, Professor, give 'em hell."

Stevenson's speech delighted the Gridiron audience.

"A funny thing happened to me on the way to the White House." he began.

"While I did not carry many states, I seem to have run way ahead in the Fourth Estate, excluding, of course, you publishers."

Then he made a pitch which never offends Gridiron members or most of their guests.

"I can think of no state I would rather have carried, and perhaps I should begin by apologizing to those of you who work for a living and who thought I was out in front. The fact was, of course, that the General was so far ahead of me we never saw him, and I was happy to hear that I had even placed second."

Referring to Governor Thomas E. Dewey, who sat a short distance down the head table, Stevenson said it was apparent "that I was not the first choice of a great many. But no one will say, I trust, that I snatched defeat from the jaws of victory [as had been said of Dewey]. Which reminds me that four years ago, occupying the seat I occupy tonight, was another great governor—excuse me, the governor of another great State—some say the second greatest state in the union. What has just happened to me had just happened to him. In fact, it had just happened to him for the second time. But did he despair? He did not. He said to himself—if I may take a newspaperman's license and tell you what a man says to himself—he said, 'If I cannot be

President myself, I can at least make somebody else President.' Which, bless his merry heart, he proceeded to do. And look at him now. He's as contented as the cat that swallowed the canary, or should I say the cabinet."

Stevenson recalled that at that Gridiron dinner after Dewey's defeat he had just been elected governor of Illinois, and that he "sat down there with you common people."

"I was happy and carefree and had nothing to worry about, except the organization of a new administration to clean up the state of Illinois after the long years of the usual Republican misrule. (And now I don't even have that to worry about!)

"I, a Democrat, had just been elected governor by the largest majority ever received in Republican Illinois. And here I am, four years later, and just defeated by the largest majority ever received in Democratic America.

"Wasn't it Jim Watson who said that he entered the Senate with almost *no* opposition from the people of Indiana, and that he left the Senate, with *none*?

"I feel a little the same way. But I wonder if I'm not entitled to some kind of a record. Did anyone starting from scratch ever *enter* our public life with such widespread approval and *leave* with such widespread approval—all in the space of four years? Frankly, I think the chroniclers of our times have overlooked the meteoric beauty and brevity of my political career.

"Well, I had not planned it that way. I had wished to continue as governor of Illinois, there to erect and fortify a shining temple of administrative purity and political probity. But the fates decreed otherwise after meeting in the Chicago stockyards. Mindful of the Chinese maiden's philosophical acceptance of unwanted and aggressive attentions, I concluded to accept my fate gallantly and joyfully, with consequences that were reported by most of you publishers—also joyfully.

"Now I content myself that it is all for the best. After all, didn't Socrates say that the duty of a man of real principle is to stay out of politics? So you see I'm delighted that the sovereign people have put an even higher value on my principles than I did.

"Yes, I have much to be thankful for and it would be out of character if I didn't frankly confess my happy state of mind, even here, surrounded by my late executioners."

Like many Gridiron speakers, Stevenson paid his tribute to

laughter, which, he said, "distinguishes us from the lower—or untaxed—animals." And he was relieved that the Republicans had decided not to prohibit humor by federal law and to leave "this newest threat to the Republic" for the states to deal with.

The year 1952 was the time when the word "egghead" first came into wide usage, and it was applied to many of Stevenson's more erudite academic supporters. Stevenson "bequeathed" that word to the nation's vocabulary.

"It seems to have been first used in this campaign to describe the more intelligensiac members of that lunatic fringe who thought I was going to win."

He referred to *Time* magazine, which he said he didn't read, but he understood that it had concluded "that the election showed that American intellectuals are hopelessly out of touch with the rest of the country.

"Of course," he commented, "I take considerable comfort from this authoritative admission that all the intellectuals were on my side. But being a believer in the two-party system myself, I cannot accept the totalitarian view that 27 million losers in an election, 45 percent of the voters, are out of touch with the American people!

"That figure, 27 million, still staggers me. But I need a much stronger verb to describe what is done to me by the still larger number of those who like Ike."

Then, speaking of President-elect Eisenhower, he said he hadn't compared notes with the President-elect on how he enjoyed the campaign.

"Indeed now that the affair is over," said Stevenson, "I hope some time to know him, which recalls many editorials and articles you gentlemen wrote last spring about how I wanted to run against Senator Taft but not the General who was my old time friend. It has seemed to me odd that the simple truth that I did not want to run against anyone had too little apparent news value.

"I would tell him that for my part I enjoyed the campaign— in spots. There were times, I confess, when I was afraid I wouldn't die, times when I felt I wouldn't do it to a dog. Let me add, by the way, that, like every red-blooded American patriot, I own a dog. It was not a campaign contribution. And I think the General would say to me that there are times when he wished he was in my shoes—you see I had them fixed." [This was a reference to a picture taken of Stevenson and widely reprinted during the campaign, in which he had his legs crossed and showed a big hole in the sole of his shoe.]

Proceeding to describe his reactions to the campaign, he referred to those who shouted "Good old Ad-lie!" and advised his audience that if any of them decided to run for public office and had a slightly unusual name, to change it before they started. He told about his travels of tens of thousands of miles up and down the country, "and all free," he said, "free, that is, if blood and sweat, money and deficits don't count."

He managed to get several hours sleep a night, he told the audience, and was fed pretty regularly, even if it was usually cheese on rye sandwiches and coffee in cardboard containers.

Then Stevenson referred to the disclosures of personal life and finances which have been demanded so frequently in all recent campaigns. But he had a new twist for it this time.

"Although I clearly won the bosom-baring and public stripping contest of last fall, I am now prepared to go a step further and disclose my pre-nomination expenditures in full.

"Before the convention:

1. 3-cent postage stamps to explain, mostly to the press, why I was not a candidate for the nomination .... $ 150.00

"After the convention commenced in Chicago, a large number of persons took up their residence on the street and lawns around my house—and you know who they were—and the following expenditures were incurred before I could escape:

2. 68 cases of beer—*for* the press .... $ 272.00
3. 16 cases of non-acoholic beverages—*for* the press   34.00
4. 8 cases of other beverages—*for* the press 480.00
5. Hire of truck from house to Convention Hall *for* the press 30.00
6. Hire of bus from house to Convention Hall—*for* the press 50.00
7. Special police assigned to protect house— *from* the press...   500.00

Total $1,366.00

"There is a further item, not yet available, for restoring lawns destroyed, if not permanently scorched—*by* the press.

"The eggheads present, if any, will identify and understand, then, why I think of those words, 'How sharper than a serpent's tooth it is to have a thankless—press.'

"Of course I make this further and positively *final* revelation with no expectation of political reciprocity, but merely to suggest, with characteristic delicacy, that the American Newspaper Publishers Association can send its check to me.

"And now that the tumult and the shouting have died, and Walter Lippmann and Joe Alsop have gone back to writing the next chapter of the Doomsday Book, how does the defeated hero feel, and what of the future?

"Well, gentlemen, there are certain pleasurable aspects of defeat. Although there seemed little perceptible editorial enthusiasm for me during the campaign, except in some of the better papers, I have been stirred by the virtues which so many essayists discovered in me the moment it became clear that the outs were in. Much of this comment seemed to suggest that it couldn't have happened to a nicer guy. And, lest you get ahead of me, I say that I couldn't have lost to a nicer guy. And I'll still think so, even if the boys are not out of the trenches by Christmas!

"Then there were the letters. We gave up counting before long and began to weigh them. So many of them were from people who voted for the General, and evidently felt that they owed me an explanation; curious why people will go to all that trouble to write a long letter when a little X in the right place would have been so much easier.

"But I am grateful to them all, and I wish there was some refined way befitting my station to explain to each of them that we spent a lot of money we didn't have, etc. But I suppose if I did they might write again, in less friendly vein, and say, 'Just like a Democrat.' "

Shifting at this point to his own future, Stevenson said there were some who felt "that I should devote my classic talents to the welfare of mankind by frequent talking; then there is another smaller group who insist that God and/or the election has appointed me the scourge of the Republican party; and finally there is the much smaller group that feel that it is not wholly unworthy or improper to earn a living. My sons are numbered in the latter group.

"But despite anything you may have read or written, there are some future plans of action that I have definitely rejected. I have declined an invitation to become President of the National Association of Gagwriters. And I will not go into vaudeville. It is equally definite that I will not become manager of the Washington Senators—I mean Clark Griffith's, not Mr. Taft's."

Then, turning to the role of "those of us who constitute what

I trust will be known as the responsible opposition," he said that these were times of unusual complexity. "Mention of Mr. Taft suggests, for example, that for the moment, at least, we Democrats are intruders in a family quarrel. Indeed it is difficult to be certain for the present whether we Democrats will be disagreeing with the new President, or acting as his bodyguard.

"But whatever happens to the Republicans, the Republic will survive," he declared. "I have great faith in the people. As to their wisdom, well, Coca Cola still outsells champagne. They may make mistakes. They do sometimes. But given time they correct their mistakes—at two or four year intervals.

"I have faith in the people, and in their chosen leaders: men of high purpose, good will and humble hearts, men quite prepared to stand aside when the time comes and allow even more humble men to take over."

Stevenson closed with a last word to the press.

"It is the habit of journalists, as of politicians, to see the world in terms of crisis rather than continuity; the big story is turmoil and disaster, not the quiet spectacle of men working. I trust that there will be none among my party who will hope for just a small, dandy little catastrophe to vindicate us. I am aware of the thesis that bad news sells papers. But neither politicians nor publishers have the right in this age to hope for the worst. Every newspaperman has talked at one time or another of how to handle the story of the end of the world; but who will be around to buy the extra?

"Every lesson of history is that democracy flourishes best when speech is freest. No issue is more important—and more troublesome—in this time of conflict with massive repression than the preservation of our right even to bore each other.

"Never was the responsibility of the majority press greater to make clear that it is concerned about the freedom of all Americans, and not merely about its own liberty to agree with itself. Your typewriter is a public trust. Its sound may be the most beautiful noise you know, but it has meaning and justification only if it is part of the gloriously discordant symphony of a free society."[11]

Immediately afterward, the dinner closed with the drinking of the toast to the President and the singing of "Auld Lang Syne." Thus, so far as the Gridiron Club was concerned, the Truman era passed into history.

But no account of President Truman and the Gridiron Club

would be complete without the recital of some subsequent events which are related by Edward T. Folliard of the *Washington Post* in a memorandum for the Gridiron archives, telling how the club was an instrument in bringing about an end to a bitter feud. He wrote:

"In 1956, the then president of the Gridiron Club, Roscoe Drummond, decided that our 'little dinner' of that year, to be held on December 8, would be in honor of men who had served as Vice President of the United States and men who had run for that office. Mr. Drummond assigned me to invite Mr. Truman, who of course had served as Vice President under FDR.

"By the time Mr. Truman replied to my letter, November 20, the national election of 1956 was over and the Eisenhower-Nixon ticket had been re-elected. That meant, of course, that Vice President Nixon would certainly be at our 'little dinner.'

"The prospect of breaking bread with Nixon was abhorrent to Truman. He told me in his letter that he would not 'sit with that fellow or with his boss either'—meaning President Eisenhower.* Truman, as you can see by his letter, accused Nixon of calling him a 'traitor.' He was sore with Ike because of Ike's failure to stand up for General George C. Marshall in the '52 campaign.

"According to Associated Press stories on October 27, 1952, the then Senator Nixon spoke in Texarkana and said that Truman, Dean Acheson and Adlai Stevenson were 'traitors to the high principles in which many of the nation's Democrats believe,' and added, 'Real Democrats are outraged by the Truman-Acheson-Stevenson gang's toleration and defense of Communism in high places.'

"Earl Mazo, a biographer of Nixon, has quoted Nixon as saying that all he did was to question the judgment of Truman, Acheson and Stevenson, not their patriotism.

---

*The full text of Truman's letter to Folliard is as follows:

November 20, 1956

Dear Eddie,

Your letter of the 16th was highly appreciated, and I am sorry I cannot be present at the Gridiron Club's private dinner on December 8. The reason is that I will not sit down at the same table with Nixon. He has never refuted his statement that I was a traitor; but even if he did, my feelings about him would remain the same.

Therefore, please do not count on me for the private dinner or for your annual dinner in March. I regret it very much for there is nothing I would like better than being there, but I just cannot sit with that fellow, or with his boss either.

Sincerely yours,
/s/ Harry S. Truman

"In 1964, when Fletcher Knebel was president, I invited Mr. Truman to the Gridiron Club's annual dinner of April 25. I was quite honest with him, telling him that Nixon, then out of office, would be a head table guest.

"Recalling his earlier refusal to 'sit with that fellow,' I told Mr. Truman:

" 'All I can say is that your many old friends in the Gridiron Club—fellows like Pete Brandt, Arthur Krock, Fletcher Knebel and myself—sure would like to have you at the dinner. I know that President Johnson would, too.'

"To the delight and astonishment of us all, Mr. Truman accepted our invitation.

"President Knebel, knowing that I was rather close to Mr. Truman because of my long White House coverage, assigned me to be his escort on the night of the dinner. Accordingly, I met Mr. Truman at the 16th Street door of the Statler and took him to the Continental Room, where a bar had been set up for the head table guests.

"As I guided Mr. Truman into the Continental Room, I was horrified to see directly in front of us the last two men I wanted the old Missouri warrior to meet. They were Nixon and James F. Byrnes, who had quit as Secretary of State after a quarrel with President Truman. The two were talking.

"There was no way in which I could divert Mr. Truman; an encounter was unavoidable. To my surprise, Truman went up to Byrnes with outstretched hand and said, 'Hi, Jim.' Byrnes accepted the handshake, smiled, and said, 'Hi, Harry.'

"Truman completely ignored Nixon, but it wasn't clear to me whether he was being deliberately rude or just failed to see him or recognize him. Nixon then showed what a resourceful guy he is. He walked over to the bar, which was but a step away. Returning with a highball, he said, 'Mr. President, here is your favorite drink, bourbon and water.'

"Truman took the highball with one hand, extended the other to Nixon and said, 'You are a gentleman.'

"That seemed to end the Truman-Nixon feud, right there and then, but there was more to come, all of it pleasant.

"Nixon was the Republican speaker at the 1964 dinner, the theme of which, in the words of the opening song, was 'Love is bustin' out all over.' In the spirit of the evening, Nixon told in his speech of his encounter with Truman in the Continental Room. He told how he had fetched him a bourbon highball, and how

Truman had downed it 'without even having it tested.' This evoked about the biggest laugh of the evening.

"There was a sequel to this at the Gridiron Club's 1969 dinner, by which time Nixon was President. In my role as deputy chairman of the Reception Committee, I took the club's guest book to the Continental Room.

"When I handed President Nixon a pen with which to sign the book, I said something like this, 'I was thinking, Mr. President, of the last time I saw you in this room.'

" 'It was the night I brought President Truman a drink,' he shot back, laughing.

"I reminded him that Mr. Truman would be eighty-five on May 8, and that it would be nice if he could do something about it.

" 'I have a plan,' Mr. Nixon said, and after a pause, he said, 'Would you like to go with me?'

"I didn't know what he had in mind, but I said something like, 'You're damn tootin' I would.'

"Later in the evening, at a post-dinner gathering in the Cowles Brothers suite in 1240, President Nixon summoned me and told his military aide, Colonel Don Hughes, U.S.A.F., to make arrangements for me to accompany him on Air Force One when he went out to Independence, Missouri, to see Mr. Truman.

"On the appointed day, late in March, a White House car called for me at home, took me to Andrews Air Field, and off I went in Air Force One as a representative of the Gridiron Club.

"Before the plane got to Kansas City, Mr. Nixon invited me into his private cabin. Secretary of State William Rogers and Foreign Affairs Adviser Henry Kissinger were with him. The President recalled all that had happened that night he got the drink for Mr. Truman in 1964, treating it as a prologue to what was to happen later that day in Independence.

"What happened in Independence was that, along with President Nixon, I greeted Mr. and Mrs. Truman at their home, and then drove to the Truman Library. There President Nixon presented to Truman the Steinway he used in the White House, and then Nixon sat down and played the 'Missouri Waltz.' "

XVI

Dwight D. Eisenhower

1953-1956
Republicans and Democrats Laugh
and Work Together
and the Gridiron Burns Neither

President Eisenhower attended Gridiron dinners regularly until he suffered his first heart attack in 1955, and irregularly after that. The first dinner at which Eisenhower was present as President on April 11, 1953, three months after he had taken office, was to a considerable extent a welcome to him. He had always been very popular with the newspapermen, who could not resist his geniality and his smile any more than other people could. The welcome, however, came with considerable banter to him and his administration, some of it rather biting.

Eisenhower was an avid golfer and belonged to Washington's famous Burning Tree Club, where he played golf as frequently as he could.

So 1953 Gridiron President Duke Shoop, Washington correspondent of the *Kansas City Star*, in his speech in the dark, welcomed the guests of the Gridiron Club "and fellow applicants for membership in Burning Tree."

"The watchword of the hour in Washington," said Shoop, "is try, try again. Our guest of honor is trying to break ninety— the rest of us are trying to break even. . . .

"Government by businessmen has been a smash success. It has been in office almost three months without a depression— and with only two major stock market reverses.

"Everybody's working on the budget. One half of the administration is working to balance it. The other half is working to alibi it."

The opener consisted of several of the Eisenhower songs from previous dinners, beginning with the one in 1947, "Ask Me, Ask Me Again"; the one in 1948; "Nomination I Refuse It, but I Thank You So"; the one in 1949, "Some Enchanted Evening, I Will Pick a Party"; and ending with the one in December, 1952, "This Ain't the Army, Mr. Ike."

With the coming of the Republicans, there developed, especially among the Democrats in Congress, great concern over possible conflict of interest. All of the cabinet members, before confirmation, had been required to sell stock which they owned. The most notable instance was that of Secretary of Defense Charles E. Wilson, who had had to sell several million dollars worth of General Motors stock at a time when it was at a depressed price.

Consequently, as the Republicans took over the stage, they appeared in rags and tatters, while the Marine Band orchestra played "Brother, Can You Spare a Dime?" and an impersonator of Secretary Wilson sang:

> Once I built an auto, made it run,
> Made it race against time.
> Once I owned the business, now that's done—
> Brother, can you spare a dime?
> Once I built an empire, it was fun,
> No one thought it a crime;
> Once I got a bonus, now that's done,
> Brother, can you spare a dime?

There was a golf skit set at the Burning Tree Club. Prior to it, the chief Washington representatives of various businesses, who customarily played there, were asked to stand.

The scene opened on a row of lockers above one of which hung a huge five-star flag. Several golfers, in various stages of undress, were conversing.

1st golfer: And that isn't just my opinion—it's *His.*
2nd golfer: What were his exact words?

1st golfer: Well, it wasn't what he said as the way he waved to me from the thirteenth tee. I could see him just as plain from the first green.

3rd golfer: But I talked to him face to face.

4th golfer: You did?

3rd golfer: Yeah, he asked me if I had any spare tees. Six other guys offered theirs too, but he took mine.

1st golfer: He did?

3rd golfer: Yep, and you know he never does anything without a reason.

2nd golfer: Say, that's hot. I'm gonna phone the boss.

Then he went to the phone and told Ben Fairless, chairman of U.S. Steel, all about it. At this point an impersonator of the President's caddy, Cemetery Poteet, came into the locker room, and all the golfers jumped to attention. They quizzed Poteet at length about what HE said. One of them asked if he mentioned anti-trust, and Poteet replied scornfully, "Anti-trust? Why dey ain't no anti in dat man. He trusts everybody."

The skit ended at the conclusion of the questioning when one of the golfers said he'd heard and seen everything: "William H. Mylander of the Du Pont Company practicing to be a dub."

Poteet: (*Turning to the audience*) So would all of you iffen you were going to play with (*pointing to head table*) Him tomorrow.

Before President Truman left office, he had put into civil service a large number of Democratic officeholders, including postmasters, a considerable number of government information people, and various others.

This served as the idea for the opening of the Democratic skit, which was located in the bar lounge of a palatial ocean liner, "the luxury cruise of the U.S.S. *Loyal Opposition*."

A group of postmasters recalled one after the other how "Jim Farley put me on," "Frank Walker put me on," "Jess Donaldson put me on," and the last one, "Benjamin Franklin put me on."

They thought Civil Service was wonderful because nobody could now put them off, and one of them sang, to the tune of "They Say That Falling in Love Is Wonderful":

It's wonderful, wonderful Civil Service,
Merit is all that's required.
Once the job is mine,
I will ne'er resign.

Dear old Civil Service,
Wonderful, wonderful,
I just cannot be fired.

"Captain Harry" and a few other first-class passengers, including "Senate Democratic Leader Lyndon Johnson," then came on the stage, proclaiming that this is the life—"I even like old Ike!"

Johnson asked Captain Harry if he had started to write his memoirs yet, and the Captain replied, "Not yet, but I'm going to make 'em dignified."

"Like those letters you used to write before breakfast?" teased Johnson.

Captain Harry told the boys that they needn't try to forget him; he was their rabbit's foot, the Democrats' lucky star. And then he sang a parody of "(You Are) My Lucky Star."

I was your lucky star,
Winner spectacular.
We always won with me nominated.
We rated!
Dominated!
I'm all your lucky charms
In cities and on farms,
I opened White House portals in this town to you poor mortals,
Truman's your lucky star!

They had some fun with Senator Wayne Morse, who had recently joined their party, and who, in a riding escapade, had been kicked in the head by his horse. The injuries were not so serious that they could not be laughed about. "Morse" was riding around the deck on a costume horse, and Johnson asked, "You said the horse kicked Morse?"

A sailor replied, "No sir, Morse kicked the horse."

Morse asked the assembled multitude to "lay off, fellows. I'm on your side at last." Then, an impersonator of Democratic National Committee Chairman Stephen Mitchell noted that "we always knew we had you," but that "what worries us is getting men like Dick Russell to admit we don't have a Democratic President." He appealed to "Senator Hubert H. Humphrey" to "tell old Dick" (who was the most powerful of the southern senators) "just how much the Democratic party needs him," and Marshall McNeil, as Humphrey, sang his own parody of "High Noon."

Do not forsake us, O Dick Russell,
Come next election year,

Without the South we're lost, Dick Russell,
Come—come along.

I do not know what fate awaits us,
I only know we must agree
That we will face a man who beat us . . .
A smilin' General,
A winnin' General,
A five-star General—not named Lee.

O, to be torn 'twixt you and Adlai,
Millions still gladly love him madly,
Think of his big vote in the cities
November last.

I made a vow the last convention
Vowed I would end all this dissension.
I'm not afraid we'll lose, but O what will I do if you leave me.

Do not forsake us, O Dick Russell,
You made that promise just last year,
Do not forsake us, O Dick Russell,
Although you're grievin', don't think of leavin',
Now that we need you
On our side.
Come along, come along.

An impersonator of Adlai Stevenson entered, very carefully dressed, swinging a light cane, carrying a snappy traveling bag, and wearing a Panama hat, all of which he handed one at a time, very deliberately, to a steward. Johnson identified him as "the eggheads' William Jennings Bryan," and Stevenson replied, "And maybe the poor man's Thomas E. Dewey."

Then, to the tune of "Anywhere I Wander," he sang:

I took the job most reluctantly,
I feared I'd surely lose,
But then I knew what my path must be
Through the ever-haunting blues.

Oh, those twenty-seven million votes,
Of love they gently told,
And in each vote was the tenderness
I may never more behold.

Anywhere I wander,
Anywhere I roam,
'Till I get elected to office again,
My heart will know no home.

Senator Estes Kefauver of Tennessee had become prominent through a Senate investigation on crime. Under television cameras he had questioned such an eminent practitioner as Frank Costello and qualified himself for an investigation of the drug industry later on. His trademark was a Tennessee coonskin cap, and some three years after this dinner he was to be nominated as Adlai Stevenson's second running mate. His impersonator came on the stage and sang:

You must remember this

(At this point he brandished his coonskin cap and put it on)

You must remember this,
I wore it last July,
And fundamental things don't die,
As time goes by.

TV and hand-shakes never out of date,
In Fifty-six will help to stimulate,
Streets full of voters I will captivate,
That no one will deny.

It's still the same old story,
A fight for votes and glory,
A case of do or die,
Primarily I'll be the winner,
As time goes by.

He grabbed Captain Harry's hat, put it on, told the captain that he was through and said, "Set 'em up, bartender. Have a drink on me—on me and the CIO, ADA, TVA, FEPC—and the NBC and CBS television networks."

The skit ended with an impersonator of Senator Stuart Symington summing up the views of the Democrats to the tune of "Blow High, Blow Low":

We never can understand
Why people of this land
Took a likin' to Ike in 1952,
For we served them well you see since 1933,
And I ask you what more a friend of the people could do.

Blow high, Blow low,
Republicans must go,
We've got a mandate to chase them away.
We'll fight our foe,
Blow high and low,
For many and many a long, long day.

At its conclusion, the Gridiron president presented to speak for the opposition, "a new and important figure in American national politics, Senator Lyndon B. Johnson."

Senator Johnson's standing among the Democrats had been dramatically indicated by his unanimous election as minority leader, although he was himself still a first-term senator and had been elected to the Senate by the narrowest of margins. However, he had been in Washington for sixteen years, first as secretary to Representative Richard M. Kleberg, whose family owned the King Ranch in Texas, and then for almost six terms as a member of the House.

He and President Eisenhower got along very well, and Johnson was the epitome of a "loyal" opposition, but the philosophy of the opposition which he expressed in this speech was quite different from the character of the later opposition that Presidents Nixon and Ford encountered.

Johnson began by gently ribbing the President about his "excellent relations" with Congress.

He was basking, he said, "in the warm peace and harmony that characterizes this eighty-second day of the Great Crusade."

Then he analyzed the "string of unbroken victories" that the President had had in Congress.

"He has defeated the Republicans," said Johnson, "who wanted to repudiate our foreign policy.

"He has defeated the Republicans who wanted to cut taxes before balancing the budget.

"He has defeated the Republicans who wanted to reject "Chip" Bohlen* because of his association with John Foster Dulles.

"I expect to hear any day now that the President can muster a majority in the Senate. All he needs are two more Democratic seats."

He remarked that the President had gone ahead on his promise "to clean out the mess in Washington," and said that "we Democrats watched in awe as the Cadillacs replaced the Lincolns."

"We recalled," he said, "that the first Republican President, Abraham Lincoln, was famous for throwing out the generals. We were amazed when we saw a Republican general throwing out the Lincolns."

---

*American ambassador to the Soviet Union.

Then, referring to the election, he noted that the impression had been around last fall that taxes were going to be cut if the Republicans won, and the budget was going to be balanced.

"I do not say that any candidate, living or dead, successful or unsuccessful, really promised these things," he said.

"But I must say . . . that impression certainly got around among the voters.

"So what happened?

"Well, recently a famous statesman-general—newly elected to high office—declared, and I quote, 'If it weren't difficult, the budget would have been balanced long ago.'

"It's really been tough on the Democrats, Mr. President. We would like to be the loyal opposition. We have had no trouble being loyal. But you have made it almost impossible to be opposition.

"We thought we might blast some of your appointments, but some trigger-happy Republican always fired first.

"Nevertheless, the team is ready to go.

"The President has a secretary of state and a mutual security administrator anxious to negotiate a treaty with any foreign nation. Maybe some day they'll beat Senator McCarthy to it."

All was peace and harmony and unity, Johnson noted, and the Republicans were very well organized.

"Hardly a day passes," he said, "that the President doesn't find a new Republican party organized on his White House doorstep.

"They have the Republican party of President Eisenhower. They have the Republican party of Senator Taft. They have the Republican party of Senator Morse. And somewhere—way out behind the Chicago Tribune Tower—is the Republican party of Senator McCarthy, with one foot heavy in Greece and the other foot in Secretary Dulles' security files.

"It makes bipartisanship right difficult. We Democrats need to know which one of the Republican parties to be bipartisan *with* and which one of the Republican parties to be bipartisan *against*."

It was beautiful satire, directed to a Republican President who laughed as loudly about it as anyone else.

Then Johnson, quite seriously, and quite eloquently, stated his philosophy as the Democratic leader of the Senate.

"For the next four years President Eisenhower will be our

Commander-in-Chief, the only Commander-in-Chief we will have.

"Many things—things that are not pretty—could happen to us in those four years.

"We could lose our freedom to a foreign foe.

"We could lose our freedom by pitting American against American; neighbor against neighbor.

"Freedom is all that we have and all that we are—for this, all our exertions; for this, all our prayers.

"Freedom is being chipped away by the knives of malice; by infiltration; by irresponsibility.

"To protect freedom there is the government of the United States, and the government of the United States stands upon its three great pillars: a legislative that is a deliberative body and not a free-wheeling grand jury; a judiciary that determines the guilt or innocence of those accused of breaking the laws; an executive who conducts the business of the United States and its relations with foreign countries.

"If one of these pillars wages guerrilla warfare against the others, our freedoms are weakened. If one surrenders its rights and authority to another, our freedoms are gone.

"As Democrats we will oppose the President in principle when we think he is wrong. But as Americans we will reject the jungle tactics which seek to tear down the President by tearing down the institution of the Presidency.

"This, I believe, is the role of the opposition—to fight on principle, but to fight in a principled manner.

"There is also a role for the majority—to present a constructive program, to rally the people to its support, to lead the nation. Unless leadership flows from the constitutional leader, there will be a vacuum. Arrogant and selfish men will fill that vacuum. Our traditions of tolerance and our systems of checks and balances will be destroyed.

"To the President, so recently and gladly elected, to the President who once fought so nobly against a foreign enemy, we Democrats say:

"You have an opportunity unparalleled in our history. You have a resounding mandate from the people. Your administration is regarded with good will. Your political opposition is determined to be responsible.

"Ours is a nation of free people. Lead it to a future of ever-expanding peace and freedom, Mr. President, and your place in the heart of America will be secure forever."[1]

Johnson received a standing ovation. Most in the audience regarded this speech as an outstanding example of responsible opposition leadership.

The foreign affairs skit was set in a desert, where a party of State Department archeologists, headed by Secretary John Foster Dulles, were busy digging, "looking for a Republican foreign policy." They produced an array of bones and finally turned up the skull of a jackass. An impersonator of Secretary Dulles staggered back in dismay and sang a parody of "How Much Is That Doggie in the Window."

> How much does that fossil there remind me
> Of one that I knew months ago?
> How much do I wish someone would find me
> One that won't embarrass me so.
> I promised a trophy to the Senate,
> With teeth that were sharp and could bite;
> If I bring this thing or if I sent it,
> Then—John Foster Dulles, good night!

> I don't want a Yalta or Teheran,
> I don't want a Teddy's Big Stick.
> I don't want a Truman's red herrin',
> I want one that bites and can kick.
> What price for a policy that's hearty,
> A cross twixt the tiger and dove?
> A policy pleasing to McCarthy
> That Taft, Lodge and Bridges can love.

This was the time when the McCarthy investigation was digging into alleged Communist infiltration of the State Department. In the skit, characters representing Senator Joseph McCarthy and his colleague, Senator William E. Jenner, arrived on the scene. On behalf of McCarthy, Jenner sang an adaptation of "Don't Let the Stars Get in Your Eyes" to the archeologists.

> Don't let the State Department spies
> Pull any wool o'er your eyes.
> It's all a plot, so I'll put you wise;
> Don't let that Dulles fool you guys.
> So keep your trust in me,
> But if you don't agree
> Why, then my third degree will take you by surprise!

Too many thoughts,
Too much fair play,
Too much free speech will wreck your mind.
If you think I'm wrong,
Just where will you belong,
When my television cam'ra starts to grind.

"Senator Everett McKinley Dirksen" was the next arrival on the scene, and after some inquiry he announced that he didn't like what they were finding here, "all those old Acheson fossils." One of the diggers sang:

It will take more than a pack o' wild horses,
Pullin' and pushin', to give you your way.
That will take all sen-a-tor-i-al forces,
Even the Rooshin thinks your way will pay.

The skit ended with a song to the music of "I Believe," by an impersonator of Senator Alexander Wiley, chairman of the Senate Foreign Relations Committee:

We believe that freedom, peace and dignity,
Are man's estate.
We believe that truth and light and confidence
Will banish hate.
We believe that strength of men who would be free,
Forever lies in unity.
We believe.
We believe.
We believe that out of strife a peaceful world
Will come one day.
We believe that destiny has called this land,
To show the way.
Every time we feel the spell of men who try,
Whose faith is strong,
Whose hopes are high,
Then we know why
We believe.

The toast to the President was proposed and President Eisenhower responded extemporaneously with remarks that are recalled by those present as just as felicitous to Johnson and the Democrats as Johnson's were to him.

Except for a couple of Gridiron occasions, during his entire Presidency, Eisenhower spoke extemporaneously from very abbreviated notes, none of which exist in his papers at the Abilene

Library. Neither Mrs. Eisenhower nor the President's press secretary, James C. Hagerty, have any such notes or know of their location.

Partly because of their extemporaneous nature, Eisenhower's speeches, as recollected by Gridiron members present at the dinners, had a delightful quality of informality, mixed in with occasional serious thoughts about the foreign, economic and political problems of the country.

• • •

Before the December 12, 1953 dinner, President Eisenhower had repudiated Wisconsin Senator Joseph R. McCarthy and his "witch hunting" for Communists in government. He did so, not because of the purposes of the investigation, but primarily, because of Senator McCarthy's slam-bang methods.

Reference was made to this in the speech in the dark by Gridiron president Shoop.

"The Republicans promised they wouldn't turn back the clock. They haven't. The works are missing, that's why. The President and Secretary Dulles gave the works to Joe—in Wisconsin, at last!"

Then he took a crack at what many people regarded as the rather weak Eisenhower leadership of the Republican party.

"The Eisenhower team," he said, "has had its flashes of brilliance. The quarterback went to Ottawa and spoke to the Canadian parliament in French—thus confirming the suspicion that he has been calling the team's signals in some foreign language with no interpreter present. Then he went before the United Nations and spoke in all languages."

In the guest skit, Lyle C. Wilson and Walker S. Buel poked fun at the tendencies of Gridiron members to invite people in power rather than those out of power. Wilson announced that the vehicle for the stand-ups would be "a new look at politics and politicians through the unexplored medium of Three-D."

"Three-D!" said Buel in amazement. "You can't mean three Democrats. There aren't that many in this room."

There were. Wilson asked former Attorney General Homer S. Cummings, former Secretary of Commerce Jesse H. Jones, and former Postmaster General James A. Farley to stand.

They also took a swipe at Sherman Adams, head of President Eisenhower's White House staff, by simultaneously asking Mr. Adams and Joseph N. Pew, Jr. of Sun Oil to stand. "Just proves," commented Wilson, "that oil and ice water can mix."

The scene of the Democratic skit was a drugstore counter in Smalltown, U.S.A., where the citizens had gathered to discuss the sad case of "Miss Demmy," whose lover had gone away. The lover who had gone away was identified as "that city slicker who'd rather be bright than President," and "who had sure sweet-talked her in Chicago."

The city slicker, "A-da-lie," came on stage with his new girl friend, Miss Ada [Americans for Democratic Action], and sang a parody of "Bali Ha'i."

> Most people yearn for their former i-dol,
> Lost in the middle of a foggy sea.
> Most people long for another i-dol,
> One they know that he would like to be.
>
> A-da-lie may call you any night, any day.
> In your heart you'll hear him call you;
> Come away, come away.
> A-da-lie will whisper on the wind of the sea:
> "Here am I, your special i-dol!
> Come to me, come to me!"
>
> Some day you'll see me, floating o'er Chicago,
> My head sticking out from a low flying cloud.
> You'll hear me call you, singing in Chicago,
> Sweet and clear as can be.
> Come to me, here am I, come to me!
> Come to me, A-da-lie.

An impersonator of Senator Stuart Symington volunteered that if A-da-lie didn't want Demmy, he'd take her, whereupon a character representing Lyndon Johnson sang a parody of "You, You, You."

> Stu, Stu, Stu
> Symington, no one's like you,
> Male Missouri ingenue,
> Will you run, O, tell us, do!

Impersonators of Governor James F. Byrnes of South Carolina and a character identified as "Harry S., who has come all the way from Missouri," then rushed on the stage to defend Miss Demmy, who, they had heard, was being abused.

"Harry S." carried a shotgun, which he shook as he told A-da-lie, "You proposed to this woman, and by gollies, you're gonna marry her." A-da-lie pointed brightly to Miss Ada and said, "This one?" Whereupon Harry S. responded sharply, "No, not Miss Ada, this one."

He grabbed Miss Demmy's hand and was standing between A-da-lie and Miss Demmy when the orchestra softly began playing "Happy Days Are Here Again." The whole cast, including Harry S, was spellbound.

Then "Enoch Arden Roosevelt," Jr. came on stage and Miss Ada and Miss Demmy broke away and flew into his arms. Harry S., amazed, demanded to know who this fellow was, and Enoch replied, "I'm their first love come back to them." The skit closed with Enoch singing a new version of "Joshua Fit de Battle of Jericho."

> Roosevelt, Roosevelt, Roosevelt,
> Roosevelt, Roosevelt,
> And the votes come tumblin' down.

> Frank'll fight de battle ob Washington
> Washington, Washington,
> Frank'll fight de battle ob Washington,
> and de votes come tumblin' down.

> You may talk about yo' kings and emperors,
> You may talk about yo' man ob steel,
> Dere's none like our little Frankie
> at de battle ob Washington.

> Up to de walls ob Washington, he'll march
> wid spear in hand.
> "Go blow dem ram's horn," Frank'll cry,
> "kase de battle am in my hand."

Franklin Delano Roosevelt, Jr., representative in Congress from a New York congressional district, was the Democratic speaker. He tied his speech to the skit by saying he loved both Ada and Miss Demmy dearly, but that he wanted to set the record straight; he'd been married for the last five years "to the sweetest little congressional district this side of reapportionment."

"I'm no eligible bachelor and couldn't compete anyway with those other fellers—they're dark and handsome and, by heavens, tall too. Any one of them would make Ada and Miss Demmy a wonderful husband in '56. Also, I've got other wooing to do.

"If Tennyson's Enoch Arden had any idea that on his return home he would find himself in competition with the senior senator of a great state [a reference to the fact that the Republican speaker was to be Senator Knowland of California], in the presence of the chief justice of the United States, and the President, I guess he'd have stayed away for good.

"I am flattered, if somewhat abashed, to be the only Democrat asked to speak here tonight. To tell the truth, I am the only one they could get; the rest of the team, you should forgive the expression, is up in Philadelphia, trying to raise money. They seem to have picked the wrong place. Near as I can figure out from looking around, all the big money that's not in Texas is right here. Actually, I was a bit surprised when that Enoch Arden character turned up in the skit. Enoch Arden, you will remember, was supposed to be lost at sea and was missing for ten years when he made his reappearance. My goodness, does it seem like ten storm-tossed years since the Republicans took over?"

Then Roosevelt took a crack at his brother John, a Republican.

"There has always been some confusion in the mail room at 1600 Pennsylvania Avenue. Why, I can remember getting a letter from a girl who had met my brother John at a dance and she thought he was Franklin. After a while, John got tired of being taken for me, so he turned Republican."

Turning to the political situation in Washington, he noted that "we Democrats seem to spend an awful lot of our time debating with Republicans and sometimes with ourselves, but I must admit we've been drowned out lately by the brawls within the GOP. . . .

"We Democrats, too, I am proud to say—however sharp our disagreements with our political opponents may have been—do not let these disagreements affect our conviction that the interests of our whole country must come first [and] that America cannot go it alone.

"Yet you have heard cocksure voices raised lately in dispute of this basic principle. These are the voices of men who, out of ignorance or selfishness, would have us dismiss our allies, or debase them, or stand them in the corner like naughty school children who have disobeyed their master. When we treat our friends abroad with less than respect, our own dignity is tarnished. When we treat them unfairly, it is our own heritage of justice that suffers. When we treat them as subservient beings, it is our own freedom that is threatened. When we treat them like children, it is we who seem adolescent. If we lose them, it is we who are lost.

"It is a testimonial to the staunch American belief in the unfettered exchange of ideas—and even of jests—that on an occasion such as this, men of divergent views may differ with one another openly, not in a spirit of rancor but in a spirit of fair play, undismayed by the irresponsibles who confuse the difference and dissent of honest men with treason and disloyalty.

"Let us never lose sight of the fact that no matter how much we may disagree among ourselves, we must remain in our relations with the world one nation, indivisible, a nation unafraid, a nation that knows how to make and keep friends even as we advance, throughout the world, the peaceful influence of a strong America."[2]

President Eisenhower had recently made a visit to Mexico, so the Gridiron Club explained that they were transplanting the administration to that "happy land of Mañana," because its tempo seemed in conformity with the fulfillment of the administration program. The scene opened with "Secretary of Agriculture Ezra Taft Benson" sleeping peacefully outside a hut, where "Representative Daniel A. Reed" woke him up with the news that "we're in trouble." To the tune of "Mañana Is Soon Enough for Me," Reed sang:

> Our program isn't working, and we don't know what to do;
> The old umbrella seems to let a lot of water through.
> The leaders up in congress shout for action right away—
> We'll go to work *tomorrow*, but we really can't today!

> Our budget isn't balanced, but Ike doesn't seem to care,
> Our plans for cutting taxes are not getting anywhere.
> The Humphrey solid dollar will not buy a beefsteak now,
> But sometime in the future, we will fix it up somehow!

> Our Mister Ezra Benson and the farmers can't agree,
> The cowboys are yelling, just as mad as they can be;
> But give us just a little time—we cannot say just when—
> We'll surely please the farmers—if they'll only wait till then!

> Now there you have our story, it is easy to be told;
> We still are making studies how our program to unfold.
> Just wait until tomorrow, when we add up all the sums,
> Then you'll know what we're doing—if *tomorrow* ever comes!

The Republicans in New York had been having trouble, and one of them, a former state chairman, had been sentenced to the state prison at Danemorra. This was the cue for an impersonator of Dewey to sing:

How are things in Danemorra?
Are the party leaders calling there?
Do they still run down to see their friends
Through iron bars,
Or do they longer dare?
How are things in Danemorra,
Are the politicians meeting there?

This was about as subtle as a Caterpillar earth mover, but it did point out, with less than the usual Gridiron obliqueness, a serious Republican embarrassment.

"Senator Joseph R. McCarthy" then strode in to explain what was wrong with the administration. It couldn't even count telegrams. Directly to President Eisenhower, who had denounced him, he sang his advice to the tune "I'm Walking behind You."

I'll sometimes support you,
I'll sometimes stand by,
But voices are calling
For me to climb high.
I'll never forget you,
You're much on my mind;
Look over your shoulder,
I'm walking behind!

The skit ended with "William F. Knowland," the Senate Republican leader, saying that they couldn't "get me in the dog house as long as I have that man in the White House," and in a parody of "I'll Get By," he sang again directly to President Eisenhower:

Senators crave for power,
But if you will say I'm fine,
Whatever they say, whatever they do,
I'll keep them in line,
　　For—

I'll get by, as long as I have you.
Though there is Morse, and Capehart too,
I'll hold the fort, I'll see it through.
Senators may roar at me, that's true,
But what care I, say,
I'll get by,
As long as I have you!

The dinner closed with a foreign affairs skit, traditional at that time. The scene was in Bermuda at a Big Three Conference between Secretary of State Dulles, Britain's Foreign Minister Anthony Eden, and France's Foreign Minister Georges Bidault.

The announcer explained that "at this enchanted island, frolicking among the Frangipanis, are 275 newspaper correspondents, 107 radio commentators, 23 television crews, and—oh yes—some diplomats."

"Dulles," "Anthony Eden," and "Georges Bidault" entered, shook hands, and sang:

> Three of us! Three of us!
> Small exclusive coterie of us.
> World-wide crises are the misery of us,
> Yet the three of us must solve them all alone.
>
> Glorious! Glorious!
> Winnie wishes there were four of us,
> Glory be that there are no more of us!
> Cause the three of us can louse it up alone!

"Prime Minister Louis St. Laurent" of Canada, accompanied by "Lester Pearson," entered, and Pearson demanded that the Big Three be increased to the Big Seven, and that there should be included Quebec, Saskatchewan, Medicine Hat and Igor Gouzenko.* St. Laurent sang:

> It's beginning to look too much like Christmas
> Everywhere we go.
> For there's Ike in a grand hotel,
> Winston, Monsieur Laniel,
> There's Foster D. and Eden and Bidault.
> It's beginning to look too much like Christmas,
> As the Big Three steal the show,
> But a lovelier sight you'll see
> When we add our four to three
> In the far north snow!

Dulles responded that he had a tip that a fourth was about to arrive—Santa Claus. The Santa Claus proved to be Georgi Malenkov, Stalin's successor, dressed up as Santa Claus but with two pistols at his belt. The chorus fell back in dismay and sang:

> Dashing through the snow
> In a lend-lease Chevrolet,
> Clad in *status quo*,
> Jeering all the way;

---

*Cipher clerk in a Soviet embassy, whose defection to Canada with a briefcase full of secret documents caused quite a stir.

Bells no longer ring,
Making spirits bright,
How dull it is to jest and sing
Of a man who is always right.

"Malenkov" announced that he was the spirit of Christmas.
"To war mongering, ruling circles, I bring the gift of peace—at
my price. But who are these members of the leisure class not
fulfilling their norms?"

"These, Santa Claus," said Bidault, "are representatives of
the corrupt western allies. These gentlemen are consuming their
expense accounts and their per diems."

"Bourgeoisie! Fascist pigs! Counter-revolutionists! Lucky
dogs!" loudly sighed the envious Malenkov.

They then proceeded to talk about the joint communique
and ended up with one of the diplomats singing:

We're dreaming of a bright Christmas,
Just like the ones we used to know,
When the bells were ringing,
And choirs were singing,
Of peace on earth to men below.
We're dreaming of a bright Christmas,
When ev'ry fear is put to flight,
And the dawn of freedom's in sight,
That's our wish for Christmas-tide tonight!

This was the end of the skit, the toast was drunk to President
Eisenhower, and his extemporaneous response closed the dinner.

• • •

Two regular dinners a year, which had been feasible in the
days of a quieter Washington, had become too onerous for the
fifty active members of the Gridiron Club to prepare and stage,
so in 1954 they decided to revert to one full-scale dinner a year
and substitute for the other one a private dinner for Gridiron
members only, plus a few guests invited by the Club. The first of
these small dinners was held on April 10, and was in honor of the
congressional leaders of both parties.

The entertainment consisted largely of the chorus re-singing
some of the better Gridiron songs that had been used in past
dinners and which were applicable to guests who were present.

There were no original skits produced, and the major
speeches, in a typical Gridiron twist, were made by Senator

Everett M. Dirksen, Republican of Illinois, who spoke on "The Future of the Democratic Party," and by Senator Stuart Symington, Democrat of Missouri, who spoke on "The Future of the Republican Party" and said he was sure the party had a future "provided the voters forget the past."

The only other speaker was Arthur Krock, who was again called upon to address himself to the sins and virtues of the Gridiron Club.

He described the "power" and "tyranny" exercised by Gridiron presidents and said that "many long years under this oppression enabled me to give you the explanation."

"The outrage, and the submissiveness with which it is accepted," he said, "are attained by tyrannies expressed through censorship of talent, favoritism in the casting of the actors and the singers, and monopoly of the song-writing—these in addition to the rewards and punishments of offices given and withheld by the hard-hearted cabal that runs the Gridiron Club. And, piled like Ossa on Pelion, is the final cruelty of rewriting the skits submitted by the rank-and-file. This can be positively Florentine in its malevolence."

He told how under one Gridiron administration one of his skits had been turned over for rewriting "to a beardless boy of forty-five or so, a syndicated writer of humorless humor—and he bollixed it up—but good! And the one member who ventured to join me in protest was assigned thereafter to play female parts exclusively."

Formats similar to this have been followed for the small dinners from that time on.

• • •

The major dinner, held December 11, 1954, was opened by Gridiron President Marshall McNeil of Scripps Howard. He began by commenting on the "confusion of a nation dedicated to the proposition that the Senate can survive half Lyndon Johnson and half Bill Knowland . . . half-hearted and half-cocked."

"Old Guard Republicans," he said, "are trying to elbow their way back into power. But Democrats say they are more to be pitied than censured.

"Censure—that's when Joe writes on his slate, 'I love me, Joe; I'm only a loud-mouthed kid.' "

But, following the formula of many Gridiron speeches, a few gibes, a little raillery, and then a serious note at the end, McNeil used his close to pay tribute to President Eisenhower.

"Seriously," he said, "we meet at a solemn time. The Free

World has full notice that this nation starts from strength, remains strong and continues toward but one single unchangeable goal—world peace.

"We have at the helm a man who gets humanly angry at the irritations, the below-the-belt punches from Peking and Moscow, but whose temper cannot be carelessly aroused—a man who knows war, won a war, and with God's blessing will keep us out of another."

This was followed by the Marine Band, which McNeil noted was "for sixty-five years first in war, first in peace and first on the program at Gridiron dinners."*

Averell Harriman had just been elected governor of New York, and the scene for the Democratic skit was "Harriman's Hideaway" in the Sun Valley resort owned by the Union Pacific Railroad. Harriman's father had been one of the creators of the resort and the Harriman family still held substantial interests in the railroad.

The scene opened with the Speaker-to-be of the new Democratic Congress, "Sam Rayburn," and "Lyndon Johnson" together on the stage with a Union Pacific porter. Johnson and Rayburn were dressed in skiing costumes, and the porter told them how fine they looked.

Both were angry and said they wouldn't be caught dead in such outfits in Texas, but the porter told them how "Mr. Averell" had gone to Moscow and captured Russia, and to Yalta and captured Yalta, and that just last month he had captured New York, and now he planned to capture the whole Democratic party.

"Yeah," said Rayburn scornfully, "but he ain't captured me and Lyndon," to which the porter replied, "Well, he got you and Mr. Lyndon in them monkey suits, ain't he?"

"Harriman" and the chorus entered to the music of "Hernando's Hideaway," and Harriman sang:

> This is the place where Democrats
> Can laugh and play like plutocrats,
> And even meet some diplomats,
> We call it Averell's Hideaway . . . O-lay!
>
> Way out here in Idaho,
> Our Ave has lots and lots of dough,
> And we can help him watch it go,
> Out in our Averell's hideaway . . . O-lay! *(Castanets)*
>
> If you're tired of politicians pounding at your door *(Castanets)*

---

*The band was led by Col. William F. Santelmann and played "The Gridiron March."

Of if the common man is something of a bore *(Castanets)*
Then if you come to the spot where all is peace and joy,
You may not crave . . . to gaze at Ave,
But he's our boy!

And the chorus came in at this point:

He may not be so eloquent,
He may have won by accident,
He thinks he MIGHT be President,
And that's our Averell's hideaway . . . O-lay!

"Carmine DeSapio," leader of Tammany Hall, had brought a political brother act to Sun Valley. He asked "G. Mennen ('Soapy') Williams," who had just been elected to his fourth term as governor of Michigan, to tell them about it, and Williams sang:

Frankie and Jimmy were brothers,
Oh, what a couple of kids.
Frankie was aimed for the White House,
When his career hit the skids.
He had a plan. He's an also ran.

Tammany didn't like Frankie,
And Frankie said he didn't care.
He said his initials were F.D.R.,
But, that Tiger wouldn't scare.
Frank had his plan, now he's an also ran.

Jimmy, the brother of Frankie,
Wandered around for a spell.
Jimmy was loyal to Jimmy,
Jimmy sure wished Jimmy well.
Jim was Jim's man. Jim has him a plan.

Jim got elected to Congress,
He wants to be Governor soon.
He says his initials ain't F.D.R.,
But he sings that Roosevelt tune.
Jim's got a plan for Jimmy's favorite man.

This is the end of Frank's story.
This is the start of Jim's song.
Frankie is out in the dog house.
Jimmy may be there ere long.
What is a Plan, without their old man?

"Governor James F. Byrnes" of South Carolina arrived on the scene, accompanied by an impersonator of his "write-in winner," Senator-elect J. Strom Thurmond.

Harriman laughed that off. "We didn't realize so many in South Carolina could write."

Byrnes restrained Thurmond and asked him not to answer, because "the Southern governors who came with us will tell him where we learned to write."

This was the year the Supreme Court had issued its first desegregation decision, and the Dixie governors and Thurmond sang:

> We're dreaming of a white schoolhouse
> Just like the ones we used to know.
> Before integration in education
> Laid our dear traditions low.
>
> We're dreaming of a white schoolhouse,
> Nuts to our party in the north;
> We would rather throw a campaign
> Than pollute our lily-white domain.

"Senator Hubert Humphrey" protested and appealed to Lyndon Johnson to "kick these guys out," but "Patrick McNamara," newly elected senator of Michigan, stepped forward with another idea and sang:

> Me name is McNamara,
> I'm the leader of the band.
> Although we fear the recounts,
> We're the finest in the land.
> We play for jobs and taxes
> And the creeping welfare state,
> And when we march on Washington
> We play both loud and late.
>
> Right now we are rehearsin'
> For a very swell affair,
> The ann-yul clip and shearin'
> Of every millionaire.
> When General Mills and Motors howl,
> They tear and rend the land,
> They say, we never saw the like of McNamara's band.

Rayburn thought the party needed a good piano player, and Johnson commented wistfully that there must be somebody besides Harry who could play the piano. All the lights were dimmed, and to tinkling piano notes from the orchestra, "Adlai Stevenson," made up to resemble Liberace, came in with two attendants who placed candelabras on the piano. Stevenson played a few notes and rose to sing his version of "I'll Be Seeing You," somewhat prophetically for 1956:

You'll be seeing me in all the old familiar places,
With my wit and charm and graces polished new,
Loved in Harvard's yard and on the boulevard,
Admired in old back bay and also by the ADA.

You'll be seeing me on every lovely rampart gay,
My every fight's a matinee,
With spirit born of old croquet.
You'll find me on the campaign stump and at the jubilee,
You'll be searching for new stars,
But you'll be seeing me.

Governor Williams was introduced at the end of the skit to speak for the Democrats, but no copy of his speech is in the Gridiron files.

The Republican skit was set at President Eisenhower's farm at Gettysburg, Pennsylvania, where the Republicans had gathered for discussion of their problems and prospects. "Speaker Joseph W. Martin," who was to lose his Speakership the next month as the Democrats took over both Houses of Congress, opened the act by singing:

This ole house has gotten shaky,
Shakin' out the GOP
This ole house was home and comfort
When we fought for liberty.
This ole house once rang with laughter
At the sound of roll-call bells,
Now it trembles in the darkness
At the sound of rebel yells.

Ain't a-gonna lead this house no longer,
Ain't a-gonna lead this house no more,
No more goin' to bang the gavel,
No more goin' to rule the floor.
No more goin' to run the business,
Democrats will have the say,
Ain't gonna lead this house no longer—
I'm a-gettin' ready for judgment day!

A Gridiron member, acting the part of Senator Everett M. Dirksen, who was rising to leadership in his party, summed up the Republican problem in a song directed to President Eisenhower at the head table:

If we ever needed you, we need you now;
I can't remember when we've ever been so blue.
If we ever needed help, we need it now.
We feel so all alone, we don't know what to do.
Before election day,
You seemed so far away,
You say "cooperate," but that's not new.
It has never worked before—
We don't know how—
If we ever needed you, we need you now!

A character impersonating Sherman Adams, assistant to the President, undertook to explain how President Eisenhower reacted on the congressional election night and told the audience what he had heard him say on that historic evening:

I'm all alone here this ev'ning,
All alone, calling you,
Asking *where* you vote, and *how* you vote,
And *will* you vote straight tickets too!

A character representing James Hagerty, press secretary to Eisenhower, was asked to tell the group what President Eisenhower's *real* reaction was to the congressional election.

"As usual," he replied, "I can tell you what I *think* the President *thinks*. This is released for direct quotation from Mr. Eisenhower."

And in a parody of "Gee, I Wish I Was Back in the Army," he sang:

In nineteen-fifty-two, I thought that I was through
With all the heavy cares of storm and strife.
I thought that politics had lots of happy tricks—
But after months of tough civilian life—

Gee, I wish I was back in the army,
I'd like to hang my homburg on the wall,
Walk with a snap, in my five-star cap,
Uniforms in winter, spring and fall.
There's a lot to be said for the army,
A life without responsibility.
But now when I get stuck, I'm really out of luck,
There's simply no one higher up where I can pass the buck—
Oh, Gee, I wish I was back in the army!

The Gridiron program closed with the traditional foreign affairs skit. An announcer pointed out that "since he was sworn in, Mr. John Foster Dulles has been up in the air more than any other secretary of state," and that he had already flown a record-breaking 376,000 miles.

"It has seemed only sensible, therefore," he continued, "to move the State Department from Foggy Bottom to the National Airport—and off we go!"

The band struck up the Air Force song, while the principals and chorus moved onto the stage, and "Herbert Hoover, Jr.," under secretary of state, stepped forward and sang, to the tune of "Dawn":

> The squawk-box is sounding its warning,
> To waken Attaches from sleep;
> The clock stands at six in the morning,
> The sun lightens jet plane and jeep.
> The code clerk deciphers the cable,
> The Chargé his chapeau has doffed,
> We're diplomats willing and able,
> To write our dispatches aloft.
> When we're away we're up there trying,
> When we're at work, we're far out of sight;
> When we're away our program is flying,
> When we are near even Knowland seems bright.

There was a sound of airplanes overhead, and as it ceased, "Dulles" came in breathlessly and gave "an agonizing reappraisal of his experiences as a Happy Wanderer."

> They call me Faster Foster now,
> The dullest man can see
> That as I wing across the world,
> They all give in to me.
>
> Bases here, dollars there,
> Atoms free, wait and see.
> Co-exist—they all give in to me.
>
> A real slap-happy diplomat,
> I fly the con-frence track.
> And as I fly,
> I love to tote
> The whole world on my back.
>
> I am your foreign minister
> As foreign as can be.
> I'm never home,
> I always roam
> O'er every shining sea.

Bases here, dollars there,
Atoms free, wait and see.
Co-exist—o'er every shining sea.

"William F. Knowland," Republican leader of the Senate, entered and to the tune of "Lullaby of Broadway" he warned them all against the "Russian Lullaby."

Every day they croon to you
That Russian lullaby,
Every day the same old tune,
That Moscow alibi.
Dream of peace, they tell you,
False hope they sell you,
There's no recall for those who fall
For a Russian lullaby.

There was a whirr of airplanes again, and this time it was "Malenkov" from Moscow and "Mao Tse-tung" from Peking who had come on behalf of the Russian and Chinese people to make protest.

"We protest," said Malenkov, "that we are the only statesmen in the world Mr. Dulles has not visited."

This was back in the days of the Cold War, and Dulles replied to them, "You know you're not on my calling list." He asked an impersonator of Admiral Arthur W. Radford, chairman of the Joint Chiefs of Staff, to tell them why, and Radford closed the program by singing:

Hey, there, you with the wars in your eyes,
Peace you can't take away from us.
For once, can't you be wise.

Stop, there, Red in the tall Kremlin tow'r,
Don't ever think we're soft again,
Or atoms our only power.

Better forget it.

We have the ships and the air,
We have marines and army, too,
And back of them our will to do.

Won't you take the advice I hand you and all others:
In our might we have but one aim,
And if you will make yours the same,
We can keep this old world at peace
And live like brothers.

At the invitation of the Gridiron president, the entire group rose and drank a toast to the President of the United States, after which Eisenhower responded extemporaneously.

• • •

The dinner on May 7, 1955 celebrated the seventieth anniversary of the Gridiron Club, and the technique for the inauguration skit for its president that year consisted of a group of Washington sightseers on the Gridiron stage, whose guide, after commenting on various other Washington phenomena, took the crowd to Washington's Foggy Bottom district, where he told the group the president used to play as a boy.

"Which president?" someone wanted to know.

The guide turned nonplussed to the head table, and President Eisenhower, who had been prompted about the skit beforehand, answered, "Everybody knows that. It was Edward T. Folliard of the *Washington Post*, the president of the Gridiron Club."

Folliard, in his speech in the dark, noted that in this spring of 1955 President Eisenhower was looking hopefully to the Far East, but that "some of his Republicans on the Hill are not very happy. Senator Knowland and others say that the only thing we have to fear is peace itself.

"That's the way things are going around here," Folliard continued. "The Democrats are afraid to attack the President, and the Republicans are afraid to support him."

He noted that in this country we'd lost interest in Red-hunts, "but that hasn't stopped the Democrats," he said. "They turned to Wall Street and investigated prosperity."

The scene for the Democratic skit was set in Never-Never Land, where the announcer said, "You will now see Peter Pan Harriman. He has flown down from Albany to teach these hopeful but still earthbound Democrats how to take wing and soar."

"Harriman" was pushed on stage in a baby buggy by "Perle Mesta," and behind him came prancing, costumed as the pirates of Never-Never Land, a group led by "Captain Hook Truman."

"I'll mow 'em down," shouted Captain Hook. "I'll pour it on. I'll give 'em hell. Just like '48. And here's my man!"

His man was pirate "Adlai Stevenson," who sang:

Mister Truman, you've got a dream
Of an election that's right on the beam.
But I don't know that I'd be in clover—
Perhaps the time for me to run is over.

Yes, no—what shall I do?
Whether to wisecrack, or to look blue?
So turn on your magic gleam,
Mister Truman, go on and dream!

Then Captain Hook presented another Democrat whom "you could teach to fly, Peter Pan. He's a Texas pirate who operates three miles offshore."

Mrs. Mesta introduced him: "You don't mean Larrupin' Lyndon Johnson, the marginal Democrat from Texas?" And the character representing Johnson responded with a paraphrasing of "The Surrey with the Fringe on Top."

Speaker Sam must watch, look and listen,
After all this party ain't his'n,
I just live by one proposition,
I'm the man on top.

In his House the boys always mutter,
Senate loyalties never flutter,
Unity's our theme, full and utter, to the Man on Top.

I stand near center, neither left nor right
And tread on nobody's bunions,
I rally my troops, but I'd rather not fight.
At stalling I sure know my onions.

This boy here is wheelin' and dealin'
Fifty-six will be most appealin'
Course right now I must be concealin'
That I'd like to swap
The Democratic leadership for one job—on top!

Another of the pirates was "Carmine De Sapio," who had been one of the principal figures in putting Harriman into the governor's office in New York. He sang a parody based on "The Ballad of Davy Crockett."

Got him elected with some votes to spare,
Ditched young Roosevelt to clear the air.
This railroad man's got political flair,
Especially since he's a millionaire.

I got the delegates, he's got the dough,
Forget about Yalta, say he didn't go.
Albany's behind him, I'll make him grow,
I teach him easy, but he learns so slow.

And the chorus chimed in:

Carmine, Carmine De Sapio,
Chief of Tammany Hall.

"Senator Estes Kefauver," costumed in Daniel Boone attire and carrying a rifle, was brought forth to sing, as "a leftover from the 1952 convention."

I'm wild again, beguiled again,
But when it's time, I will be filed again,
Bewitched, bothered and bewildered am I.

Another of the aspirants was "Mayor Robert F. Wagner" of New York City, who sang:

Sincerely, oh, yes, sincerely,
I'm forever for you, Adlai,
You're first—after me.

Harriman announced that he'd teach them all how to fly. "It's simple," he said. "You take a million dollars—and just spread it out like this."

He spread out his arms, which raised up diaphanous wings with dollar signs affixed. Then, mounting a small platform and posing, he waved his wings gently and cried out, "I fly! I fly!"

Whereupon he fell flat on his face. As he got up, Captain Hook said, "That's all right, Peter Pan Harriman. A good flight is one you can walk away from. We'll outfly those snollygosters yet. They think they can win next year with Ike and a tax cut. We'll win with Nobody and a bigger tax cut. You tell 'em, Speaker Sam Rayburn."

And "Rayburn" closed the act by singing: to the tune of "The Darktown Strutters' Ball":

We'll be down to get you with a tax cut, brother,
We'll dish it out, I'm here to state,
So sorry to be late;
But we'll produce before the campaign's rollin'.
Remember when you get it, brother,
The Democrats were on the ball.
We may get George Humphrey's goat,
But we'll win that White House vote
With that free-for-nothin' dough for one and all.

There was much speculation at the time whether President Eisenhower would run for reelection the following year. There had also been newspaper stories about a squirrel running across a green and disrupting Eisenhower's putt on the White House lawn. Therefore, the scene for the Republican skit was a putting green on the south lawn. The flag on the pin said '56.

"Senator Knowland" had called a special meeting of the greens committee to look into the squirrel problem. The committee consisted of various Republican leaders, and the skit began with an impersonator of James C. Hagerty carrying the President's message to the squirrels in song:

> A little grass that slowly grows and grows,
> Not some that comes and goes,
> That's all I want from you.
> A sunny day, upon the White House ground,
> A putt that goes right down,
> That's all I want from you.
> Don't spoil my score, I like to putt with care;
> And at the nineteenth hole, I want some time to spare.
> Don't spoil my game, and squirrels, keep away—
> I may not stay here long, upon this lawn to play.
> A little grass that slowly grows and grows,
> Not some that comes and goes,
> That's all I want from you!

Knowland, ambitious for the Presidency himself, remarked that he wanted the President "to have just what he wants—down Gettysburg way," where the President had bought a farm to which he liked to go occasionally on weekends. Then he sang:

> How'm I gonna keep him down on the farm,
> After he's seen D.C.?
> How'm I gonna keep him from his stag dinners,
> Folks with big names, and opening games?
> How'm I gonna keep him down on the farm
> Far from Burning Tree?
> He soon won't want to see a rake or plow;
> And who can use a niblick on a cow?
> How'm I gonna keep him down on the farm,
> And leave a chance for me?

"Leonard Hall, "chairman of the Republican National Committee, decided he ought to address some remarks to every *good* Republican, and "most of them," he said, "are right here in this room." To them he sang:

> We need lots of money,
> We're in an awful fix.
> It's sure to cost a-plenty
> If we win in fifty-six.

So join the party angels
If you're well supplied with tin,
Just open up your hearts and let the sunshine in!

So let the dough roll in,
Give it with a grin,
Spenders never lose and tight-wads never win.
So let the clouds roll by,
Let the sunshine in—
Open up your hearts and let the dough roll in!

This skit ended with "Governor Goodwin Knight" of California asking an actor impersonating Vice President Nixon "what would happen if President Eisenhower did not run again?"

"I've given that quite a little thought," answered Nixon. "I'll express my ideas right to the President himself." Then he parodied "After You've Gone":

Now won't you listen to us while we say
How could you tell us that you're goin' away
And leave the GOP without a nominee?
You know we've backed you well since fifty-two,
Backed you night and day.
How could you leave us now when we ask you,
"Please don't go astray"?

After you've gone, if we should break up,
After you've gone, you're gonna wake up.
GOP might name *me*,
And what a party prospect that would be!
There'll come a time, now don't forget it,
There'll come a time when you'll regret it.
Some day in some November,
The pleas of GOP's you all will remember,
Only too late,
After you've gone away!

The foreign affairs skit was set on the summit of Mount Everest, with the cast costumed in parkas with fur-trimmed hoods, and carrying ropes and ski poles. The exploratory Big Four talks were under way at this conference at the summit.

One of the characters wanted to know what "we are doing up so high," and "Senator Walter George," chairman of the Senate Foreign Relations Committee, replied, "We went to Yalta and gave away Asia. We went to Potsdam and gave away Europe. There just ain't much left below timber-line."

A newsboy came through shouting, "The Daily Leak, the Daily Leak! Get the inside secrets of the Everest conference!"

"Molotov," the Russian Foreign Minister, came pushing through the crowd, announcing that Marshal Georgi Zhukov was the fastest climber and said, "Tell 'em how you feel about the American President, Zooky."

"Zhukov" sang:

Don't throw bouquets at me,
Don't praise my name too much,
Don't boast of my fame too much,
People will say we're in love.
Don't take my part too much,
Your rank was so like mine,
Your stars shouldn't glow like mine,
People will say we're in love.
Don't start suggesting things,
Give me my sword and my glove,
Khrushchev—he's suspecting things,
Praaaavda will say we're in love.

Harold Stassen had been appointed special assistant to the President with cabinet rank, to direct studies of United States and world disarmament.

This placed him in a position to offer rather generous aid to countries which cooperated. An impersonator of Stassen came on the scene and sang:

Everything is rosy, I work night and day,
I have the most fun, giving things away.
Once I was lonely, friends I had not,
Then I pulled the lever on the old jack pot!

They call me generous Hal,
A liberal sort of a pal,
With a smile that is sunny
And a pot-full of money,
That's your pal, Hal.
For ev'ry one there's enough,
We will write it down on the cuff,
From far lands they holler,
They like Yankee dollar
From their pal, Hal.

As characters representing Chou En-lai, Anthony Eden, and Secretary Dulles came on the scene, Senator George expressed his surprise that Dulles was using snowshoes.

"You have a hard enough time covering your tracks as it is," he said.

"Herbert Hoover, Jr." protested, "Now don't be too hard on the secretary. He has just come from a meeting of the National Security Council. They took a great step toward peace.

"What did they do?" asked Senator George.

"We adjourned," replied Dulles.

Eden suggested that Chou En-lai and Secretary Dulles discuss the situation and they did, in song:

Dulles:

    I could be happy with you, Chou.
    If you could be happy with me.
    I'd be contented to give up Matsu,
    That's what I'd do,
    Would Knowland do it too?

Chou:

    I could do business with you, John.
    For one thing's as clear as can be.

Both:

    I know that I could be happy with you, my darling,
    If you'd give Formosa to me.

Eden commented that they were making progress: "We're getting nowhere faster than expected. Let's issue the final communique."

And "Henry Cabot Lodge," ambassador to the United Nations, called on "Secretary General Dag Hammarskjold" to issue it:

    There's a bright golden haze on the mountain.
    There's a bright golden haze on the mountain.
    Can this light signify
    That mankind will not die?
    Is it writing a message of peace in the sky?
    Oh, what a beautiful morning,
    Oh what a beautiful day.
    I got a beautiful feeling
    Peace, now, is coming our way.

    Now the shadows will flee with the sunrise.
    Now the shadows will flee with the sunrise.
    The war flags are furled,
    And the hopes of the world
    Are as bright as the light

That the sun's rays have hurled.
Oh, what a beautiful morning,
Oh what a beautiful day.
I got a wonderful feeling
Peace, now, is coming our way.

The dinner ended with the toast to the President and President Eisenhower's extemporaneous response.

• • •

Considerable light is thrown on President Eisenhower's reactions to the dinner and some individuals, in a memorandum for the Gridiron records written immediately afterward by Gridiron President Folliard, relating his conversations with President Eisenhower during the dinner.

Folliard told how he had met the President at the side entrance to the Statler Hotel and escorted him to the Continental Room for a predinner drink with other head table guests. When the signal came to move in to the head table, the other guests moved on and Folliard remained with the President. He told him that he might be interested to know that the other speakers were Governor Averell Harriman for the Democrats and Governor Goodwin Knight for the Republicans.

"Ike said something about political speakers being all right," says the memorandum, "except that they were too brutal. I didn't catch his words exactly, but what he then said was engraved on my mind.

" 'Now you take Truman,' Ike said. 'He invited me to run for President twice and for Vice President once, and yet he accused me (in 1952) of trying to misrepresent things, of saying things that weren't so. What do you think of that?'

" 'Well,' I said, 'I think you and Mr. Truman have different codes.'

" 'I'll say so,' said Ike."

They moved on into the banquet hall as the Marine Band orchestra played "Hail to the Chief." Then the full Marine Band came in for its march-on.

"Ike," said Folliard, "was as much thrilled by the march-on of the Marine Band as anybody in the hall. He drummed on the table in time with the music.

"He was fascinated by the Seventieth Anniversary seating chart prepared by George Rothwell Brown. He went along looking at Cliff Berryman's cartoons of the notables who had been club guests over the years, and paused over the sketch of Theodore Roosevelt.

" 'I've heard he raised hell here one night and broke up the dinner.' Ike said.

"I told him what I knew of the brawl between T.R. and Senator Joe Foraker, and promised to send him an account of it, as given by Sam Blythe at a 1931 dinner. . . .*

"Ike talked a good part of the time to Chief Justice Warren, addressing him as 'Earl.' But he also paid close attention to the skits.

"After Harriman spoke for the Democrats, Ike said he thought Averell had done pretty well—that is, after he got going. He was referring to the last part of the talk, in which Harriman spoke up for bi-partisanship in foreign policy.

"Ike was delighted by an entertainment skit, which was a broadcast of bits and pieces from his recorded press conferences.

" 'Where in the world did you get that stuff?' he asked.

"I explained that NBC got it up, and told him that it was not supposed to make him look good.

" 'You don't have to tell me that,' he said, and laughed heartily.

"Ike ate like a horse, cleaning up everything put in front of him. However, he turned all of his wine glasses upside down—all, that is, except one. Toward the end, when the time was nearing for him to speak, he accepted a glass of champagne. Having drunk it, he asked for seconds, and I had to ask Robert, the Maitre d', to chase after the bottle and bring it back.

"Ike showed that he was thoroughly familiar with the pattern of the Gridiron dinner. When Walker Buel and Lyle Wilson walked onto the stage for the guest skit, he turned to Chief Justice Warren and said, 'This will be good.'

"The line he enjoyed most was the one inspired by the death of Colonel Robert McCormick of the *Chicago Tribune*. Three Tribune officials were asked to stand, and then Wilson said, 'They are not running for President, but for Colonel.'

"Ike said, 'That's the best yet.'

"Ike was all attention when the curtain went up on the Republican skit. At this point, as usual, our guests swung around to see how he was going to 'take it.' The song he seemed to enjoy most was the one sung by a character portraying Senator Bill Knowland, who, everybody knew, was watering at the mouth for the Presidency and was hoping that Ike would forego a second-term race and retire to his Gettysburg farm."

---

*See pages 50-54.

'After the chorus had sung the "How'm I gonna keep him down on the farm" song, Folliard reported that "Ike leaned over toward Vice President Nixon and myself, laughed, and said, 'I assure you, that would be easy.'

"Looking back, I'm glad I didn't take that literally.

"Ike was delighted by Goodie Knight's speech poking fun at the Democrats. It was clear that he thought Knight had taken Honest Ave, [Averell Harriman] and I suppose he had.

"Ike's attitude changed when the foreign affairs skit came on. He stopped talking, and followed every song closely. He seemed to be charmed by Zhukov and the song, 'Don't Throw Bouquets at Me.'

"But he was most moved by the curtain song, the parody on 'Oh, What a Beautiful Morning,' as sung by Gene Archer. . . .

"In a moment of soaring optimism (unfounded, as it turned out), I said, 'Mr. President, I don't know about you, but I believe that song.'

" 'I do, too, Eddie,' Ike said. 'That's what I tried to tell you fellows at the press conference.'

"A moment later he said, 'You know, pessimism has never yet won a battle, in war or in peace.'

"The Summit Meeting at Geneva was then being arranged. There is no doubt that he had convinced himself that Khrushchev and Company were ready to do business with the West. As it turned out, of course, he was wrong."[3]

• • •

James C. Hagerty was one of the most competent press secretaries the White House had ever had, and he was also one whom the newspapermen liked and respected greatly. Consequently, the small December 1955 dinner was in honor of Hagerty, and it was notable primarily for a speech by Clark M. Clifford, who for five years was special counsel to President Truman and was later to be secretary of defense in the Johnson cabinet, and one of the real wits in the Democratic party. A portion of this speech was given at the end of Chapter One.

Clifford also paid a high tribute to Hagerty:

"The best White House press secretary I ever knew was Charlie Ross, a sincere, honest, greatly beloved man. Honesty prompts me to state, however, that that accolade must now be bestowed upon Jim Hagerty. You have brought dignity, skill and fairness to a difficult task and your handling of the unfortunate developments of these last weeks has been nothing short of monumental. [He was referring to the situation after President Eisenhower had had his first heart attack.] I honor you, Jim, for the great service you have rendered to the American people."

• • •

The Gridiron dinner of May 12, 1956 was the first time that President Eisenhower had gone to any dinner outside the White House since his heart attack in 1955.

Gridiron president Roscoe Drummond, then head of the *New York Herald Tribune* bureau, took note of this in his opening remarks in the speech in the dark.

"I know that I speak for this distinguished assemblage," he said, "in saying, in your behalf and mine, that President Eisenhower's continued health and vigor is something we all, regardless of party, prayerfully cherish."

But from that point on, the Gridiron style took over, as he pointed out that "surely the President must be very pleased tonight to see among us so many fine conservative humanitarians, those Republicans eager to march forward with Eisenhower—protesting every step of the way."

As to the Republican party, Drummond commented that "all the Republicans know what they want—just an unshakable grip on those coattails, and then they can soar above principle."

Directing his wit toward the Democrats, he noted that moderation was the spirit of the times, and that Adlai Stevenson had openly visited the Guggenheim estate in Georgia to shoot quail.

"In the old days the New Deal candidate would have given the estate to the birds—and shot the Guggenheims."

Referring to the internal Democratic problems, he commented that half the Democratic party was intent on secession. "The other half seems to prefer suicide. Republicans say that if the Democratic politicians were laid end to end—they would point in all directions."

Since the party conventions were only a short time in the future, it was natural that the skits should concentrate heavily on the forthcoming Presidential campaign. The opener consisted of Democrats singing:

Chicago, Chicago, that big windy town,
Chicago, Chicago, where stockyards abound,
We'll go there,
Bet your bottom dollar we will throw the bull in
Chicago, Chicago,
The town that even the Democrats can't shout down.

And the Republicans sang:

San Francisco, here we come,
Blow the bugle, beat the drum
Where banners and badges shine in the sun,
Each morning at dawning
You'll see the GOP
Building up a running mate,
Old Cow Palace, we can't wait,
Open wide that Golden Gate—
San Francisco, here we come!

The scene for the Democratic skit was a Midwestern farmers' barn dance, and impersonators of all the possibilities for the Presidential nomination were trotted out. At the outset, summing up the general party attitude, "Senator Sparkman" reworded in song, "Memories Are Made of This."

Take one dash of F.D.R.
Add one Happy Warrior,
We'll win once more with-out war,
Vict-o-ries are made of this.

Let's forget the ADA,
Throw the Dixiecrats away,
Tax-es are low-er, spend-ing high-er,
Vict-o-ries are made of this.

In the New Hampshire primaries a few weeks before, Senator Estes Kefauver had done very well and Adlai Stevenson rather poorly. "Stevenson" sang:

Hot diggity dog ziggity *Boom* what you did to me.
It's so new to me . . .

Never dreamed anybody could slug thataway,
Yank a rug thataway,
Pull a plug thataway,
In New Hampshire you acted like thataway
Don't you know you're blighting my life.

And a few moments later "Kefauver" answered by singing a parody of "All the Things You Are."

I am the promised breath of victory
That makes all southern comfort depart;
I am the Yank from Chattanooga
Who made the grade with his hand—not heart;
I am the winning glow that lights the west,

The dearest thing you know;
Estes is best!
Some day my happy arms will hold it
And it means the job Ike has for a time—
Some day I'll make it mine—all mine!

"Mayor Wagner" of New York assessed the situation of Governor Harriman.

Ave and Harry, Ave and Harry,
Go together like a Tom and Jerry,
This I tell ya, brother,
You can't have one. Who wants the other?

Ave and Harry, Ave and Harry,
If you take Ave, you will still get Harry;
DeSapio will tell you
Walter Reuther goes along too.

"Speaker Rayburn" complained that "this barn dance is getting as forlorn as a Democrat trying to get a job under Governor Frank Lausche in Ohio," and he decided that what was needed was "a real country slicker." "Lyndon Johnson" had "just the man," and Senator "Stuart Symington" came forward to sing:

Let the rest have fun.
I'm the only one.
Sweet Stu
For you.

Adlai's lost his steam,
Estes' off the beam,
And Ave knows now that he never will come through.

I'm a glamor boy,
Though a wee bit coy.
Sweet Stu
For you.

After such "farmers" as Dean Acheson, Hubert Humphrey, Jake Arvey and Carmine De Sapio had had their say, an impersonator of former President Truman, who at that time was doing a considerable amount of writing, part of which proved to be quite controversial, sang a rollicking song to the tune of "Sixteen Tons" that was not designed to flatter either Truman or his publishers.

Some people say a book is wrote to be sold,
A book is made out of fiction for gold,

Fiction and gold and friend and foe,
If the verbs are weak, get a ghost that's strong . . .

So I start one morning to find out the proof,
I ransacked the White House from cellar to roof,
I loaded sixteen tons of fiction and fact.
Hauled it to Missouri on my back.

I arose one morning. I was fightin' mad.
Said that Doug MacArthur was a sack that was sad.
Sad Sack Mac, he tried to talk back.
I decided I would have to give him the sack.

If you see me comin', better step aside.
A lotta men didn't. A lotta men cried.
One fist of iron and the other of fire.
If a man says that he beat me, he's a low-down liar. I wrote—

Sixteen tons. What have I got?
Some facts that are true and others that are not.
Saint Peter, if you want me, best use a noose,
I owe my soul to Hen-er-eee Luce.

Walter George, the much respected southern senator, had been scheduled as the Democratic speaker, but a couple of days before the dinner he phoned Drummond and explained that because he had just signed the "Southern Manifesto" on racial policy, he felt that the Gridiron Club would not wish to have him as its speaker. He was told by Drummond that the Gridiron Club did not base its choice of speakers on political policy and that they would like to have him stand by his acceptance. But he said no, he felt he shouldn't speak and that the decision was his, not the Gridiron Club's. So about thirty-six hours before the dinner, Senator Lyndon Johnson was asked by Drummond to substitute for George.

After appropriate complimentary remarks about Senator George, Johnson began expounding on Texas Democratic precinct conventions, on which, he said, both he and President Eisenhower were experts. [He was referring to the "Texas steal" in the 1952 convention, which, when resolved by that body, assured Eisenhower's nomination.] But he said that he and the President weren't similar just because they both favored Texas precinct conventions—"in different years."

They were also both native-born Texans, they were both cattle raisers, and they were both experts on the farm problem. But there, Johnson said, the similarity ceased. He quoted one of the columnists as saying, "Johnson can never be a serious candidate because he has had a heart attack."

He earned his living, he said, "trying to get along with ninety-five Senators and the Speaker of the House. That's so exhausting that I felt I had to give up my membership in Burning Tree."

He referred to the bipartisanship of the last three years and said that it was "a little hard to break the code as to what bipartisanship means. As nearly as I can make out, it means that the Democratic majority leader has the duty of protecting the President's foreign policy—particularly from the Republicans—whenever he has a free moment in defending himself from Republican charges that he is obstructing the President."

A big public controversy had blown up in the months before the dinner, when, just as the Senate was ready to pass a natural gas bill much wanted by the oil industry, Senator Francis Case of South Dakota rose in the Senate and announced that he had been sent a check for $2,500 for "campaign expenses" by Howard Keck, president of the Superior Oil Company. He announced that he was returning the check and voting against the bill, although he had originally planned to vote for it. As a result of this disclosure, President Eisenhower, a man of unquestioned integrity, reluctantly vetoed the bill.

Senator Johnson had been an ardent advocate of this legislation, which would have been much to the advantage of his state. He referred to this and said that the columnists had called this a "courageous" thing when the President vetoed the bill. Then he voiced the suspicion that the President might have told the gas producers he would let them have the bill—after November.

"I said to myself," said Johnson, "well, since ladies are always present at the Gridiron, never mind what I said to myself."

Congress had also passed a farm bill that President Eisenhower vetoed. Again, Johnson said, the columnists had called the veto "courageous" and had called him a "political demagogue" for attacking the President's veto.

"Well," he said, "with the help of Senate economists, I found the answer. You see, I was—I am—for 90 percent of parity. The President was—and, I presume still is—for 86 percent of parity. Courage, the economists assured me, was a matter of four percentage points."

Johnson noted that he'd also wanted a tax cut, and the President had opposed it.

"But, I'll tell you, gentlemen, I'm an experienced man now. I have a feeling that before November, General Ike's Mr. Humphrey is going to be for that tax cut—say about four percentage points lower than the one I wanted."

He closed with an appeal to unity and direct advocacy to those in the room to promote it. The haters, he said, would try to divide "brother against brother, friend against friend, Northerner against Southerner, Westerner against Easterner."

"They will not win if you, the leaders of this nation who sit in this room tonight, will resist them to the hilt.

"Our people are a reasonable people. They *are* men of good will. If they receive from you the kind of leadership they deserve, they will listen.

"This burden of leadership falls on you, the leaders of government, of the press, of business.

"For we must have unity—the unity of free men. Mr. President, gentlemen, there is no greater problem before our nation tonight. Together we can solve it.

"Earlier this evening, I talked about the similarities between myself and the President. There is one other similarity between us. We both hope all the bipartisan efforts for a positive peace will come true and stay true."[4]

One of the perennial Senate lobby investigations which come along every few years was on at the time of the 1956 dinner, and the Republican skit was entitled "Lobbyists in Paradise," with "Senator Francis H. Case" of South Dakota one of the principal figures, and the chorus dressed as angels, some of them with harps.

"Hidden away," said the announcer, "far from the Black Hills of South Dakota, is the politicians' Garden of Eden. It is a paradise where all contributions are large, there's no conflict of interest, and they pass nothing but gas bills. But hark, there's a revolt of the angels . . . trouble ahead, in Paradise!"

The scene opened with an impersonator of Senator Case's campaign manager singing:

> Cross my palm, I'm a stranger in paradise,
> All lost in a wonderland
> Where lobbyists fraternize.
>
> Sure there's gold in those old Black Hills,
> But a stranger in Paradise
> Now wonders who'll pay the bill,
> Six more years in Paradise.

Among the lobbyists who were satirized were impersonators of Walter Reuther and George Meany, who sang their new version of "I Found a Million-Dollar Baby."

Taft-Hartley hasn't changed a comma;
The gas bill passed—we knew it would.
We got a billion dollar lobby,
But it don't do us no good.

We take the dues; we turn the heat on.
We put our pals on TV screen.
We got a billion dollar lobby,
But the pickin's mighty lean.

"Howard Keck" was a sobbing character claiming he was an outcast and that "nobody loves me any more; nobody will take my money."

Four other characters who had been dismissed or eased out of the administration because of improprieties expressed their feelings in a parody of "I'll Be Seeing You."

We just helped ourselves in all those old familiar places,
In the Air Force, planning bases, making deals
Inside GSA.
We had a friendly way,
The job in ICC
Was simple, clear for all to see.
You'll be missing us as Ike's campaign bills start to climb,
Don't ask us, we won't give a dime
Since GOP thinks trade's a crime.
We all got letters, sweet, from Ike,
But when we read them through
We discovered we'd been fired—
So—we'll be seeing you.

"Senator Robert S. Kerr" of Oklahoma wanted to "hang Brother Case from a sour apple tree," to which all of the angels yelled "Hallelujah! Amen!" and Kerr announced he was there to lead the group.

"How we gonna be statesmen if we don't come back?" Kerr asked.

The act closed with an impersonator of Senator Homer Capehart of Indiana singing:

Oh, them golden slush funds,
Lovely golden slush funds,
Happy statesmen we cannot be
Without seniority.

This was all a little rougher than usual for the Gridiron Club, but it didn't seem to bother President Eisenhower.

Governor Christian A. Herter of Massachusetts—in a very difficult spot—rose to speak for the Republicans. No copy of his speech could be obtained.

For the foreign affairs skit, the Gridiron Club transported its guests to the construction site of the Aswan Dam, where Nasser and Nehru, in native dress, and a group of American officials, in customary cutaways, discussed the situation with a chorus of shieks, desert construction workers, natives, and dancing girls representing "The Gaza Strip."

The announcer noted that "the State Department has at last achieved its goal of massive retaliation. It has forced our foreign friends to accept a new and more expensive version of our own late lamented WPA," something that had been accomplished "against the greatest imaginable competition."

"Nehru" invited everybody to participate.

> Oh, this great come-and-get-it day,
> Isn't it fun, our worry is done and money is hay,
> Now's the time things will come our way
> On this great, great come-and-get-it-day.
> Just dip right in—there's surely enough,
> Now don't hold back, it's all on the cuff,
> 'Cause the word has come from across the sea,
> The U.S.A. somehow is a-givin' and now it's free.
> Glory time's with us for to stay,
> On this great, great come-and-get-it day.

"Secretary of State Dulles" arrived with great fanfare and sang, to "The Desert Song":

> Blue heavens are calling me,
> I fly over the moon-lit sea,
> The desert breeze whispers a melody,
> I may land in China, or South Carolina.
> Oh, give me a plane that's new,
> I may turn up in Timbuktu,
> You'll find me there, lending,
> And they'll be sending
> An IOU

Then the Russians, "Bulganin" and "Khrushchev," arrived to dedicate "our dam." A flunky named Ivan who accompanied them sang:

Whatever Ivan wants, Ivan takes,
And little men, little Ivan takes you.
Make up your mind, we make no mistake,
Recline yourself, resign yourself, you're through.
We're sure to get what we came for,
And between the eyes is what we aim for.
Whatever Ivan wants, Ivan takes,
Call off your plans.
Don't you know you can't win.
You're no exception to the rule,
We're irresistible, you fool . . . *Give In!*

The skit ended with the arrival of "The Reverend Billy Graham," shouting "Judgment day's a-comin! Hallelujah!" and singing:

I been watchin', seen the Commies launchin'
Trouble all over the land.
I'm a-sayin', got to do some prayin'
Join the happy band, then you'll understand
Why I give to all this one command.

Sing hallelujah, hallelujah, and you'll shoo those Reds away.
When they pursue ya, hallelujah will skidoo them on their way.
Stalin was a jerk-ski, did dirty work-ski, so they say;
Sing hallelujah, hallelujah, and you'll shoo them all away.

Following its policy that "the Gridiron glows, but it never burns," the club closed the dinner with a very pleasant and complimentary skit on President Eisenhower. An impersonator of Dr. Paul Dudley White, the celebrated heart specialist who had been called in after President Eisenhower's heart attack, announced that "President Eisenhower is the first Republican candidate in history who can give medical proof he's got a heart."

The scene was set at a country club which was to be "the Republican front porch." One after another, various Republican leaders proclaimed their loyalty to the President. "Senator Knowland," in a parody, sang:

You made me love you,
I didn't wanna do it, I didn't wanna do it,
You made me feel blue,
And all the time you knew it,
I wouldn't want to do it.

An impersonator of Vice President Nixon sang a parody of "Suddenly There's a Valley."

When I've climbed the highest places,
But a cloud holds the sunshine in,
Suddenly there's the White House
And I'm all at peace again.
When a storm hides the distant rainbow
And I think I can't find a friend,
Suddenly there's the White House
And my trouble's at an end.
When people said you'd dump me
And thought that I wouldn't do,
And things seemed to be the darkest,
It was then the sun came through.
When I think there's no bright tomorrow
And I fear I can't try again,
Suddenly there's the White House
Where you—and hope—remain!

"Secretary of Agriculture Benson" mused in a song reminiscent of "The Yellow Rose of Texas":

Oh, the good old state of Texas
And California too,
Together form a ticket
That's good enough for you.
And the native sons of Texas, and
The golden state so free—
With the farm-bloc team of Ike and Dick—
What will the harvest be?

"Republican chairman Hall" closed the dinner with a song telling the President that it all depended on him.

You alone, could make it known,
You alone could make the decision,
You said "yes" in happiness,
We're making plans for tel-e-vision.
We don't have a lot to tell,
And you're the one who must sell the nation,
With your grin and magic name to win—
It rests with you alone!

The Gridiron show script for the dinner has a rather unusual stage direction at the end of this skit, written by the music chairman of that year, Fletcher Knebel. "Get the hell off the stage," he wrote, "so the man can get back to his bridge game."

President Eisenhower closed the dinner, in response to the

toast to the President, with some brief but pertinent off-the-cuff remarks.

Never much of a humorist, he drew his only laugh at the opening, when he addressed Drummond, the Vice President, the chief justice, Governor Herter, and "My Fellow Cardiacs." But he was always gracious, and through his speech shone the unforgettable appeal of the personality exhibited in his later years at Gettysburg College, when he threw his arms around Perle Mesta and said quite audibly before a crowd of thirty people, "I love you, Perle, even if you are a Democrat."

Eisenhower thanked the Gridiron Club for "an evening of scintillating entertainment. It is," he said, "one of the most successful performances I have ever seen."

He had little to say, he added, other than expressing his thanks to the members of the club. Then he closed with a simple appeal for unity.

"I should like to refer just briefly," the President said, "to the last sentence of Senator Johnson's speech. We are all Americans, all Americans working for peace.

"I submit that the time has come to rather forget the words bipartisan and unpartisan. When we talk about this great aspiration, I think we should accept among ourselves—the American businessman, farmer, laborer, the professional man, and even the politicians—we want peace. We want it with all our hearts because we know that the foreign situation either causes, or certainly deeply colors, every single domestic problem. It fixes our level of taxes, it disturbs our minds, it keeps us continually concerned. This is an American problem. How does America meet it? By joining ranks together, joining hands.

"No one man, no one party, could possibly do anything about it unless all were very definitely joined in this great effort. It is my faith, my conviction, that with the joining of hands that Senator Johnson mentioned, we cannot fail. The truth and decency of free government is bound to prevail over the lies and deceit of dictatorship in the long run.

"We are blessed with countless friends throughout the world. With not all of them do we always agree. In fact, I think it is safe to say, with each of them on some one subject we disagree. But I am equally certain that all of these friends know that America is honest in this great search for peace.

"They know that America also realizes this," Eisenhower

said, "there can be no peace for us unless it is shared by all. Therefore, their fortunes and ours are in the same basket. So we do each join hands among ourselves and lead forward, never defeated in this greatest of all efforts and aspirations of men. Let us remember that those abroad—all races or color or creed or language—that they, by the millions, are marching with us to make victory doubly certain."[5]

XVII

Dwight D. Eisenhower

1957-1960
"Just don't disturb the table
too much. . ."

The spring dinner, held on March 2, 1957, was the first major dinner after the overwhelming reelection of President Eisenhower and Vice President Nixon by an electoral college vote of 457 to 73. But neither Eisenhower nor Nixon were present at this dinner. Eisenhower was conserving his strength and Vice President Nixon was in Africa. The two principal guests were Chief Justice Earl Warren and the former king of England, the Duke of Windsor.

Marquis Childs of the *St. Louis Post-Dispatch*, Gridiron president, welcomed the guests with "special warmth . . . because we are a lonely little band in Washington these days." The exodus from this capital city had begun, Childs noted, and Vice President Nixon was off in Africa, perhaps running for president of the Gold Coast, "and all his good friends," said Childs, "including Senator Knowland and Governor Knight, wish him well. They can't think of a better place for him to be President of."

Stassen, he said, hoped to run the following year for governor of Pennsylvania, and Senator Knowland was going back to

California. "That famous victory of last November," he said, "seems a long way off. Everybody got something. Flushed with his great triumph over both Democrats and Republicans, the President has by now completely recovered—from a tendency to slice his tee shots."

Treasury Secretary George M. Humphrey, he noted, was getting some new printing presses "to print money twice as fast as ever before," and by doing so he estimated that "they will just about keep up with the $72 billion budget."

And Adlai Stevenson, whom Eisenhower defeated for the second time, "got the material for another book. I can't think," said Childs, "of a harder way to be an author."

The opener was a chorus of half Republicans and half Democrats. Two soloists representing each party delivered the Gridiron Club's message on the state of the union in a parody of a song from the musical *Li'l Abner*.

Democrat: Republicans and Democrats are pretty much alike.
Republican: Though only some of us lives in the sticks.
Democrat: We orate at each other.
Republican: We're fierce with one another.
Both: But we plays the same old game of politics.
Chorus: With us the country's in the best of hands.

In the final weeks of the Presidential campaign, war had broken out in the Middle East. Stevenson had made the political mistake of viewing this with great alarm and blaming the Administration for diplomatic failure. But the more people became scared over the situation there, the more they turned to the general who had won World War II. So the skit closed with these words:

Democrat: The President asked Congress to let the Rooshians know
Republican: That if they took the Middle East we'd cut in on the show.
Both: But when we asked him how and where he told us to go slow, Keep out of what no Congress understands.
Chorus: The country's in the very best of hands.

Republican resurgence in the South had begun again in the 1956 election, and Arthur Larson, special assistant to the President, had written a book entitled *A Republican Looks at His Party*. Consequently, the scene for the Republican skit was a New Orleans Mardi Gras, and the Gridiron guests were taken there to one of the "new hotbeds of the new Republicanism in some unexpected locations," where the Republicans were "exploring their newly discovered territory."

An actor impersonating Republican National Committee Chairman Meade Alcorn sang his reactions to the tune of "Waiting for the Robert E. Lee."

> Watch them shuffle along,
> See them votin' so strong,
> Down New Orleans way, they say
> We'll vote the straight ticket, the GOP ticket,
> And we'll join that shufflin' throng,
> Hear that *Civil Rights* song—
>
> Hah Hah!
>
> It's simply great, mate, votin' on the levee,
> Votin' for the GOP!

Secretary of Defense Charles E. Wilson had once said, "What's good for the country is good for General Motors, and vice versa." However, this was easily reinterpreted by political opponents into a single quotation, "What's good for General Motors is good for the country." This caused great discomfiture to Secretary Wilson. Thus, an impersonator of him sang:

> I'm forever making boo-boos,
> Pretty boo-boos in the air.
> The bird dogs first, then th' National Guard,
> They're so unjust, they hit me hard.
> I'm a man well-meaning,
> Trying to be fair,
>   BUT
> I'm forever making boo-boos,
> Pretty boo-boos in the air!

The aspirations of Vice President Nixon to succeed President Eisenhower in 1960 were voiced in a solo by "Leonard Hall," former chairman of the Republican National Committee:

> On a perch in the Senate a Dicky bird sat,
> Singing Dicky, Oh Dicky, Oh Dicky!
> Every thought in his head was entirely on that—
> Just on Dicky, on Dicky, on Dicky!
> He was thinking of sixty and what he might do

In the four coming years to help carry him through
To the big nomination he thinks will be due
For Dicky, for Dicky, for Dicky!

"Larson" came on the scene and was told by "Senator
Leverett Saltonstall" that since he'd rushed into print the admin-
istration had lost young Herbert Hoover, Harold Stassen, Senator
Knowland, and it looked like others might be leaving.

"Yep, soon there'll be nobody here but us modern Republicans," replied Larson. "Just me and Ike. And sometimes I wonder about me—and about Ike."

This led to a song by an impersonator of Senator Styles
Bridges of New Hampshire.

Not a soul down on the corner,
That's a pretty certain sign
That Eisenhower is breakin' up that old gang of mine.

There goes Jack,
There goes Jim,
To buy that Larson line,
Now and then, we meet again,
But it ain't like Auld Lang Syne.
Oh, I get a lonesome feeling,
When I hear the word, "resign,"
That Eisenhower is breakin' up that old gang of mine.

Arthur Larson was then introduced as the Republican
speaker, but no text of his speech is in the Gridiron files.

The Democratic skit was notable for the entrance of two
characters new to the Gridiron stage, Senator John F. Kennedy of
Massachusetts and Governor Edmund S. Muskie of Maine.

The scene was Dr. Lyndon Johnson's Jolly Pill Pharmacy in
Milltown, U.S.A. "Senator Hubert H. Humphrey" announced
that he loved the South because the South is what he runs against
in Minnesota, and "Senator Herman Talmadge" announced that
he loved the North because the North is what he runs against
down in Georgia. But the pharmacist, Dr. Johnson, had other
ideas, and Ned Brooks, impersonating him, sang:

I dreamed a Texas resident
Was drafted to be President,
And I don't mean my colleague, Mr. Sam.
I dreamed I had the votes to pass
Free enterprise for natural gas,
Despite a Presidential double-wham.

We have control in both our branches
Practically by avalanches,
Listen to that old steam-roller roar!
Anything we want we're takin'
And if you should think I'm fakin'
Watch me pick myself up off the floor.

An impersonator of Governor "Soapy" Williams of Michigan surveyed the Presidential scene and announced in song that "we ain't got nobody, unless that nobody's me."

But "Muskie" had other ideas. He thought they needed "a young, romantical type," and as "Kennedy" entered announcing that he was "young, rich, romantical, and courageous as a lion," the conservative "Senator Eastland" of Mississippi sang his praises, somewhat prophetically but not exactly in terms designed to please Mr. Kennedy.

Ivy League and Harvard A and curly hair,
We're raving 'bout our newest find,
Got a little lettuce here and lettuce there,
Don't want to run without him.
We need him, goodness knows,
When that campaign gets going
How papa's money flows.

Baby face, you've got the cutest little baby face,
There's not another one can take your place, baby face,
All the girls are jumpin'
You sure have started sumpin'
Baby face,
We'd be in clover if we got you in the race,
No voter'd need a shove,
'Cause they'd just fall in love
With your pretty baby face.

A forlorn "Adlai Stevenson," attired as court jester, with tinkling bells on his high pyramid cap, announced that he had been everybody's sweetheart not so long ago, but that things were different now.

I'm nobody's sweetheart now,
They don't vote for me somehow
Cast aside, so unkind,
Who would ever think I'd run so far behind.

When I rode down the avenues,
The egg-heads thought I couldn't lose,

Tried to act—like a lion,
I'm all washed up like William Jennings Bryan,
It all seems wrong somehow,
But I'm nobody's sweetheart now.

The skit ended with Democratic Chairman "Paul Butler," singing:

Somewhere over the rainbow, there must be
Votes that give us the right to ask for the White House key.
Sometime, some bright November, we'll get in;
We can spend more than Ike can; spending's not now a sin.
That day we'll have our own Humphrey
And Democratic Montgomery*
To guide us;
We'll play the golf, we'll shoot the quail,
We'll give you even slower mail—
That much we promise.
Maybe in nineteen sixty, we can do
Do what Stassen has tried, and tried—
     but just could not do.
If Nixon just to run is told
At rainbow's end we'll find our pot of gold

Stevenson made the Democratic speech.

"After that sad song about my present friendless state," he said, "I am very grateful for your friendly greeting. I feel a little like that famous cow on the cold wintry morning who looked at the farmer and said, 'Thanks for that warm hand.' I only wish it had been as warm and friendly last November!"

He had hesitated, he said, to come back four months after the election "to rake among the embers of my funeral pyre, a bonfire which most of your publishers fanned so vigorously and a funeral at which so few of you mourned!

"Yet good taste prescribes," he continued, "that I greet you humbly, contritely, as a man who has twice been tempted, and twice suffered the consequences of his weakness. Just what made me think I could do better the second time escapes me now."

However, it wasn't so much of the President as it was of the campaign and himself that he said he was supposed to speak. He didn't want to discourage any of his audience from running for President, he said. "It's a wonderful way to meet a lot of people you wouldn't meet otherwise—at any price!"

---

*Robert Montgomery, who coached Eisenhower on his television appearances.

"Besides, as I have often remarked, it is fine exercise for the hands, feet, stomach and vocal chords. And I am told that it is not too hard on the head, if you use good judgment. You don't even have to read or write; someone will do it for you."

Turning then to Arthur Larson, Stevenson said he was happy to meet "the *Republican* egg-head" and added, "I hope you are enjoying your missionary work among the heathen."

He had had some experience, he said, "in the perils of writing my own speeches.

"The price of being yourself in American politics is ruinous; Your speeches are always late, the reporters are harassed, you miss their deadlines, and these things are evidently far more important than what the candidate really thinks, writes and says. And worst of all, when I added what I insisted on saying to what my staff said must be said, I couldn't possibly get off the air before the television time was up.

"And, extravagant Democrat that I am, I could never allow for any spare time at the end of a speech because I couldn't reconcile myself to paying $5,000 a minute for an ovation from the faithful.

"You know that wonderful song from *My Fair Lady*, 'Get Me to the Church on Time.' Well, it wasn't until afterward that I discovered that the theme song of my staff was 'Get Him Off the Air on Time.'"

Referring to the Middle Eastern war, which had had such a tremendous effect upon his campaign, he said that the Republicans hadn't counted on the explosion in the Middle East just before the election.

"Neither did I," admitted Stevenson.

"Now I don't say that the administration planned it all; indeed I see no evidence of any planning in the Middle East. But in 1952 General Eisenhower at least had to say, 'I will go to Korea.' This time the Middle East came to him! . . .

"After witnessing the magic, the alchemy, by which a foreign policy failure is converted into a political success, I have concluded that we poor Democrats have a lot to learn from you Republicans."

Stevenson commented that it didn't look so bad for "us Democrats" as it did for Mr. Larson's New Republicanism. "Now I haven't yet had an opportunity to read your book about the Republican party, Mr. Larson," he said. "I have been waiting for the revised edition after you have been here a little longer.

"As I have said before, I'm not quite sure just what the New Republicanism is, but from what I've observed in the past few years, especially around election time, the New Republicanism looks to me a good deal like the old New Deal at its twenty fifth reunion.

"But clearly we Democrats should not complain too much. We've been asking you Republicans to *adopt* our liberal reforms for many years, although we didn't ask you to *steal* them. And I suspect that the greatest contribution of the Eisenhower administration to political science is the accomplishment of this theft with a fresh and wide-eyed innocence which has all but ennobled larceny—even if it hasn't convinced many of the Old Guard."

Toward the close of his speech, Stevenson commented that several years ago when he spoke at a Gridiron dinner he had "preached" a little bit about freedom of speech and the responsibility of the newspapermen toward it.

"I seem to have lost my license as a preacher," he said, "but hope you will indulge me all the same. You see, it may be my last chance.

"It has been well said that we spend too much time on Presidential elections *before* they take place, and too little time on them *after* they are over. This one is now over, but our job isn't. The great imperative of press and politics remains—to serve the truth. . . .

"Your job is truthful, merciless appraisal. But it is even more, I think, in this time when moral and mental fatigue seem to be overcoming mankind, when the resourcefulness that is part of the will to survive in a meaningful way seems to be fading, when so many retreat before complexity, too tired to do more than cling to their own.

"I don't know where we go from here. But it seems to me that the best place to begin is with a new mood—a mood of reverence for truth about our friends, our enemies, and above all, ourselves.

"This is the toughest work in the world, this business of inspiration, but it is the most essential. And it is business for thinkers, for writers, for speakers—for the press and politicians especially. . . .

"But what needs saying most right now is that I gladly accept the people's verdict, indeed I am getting used to it! I wish President Eisenhower and his administration the best of luck. I will gladly help them in office; and, of course, I will gladly help them out of office.

"And to the Gridiron I say thanks, and long may you wave!"[1]

Christian Herter, former governor of Massachusetts and former congressman, was then assisting Dulles as under secretary of state. The 1956 war in the Middle East was still in the negotiating stage at the time of the dinner. Impersonators of Prime Minister David Ben Gurion of Israel, former Prime Minister Anthony Eden of England, and Prime Minister Guy Mollet of France each sang in the foreign affairs skit their own version of what might have happened there "with a little bit of luck." Mollet summed it up at the end with a parody of that *My Fair Lady* song.

> We bungled the landing at the Suez,
> We didn't topple Nasser at the start,
> And in Algiers we couldn't stop rebellion,
> But—with a little bit of luck,
> We might well have taken him apart.

And then, looking to the future, the chorus sang:

> Onward Christian Herter,
> Smartest of them all,
> He who yields to Ni-i-ix-on
> Gets paid off by Hall.
> Overseas diplomacy
> Strikes him as a bore,
> Making time with Co-o-on-gress
> Is his major chore.
> Onward Christian Herter,
> Pounding to the gate,
> Ready to be drafted
> Should
> Dulles ab-di-cate.

The skit and the show ended with "Dulles" singing, somewhat cynically:

> When I pretend I'm gay, I never feel that way,
> I'm only painting the clouds with sunshine;
> When I say Russia's sunk, and all that kind of junk,
> I'm only painting the clouds with sunshine.
> At every chance, vive la France,
> Cheerily, sweetly I cry,

Gay even though good old Pineau's
Thumb's in my eye.
When I say ties are tight
With England, that's not right,
I'm only painting the clouds with sunshine.

When I say Nasser's fine, that's just the party line,
I'm only painting the clouds with sunshine;
We'll save ten billion clams, not building Aswan Dams,
That's really painting the clouds with sunshine.
Every fez, near the Suez
Covers a hat-full of hate,
But I report
Naught of the sort,
Everything's great.
The Arab news I hear
I say is full of cheer,
I'm only painting the clouds with sunshine.

• • •

Although Eisenhower was nearly three years away from the completion of his second term, there was already great interest in the country concerning his successor. The Gridiron dinner of March 15, 1958 was focused quite heavily on this subject, and on the approaching congressional elections in November. Eisenhower was not present at the dinner, but practically all other administration, judicial and congressional leaders were.

"We meet here this evening," said Benjamin M. McKelway of the *Washington Star*, Gridiron president, "on another fateful Ides of March. And we find ourselves, as in Washington we so often find ourselves, completely in the dark."

Referring to some overlapping of functions between Secretary of State Dulles and Presidential Assistant Harold Stassen, he continued, "This is an age of great discoveries. Jim Hagerty, on a quick trip to Washington from Georgia via Arizona, discovers Elizabeth Arden vanishing cream. He presents it to Harold Stassen, with the compliments of the secretary of state.

"Discontented Republicans discover that if they can bypass Sherman Adams they can take their troubles directly to the President—provided, or course, they can discover just where the President is.

"The Democratic leader of the Senate, Mr. Lyndon Johnson, discovers the potentialities of outer space and plans to annex it to Texas, as a new congressional district.

"All of us discover the new Nixon, only to discover that nothing has happened to change the old Truman.

He also had a barb for Chief Justice Warren and the Warren Court.

"Led by the chief justice," he said, "the Supreme Court discovers things in the constitution that nobody knew were there before. . . .

"But, Gentlemen, keep your chins up. For at last the light is dawning in the mellow glow of the Gridiron." And as it flashed on, he said, "It can only shine as it has been shining for nearly seventy-three years in a free country, a strong country, a country that knows no fear."

One of the big television hits of that period was "Gunsmoke." The Gridiron Club used its version of this drama as the vehicle for the Democratic skit.

Into a terrorized town in the Old West came "Marshal Lyndon Johnson" and "Deputy Marshal Stuart Symington." The chorus was a posse and they had brought in prisoners. Symington inquired of Johnson, "After the jury trial, who do you want to hang first?"

Among those brought in were impersonators of former President Truman, Hubert Humphrey, Adlai Stevenson, "Soapy" Williams, Walter Reuther, Estes Kefauver, Governor Orval Faubus of Arkansas, Averell Harriman, and John F. Kennedy.

Truman was the first to be tried. During his Presidency he had written some fairly vigorously phrased letters to various people who did things he didn't like, including music critics who found Margaret Truman something less than equal to Lily Pons.

In defense, Truman sang:

I'm gonna sit right down and write someone a letter
And give 'em hell in words of yore.
I'm gonna write words, oh, so tough,
They're gonna knock off all that guff.
A lot of postscripts on the bottom,
Red-hot as I jot 'em.
I'm gonna smile and say, 'I hope you're dropping deader,'
And where you fall, there ain't no floor.
I'm gonna sit right down and write someone a letter
And tell 'em all that I deplore.

The marshal sentenced him to "ten years on bread and water. And not too much water—or bread."

Soapy Williams and Walter Reuther were next, but Reuther took over for them and sang, to Soapy Williams:

> Button up your union suit on a stumping spree,
> Take good care of yourself, you belong to me.
> If by chance the Democrats vote you nominee,
> Make sure they understand, I've a share in thee.

Marshal Lyndon ordered them to shoot Williams, because "he's the one without the delegates."

Adlai Stevenson, attired as a city dude, and Hubert Humphrey, as a cowhand, came forward, and to the melody of "Poor Butterfly," Humphrey sang to Stevenson:

> Poor Ad—a—lie,
> Once his hopes were fading.
> Poor Ad—a—lie,
> For we loved him so.
> His moment passed into hours.
> The hours pass into years,
> And as we smile through our tears,
> We murmur low:
> Poor Ad—a—lie.

Symington said that for him "Marshal Lyndon has ordered maximum punishment—put Stevenson in the same cell with Harry Truman."

The next pair were Estes Kefauver and Governor Faubus, a violent opponent of the Supreme Court's integration decision. Rudolph Kauffmann II, impersonating Faubus, played a guitar and sang:

> An unreconstructed rebel. Now that's just what I am. . . .
>
> I fit them paratroopers. I showed them war is hell.
> Went flyin' down to Newport and sassed that ol' Brownell.
> They snitched my Central High School. They conquered all my
>   land,
> But they didn't get my statehouse. I'm Dixie contraband.
>
> I hates the Yankee nation and ev'rythin' they do.
> I hates the Declaration of Independence too.
> I hates that Yankee eagle, with all his scream and fuss.
> But them ever-growin' Yankees, they hates me even wuss.
>
> I can't take down mah musket and fight with them no more.
> But o' one thing I am sartin' and one thing I am shore:
> That I won't git no parden for what I been and am,
> But I might git reelected—so I don't give a damn.

To that, Symington reported that Marshal Lyndon said, "No comment. On matters interracial, he's strictly outer-spatial."

But perhaps the song directed most to the future was that sung to the tune of "My Heart Belongs to Daddy" by an impersonator of John F. Kennedy, who was running for reelection to the Senate from Massachusetts in November.

> I'll have a ball and votes this fall
> Will crown this Bostonian laddy.
> Then I will run for the top-most gun—
> And I learned it all from daddy.
> Now some hob-nob with Brother Bob,
> The boy who drove old Dave Beck batty.
> But Bob will chime that it ain't no crime
> For to take our cue from daddy.
> Yes I'll do it just like daddy,
> And I hope he will not be mad
> When I send the bill to daddy,
> Da-da, da-da-da, da-da-da-dad!
> So don't try to beat this laddy,
> Though your aim be perfectly swell.
> For the bill belongs to daddy,
> Cause my daddy, he pays it so well.

The marshal's verdict on him was, "Get his contribution. Then hang him!"

Now that all the "bad element" had been taken care of, the marshal sang:

> I'm a Texas Doodle Dandy.
> A Texas Doodle, do or die.
> A real live nephew of ol' Speaker Sam.
> I've got my goal in the sky.
> I man the outer space-es ramparts,
> Super-sonic pride and joy.
> Lyndon Johnson comes a-flyin', oil and gas forever.
> I am your Texas Doodle Boy!

That closed the skit and Kennedy was introduced as the Democratic speaker, to make the first of several great and witty Gridiron speeches.

Referring to the "Daddy" song, he opened his talk by pulling a "telegram" from his pocket and saying, "I have just received the following wire from my generous Daddy: 'Dear Jack—'Don't buy a single vote more than is necessary—I'll be damned if I'm going to pay for a landslide.' "

Although the dinner speeches were off-the-record, this Kennedy response was widely quoted and widely printed.

"I am grateful to my father for his support," went on Kennedy, "but I am even more grateful to 'Mr. Sam' Rayburn [who had presided over the 1956 Democratic Convention when Kefauver was nominated for Vice President in a close race with Kennedy]. At the last Democratic Convention, if he had not recognized the Tennessee and Oklahoma delegations when he did, I might have won that race with Senator Kefauver—and my political career would now be over."

Then he turned his barbs toward the Gridiron Club itself.

"I have been told tonight that if I will only not reveal the truth about the members of the Gridiron Club in front of their bosses, they in turn can insure me the Democratic Presidential nomination.

"I am not the first politician to be thus tempted by the newspaper fraternity. When Speaker Joe Cannon half a century ago was told by the ANPA [American Newspaper Publishers Association] that, in exchange for his opposition to the newsprint tariff, the publishers would deliver him the Presidency, Speaker Cannon removed his cigar and replied, 'You know, 2,000 years ago or so, another fellow was tempted like this. And the tempter led him up on the highest mountain top; and showed him all the kingdoms of the world, and all the valleys of milk and honey, and he said, "If you will fall down and worship me, all of this will I give you." But the truth of the matter is,' Speaker Cannon went on, 'he didn't own one damn inch of it.'

"I am not sure that the members of the Gridiron Club do either."

Then, with a deft and amusing reference to the religious issue, which many people feared would make the election of Kennedy as President impossible, as it had that of Al Smith thirty years before, he said, "Frankly, I am not now making any plans for the Presidency. Should I be elected, I do hope that Methodist Bishop Bromley Oxnam will be my personal envoy to the Vatican—and he's instructed to open negotiations for that Trans-Atlantic tunnel immediately.

"Otherwise I am not campaigning. It is true that I have travelled some—because I told Paul Butler that I would be willing to go to *all* states with promising Democratic candidates. I should have known that we have no other kind."

Coming back to the Gridiron Club itself, Kennedy said that

he'd understood that the Gridiron files had recently been broken into and that someone had stolen "your officers' election returns for the next six years."

He said he had been told that the club was a "Republican organization," but he was there "bearing an olive branch," inviting newspapermen and Democrats to unite.

"Under our regime," he said, "all reporters can go to Communist China *without* official protection—in fact, I'm drawing up now a list of those I want to see go first."

He thought the club could help in a number of ways, the first being "to screen all our potential candidates for 1960." This enabled him to get his barbs in at some other Presidential aspirants.

"I dreamed about 1960 myself the other night, and I told Stuart Symington and Lyndon Johnson about it in the cloakroom yesterday. I told them how the Lord came into my bedroom, anointed my head, and said, 'John Kennedy, I hereby appoint you President of the United States.' Stu Symington said, 'That's strange, Jack, because I, too, had a similar dream last night, in which the Lord anointed me and declared me, Stuart Symington, President of the United States *and* outer space.' And Lyndon Johnson said, 'That's very interesting, gentlemen; because I, too, had a similar dream last night—and I don't remember anointing either one of you!' "

The Democratic party had lots of candidates, and Kennedy talked about a survey which, he said, had "asked each senator about his preference for the Presidency—and ninety-six Senators each received one vote."

"One possible ticket," he continued, "would be Soapy Williams and Orval Faubus—that way the voters could hear a real debate of the issues without ever tuning in the Republicans."

Turning to the internal difficulties of both parties, he commented that "the Democratic Advisory Council has succeeded in splitting our party right down the middle—and that gives us more unity than we've had in twenty years.

"But we want you to help," he told the Gridiron members, "by reporting all Republican feuds in full. Some of them are diminishing, I must admit. Vice President Nixon and Sherman Adams, for example, decided to bury the hatchet—in Harold Stassen.

"Mr. Stassen announces he will run for governor of Pennsylvania. He has already been governor of Minnesota—that leaves only forty-six states still in jeopardy."

And, as though recognizing who his opponent would be two years hence, Kennedy described the key Republican, "my old friend, Dick Nixon, the most popular man in his party. Some people used to say that Mr. Nixon was doing the basement work over at Republican Headquarters. But now they've given those janitorial duties to Sherman Adams, and moved Dick upstairs to teach the men's Bible class."

Turning then to a current recession, he said, "As I interpret the President, we're now at the end of the beginning of the upturn of the downturn. Every bright spot the White House finds in the economy is like the policemen bending over the body in the alley who says cheerfully, 'Two of his wounds are fatal—but the other one's not so bad.'

"No anti-recession program for the farmers has been announced except Mr. Benson's hope to get the government out of the farming business. The farmer's program is to get Mr. Benson out of the governing business."

As is so often the case with Gridiron speakers, Kennedy closed on a serious note.

"But whatever our failings as Republicans and Democrats— and they are many—the fact remains that we together are the only instruments of popular government that the American people possess. We are all they have.

"The question is whether a democratic society—with its freedom of choice, its breadth of opportunity, its range of alternatives—can meet the single-minded advance of the Communists.

"Our difficulties are compounded by the subtlety of the decisions we must make, by the complexity of our interests, by the insoluble nature of so many of our crises.

"Can a nation organized and governed such as ours endure? That is the real question. Have we the nerve and the will? Have we got what it takes to carry through in an age where—as never before—our very survival is at stake, where we and the Russians have the power to destroy one-quarter of the earth's population—a feat not accomplished since Cain slew Abel? Can we carry through in an age where we will witness not only new break-throughs in weapons of destruction, but also a race for mastery of the sky and the rain, the ocean and the tides, the inside of the earth and the inside of men's minds?

"We are moving ahead along a knife-edged path which requires leadership better equipped than any since Lincoln's day to make clear to our people the vast spectrum of our challenges.

"In the words of Woodrow Wilson, 'We must neither run with the crowd nor deride it, but seek sober counsel for it—and for ourselves.' "[2]

The speech made a profound impression upon the Gridiron audience, many of whom were seeing and hearing for the first time the man who two years later would be elected President of the United States.

In addition to the usual Democratic, Republican and Foreign affairs skits, the Gridiron Club had another brief one at this dinner, satirizing the Supreme Court, seven of whose members, including the chief justice, were present.

Under the leadership of Chief Justice Warren, the Court by 1958 had started on its long course of decisions revising the rules of evidence and procedures. One result of this was the setting free or ordering of new trials for numerous convicted criminals.

On the Gridiron stage, nine unidentified men appeared in long robes and wigs. All wore black robes except the one in the center; his robe was red. They sang a song parody written by Marshall McNeil, who played the red-robed individual.

> Mine eyes have seen the glory of a civil rights decree.
> We have trampled on the Democrats and also GOP.
> As for who is going to make it work, I'm glad it isn't me.
> Oh, boy, this job is fun.
>
> We've opened up the files of FBI for all to see.
> We have emptied all the prison cells from Maine to Kankakee,
> And any hood can take the Fifth with equanimity.
> Oh, boy, this job is fun.
>
> Oh, critics say we write the laws, from this I won't dissent.
> We tell the Constitution's authors what they should have mean't.
> Results of each election, we will never circumvent.
> Oh, boy, this job is fun.
>
> Glory, glory, always justice,
> Five to four it's always justice,
> We give double scoops of justice
> For just the price of one.

The Republican skit was set in "Sherman Adams Last Chance Feed Lot." The announcer explained that "in 1960 somebody may get slaughtered. Just in case that somebody is the Republican party, the Eisenhower team is fattening up—while there's still time."

All the characters on the stage had pillows under their costumes to make them look fat. There had been some criticism of the granting of television licenses by the Federal Communications Commission, and as the skit opened, "Secretary of Health, Education and Welfare Marion B. Folsom" declared that he was fresh out of welfare and that if anybody wanted any they had to go to the FCC. Then he sang:

> Sugar in the mornin', sugar in the evenin', sugar at supper-time.
> FCC's our baby,
> And TV ain't no crime.
> Honey in the mornin', honey in the evenin', honey at supper-time.
> Sherm will write a letter
> And it won't cost you a dime.
> Grab a TV license, then your future's made.
> Careful, don't tell Congress you're on the hit parade.
> Sugar in the mornin', sugar in the evenin', sugar for GOP.
> If you know the system,
> It comes to you for free.

There was a great deal of speculation in March 1958 as to who would succeed President Eisenhower as the Republican candidate. One aspirant was Governor Goodwin ("Goody") Knight of California, whose impersonator sang:

> In the ring I've thrown my hat,
> And it's there to stay, that's that.
> Who cares if I have in me a streak of Democrat.
> Now you lie awake just figgerin' ways to beat.
>
> Goody! Goody!

Another aspirant, "Senate Minority Leader William F. Knowland," also of California, sang:

> When you're making plans for nineteen sixty
> Do you ever think of me?

Harold Stassen, who was unsuccessfully seeking the nomination for governor of Pennsylvania, sang:

> The last time I saw Pittsburgh, I heard from GOP.
> Go back to Minnesota, boy, we want no part of thee.
> The last time I saw Pittsburgh, the climate sure was hot.
> The voters carried signs that read, "For Stassen we are *Not*."
> I'll try my White House politics
> That I have used of late.
> I'll tell them how I won the peace
> And how I got the gate.
> I'll see you all in Pittsburgh and when the race is done,
> What matters how they treat me cause—I just like to run.

There was talk in those days about "the new Nixon," and an impersonator of the Vice President sang:

Getting to know me, getting to know all about me.
Getting to like me, now that I'm something new.
Getting to know me, doing it my way, but nicely.
I am precisely your dish of stew.
Getting to know me, now that I'm free and easy.
When I'm campaigning, getting to know what to say.
Haven't you noticed, suddenly I'm bright and breezy,
Because of all the beautiful and new
Things I've added for you, day by day.

"Attorney General William P. Rogers" and "Sherman Adams" entered, the latter preceded by a valet who shouted, "Make way for Sherm the Firm! He's very, very busy. Breakfast with the FCC today! Lunch with the CAB tomorrow. He's the workin'est man!"

Rogers, who thought everybody had "dropped out of the crusade except me—and sometimes I wonder about me," inquired about "our big boss, Mr. Eisenhower." Adams replied that "he works even on holidays. Except, of course, for Labor Day."

The skit closed with Adams singing:

Every day is Labor Day with him.
His problems often seem so very grim.
And indeed it is a pity, so we form a new committee.
Just to help him as he climbs down off the limb.
If business slumps and gets a case of cramps,
That's the very time to raise the price of stamps.
When the farmers want to use a gun,
There's nothing like a hole-in-one,
So——every day is Labor Day with him.

This was the cue for the introduction of Attorney General Rogers to make the Republican speech.

He began by commenting that these dinners were wonderful affairs with so many political leaders from all over the world, and so many prominent businessmen from all over the country. "In fact," he said, "there are several businessmen here tonight that I've never seen in court."

Referring to the fact that publishers were suspected of picking up Gridiron dinner expenses for some Gridiron members via expense accounts, Attorney General Rogers suggested that the Gridiron Club revise its admonition at the beginning to read as follows: "Ladies are always present, reporters never present—just publishers."

"There is one disturbing development," he continued. "As you know, the Internal Revenue Service is still considering adding Line 6A to the tax returns, and this requires some taxpayers to file a very detailed expense accounting. We might just as well face it, if they rule that Line 6A applies to publishers this may be the last Gridiron dinner."

Rogers had had a lot of fun with some of the other political figures in the country and said, with tongue in cheek, that in preparing his speech he'd asked several political figures in Washington if they'd be willing to give their comments on it after they'd read it.

"I found they were glad to," he continued, "and it was interesting to me that all of them said they didn't need to read the speech to comment on it."

Then he proceeded to give some of their comments:

"Senator Lyndon Johnson said, 'As a statement of general principles Rogers' speech was all right, but the big question that I am sure must be in your mind is "Who will provide the leadership?"'

"Ambassador Menshikov [of the Soviet Union]: 'It was a delightful talk. In fact, I think all officials of the American government are wonderful.'

"Senator Wayne Morse said, 'At a time when bipartisanship and good will are vital it was a brazen, unholy, deceitful Republican speech by another ignorant Republican.'

"Former Governor Adlai Stevenson: 'It wasn't bold and it lacked a sense of urgency. I propose that we immediately call for a space age summit conference made up of the heads of planets—I can't be there myself but I will be glad to act as an advisor.'

"Speaker Rayburn and former President Truman jointly made this comment: 'Rogers is a man of considerable inability. The speech was amusing enough as an after dinner speech for laymen—but it certainly didn't appeal to us lawyers.'"

Rogers followed with comments about the political picture in 1960 and, pointing out that "both parties have their problems," he said that "we Republicans have all of our eggs in one basket. Although Mr. Stassen may not agree, we have just one real prospect. . .

THE GRIDIRON CLUB.

MENU

Little Neck Clams.

POTAGE.
Consommé Royal.

HORS D'ŒUVRES.
Bouchées à la Reine.

POISSON.
Truite, Sauce Geneveise.
Salade de Concombres.

RELEVÉ.
Côtelettes d'Agneau, Petits Pois.

ENTRÉES.
Pâté de Foie-Gras en Belle-Vue.
Asperges en Branches.
Salade de Volaille Mayonnaise.

DESSERT.
Fraises et Crème.
Vanilla et Water Ice.
Fruits.   Fromage.
Café Noir.

Dinner Committee.
Chas. T. Murray,   O. O. Stealey,   Geo.
Welcker's, May 23, 1885.

1885   The Gridiron Club   1976
Annual Spring Dinner
Saturday, April 3, 1976

Menu

Prosciutto and Melon

Diamond-Back Terrapin, Maryland
Hot Corn Sticks

Chesapeake Shad and Roe

Filet of Beef, Richelieu, with Mushrooms
Cauliflower   Carrots
Kentucky Wonder Beans

Bibb Lettuce or Boston Lettuce
Lemon and Olive Oil Dressing
Brie

Cannoli Volante
Demi-Tasse

THE STATLER HILTON, WASHINGTON, D.C.

Mr. Beardsley

Menus of Gridiron dinners. Above: One from the first dinner in 1885 and another from the most recent affair in 1976.
Right: The bill of fare of a dinner during World War I approved personally by Herbert Hoover, who was food administrator at the time.

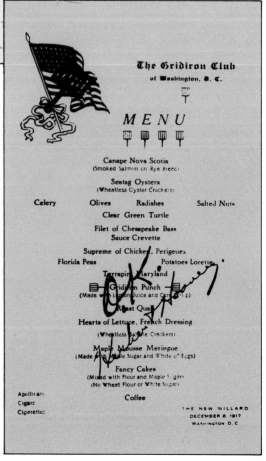

The Gridiron Club
of Washington, D. C.

MENU

Canape Nova Scotia
(Smoked Salmon on Rye Bread)

Seatag Oysters
(Wheatless Oyster Crackers)

Celery   Olives   Radishes   Salted Nuts

Clear Green Turtle

Filet of Chesapeake Bass
Sauce Crevette

Supreme of Chicken, Perigueux
Florida Peas   Potatoes Lorette

Terrapin Maryland

Gridiron Punch
(Made with Lemon Juice and Corn Syrup)

Roast Quail

Hearts of Lettuce, French Dressing
(Wheatless Saltine Crackers)

Maple Mousse Meringue
(Made with Maple Sugar and White of Eggs)

Fancy Cakes
(Mixed with Flour and Maple Sugar)
(No Wheat Flour or White Sugar)

Apollinaris   Coffee
Cigars
Cigarettes

THE NEW WILLARD
DECEMBER 8, 1917
WASHINGTON, D.C.

Be it ever so humble,
there's no place like home.

Gridiron dinner menus often carry cartoons as represented by these dealing with Presidents Kennedy and Nixon.

....BUT, BILL, HOW CAN YOU BE PRESIDENT OF *ANYTHING* WITHOUT A FEW *BROTHERS*?

"GET THE NAME OF HIS TAILOR"

"THEY WENT THEN TILL THEY CAME TO THE DELECTABLE MOUNTAINS"

More cartoons ribbing political figures which embellished Gridiron dinner menus.

"....But, Mr. President, THIS...."

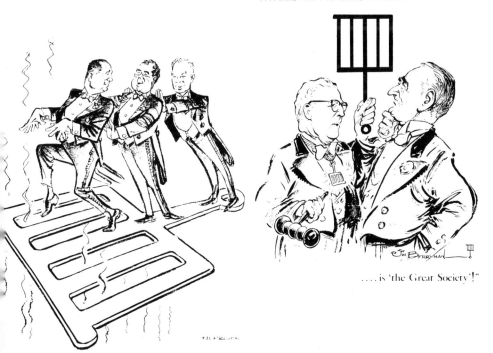

"FORWARD ———— TOGETHER, OF COURSE"

....is 'the Great Society'!"

THE SECRETARY OF STATE
WASHINGTON

November 20, 1922.

My dear Mr. Cunningham:

I have received your letter, enclosing invitation to The Gridiron dinner for December ninth. It will give me much pleasure to be present and even greater pleasure to be able to listen to others with no thought of being a burnt offering.

Sincerely yours,

[signature: Charles E. Hughes]

Mr. J. Harry Cunningham,
    Secretary,
        The Gridiron Club,
            48 Post Building
                Washington,

In letters accepting Gridiron Club invitations, many in public life responded with wit and humor.

THE SECRETARY OF THE NAVY
WASHINGTON

14 November 1945

Dear Lew:

Thank you for your note about The Gridiron invitation. It is encouraging to note that bureaucrats still have some chance of getting to eat free.

I thank you and all hands for the invitation, which I am of course accepting.

Sincerely yours,

[signature: James Forrestal]

James Forrestal

Lewis Wood, Esq.,
The New York Times,
Albee Building,
Washington, D. C.

OFFICE OF THE VICE PRESIDENT
WASHINGTON
March 23, 1945

Mr. Charles G. Ross
St. Louis Post-Dispatch
Kellogg Building
Washington, D. C.

Dear Charlie:

     Thanks a lot for the invitat[...]
the Gridiron Club.

     I shall certainly be there u[...]
I get crippled or something.

     The invitation is most high[...]
appreciated.

     Sincerely yours,

     harry S. Truman

March 21, 1945

The Hon. Harry S. Truman
Vice President of the United States
240 Senate Office Building
Washington, D. C.

My dear Mr. Vice President:

     Your invitation to the Gridiron Club's 60th
anniversary dinner at 7:00 p.m., Saturday, April 14, at
the Statler Hotel is in the mails and probably already
has been received. My spies inform me that you were
properly apprised sometime ago of the place and date.
I would like to impose on you for some very brief remarks on the night of the dinner, only two minutes.
Would you drop me a line, please, if you are willing to
undertake such a chore in our behalf?

     Sincerely yours,

     Lyle C. Wilson

The sequence of letters between the Gridiron Club and Vice President Truman for a dinner in the Spring of 1945 which was cancelled because of President Roosevelt's death a few days before it was to be held.

OFFICE OF THE VICE PRESIDENT
WASHINGTON
March 23, 1945

Mr. Lyle C. Wilson
United Press Associations
Manager, Capital Bureau
National Press Building
Washington, D. C.

Dear Mr. Wilson:

     I'll be glad to take the two minutes
which you suggest at the Gridiron Club if you
will tell me exactly what you want. This will
be entirely new to me and I don't want to make
a mess of it.

     Sincerely yours,

     Harry S. Truman

April 9, 1945

Dear Lyle:

From my hideout in Georgia, I just want to say hello to you and all friends in the Gridiron Club. I wish I could be with you but unfortunately I shall not be back in Washington until sometime next week -- when the stiff shirt season is over. I write this line with mixed emotions. What's this I read on my card about "black tie"? Has Gridiron conservatism surrendered to the spirit of modernism or is it that those mossy green tailcoats have finally fallen apart?

The best of luck to all and a merry evening, too.

Very sincerely yours,

Franklin Roosevelt

Lyle C. Wilson, Esq.,
President,
The Gridiron Club,
National Press Building,
Washington, D. C.

The letter written by President Roosevelt from Warm Springs, Georgia, three days before his death.

HARRY S. TRUMAN
FEDERAL RESERVE BANK BUILDING
KANSAS CITY 6, MISSOURI

November 20, 1956

Dear Eddie:

Your letter of the 16th was highly appreciated,
and I am sorry I cannot be present at the Gridiron Club's
private dinner on December 8th. The reason is that I
will not sit at the same table with Nixon. He has never
refuted his statement that I was a traitor; but even if
he did, my feelings about him would remain the same.

Therefore, please do not count on me for the private dinner or for your annual dinner in March. I regret it very much for there is nothing I would like better than being there, but I just cannot sit with that
fellow, or with his boss either.

Sincerely yours,

Harry Truman

Personal

Mr. Edward T. Folliard
The Washington Post
1515 L Street, N. W.
Washington 5, D. C.

Former President Harry Truman, with
extraordinary candor, declined in
the above letter a Gridiron Club
invitation.

Deputy in Full Dress 'Crashes' Gridiron Dinner With Subpoenas

Sickler Used Frat Grip to Serve Doherty

Gerald W. Sickler, former cheer leader, amateur actor and psychology student at George Washington University, was the "Sweetheart of Sigma Chi" last night.

In the eyes of his fraternity brothers he loomed a hero deserving a medal or something as the only person extant who had ever crashed a Gridiron Club dinner.

Gave Frat Grip

He did it with his Sigma Chi grip, and for a purpose—to serve a stack of 14 subpoenas on Henry L. Doherty, multimillionaire utilities magnate.

Not that subpoena serving is a part of the fraternity ritual or

HENRY L. DOHERTY
'Served' at Dinner.

anything like that, but being a "Sig" enabled the young ex-collegiate to get away with his job in first-class fashion.

And Frat Brother Patrick J. Hurley, former Secretary of War, unwittingly aided and abetted the performance.

It was like this:

How He Did It

For some time regular Deputy United States Marshals had tried in vain to serve the subpoenas on Doherty in suits filed by fourteen purchasers of stock in an oil company which the utilities magnate heads. Three weeks ago Justice Jennings Bailey of District of Columbia Supreme Court, in which the suits were brought, deputized Sickler and he was given the papers to serve.

One of the lawyers interested in the case, knowing Doherty was to be here for the Gridiron dinner, conceived the idea of obtaining service there. He went along with Sickler to see the job through.

Sickler dressed for his role in tails, white tie and all. The lawyer went in business garb. Secret

GERALD W. "CRASHER" SICKLER
He shows how, dressed in swallowtails, he handed Colonel Doherty 14 subpoenas.

Service men spotted the lawyer and hustled him out, but Sickler in his formal dress and looking the part of an energetic young newspaper correspondent dressed up for the evening, managed to stroll by the guardians at the door.

Hurley "Taken In"

Once inside Sickler recognized Brother Hurley, strolled over to him, gave him the frat grip and renewed an acquaintance formed at a Sigma Chi function. Brother Hurley returned Brother Sickler's greeting in kind and they chatted together several moments.

From then on it was easy going.

Hobnobbing with Pat Hurley was all the entre the young man needed so far as the Gridironers and the other guests were concerned.

From another guest Sickler borrowed a seating diagram and spotted Doherty's table and seat. And then he nonchalantly walked over to Doherty, introduced himself and handed him "the papers."

Doherty good-humoredly took the subpoenas and stuffed them in his pocket.

By that time Sickler's nerve was beginning to weaken, and with a bad case of "jitters" he "ducked the party." Now he's sorry he didn't stay for the show.

August twenty third
Nineteen fifteen

The Gridiron Club,

Washington.

Gentlemen:-

On the tenth instant I paid one hundred dollars to your Mr. Patterson and received a receipt numbered eighty four as an Associate member. I write to know whether I am to receive anything more formal in acknowledgment, and take this opportunity because I am about to leave for the Pacific Coast to attend the Bankers Convention and want to attend to any matter requiring it before leaving. Awaiting your advices with interest, I am

Very truly yours,

Below: "Dr." Jules Waterbury who, under various aliases, sold phony memberships in the Gridiron Club and (left) a letter from one of his victims.

Left: The Washington (D.C.) Herald story of December 16, 1935, recounting the incident of the white-tied gate crasher who served subpoenas on Henry L. Doherty.

'WATERBURY SMILE WINS 'DOC' A PAROLE

Noted Confidence Man Admits Crooked Deal, but Says He's Reformed.

JUDGE OFFERS CHANCE

Auburn Warden Says Swindler Has Been Hard Working Model Prisoner.

GOES HOME TO PARENTS

Crook Refuses to Talk on Morality Calling It 'Mawkish Piffle.'

FEB 21 1923

You would never have known Doc Waterbury as he stood before Judge Rosalsky in General Sessions yesterday, brought from an Auburn cell to answer to an old indictment of grand larceny. He was still spruce enough—as spruce as his somewhat worn clothing permitted—and there was something of the old suavity. But it wasn't the Doc Waterbury of the days when We Boys were one of the sights of

the city, sunning themselves on Broadway just above Forty-second street.

Somewhat stooped, dull of eye and with his intelligent face deeply lined, the Doc looked licked. When they sent him to prison in the fall of 1919 the Doc was most debonair. He wore a carnation in his buttonhole. A gray derby sat upon his head at a slight angle. He wore gray spats and gloves. The Doc was the very last word in sartorial correctness. Yes, come to think of it, the Doc was not chic. But yesterday the Doc was chic.

For the benefit of the few who have not known of Doc Waterbury, it is explained that he is Jules Howard Ford—Mr. J. Howard Ford of New York, London, Monte Carlo and one or two equally famous though smaller towns where penal institutions are located. The Doc was a confidence man. He could sell you something he didn't have in a manner so pleasing as to extract some of the sting. The Doc insists that he has not theories. Maybe he is right.

Sold Gridiron Membership.

Well, Doc Waterbury, to use the old familiar name, was arraigned before Judge Rosalsky yesterday charged with grand larceny. The charge had grown out of the Doc's sales of memberships in the Gridiron Club, the dining organization of the newspaper correspondents in Washington.

Doc knew that memberships in the Gridiron Club were not for sale. It would seem that everybody should know it. But there were men who didn't know it and the Doc took them in with the graces of a courtier lobbing the time of day to the most beautiful lady in waiting. There were many gentlemen who couldn't be swindled by anybody but the Doc. They were, so to speak, the Doc's regular customers.

At the Doc's side yesterday in court stood Assistant District Attorney Pecora. Mr. Pecora had in his hand a letter from E. S. Jennings, warden of the Auburn prison. Briefly Mr. Pecora said that it was his opinion that this was one of those times when prosecutors and courts should take a flier in human nature. Here, he said, was a man who showed all the signs

of being tired of playing jokes on the law. The letter had it that the Doc had been paroled to his father's home in Ithaca; that the father has but a little while to live and that the Doc's mother is surrendering to her age and her troubles.

"This man," read the letter, "has done his time at this prison in a very satisfactory way; in fact, he has been very valuable to us by giving his honest conscientious effort to work in our Bertillon office. He desires to go home to live with his father, who undoubtedly has only a short time to live.

"The Parole Board took favorable action in his case after careful investigation. I believe he has been punished sufficiently for the several crimes that he committed, and feel that if he is given a chance he will become a law abiding citizen and will try to live down his past unfortunate record. He now has an additional responsibility, as his father is dying and his mother is in feeble health and very old. He will be needed at home to manage the affairs of his family."

Not the Same Old Smile.

Doc Waterbury smiled at Judge Rosalsky. It was not the refulgent smile of the days when he was floating a grand scheme to supply libraries for the American Army in France (for which he went to Auburn prison), and it had none of the reassuring brilliance that it had when he played his smile so successfully upon credulous ladies and lords in London twelve years ago. It was just the smile of a man who finds it hard to believe that any one is going to take seriously his protestations of reform.

"I am guilty of this charge, your Honor," said the Doc quietly. "I shall never trouble you again. Times have changed and I have changed with them."

And then Judge Rosalsky suspended sentence and told the Doc to go home to Ithaca and the old folks. The Doc left court with that foolish smile still on his face. A couple of reporters stopped him. The Doc paused, seemed about to launch forth upon a lecture upon the futility of being a crook, and then shook his head.

"Nope," said the Doc. "I guess not. I was about to get sentimental and give you a sermon on morality. But what's the use. It would only be a lot of mawkish piffle. All I have to say is that I'm going home."

The Doc is 45.

This is the text, handwritten and typed, of a talk by President Truman elaborating on his decision to drop the first atomic bombs on Japan. After the dinner, Lyle Wilson, president of the club, asked for and obtained the typed text on which President Truman added a penned note.

THE WHITE HOUSE
WASHINGTON

This is a great privilege. I have been here before as a United States Senator, - a Junior United States Senator

It was my good luck on those occasions, to hear President Roosevelt express himself at his best. He told you gentlemen of the press exactly what he thought of you - and made you like it.

I haven't his ability of expression, but I shall be

wishes Roosevelt was back -

THE WHITE HOUSE
WASHINGTON

You know the most terrible decision a man ever had to make was made by me at Potsdam It had nothing to do with Russia or Britain or Germany. It was a decision to loose the most terrible of all destructive forces for the wholesale slaughter of human beings. The Secretary of War, Mr. Stimson, and I weighed that decision most prayerfully. But the President

THE WHITE HOUSE
WASHINGTON

had to decide. It occurred to me that a quarter of a million of the flower of our young manhood were worth a couple of Japanese cities, and I still think they were and are. But I couldn't help but think of the necessity of blotting out women and children and non-combatants. We gave them fair warning and asked them to quit. We picked a couple of cities

THE WHITE HOUSE
WASHINGTON

where war work was the principle industry, and dropped the bombs. Russia hurried in and the war ended.

Now we are faced with equally grave decisions. On these decisions rest either peace and the greatest age in history or another armament race and total destruction of civilization as we know it.

Now my friends it is

THE WHITE HOUSE
WASHINGTON

time for prayer and most solemn thought.

Sherman was wrong I'm telling you I find peace is hell and repeat

You know that the most terrible

decision a man ever had to make was made by me at Potsdam - it

had nothing to do with Russia, or Britain or Germany. It was a

decision to loose the most terrible of all destructive forces

for the wholesale slaughter of human beings. The Secretary of

War, Mr. Stimson, and I weighed that decision most prayerfully.

The President had to decide. It occurred to me that a quarter

of a million of the flower of our young manhood was worth a couple

of Japanese cities, and I still think they were and are. But

I couldn't help but thing of the necessity of blotting out

women, children and non-combatants. We picked a couple of cities

where war work was the principle industry, and dropped the bombs.

Russia hurried in and that war ended.

Now we are faced with other equally momentous decisions.

On them rest either peace and the greatest age in history or

another armament race and total destruction of civilization as

we know it. Men, friends, it is a time for prayer and solemn

thought. Sherman was wrong. I'm telling you I find"peace is

hell" xxxxxxxxxx - and repeat.

In fear & trembling

12/15/45   Harry Truman

1.

Mr. Mckelway, Mr. Vice President, Mr. Chief
Justice, Gentlemen of the Gridiron:

I have just received the following wire
from my generous Daddy: "Dear Jack -- Don't
buy a single vote more than is necessary --
I'll be damned if I'm going to pay for a
landslide."

2.

I am grateful to my father for his
support -- but I am even more grateful to
"Mr. Sam" Rayburn. At the last Democratic
convention, if he had not recognized the
Tennessee and Oklahoma delegations when he
did, I might have won that race with Senator
Kefauver -- and my political career would
now be over.

Excerpts from texts of talks at
Gridiron dinners, with the
speaker's own editing.
Left:
President Kennedy;
Below:
Senator Robert Kennedy
Upper right:
Senator Barry Goldwater
Lower right:
President Ford, when he was in the
House of Representatives.

Another false story I would like to clear up is the
report that J. Edgar Hoover used to get me upset when I was in
the Justice Department. He never upset me . . . of course,
sometimes he bugged me a little . . .

There's only one way to keep J. Edgar Hoover friendly
. . . I don't know what it is, but (there must be some way).

Although Mr. Hoover has been worried about our contacts
with the Soviet Union, President Johnson has just announced a
new cultural exchange -- Stalin's daughter for George Hamilton.

I'm glad to see Governor Reagan here tonight. He
is really shaking things up in California. He has even adopted
a new motto for the State seal: "Lights -- Camera -- Reaction."

Governor Reagan has the University is being very generous
about the whole thing and has decided to award him an
honorary L.S.D.

I'm serious about this...I like the address of the White House... anything with 1600 in it strikes my fancy.

And, Mr. President, I look forward with great anticipation to this race...While I know it will be a tough one (there are more Kennedys than Goldwaters) I have every confidence that I will be declared the winner when the votes are counted -- IF THEY ARE COUNTED.

I have already launched my campaign...I have resigned from all my clubs...~~I have made my promises to Reuther~~...~~I have written a book called "Practice of Confusion"~~...I salaam 5 times a day in the direction of Harvard and 10 times a day towards the United Nations....~~I'm well on my way in Illinois — I already have the results from Cook County in my pocket.~~

Mr. President, I believe in copying success. So you will find that my campaign plans cover ^MUCH OF the same areas that your own touched on in 1960. ~~This leaves only the problem of how to get Caroline in my act yet to be decided. On this, we'll have to consider carefully and reach a judgment.~~

But allow me to discuss my plans. And again I say, Mr. President, if some of the more enticing phrases strike a familiar note you will know that I borrowed them in the firm conviction that you can't argue with success.

HAVE ABSOLUTELY NO DESIGNS ON HIS JOB.

HOW MANY OTHERS IN THIS ROOM CAN MAKE THAT STATEMENT?

I'M SERIOUS. I'M NOT AT ALL INTERESTED IN THE VICE-PRESIDENCY.

I LOVE THE HOUSE OF REPRESENTATIVES, DESPITE THE LONG, IRREGULAR HOURS.

SOMETIMES, THOUGH, WHEN IT'S LATE AND I'M TIRED AND HUNGRY -----

ON THAT LONG DRIVE HOME TO ALEXANDRIA ----- AS I GO PAST 1600 PENNSYLVANIA AVENUE, I DO SEEM TO HEAR A LITTLE VOICE SAYING:

"IF YOU LIVED HERE, YOU'D BE HOME NOW."

Club members, who write, produce and act all the skits, are shown here at various dress rehearsals.

"The Democrats have an advantage in having a lot of candidates. Their leading prospect seems to be the distinguished senator who spoke so ably a few minutes ago. He writes well too, but as a writer he is gentle and sincere, not sarcastic or flip. He was able to convince Drew Pearson that he wrote that book* himself, but he'll never convince me that he wrote that speech himself.

"Although Senator Kennedy looks good now, there are a lot of people who have doubts. They think he will turn out to be just part of the count down when Explorer Lyndon Johnson is launched.

"Mr. Truman continues to remember more and more about what never happened. No Democratic candidates are under Mr. Stevenson's influence—including Mr. Stevenson. Basically though, the Democrats have the same serious difficulties they had in 1952 and 1956. They have the same old shape—but they're trying to give it that new chemise look.

"Actually all of the Democratic possibilities have serious drawbacks: Some are too old, some too young—some are too rich, others are richer—some are not known, others are known. So as I see it, the big question the Democrats will have to decide is, 'Which one are they willing to get stuck with?'

"So you can sum up 1960 this way—our problem is one of preservation and the Democrats' is one of elimination."

Noting that he liked Gridiron dinners because "somehow they make our differences seem less important," Rogers commented that "later when the Vice President speaks for all of the guests of the Gridiron Club there will be no differences, and at the close of the dinner we will walk out of this room proud of our free system that makes such an event possible. . .

Then he closed with a few notes about the future.

"I believe the word 'responsibility' will assume greater importance," he said. "The stakes will be too high to pardon irresponsible attacks such as some of the attacks we see made today on the President, the courts, and the Congress.

"We will have to have a better sense of values and a more accurate way of judging character. Persons who exploit trouble and stimulate alarm for political purposes must stand condemned.

---

*Profiles in Courage

"We will need to develop greater respect for our system of government—a system which has made it possible for the American people today to enjoy the highest wages, the best housing, and the greatest freedom that any people have enjoyed in the history of the world.

"We will need to foster greater mutual regard among the people of our country. Ours is a competitive society and a man who has respected the rules of the game and succeeds should be considered a success—not a vested interest.

"A free people, proud of our fundamental belief that all men are created equal, must wipe out the few remaining pockets of prejudice. We should do this not so much because our friends in other lands don't understand—although that is an important factor—we should do it because it is right.

"And, finally, our greatest mission of all is to take the lead in the cause of peace. The ultimate goal of the American people and of the American government is peace in the world. With that goal in mind we can all take pride in knowing that for the next three years we will have as the President of the United States the most dedicated, respected and wise crusader for peace in the world today."[3]

The scene for the foreign affairs skit was set in the"Hotel Cosmos Hilton" in outer space, where a conference was taking place.

In spite of President Eisenhower's effort to unify the defense establishment under Secretary Neil McElroy, who had joined the administration from Procter and Gamble, there was still considerable rivalry among the air force, the navy and the army. Impersonators of the three chiefs of these services, General Thomas White of the air force, Admiral Arleigh Burke of the navy, and General Maxwell Taylor of the army, sang, to the tune of "We Three Kings of Orient Are":

White:
> Oh, up the air force, wing-ed might.
> SAC is poised for costly flight.
> Army's cheating, Navy's bleating.
> Atlas some day may fly right.

Burke:
> Oh, trust the Navy day and night.
> Missile submarines we fight.
> Soldiers squawk and airmen talk,
> While victory, we expedite.

Taylor:
> Oh, let the air force fly its kite.
> Army gadgeteers shine bright.
> Down Polaris! Up Medaris!
> Take a look (*gestures up*)—our satellite.

Together:
> We three chiefs of services are.
> Each of us an absolute czar.
> Ne'er unitin', feudin', fightin'
> Three diff-rent wars—hurrah!

The Cold War was still continuing, and an impersonator of Secretary of State Dulles sang a parody of "No, No, a Thousand Times No."

> I am a vet-ran of statecraft,
> My grandpappy showed me the ropes.
> And practice since then has convinced me
> That in this business good guys are dopes.
> Khrushchev would like me to take down my guard,
> But I am wise to his game.
> Each time he threatens, "The Summit—or else,"
> Here are the words I'll exclaim:

> No, no, a thousand times, no.
> Quote me on this for the press.
> No, no, a thousand times no.
> I'd rather die than say yes.

An impersonator of McElroy wasn't interested in putting a man on the moon. He had "higher ambitions."

"I'm gonna hit the White House," he said. "Ask yourself—how many divisions has Nixon got? Why, I've got enough assistant secretaries to stack the 1960 convention."

Then one of them sang to the tune of "Danny Boy":

> Oh, McElroy, the White House is a-calling.
> That ain't the phone—that's destiny you hear.
> You conquered soap, you stopped the service brawling.
> There's just one job to top off your career.

But like nearly all Gridiron foreign affairs skits in those days, this one closed on a note of unity and hope, sounded by an impersonator of United Nations Ambassador Henry Cabot Lodge.

"Gentlemen, we've had our fun. But as we close another Gridiron dinner, here is the real message America has for the world. 'Senator Green,' the chairman of the foreign relations committee, will sing it."

> Around the world we search for peace.
> Our goal is clear. We'll persevere.
> Our hope shall never cease.
> We know somewhere, sometime, somehow
> Mankind will know the bless-ed glow,
> he deeply prays for now.
> Where hate and strife and fear now reign
> Let men and nations join their hearts and
> hands as one again.
> And pledge their vow that all around the world,
> We'll always find our world at peace.

Vice President Nixon responded to the toast to the President. He complimented both of the other speakers and noted that both of them were winners, but as to Kennedy he wanted to note also that he was referring to being a winner in 1958.

"In these trying times," he said, "what we need is people who do not lose their sense of justice and their faith. . . .

"Tonight I would suggest that in these times which are difficult economically, from the standpoint of foreign policies, and in other areas, that we praise instead of complaining about leadership. Consider the power in this room—in the press, the business community, the power in government, the leadership which can be provided by America working together toward this great objective."

He said that Americans were not interested in dominating other people or acquiring an acre of territory belonging to anyone else, but that we were interested in "providing that others may enjoy the same rights and, if possible, the same prosperity which we enjoy."

He closed with a tribute to Ben McKelway and got a laugh by saying he was the first Gridiron president in his memory who closed the dinner by 11:30 at night.[4]

$ $ $

At the time of the March 14, 1959 dinner, the chief public interest was the upcoming 1960 Presidential race. Gridiron President Paul Wooton of the *New Orleans Times-Picayune* summed it up in his speech in the dark, by saying that in 1956 there had been Eisenhower and Nixon. Now, he said, "Ike can't wait to get out. Dick can't wait to get in. Kennedy can't wait, period. . . .

"An anti-barber shop ticket for 1960 has been suggested—Fidel Castro and Yul Brynner."

He referred to some comments by former Secretary of State Dean Acheson. His appraisal of Presidential candidates, as Wooton interpreted them, "eliminated all of them except himself. Now, however, he has added Lyndon Johnson."

But, except for Acheson, "everyone," he said, "seems to be avoiding something. Rockefeller is avoiding Nixon. Nixon is avoiding another good-will trip to Venezuela [on his previous one he had received uncomplimentary treatment]. Khrushchev is avoiding any more American Presidential candidates.

"Governor Williams wants out of Reuther's pocket. Senator Symington is avoiding too close a link with Lyndon Johnson.

"Johnson is avoiding anything that will take him out of the limelight.

"Everyone is avoiding Carmine DeSapio."

The Kennedy speech the year before, in which he had said that he had polled the Senate on their choice for President and that each senator had received one vote, was the inspiration for the opener at the dinner. The chorus was introduced as the hopeful candidates and, to the tune of "Seventy-six Trombones," they trooped in and Dwight Rorer sang:

Ninety-eight lined up for the White House race,
With the flush of a candidate on each face,
Nominees by the row and row
Of political virtuosos
Running madly for first place.

Ninety-eight who wait for a Gallup trend
With an axe for the back of each rival friend.

The inauguration skit was used as the vehicle to poke fun at members of Congress who put relatives on their staff payrolls. The new president of the Gridiron Club was revealed to have very few relatives, and thus did not seem qualified for office. But an impersonator of a congressman suggested that they had a list of relatives who could be supplied, and Ned Brooks sang:

Pack all your fam-ly on the old payroll and smile, smile, smile.
If you've a son or two that aren't too old, Hire, boys, it's the style.
Wives and moms come scurrying. We've cousins too on file,
So pack all your fam-ly on the old payroll and smile, smile, smile.

Eisenhower, while in Washington, attended the National

Presbyterian Church, whose pastor was Dr. E. L. E. Elson. In the guest skit, Lyle Wilson called to their feet Dr. Elson, Meade Alcorn, Republican National Committee chairman, and the President's brother, Dr. Milton S. Eisenhower, the president of John Hopkins University.

Richard Wilson commented, "Dr. Elson is the man who has to pray for the President of the United States after Dr. Eisenhower and Mr. Alcorn get through advising him."

The scene for the Democratic skit was "Senator Johnson's Big Chance Casino in Las Vegas, where hopeful candidates for the Presidential nomination are studying the winter book odds on their chances." On the stage were slot machines, a dice table and a tote board, giving winter book odds on President, the lowest being 100 to 1.

"Former President Truman" advised all candidates to:

Put your head on my shoulder,
You need some one who's older,
Be Missouri's favorite son.

And "Adlai Stevenson," in song, pleaded for:

Just one more chance
To gain the triumph that eludes me,
To win a vict'ry that includes me
Just one more chance.

Just one more chance,
When Ike is not my competition,
When Dick or Rock's the opposition,
Just one more chance.

Almost as if the Gridiron Club already knew the 1960 ticket, the major songs of the skit related to Kennedy and Johnson. At one point, the whole "Kennedy family" entered, led by "Papa Joe" and his three sons, and the family patriarch sang a song written by Fletcher Knebel.

All of us,
Why not take all of us?
Fabulous,
You can't live without us.
My son Jack heads the procession,
Then comes Bob,
Groomed for succession.

We're the most,

We stretch from coast to coast.
Kennedys
Just go on forever.
I've got the dough,
You might as well know
With one—
You get all of us.

When "Senator Johnson" was asked to give his views, he sang, to Cole Porter's tune:

I'm the top,
I'm the U.S. Senate.
I'm the top,
Take a vote—I'll win it.
In particular, I'm spectacular—
with grace!
I'm a Titan rocket,
Just watch me sock it,
I'm outer space! . . .

I'm the top,
I'm atomic fission;
I'm the top,
Just to lead's my mission.
On your civil rights
I've set my sights—this year.
I'm a Treas'ry surplus,
A man with purpose
No one need fear.

I can't lose,
I'm a Texas gusher;
If I choose
I can out-talk Russia.
I will reach the moon sometime in June—non-stop.
There'll be many at the bottom—I'm the top.

The Democratic speaker was Governor Edmund G. Brown of California, who had been elected by an impressive majority. The governor said that he was appearing that night through the courtesy of Nixon, Knowland and Knight.

"They were imprudent," he said, "but I needed them."

Senator Knowland, who had retired to California to edit the *Oakland Tribune*, which he and his family owned, was answerable, said Brown, "only to himself, to his God—and the Newspaper Guild."

He also commented that "out in our state, the Republicans are still not sure whether Knowland and Knight leaped into oblivion—or the Vice President pushed them."

Turning to the forthcoming Presidential election, he declared that in order that there be no question of any availability he would like to declare, courageously and unequivocally, that "I am not a candidate for President in 1960."

"If this doesn't put me in the thick of the race, I don't know what will."

The Democratic Convention was to be held in Los Angeles the following year, and the next section of Governor Brown's speech dealt with what he called "local sentiment on the various non-candidates.

"Let us begin with Adlai Stevenson," he said. "We have begun with him twice before. It is really too bad that the Third Term Amendment keeps him from trying for the nomination again.

"Turning from youth to experience, we have Jack Kennedy. If Mrs. Roosevelt would just stop endorsing Jack's father, I think a lot of people would forget about whether Jack is old enough. . .

"That brings us to the taciturn Hubert Humphrey. Hubert got a big lift when Khrushchev denounced him and ignored the rest of the Presidential hopefuls. When Comrade Mikoyan was in San Francisco, I spent several hours trying to get him to say something nasty about me. He flatly refused. This shows how hard it is to do business with the Russians.

"Senator Lyndon Johnson, I understand, will soon make a public denial that he believes in the divine right of kings. This should drive back to the hills that well known rebel—Fidel Proxmire.

"Whatever you may think of Senator Proxmire's criticisms of Lyndon Johnson, you have to admit that, like Notre Dame, Proxmire plays a tough schedule.

"I was going to say something about Senator Symington but I had lunch with Clark Clifford and he assured me that the senator was not in the race."

Turning to the Republican candidates, he said that the three leading ones out West were Harold Stassen, Ezra Taft Benson and Alf Landon, but that when he came East he found there was a good deal of talk about the Vice President and Governor Rockefeller.

"It would be a tough decision for me," he declared, "if I had to choose between the two. The Vice President was a tower of strength to me in 1958 [when Brown won his landslide election as governor over Senator William F. Knowland]. If the opportunity should arise in the future, Mr. Vice President, be assured that I shall be prepared to do *for* you all that you so kindly attempted to do *to* me."

As for Nelson Rockefeller, he noted that Americans had traditionally admired the self-made man. Charles A. Halleck, who was to speak for the Republicans, he described as "that brilliant young radical.

"He is the kind of rebel who can succeed in the Republican party," he said. "You certainly can't underestimate a man who is clever enough and persistent enough to win the minority leadership despite White House support."

To the Republican party in the election campaign, he recommended "agreement on a positive program of negative thinking."

Then, speaking more seriously, Brown sounded a note that was later to become the keynote of the Kennedy campaign. He said he heard the people saying that "America must be on the move again." He called for new vision and new ideas and the courage and confidence to act on them.

"Give us, America is saying, leadership which is fresh and flexible, pioneering and practical. Let us stop being slaves to outdated symbols and overworked dogmas, and let us start being creative again.

"When the people ask for leadership, they speak in a bipartisan voice. They place their order without party label, and they will respond without reservation, just as all of our nation has responded to the President's firm hand in the Berlin crisis. We will serve both our people and our parties if we will remember that the enlightened leadership of free men is our high privilege and our solemn duty.

"I have greatly enjoyed my visit here. It has been a delightful experience to meet and visit with the leading Democratic candidates for 1960. They are able and outstanding men.

"I believe I can say, without fear of successful contradiction, that each and every one of them would make a satisfactory running mate."[5]

The Republican skit was set at a construction site for the "Bridge on the River Quail." It was explained that this bridge extended from Gettysburg to George Humphrey's plantation in Thomasville, Georgia, so that the Republicans could bypass Washington because "it's so lonesome for them there."

Asked what direction "our boss" is heading, an impersonator of Jim Hagerty sang his new version of "Left, Right, Out of Your Heart."

> He tried to find the middle road,
>   he told them it was best.
> He didn't know just what it meant
>   but never ceased his quest.
> He tightened up the budget, he said
>   we shouldn't spend,
> But Congress it thought diff'runt and
>   he found that he was—

> Left right out in the cold,
> He had no left right place to take hold.
> He kept his eyes right like he was told,
> Now he is left right out in the cold.

In the newly organized Congress, Charles A. Halleck, who had been reelected in Indiana, had unseated Joe Martin as minority leader. The Republicans wondered where they had made their mistake, and an impersonator of Barry Goldwater answered, "It's very simple. We invited the voters to examine our record."

"Charlie Halleck" was asked how he was getting along in his new job, and he sang:

> Charley, my boy, oh, Charley my boy,
> It thrills me, it chills me,
> With shivers of joy.
> In grabbing Martin's job I showed off a knack
> I learned from feeling Dewey's knife in my back.

Taking a dim view of the Republican congressional future, the Gridiron Club had "Thomas E. Dewey" tell "Senator Kenneth Keating" that they were offering the Republican Presidential nomination to anyone who could wake the elephant up.

"Oh, no," said Keating, "you must be confused—the nomination is *second* prize."

Dewey: What's the *first* prize?
Keating: Two dollars and a half.

Next came an impersonator of Vice President Nixon, "the nice man cometh," and he sang, somewhat more prophetically

than most of the Gridiron members probably realized a year and
a half before the 1960 election, a revised version of "This Nearly
Was Mine."

> One dream in my heart,
> One goal I was striving for,
> One chance I was living for,
> This nearly was mine.
>
> One vote by acclaim,
> One roar for the nominee,
> One choice for the GOP,
> This nearly was mine.
>
> Close to my grasp this came,
> Only to fly away,
> Only to fly as they
> Cry for Rocky—
>
> Now, now I'm opposed,
> Now, now when the fight begins
> I dream of the might-have-beens,
> This nearly was mine.

Although Representative Martin had been deposed as
leader, he was left with one of the perquisites of the leader—a
chauffeur-driven Cadillac. He acknowledged that while "they
gave me a broom closet for my office," he nevertheless still rode
to work in style.

> Thanks for the Cadillac . . .
> Some said I should have thundered
> And some said that I should have blasted,
> Well it was good while it lasted.
> It leaves no scar—
> I've got my car.

Reluctantly ("It's like losing my right arm"), President
Eisenhower had dismissed his most important assistant, Sherman Adams, because Adams had accepted gifts of a vicuna coat
and a Persian rug from people whom he had helped. "Adams"
sang:

> A soft vicuna coat,
> A Persian rug of note,
> These things I sadly tote
> Among my souvenirs.

The skit closed with a Rockefeller song:

Rock! With Rock a fella,
The ladies love my smile,
I'm a charming fella.
I've got that winning style.
The voters know my love is true,
The wolves of Wall Street love me too,
Rock a fel la!
Just hear that cry!

Buy young Rock a fella,
Accept an inside tip,
I'm the man who has the White House in his grip.
I'll pitch my tent
Where Richard Nixon thought he should of went.
Love that Rock a fella,
A really true blue chip.

Charles Halleck was introduced to make the Republican speech with the comment by Gridiron President Wooton that "he takes the hide off of an opponent one day and bends over backward to reconcile him the next day."

The Republican congressional disaster in the 1958 elections had been overwhelming. The Republicans lost 47 seats in the House and 13 in the Senate, to leave them with a House lineup of 153 Republicans and 283 Democrats, and a Senate line-up of 34 Republicans and 64 Democrats.

Halleck began by laughing at himself and at the Republicans. "Speaking as one interested in conservation," he said, "may I say that Republicans should no longer be considered fair game.

"We have joined the limbo of the whooping crane.

"Those of us left," he continued, "are still laying eggs—but we haven't figured out a way to get around the Hatch Act [which governed campaign activities and contributions at the time].

"The slaughter was terrific out in Indiana last November. People ask me what I did during the debacle.

"I survived.

"I'm not a fatalist, but as I look back I think destiny must have ordained me to be the Republican leader in 1959.

"What else could happen to a guy who thought he was going to be Dewey's running mate in 1948? . . .

"I've heard it said that Gridiron speeches have nipped some promising political careers in the bud.

"I wouldn't say that I've had a promising career—but I have made a career of promising.

"The Gridiron powers were more cagey with me. They waited until they were sure I had no place else to go and then gave me this assignment."

He also had a word for the publishers.

"I have read about half of your political editorials—and buried the other half in the *Congressional Record* so nobody else will see them, including your own reporters."

And for the Gridiron Club:

"I've been coming to Gridiron dinners for years, and many of the members are my old friends—in spite of it. . .

"Only one thing bothers me tonight—I'm not mad at anybody. I wonder if I'm slipping or if it's just that writers couldn't find anything to rhyme with Halleck.

"Actually, though, I don't know what I'd do without the press. They keep my home folks informed about my really important accomplishments in the Congress, right down to the latest addition to my fleet of Cadillacs. According to the last press report, I've got more Cadillacs than General Motors."

Then Halleck noted that there were a lot of new names and faces around Congress that year. "But," he said, "the Democrats are having their face troubles too. We're trying to lift ours, they're trying to save theirs.

"Right now, for instance, they're sweating out support from union ranks on one hand and evidence of something rank in unions on the other.

"We can't get a labor reform bill out because they've stacked the committee with too many Democrats who have other bills to worry about—all from COPE for services rendered in the last campaign.

"And look at Lyndon Johnson's dilemma. He's caught between Proxmire and the Solid South.

"I've known Lyndon for a long time and he's really a cautious fellow. At the moment he's not sure which way to turn. He's waiting to see which way the people are going, so he can lead 'em.

"There was a time when one of the big tourist attractions in Washington was the White House. But after you've seen Johnson's acreage in the new Senate Office Building, the State Dining Room looks like something out of a low-cost housing project."

Shifting to the forthcoming 1960 campaign, he commented that "the voters will decide whether they want to elect a Republican with Democrat ideas or a Democrat with Republican money.

"At the latest count the Democrats have at least ninety-nine hopefuls. That includes sixty-four Senators and thirty-four Governors. Plus Adlai Stevenson. They had an even hundred until Michigan went broke.

"I understand Kennedy is out in front. That's not hard to figure—his dad named him John and then gave him the Jack to run for President."

Remarking that he hoped he had kept within the bounds of Gridiron tradition and not really offended anyone, Halleck said that while it is true "we should never take ourselves too seriously, it is nevertheless vital that we look to our responsibilities in these trying times.

"Certainly the right to dissent is the essence of freedom. Over much of the world it has been lost.

"We can keep that priceless privilege alive for those who follow in our footsteps only if we use it judiciously ourselves.

"In domestic matters, therefore, may we—as advocates of principles and policies—always distinguish between honorable contention and reckless abuse.

"And, having in mind Berlin, may we—to whom the free world looks for leadership and the slave world looks for salvation—recognize that partisanship is a luxury we shall enjoy only so long as we close ranks as Americans all in the face of challenge from beyond our shores."[6]

The situation with the Soviet Union in March 1959 was still tense. The dinner came after Senator Hubert Humphrey had gone to Moscow and had had an eight-hour conference with Khrushchev during which Humphrey had apparently done most of the talking, leading Washington wags to comment, "Poor Khrushchev."

The scene for the foreign affairs act had most of the cast in revolutionary costumes and was set on the battlefield of Bunkum Hill, with strong emphasis on the "Bunkum." It began with an impersonator of Soviet Deputy Premier Anastas I. Mikoyan, the "merry Marxist minstrel," singing to the tune of "Playmates":

Come on, my playmates,
Why can't we co-exist,
Relax each iron fist,
Strike rockets off the list.
You send us pipe lines,
Put vodka in each bar,
Live like a Commissar
On caviar.

Senator J. William Fulbright was the new chairman of the Senate Foreign Relations Committee and his mouthpiece, his impersonator said, was Senator Hubert Humphrey. "Senator Humphrey,"he emphasized "doesn't talk *with* people. He talks *at* people. Hubert—declassify!"

Then the character representing Humphrey sang:

I could have talked all night,
I could have talked all night,
And still have talked some more.
I couldn't talk enough,
I told him jokes and stuff
He'd never heard before.

I could have made our little chat exciting,
The things I had to say were biting.
I could know when he
Began to talk to me,
I could have talked, talked, talked, talked, talked
All night.

In those times, as today, there was substantial pressure to cut down defense expenditures, and an impersonator of Robert B. Anderson, secretary of the treasury, expressed this view with a parody on the song "Side By Side":

Oh, our troops may be ragged and funny,
But we've got a barrel of money,
And we'll travel along
Singing our song,
Save that buck.

Through all kinds of warfare
Even if rockets fall,
As long as the budget's balanced
It doesn't matter at all.
And when all of the battles are ended,
We'll bank what we might have expended—
Though we end in the ditch
We still will be rich,
Save that buck.

But, like all foreign affairs skits of the 1950s and most of the 1960s, it ended on a hopeful note, with an impersonator of Acting Secretary of State Christian A. Herter singing:

The world awaits
A peace that's just
And fair to all.

Confer we must,
We cannot fail
To heed Mankind's urgent call.

Let's end this race,
We'll find in space
Glory unfurled.
One Happy Day
We'll find the way
To banish fear
From the World.

On that note, the toast was drunk to the President, and Vice President Nixon responded, with a short, rather amusing account of the life of Paul Wooton, the Gridiron president, in which he noted that he had not stopped at being "a mere vice president, as I have—or probably have."

● ● ●

The March 12, 1960 dinner was Eisenhower's last as President. And the Gridiron Club, most of whose members had always liked Ike very much, made a special occasion of it, not only because of this but also because it happened to be the Gridiron Club's seventy-fifth year.

The dinner was opened by Gridiron President John C. O'Brien of the *Philadelphia Inquirer*, who referred to the club's seventy-fifth year and said that "some say it has mellowed with age."

"Others retort," he said, "that our forebearance is not charity. It's merely oversight."

He assumed in his speech in the dark that Vice President Nixon would be the Republican nominee and said that Mr. Nixon was worried "because things look too good for him."

The Wisconsin primary was coming up, in which both Humphrey and Kennedy were candidates.

"If Humphrey wins," said O'Brien, "it's the end of Kennedy. If Kennedy wins, it's the beginning of Symington."

For the Presidential campaign, Kennedy had bowed a little to public opinion and had had his hair cut a bit shorter than before. This led O'Brien to remark that "Senator Kennedy has discovered that a candidate's best friend may be his barber."

And as for Lyndon Johnson, he said that he had discovered "that he is the only candidate who can whistle Dixie while humming the Battle Hymn of the Republic."

The opener was a parody on "Wintergreen for President."

The chorus came on stage carrying all kinds of funny campaign placards, such as "More Payola," "Home Rule for Husbands," "Gridiron Dinners Every Month," and "More Whiskey Breaks." They sang:

> Anyone for President!
> Anyone for President!
> Who's the man the people choose,
> To fill Eisenhower's shoes?

Walter Trohan, the announcer for the skit, then stepped forward and got nearly everybody at the dinner to their feet by asking everyone who had ever been called "Mr. President" to please rise.

"Stand up," he said, "if you were President of the United States, the James G. Blaine Fish Chowder and Marching Club, the Old Settlers of the District of Columbia, your high school class, your corporation or your union."

And then the chorus sang:

> Everyone's a President!
> Everyone's a President!
> We're the men the lightnin' struck.
> So let's keep pressin' our luck.

Reversing the traditional order, the foreign affairs skit came first, the scene set in the "command post" of the Central Intelligence Agency, which had finally been located in "a sewer in old Vienna."

Here "Allen Dulles," its director, presided. But he didn't know what the latest was from his agents in Russia, because "our copy of *Pravda* is late today and somebody stole our scissors."

After a couple of songs relating to the missile buildup, "Charles de Gaulle" arrived on the scene, announcing that he had just walked across the Mediterranean. He had also just exploded the first French nuclear weapon. This was the cue for the de Gaulle song.

> From the sands of the Sahara
> To the mountains of Savoie,
> Insurrection's out of fashion,
> For they know "L'etat, c'est moi."
> We explode our nuclear weapon with a Boom that's loudest of all,
> And the world will know it's dealing
> With General Charles de Gaulle.
> On the desert sands I shoot my bomb and *Boom*,

Catch up with the rest.
And now I'll climb the summit—
And stand firmly with the West.

"Selwyn Lloyd," Britain's foreign minister, thought there were fine things about a summit and sang:

There's something about a summit
That is fine, fine, fine!
All the heads of state who meet there
Have press advisers meet there
To help them to compete there
For the Big Headline.

With diplomacy that's charming
They talk about disarming:
"If you reduce your military, I'll cut mine."
Oh, it's "After you, Alphonse,"
"No, you first" is the response.

There's something about a summit
That is fine, fine, fine.

Other characters representing Khrushchev, Mikoyan and Chancellor Adenauer of Germany contributed their bits, and with a deep, booming voice Gene Archer as Secretary of State Christian A. Herter sang of the shuttling back and forth of foreign ministers and heads of state in those days:

Take me somewhere east of Suez,
Where the worst is pretty bad,
Where the population's poppin'
Thanks to every mom and dad.
For I feel a yen to travel
While the government will pay,
And I'd like to get some time in
On the road to Mandalay.

On the road to Mandalay,
Which was paved by CIA,
Can't you hear those neutrals chucklin' from Kabul to Mandalay?
On the road to Mandalay,
Where the counterpart funds ain't hay,
And the coexistence rises out of China 'cross the bay.

It's the old Moulmein payola
For the folks across the sea,
All the neutrals are awaitin'
Just to put the bite on me.

Oh, I don't begrudge the handouts,
It's the old American way,
But I wish they'd get less neutral
On the issues of the day.

The scene for the Democratic skit was a gang war in "an alley behind that famous Kennedy department store—the Merchandise Mart!" "Humphrey," heading the gang, sang:

I ain't nothin' but a hound dog,
Runnin' all the time.
I ain't nothin' but a poor boy,
Haven't got a dime.
But you ain't gonna win Wisconsin,
And you ain't no friends of mine.

"Truman" and his gang had no use for primaries. He sang:

The primaries are pure eyewash,
It's politicians who count, by gosh,
It's delightful, it's delicious, it's DeSapio.

So, keep repeating, you candidates,
It ain't the voters who name the slates,
It's de-Lawrence, it's de-Arvey, it's de-Ribicoff,
It's de-Pendergast, it's de-Truman, it's de-Meany, it's Disalle, it's
    disastrous.

"Kennedy"—with "so many Kennedys coming along that we're going to run 'em in platoons on both tickets"—sang:

Darlings, I am growing old.
Silver threads among pop's gold.
Youth so fair I've put away.
Age I'm courting for today.
And, my darlings, you can see, can see,
What a hair cut did for me.
Yes, my darlings, can't you see
No more boyish charm for me.

Darlings, I am growing, growing old.
Reaching for the prize I'd hold.
Snow upon my crest will lay
When they ballot at L.A.

But here the gangs all shouted, "Make way for the Big Wheel," and an impersonator of Lyndon Johnson, to the tune of "That's What I Like About the South," sang:

I'm Lyndon
From the South,
Don't say that
Shut ma mouth,
'Neath this vest
Heart's in the West,
That's what I like about the South.

Oil and gas
Ain't good t' eat,
But to me
It's red meat.
It is easy
To de-plete,
That's what I like about the South.

Chorus:

Lyn-don,
The pride 'a Tex-as, Al-a-mo, Old Black Joe,
Lyn-don,
The pride 'a Broadway, Chi-ca-go, Ko-ko-mo.

'Comes ol' Jack,
Love his Dad;
At Ken-nedys
I ain't mad.
With that Jack
They can't be bad,
That's the way they like it in the South.

Hubert's smart,
Knows all the news,
Tells you quick
All his views,
And he's all caught up
In his Union dues,
They won't like him in the South.

Stu's my pal
From Miss-oury,
Dark, dark horse
He thinks he'll be.
When they're through
You'll find
It is me.
That's what I like about the South.

Since Stuart Symington was to be the Democratic speaker

immediately after the skit, tradition, which is usually respected in the Gridiron Club, required that the skit had to end on a song by him. He was brought forward by an impersonator of former Missourian Clark Clifford, who said "Stu doesn't stand on issues. He kind of leans on them." Then an impersonator of Symington sang, to the tune of "St. Louis Blues":

> Saint Looey Stuie,
> With my power and flair,
> Got my missiles,
> Least a coupla pair.
> Got de po' folks
> And de rich wid me.
> Un-ion labor
> And A.T. & T.

Chorus:

> I'm your Saint Looey Stu just as true as ah can be,
> Truman gonna help me be boss of all I see,
> Also I gonna have N double-ACP.
> You'll love dis man like an egghead loves Ad-lie.
> Like Eleanor Roos-velt loves the common guy.
> You'll love your Stuie till the day you die.
> You'll love your Stuie till the day you die.

Symington expressed his pleasure at being there, because he had "few opportunities to address Republican meetings." With a gentle dig at the Gridiron Club, he noted that next fall there was going to be an election. "I guess you know this," he said, "it has been in all the papers.

"Now, frankly, I have been soliciting advice on how to win the Presidency.

"I think I have talked to all the right people—Alf Landon, Tom Dewey, Harold Stassen. And I have drawn a number of confusions—conclusions."

Then he launched into a discussion of his plans for both the convention and the election.

The first step, he said, would be to get a good speechwriter, and he'd found just the man—a "bright, new literary genius, that wonder of wonders, that master of the written word—the author of the Air Force Manuals.

"I was lucky to get him," he continued. "Until recently, he has been writing off-color jokes for Jack Paar. Upon investigation I found out that he is a bachelor, as was his father before him."

He said that his next move would be to follow faithfully the advice his good friend Jack Kennedy had given him: "Avoid the danger of 'over-exposure' to the people."

He would enter no primaries, in spite of the fact that "Jack keeps challenging Lyndon Johnson and me to run in certain primaries." Instead, he insisted that they were "running good old Hubert Humphrey.

"And Lyndon and I will be in there fighting," he said, "shoulder to shoulder, as long as there is a breath in Hubert's body."

His strategy for the convention, Symington explained, would be "simplicity itself": Kennedy would knock off Humphrey in Wisconsin and Humphrey would knock off Kennedy somewhere else.

"Governor Brown," he said, will veto Lyndon Johnson on the ground that he wouldn't take California. Johnson will veto Brown on the ground that he wouldn't take orders.

"At this crucial juncture, the more advanced liberal group of our party—a group, incidentally, with which I am proud to be confused from time to time—will come out for me.

"This will infuriate Governor Wesley Powell of New Hampshire. He will call a press conference and announce publicly that 'Symington is soft on Communism.'

"That will turn the trick—quick! I will be nominated on the next ballot.

"Thereupon Jack Kennedy will go into a conference, called by 'Big Daddy.' Three thousand people will be present—all relatives. Out of it will come a marvelous combination—*Miss*ouri and *Mass*achusetts.

"We will call it the 'Mish-Mash' ticket.

"And then Hubert Humphrey will issue a five thousand word statement, refusing comment."

Symington revealed that the strategy for the campaign would be for him to make three major policy speeches. He would open with a Labor Day speech in Detroit, then would come a farm speech in Des Moines, and "my speech on civil rights will be in Fairbanks, Alaska."

"But the big question is—how do we beat Dick Nixon? I will be in Room 1240 after dinner [Richard L. Wilson's suite, where the major afterparty is held each dinner], and any suggestions will be gratefully received.

"One plan we have is to furnish the Vice President with television time for a debate in the Lincoln-Douglas tradition. . . .

[Let no one say that Gridiron speakers don't possess crystal balls.]

"But putting Dick on TV has a certain danger, however. That damned dog might get in the act again."

In the serious part of his speech, Symington pointed out that "the transcendent and overriding question of our day is that our nation faces a clear and imminent threat to its survival.

"Unfortunately," he continued, "I am convinced that the American people have not awakened to this alarming and unpleasant fact.

"Part of the explanation is that our people don't understand the profound change that has taken place in the conduct of this world's affairs. They believe that if we are not in a shooting war, then we are at peace. Not so with the rulers of the Kremlin.

"They view their relationship with the West as a struggle to be waged day by day and year by year, until they achieve final victory. In the minds of those who rule from Moscow and Peking, we have been at war since 1946.

"We didn't ask for this contest. We don't want it. But we cannot wish it away. We have but one alternative. Either we outperform them, or we pay the price. And the price, based on the record, is either annihilation or slavery. We cannot proceed with 'business as usual' and hope to prevail.

"More of the strength of our economy must be thrown into the contest, and every thoughtful citizen, regardless of party, who has been brought in to study this subject has emphasized that fact.

"We must meet the challenge whenever and wherever it occurs. This is not simple, for it is a departure from our usual way of life.

"Those of us who are serving in public life have an urgent responsibility. The American people must be told the alarming truth about their world, the nature of the forces arrayed against them, and the steps that must be taken, at whatever cost, to survive and preserve our freedom.

"I do not claim greater competence, or greater loyalty, than the high-minded men who lead the present administration. I say only that I see the danger increasing at a terrifying rate. And I shall try, in every way possible, to persuade the American people to make a greater effort than now is being made."

Then, becoming light in his final words, Symington said he wouldn't want to close without a word of praise for the next speaker, "my good friend Senator Dirksen, the modern Abraham Lincoln, 'Honest Ev,' the hairsplitter from Illinois.

"At a dinner the other evening, the hostess leaned over to Ev and said, 'You know, senator, I've heard a great deal about you.'

" 'That's possible,' Ev replied, 'but you can't *prove* anything.' "[7]

The Republican skit, the Peace and Prosperity Travel Bureau, opened with "George Allen," confidant, and some said "court jester" to several Presidents, and one of Eisenhower's favorite golfing campanions. In song, Allen referred to the tendency of the President to slip away for a little golf now and then.

> Every morning, every evening,
> Ain't we got fun,
> Travel hither, travel thither,
> Ain't we got fun.
> Down to Augusta, by train or by car,
> You've no idea how happy we are.
> Millionaires go on a frolic,
> Don't we have fun.
> Who can say it's diabolic
> When we have fun.
> Those folks who tell us
> We shouldn't play—they're only jealous.
> In the meantime, in between time,
> Ain't we got fun.

Ezra Taft Benson, the secretary of agriculture, was trying to cut back government subsidies to farmers, which had been started in the Roosevelt administration and seemed never to end. Consequently, he wasn't one of the most popular members of the Eisenhower cabinet, especially among the farmers. As his impersonator came on the stage to make an important announcement, one of the travelers shouted, "Hurrah! He's gonna resign." But Benson answered in song:

> I'll be hanging 'round—always,
> Here's where I'll be found—always,
> When the farmers mourn,
> When their hopes are torn,
> I'll supply the corn—always, always.
> Ezra's right as rain—always,
> Goes against the grain—always.
> I am here to stay,
> Not for just a day,
> Not for just a year—but Always.

Later, there was a duet between Rockefeller and Stassen, both of whom had been caught in the same blizzard and found it was very cold outside.

Rocky: We ought to stop pacing the floor.
Stassen: Maybe we should try it some more.
Rocky: My head is all in a flurry.
Stassen: Your smile is like Arthur Murray.
Rocky: Well maybe I should try sixty-four.
Stassen: Can't we break down that White House door?
Rocky: Don't say that I'm through.
Stassen: But brother, it's cold outside.

By March 1960, most people were conceding that Nixon would be a shoo-in for the Presidential nomination, and the skit ended with a Nixon impersonator singing:

I've got the White House in my hands.
I'm kissin' babies across the land.
I want your vote, brother, in my hands;
I want everybody's vote in my hands.

I've got the White House in my hands.

Governor Hatfield of Oregon had been scheduled to be the Republican speaker, but was unable to do so, and Republican Senate Leader Dirksen substituted for him in a speech that was the typical Dirksen combination of friendly ridicule and exaggerated oratory. He began by explaining that he was not Irish and was therefore a "poor substitute for the Governor of that great Irish state of Oregon."

These were "bewildering days," he said, "but we'll simplfy it all—do it with Dick, a half-Nelson is all it will take."

But then we had Symington, he said. "I love my neighbor from Mighty Mo. He is the first in history to keep the fire unlit so long." He described him as a "horseman of preparedness.

"Missouri," he said, "is always at war. When there is no ready foe, even Truman feuds with himself." He proclaimed his love for Symington's "universality—one foot in the South, one foot in the North, one hand on the West, one hand on the East, one eye on Atlas, and one eye on Ezra."

Referring to the obvious preoccupation of Symington with military strength, Dirksen described his Presidential slogan as "Two missiles in every pot, a launching pad in every backyard, a bomb shelter in every basement, and free rides on Atlas every Sunday afternoon."

One by one he took on the various Democratic possibilities.

"And Hubert is here," he said, "and there, and everywhere. Compared with Hubert, Kilroy is a bedridden old soldier. Hubert is the only living thing that filibustered Khrushchev. It was great contest—Minnesota larynx versus Moscow lynx. He's the only candidate whose launching pad was 6,000 miles from home."

Then Kennedy: 'I'm wild about Jack, but with inflation, who isn't? We used to say 'All work and no play makes Jack a dull boy.' But how ancient can I get? Today it's 'All jack, some play, lots of work, makes Jack—and maybe a nomination.' Take note, I did not say election. It's the first time since Lincoln that hair has become an issue. Then it was a beard, now it's a hairdo."

And of Johnson (*in mock cowboy language*): "Now podners, pull up your firesides. Here's my pal Lyndon. . . . It's a front ranch campaign, you know. Think of a stable full of candidates and how to handle them. Lyndon is like Lincoln. Every member of Abe's cabinet was a candidate. Someone said he should fire them, and Abe said, 'Then how can I watch them?' Abe had no live quorums to count on. Lyndon can not only watch them, he can embarrass them."

He pictured the scene at the Los Angeles convention, when all the boys from Texas arrived.

"What a spectacle as some sturdy, eloquent Texan with the right mixture of the spirit of the Alamo and a little corn tranquilizer in his fevered veins moves into the nominating peroration, strikes the right rhetorical pose and says, 'My friends, who can lead us into the land of milk and honey? Who can lead us to that big white Texas mansion on the Potomac with the Treasury only a block away? Who but that tall, towering, tanned, terrific, titillating, Texas toreador—LBJ.' . . .

"Up the sombreros, Stetson stock will jump twenty points."

Dirksen had other similar remarks for Adlai Stevenson and the Republican-gone-Democrat Senator Wayne Morse from the Beaver State—"the beavers got into his blood—the eager variety."

To all of them he raised his glass and drank a personal toast: "May you achieve everything except what you want most. We love you for what you are—logically illogical, regularly irregular, frugally unfrugal. We love you best in your traditional pose—

looking backward. . . . We love the constancy of your devotion to doom and gloom. . . . And we love the symbol of your party—the jackass, a noble beast, but with no pride of patrimony and no hope of a future."

He pictured the future after the election.

"Lyndon will still have Wayne, Jack will still have jack, Hubert can again commune with Ezra, a special Space Committee will explore the missile gaps to find Stu, and Adlai should by then be checking the precincts in Singapore."

Then, turning to Eisenhower, he paid his respects to the President with typical Dirksen oratory.

"And now, Mr. President, when the Gridiron sizzles a year hence, you will have laid aside the cares and burdens of high office. You will think of us, and we shall think of you.

"In the quiet moments, Mr. President, there will flash across the inward eye the image of a gentle, patient, kindly man with an understanding heart whose fidelity was to America and what was good for her.

"We'll think of you as a father and a grandfather who found the peace of infinity in your grandchildren, and in whose heart was the desire to leave them and to all children and grandchildren, who will be the citizens of tomorrow, a legacy as good as what you got.

"We shall think of you as a soldier in war and in peace, with a spirit dedicated to the noblest of all man's achievements—the cause of human peace.

"And we shall think of you as one in whom the healing of laughter has been fully preserved when the lampoon comes forward. And when you think of us, Mr. President, the many sweet associations of these years will come tumbling out of the wells of remembrance.

"You can laugh a little as you think of that proposal to make ex-Presidents members of the Senate, and the terrible chore of having to learn the rules of the Senate—that you escaped Lyndon's lecture on that most amazing of all weapons, the veto-pistol, or Wayne, falling into some legal morass, or Jack, coaching Charlie deGaulle on how to cope with the Casbah, or Stu, extricated from the missile gap but still trudging like old man Atlas with the world upon his shoulders, and Adlai—Mr. President, you'll have to send him a post card from Gettysburg. . . . Just address it care of Paul Butler, South Bend."[8]

The dinner closed with a Seventy-fifth Anniversary skit,

presided over by Arthur Krock, who had belonged to the Gridiron Club for nearly fifty of its seventy-five years.

"We have sung to, and satirized," he said, "Presidents and
potentates, statesmen, malefactors of great wealth, philan-
thropists, and just plain politicians and editors.

"All the Presidents of the United States for seventy-five
years have graced our head table—with one exception. Grover
Cleveland never came. He ruefully regretted this after he left
office. It would have been easier, he said, if he'd have come."

Against the background of those seventy-five years, the
Gridiron soloists resang, one after another, a few lines from
many of the best songs that had been used in Gridiron skits,
including several like the "No Third Term" song, in which the
Gridiron Club had guessed completely wrong.

Krock then pointed out that in 1949 the Gridiron Club had
sung a parody of "Some Enchanted Evening," "before Dwight D.
Eisenhower, or any of us, knew to which party he belonged."

After the club sang the song once more to Eisenhower, Krock
stepped forward again. "Now," he said, "just as we have from
Benjamin Harrison to Harry Truman—we salute President
Dwight D. Eisenhower and bid him our Jubilee farewell." Then
the Gridiron members sang:

> From the White House you soon will be going,
> Where for eight years you lived—now and then.
> You can golf without prying reporters,
> Asking who, why, whether or when.
>
> Wherever you go we will miss you,
> Do not hasten to bid us adieu;
> Now forget all those press conference questions,
> From here on "No comment!" will do.
>
> Please don't pine for the White House you're leaving,
> When at ease on your Gettysburg farm,
> Don't let talkative generals still haunt you
> Or the party you tried to reform.
>
> Wherever you go we will miss you,
> Do not hasten to bid us farewell.
> We're left here with Congress as us'al,
> What they'll do without Ike, who can tell?
>
> We've toasted McKinley and Hoover,
> Sung to Coolidge and Roosevelt, too.
> In the Jubilee glow of the Gridiron
> We hail Ike and bid you adieu.

Each of the members and guests at the dinner that night, in observance of the anniversary, received a sterling silver money clip decorated with the Gridiron emblem; a special one in gold and inscribed was presented to President Eisenhower.

The toast to the President was proposed, and Eisenhower rose to respond.

Obviously moved, he did not speak at all in the Symington or Dirksen styles. He thanked the club for the many occasions when he had been present, some as President, some before that.

And then he made what many regarded as his endorsement of Richard Nixon as his successor, saying that one of the duties of the President was to speak for the guests of the Gridiron in thanking the club for enjoyable evenings. He referred to this as "a great privilege."

"And I might add," he said, "that after listening and seeing the antics on the stage, I understand there are a number who would like to succeed to this privilege, which I assure you is a very pleasant duty.

"Now it occurs to me, as we look at this table and its seating [with the President on the Gridiron president's right and the Vice President on his left], that it would be far less bother just to move a man to this seat very easily and very simply by moving two chairs than making any big fuss around the table.

"But, in any event, of the characters who've been portrayed on the stage this evening, one is going, of course, to be lucky—he thinks. Frankly, after the excitement of picking his cabinet, getting settled, and the first batch of world intelligence reports come, brought up possibly by Mr. Dulles or one of his associates, possibly accompanied by some of the chiefs of staff, and picturing three or four situations that are not easy to straighten out, he will begin to wonder about this luck.

"Now some staff officer about this moment will come back and remind him that if he will listen to some of the advice in the papers, he will know exactly how to make his decisions, he will try to find out whether there is 100 percent agreement among his associates, and therefore, he won't have to do anything (I've never seen that occur, but that could be one solution), but he is going finally to begin to walk up and down that hall and look around at the walls that are not yet decorated and his family pictures are not up, and he's going to be wondering what in the devil to do. And about this moment, it's probably going to occur to him, 'How in the world did I ever get in this place?' The only thought I want to leave with this man, whoever he may be, and I of course reserve my own hopes, but whoever he may be, I want to assure him, he's going to have my prayers for his success. . . .

"This country does face great problems, as one of our speakers reminded us," Eisenhower continued. "And they are not all military. If America is going to set its course forward, to that goal of peace and where all humankind is going to have the great satisfaction of seeing families raise their living standards, their cultural levels, and getting greater satisfaction in their spiritual devotions and freedoms, then America must think of more than just weapons.

"I have been a soldier all my life and I do not decry weapons. We need them and we must always keep them; but we must never forget that man is a spiritual being, he's not preserving just his wealth, just his homes, even his existence. He's preserving great, priceless values. We've got to think of these things at home as we look at our domestic problems, we've got to think of them when we think of Pakistan or India or Burma or any other corner of the world. We've got to remember in their betterment we become stronger. We come closer to the realization of our own ambitions as a free, proud, progressive people.

"These are the kind of things that are going to weigh on that man's heart. Whether he's on the golf course, or whether he prefers to shoot, or whether he just likes to sleep, or whether he'd just rather sit in his office.

"But I repeat, that I believe every true American will be praying for his success. This does not mean that all of us, although I doubt that I shall be one of them, will not have the privilege of criticizing, and they should criticize and differ with him, but I do say, if we can help in those years to come, because the next stages are going to be just as tough as this past stage, there's no question about it. And I say, God bless him.

"And now my friends of the Gridiron Club, the members, I am deeply touched by the little remembrance your president handed me this evening. I didn't need something material to remind me of the pleasant evenings I've spent with you, but I am very proud that you would have thought to give me something like this, and indeed I'm proud of that song that was sung last as we closed the evening.

"Good night, and again, don't forget, just don't disturb the table too much."[9]

It was an impressive final word to the Gridiron audience of a rather nonpolitical President, whose decisions had not served at all to entrench the power of either the Republican party or himself, and had not always necessarily been those of the greatest wisdom, but which were, as Emmet John Hughes later wrote, "overwhelmingly honest, untainted by fright for self or greed for power."[10]

XVIII

John F. Kennedy

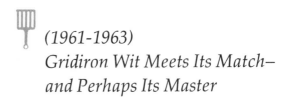

(1961-1963)
Gridiron Wit Meets Its Match—
and Perhaps Its Master

After the election in 1960, in which John F. Kennedy won a very narrow victory over Vice President Nixon, Washington was all abuzz with discussion of the activities of the glamorous Kennedys.

The dinner held on March 11, 1961, was the first which Kennedy attended as President. Gridiron President Robert L. Riggs of the *Louisville Courier-Journal*, said in his speech in the dark, that the Gridiron Club had invited Mr. Kennedy here "for our own protection."

"The way he rushes around town, dropping in at newspapermen's homes for meals, no reporter's larder is safe."

Kennedy had installed a new chef in the White House, and this led Riggs to remark, "Besides, there's danger your cook will be kidnapped. . . .

"Servants at the White House are required to promise they won't write memoirs. But what precautions are being taken about three-year-old Caroline? She's already peddling inside stuff such as, 'Daddy's just sitting there with his shoes and socks off, doing nothing.' Her father and Uncle Bobby will find her stiff competition in the hunt for publishers."

Referring to the business worries about the new administration, Riggs said that "it's a pleasure to see big business executives able to relax in this presence. We're glad so many are out on parole. . . .

"The life of the lobbyists gets harder and harder. Now they have to load up several barrels of extra foxes and dump them out at Middleburg, Virginia."*

Edward R. Murrow had been appointed head of the U.S. Information Agency, and Riggs dubbed its headquarters "Murrow Castle."

"This administration wants us to believe it's as middle road as was the Eisenhower regime. We'll never see much resemblance until George E. Allen shows up as a Presidential crony."

The opener was a parody on the song "Good News." It was introduced by Fletcher Knebel imitating the wartime broadcaster Gabriel Heatter, who had always begun his broadcasts with, "There's good news tonight."

"Mr. President," said Knebel, "there's wonderful, wonderful news tonight—all bad. They're fighting in Laos, they're fighting in the Congo, in the United Nations, in Congress. Unemployment is up. Revenues are down. Half of General Electric is in jail.** Soapy Williams is on the loose again. There's bad news tonight."

Then the chorus sang:

Bad news! Everything's awful bad;
That's how we like it, bad news!
Danger! Think of the gold we lose.
We love to holler the blues.

In somewhat of a forecast, Richard Wilson asked several of the new Kennedy intimates to stand for the guest skit, among them Kenneth O'Donnell, Theodore Sorensen, McGeorge Bundy and Arthur Schlesinger, Jr. Then Lyle Wilson requested, "Will the Secret Service agents please move among these gentlemen and confiscate their diaries?"

The Washington baseball team was rather low in its league

---

*In fox-hunting country, where a Kennedy estate was located.

**Three General Electric officials had been given jail sentences in an antitrust prosecution.

standing at that time. Two more guests were introduced, "the chief of muzzle operations, the press secretary to the 1960 Republican Presidential candidate, Mr. Herbert Klein, and the head of the newly reorganized ball club, General Elwood (Pete) Quesada."

Richard Wilson cracked, "In General Quesada's league, Mr. Klein is a genius. His team finished second."

Buoyed by the Kennedy victory, labor leaders were riding high, and a trio was asked to stand consisting of John L. Lewis, Secretary of Labor Arthur Goldberg, and the president of Du Pont, Crawford Greenewalt.

"Mr. Greenewalt says of Secretary Goldberg and Mr. Lewis, they are the perfect examples of Professor Galbraith's Affluent Society," commented Lyle Wilson.

At the time of the dinner, former President Eisenhower was golfing in Palm Springs. The announcer for the Republican skit, Julius Frandsen, said the Republicans were in desperate straits; "down and out, and short of everything—everything except volunteers for the title of leader."

"To solve their problem," he said, "these down-and-outers are gathering in the world's most luxurious hobo camp outside Palm Springs, California, where a distinguished citizen is enjoying his retirement. Let's join the meeting."

The scene was a "hobo jungle," with stew cooking over a campfire and most of the characters asleep. A servant entered and said to one of the hoboes named "Ike," "Come on, Boss, git up. Those Republicans are comin' here today to pick a new leader."

"Wasn't that the job I had?" yawned Ike.

"Yes, but thank goodness y'never got involved in it," answered the servant.

An impersonator of Thruston Morton, chairman of the Republican National Committee, led on the chorus and asked Ike if he had anything to say.

"Yes, indeed," was the response. "I'd like to address my remarks to Mr. Nixon." And he sang:

Don't blame me! I did what I could for you.
I trained you to be the leader like me, so
Don't blame me!
I campaigned—I did lots of good for you;
Made speeches galore; at least three or four, so
Don't blame me!
I played golf with very influential men—

Told them all, you were my special friend.

I fought hard, I did what they told me to.
You met your fate, in TV debate—
So don't blame me!

A strong Nixon supporter in the campaign had been Dr. Norman Vincent Peale, and his impersonator emerged from the chorus to sing:

Hold an election ev'ry autumn.
Ding, dong, the campaign bells can chime.
Say you are fixin' vic-try for Nixon,
But leave me in the church next time.

"Nixon," described as "our 49 99/100 percent leader," came forward and sang:

I thought I would win the White House race,
I didn't expect just second place,
Say, who put that make-up on my face?
I'm beginning to see the light.
My victory special jumped the track,
For I ran with Rocky on my back.
Reporters, they were a claque for Jack,
I'm beginning to see the light.
Texas and Chicago too
Did their tricks to you-know-who,
Finally I was taboo,
For I never knew just what hit me.

Electoral college, it's the bunk,
Hip-hip-hooray and all that junk,
Why in the world did I have to flunk?
I'm beginning to see the light.

Republican "stand-patism" was satirized in a "Tit-Willow" song on former Senator John Bricker of Ohio, former Senator George Bender of Ohio, and Ray Bliss, former Republican chairman.

On a fence in Ohio three dickey-birds sat:
I'm Bricker.
I'm Bender.
I'm Bliss.

And they longed for the days when the party stood pat,
With Bricker,
And Bender,
And Bliss.

Oh, bring back the years of the old GOP.
The words of McKinley are music to me.
By a nod of your heads I am sure you agree
With Bricker,
And Bender,
And Bliss.

"Nelson Rockefeller" was presented as "the only Republican who can stand on the Democratic platform without blushing," and he sang:

Come on along and listen to
The Rocky boy of Broadway.
With hip hooray and ballyhoo,
The Rocky boy of Broadway.
The whistle of the campaign train,
With all the voters mixin';
And then perhaps a midnight chat
With Richard Milhous Nixon.
When your Rocky Baby hits the trail,
You'll hear the dollars jinglin';
You're gonna hear the voters wail
Their fav'rite song:

"We want Rocky, we want Rocky all the way."
You'll cheer Rocky, you'll say—
Let's call it a day.
Listen to your lovin' Rock—
Of old Broadway!

Then, in a forecast of the long future, which turned out to be partially accurate, "Barry Goldwater" closed the skit by singing, to a tune written by Vincent Youmans, a guest at numerous Gridiron dinners, "Great Day":

Let's move to the right,
I'm here to lead your fight,
There's gonna be a great day.
Put away your fears, watch me roll back the years,
Then it will be a great day.
No left turn today, boys,
Those ADA boys can go that way.
Barry's here to stay, no middle road,
    hooray!
There's gonna be a great day.

Barry's here to stay, no middle road,
    hooray!

There's gonna be a great,
There's gonna be a great eighteen ninety-eight day.

Senator Thruston Morton, the Republican speaker, began by recalling that Kennedy, at the 1958 dinner, talked about a supposed telegram from his father, asking him not to buy "a single vote more than is necessary," since he didn't want to pay for a landslide.

"He didn't," said Morton.

President Kennedy had appointed his brother Bobby as attorney general, and it caused considerable criticism. Morton, in expressing his gratitude for being invited to talk to "this top-drawer assembly of opinion-makers," said that it gave him a perfect forum "to put a nasty whisper to rest.

"I hereby deny that we Republicans are responsible for the rumor that the initials J.F.K. means 'Jobs For Kinfolk.'"

President Kennedy had sent former Governor G. Mennen ("Soapy") Williams to the Congo on a special mission. Williams had not distinguished himself by his diplomatic touch and had raised many African hackles. Morton said that, in discussing the accomplishments of the new administration, he was tempted to entitle his remarks "Empty Saddles on the New Frontier.

"But I rejected this," he said, "because the administration does have some notable accomplishments. It got Soapy Williams out of the Congo alive. . . . In Africa, Soapy proved this new frontier quiet-diplomacy can efficiently get all sides blazing mad at each other. And Soapy is learning fast. It took him only twelve days to do to Africa what he did to Michigan in twelve years.

"Soapy should tour Russia and China—that would bring the Khrushchev-Mao rivalry to a head in a week."

With a degree of good-natured whimsicality, Morton stated his political principles as chairman of the opposition party. He supported the President's version of helping depressed areas, "if the Republican party can qualify," and announced that "we Republicans have as much concern as anyone else—perhaps more concern—for the unemployment situation.

"But above all," he said, "we intend to be affirmative and responsible while pressing the views of the 34 million plus Americans who voted for us. World peace, the national security and domestic prosperity continue to be the responsibility of the Republican party just as much as of the President and his party.

"We believe that in 1961 it is up to the party of Lincoln to demonstrate to the world, that this nation divided against itself—half Kennedy and half Nixon—can and will endure."

Referring to the Lincoln-Douglas debates and the Douglas candidacy for the Presidency in 1860, he said that as soon as the election was over Douglas had moved to solidify the nation behind its President and even held Lincoln's stovepipe hat while the Great Emancipator delivered his historic First Inaugural.

"Mr. President," said Morton, "we Republicans envision a greater role for ourselves than holding your hat—you always hold it yourself—and you never wear it anyway.

"But I pledge that you can always count on us for loyal support whenever that national interest is at stake—be it in Laos—or in layoffs.

"The voice of opposition will not be stilled, and in speaking out we will be fulfilling the promise of our great two-party system.

"This is the system which brings the very best of American thought to bear on our problems.

"It is the system that has enabled America to prevail while governments of a single philosophy have crumbled in the dust.

"It is the system that makes our political structure uniquely representative of all the people.

"So when our principles are stepped on, you'll hear me sounding off about it—as soon as I check with Eisenhower, Nixon, Rockefeller, Goldwater, Dirksen, Halleck, Keating and Javits, to find out *why* we oppose it—and what we are *for* instead. And to maintain our bipartisan pledge, I will also consult with Harry Byrd, Jimmie Byrnes and Alan Shivers."[1]

The scene for the Democratic skit was Glen Ora, the President's weekend estate at Middleburg, Virginia, where the Democrats were having a hunt breakfast with the fox and hounds set, and were beginning the Spartan practice of self-denial and sacrifice.

One of the characters, "Secretary of the Interior Stewart Udall," commented that he had had to give up a week's salary "just to rent this outfit."

The first problem was about "that French chef" to whom President Kennedy had offered a job at the White House. To the tune of "I Love Paris," the character representing Agriculture Secretary Orville L. Freeman sang:

Every time I recall what they tried to do,
I get all goose-pimples and tense;

Now to nightmares I'm prone, and I awake with a groan,
For we nearly had war with the French.

All the Democrats involved, including House Speaker Sam Rayburn, were on a culture jag. "Rayburn" said that every night he was reading T. S. Eliot, Huxley, Toynbee, and "all that jazz. The President has decreed culture and I'm a loyal Democrat." Kennedy's "tutors" were Robert Frost and Frank Sinatra, Frost having been invited to the White House to read his poetry and Sinatra to sing. "Frost" introduced his "cultural protege," an impersonator of Frank Sinatra, and Sinatra sang a parody of "Friendship."

If you ever want a man,
I'm your fan.
If you want a little song,
Ring the gong.
If you ever want Sinatra to run the show,
Let me know.

It's culture, culture,
I'm a culture vulture.
When other culture has been forgot,
Ours will still be hot.

A character representing Senate Majority Leader Mike Mansfield wondered "when do our relatives get in the big picture," and asked "Senator Hubert Humphrey" to sing. He did, in a new version of "I Am the Monarch of the Sea."

For fourteen years he sought the top
With much encouragement from pop.
It was a happy circumstance
For him and his sisters and his cousins and his aunts.

From one rung to the next he went,
And now he is our President.
He wields the pow'r the office grants,
And so do his sisters and his cousins and his aunts.

He brought his brother Bob along
To punish people who do wrong,
And learn to practice law perchance,
And care for his sisters and his cousins and his aunts.

The election had swung on the votes of Illinois and Texas, both of which were very slow in coming in. This was handled by the presentation on the stage of impersonators of Jake Arvey,

Democratic leader of Cook County, and Mayor Richard Daley of Chicago. Arvey explained that success was a simple matter of vote propagation.

"Explain how it works," said Daley, and Arvey sang to the tune of "Tea for Two":

> Two for you and three for me,
> And here's a few; they all are free—
> And counting fast, I see they're cast for Jack.
>
> Nobody's near us to see us or hear us;
> No cops or computers to stop or refute us.
> The vote will be mounting, for we'll do the counting out back, so—
>
> Let's don't wait, the other slate
> Is working late away downstate;
> They're making votes to throw to GOP.
>
> One thing's sure you will agree
> That they can't count as fast as we;
> And that's the way to make a vic-to-ry.

"Vice President Johnson," introduced by "Navy Secretary John Connally" as "the same old humble, self-effacing public servant of yore," entered in morning coat, with a carnation in his buttonhole, and announced that "I bear my sorrows with humility." Then he sang, to the tune of "On the Street Where you Live":

> I have often walked down this street before.
> Sixteen hundred Penn-syl-va-nia is for me no more.
> All at once am I—just another guy,
> At the foot of the street where you live.
>
> Now no high-heeled boots tread the heart of town.
> Beacon Hill and not the Alamo has won renown.
> For enchantments pour out of just one door—
> And that's down on the street where you live.
>
> People stop and stare, and they bother me;
> For instead of standing here, there's where I'd rather be.
> And as time goes by, I will show them I
> Still belong in the street where you live.

At this point, "Attorney General Robert F. Kennedy," in a ski costume and with his leg in a splint (he had broken it skiing a week before), entered as "cruise director for this fox hunt," followed by all the Kennedy family except his older brother. With recognition of the Kennedy family fervor for touch football and similar sports, his sister Eunice proclaimed that it was a terrific day for a game, and an impersonator of Bobby sang a parody of "There Is Nothing Like a Dame."

You got muscles that are soft,
You got sinews like a gnat.
You got biceps that are scrawny
And your stomachs are too fat.
You got politics and culture;
You got high-falutin' names.
What ain't you got? You ain't got games.

New Frontiersmen here's your cue
From our first-string quarterback:
You play touch, lacrosse or even squash,
You'll be okay with Jack.
Even indoor games like scrabble
Are all right when played with vim—
You must play hard, to be like him!

Senator Eugene J. McCarthy of Minnesota, the Democratic speaker, said he guessed he was the spokesman for the liberal Democrats, because they hadn't really accepted this administration yet. But he thought there might also be a better reason.

"I like to believe," he said, "that the head of the Democratic party—that is the President—may have concurred in my choice. He and I have much in common: Both of us nominated Adlai Stevenson for President. He in '56, and I in '60. There was some difference in our timing. As a matter of fact we had a lot in common even at the 1960 convention: We had the same set of candidates for both offices. We just didn't sort them out quite the same way."

Describing his own campaign for the Senate in 1958, he quoted from "astute newspapermen who said I was a kind of precursor, that I was John the Baptist making straight the way. They said that in Minnesota I as a Catholic had won over a Lutheran."

Relating how two weeks before his election the Archbishop of his home-town diocese had denounced Martin Luther, McCarthy recalled that he answered by protesting that "he [Luther] had been around, or at least his reputation had been around, for 400 years and I thought he could let it live for two more weeks."

But he overcame the handicaps, and after the election, he

said, the astute newspapermen wrote articles saying that he had proved that one with all these handicaps could win.

"I was quite set up, until I overheard someone say, 'Well, it might just prove that, but it might have proved that anybody could win.'

"Well, I think that once we're elected we shouldn't look too closely at the votes we get or to the reasons why people do vote for us."

As for the Republicans, he thought most Democrats hated to see the Eisenhower administration go.

"They were a moving target—just barely. But in any case, it was a target, and Democrats generally are rather sporting fellows."

The Republicans had "a gift of survival," he found. "Even at their high points of life, they're not very vigorous. But in the period of decline, they are like the lower forms of plant and animal life: It's really hard to destroy them." [2]

The show closed with a foreign affairs skit which ranged from the gold drain and the balance-of-payments problem to the controversy over whether there was a missile gap, as Kennedy had charged during the campaign.

The scene was laid in the "Fool's Gold Saloon" in the Yukon and was entitled "The Gold Rush."

"Roving Ambassador Averell Harriman" arrived just as an actor portraying Secretary of the Treasury Douglas Dillon was bounced out.

"Man, I'm busted," moaned Dillon, as he went. "When I tried my Diners Club card at the bar, I got the bounce. What I need is gold, gold, gold."

The supposed luxurious life of diplomats was satirized in a song by an impersonator of Congressman John J. Rooney of Brooklyn, who wanted to "slash the booze fund of diplomats," and sang:

> Another drink,
> Another brunch,
> Another five-Martini lunch,
> Your taxes go up,
> But they won't slow up,
> They're making whoopee.

The club made merry over the administration's embarrassment over the question of whether there was or wasn't a missile gap. Alluding to Secretary of Defense Robert S. McNamara's background remarks that there was no gap, a character portraying Senator J. W. Fulbright asked another playing the role of General Lyman Lemnitzer, chairman of the Joint Chiefs of Staff, just how wide the missile gap was, and he was told it was "approximately the distance from Assistant Secretary Arthur Sylvester's mouth to Mr. McNamara's foot."

"McNamara," a former director and president of Ford, told the sad story in song, to the tune of "Cockles and Mussels."

> Now Detroit's a fair city
> Where the Fords are so pretty—
> And the Edsels lie buried there row upon row.
> I wish I had stayed there
> And worked at my trade there,
> And not counted missiles alive, alive-oh.

> For Jack wasn't happy
> When I said the gap he
> Had claimed in our missiles had melted like snow.
> Now I'm on the rockpile
> For counting the stockpile—
> Finding too many missiles alive, alive-oh.

After the fun, the show ended with an impersonator of Secretary of State Dean Rusk singing:

> Hey, look us over,
> Lend us an ear.
> Please note the peace pipe,
> Don't miss the spear.
> Here's where we stand, folks,
> We testify
> We'll listen whenever you want to talk—
> And keep our powder dry. . . .

> We're a little bit new at diplomacy,
> But we will make things hum,
> So look out, world—here we come!

The President was toasted, and he began his brief speech by saying that he was delighted to pay tribute to the newspaper industry. The *New York Times* had supported him in the election, and he commented, "I am at least one person who can say I got my job through the *New York Times.*

"I resolved long ago," he continued, "that when I reached national office I would always go to these dinners with influential members of the national press. After all, Dick Nixon came to the Gridiron every year, and look what it did for him."

Then, with the disarming Kennedy touch, he kidded himself and his associates.

"I was glad to see that there weren't any skits accusing me of recklessly spending the taxpapers' money," he said. "At least I am doing my best to keep it all in the family."

He said that the first mission of the Peace Corps would be to rescue Soapy Williams.

"I do want to report that Soapy is on his way home," he added. "I had received a cable from him a few days ago, asking permission to stay a few more weeks, but I sent one back saying, 'Africa is for the Africans.'"

Talking directly to the newspapermen, Kennedy said he expected there would be occasions when he would be criticized, and properly. He welcomed such constructive criticism, but he thought that the critics should always base their comments on a thorough understanding of the facts.

"For example," he said, "I've been criticized by quite a few people for making my brother Bobby attorney general. They didn't realize that I had a very good reason for that appointment. Bobby wants to practice law, and I thought he ought to get a little experience first."

Being in the White House, he said, was in many ways "just like the campaign—long hours, great debates over economic growth, the same fight with new teams over religion. As all of you know, some circles invented the myth after the 1928 campaign that Al Smith sent a one-word telegram to the Pope saying, 'Unpack.' After my press conference on the school bill, I received a one-word telegram from the Pope which said, 'Pack.'

"I want to thank you all, wish you all goodnight, and to wish you another happy year until we are exposed to the warm glow of the Gridiron again." [3]

• • •

At the dinner on March 17, 1962, Julius Frandsen of the United Press was president of the Gridiron club, and in his opening speech in the dark he referred to Jacqueline Kennedy traveling in India at the time, unaccompanied by Caroline.

"And so we are honored by having with us tonight the world's highest-paid baby-sitter."

The dinner was held a week later than the customary time because this was more convenient for President Kennedy, and

Frandsen referred to this postponement, saying that the President had had to go to Florida on the previous weekend to help the party raise money.

Referring to the Democratic party's money raising difficulties, he said, "It seems the Democrats' big contributors have been suffering from shell-out falters."

That was the year of the first major space flight, commanded by Lt. Colonel John H. Glenn, Jr., now Senator from Ohio. President Kennedy, said Frandsen, had made a wise decision to keep Colonel Glenn on the job. "The last time a Democratic President let a national hero go on tour, the Republicans kidnapped him and put him in the White House. . . .

"Both political parties have denounced the extreme right and the extreme left. Mr. Kennedy didn't let it go at that. He became an extreme middle-of-the-roader. His middle of the road stretches from curb to curb. That leaves the sidewalk for Senator Goldwater—the barefoot department store owner. . . .

"But it's a great country. All systems are *GO*—Bobby is *GO*—Jacqueline is *GO*—and Chester Bowles is gone."

Since the dinner was held on the night of St. Patrick's Day, Robert J. Donovan, then of the *New York Herald Tribune*, pointed out that the Irishmen all over the world were gathered on this night to salute Ireland's favorite son—"his style, his manner, and his prose." Whereupon the chorus poured on the stage, led by George Myers and William F. Raymond, and sang the Gridiron version of "My Wild Irish Rose."

> His wild Irish prose,
> It sparkles as it glows.
> It fulfills all the needs
> Of words—if not deeds,
> In the best Em-rald prose.
> His fine Harvard syle
> Beats FDR a mile.
> And if Cuba we lose,
> We can heal up the bruise
> With the charm of his fine Irish style.
>
> His wild Irish prose,
> It reaps not, but it sows.
> We hate sacrifice,
> But still it's so nice
> With his green ivy pose.
> His wild Irish prose,

It humbles all our foes,
And make no mistake
There's nothing can take
The bloom from that wild Irish prose.

These verses became even more pertinent several weeks after the dinner, when President Kennedy's confrontation with the steel industry over a price increase occurred.

The title of the Republican skit was "How To Fail in Politics Without Really Trying," and the scene was a soup kitchen in Newburgh, New York.

The first characters to enter were "Eisenhower" and "Rockefeller." The latter announced that "our motto is A.O.K.—Always Outpromise Kennedy."

A wall was being built around the soup kitchen "to keep the John Birchers out and the Republicans in." An impersonator of Robert Welch, leader of the Birchers, led them on stage, and "Welch" announced to "Senator Goldwater," "Barry, this is your last chance. You join us or we'll join you."

So, to the tune of "The Best Thing for You," Goldwater sang:

Please let me say from the start,
You're not politically smart.
I just suggest, what I think best,
Having your in-t-rest at heart.

I on-ly want what's the best thing for you and the best thing for
   you would be me.

Republican minority leaders Everett Dirksen of the Senate and Charles Halleck of the House were at the time putting on a weekly television commentary dubbed "Ev and Charley," so their impersonators were introduced.

Ev:
   Me and my shadow
   Showing on your TV screen,
Charley:
   Me and my shadow,
   Greatest lot of corn you've ever seen.
Both:
   We haven't long to run,
   Our sponsor's done,
   But while we last,
   We're just havin' fun.
   Just me and my shadow,
   Ev and Charley on the job.

Thinking of 1964, "Senator Hickenlooper" of Iowa thought that "we can beat Jack all right. It's Caroline I'm worried about. If we only had her on our side." Then he sang:

What we need is a Caroline,
Sweet young lady with manners fine,
With two big eyes that shine,
Oh, wouldn't it be loverly?

Someone new with vote appeal,
Someone charming, someone real,
Outshines the whole New Deal,
Oh, wouldn't it be loverly?

We need votes, you will all agree,
Caroline, you're the girl for me,
Come join the GOP.
Oh, wouldn't it be loverly?

Little "Caroline" came out, marking the first time a non-Gridiron member was used onstage in a skit. She was Walter Ridder's little daughter. She whispered to Hickenlooper, and Hickenlooper said, "She wants me to ask the astronauts—where are the monkeys?"

"Senator Margaret Chase Smith" thought all the candidates were cowards, because they were all afraid of Kennedy, and she sang, to the tune of "Dear Hearts and Gentle People":

The Gallup Poll cats have got them shaking,
There isn't any doubt.
It looks like Rocky and Dick are faking,
They really want to sit this out.

I feel so helpless each time that I detect
That they're hanging poor old Romney on the mast,
We've got those faint hearts and timid people,
They keep our party running last.

"Nixon" was asked how it felt to be running again (for governor of California), and he sang:

Running's wonderful, the second time around,
Head up in the clouds and one foot on the ground.
It's that second time you hear the starting gong,
Makes you think perhaps
That half the voters now know they were wrong.

Life's so comf'table 'way out there in the West,
Should I play it safe, give TV fans a rest?

Who can tell what leads me to this miracle I've found,
There are those who'll bet
I'll take a fall and yet
I'd be so glad to get a second time around.

Whereupon Senator Goldwater was introduced to make the Republican speech. He began by apologizing "if this announcement comes as a shocking surprise," and then, in mock seriousness, he read:

"Having talked with Nelson, Dick, Ike and George [Romney]; having checked with U.S. Steel, General Motors, the New York Stock Exchange, the NAM and the DAR; having taken favorable polls in West Virginia, Wisconsin, East Palm Beach, Hyannis Port, and Bellevue Avenue in Newport; I have decided to accept this authentic draft, the first in history, from the leaders of my party and become the Republican candidate for President in 1964.

"I'm serious about this. I like the address of the White House—anything with 1600 in it strikes my fancy.

"And, Mr. President, I look forward with great anticipation to this race. While I know it will be a tough one (there are more Kennedys than Goldwaters), I have every confidence that I will be declared the winner when the votes are counted—*if they are counted.*"*

Then Goldwater announced a campaign program—a satire on some of the things that President Kennedy had done.

"I have already launched my campaign," he said. "I have resigned from all my clubs. I salaam five times a day in the direction of Harvard and ten times a day towards the United Nations.

"Mr. President, I believe in copying success. So you will find that my campaign plans cover much of the same areas that your own touched on in 1960.

"But allow me to discuss my plans. And again I say, Mr. President, if some of the more enticing phrases strike a familiar note you will know that I borrowed them in the firm conviction that you can't argue with success.

"Here we go:
CIVIL RIGHTS

"Here, I will continue the present administration practice of playing footsie with the Southern Democrats for legislative reasons. . . .

---

*Goldwater was referring to vote counts that were questioned for both Chicago and Texas.

"And when my administration takes office in January, 1965, I will use the full powers provided in the Civil Rights Acts of 1957 and 1960 to secure for all Americans the right to vote.

"But, like your administration, Mr. President, I will *not* set any specific date for this action. I will, at the proper political moment, insist that my attorney general invoke the letter of the law—if he happens to be in the United States.

NATIONAL DEFENSE

"I shall begin by continuing nuclear tests in the atmosphere, as you so correctly have resumed. I will expand our program for sending jets to Tito by sending U-2 planes to Khrushchev. I will disarm to the teeth and blame it on the Radical Right if anything goes wrong. In true bipartisan fashion, I will provide fall-out shelters for the ADA and fox-holes for the Minutemen."

He proposed to retain in his administration "that distinguished linguist, whose broad Sengalese I deeply admire, Mr. Soapy Williams." And he would also keep "the multi-lingual and equally facile Chester Bowles. Also John Galbraith, who has mastered not only the art of distributing our earnings, but also the poetic languages, cultures and politics of the Far East."

Goldwater said he would try "a bold new approach in foreign policy. . . . And that is to use the distasteful idea that we can win in this ideological war with the communists.

"I know," he said, "the whole idea drives Bill Fulbright and Walter Lippmann half crazy. They think I want to turn back the clock to that day when all Americans understood victory, fought to win and were willing to make any sacrifice to reach their objective. I want to say just once to the American people that we do not intend to be buried by communism and that because our ideas are better than theirs we intend to win. They need to hear it from someone."

Referring to the Democratic platform in 1960 and addressing President Kennedy directly, he said he liked "the way it rolls off my tongue and the way it has rolled away from your mind."

"I will promise," he said, "a balanced budget and act like I mean it by not accompanying it with a bagful of government goodies for every economic group with the power to vote."

He would offer industry incentives by liberalizing the depreciation write-off, and he said, "I pledge that when I appear before the NAM and 'stress' the need for wage restraint I won't merely 'hope' for it two days later when I confront the AFL-CIO.

"And I will warn my secretary of labor not to follow up my

remarks with a statement that 'there is plenty of room for further wage increases.' . . .

"There will be none of this creeping stuff in my administration. If we must have socialism, let's go whole hog or none. If we must have federal aid why discriminate? (I propose to extend the boundaries of humanitarianism and welfarism and, in the process, pick up a sizeable number of votes.) My program will include federal aid to race tracks, gambling casinos, bookmakers, slot machine emporiums and brothels. After all, let's not forget the underprivileged."

He would create a counterpart to the Rhodes Scholarship and call it the Harvard-Fulbright scholarship and dedicate it to the purpose of keeping America from rejoining the British motherland.

"I realize," Goldwater said, "that this platform has some deficiencies and, in places, doesn't make a lot of sense. But you must remember this wasn't written in Rocky's office with Dick taking dictation. Nor was all of it hammered out under the boxing ring in the sports arena in Los Angeles. But a lot of Americans will recognize it for the fine Fabian document which it is." [4]

There had been several resignations from Washington clubs by Kennedys and people in the administration because the clubs were alleged to be discriminatory on account of having no blacks in their membership. The Democratic skit was set in the fallout shelter of a famous club from which many had just resigned.

Abraham A. Ribicoff, Kennedy's secretary of health, education and welfare, was a candidate for the Senate in Connecticut because, according to a statement of his impersonator in the skit, "it's the one state where they aren't running a Kennedy yet." He presented "Harry Byrd, Jr.", then a Virginia state senator, to sing:

> I want a club just like a club
> That took in dear old dad.
> Good Old-fashioned clubs like days of yore,
> Not new-fangled clubs with open door.

This dinner occurred after the abortive Bay of Pigs invasion of Cuba, and "Theodore C. Sorensen," special counsel to the President sang, to the tune of "Just an Honest Mistake":

> Anyone can make an honest mistake,
> An honest mistake from the heart.

CIA invaded Cuba,
It was sure to be a snap,
But Rusk said whoa and Fulbright no,
And the White House took the rap.

Stu said there's a missile gap,
We had dropped behind by years.
In seven weeks we found the facts,
They are coming out our ears.

It was just a tiny little slip up,
Anyone is bound to trip up,
Anyone can make a slight mistake.
It was just a little tiny, teeny,
Just an eenie, meenie, weenie,
Just an honest mistake.

The position of Vice President Lyndon Johnson was particularly difficult. Asked how he walked the fine line of authority, "Johnson" sang:

Tip-toe like a Texan of discretion
Who is not of kin,
I tip-toe through the White House to him.

The most rollicking song of the skit was sung by Rudy Kauffmann with his guitar, impersonating Senator John Stennis. He sang about the Democrat-turned-Republican, Senator Strom Thurmond of South Carolina, to the tune of "Big Bad John."

Ever' mornin' in the Senate you could see him arrive.
He stood six foot tall and weighed one-seventy-five.
Kinda broad in the shoulder, narrow at the hip,
An' ever'body knew you didn't give no lip
To Big Strom.

Nobody seemed to know what Strom could do.
He just ran for office like the Dixie dew.
He didn't claim much, not like Russell nor Byrd,
Runnin' once for pres-dent, he came in third.
Big Strom.

Then one day he found the military,
Where he got in a fight with the sec-re-tary,
An' a crushin' blow from a huge right hand
Sent McNamara to the promised land.
Big Strom.

Then came the day at the bottom of the deal
When the GIs came by foot and by wheel.
Marines were landin' and hearts beat fast
An' ever'body thought that he'd breathed his last—
'Cept Strom.

Through the dust and smoke of this man-made hell
Strode a tower of a man with a hand-grenade shell,
Threw a questionnaire and a double-barreled quiz,
An' by the sorta questions, they had to be his.

Big Strom, Big Stro——om.
Big Bad Strom.
Big Strom.

The skit ended with a big hullabaloo, as a loud-voiced chorister yelled: "Make way! Make way! For his royal highness, secretary of the exterior, the interior, the anterior, the superior! Grand vizir of the realm! First lord of the admiralty! Exalted cruise director!—*Robert Francis Kennedy!*"

"Bobby" entered and somebody shouted, "Let's storm the Alamo! Bobby replied, calmly and sweetly, "Gentlemen, my role in this government is very simple."

Then, in a parody of "You're My Everything," he sang:

I'm his everything,
Diplomat and sleuth,
I'm in everything,
Cellar up to roof.
I'm his private eye, his only true prime minister.
In fact, I'm the guy who some day will administer
All of everything,
Everything you see.
I'm the CIA.
And the AEC.
I'm the sub commander-in-chief,
Your welfare and relief,
In the winter, summer, spring, your everything.

Ribicoff, the Democratic speaker, began by addressing the president of the Gridiron Club, and then: "Mr. Attorney General, Mr. Brother of the Attorney General, Relatives of the Attorney General, and friends—of the attorney general."

He said he thought Barry Goldwater's speech was "really great," even better than one he had made two months before, accepting the presidential nomination at the Alfalfa Club.

"That one was a classic in its own right," said Ribicoff. "It may very well become a collector's item. It may go down in history as Barry Goldwater's only acceptance speech."

Referring to his own announcement of candidacy for the Senate, he said that he really liked Barry, and "besides, he's a senator and I'm only a cabinet member. A few weeks ago I would've said I'm a cabinet member and he's only a senator. But since then my plans have changed and now I'm able to see these things in proper perspective."

Ribicoff said there was one thing he liked about the John Birch Society—they were trying to create a vacancy on the Supreme Court. [The John Birch Society had been calling publicly for the impeachment of Chief Justice Earl Warren.]

"But, Barry, you'll have to admit I'm doing it the hard way. After all, I could've just moved to Massachusetts and announced for the Senate against Teddy. That way, I'd be assured of a judgeship."

He said that he'd like to be a senator, that since his appointment to the cabinet, he had attended a great many congressional hearings as to his qualifications, his activities, his views, his programs, "and I'd like a chance to sit on the other side of that table and ask a few insulting questions myself. . . .

"But I know this is a perilous course. I'm showing my profile in courage by standing alone as the only New Frontiersman to apply for membership in an exclusive club from which the President has resigned."

He ribbed former President Eisenhower, "the only President in history who got into politics after he left the White House. Then there's Dick Nixon, out in California, collecting fire insurance and hoping he's still hot. And Rambling Romney, the 1964 Sacrificial Lamb," who had many things in his favor.

"Only a guy who drives a small car has even an outside chance," said Ribicoff, "the way the President hogs the middle of the road.

"Then there's Nelson Rockefeller. Republicans don't really know what to make of him. In New York, if he moves any further to the left, he'll fall off the Democratic platform. But whenever he speaks in Des Moines he wears his McKinley button—he can't decide whether to be Grover Whelan or Roswell Garst. [The Iowa farmer who entertained Khrushchev and showed him his farm.]

"This brings us to Doctor Goldwater, I presume. Barry has

one great distinction this year. He's the last of the unmuzzled generals.

"We're all familiar with the expression, 'I'd rather be right than President.' In Senator Goldwater's case, I'm sure he will be.

"Well, there's the list. What a forward looking group! They're all looking ahead—to 1968. You know, as you listen to these Republicans, you hear so many different voices it's sometimes hard to tell whether your're listening to the Tower of Babel or the Babble of Tower [Republican Senator from Texas].

"But I see the Republicans have now decided to speak with a single voice. They've formed a special Policy Committee to get the Republican Bandwagon rolling. The Republican Bandwagon, you know, is the surrey with the lunatic fringe on top.

"The reason I'm dwelling on the possible Republican candidate is that you correspondents have a great interest in who he might be, you'll have to travel with him, spend a lot of time with him.

"If it's Rockefeller, you're going to save money: You'll go by pipeline. If it's Barry, you'll go by jet.

"As for Romney, I'm sure you'll enjoy the trip. Because George Romney's a gentleman. He doesn't drink, smoke, or swear, which makes him ideal company for you newspapermen.

"Finally, Mr. Nixon—a lot of you fellows have already traveled with him. You know him and he knows you. So I can tell you that if Dick Nixon is nominated, you'll have no problem about traveling. He's not going to take any of you."

To the correspondents, Ribicoff said, "I hope this advice has been helpful to you. I'm very fond of the press. I admire Washington correspondents especially. A Washington correspondent is the only newspaperman I know who will devote all his time and energy to the careful and honest checking of the truth of a rumor which he started himself." [5]

The foreign affairs skit utilized an artist's studio in which several new painters, among them Edward R. Murrow, Sargent Shriver, and John Kenneth Galbraith, had just finished a new portrait of the "Handsome American."

"Secretary Rusk" came on the scene for the unveiling, and "Murrow" pulled the cord to reveal a huge blowup of President Kennedy.

"Bowles" inquired of Rusk how things were on the home front. "They could be worse, Chester," responded the impersonator of the secretary, "and with you back, they soon will be."

Some of the songs were by "Sargent Shriver," head of the Peace Corps ("Peace Corps's a comin' to save them all"), and "Fidel Castro," the first and only occasion he had been a character on the Gridiron stage. Picking the feathers off a chicken, (as he had been photographed doing on his one visit to New York), Castro sang:

> Yes, we have no Havanas,
> We sell you no seegars today.
> Tamales and fritos
> For Khrushchevs and Titos,
> And all sorts of Reds and say,
> We have a true Communistic ardor,
> And tons of fruit to barter, but
> Yes, we have no Havanas,
> We sell you no seegars today.

There was some disillusionment about Jawaharlal Nehru, and an impersonator of John Kenneth Galbraith, Ambassador to India, introduced him and told the group that he had just undergone an operation: "He had his conscience out."

So "Nehru," who had just seized the Portugese colony of Goa, sang, to the tune of "Chloe":

> Go—a,
> Go—a,
> Principles will have to wait,
> Neutral guns will liberate
> Go—a,
> Go—a,
> Peace is yours, as bef-o-ah,
> Uncle Nehru now runs Goa.

> Through the black of night,
> I follow my pale pink star,
> If it's wrong or right,
> I follow it near and far.
> I lead all the friendly neutrals,
> I got it made!
> Be it war or peace, I'm bland,
> Ain't I grand!

> Never doubt me, Goa,
> And as heretofo-ah,
> On Aggression Day,
> Ole Nehru will be on hand.

Khrushchev was lampooned in the song which a character representing him sang:

I may be wrong but
I think I'm wonderful,
I may be wrong but
I think I'm swell.

I like to shout,
Pound my shoe for emphasis,
Give 'em cold chills
And raise lots of hell.

I like a nice vodka toddy,
A dozen will set me right off,
I've hidden Uncle Joe's body,
Demoted Old Molotov.

Oh, come along,

Gee, I think I'm wonderful,
I think I'm grand,
But I may be wrong.

At this point, Gridiron president Frandsen pounded his gavel, stopped the music, and introduced James E. Webb and other officials of the National Aeronautics and Space Administration, and five of the Mercury astronauts, closing with Lieutenant Colonel Glenn.

"Gentlemen of space—the Gridiron Club, its singers, its chorus, now salute you," said Frandsen.

And the skit closed with an adaptation of "The Battle Hymn of the Republic."

Our eyes are on the wonder
Of the worlds in outer space.
We will orbit Mars and Venus and
We'll make the Moon a base.
We will claim the distant planets
For the restless human race.
The age of space has come!

After the customary toast, President Kennedy rose to reply.

Edward Kennedy was running for nomination to the United States Senate in Massachusetts, against Edward J. McCormack, Jr., nephew of the Speaker of the House.

President Kennedy said it wasn't true that his brother was

getting any help from home. "We're not sending in any troops, just a few training missions."

Referring to Gridiron President Frandsen's comment about his being "the world's highest-paid baby sitter," Kennedy observed, "I know my Republican friends were glad to see my wife feeding an elephant in India. She gave him sugar and nuts. But, of course, the elephant wasn't satisfied!"

To help the milk people, Kennedy had issued a proclamation asking people to drink more milk, and of course he had to set the example. "I am certainly enjoying being with you newsmen this evening," he said. "None of you know how tough it is to have to drink milk three times a day."

He explained that he'd had some trouble disengaging himself in order to be at the dinner, because he had really been supposed to be at a meeting in South Boston that night, but he said he had telephoned the people running the South Boston meeting to say that he had to go to a dinner in honor of Secretary of Health, Education and Welfare Abraham Ribicoff and Republican Senator Barry Goldwater.

He said he could hear a voice in the background yelling, "Hey, what Cardinal Spellman says about that guy must be right."

Princess Lee Radziwill, Jacqueline Kennedy's sister, was traveling with the President's wife in India, and the President commented that "there is no truth in the charge that we're going to change the name of Lafayette Square to Radziwill Square—at least not during my first term anyway."

He told how Master Robert Kennedy, Jr., age seven, "came to see me today—but I told him we already had an attorney general."

The Metropolitan Club in Washington was one of those from which several Kennedy administration people had resigned because its membership included no blacks, and Arthur Krock, one of its prominent members, had written a few pieces about the Democrats that were less than laudatory of some of President Kennedy's policies.

"Krock criticized me," said Kennedy, "for not letting President Tshombe of Katanga come here, so I told him we would work out a deal. I'll give Tshombe a visa and Arthur can give him a dinner at the Metropolitan Club."

Other Presidents had been irked by some of the questions of

Texas newspaperwoman Sarah McClendon at press conferences, and Kennedy was no exception. She was his last target.

"I saw my wife's picture," said Kennedy, "watching a snake charmer in India. As soon as I learn Sarah McClendon's favorite tune, I'm going to play it."

Kennedy closed by saying that he wished to thank everyone again and to wish everyone a good night and a good year "until we all meet again under the friendly glow of the Gridiron." [6]

• • •

The 1963 dinner was held on March 9, after the Supreme Court had issued its controversial decision prohibiting prayers or the reading of the Bible in public schools, and Gridiron President William L. Beale, head of the Associated Press bureau in Washington, opened his speech in the dark by saying that "in deference to the presence here tonight of the chief justice of the United States, we shall omit any invocation.

"Instead," he said, "we take you to the newest New Frontier, where the fiscal program is handled on a pray-as-you-go basis. Our plea is: Forgive us our debts. Our aim is representation without taxation."

The Kennedys, he noted, were "on the move, and in the best St. Patrick tradition, the President is moving to Rattlesnake Mountain in old Virginia. But St. Patrick never had to battle the Harry Byrds."

Beale said that Robert Kennedy had finally begun the practice of law by trying a case in the Supreme Court. "And Baby Teddy," he added, "moved into that famous nursery of presidential ambitions—the United States Senate. Teddy wants to stay out of the limelight. No flashbulbs, please, when you shoot his picture."

He also had a word for "the White House News Management Bureau," consisting of Pierre Salinger, press secretary to the President, and Arthur Sylvester, assistant secretary for press relations in the Defense Department. "When Arthur says he's fibbing, he sounds like he's telling the truth. When Pierre says he's telling the truth—well, you know what he sounds like."

The opener was based on the many Kennedy moves to win over the cultural forces of the country: the elaborate White House dinner for all American Nobel Prize winners, and the numerous invitations to people in literature and the arts to White House dinners. The chorus, all dressed in artists' costumes, paraded on the stage and sang:

Culture's sweeping the country,
Art now wins at the polls.
Since Beethoven
Is interwoven
With patronage and pap and doles.
Now as voters all twist
Past Mona Lisa's smile,
We get so woozy
When we play Debussy,
But culture's here to stay;
Jackie wants it that way.
Culture's sweeping the country
There never was so much . . . art.

The scene for the Republican skit was Camelot, where the Republican leaders had gathered "in a round table strategy conference, searching for a plumed knight to rescue them in 1964."

The explanation for the setting came in the first lines, when an impersonator of William Scranton, governor of Pennsylvania, asked the chairman of the Republican National Committee what the Republicans were doing here in Camelot and was told, "Well, Governor Scranton, we camelot closer in 1960 than we ever will in 1964."

The Kennedy confrontation with the steel industry had still not been forgotten, and the first solo in the act was sung by an impersonator of Roger Blough, then chairman of United States Steel.

There's no business like steel business,
You're up, then you are down;
First you get a rabbit-punch from Bob,
Then a playful sock from Brother Jack . . .

"Goldwater" announced that if he could get equal time in '64 he would defeat Rockefeller "in four straight debates," whereupon the character representing Rockefeller sang, to the tune of "Why Do I Love You?":

Could I run with you?
Could you run with me?
Could we win with two
Different as we?
We're a ticket they would care for,
We're a slate they-d say a prayer for.
You are on the right,
On the left I'll be.

With the two of us,
Hopes bright will be.
Robert Welch will surely love you,
Liberals will go for me.

In one of the few instances when the chief justice has been impersonated on the Gridiron stage, an actor playing Associate Justice Potter Stewart explained why the chief justice was so unhappy: "He just caught a school boy playing hookey and trying to sneak into the President's prayer breakfast." Then "Warren" sang:

School days, school days,
No one in the room prays.
Pupils can't mention the Lord no more,
The High Court has held it's against the law.
Old and New Testament must go
Prayers are the instruments of woe.
So they should have been ruled out long ago,
Now praying can't ruin our kids.

For the second time at a dinner, there was an "Ev and Charlie" duet.

Both:
Here we are, all prepared to grouse.
Dirksen:
Dirksen in the Senate,
Halleck:
Halleck in the House.
Both:
Two sleepy people with not much to do,
And nobody saying, "I love you."

The skit ended with the introduction of "Representative Gerald Ford" of Michigan and recently elected "Governor George Romney," whose Presidential boom was then being pushed. Ford gave Romney some advice in the closing song of the act, to the tune of "Buckle Down Winsocki."

Buckle down, George Romney, buckle down,
You can win, George Romney, if you knuckle down.
If you do your job,
You can lure the mob,
You make all hearts throb,
So buckle down . . .

If you fight, we'll triumph at the polls,
If you fight, we'll realize our goals,
Knuckle down, George Romney, knuckle down,
You can win, George Romney, if you buckle down.
In the race count-down,
You can go to town,
You can wear the crown,
If you will only buckle down.

Governor Romney, as the Republican speaker, said he was glad to be at the Gridiron dinner which "doesn't cost us anything. I know you have all heard of that recent dinner given by the Democrats where if you paid $1,000 you got something to eat, but if you paid only $100 you went without supper."

He was honored, he said, to be a speaker at "this cannabalistic cook-out," particularly because his wife Lenore "tells me that the only time I'm really funny is when I'm trying real hard not to be funny."

He had a gibe for the Humphrey-Kennedy relationship and said he was looking forward that night to "Senator Humphrey's first uncensored remarks since the West Virginia primary [in which Kennedy had soundly trounced him]."

Turning to President Kennedy, Governor Romney said, "Mr. President, you have quite a family. A lot of people grumble about it but, as usual, there's a basis on which even they can count their blessings. The way the Kennedys are overrunning Washington, it's a good thing it was the Mormon Church and not the Catholic Church that practiced polygamy.

"But I have quite a family, too. Both my grandfathers, you know, had four wives and thirty children. As a result, my father and mother had a great many brothers and sisters and recently when we counted them I still had 237 living first cousins. Mr. President, if you thought it was tough finding jobs for Bobby and Teddy and Sarge Shriver and the rest, just think of having to find jobs for dozens of uncles and aunts and 237 cousins!

"We Mormons haven't practiced polygamy for a long time, of course, but I still admire the position Senator Boies Penrose took in settling the seating of Senator Reed Smoot. Smoot's qualifications were challenged on the basis of a polygamous background even though he himself had only one wife. When it became apparent Penrose's position was going to be decisive, he was asked how he was going to vote. Senator Penrose said: 'Well, I've decided I'd rather vote for a "polyg" who "monogs" than for a "monog" who "polygs".'

"I note," Romney said, "from glancing through this year's proposed budget that some of the financial ideas that wrecked Michigan have been catching on down here. This new pray-as-you-go fiscal program seems to be based on the principle that it's unwise for both the government and the people to go broke simultaneously."

He had a new idea for his own party.

"We Republicans should nominate Attorney James Donovan. If he can get Gary Powers back from Khrushchev and the Cuban prisoners back from Castro, perhaps he could get the United States back from the Kennedys."

He referred to the curiosity about his own future plans. "My own reaction is, how could one compete with a man from such a fabulous family, whose philanthropies are so extensive, whose able brothers add such luster to his own image, whose sound conscience is so well known and whose popularity is so well established—I mean Nelson Rockefeller, of course."

Remarking that "a serious thought or two is allowed at this dinner where a cat may not only look at a king but can dine with him as well, let me assure you that this particular cat has no desire, nor ambition, to become the king.

"Quite the contrary. I have a lot of sympathy for the gentleman who, as our President, sits at the center of our head table tonight. His problems are multitudinous. . . .

"While I'm a Republican and I'm proud to be here tonight speaking as a Republican and while I specifically oppose certain current Democratic philosophies, I do not endorse the thinking that causes some to recoil from anything just because it comes from the opposition party.

"I have a deep and abiding faith that to play strictly partisan politics with the public good is not only bad business but bad politics."

The great issue of one hundred years ago, he said, was whether "excessive state sovereignty was to fragment and destroy the union and the Constitution; the great issue of today is whether excessive federal sovereignty is going to be so concentrated that it will nullify state, local and individual responsibility and thus destroy the nation and the Constitution."

Romney closed by directly addressing President Kennedy.

"All of which, Mr. President, leads to a statement of my assurance to you of whole-hearted support in your efforts to handle the delicate and perilous international problems which face us. And at the same time may I assure you in matters on which we may differ of my loyal opposition.

"All Americans, in my opinion, should accept a simple truism that the late Alben Barkley used to expound: 'We have never had an American President with an ambition other than to be America's best president. Because this is the kind of country it is, I don't believe we ever will.'" [7]

The scene for the Democratic skit was "the humble little Kennedy lean-to on Rattlesnake Mountain in Virginia, which, believe it or not, is shown on official surveys to be bounded by a road named Segregation Road."

The cast was in hiking clothes, having just returned from a fifty-mile hike. Among the actors were impersonators of the President's two brothers. "Treasury Secretary C. Douglas Dillon" announced triumphantly that "Bobby can raise more money faster from Republican industrialists than George Humphrey."

Teddy replied, "Yes, isn't he clever? Bobby, tell them how you do it," and Bobby sang, to the tune of "When I Kiss Your Hand, Madame":

> The twister of the arm, gendarme,
> I twist their finger tips.
> And when I twist the arm with charm,
> They shower me with chips.
> I haven't any right, my friends,
> To do the things I do.
> But when I put the bite, my friends,
> They cough up out of fright, my friends,
> With dollars shiney bright, my friends,
> Some day I'll ransom you.

This was followed by a song about the Kennedy family to the tune of "Frère Jacques," which was done by George Myers as David Powers, a Kennedy aide and family friend, and Rudy Kauffmann with his guitar, as Peter Lawford.

Powers:
> How's your acting, Lawford?

Lawford:
> Better than Joan Crawford.

Powers:
> How's your in-law Teddy?

Lawford:
> Younger than he's ready.

Powers:
      How's your in-law Bobby?
Lawford:
      Hoffa is his hobby.
Powers:
      How is little Care-line?
Lawford:
      Probably on some air line.
Powers:
      How you count your cousins?
Lawford:
      Cheaper by the dozens.
Powers:
      How about Princess Radziwill?
Lawford:
      She will never stand still.
Powers:
      Where is sister Eunice?
Lawford:
      Think she's gone to Tunis.
Powers:
      What became of Shriver?
Lawford:
      Overseas skin diver.
Powers:
      What tour is booking Jackie?
Lawford:
      Italian or Iraqui.

"Senator Humphrey" wanted to know where Lyndon Johnson, the Vice President, was and said that "to hear him tell it, if it weren't for him, we wouldn't be where we are today."

Dillon replied that "I don't cotton to that guy. Once I heard him say a kind word for solvency."

An impersonator of Johnson then appeared on the scene announcing that he had troubles. He sang:

O bury me not on the New Frontier,
Where my sheltered life has been so austere;
I open shows—auto, home, or ship—
Write me one more speech and my lid will flip.

O bury me not on the New Frontier,
Where you seldom hear any Texan cheer;
Gimmie back my spread on the Senate floor,
Lemme wrangle votes as I did before.

I can't forget sixty-four is near.
I'll try real hard not to interfere.
But in sixty-eight, I'm a tellin' them all:
I'm the fastest gun in convention hall.

There was considerable comment in those days about "management of the news," and the two principal characters involved in the hassle were brought on the stage by a courier who entered shouting, "Make way. Make way. Make way for the royal, imperial public relations, the potentates of flak, the keepers of the image—the Assistant Secretary of Defense, Mr. Arthur Sylvester, and the White House Press Secretary, Mr. Pierre Salinger."

As they entered, Humphrey asked the character representing Sylvester to "tell us about this management of the news. Do you ever fib to us?"

"Let's put it another way, said Sylvester. "I frequently tell the truth."

"The truth?" retorted Humphrey incredulously. "Thank God it's not a campaign year."

Then "Salinger" stepped forth to explain:

Veracity's a-glow
And honesty's in our eyes,
At night when we tell you
Those little white lies.

We try, but we can't help fibbing
When evening appears.
We cry, but we can't help cribbing
In spite of our tears.
You may not believe our lips,
But try to believe our eyes
At night when we tell you
Those little white lies.

But "Teddy Kennedy" had the solution: "What's good for the Kennedys is good for the country." And the skit closed with "Theodore Sorensen" singing:

Consider yourself our own
Consider yourself one of the Kennedys,
We've taken you in so long
It's clear we never have been wrong.

Consider yourself well snowed,
Consider yourself part of the scenery.
There's no other part you play,
We cares? We say all there is to say.

Consider yourself our meat,
We don't want to have no fuss,
For after some consideration you are beat
Unless you are one of us.

Senator Hubert Humphrey, the Democratic speaker, greeted the assembled crowd as "fellow managers of the news" and recalled that Adlai Stevenson, in his speech to the Gridiron Club after he had been defeated by General Eisenhower, used as an opening line, "A funny thing happened to me on the way to the White House."

"You know," said Humphrey, "ten years ago I thought that was very funny." He made a long pause.

"And then came West Virginia.

"You may remember," he continued, "that the President and I travelled together quite a bit in 1960. It was a good scrap, and I have no regrets. Frankly, gentlemen, I think I did pretty well for a Protestant.

"So here we are today. I have Strom Thurmond, and he has Charles deGaulle. Let the punishment fit the crime.

"But if our President sometimes has his difficulties with the deGaulles and Diefenbakers of the world, let us never forget that he is the first President within the memory of man to have the last word with May Craig."

[May Craig at that time was a celebrated correspondent of New England papers, who appeared regularly on "Meet the Press" and at White House conferences, and whose questioning, while always polite, was also very penetrating.]

Turning to Romney, he noted that he had read recently that Romney had announced he would not be a candidate for President in 1964.

"Governor," said Humphrey, "that makes two of us.

"Now my advice to you Republicans is to remember the immortal words of that apostle of stand-pat Republicanism, Calvin Coolidge. Permit me to paraphrase and update—I do not choose to lose."

He told of a conversation he had had in Minnesota with a Republican friend, to whom he had pointed out that the Democrats had a big edge in registration, and that they were just the bigger party. The friend asked if he didn't believe it was possible once in awhile for a good little man to beat a good big man.

"Yes," said Humphrey, "it's certainly possible. After all

David did defeat Goliath. But it was so unusual that three thousand years later, people are still talking about it."

The Internal Revenue Service was putting on a campaign at that time against expense account deductions that they thought were excessive.

"So let us eat, drink and be merry," said Humphrey, "for tomorrow we shall have tax reform. France may have the Mona Lisa, England may have the Cheshire Cat, but we have the only smiling tax collector in history—Merry Mortimer Caplin.

"The new frontier has arrived—ask not what you can deduct for business expenses. Just eat at Howard Johnson's and go Greyhound.

"Mr. President, I'm loyal. I support most of your tax proposals. But really, Mr. President, things are going too far. Do we have to give up those dinners at Twenty-One? Do we really have to report her *name and address?*"

But he told his audience not to worry about the tax reforms. He would be "pleading our case every Tuesday at the White House breakfasts," and "by the way, two or three years ago I counted on having most of my meals over there."

Humphrey said he had been talking to the President about the fact that most of the big defense contracts had been going to the West Coast, leaving nothing for the Midwest.

"My argument," he said, "has been overwhelmingly persuasive. The tide of defense contracts has been reversed. Completely reversed!"

Then, with arms outstretched dramatically to Senator Edward M. Kennedy, he said, "Teddy, for God's sake, leave something for the Midwest!"

He wasn't suggesting that President Kennedy and his White House associates were giving out any special favors, but he had noticed, he said, "that Ireland just received its first sugar quota in history."

Picking up the cue about managing the news from the end of the preceding skit, Humphrey said he'd heard that the newsmen and publishers had been "complaining about the White House managing the news. Shame on you," he said. "When did professionals ever lower themselves to worry about amateurs!"

He recalled that he had been the target of a "few journalistic darts" himself, and that he had read "the farewell comments of our former Vice President at the end of the California gubernatorial campaign" [when he told them they wouldn't have Dick

Nixon to kick around any longer], and said he understood that most of the newspapermen were "secret Democratic agents.

"How wonderful it is," Humphrey exclaimed, "to be in this hotbed of the Democratic underground tonight."

He hoped the Bobby Kennedy hiking craze wouldn't catch on with the Republicans, because "it would be just too painful to see Ev and Charlie walking fifty miles—backwards."

Then, in mock seriousness, he said he wanted to leave one last thought about the 1964 elections.

"Do you really think that the American voters would elect a President who might appoint his brother David as attorney general, his brother Winthrop as head of the Peace Corps, and then turn around and support a third brother, Lawrence, for the United States Senate?

"Gentlemen, we of the Kennedy administration do not believe that this country will stand for a dynasty."

He bowed to the tradition that speakers on these occasions should strike a serious note before they close. It was a good tradition, he said, and he was glad to observe it. But his message, which he addressed to both Republicans and Democrats, could be compressed in one sentence from Abraham Lincoln, uttered at "another trying period in our history."

" 'In times like the present, men should utter nothing for which they would not willingly be responsible through time and in eternity.'

"It seems to me that advice is just as good today as it was 100 years ago."[8]

The confrontation between President Kennedy and Nikita Khrushchev over missile sites in Cuba was the main theme of the foreign affairs skit. An impersonator of John McCone, director of the CIA, "The Cuba Invasion Agency," sang a parody of "Rum and Coca Cola":

Before the revolution they used to sing and toil,
But now they're drinking Red Castro oil,
And the ruble talks, not the Yankee dollar,
Since the Bay of Pigs made us Yankees hollah!

Fidel drank some oil when us Yankees go;
It went right to his head, you know.
He woke up in bed, and he wasn't alone,
But with Khrushchev givin' him lend-lease loan.

We were all in the dark when the missiles came,
But election day and a U-2 plane

Tip us Yankees off what it's all about,
So we hollah with Vigah and he pull them out.
    Pfui on Castro oil!
    Pfui on Castro oil!

To this, "Rusk" commented, "Well, our blockade worked so well last fall, we may try an invasion for the '64 election."

Next on the scene was "Mao Tse Tung, poison pen pal of the Kremlin," who explained that only Fidel Castro and he understood Marshal Enver Hoxha, chief of state of Albania. An impersonator of Hoxha sang that his lot was not a happy one.

Our feelings we with difficulty smother—
When Moscow snarls at us for what they've done,
Ah, take one consideration with another,
An Albanian's lot is not a happy one.

At the time, Sargent Shriver was toying with the idea of running for governor of Illinois, and Richard J. Daley of Chicago had coined a slogan for him—"Out of the Congo and into Chicago."

"The Peace Corps is going to help me teach those voting machines how to count," said the character representing Daley. "You tell 'em, Sarge."

"Shriver" welcomed the attitude of Chicago's mayor and sang:

The peace corps' marching back home
To look for its own.
Back in its own back yard.
We'll fix those voting machines,
Beyond Daley's dreams,
Back in his own back yard.

No foreign affairs skit would have been complete in the early 1960s without "Charles deGaulle," who came on stage with "Prime Minister Harold MacMillan" of Great Britain, whose entry into the Common Market deGaulle opposed. deGaulle announced that "everyone is out of step but me," and asked MacMillan to tell them about it. "MacMillan" sang:

Napoleon from old Lorraine, parlez vous,
Napoleon from old Lorraine, parlez vous,
He wants to keep the market clear
Of Anglo-Saxon atmosphere,
Hinky, dinky, parlez vous.

He's sure that he's a modern day Joan of Arc
Whose vision has a supernatural, saintly spark,
But if he keeps up this mistake,
We'll have to burn him at the stake,
Hinky, dinky, parlez vous.

He's out to prove he's got the power, parlez vous.
He's growing stronger every hour, parlez vous.
He fought with Winston and Eisenhower,
And now he's taking on Adenauer,
Hinky, dinky, parlez vous.

If you want him, you've got to speak, parlez vous,
With just the proper magnifique, parlez vous,
If anyone gets in his way,
He'll squelch them with a communique,
Hinky, dinky, parlez vous.

Rusk commented that "there's been enough disarray for one evening. He wanted McGeorge Bundy, White House adviser on national security, "to step up and lead us in some positive thinking." And the skit ended with Bundy's impersonator singing to the "Song of the Vagabonds":

Here's to toil and trouble,
Bring them on the double,
We shall find a way to win.
Brotherhood will win out,
Racial strife will thin out,
As we drive along the way.
    Onward! Onward!
    Sails the Ship of State.
    Forward! Forward!
    Masters of our fate.
Mankind's pace is gaining,
Cuba's drive is waning,
And to hell with Muscovy.

President Kennedy addressed the audience as "fellow managing editors." Then he said: "I have tonight, a very grave announcement. The Soviet Union has once again recklessly embarked upon a provocative and extraordinary change in the status quo in an area which they know full well I regard as having a special and historic relationship.

"I refer to the deliberate and sudden deployment of Mr. Adzhubei [Premier Khrushchev's son-in-law] to the Vatican.

"I am told that this plot was worked out by a group of Chairman Khrushchev's advisers, who have all been excommunicated from the church, known as Excoms. Reliable refugee reports have also informed us that hundreds of Marxist Bibles have been unloaded and are hidden in caves throughout the Vatican. We will now pursue the contingency plan of protecting Vatican City which was previously prepared by the NSC—the plan known as Vat 69. We are, in short, eyeball to eyeball over the Holy See. They're cross-eyed.

"Speaking of the religious issues, I asked the chief justice whether he thought our new educational bill was constitutional. He said it is clearly constitutional—it hasn't got a prayer."

President Kennedy said that he wished he could stay after the dinner and visit everybody individually, "but I must get back to the office because Adam [Clayton Powell] and I are planning my trip to Europe this summer. Tomorrow I will be spending the day in the country with Ken Keating up on Rattlesnake Mountain.

"The Vice President complained to me," he continued, "that Doris Fleeson [a correspondent] was still criticizing him. But I told him he didn't know how lucky he was—I'd rather be Fleesonized than Krocked."

Then, for the first time in a Gridiron speech as President, Kennedy had a serious moment after expressing "on behalf of all of us, our appreciation to the Gridiron Club, and to the profession which they ornament with such distinction.

"I suppose any visitor to the U.S. coming here would have a picture of a country strongly divided," he said, "a good deal of movement to and fro, a press filled with headlines. But I would think they'd make a mistake, as has been made on many occasions, if they forgot that the strong right arm of any President of the United States is the fact that in great numbers, and in the more difficult moments, this is a strong and united country. It has been a source of strength to me, particularly last fall, and will be a source of strength to my successor.

"This is a great country. The press contributes to it. Transcending, I think, all of our momentary differences is the fact that all of us, on whichever side of the aisle we sit, are commonly committed to the maintenance and freedom of our country, the United States.

"Thank you, gentlemen. Once again, the Gridiron glowed but did not burn. Thank you." [9]

Probably no President, with the possible exception of Theodore Roosevelt, enjoyed the Gridiron dinners as much as Kennedy did. The cracks at him and his associates didn't bother him, and truly for him the Gridiron "glowed but did not burn." He never exhibited, so far as can be learned, any annoyance about any Gridiron skit, and he fitted into the format of Gridiron dinners, which emphasize wit more than seriousness, very well indeed. He had the wit, and he exhibited some of the best of it at these dinners, especially when he laughed at himself.

This was John F. Kennedy's last appearance at a Gridiron dinner. The one scheduled for December 23, after the assassination, was canceled out of respect for him.

XIX

Lyndon B. Johnson

1964-1966
"I am a free man first . . ."

And Richard Nixon, Barry Goldwater, and
Hubert Humphrey also Speak.

The spring dinner of 1964 was held later than usual, on April 25, by which time President Lyndon Johnson had been in office five months.

During this interval, he had had a group of newspapermen visit the White House one night, and in showing them around the various rooms of that magnificent residence, he had been very careful and somewhat ostentatious about turning off the lights in each room as they left it, presumably to indicate his devotion to economy. This had elicited wide press comment.

Consequently, Fletcher Knebel, 1964 Gridiron president opened his speech in the dark with the words, "Mr. President, fellow enemies of illumination:

"The Gridiron Club is far ahead of the Johnson administration. For seventy-nine years, we've been operating in the dark—on purpose.

"These are strange times. . . .

"Treasury Secretary Dillon reports that the run on gold has finally stopped. And for good reason. There is no more gold.

"Adam Clayton Powell may soon be off to Europe again with

his female secretaries. When reporters asked him what for, Powell said no, five.

"Republican Chairman Miller says his party has more issues than it knows what to do with. That's not news. It has been years since the Republicans had an issue they knew what to do with.

"Senator Goldwater confesses that he made some campaign mistakes in New Hampshire. But he shouldn't blame himself. A man can't always get laryngitis when he needs it. . . .

"Dick Nixon accuses President Johnson of a leadership gap. Whereas what troubles Nixon is a followership gap."

Press Secretary Pierre Salinger, a native of California who lived in Virginia, had announced his candidacy for U.S. Senator from California, and a member of the opposition out there had remarked that "Pierre isn't a carpetbagger. He hasn't had time to pack a bag."

Knebel commented that "Pierre Salinger is a one-man reapportionment act. If elected, he will give California one senator—and Virginia three. . . .

"Democrats shut down the Bobby Baker investigation. They say it didn't prove a thing—and just in the nick of time, too. . . .

"But all is not to be lamented.

"Fidel Castro misjudged American fighting men when he cut off their water [at Guantanamo Bay]. Most of them haven't touched the stuff in years."

President Johnson, while at his ranch near Austin, Texas, had taken a group of newspapermen around on a tour, and one of them had ungraciously reported that at one point the speedometer had gotten up to 90 mph.

So Knebel finally came forth with a "word of protocol for the users of the nation's highways.

"If anybody passes you doing ninety, don't call the police—call the Secret Service."

The announcer for the opener recalled that President Johnson, in one of his first speeches, had said that "we of the United States are the most beloved people on earth.

"Greatly impressed by his discovery, the Gridiron Club tonight takes love as its theme—the world's love for us, our love for one another, Harry Byrd's love for Soapy Williams, anybody's love for everybody."

The chorus came on with two soloists dressed as cupids, and the rest of the cast in white tie and tails with great big pink hearts pinned on their lapels. They sang:

Love is bustin' out all over,
All over the Congo and Brazil.
Love is bustin' outa As-yuh
In a way that would amaze yuh.
All our friends and foes are bloomin' with good will.

Love is bustin' out all over.
The feelin' is getting warm and gay.
Oh, the Arabs and Israeli
Do not shoot each other daily
'Cause they're savin' all their shot for U.S.A.

Love is bustin' out all over,
E-mo-shun is getting out of hand.
Ev'ry throbbing foreign nation
Has been mobbing our legation.
We are getting too much love for us to stand.

In the guest skit, George Reedy, White House press secretary, was asked to stand and it was announced that "Mr. Reedy says in every other administration the President has had advisers; in this administration, the President has listeners."

A Texas guest was quoted as saying that "this week Texas is celebrating the anniversary of the battle of San Jacinto. Mr. Dobie says that if only Sam Houston had lost that battle, Lyndon Johnson would now be emperor of Mexico—and we'd all be free."

But it was for the Democratic skit that the club reserved most of its gibes about the administration, and President Johnson's well-known facility for making sure that things went the way he wanted them to go.

There is a story told when he was Senate leader. At a luncheon one day he had boasted to Republican leader Dirksen that he was going to get an amendment to a certain bill adopted on the floor that afternoon. Dirksen said he had enough votes to defeat him, and they made a ten dollar bet. The roll call came and when the last name had been called, the Dirksen forces were ahead by one vote.

Dirksen smiled smugly across the Senate floor to Johnson, whereupon Johnson raised his hand and snapped his fingers four times. The cloakroom doors opened and in walked four Democratic senators, which changed the vote and gave the victory to Johnson.

The scene for the Democratic skit was on the Pedernales River, where the Democrats were gathered at the LBJ ranch, and where the Gridiron Club would "continue our exploration of America's state of belovedness—and nowhere is love more honored in the breech than in the Democratic party."

An actor playing Representative Carl Albert, majority leader of the House, was presiding over this gathering of Democrats, all in bright white chaps, boots, sombreros and crimson cowboy shirts. The act opened with "Sargent Shriver" singing, "Everything's up to date in Johnson City."

At that time Shriver was head of the poverty program, and Albert asked him, "As the only Yale man who has ever loved poor people, do you think you can abolish poverty?"

Shriver replied, "Abolish it? Man, we're promoting it."

Then an impersonator of Jack Valenti, one of President Johnson's closest associates, sang to the tune of "Tammany":

> There's an issue that's unequalled in this campaign year.
> Just its mention 'round the country all will shed a tear.
> Sargent Shriver is our leader, he's a lucky guy.
> He will make vice president with this new battle cry:
>
> Poverty, poverty.
> It's no good for you and me,
> But it's fine politically.

There was considerable adverse comment then about the ages of Speaker John W. McCormack of the House and Senator Carl Hayden, president pro tem of the Senate. Their impersonators sang a duet:

Both:
> Younger than springtime are we,
> Bursting with vi-tal-i-ty.
> Where did you get the idea that we're too old to serve?

McCormack:
> I'm not yet seventy-three.

Hayden:
> And eighty-six suits me.

McCormack:
> Younger than spring-time am I.

Hayden:
> Gayer than laughter am I.

Both:
> Brimming with spirit, gallant and strong, so young are we.

Next to step forward from the cast were "the Vice Presidential Beatles," impersonators of Senator Hubert Humphrey of

Minnesota, Governor Pat Brown of California, and Senator
Eugene McCarthy of Minnesota. Shriver came pushing in, saying
"I want in on this act," and Albert asked Humphrey, "What do
you boys have in mind?"

Humphrey pointed to President Johnson and said, "He
knows, but I'm not sure he's paying attention. We'll tell him
again." Then the four sang their version of a Beatles song.

> Oh yeah, I say to Lyndon,
> I think he'll understand.
> When I say to Lyndon,
> I wanna hold your hand.

There had been talk among the Kennedy followers that
Robert F. Kennedy, the attorney general, would make a good
running mate for President Johnson, but Johnson had squelched
this by announcing publicly that he would not select any member
of his cabinet for the Vice Presidential post. An impersonator of
the attorney general was the next principal to speak. He lamented
that "Lyndon took me out of the ball game," and sang:

> Take me out of the ball game,
> Put me back in the crowd.
> Up in New Hampshire with song and shout,
> They wrote me in, and he wrote me out.
> So take me out of the ball game.
> Gee, I could win, it's a shame.
> But it's one, two, three states and out
> Of the old ball game.

The Johnson administration was already embarrassed because of the revelations that Bobby Baker, Johnson's principal
assistant while he was majority leader of the Senate, had been
engaging in some legislative activities which had led people to
make handsome gifts to him, some of which had been invested
in the building of an elaborate resort at Ocean City, Maryland,
named the "Carousel." Baker's lawyer was Edward Bennett Williams.

When "Baker" came on the stage and Albert asked him what
he had to say, Bobby replied, "Ah, it's a great country when a
poor kid from South Carolina can come up north and fleece the
Yankees out of enough to pay Edward Bennett Williams' legal
fees."

An actor representing Senator B. Everett Jordan of North
Carolina, who had headed the Senate's embarrassed inquiry into
Baker's activities, was introduced as "the great investigator of

sin." He announced, "I come not to bury sin, but to praise it,"
and sang:

> Hello, Bobby. Well, hello, Bobby.
> It's so nice to see that you are still about.
> You're looking hale, Bobby.
> What's for sale, Bobby?
> Any stock tips, any blue chips you can do without?
> You were a free wheeler,
> And a big dealer,
> At the Carousel and Quorum Club back then.
> So—glad you're back, Bobby.
> We'll let you keep your stack, Bobby.
> You'll never have it all that good again.
>
> Hello, Bobby, well, hello, Bobby.
> Don't you wish you had the job you had before?
> It was your niche, Bobby,
> Made you rich, Bobby.
> You were swingin', you were wingin' on the Senate floor.
> But now your slip's showin',
> GOP's crowin'
> 'Bout that hi-fi for your friend from way back when.
> Oh, 'twas a gift, Bobby,
> No need to take the fifth, Bobby.
> Sin will never be the same,
> Sin will never be the same,
> Sin will never be the same again.

The act closed with a reference to President Johnson's turning out of White House lights and his penchant for phoning
people—sometimes rather late. To the melody of "Penthouse
Serenade (Just Picture a Penthouse)," the chorus sang:

> Every night at sundown,
> Lyndon wants a rundown
> On the day's electric bill
> And how much he's saved the till.
> The lights in the White House show nary a spark,
> But Lyndon can still find the phone in the dark,
> And dial by the glow from the lights in the park.
> Cut those lights.

Carl Albert, majority leader of the House, was introduced as
the Democratic speaker. He began with a salutation.

"Mr. Knebel, President Johnson, Mr. Chief Justice, my colleagues of the Congress, distinguished members of the press and other writers of fiction, distinguished publishers and other Republicans."

He quoted Mark Twain as saying that "the only way for a newspaperman to look at a politician is down," and commented that the authors of the last skit took Twain at his word.

He mentioned a remark in the skit about himself as being from "Bug Tussle, Oklahoma," and said that its inference was that this was his only claim to fame.

Albert, a person of small physical stature, commented, "I can tell you that visitors to the House Gallery think otherwise. They think I'm a junior page boy."

With reference to the Democratic skit, he said, "The last skit reminded me of a spectacle in the coliseum in ancient Rome. The only difference was that in those days, the senators watched while the Christians were fed to the lions. But it's great fun tonight—for the Christians."

Then he turned to other matters. First, the Congress.

"The present session," he said, "is expected to be short. About two billion dollars short.

"There was one advantage in last year's twelve months session; we didn't have time to go home and explain it to the voters.

"But this year we're moving faster. Did you notice how quickly the Senate wound up the Bobby Baker investigation?"

He referred to the talk among some members about major reforms in the way the Congress operates, particularly the House.

"A lot of people," said Albert, "want to do things with the Rules Committee. The smart ones just want to get on it."

Shifting over to the Presidential election, he said he was happy to welcome back to Washington former Vice President Nixon—"temporary though it may be."

"President Johnson happily goes from day to day, just doing what comes naturally—and 77 percent of the voters approve. Things are going so well for him that they tell me he opens cabinet meetings with the prayer that Divine Providence remain under the protection of the administration."

On the Republican side, he found the situation to be "mildly confused and even puzzling."

"I have followed the positions Senator Goldwater has taken these past few months," he commented. "He's the only bull I ever saw who carries around his own china shop."

Of Nelson Rockefeller: "He is a man who has risen to immense wealth in just three generations."

Of Ambassador Lodge: "If you believe the polls, nothing stands between Lodge and the top of the ladder—except the ladder."

And of George Romney: "My opinion is, he's being kept under wraps in case the Republican kingmakers at San Francisco need a stop-Stassen candidate.

"As I conclude," Albert said, "I cannot miss this opportunity to get in a plug for my party. I say to you, gentlemen, that all my party wants is the chance to complete its program. And what is its program? To stay in office another four years."[1]

It was the perfect combination of laughing at oneself, one's own party and the opposition, which goes over so well at Gridiron dinners.

The Republican skit, opened with the announcer, saying that "the Republican party is truly beloved. Everybody loves the under-privileged. Tonight we find the Republican party gathering in the ABC television studio at San Francisco, where their famous non-leader, General Eisenhower, is manifesting a sudden strange and alarming interest in politics."

An impersonator of Eisenhower, described as a "kind of Huntley-Brinkley after taxes," was at a broadcasting desk. "Senator Dirksen" asked him what he thought about the Executive Mansion being all in the dark. Eisenhower didn't want to take sides, so he let James Hagerty answer for him, and "Hagerty" sang:

> When the lights go on again all over the land,
> If the GOP could win, it sure would be grand.
> But all our candidates, seem a little less than a threat.
> They're all scarred up or else playing hard to get.
>
> What we need to light the lights is this kind of bird:
> One with grin and name and rank, who's a household word.
> But all we've got to choose is guys that lose,
> And they'll blow the fuse.
> When the lights go on again all over the land.

Henry Cabot Lodge, who had been appointed ambassador to South Vietnam, and who had just won the New Hampshire Republican primary on a write-in vote, was introduced to prove "that the most popular Republican is always the one who's furthest away."

"Lodge" expressed pleasure at the New Hampshire result, but said, "I'm afraid of Goldwater and Rockefeller when we get into those big cities where people can't write."

"George Romney," who by this time had retired from the campaign, sang:

Won't you come home now, Cabot?
Won't you come home? You've been away too lo-ong.
Excepting in New Hampshire, things don't look good;
But you are going stro-ong.

How can we fight old Lyndon, about Vietnam?
Why can't you get it through your dome?
You're spoiling our aim, and it's just a shame!
Oh Cabot, won't you please come ho-ome?

After the New Hampshire primary, some of the other candidates had had difficulty raising funds. At this point impersonators of former Senator Knowland and Senator Goldwater, dressed as beggars, came on the stage, announcing that they were dead broke and that since New Hampshire they'd been "reduced to begging on the streets." Goldwater, the man who three months later was to be selected to run against President Johnson, sang:

Once my wealthy backers coughed up dough.
Thousands coughed at a time.
Ever since New Hampshire they've been slow.
Brother, can you spare a dime?

Guess we'll have to sell the TVA,
It was always a crime.
Even the post office doesn't pay,
Brother, can you spare a dime?

There is only one place that's still got cash.
Now those dollars do chime.
Gee, I hate to do it, but I'm rash:
Rocky, can you spare a dime?

One by one, characters representing the other Republican personalities were introduced. "Rockefeller," who had been divorced and had remarried, told "Governor Scranton" that he had "stumbled on the chapel steps," and sang:

Not a leader in my corner,
That's a pretty certain sign,
Those wedding bells have broken up
    that old gang of mine.

All the pros are looking elsewhere,
They use to like me fine,
Those wedding bells have broken up
  that old gang of mine.

The skit ended with the entrance of "Nixon," and Dirksen acknowledged that "no gathering would be complete without his strong aroma of sacrifice." He commented further that they wanted him back in San Francisco, where the Republican Convention was to be held, "because it's an awful lot of work to break in a new loser."

Scranton told Nixon to speak up, and his impersonator sang, to the tune of "I Left My Heart in San Francisco":

I'll sacrifice in San Francisco,
For GOP I'll try to find
The Presidential candidate,
Or even running mate.
It may be hard,
But can't you guess
Who'd say yes?

Here's my address
In San Francisco.
And in that blue and smoke-filled hall,
When I come back to you,
San Francisco,
However soft,
I'll hear your call.

Knebel then introduced that "good friend of Cartoonist Herblock, the titular leader of the Republican party, Mr. Richard M. Nixon."

"Prime Minister Menzies once told me," Nixon began, "that after he had been worked over at the Australian version of the Gridiron dinner, he responded by proposing this toast to the press: 'To the most overpaid, unskilled labor in the Commonwealth.'

"I can assure you that I shall not respond that way tonight. One blast at the press in sixteen years is enough!"

"Since reporters are never present at a Gridiron dinner, it occurred to me that this would be a good time to give some forthright answers to some of those loaded questions many of you would like to ask me.

"Why, instead of moving to New York, didn't I have the good sense to do what Cabot Lodge did?

"I will have to admit he certainly has found the secret of success. He wins where he isn't and he loses where he is.

"I tried to get an ambassador's post, and Lyndon Johnson was willing to give me one. But he wanted to send me to Caracas. If I'm going to get stoned again, it's going to be at the Gridiron dinner and not in Caracas.

"Why did I make that statement about running for office being a sacrifice?

"Here I must go into a little background. As titular leader of my party, I must think of the party first and myself second. Now let's look at the plight of our party. The Republican party today has only 16 governors out of 50, 33 senators out of 100, 1 ambassador out of 109. It is crystal clear that the Republican party needs Nelson Rockefeller as governor of New York, George Romney as governor of Michigan, William Scranton as governor of Pennsylvania. And the party certainly needs Barry Goldwater, Margaret Chase Smith and Thruston Morton right where they are in the United States Senate. There can be no question that the Republican party needs Cabot Lodge in Vietnam (and come to think of it, the Democratic party needs him there too).

"Now, I realize that leaves only one man. But look at his qualifications: a lawyer in a populous eastern state, holds no office, willing to run for any office, has had years of invaluable experience in Washington under Dwight D. Eisenhower. There can be no question but that the logical candidate is—Harold Stassen of Pennsylvania!

"And I still say it would be a sacrifice for me to run as Vice President on a ticket with Harold Stassen.

"Incidentally, just to clear up that remark about being willing to run for Vice President. I misunderstood the question. I thought they were asking me if I would run on the ticket with Lyndon Johnson. Of course, I said yes.

"If Bobby Kennedy can get along with him, I can.

"But now let's turn to the big question.

"Can anyone beat Johnson?

"We could beat him if we could ever catch him.

"If he'd only take the bus and leave the driving to us! Of course, he's riding high now, and pretty fast too."

But President Johnson had troubles coming up, Nixon noted. It was easy to get along with Mr. Khrushchev when you were five thousand miles away, "but wait until he meets him face-to-face.

"I recall my experience. Ambassador Thompson had

suggested I might get on a good footing with him by telling him how I had worked for a living as a boy.

"So when I showed him the supermarket at our American Exhibition in Moscow, I said, 'Mr. Khrushchev, you may be interested to know that my father once owned a grocery store and I worked in it as a boy.'

"He replied, 'All shopkeepers are thieves.'

"Now what do you think he is going to say to somebody whose wife owns a TV station!"

It is interesting that President Nixon's speech up to this point had been prepared, and the Gridiron files contain typewritten copy, but the rest of it is in his own handwriting on the backs of the pages that contained the original speech, and was evidently written at the dinner as he listened.

He noted that the worst thing a Republican could say about anybody is to call him a me-too-man. "Look where that leaves President Johnson." he said.

"He took his welfare program from his Democratic predecessor, his legislative program from his Republican predecessor, and now he promises to spend more than JFK and save more than Dwight D. Eisenhower.

"That makes him a double me-too candidate.

"He's getting pretty good mail now," continued Nixon. "But just wait. He should see some of my mail. I received a letter the other day which said, 'The Republicans should nominate you. They're going to lose anyway. Why not choose an expert in losing . . .

"If he [Johnson] refuses to debate, Bill Miller tells me that we won't use that empty chair routine. He has some old TV clips and is ready to put on the TV debate of the century—President Johnson vs. Senator Johnson on civil rights.

"Now, despite the remarks I have made, I want to express my personal respect and admiration for President Johnson, not just as President, but as a man.

"After all, we have a lot in common!

"We both served in the House.

"We both served in the Senate.

"We both served as Vice President.

"We both ran for President against John F. Kennedy—and lost!

"I have to admit the odds against any Republican are great when it comes to winning against one of America's most resourceful politicians backed by the tremendous power of the Presidency.

"But because the odds are great, I think this can and should be the Republican party's finest hour.

"Nations, organizations and men rise to greatness, not when the going is easy, but when it is hardest.

"The Republican party in 1964 can go down to its most humiliating defeat if it consumes itself with cannibalism, becomes frustrated with defeatism, offers only nit-picking negativism, or decides to rubber stamp the administration's policy with a caretaker candidate and wait until 1968.

"On the other hand, the Republican party can rise to its greatest heights by inspiring America with the challenge of new leadership which will rebuild the grand alliance, reverse the tide of defeat in Asia, deal with the cancer of Communism in Cuba, and establish new confidence and respect for American leadership throughout the world.

"Such a campaign will be good for the Republican party, for the nation and for Lyndon B. Johnson.

"One of President Johnson's favorite expressions is that he always does his best.

"I do not doubt that that is the case. I think history will record that no President in this century has worked harder and longer on the job than Lyndon B. Johnson.

"But forty years ago, a great distance runner, Paavo Nurmi, ran against the clock because he had no competition. He wore a wristwatch on his wrist and looked down at it as he finished each lap. He did as well as he could. But sports experts agree he could have been the first man to break four minutes if he had had competition.

"May 1964 be the year when no one runs against the clock, when both Republican and Democratic candidates, because of the challenge of competition, will rise to heights they might never otherwise have achieved.

"America under the man elected President in such a campaign will answer the call to greatness which is her destiny."

Then Nixon turned to Gridiron President Knebel and said he would like to conclude with a personal note, relating to the theme of this dinner, which was love.

"Tonight at the reception for head table guests, preceding the dinner, I saw a dramatic demonstration of that theme. I met President Truman, and we shook hands for the second time in fifteen years—there were no photographers present! Then, because I happened to be standing between him and the bar, I handed him his drink, at the request of the bartender.

"Now, when Dick Nixon can hand Harry Truman a glass of bourbon and water, and he drinks it without having it tested first, that, gentlemen, is love!"

There was a difficult situation in the underdeveloped countries of Africa, with demonstrations and mob scenes in front of various American embassies and even attacks on some with attempts to burn them down. Frederic W. Collins of the *Providence Journal* introduced the foreign affairs act by reading to the president of the Gridiron Club a letter "to your lovelorn editor:"

"Dear Miss Lonelyhearts: I am a small African nation deeply in love with a great big North American country that doesn't seem to know I exist. How can I attract his attention?

Signed: Wistful."

Knebel answered from the head table.

"Here is the proper reply. 'Dear Wistful: The answer is simple. Take his money, burn down his embassy, flirt with the Communists, and then sue him for non-support.'"

The orchestra broke loose with the sound of rockets, gunfire, breaking glass and pandemonium, as the curtains parted to show a sand-bagged command post, manned by two men in battle dress, "Secretary of State Dean Rusk" and "General Maxwell Taylor," chairman of the Joint Chiefs of Staff.

General Taylor wanted to know why the people of the whole world "love us to death like this." As the chorus entered in bright uniforms and berets, Rusk thanked heaven that help had arrived and asked "Assistant Secretary of State G. Mennen (Soapy) Williams," "what do you hear from your love nest?"

To the tune of "Wunderbar," Williams sang:

Zanzibar! Zanzibar!
Where they gave us all their love,
But it may leave a scar
—Our romance in Zanzibar

Oh they care there for us greatly.
They wave at us so grand.
But we've noticed one thing lately:
There's a pistol in each hand.

Zanzibar! Zanzibar!
We're as close as hand-in-glove,

> Or as feathers-and-tar
> With our pals in Zanzibar.

There had also been trouble in Panama, where the local government had been grousing about the Panama Canal. "Assistant Secretary of State Thomas C. Mann" arrived with what "Rusk" termed good news: that President Chiari had turned the water on again in the Panama Canal. Mann sang:

> It's a grand old flag,
> It's a high-flying flag,
> Hip-hooray, hip-hooray, hip-hoorah!
> Let it be unfurled
> 'Round all the world,
> Excepting, of course, Pan-a-ma.

Britain had been rocked by the scandal of Christine Keeler, a "call girl" who had been called by some high British officials. As an impersonator of British Prime Minister Sir Alec Douglas-Home came on the stage, General Taylor commented that "our Bobby Baker is a match for their Christine Keeler. But maybe we're not as slick as the Tories about handling it."Then Home sang:

> We're still the same old Tories.
> We lived through Christine's glories
> A case of doll and guy—
> The world will always pardon love
> As time goes by.

> You must remember Chris,
> Her kiss our nemesis,
> Her sigh reached persons high,
> And John Profumo told a lie
> As time went by.

The Gridiron Club could never resist satirizing Charles de Gaulle. As he came on the stage, played by Phelps H. Adams, with regal costume and scepter and seven stars in his crown, he shouted, "After me, the deluge. Any minute! Tell them, Couve de Murville, about my painful modesty." Whereupon "de Murville" sang, to the tune of "I Love Paris":

> He likes Castro in the springtime,
> He likes Mao in the fall.
> He likes Saigon in the winter, he's its savior.
> He likes Allies when they're on their good behavior.

These are only mild flirtations.
Some day they are bound to pall.
But sincerely, there is one that he loves dearly:
His name is Charles de Gaulle.

The skit ended with Secretary Rusk announcing that "We are truly a beloved people. These uprisings of affection would stir the hardest heart. Honest, world, we're on your side. Tell them, Under Secretary of State George Ball."
And "Ball" sang:

Climb ev'ry mountain, hoist any load.
Always keep us moving, down that peaceful road.
O'er ev'ry hilltop may be at hand
A view that is brilliant of the Promised Land.

It may be a dream that is still far away,
But if we persevere it will come true some day.
Peace is our lodestar; freedom our grail.
Follow ev'ry prospect, and we cannot fail

The curtains on the stage closed and the guests drank the toast to the President, who began by addressing his remarks directly to Knebel.

"After spending Friday in the midst of poverty, here I am tonight in a pocket of prosperity," Johnson said. "With your President Knebel, that's exactly what it is. He's the only man I know who made a million dollars in seven days in May!" (*Seven Days in May* was Knebel's and Charles W. Bailey's best-seller, published shortly after the Cuban missile crisis.)

He commented that he hoped nobody would "think it significant that I am running behind Dick Nixon on this program. Obviously, the order of this program was not arranged by me—or Dr. Gallup!"

Then, with reference to the fact that several of the more aggressive Washington newspaperwomen were agitating for election to the Gridiron Club, he said, "after what I've seen here tonight, I am immediately appointing fifty women to the Gridiron Club.

"I wish, in addition," Johnson went on, "to appoint a new commission to study what happened to the governor on my Lincoln Continental during the Easter weekend. The governor is supposed to keep me from going more than sixty-five miles an hour. The commission will be headed by Henry Luce. But until the report is in, there will be a new policy at the LBJ Ranch: Everybody walks—and drinks Pepsi-Cola.

"After this evening—and some experiences of my own—I'm none too sure which is more hazardous: being a guest of the press or having the press as your guest.

"Someone asked me about my relationships with the press. Tonight I thought I'd explore getting along with the press with an expert in that field who is here tonight—my old colleague Dick Nixon. However, Dick's solution may not be entirely satisfactory with me: he moved away to another state; to another job.

"But, throughout my life I have determined that things usually happen for the best—particularly when the Lord is on your side. For example, Lady Bird was flying to Cleveland the other day and her plane was struck by lightning. But even that had one salutary effect. Now, she's willing to drive with me again.

"Gentlemen, I am happy to be here. I'd like to leave you with one thought.

"I came into this office under the cruelest of circumstance. There were things to be done; and somehow God gave me the strength to try to do them. I am grateful for the help and prayers and the support of all my countrymen, Democrats and Republicans. But whether I am in this office one year, or more, I want to leave my country a little less frightened, a little less hungry, and a little more hopeful.

"And I would pray that future historians may speak of my appointed time in the White House in the words of Isaiah: 'There shall be peace and truth in my days.' "

• • •

In the 1964 election, President Johnson really earned his nickname of "Landslide Lyndon." He carried all states except Arizona, South Carolina, Louisiana, Mississippi, Georgia and Alabama, which led Dean Burch, chairman of the Republican National Committee, to comment that "the Democrats have really goofed—they overlooked six states."

And John Bailey, Democratic chairman, commented that as long as he held that position, "I want Dean Burch to be my counterpart—we make a winning team."

President Johnson was at his Texas ranch and missed the March 20, 1965 Gridiron dinner, but the Gridiron darts did not miss him.

There had been considerable comment about a picture of the President at the ranch, lifting up a dog by the ears. Gridiron president Frederic W. Collins, in his speech in the dark, made reference to this.

"Let us take as our text tonight a Biblical quotation President

Johnson seems to have overlooked. It is found—really found—in Proverbs, Chapter 26, Verse 17: 'He that passeth by, and meddleth with strife belonging not to him, is like one that taketh a dog by the ears.' "

America was somewhat mixed up, Collins said, but there were signs of progress. "All believers in free competition welcome that second TV station in Austin. It is called Radio Free Pedernales."

The Gemini flight into space had been put off toward mid-week, he said, "to take advantage of the family fare plan. Our Moon Men train for a landing, carrying top secret White House orders: 'Be sure to turn it off when you leave.' "

On other matters, he quipped that "the United States continues to cooperate with even its worst enemies. It is building embassies only a stone's throw from Riot Headquarters. We've finally abandoned the No-Win policy, however. Now, it's No Windows."

The opener noted that "the vision of a Great Society described by President Johnson has gripped the imagination of all Americans. The Gridiron Club therefore takes the Great Society as its theme this evening, examining the architecture, engineering and goals of this project for building the kind of life we'd all like to become accustomed to."

The chorus trooped on the stage, bearing a litter topped by an elephant ridden by Roscoe Drummond, who appeared as a Pharaoh wearing a Texas cowboy hat. Then, to the strains of the "Triumphal March" from Verdi's *Aida*, the chorus sang:

> All Hail!
> The Great Society in LBJ's great name!
> Cradle to the grave
> For all,
> For all, from him-m-m.
> We'll share
> Money and love and fame,
> Everything grand and free,
> Bizness will boom in this land of the brave.
> We'll have a ball!
>
> Ev'ry variety,
> Goodies from A to Z,
> His Great Society.
> O! Happy day!
> So come

To the millenium,
Saving is out of date,
Deficits are great.
LBJ
Hail to him!
Hail LBJ!

Among the stand-ups in the Republican skit were Senate Minority Leader Everett McKinley Dirksen, House Minority Leader Gerald R. Ford, and Ray C. Bliss, the new chairman of the National Republican Committee.

Walter Ridder, the announcer, said that "the Republican party in the last election based its strategy upon all—or nothing. It almost achieved one of those objectives."

The scene was at Peachtree Street and Magnolia Avenue in a war-torn town in Georgia, with ruined buildings in the background, and a paper moon and the stacked rifles of a Union Army bivouac. Soldiers were lying around at rest.

" 'Ten-shun!" snapped an officer, as three gold-braided generals entered, with General "Knowland" commenting that the southern strategy really worked and that they'd made a clean sweep of six southern states.

General "Nixon" noted that he'd been campaigning everywhere else but in the South. "It's been a rich experience," he said, "but let me tell you, the Democrats have more people out on bail than there are in the whole Republican pary."

But General Knowland wanted a celebration, and the chorus came forth to sing, to a tune that sounded suspiciously like "Marching through Georgia":

What a happy day for the triumphant GOP!
Twarn't no loss we suffered, but a brilliant victory.
Just like Sherman did before, we've set the Southland free,
While we were marching through Georgia.

Hurrah, hurrah, the South has seen the light.
Hurrah, hurrah, we're steady on the right.
While we lost the North, it's true, we sure stayed lily white,
While we were marching through Georgia.

We have brought two parties to a section that had one.
Democrats throughout the South are really on the run.
Although our total in the North fell all the way to none.
While we were marching through Georgia.

Impersonators of three unsuccessful aspirants for the Republican nomination, Governor Nelson Rockefeller, Governor George Romney, and Governor William Scranton, sang together of "a little bit of luck."

> The GOP last year was made for Barry,
> To share his views, although his goose was cooked,
> The GOP had more than it could carry,
> But—with a little bit of luck,
> Not a single one of us got hooked.

The casualties of the battle included "former Republican Chairman Dean Burch." Burch had been chairman only from the time of the Republican Convention through the election, and to the tune of "A Woman Is A Sometime Thing," he advised his successor, Ray Bliss of Ohio, not to give up his house in Akron.

> Lissen to some words to ta-ame you,
> 'Fore you start to think you're king:
> Bosses will name you,
> Frame you and blame you,
> For—a chairman is a sometime thing.

> If the left wing or the right wing selects you,
> The middle's going to make you sting,
> Suspects you and rejects you,
> And polite-like dis-elects you,
> 'Cause—a chairman is a sometime thing.
> Yes, a chairman is a sometime thing.

The song ended with an impersonator of Nikita Khrushchev, who had just been deposed in the Soviet Union, coming in and announcing that he "vished to seeng."

"What do you want to sing," asked "Bliss."

Khrushchev mournfully replied, "A chairman is a sometime theeng!"

Since Goldwater was to be the Republican speaker, according to the traditional Gridiron style his impersonator closed the skit with a parody based on "Pass Me By."

> In your heart you know yours truly was so right.
> I have just the ticket, give the world a fright,
> I'll cas-ully mention that I may renew the fight,
> Speculatin' really can be fascinatin'.
> Meantime Lyndon's welcome to the job;
> He can fret and cuss while I
> Can tell the whole darn world I am off the Great Society,
> Deal me out,
> Thank you kindly, pass me by.

As the chorus marched off and the curtain closed, Collins, from the head table, introduced Goldwater by saying, "And now we hear, speaking for the Republican party, an extremist in the defense of liberty, in the pursuit of justice, in hope for high office—and in his determination, just now, to relax."

"Mr. Chairman and gentlemen of the Gridiron Club," Goldwater said, "in your hearts you know I lost." (A Goldwater campaign slogan had been In Your Heart You Know He's Right.)

As one who was unemployed, he said, he felt it was necessary to identify himself.

"I am that trigger-happy, war mongering S.O.B. who last year and the year before called for the bombing of the supply routes into South Vietnam [which had been done by President Johnson after the election]. My name is Barry Goldwater—sometimes known as the Brand X of the Republican party.

"And I must say it's wonderful to see so many friends here tonight—and some Republicans, too!"

Then, with a delicate swipe at the white tie and tails and red roses and champagne and music of the rather splendiferous Gridiron dinner, he said; "Having thus made myself known, let me tell you it is a real thrill for me to be here with you again in this foxhole in the war on poverty."

President Johnson did not always get along too well with the press, and Goldwater made an oblique reference to this.

"To be able to sense and feel the warm comradeship that permeates the relationship between the members of the press and the White House revives and strengthens my complete confidence in the infallible accuracy and objectivity of what I read in my local papers so far away from this fountain of fact and news.

"Gentlemen, I realize," he continued, "that the purpose of the Gridiron Club is annually to put Americans on the griddle. Sometimes I think the members forget, in their ranting at politicians, that it is likely that if Mr. Johnson and I weren't in politics you'd have to support us some other way.

"However, the club does perform an invaluable service in teaching us there's nothing wrong with a good political joke—unless he gets elected."

Referring to his assignment to speak that night, he told his audience that it was not an easy one.

"What do I talk about?" he asked. "It's easy to be humble when you're a success, but it takes real talent to be arrogant when you're a flop.

"Certainly I am not important. The President is important, but he is far better discussed by you than by me. . . .

"So the country—our country—and what you and I as citizens can do for her becomes, by far, the most important object of discussion I can think of."

But before embarking on that, he wanted to discuss his own reactions a bit. He and Mrs. Goldwater, he said, had been "sitting on our hill in Phoenix, watching the sunsets and humming 'Hail to the Chief.'

"We were watching television the other night and saw a commercial that claimed twenty-seven million people switched to a new remedy to get rid of their headaches.

"I said to Peggy, 'Isn't that ridiculous? What could twenty-seven million people get a headache from?' "

There was a long pause, and then he said, "Then I remembered!

"It's a fascinating experience being a losing Presidential candidate. On November first when I walked into my office there might be three or four hundred messages waiting. By December first even the Fuller Brush man had stopped calling. And by January first I was thinking of going to Hertz Rent-a-Friend. . . .

"But the one thing a defeated candidate has to learn is how to adapt. And my idea of adaptability is the Arizona supermarket that had six thousand cans of a soft drink in stock on November fourth. Now, ordinarily, this wouldn't be much of a problem—but this particular soft drink was called Goldwater.

"And here's where the adaptability comes in. They made a big pyramid of the six thousand cans and on the top put this sign: In Your Heart You Know It's Ginger Ale. . . .

"I've thought of getting a job, and I'll admit it's a revolting thought after twelve years in the Senate. . . .

"The President offered me a job with one of his radio stations, and I hadn't even known he had one in the Baffinland. . . .

"Dean Rusk called the other day and suggested a key administrative post for me—librarian in Indonesia [where rioters had burned a U.S.I.A. library].

"I know a lot of people have been curious why I've been spending so much time in Washington lately. Well, somebody's gotta keep Hubert company, and extremism in the pursuit of a job is no vice."

Goldwater said when he heard that the budget was ninety-nine billion dollars, "I called the White House and said, 'Mr. President, ninety-nine billion dollars? Who buys retail?'

"Ninety-nine billion dollars and the President calls it a bare-bones budget. Bare-bones! In Texas that's what they call Jayne Mansfield!

"And the Great Society! Personally, I think the President is carrying this too far. Like I just saw a picture of George Washington crossing the Pedernales River."

For the serious part of his speech, Goldwater stated what might be interpreted as his personal creed.

"I believe that we, as individuals, must promote a respect for morality, for law and for order. I believe that each of us in our own individual way, working in the sphere we occupy, should speak of the greatness of the American dream and the American achievement and not belittle or downgrade the magnificence of our country or of our purpose.

"I believe that, as individuals, we should eliminate hate and misunderstanding from our daily lives and replace them, instead, with love and understanding.

"And, lastly but certainly not least, we should hail our President when he is right and pray that he is right all the time—for he is *our* President and our help must be always his to ask.

"In closing, let me tell you that my twelve years of li e in this great city have been years of enjoyment, friendship and of pride—so often because many of you have made my life here that way.

"I do not suffer in defeat. I have pride in the knowledge that I have been privileged to serve my country as a citizen, a soldier, a United States Senator and as a candidate for the highest office in the land. And, as a citizen, I shall continue to serve.

"It is a real pleasure to be with you—only in America can we mirror ourselves in the warm glow of the Gridiron.

"May God keep it thus."[4]

The speech was a terrific success, and Betty Beale, in a newspaper column, quoted an unnamed Gridiron member as saying, "If Barry Goldwater had talked like that during the campaign, he might have won."[5] This was obviously an overstatement, but the speech did have the effect of creating a warmth toward Goldwater that had been lacking in the campaign.

The Poverty Program was the motif for the Democratic skit, which was set at "Budgetary Gap" in the New Appalachia, where the Poverty Committee of the Chamber of Commerce was meeting on the grave problem of "how to stay poor enough so that Washington can make you rich."

A committeeman who wanted to "get the dough before they

sober up in Washington" asked "Sargent Shriver," director of the Peace Corps, "how do we cash in and make Budgetary Gap a better place to live?" Shriver sang:

There's a bright yellow haze o'er the mine shaft,
There's a bright brownish cast in the river,
The corn in the jug makes us snug as a bug,
And if we play it right they will think we are bright.

Oh, the Job Corps will work on the highway,
Oh, they'll stand there just like they were statues,
They won't even try till Sarge Shriver rides by,
Then they'll sing my praises right up to the sky.

Oh, what a beautiful junk yard,
Oh, what a beautiful dump.
I got a beautiful feeling,
Soon they'll start priming the pump.

A delegation arrived from Washington, comprised of "Tommy Corcoran," "Abe Fortas," "Clark Clifford" and others. Clifford announced that "we consent to anything we advise. We advise you now there's nothing more durable than old New Dealers."

Tommy the Cork responded, "Right. If you can't lick 'em, outlive 'em. Tell them how it is Abe Fortas."

"Fortas" announced that "we're not black sheep any more" and sang, in his new version of "The Whiffenpoof Song":

To the New Deal coalition,
To the happy common man,
To the taxing and the spending and the rest.
We have brought a new dimension
Of the splendid way of life,
And a program that will surely meet the test.
Yes, a program that will get us
All the votes we need to win
When we promise them those things they like the best.
We will rally 'round our leader and hold the banner high,
And we'll end up with a nicely feathered nest.

We're old New Dealers who've found our way,
Baa, baa, baa.
Back to the White House with LBJ
Baa, baa, baa.
Gentlemen barristers out for a fee
Helping the Great Society

End corruption and poverty,
Baa, baa, baa.

Impersonators of George Reedy, press secretary to the President, and Jack Valenti, one of the President's White House assistants, came on the stage. Reedy commented, "You think you've got trouble. At the White House they don't even tell me what day it is—but he does make it clear what administration it is."

Then Valenti told him in song what the situation was at the White House.

Oh, he gets Valenti for nuttin',
Valenti is plenty, you see.
He's got Bill Moyers,
Got his lawyers,
Got Abe and Clark for free.

Next came a character representing Robert F. Kennedy, "a real expert on poverty," who said he was having trouble because he couldn't "quite talk that Texas talk."

"Oh, we'll teach you," answered a committeeman, played by Walter Ridder, who had written the song. "Come on, try now. Today Ah'm all the way with LBJ."

Kennedy: Today, I'm—
Committeeman: No, no. Not I. Ah'm. You know, like your arm.
Something that gets twisted. Now try again.
Kennedy: (Slowly, to the tune of "The Rain in Spain"). Today, Ah'm
all the way with LBJ.

He repeated it two or three times, and a committeeman inquired of him, "How long are we to stay?"

"All the way, all the way," said Kennedy, who began to dance a fandango and closed the song by repeating again, "Today Ah'm all the way with LBJ."

"Olé," shouted the committeeman, and Kennedy sidled up to the microphone looking furtive, and said, "Well, anyway, halfway."

"Vice President Humphrey" introduced "Bobby Baker," who, he said, had "signed up for the war on poverty as a conscientious objector." The committeeman announced to Humphrey that "we're all with you. If you can't make us poor, nobody can. Tell us why, Hubert."

And Humphrey sang:

I'm an old cowhand with the Johnson brand,
And I take my stand in the promised land.
Never rode a hoss, 'cause I don't know how,
But you know darn well I'm gonna learn to now,
'Cause it sure beats walkin' behind a plow,
Yippee-yi, LBJ.

I'm a maverick stray from the ADA,
And I used to play Walter Reuther's way,
But I'm steppin' out in diff-rent comp'ny now,
Henry Ford, Fred Kappel and Roger Blough,
We're saddled up with businessmen somehow,
Yippee-yi, LBJ.

I'm the quietest man in all the land
Since I got the word to be seen—not heard.
I could talk all day if I had my way,
But I'd better not, there'd be hell to pay,
I may do tomorrow what I can't today,
Yippee-yi, LBJ.

Collins introduced Vice President Humphrey as "the co-pilot on the Great Society's dizzy flight into the future," to speak for the Democratic party.

President Johnson had made it plain, as the Democratic Convention approached in 1964, that he was going to choose his running mate as all previous Presidents had done, but he let the speculation go on for months as to who it would be and finally announced, after the Democrats had gathered in Atlantic City, that his choice was Senator Hubert Humphrey.

Humphrey began his speech by giving his version of how this came about.

"You recall I never sought the job," he said. "All those meetings last summer with businessmen, bankers, and oil tycoons, editors, governors, mayors had but one objective, to help President Johnson. I was the most surprised man in Atlantic City when I got that call from the White House."

He described the call from Johnson as beginning " 'Hubert, do you think you can keep your mouth shut for the next four years?' I said, 'Yes, Mr. President.' And then he said, 'There you go interrupting me again.'

"And then came the campaign—extremely interesting, extremely long, extremely expensive, but ending up extremely well. And Barry, you were extremely helpful.

"Barry, we met only once during the campaign, and appropriately at the cornpicking contest. And you may recall I said, 'Barry, you'd better lay off that Social Security issue.' And you replied, 'Listen, Horatio, you run your campaign, and I'll ruin mine.'

"But Barry's doing all right. He has a new TV network show. It runs from 6 P.M. to 5:30 every night. He is writing a syndicated column that reads from right to right.

"But Barry's a smart man. If you can't beat those sensation-seeking columnists, join them."

Then Humphrey turned to Nixon, whom he described as "another friend of the President here tonight."

"After being elected," he said, "I immediately sought his advice. I said, 'Dick, what do I need to do to be a good Vice President?'

" 'Well,' he said, 'get yourself a good dog.' 'Anything else,' I said? 'Oh, yes, you need a crisis. In fact, you really need six crises.' 'And what else,' I asked him? He said, 'Stay out of South America.'

"But being Vice President is not all one happy rose garden. For one thing I had to declare all my assets. Up until then, I had Muriel thinking we were broke. She even made her own dresses.

"President Johnson is an amazing man," he continued. "The President believes in on-the-job training. I remember the President saying to me after that 1960 West Virginia Primary, 'Hubert, that was the poorest campaign I have ever seen. If ever this country has a poverty program, you ought to be in charge of it.' "

Then he mentioned the discussions that had occurred about building an official residence for the Vice President.

"The President asked me about that," Humphrey related. "I said, 'Mr. President, I kind of go for those big old houses with the columns on them.'

"He said, 'Yes-s-s-s.'

"I said, 'Mr. President, I like a house that is close in. I like a lot of yard, a lot of trees and squirrels and a lot of driveway. I like a lot of bedrooms in different colors.'

"The President said, 'Yes-s-s-s.'

"And finally I said, 'Mr. President, I think I have my eye on just the right place.'

"The President said, 'Hubert, you have had too much time for reflection.'

"And that's when he assigned me civil rights, poverty, mayors, travel–See-America, Peace Corps, ambassadors, agriculture, legislation, and diligent attention to my duties as a trustee of the Board of Regents of the Smithsonian Institution.

"Now I'm not complaining. I really like my job—I mean jobs! Why, I will go any place I am asked to go. I will do anything I am asked to do at any time. You see, I try harder. I have to. I'm only No. 2."

He recalled an imaginary conversation he had had with George Reedy.

"One of the real pleasures has been working with the White House Staff. The other day I called George Reedy and asked him about that dinner for Princess Grace of Monaco.

"He said, 'I'm sorry, I don't know about any dinner.'

" 'But, George, you announced it to the press at Monday's briefing.'

" 'I don't remember having a Monday briefing.'

" 'But, George,' I said, 'there's a dinner tonight for Princess Grace.'

" 'I don't have any information on that. I have to check it out.'

" 'George, ' I said, 'do you know who you are talking to.'

" 'I am not sure.'

" 'This is the Vice President of the United States.'

"And he said, 'Could you give me a few more details.' "

That ended the humorous part of Humphrey's speech, and his serious close concentrated on the need for both individuals and nations to search their souls for the answers to the vital questions of life.

"Who am I? What do I believe? What really counts in my life?" he asked.

"To confront such questions forthrightly is never easy.

"To answer them honestly is often painful.

"Yet a determination to do this is the true test of one's courage and conviction—and of one's humanity.

"And so it is in the life of a nation.

"Do we, as a free people, possess the courage, the conviction and the humanity to ask: Who are we? What do we believe? What does America stand for?

"I believe that today America is searching her soul for these answers. She is doing it on the highway between Selma and Montgomery, in the marbled halls of Congress, in the barren valleys of Appalachia, in the poverty-stricken slums of Harlem and South Chicago, and on the distant battlefields of Southeast Asia.

"And, as in the life of an individual, this process in the life of a nation is never easy.

"It is not without great pain and sacrifice. Yet to avoid these questions, and to evade these answers, would be to forfeit the legacy of freedom given to us by generations of compassionate and courageous Americans.

"President Woodrow Wilson was one of these Americans. Speaking in Philadelphia in 1914, he gave his vision of where America should be going:

" 'My dream is that America will come into the full light of the day when all shall know that she puts human rights above other rights and that her flag is the flag not only of America but of humanity.'

"This is Lyndon Johnson's dream. It is my dream. And it is surely yours. This is the Promise of America."[6]

The speech, like Goldwater's, was a great success.

The closing skit dwelt on the international situation and was based on the fact that 1965 was International Cooperation Year at the United Nations.

J. Russell Wiggins, then editor of the *Washington Post* but later to become U.S. Ambassador to the United Nations, announced to the audience that "so you may see this great organization before it is cooperated to the brink of nonexistence, the Gridiron Club takes you to the harmonious confines of the United Nations' Deadbeat Club."

The scene was the "Deadbeat Bar, U. Thant, proprietor," and various international characters appeared. The first ones were "Nasser" of Egypt and "Sukarno" of Indonesia. Side by side, they sang a duet:

> Oh, our people are ragged and skinny,
> The rich ones haven't a guinea.
> So we riot along, kicking the gong,
> Side by side.
> Our only export is static,
> We are both of us charismatic,
> So happy are we,
> Off on a spree,
> Side by side.

"Chancellor Ludwig Erhard" of Germany and a group of his

sailors described how they were going to run the "multilingual, multilateral, multinuclear fission boat."

> A capital ship for an ocean trip
> Was the multilingual force.
> No two in the crew quite ever knew
> What the other one said, of course.
> The mate this week is a Cyprus Greek
> But the second does the work.
> While up in the sails is a lad from Wales
> And the engineer's a Turk.
>
> A capital crew on the ocean blue
> Is our multilingual might.
> No more than two quite ever knew
> Where the blasted missiles light.
> What the Captain said when the course was read
> Was Greek to a second mate.
> A lad from Rome drove the charges home
> And he left the rest to fate.
>
> Then blow ye winds, heigh-ho,
> A-sailing we will go.

An actor playing deGaulle, with whom President Johnson had found it somewhat difficult to deal, accepted the homage of his subjects and sang:

> I'm an ordinary man,
> Who prefers to spend his evenings in the glory of my praise,
> Where he can hear a grateful nation singing out the Marseillaise.
> An ordinary man am I, a most beloved one,
> Whom Frenchmen venerate, decorate
> And call the greatest figure under the sun.
> Just an ordinary man.
>
> I am a man so shy and timid,
> One who has one idea to convey,
> Just a simple little Europe,
> One where France has all the say.
>
> But, let a Yankee in your life,
> He'll try to crowd you off your throne,
> First they spend and then they lend.
> Will Dean Rusk's visits never end?
> I would rather take a beating than attend another meeting
> With a Yankee that I'd let into my life.

Carl Rowan, later a Gridiron member, was at that time head

of the United States Information Agency, and some USIA libraries abroad had been burned or stoned in riots. His impersonator was the next character on stage. He sang, to the tune of "Smoke Gets in Your Eyes":

> They asked me how I knew
> True friends are so few.
> USIA tries
> 'Midst our tears and sighs,
> But smoke gets in our eyes.
> Someday the tide will turn
> And our books won't burn,
> When your film's on fire,
> You must realize
> Smoke gets in your eyes.
>
> Now Nasser won't repay
> The USIA,
> So I smile and say
> When a library dies,
> Smoke gets in your eyes.

The only reference to the Vietnamese War in the skit was a colloquy between "General Earle G. Wheeler," chairman of the Joint Chiefs of Staff, "General Maxwell D. Taylor," former chief, and "Robert S. McNamara," secretary of defense, who came to the conclusion that they should "let Saigon be Saigon, because, after all, General Khanh [a Vietnamese] got escalated out of there." To the tune of "Heat Wave," McNamara sang:

> We're havin' a small war,
> A hole in the wall war.
> The Buddhists are risin'
> It isn't surprisin'
> They proved that they can can Khanh.
> We're fightin' an old war,
> A very hot cold war,
> And in such a way that
> The natives will say that,
> They showed that they can can Khanh.

The skit closed with an impersonator of Secretary of State Rusk introducing an actor playing "the modern medicine man," Secretary of Health, Education and Welfare Anthony J. Celebrezze, who would "tell everybody how to get back to the Promised Land, with a song addressed to the leader of the Great Society." Celebrezze had a new version of "Oh, Promise Me."

You promised us a Great Society,
By law—and by executive decree.
Where all the lakes and rivers will be pure
And wealth will lift the burdens from the poor.
You promised every state its Pedernales
With waters gurgling Texas Über Alles,
A subway ride instead of one by bus,
You promised us! You promised us!

You promised with your promissory skill
A lot of promises you may not fill,
Because at breaking them you are adept,
We'll praise you for the promises you've kept.
There are some things we fear you won't deliver,
But we'll forgive, oh, mighty-would-be-giver!
Because all politicians have been thus,
You promised us! You promised us!

And although Lyndon Johnson was 1500 miles away down on the Pedernales, the dinner ended with the usual toast to the President.

• • •

J. Russell Wiggins, president of the Gridiron Club in 1966, set the theme for the March 12 dinner by declaring in his speech in the dark that "we live in the best of all possible worlds" and then proceeded to document his assertion.

"The country," he said, "is enjoying its prosperity so much that even the Federal Reserve Board has stopped longing for a depression. . . .

"Democracy is sweeping the world. More and more South American nations are holding elections and some of them are even letting the elected officials take office. In Africa, the last nine military coups have put into power military dictators who believe in democracy. In the Soviet Union they're giving poets and writers trials before sending them to jail. . . .

"Even the war news is good. General Sargent Shriver's brave troops are winning the war on poverty. The last of the resisting poor have been rounded up and before the year ends Sarge will have all of them beaten into submission and registered in the Democratic party."

The years 1965 and early 1966 were times when the technique of staging demonstrations to promote causes and create havoc was beginning to develop, and this was the theme for the opener.

The chorus poured onstage, and in a parody of "Freedom, Freedom," sang:

Picket, picket,
Protest is the ticket,
If it's square, man, kick it,
Pro-test!

And then several soloists, in order, began to specify:

Lie ins, drop outs,
We abhor the winners,
And we'd also like to protest
    Gridiron dinners.

(This was before the women's liberation organizations began to picket the Gridiron, to which women at that time were not admitted.)

Then there was a succession of college-song parodies:

Far above Cayuga's waters
Where the draft can't reach,
We say what we hadn't oughta.
That's what's called Free Speech.

And:

(We're)
On to Johnson, on to Johnson,
He can't fool us kids,
With his nasty war in Asia
Johnson's on the skids, rah rah!

And another:

Haircuts spurning,
Draft cards are for burning,
Leftward we are turning,
Cool!

The chorus closed it all with:

Sit-ins, lie-ins,
Frequent nights in jail,
Save us from subjections to the power structure.
Antic, frantic,
We are so romantic, the army is pedantic.
Dissenters all are we!

Prominent Republicans were asked to stand in the introduction to the GOP skit: Senate Minority Leader Dirksen, House Minority Leader Ford, and two former Republican nominees for President, Richard M. Nixon and Barry Goldwater.

The scene was Phineas T. Dirksen's Sideshow in Sock Center, Minnesota. "Dirksen" was a barker inviting people to "step right up, folks, and see the great Republican extravaganza, the Greatest Show on Earth . . . the fanciest acts of tightrope walking, political prestidigitation, legerdemain, fence sitting, vote switching and issue dodging ever exhibited on this continent."

An impersonator of Gerald Ford pointed to Dirksen as "the leader of the whole shebang," who had "syrupy tonsils, all right . . . an absolute wizard with words." Then "Ford" sang:

> We're here to see the wizard,
> The wonderful wizard of ooze.
> For he's a whiz with words, he is—
> He knows how to make the news.
> We follow old Ev and we seldom lose.
> There isn't an issue he can't confuse,
> Confuse, confuse, confuse, confuse, confuse—
> Oh, he is the kind of leader to choose.
>
> We're here to see the wizard;
> The wonderful wizard of ooze.

That phrase, "wizard of ooze," stuck with Dirksen as long as he lived.

Nixon was missing, and while the Marine Band orchestra played calliope music, Dirksen was told that Nixon was on the merry-go-round: "He's been going round-and-round ever since 1960." Nixon's impersonator was dragged in by two roustabouts, and Dirksen delivered a telegram to him from "Governor Pat Brown," who was having difficulties in California. It read, "Come back to California. I need you."

Asked what his plans were for 1968, "Nixon" sang:

> Let me go again,
> I hear the trumpet blow again,
> Don't say no again,
> Taking a chance on me.
>
> Rocky's slid again,
> And Romney's lost his bid again.
> I'm your kid again,
> So take a chance on me.
>
> I know I said I was finished,

Can't you take a joke?
With confidence undiminished,
I'm ready to go for broke.

Things are mending now.
I feel my star's ascending now.
Let's have a happy ending now,
Taking a chance on me.

"Republican Committee Chairman Ray Bliss" confided that "Harold Stassen is loose again," and Dirksen wanted everybody to cheer up because at least they had the farm vote nailed down.

"Yeah," said Bliss, "only there isn't any farm vote any more. The farmers all have moved to the city. And that's what the rest of us ought to do, too; move into the Big Town. George Romney will tell you."

Then "Romney" sang, to the tune of "Downtown":

When you're behind, you must be ready to find
The place where voters grow—*Downtown!*
Farm votes are nice, but they will never suffice.
To win we need to go—*Downtown!*

An impersonator of Ronald Reagan, who was running for governor of California, came on the stage accompanied by "Senator George Murphy" of that state, whom Nixon described as the author of Murphy's Law: "If anything can possibly go wrong, the Republicans will nominate it."

Reagan objected to the use of the word "right," because it made his public relations staff nervous and described himself as "an extreme moderate." The public relations man sang for him:

Don't throw bouquets at me.
Don't push me right too much.
With Brown don't fight too much.
People will say we're in love.

Don't call me guv-nor yet.
Don't serve birch beer for me.
Speak soft when you cheer for me.
People will say we're in love.

Don't praise my speeches so.
Don't let old ladies scream.
Please don't make me too extreme.
People will say we're in love.

The next character to come on stage represented Mayor John

Lindsay of New York, described as "our wonder boy," and "Senator Percy" of Illinois responded, "Yeah, it's a wonder he's in this Republican skit!"

Lindsay had had his troubles from the moment he took office. At the time of his inauguration, Mike Quill had called a transit strike in New York, and even before that was settled a big snowstorm had hit the metropolis and all the street cleaners had walked out. Gridiron President Wiggins referred to Mayor Lindsay as "the ringmaster of the greatest show on earth, the ruler of the city with the biggest population, the biggest deficit, the biggest thirst, and the biggest headaches in the land."

When asked how he was getting along, Lindsay's impersonator sang:

> I got elected mayor, it's a job I thought I'd like.
> They couldn't wait to swear me in to start the subway strike.
> I promised better transit and the voters have to hike.
> Everything happens to me.

> I cleaned up on the Democrats; they cleaned out City Hall.
> I asked the state for money; Rocky never heard my call.
> I made a pitch for Harlem, Adam Powell owns it all.
> Everything happens to me.

> And I suppose next spring when all the filthy snow is through
> The power will go off again, the drought will start anew.
> I feel my White House chances I had better not pursue.
> Everything happens to me.

President Johnson had declined an invitation to this dinner. But shortly after 9:00 P.M. just before the guest skit, he arrived at the Presidential Room of the Statler Hilton, dressed in a business suit, and took the place at the head table occupied by Vice President Humphrey, who had been scheduled to respond to the toast to the President. An extra chair was put in, and Humphrey was moved one notch down the table.

Johnson arrived in time to hear a couple of cracks at him in the guest skit, when Richard L. Wilson, after standing up Sargent Shriver, commented that he was "anxiously awaiting the creation of the twelfth cabinet post, secretary of transportation."

"Then," said Wilson, "there will be twelve apostles in the Johnson administration, as there ought to be."

Later on, after standing up "some prominent authors," former Secretary of State Dean Acheson, former Counsel to the President Theodore C. Sorensen, and former White House Assistant Arthur M. Schlesinger, Jr., he commented that "according to Mr. Acheson, the books written by himself, Mr. Sorensen and Mr. Schlesinger are all in the running for Pulitzer prizes in literature: one for biography, another for history, and the third for fiction."

The Democratic skit was set on a newly discovered planet, "a million light years from earth," which was the command post for the Johnson headquarters opened on Mars, Jupiter and Saturn, with the Women's Division on Venus and Bobby Baker "creaming" the Milky Way.

From this post they had proclaimed the inter-Galactic Great Society. Space Ship One was coming in and "Democratic Chairman Bailey" wanted a gathering of the beagles to greet it. A welcoming committee sang:

> He'll be plannin' brand new planets when he comes,
> Plannin' good times universal,
> For a very *small* disbursal,
> He'll be plannin' brand new planets when he comes.

But with the arrival, the crowd was disappointed. It was only "Hubert H. Humphrey" who stepped forth, proclaiming that he had come "far enough to get away from the Kennedys," only to find that "we're all Kennedys here."

At this moment, a telephone call came from the President, and Humphrey told him that "they're *all* here." "Sargent Shriver" sang:

> Bobby and Teddy are brothers,
> They always act as a pair.
> (When) one of them misses a roll call,
> The other's always there.
> Two fine young men,
> They can do no wrong.

> Bobby went up to old Broadway,
> Found there a man named Abe Beame,
> Backed him for mayor of the city,
> Dem-o-crats ain't what they seem.
> Abe was their man,
> But he done them wrong.

> (When) Bobby got into the Senate,
> (Found) Hubert H. Humphrey was there,
> Only thing wrong with old Hubert,
> He's in the Vice Pres-eye-dent's chair.

Hump' ain't their man.
And they'll do him wrong.

There is a point to this story,
Don't think it's only in fun.
With two places on the big ticket,
They will *both be* glad to run.
Oh, man. Oh, man.
Who will do whom wrong?

Humphrey bemoaned his lot in the Johnson administration by singing a new variation of "One Woman Blues."

All my jobs are cast-off,
Strictly second hand.
If I dared to blast off,
I'd be swiftly canned.
The stuff in my department's from a rummage sale,
When they draw post position, I never draw the rail.
Talk about your Avis and your Hertz,
His monogram is even on my shirts!

I've got those Second Man Woes,
Second Man Woes.
Mine is the image
Nobody knows.
Even tourists in the Senate Lobby
Look right through me while they stare at Bobby.
My eager ears
Hear only second-hand cheers,
They never flip their lids for you-know-who.
Even Richard Nixon, he's the man I abhor,
Sometimes had a chance to play at running the store.
Second Man Woes,
Oh, I've got plenty of those
On Dead End Avenue.

Then, several "members of the President's Club," which Johnson had formed for those who contributed $1,000 or more to his campaign, came in, "Roger Blough," chairman of United States Steel, "Crawford Greenewalt," chairman of Du Pont, "John Harper," president of Alcoa, and several others. Blough announced that they were all under the pressure of a few G's. "G" was described as "a measure of gravity—like one thousand bucks. One G here, another G there and we're all members of the President's Club. After that, it's easy." He invited Harper to tell them about it, and to the tune of "Did You Ever See a Dream Walking?" Harper sang:

Did you ever have your prices fix-ed?
   Well, I did.
Did you ever have both arms twisted?
   Well, I did.
Did you ever have the big Man tell you,
   you better be nice.
Oooh, it's so grand
   and it's too, too precise.

Following this, there came two long-remembered Gridiron songs about President Johnson. The first was written by Richard L. Wilson and was sung by an impersonator of Jack Valenti.

It enumerated some of LBJ's alleged favorite things:

Brown and white beagles
With big floppy ears,
Depletion allowances, and prize winning steers,
Speed boats and barbecues, Texas oil kings,
These are a few of his favorite things.

Poverty programs, and broadcasting stations,
Tax cuts and price cuts, and budget gyrations,
Something for nothing, tied neatly with strings,
These are a few of his favorite things.

Sending Dear Hubert far off on a mission,
Showing the whole world his famous incision,
Cutting up Bobby and clipping his wings,
These are a few of his favorite things.

To close the skit, "Press Secretary Bill Moyers" was introduced as "the preacher of the Pedernales," who had lost "that White House wedding job."

He explained that the reason he lost it was because he was too busy "walkin' and talkin' " to someone in the White House rose garden. Then Moyers sang:

I come to the garden with Lyndon,
   while the dew is still on the roses,
And the voice I hear falling on my ear,
   has the twang of a Texas Moses.

And he walks with me and talks with me,
And tells me I am his own,
And the news we share as we tarry there
May never, never be known.

He speaks, and the sound of his voice
Takes me back to our Texas upbringing,

and his comments on
What's written on him more often than not are stinging.

But he walks with me and he talks with me,
    and tells me what not to put out.
The stories we share as we tarry there,
    the press can do better without.

I'd stay in the garden with him,
    tho' the night around me be falling,
But he bids me go; and make it snow,
    for that he says is my calling.

And he walks with me and he talks with me,
    and he tells me I am his own,
And the news we share as we tarry there,
None other has ever known.

Then Senator Russell B. Long, a son of the spectacular Huey, was introduced as the democratic speaker and announced that he wasn't there to find fault with politicians that night.

"It has been my experience with politicians," he said, "that those with whom you find the most fault are only in that situation because you know them so much better than the other guy."

He said that he'd been accused of moonlighting, holding too many jobs, wearing too many hats. With an oblique reference to President Johnson, he commented, "All I have been doing is trying to watch how some people got ahead and pattern my conduct after them."

Then he told about a mythical leadership meeting he'd attended at the White House, and how the President had called him aside and said he was disturbed about a Vietnam resolution and wanted him to do everything he could to help get the Democrats together.

"Let's get out your whip list of Democrats and divide them up," he quoted the President as saying.

"I'll take Anderson, you take Gruening.
"I'll take Ervin, you take Fulbright.
"I'll take Harris, you take Hartke.
"I'll take Inouye, you take Kennedy.
"I'll take Lausche, you take Kennedy.
"I'll take Monroney, you take Morse."

Thus all the tough and bitter opponents of the Vietnam War were given to Long, and all the supporters or moderates were taken by Johnson.

"That's what I love about my President," said Long. "He is always there to carry the heavy end of the load!"

He continued by telling about the President's task of cutting the invitation list for Luci Johnson's wedding, from 190 million to 1,000.

"The other day," he said, "Lady Bird suggested that a good starting point would be to leave out those twenty-seven million people who voted for Barry Goldwater.

"The President wouldn't hear of this. He is counting on those votes next time.

"He said, 'After all, if they voted for Barry knowing what he promised, they certainly ought to vote for me, knowing I did it.' "

Not long before this dinner the dictator of Ghana, Dr. Kwame Nkrumah, had been dethroned by a revolution while he was away on a trip in Europe.

"That could never happen to Lyndon Johnson," said Long. "He would have sent Hubert."

Turning to his newspaper hosts, he noted that "when some fellow in the press gallery agrees with my speech, he says I was eloquent and impassioned. When he disagrees, he says I was emotional that I shouted, that I waved my arms and got red in the face, and that I waved the flag.

"Everybody knows I never do anything like that," he said, pulling a small American flag out of a pocket and waving it.

Long said he was happy to be a part of the Great Society, and made an oblique reference to his father.

"All these programs to educate everybody, to provide pensions for everybody, provide good jobs for everybody, good health for everybody, good homes for everybody, are the kind of things we were talking about in my family from the time I was big enough to lick a campaign envelope.

"Of course, we never had in mind anything so elaborate, nor so expensive as LBJ. It never really occurred to us to make everybody into high society folks.

"All we wanted to do was make every man a king."[7]

Long's speech was followed by a third skit, notable for its application to the Vietnam War. Senator J. William Fulbright, chairman of the Foreign Relations Committee, had already broken with President Johnson over the war and wanted his objection emphasized. An impersonator of Fulbright entered the scene as a tramp, looking for a handout and carrying a bedraggled white peace dove on a stick over his shoulder. He sang:

Dove for sale,
Slightly beat-up used dove for sale,
Chairman Fulbright owl-type dove,
Wayne Morse lone-wolf, growl-type dove,
Dove for sale.

Who will buy?
Who's prepared to give my line a try?
Who agrees it would be nice
To have peace at any price?
Dove for sale.

Dove for sale,
Just a few white feathers in its tail,
If you're gripped by fear and doubt,
Follow me the quick way out,
Dove for sale.

Sometimes Gridiron members get applause for their efforts from the crowd at dinners, but not from the subjects of those efforts. That was the case here. Senator Fulbright never forgave the author of this parody, Frederic W. Collins, for his devastating song.

The skit closed with Secretary of State Dean Rusk being asked to stand while the chorus ended the stage show by singing:

It seems we've stood and fought like this be-fore,
Face to face with bat-tle in the same way then
And we all re-mem-ber where and when.

A quest for peace has been our goal be-fore,
The doubts that dis-turb us, we were doubt-ing then
And we all re-mem-ber where and when.

Cou-rage for us is not a first time,
We've been here more than once before.

And so it is that when we meet a-gain,
And sing a-gain, with peace a-gain,
We'll all know where and when.

As the toast to the President was proposed, Vice President Humphrey of course yielded to him to respond, and the Vice President's scheduled speech was not heard that night.

There had been considerable griping among the newspaper corps about the scarcity of Johnson press conferences in the preceding months, and the President began by saying, "I would like for you newspaper men to know, though, that I think this should count as a press conference.

"I really didn't plan to come at all tonight, but Bill Moyers got obstreperous about it and here I am. So I gave in, came over, and especially when I heard that Vance Hartke wasn't coming.

"I also changed my mind when I picked up the *New York Herald Tribune* this morning, and I read that the President did not plan to attend the Gridiron Dinner."

J. Russell Wiggins was one of the Gridiron Club's most ardent liberals, and Walter Trohan, the vice president of the club, was its most ardent conservative. Characteristic of the spirit which has always distinguished the members of the club, Trohan, in a gesture of comradeship, had graciously stepped aside for one year to let Wiggins, who had dropped out of the line of succession several years before to go back to Minnesota to be an editor for awhile, become president.

Johnson said he had another reason for coming, too. "I thought," he said, "that I should come over here tonight to congratulate Russ Wiggins and Walter Trohan, because I think that is a combination that even Bobby Kennedy would like. And I think that kind of coalition might stand up for the weekend."

There had been a governors conference at the White House that day, which the President described as "a typical Great Society Saturday.

"All eight hours of it," he said. "I saw the governors three hours, the press saw them five. I don't know whether you have heard it or not, but Governor Rhodes [of Ohio] introduced a resolution praising my policies in Vietnam, and Doctor Berkley told me to assure Senator Fulbright that Governor Rhodes' arm would be back to normal Monday."

He picked out Frank Stanton, then president of Columbia Broadcasting Company, and brought on a gale of laughter by saying that he had been "very friendly lately." Numerous CBS commentators had been somewhat less than enthusiastic about the Vietnam War and had been given free rein by Stanton.

"I wonder," said Johnson, "if any of you have been reading that piece on how the American people love me. I think everyone knows how the *Journal* reflects the views of the man on the street—Wall Street. Somebody told me that the writer of that article is free lancing now for *True Romances*. Some of you may know, I have been very worried about the credibility gap. It's gotten so bad now that the Joint Chiefs have stopped believing Joe Alsop.

"Jack Valenti has stopped believing his own speeches and developed insomnia. And Lady Bird has stopped believing all of us.

"I wonder if you have seen the latest announcement from the Senate Foreign Relations Committee that it is going to hold hearings on the Viet Cong, and I want to deny the rumor that they intend to start those hearings in the Editorial Room of the *New York Times*. Frankly, I enjoyed those hearings that Senator Fulbright's committee has already conducted. There goes my credibility."

Johnson said that he thought Billy Graham was a good political leader, but he hadn't known how good a religious leader he was until after his daughter Luci had joined the Catholic Church.

Then he mentioned several other religious leaders who had called him about the elementary school aid bill. He remembered that "in college, they asked me what the Constitution said about education, and I wrote a theme [of] seven pages—and I got an F. The professor said, 'it says nothing [about education], makes no reference to it whatever.' "

He just wanted to close on a note of sobriety, he told the Gridiron Club, pointing out that these were days of great difficulty for all of us.

"We are on a course," Johnson said, "the final outcome of which none of us can really be certain. I do really, indeed I do, welcome your concern. I read your criticism, I listen to it, even when I do not agree with it. I try to respect the conviction in which you offer it, and on the course that I am traveling I need it, but even more than your criticism I need your hope, your hope that in the end we will be proven right, because like another friend of mine here in the audience this evening [Barry Goldwater], in my heart I really believe that I am right. I promise all of you my best until everything I have is gone.

"In the words of a great man who wrote a long time ago, 'Behind every enterprise stands one man who is ultimately responsible. The eager men around him spin golden dreams and propose new plans. And sometimes they fret while he ponders, but to him deliberation is very sweet, because he knows that success will have many shareholders, but that failure will be the sole property of the man responsible . . . '

"And so, to all of you who through the months and weeks and years have endured with us the problems that are mutual to all of us," he concluded, "I want to say tonight that we are very proud of the achievements of this country. The best efforts that we can muster have been summoned and are being concentrated to preserve our way of life and our system of government, and there are a good many men in far away places tonight that are protecting and preserving the things that we hold dear.

"A man asked me a good many years ago," he said, "to state my political philosophy, and I said I am a free man first and an American second, a public servant third and a Democrat fourth, *in that order*, but it's been a long time since I have dealt with men who have thought in terms of party labels. These days, our problems are so serious, our trials are so exacting, that nearly every man I call on is a free man first, and for that I am deeply grateful, and because of that I have complete and absolute confidence in the ultimate outcome.

"Good night and God bless you all."[8]

Vice President Humphrey had his chance the next day at the Gridiron reception, when the songs of the Gridiron dinner are traditionally resung for the benefit of those who attended the night before, plus their wives and the widows of deceased Gridiron members.

Richard L. Wilson, who each year since 1958 has acted as the master of ceremonies at this reception, introduced Humphrey at the end of it.

"Many have heard of the great mystery of the historic lost speech of Abraham Lincoln," said Wilson. "Tonight we have the lost speech of Hubert Horatio Humphrey."

It wasn't the speech that he had planned to deliver the night before, except in part, because all during the songs he had been scribbling notes in order to adapt it to the new situation.

"Thank you, Dick Wilson," he began, "the Johnny Carson of the Gridiron Club—a little overweight and a little elongated, too [Wilson is 6'3"], but he will do for a daytime show.

"You may have noticed," he continued, "that the first song rendered not by the doves or hawks but by these canaries was a protest song about sit-ins. Well, I have been sitting here since last night . . ."

He never finished the sentence, because it was drowned out with laughter.

Poking fun at his own reputation for talking, he referred to Wilson's comment about the lost speech and quipped, "No one will ever believe that about me."

"Last night was magnificent," he went on. "I had two or

three places at the head table. I never knew where I was sitting. I remember when I was second row from the back."

Laughing at himself still further, he said of the undelivered speech of the night before that he had promised President Johnson he could keep that text. "Those remarks," he said, "are under lock and key. They may be in the Johnson Library. They may be one of the few things about me he likes."

He cited the "He walks with me and he talks with me" song and commented, "I consider walking in the garden mighty nice. You ought to see what I go through sometimes."

Closing on a serious note, Humphrey paid a tribute to the Gridiron Club and said that "there isn't any country that can laugh at itself unless it has great inner strength.

"In song and in verse, it is good to take a good look at ourselves. The people of the nation are good and strong and hard working and fun loving, and they pay their own way and do what is right."

Citing the club's final song of courage, which had been deeply serious and had drawn long applause at both the Saturday dinner and the Sunday reception, he quoted Winston Churchill's feeling that courage is the "first of all human qualities because it guarantees all the others.

"As long as the nation has courage, there is hope for all mankind," he said.[9]

XX

Lyndon B. Johnson

1967-1968
"We are not going to retreat
before the future. . . ."

Robert Kennedy, Hubert Humphrey, Gerald Ford,
and Ronald Reagan Speak

By the time of the spring dinner on March 11, 1967, the attention of the country was beginning to turn again to the 1968 Presidential election. Gridiron president Walter Trohan, head of the *Chicago Tribune* bureau, welcomed the guests to "Gridiron college" and its own "political pep rally."

He revealed that the game with the College of Cardinals had been canceled, but that the big game was coming up—with the electoral college.

"They've got a tough line in the GOP—Grandfather's Old Party," he said, "and the Democrats are playing poverty for all it's worth. . . . In California, actor Ronald Reagan discovered colleges have too many drop-outs and not enough kick-outs."

Senate minority leader Dirksen, the star of the weekly "Ev and Jerry" television program [Gerald Ford having succeeded Charles Halleck as House Minority Leader], had taken out a union card as an actor, he revealed.

"Democrats," he continued, "may not have as many actors, but they have more than their share of characters, most of them

707

with one ear to the ground and the other listening to President Johnson when he says, 'It's only a suggestion, but never forget who's making it.' "

Turning to the situation abroad, he commented that "the only foreign product of which the supply exceeds the demand is crises."

The opener centered on politics, and John Hightower, chairman of the music committee, announced that the Gridiron Club, "a high-minded and unsubsidized organization," had been studying the phenomenon of politics and was ready to report.

The theme of the chorus's song was that politics is different things to different people, and various couplets to the tune of "Happiness Is" documented this.

> To George Romney, it's a White House glow,
> To Goldwater, that is no, no, no.
>
> To Mike Mansfield, it's a Senate vote.
> To Ev Dirksen, it's a golden throat.
>
> To our Lyndon, it's what looks like truth,
> But to Bobby, it is youth, youth, youth.
>
> To the Chinese, it's the thoughts of Mao,
> To Dick Nixon, it's to find out how.
>
> Politics is, Politics is, Politics is,
> Diff-rent things to different people:
> That's what politics is.

Following its habit of most recent years, the Gridiron Club set the scene for the skit in another outlandish place. This time the GOP leaders had gathered at the Delphic Oracle, where "to enrich and inspire the oracle, they have sacrificed—a fat cat."

A character representing Alf Landon, "the senior, senior leader of the party," asked the Oracle what Republicans needed to elect a President, and the Oracle replied, "A majority of the votes."

"Eisenhower," who described himself as "the only winner in thirty-five years," asked the Oracle, "How do we get that majority?" and the reply was: "Just pray that Lyndon and Bobby keep on getting along together the way they have lately."

After hearing various other replies from the Oracle, "Ike" asked "Ray Bliss," chairman of the Republican National Committee, what he thought. As the band struck up "Stout Hearted

Men," he announced that if the Republicans had the will and the money,

> And a man who's not too far out,
> You can attract quite a pack to your side!
> You can win the race,
> And at worst you'd take second place.

Then the chorus appealed for a man who could win now and then.

> Give me some men who can win now and then.
> That is really not asking for much.
> Give me a way to defeat LBJ.
> And take over in Congress, and such, O
> Please think of this, you—and give me an issue
> To put our opponents in dutch.
> Then there's nothing in this world can stop the GOP.
> When our gallant men will snatch defeat from victory.

The first candidate to appear was "Nixon," who had come "to collect some quick IOUs." To "Lara's Theme (Somewhere, My Love)," he sang:

> Someday I'll find someone that I can beat,
> It's not too late to come back from defeat.
> My law firm said: "Now please don't hesitate.
> You want time off? Take all of 'sixty-eight."
> I'll go ev'ry step of the way
> To hell and back against LBJ.
>
> Don't make me wait 'til nineteen sev'nty-two,
> And run against young Bobby-You-Know-Who.

The next candidate was "Rockefeller," and an impersonator of his brother Winthrop, governor of Arkansas, sang:

> His lips tell you No! No!
> But there's Yes! Yes! in his eyes.

"Senator Dirksen" then gave his impressions of the new junior senator from Illinois, Charles H. Percy, to the tune of "Bring Back My Bonnie to Me."

> Chuck Percy is only a freshman.
> As junior as junior can be.
> So why does he act like the leader?
> Oh, bring back Paul Douglas * to me.

---

*Paul H. Douglas, Percy's predecessor, was an aggressively liberal Democrat.

Among the possible candidates, "George Romney" came next, followed by a one-man band with drums and cymbals clashing. On Romney's back was a big poster which said, "Remember, I'm reluctant." His "sugar daddy," J. Willard Marriott, was asked to explain Romney's position, and an impersonator sang:

> No, no a thousand times no.
> Right now I can't acquiesce.
> No, no a thousand times no.
> But in the end I'll say yes.

Last of the candidates was "Ronald Reagan," ushered in by "Clark Kerr," former president of the University of California, who had been forced out of his job by Governor Reagan and was now "head of the No-Dirty-Word Club."

There ensued a duet between Reagan and "Senator George Murphy" of California, who proclaimed in song that:

> There's no biz-ness like show biz-ness
> When you're after the votes.
> Turn a handsome profile, flash a broad grin,
> Good guy image of the golden west,
> Stand for safer traffic, be against sin,
> And let the late show do all the rest.

Trohan immediately introduced "a former star of stage, screen, and television, who is one of the brightest stars in the Republican crown, the Governor of California, Mr. Ronald Reagan."

Reagan proclaimed it a great pleasure to be here and "see so many distinguished guests—members of the administration who were visitors to California during the last campaign."

"For some reason," he said, "I didn't see them then, but I hope you'll come back again and be just as successful as you were the first time."

He said he had been invited back again the following week to a White House conference on disaster planning and that he wanted to come badly, but to do so would be cheating a little because he didn't tell them that in California, "we've already gotten rid of our disaster."

Like many other speakers, he had a dig for the perennial Republican Presidential aspirant, Harold Stassen. He'd been a little surprised, he said, since he arrived in Washington "to see how everybody is speculating about who is going to be the next President. Well, *almost* everybody."

He told about being at a Republican gathering where a friend of his had announced that the next President of the United States was in the room. "I got pretty excited," he said. "I'd never met Harold Stassen."

The mere thought of being President he described as frightening.

"Imagine being the most powerful man in the world, next to [Secretary of Defense] Bob McNamara."

Then, laughing at himself a bit about his campaign promise to eliminate the budget deficit in California, Reagan said, "We're going to do it without any new taxes—we're just going to raise the old ones."

He was interested "to see the next speaker [Robert F. Kennedy]—the senator from New York, is it?" It was certainly a happy coincidence, he went on, that "tonight's affair happened during one of his infrequent visits to the United States."

Reagan mentioned Senator Kennedy's appearance in California, his delivery, his longish hair, and his "with it" style.

"He was doing great. The trouble started when he stood up on top of his car and they discovered he had shoes on."

It was wonderful to be at the Gridiron dinner, Reagan told his hosts, "and bless you for this annual night of fun and games, where we can bury the hatchet—in each other—and laugh and bleed together."

He concluded by saying that there was a great need for a change. And speaking of California, he proclaimed his own intention and that of the Republican party in that state "to see if the homely virtues, honesty, morality, frugality and patriotism, are still the hallmark for society.

"We're going to try government of and by the people, because we believe in their right to control their own destiny, to have freedom of choice, and the right to the fruits of their toil.

"We're going to call on the power and genius of our people, because we don't believe in the right of a small intellectual elite to do their thinking or plan their lives for them.

"We don't believe any bureaucracy can be big enough or talented enough to match the inherent wisdom of the people."[1]

The scene for the Democratic skit was the Mutiny on the Bounty Cafe and Pool Hall on the banks of the Pedernales, "where everything is Democratic and psychedelic," and a "hippie meditation party" was in progress.

The scene opened with an impersonator of Senator Russell B. Long of Louisiana, of whom it was said, "He ain't quite a hippie

yet, but he ain't hep to Johnson either." Long sang a parody of
"There'll Be Some Changes Made."

> There's been a change in the pol-ling,
> There's a change in the air.
> We psy-che-de-lics want a cat with flair.
> His walk must be dif-fer-ent,
> His drawl has to go.
> Pleasin' Ar-thur Schle-sing-er's the goal you know.
> We're going to move to Hippie living,
> Change that Lyndon square,
> Groom a peace-nik swinger
> With the long shag hair,
> 'Cause nobody wants to run the Old LBJ.
> We need a much changed man, to-day.
> There'll be some changes made.

In the months prior to the dinner, William Manchester had
written a book about John F. Kennedy* which had caused a good
deal of consternation in the Kennedy family and had led to controversy about its publication. At this point in the show, "the
Kennedy raiders" came on the stage, led by "Bobby" himself,
described as "the greatest daredevil rider of them all." To the
tune of "Winchester Cathedral," Bobby sang:

> Man-ches-ter's Up-hee-val,
> Is bring-ing me down,
> I thought the full st-o-ry
> 'd do Lyn-don up brown.

> I should have said no-thing,
> But I had to try,
> When Manchester quotes you
> He spits in your eye.

> Man-ches-ter's Up-hee-val,
> It made Lyndon frown,
> Bill picked up a million,
> My polls tumbled down.

Governor Wallace's term in Alabama had expired, and under
the Alabama rule that a governor can't succeed himself, Wallace
had proposed and succeeded in having his wife Lurleen elected
Governor. "Lurleen" sang:

> It's so nice to have a man around the house.

---

*Death of a President.

It's so nice to hold this office for my spouse.
Someone here just when you need him,
Who because you did succeed him
Thinks—ha ha—that you will heed him, it's so nice.
Oh, our home can be sweet home with Georgy man,
So I let him feel that it was all his plan.
If he runs a clean and right house,
He can help me win the White House,
Voting Wallace meant for Lurleen—not her spouse,
Yes, I think I'll keep that man around the house.

The widely reported antics of Adam Clayton Powell were then a major Democratic embarrassment. Once a Gridiron impersonator of the congressman from New York had strutted onstage boasting that he was moonlighting: "I have two jobs, living it up and trying to live it down."

But at this dinner, "Powell" came forward and sang a different tune.

My Mamma done tol' them
She was on the payroll;
My Mamma done tol' them that
Her man gave her small change,
But none of the big dough,
Now that the money is gone.
A woman's a two-face,
A bothersome thing
When she starts to sing
The blues in the night.

Celler said I'm cheatin'
Said I'm just repeatin', Hooey,
(My mamma don' told him).
Boy, it made her feel green
To see me with Cor-rine, Whoo-pee,
(My mamma don' like it).
On Bi-mi-ni whoo-pee
Our travel-card pack
Got caught with the sack,
The blues in the night.

From Har-lem to San Juan
And even to St. Joe,
Where-ever the four winds blow,
I'd travel with cute dolls,
We'd talk us some sweet talk,
But now there's trouble, I know.

A woman's a two-face,
A worrisome thing
Who'll leave ya t' 'sing
The blues in the night.

The skit closed with "Sheriff Hubert Humphrey" arriving and ordering the mods and hippies "to break it up and get moving." Then he sang a rewording of "King of the Road."

Change not that President,
He's to me heaven-sent,
He likes to drive fast cars,
Show off his fav-rite scars,
Ah but, he'll win in sixty-eight
If he picks me for running mate.

A man of means, by all means,
King of the Road.

Sec-ond term is his plan,
He'll be no also ran,
Won't fluff that slicked down hair
Or learn that Kennedy flair.
He's the best friend of Bobby B,
Tho' he ain't good on the TV.

He's a man who wheels
As he deals,
King of the Road.

Trohan then introduced Senator Robert F. Kennedy, whose first line was, "Gridiron President Walter Trohan—who, I might add, is the friendliest president in town."

Kennedy pulled out a piece of paper and said, "I've just been given a piece of paper and asked to announce for the press that, as soon as I begin to speak, the President is calling an immediate, impromptu press conference in the White House.

"I am sorry that the President is not here for my speech. He missed my speech on Vietnam last week while spending a quiet day at the White House catching up on his mail.

"Actually, I am speaking tonight in the hope that this speech will make some of you forget the one I made last week. I was hoping that one would make some of you forget my statement on abortion. I was hoping that one would make you forget my trip to Europe. I was hoping that trip would make you forget the Manchester lawsuit. I was hoping that would make you forget my controversy with J. Edgar Hoover. And I was hoping that controversy would make you forget that my wife Ethel was a horse thief. [She had, by mistake, taken the wrong horse out of a stall and ridden it.]

"So you can see that Life hasn't been too good to me lately—and *Look* has been even worse.

"Some of you have expressed an interest in knowing the full story about my conference with President Johnson after I returned from Europe. When I walked in, he stood up, looked me right in the eye without a smile, and said sternly: 'Bob, the time has come for you to tell me one thing, something I have wanted to know for a long time: When are you going to get your hair cut?' . . .

"You see, all those stories about Mr. Johnson and me not getting along during my brother's years in the White House simply do not square with the facts. We started out during the Kennedy administration on the best of terms, friendly, close, cordial—but then, as we were leaving the inaugural stands . . .

"Of course, I am more than anxious to settle any disputes the President and I might have. I have made it clear before, and I want to make it clear again tonight, that I am willing to go more than half-way to the White House.

"Some people said the President's press conference statement on Thursday about the sincerity of his critics was intended as a peace feeler to me—I have had better peace feelers than *that* from *Look* magazine.

"Nevertheless, I am supporting Mr. Johnson and Mr. Humphrey for reelection in next year's campaign: I will work hard for them, I will speak for them—I'll do for them what I did for [naming several losers he had supported] Abe Beame, Frank O'Connor, Soapy Williams, Pat Brown, and Paul Douglas."

His gibes at himself and the Kennedy family were numerous.

"I thought surely my brother Teddy would take pride in my speeches," he said; "then I found out that his office is distributing those pamphlets from Father Flanagan's Boys' Town showing one little boy carrying another on his back and saying to the priest: 'He ain't heavy, Father, he's my brother.'

"We brought Teddy here with us tonight—we couldn't find anyone to leave him with."

Turning to the previous speaker, he said he was glad to see

Governor Reagan there. "He is really shaking things up in California," said Kennedy. "He has even adopted a new motto for the State seal: 'Lights—Camera—Reaction.'

"Governor Reagan spoke of receiving a degree from the University of California. I wanted to tell him the University is being very generous about the whole thing and has decided to award him an honorary LSD.

"Mr. Reagan also found out that the Governor's Mansion in Sacramento is a firetrap. I understand that he moved his family out and his old movies in."

Then he turned the laughter on himself, remarking that Governor George Romney had had some trouble explaining his position in Vietnam. (This was after Romney had made the remark in a press conference that he'd been "brainwashed.")

"I think I can help him out," said Kennedy, "by calling his attention to a very clear-cut statement I made on Vietnam a year ago.

"I made it very clear then that I thought the United States should negotiate with the Viet Cong, or perhaps with the South Vietnamese, or perhaps with both of them, but at any rate that one of them should be included in the provisional government of South Vietnam, or North Vietnam, as long as there were no interim provisions for permanent representation by the Viet Cong, or the NLF, or maybe the NFL, in the transitional parliament to be provisionally elected by South Vietnam after the temporary government gives way to its interim successor as provided for in the Geneva Accords as interpreted by those nations that signed it, or some of those nations, at that time or some other time. And I don't see how anyone could misunderstand a position that is put as simply as that.

In closing, Kennedy pointed out that "we have our differences, we have our disagreements.

"But we are all citizens of a wondrous land, united by a common pride in its progress and by a common obligation to its advancement. No other nation in this history of the world has been so faithful to its word, so generous with its wealth and so restrained in the use of its military might. And no other group of men in the world has ever borne the awesome burdens that weigh down the men who lead this country. Their task is to manage the unmanageable, to reconcile the irreconcilable and in the end to save mankind from itself. For man has now learned to live in outer space and to survive in the ocean depths—but human life is not yet secure and serene in between.

"Our leaders are neither all-wise nor all-powerful. They are mere mortals doing the best they can. The rest of us, in the Congress and the press and elsewhere, must give them our patient help and our prayers. We can offer both comments and criticism; that is our right and our duty. But let us remember the ancient Greek adage, that 'None can climb the heights but those to whom the miseries of the world *are* misery and will not let them rest.' "[2]

The scene for the foreign skit was the "Toll Gate of Heavenly Peace in the Forbidden City," where President Johnson's bridge from Seattle to Communist countries had finally come down. Lin Piao's Red Guards explained who they were in song, to the tune of "A Rambling Wreck from Georgia Tech":

> We're the beatnik cats who wear the hats
> of the Guards of Mao Tse Tung.
> We're just as loud as Berkeley's crowd
> In an oriental tongue.
> We're revolution's dragons—
> Consuming friend and foe.
> We're the beatnik cats who wear Mao's hats.
> *But—*
> Even he may go!

Then, under the leadership of "Kosygin" and "Gromyko," the Russian delegates, described by a character representing Lin as "our friendly fraternal Muscovite traitors," arrived to help dedicate the new bridge. "Secretary Rusk" came on to cut the tape, handed the two ends to Gromyko and Lin Piao, and shouted triumphantly: "I've got you fellows cooperating!"

Immediately after Kosygin was introduced to "Mao," they tried to stab each other in the back. Then they sang:

Mao:
> Anything you can do, I can do redder,
> I can do anything redder than you.

Kosygin:
> No you can't.

Mao:
> Yes I can.

Kosygin:
> No you can't.

Mao:
> Yes I can.

Kosygin:
> No you can't.

Mao:
> Yes I can. Yes I can.
> Anything you subvert, I subvert greater,
>   sooner or later,
> I'm redder than you.

Kosygin:
> No you're not.

Mao:
> Yes I am.

Kosygin:
> No you're not.

Mao:
> Yes I am.

Kosygin:
> You're a nut.

Mao:
> Yes I am. Yes I am.

Kosygin:
> I bet a tin whistle you got no antimissile.

Mao:
> You with all your boasters,
>   you got no wall posters.

Kosygin:
> I can do most anything.

Mao:
> Can you dress white tie?

Kosygin:
> No.

Mao:
> Neither can I.
> Any Marx you can quote, I can quote Len-in,
> I can quote Stal-in much quicker than you.

Kosygin:
> No you can't.

Mao:
> Yes I can.

Kosygin:
> No you can't.

Mao:
> Yes I can.

Kosygin:
> China Pig.

Mao:
> Have a care, Russian bear.

Kosygin:
> I have got an airline, flying to
>   New York fine.

Mao:
> I'll show you who's master,
> > I can swim there faster.

Kosygin:
> I've got guys in outer space.

Mao:
> *You're* in the moon race?

Kosygin:
> Yes.

Mao:
> Moon will lose face.

"Leonard Marks," director of the U.S. Information Agency, was the radio announcer who described the event. He noted in the crowd "Henry Cabot Lodge," ambassador to South Vietnam, who had recently met with President Johnson at the American base of Cam Ranh Bay in South Vietnam, when the President had put down Air Force One unannounced to inspect and address the troops. Marks asked Lodge about it, and William D. Jones, impersonating Lodge, sang words written by Paul L. Martin, to the tune of "On the Road to Mandalay."

> By the old Saigon Pagoda,
> Where the market's tinged with black,
> All the money changers busy,
> All the merchants making jack.
> But I dream I'm back in Boston,
> The New Hampshire primaree,
> With the pollsters and reporters,
> And it's there I'd rather be,
> Yes, it's there I'd rather be.
>
> Than—On the road to Cam Ranh Bay,
> Where we welcomed LBJ.
> And we hailed him as he traveled from
> > Bangkok near old Cathay.
> On the road to Cam Ranh Bay,
> Where our Lyndon spent the day,
> And we listened for a signal out of
> > China cross the way.
>
> Ship me somewhere East like Boston,
> Or the beaches of Cape Cod,
> Where the Lowells speak to Cabots
> But the Lodges speak to God.
> But now I'm here in Saigon
> In the strangest companee,
> Where no one speaks my language

While I'm serving my countree,
Yes, I'm serving my countree.

On the road to Cam Ranh Bay,
Here's where Lyndon spent the day,
But we failed to get the signal out
    of China cross the way.

Justice Arthur Goldberg's arm had been mildly twisted by President Johnson and he had resigned from the Supreme Court to become U.S. Representative to the United Nations. He too was among the group at the Toll Gate, and Adon Phillips, his impersonator, sang lyrics that supposedly expressed Goldberg's innermost feelings:

Gone are the days, when I starred on Warren's team,
Gone are the days, when I warmed that bench Supreme.
My U.N. chores, would destroy the poise of Job.
I've got a deep-down yearning for That Old Black Robe.

Gone is the day when my vote was all my own.
Now LBJ gives me orders on the phone.
Life at U.N. has made me a xenophobe.
I've got a deep down yearning for that Old Black Robe.

Among the others impersonated in the cast was Richard S. Helms, director of the Central Intelligence Agency, who was scornfully introduced by Gromyko as a real poseur. "His real job," said Gromyko, "is writing schoolbooks. Probably his real name is McGuffey. Mr. Helms, describe your ideal college student." And Helms sang:

The girl of my dreams is a snake-eyed girl,
With a gift for conspiracy.
She wears her charms
Like a call to arms,
And she works for a secret fee.

The hair of her head is a copper red.
It emits a radio ray.
And she gets her man
As a lady spy can.
She's the sweetheart of CIA.

The gold of her teeth is transistorized.
Her bosom conceals a mike,
And she wears high heels
That are sharpened steels.
She's ready to kiss or strike.

The cloak on her back is a subsidized black,
And her mask is expense-paid gray.
And her bank account
Continues to mount.
She's the sweetheart of CIA.

At the conclusion of this song, the skit was interrupted by
Gridiron president Walter Trohan at the head table, who stopped
the music and introduced four volunteers from the fighting front
in Vietnam, all of whom had been decorated for heroism.

"Gentlemen of valor of the four services," said Trohan,
"please be seated. The Gridiron Club, its singers and its chorus,
salute you and all of your comrades in arms."

Led by Gene Archer, the entire chorus sang its new version,
written by Paul L. Martin, of the *Man of La Mancha* song, "The
Impossible Dream."

To live the American dream,
In space or in jungles afar.
To make a much better tomorrow,
To reach an unreachable star.

This is our quest, to follow our star,
No matter what hardship, no matter how far.
To be willing to give all that we have to give,
To be willing to fight, so that freedom
    and justice may live.

And we hope, if we'll only be true to
    this difficult quest,
That our world will be safe and secure
    for those we love the best,

That our land, without hatred or fear,
May unite, in a moment supreme,
To achieve, with magnificent courage,
Our goal—the American dream.

Vice President Humphrey responded to the toast to the President.

Taking his cue from the final skit and the closing song,
Humphrey paid tribute to "our most distinguished of all guests,
these fine gallant young men from the American forces in Vietnam.

"I am here," he said, "with a special mission this evening.
This is the time that we are all searching for peace. I have been
sitting very close to Dean Rusk in the hopes that his antenna
might get a peace feeler or two. But I want to say that we had

more peace feelers tonight than this government has heard for many a month."

Then he stuck in the knife.

"I came here with one message, stop the bombing, Bobby. . . . This is the first time that I recall my good friend from New York has spoken for all of the Democratic party, and I want to thank him for his good message."

His next references were to the previous dinner, when President Johnson had preempted his place as the final speaker.

"Before we begin this evening's festivities," he said, "before we get a start on it, I thought that there were a few preliminaries that ought to have been disposed of at once. Last year when I was here, I was ready to speak, as some of you recall. I had myself a first-class speech, which I told you later on that I had filed in the library down on the banks of the Pedernales. This afternoon I got it out of hock, and I have been revising it ever since. I'd just like to make sure now, from Walter Trohan, is he coming or isn't he? Because if he is coming, I am revising my remarks. But if you can guarantee me safe passage for a while, we can have some fun here.

"First of all, I have noticed that every place that I have been speaking of late, there's always about 50 or 100 people who find they are at the wrong meeting. No sooner do I get up to speak, [than] some of the best customers walk out. I just thought you would want to know this is the Gridiron Club's annual gathering."

Then he referred to Gridiron President Walter Trohan, the quite conservative bureau chief of the *Chicago Tribune*. Since Humphrey was the guest of honor, he was seated at Trohan's right.

"You have," Humphrey said, "an upstanding and outstanding liberal leader with you this evening as your president. This is the first time that Walter Trohan has ever been to the left of me.

"I will tell you, though, he is the kind of liberal who had his car shifted to right-hand drive just to make sure that everything was alright, and then he positioned the distinguished head of the *Chicago Tribune* to my right, and that is an accurate characterization of this gathering, I might add."

In the Trohan inauguration skit, the treasured Mark Hanna gavel had been carried from the stage to Trohan by Arthur Krock, then the senior active member of the Gridiron Club.

"When I saw the gavel passed tonight," said Humphrey, "I jotted down a note and I couldn't help but think what this meant—from Mark Hanna to Arthur Krock to Walter Trohan. I don't know what we Democrats are doing here at all. But this gavel has been used softly and impartially.

"You know, I spoke at the National Book Awards ceremony the other evening up in New York, and I listed a number of books and authors that I thought were rather pathetic and were worthy of our attention. But there was one that I forgot on that evening, and it was a book by a very fine and great man who served his country faithfully and is the father of a very distinguished family, Mr. Joseph Kennedy. It was written in 1936 and titled *I Am for Roosevelt*. And in that book there was the never-to-be-forgotten passage, 'I have no political ambition for myself or for my children.' I just can't understand what the President is worried about. I think that's about as authentic a commitment as anyone could get."

But there was also another book by William Manchester, *The Death of a President*. The advance publication of portions of this book by *Look* magazine had been quite a publishing triumph, and Humphrey commented that "it has had such an impact, my good friend Mike Cowles out here is changing the title of his magazine from *Look* to the *Manchester Guardian*. And I don't blame him, he can afford to do it."

Then Humphrey noted that for most Democratic administrations, the major source of criticism came from the business community.

"But not so for the Johnson administration," he said. "Why, just the other day he was talking with two outstanding leaders in the business world. Wealthy, progressive, hard-driving, enterprising Texans deeply concerned about the status of free enterprise in America. He had a long talk and could hardly believe what he was hearing. These tough businessmen seemed to agree with every point that he made. And when they left, the President sighed with relief and he called in his secretary and he said, 'Juanita, those are good, intelligent men. Make a note of their names, Bill Moyers and Jack Valenti.' "

Coming back to the President's relationship with Senator Kennedy, he said he happened to believe, from his position of impartiality and objectivity, "that the President does have some just cause for a grievance.

"I will give you an example. Just last Thursday, the President had a normal day's schedule. Appointments, speeches, six appointments, a short press conference, a long-awaited letter from

Prime Minister Kosygin. And it was on that very day that Senator Kennedy picked to make his speech, totally obscuring our news from the front page. It seems to me that the President does have just cause."

For Reagan, Humphrey had a word, too. He told the governor that Washington was "a nice place to visit, but you wouldn't want to live here."

And he had looked over some of the governor's comments a few years back, when he was president of the Screen Actor's Guild. "As I was reading over the former labor leader's statements, I couldn't help but think how amazing it was what a little Democratic prosperity could do to change a man's mind."

In closing, he spoke of former President Truman and quoted his statement that "I believe it must be the policy of the United States to support free peoples who are resisting attempted subjugation . . . by outside pressures."

The Truman government, Humphrey said, was formulated not for war, but as an instrument of peace. "In his time, as in ours, peace is our business. Peace means many things, and, above all, it does not mean weakness or indecision. It means, on some occasions, preventing a conflict, if it is possible. It means assuring that aggression does not succeed. It means helping nations build their strength and confidence, which makes them invulnerable to aggression, and it means trying with every resource of mind and spirit and heart and imagination to translate a conflict on the battlefield into a negotiation and an honorable settlement. That definition of peace is one that governs this nation today without regard to party.

"I have spent much of this day talking and working with our President. What we talked about were these dimensions. Just about this time a week from now, the President of the United States and his senior advisors will be on their way to the Pacific to the island of Guam. He will be conferring there with Ambassador Lodge and General Westmoreland and with the finest military and diplomatic team that this nation has ever developed to carry forward the struggle against aggression, and to find and to carefully open any avenue towards peace. He will plan there and work there to help the people in South Vietnam build their nation for themselves. I am sure that I speak for you tonight when I say that he will carry on this mission."[3]

• • •

On November 11, 1967, the Gridiron Club gave the first formal dinner in its history outside of Washington. It was at Williamsburg, Virginia. President Johnson, Chief Justice Warren and Secretary of State Dean Rusk were all in attendance, the President having left California early that day in order to be there on time—and this time in white tie and tails.

This was also the first dinner in several decades to which women were invited; the guest list included the wives of all the members and guests.

Walter Trohan, in his speech in the dark, welcomed everybody to Colonial Williamsburg, "where the Rockefellers showed God how He could have made the world if He only had the money. . .

"And speaking of politics," said Trohan, "these are exciting days in Washington. President Johnson has taken up oil painting. The other day Lady Bird found him hard at work. 'What are you doing?' she asked. 'I'm painting a picture of God,' LBJ answered. 'But no one knows what God looks like,' she protested. He answered, 'They will when I get finished.' . . .

"Congress doesn't want to go home. Members would rather prove that they can never open their mouths without subtracting from the sum of human knowledge. . . .

"Speaking of Republicans, Barry Goldwater has asked me to thank those of you who voted for him in 1964, and his wife, Peggy, asked me to thank those of you who didn't. And speaking of Barry, many of you worried three years ago that Goldwater would take you back to the eighteenth century, and now the Trohan administration is about to take you back 100 years further to the seventeenth century. What the country needs today is what it had then—more free speech that's worth listening to."

The opener set the stage for the seventeenth century show which was to follow, and John Hightower, chairman of the music committee, introduced it by saying that we would dig up the roots of our history, examine the state of our politics, and see whether we should give the country back to the Indians.

The chorus came on stage to the strains of "The Battle Hymn of the Republic" and the soloist began:

Our eyes can see the glory of our noble history,
When Williamsburg was Capitol, in 1693,
When British kings were oh, so bad,
Especially George the Three.
The days of yore are here!

From the Governor's Brick Palace

Where they danced the minuet,
To the Bruton Church and Wy-the House where
Washington had slept,
We hear the strains of yesteryear,
A Haydn string quartet,
Where freedom had a ring!

When Pocahontas saved John Smith
Along the Jamestown shore,
His cavaliers entrenched themselves
To open Freedom's door.
We date our precious liberties
From these strong men of yore.
How Tempus Fugits on!

Now it's
  Glory, glory Marijuana!
  Hail the mini-skirt and sauna!
  Burn your draft card if you wanna!
  We keep you fooled this way!

The traditional Republican skit opened with a scene on the Jamestown River, where Indian chief "Powhatan" was brandishing a great war club over the kneeling "John Smith," while lots of Indians looked on. Powhatan explained, "Captain John Smith, you are about to take a trip."

But at this point, Pocahontas Temple entered, "Shirley Temple Black," who was running for Congress in California. She had come to save Captain Smith and was escorted by "Jerry Ford," who announced that she was up to something big and asked her to tell her plans. She sang:

From the good ship Lollipop
To the House is just a hop;
An easy race:
All the voters know my dimpl-ey face.
Uncle Ronnie says I'll win
With my crinkly, twinkly grin.
For who can beat
Little girlies who are sugary sweet?

(Gridiron forecasts were wrong this time—she didn't win but was beaten by Paul N. McCloskey.)

Next was a Reagan song:

When they said that I'd be Guv-nor, then they all began to laugh.
That's exactly what I did; I'm the Sacramento kid.

Now I'm standing in the open and I think I feel a draft,
And I guess I'll soon be putting in my bid.

"Nixon" was a sad-eyed young lad, and "Senator Percy" explained that was "because he's looking ahead—that always makes Republicans unhappy."

Percy thought Nixon might have some ideas about what was going to happen the following summer at the Republican Convention in Miami and asked him about it, whereupon Nixon sang:

Doom over Miami; Reagan could bring it on.
He'd pitch his fight 'way to the right,
And the center's gone.

Doom over Miami! Our fate is plain to see.
The answer's no unless you go
Once again with me.

Governor George Romney's comment, in an unguarded moment, that he had been "brainwashed" had nearly finished his candidacy. Thus his impersonator sang the Gridiron version of "Did You Ever See a Dream Walking?"

Did you ever get a brain-washing?
    Well, I did.
With the plunger and the Duz sloshing?
    Well, I did.
Did you ever get your foot caught in
Your mouth just like me,
And gulping hard find you've choked on your knee?

Since Governor Winthrop Rockefeller of Arkansas was to be the Republican speaker, the skit ended with a song by his impersonator about "the Rockefeller problem":

The last time I saw Nelson
He said he wouldn't run.
And he was strong for Romney—*But*
Old Georgie's race is done.

And now I hear from Gotham,
This close to sixty-eight
That Nels is busy shopping for
Some new election bait.

The trouble with my brother dear,
The Rockefellers' ace,
Is that he'd like to win next year

And never make the race.

The last time I saw Nelson
He gave me a big grin;
And I gave *him* a slo-gan,
We can always win with Win.

Then Governor Rockefeller, chairman of the board of the Colonial Williamsburg organization, was introduced as "a son of the founding father of Colonial Williamsburg, who is something of a founder himself, having established the Republican party in the Executive Mansion at Little Rock."

"For better identification," said Rockefeller, "if such is necessary," he lifted one leg up on the table, so that a big Texas cowboy boot was visible.

"And just to keep everything authentic, we have some colonial Western Union suits for Price Daniel [former governor of Texas] and Marvin Watson" [one of President Johnson's principal advisors].

He explained how he was "a Rockefeller maverick," that his four brothers all had good, well-paying jobs, but that until last January he had been unemployed for fourteen years.

"Then this job turned up in Little Rock," he said. "If I had known the problems I would have thought twice before leaving the farm. Take this dinner. I was told about the white tie. Mine is so old, I thought I would rent one. But when I checked I was told there is no contingency fund in the Arkansas budget to rent white ties. In fact, my budget director said, 'What's a white tie?'

"But I have the last word, I hope! This is a night for firsts— the first Gridiron Club dinner away from Washington in recent times, and the first time ladies have been present in a half century. I must be the first guest in the eighty-two year history of the Gridiron Club who has showed up in white tie and boots! . . .

"Those lyrics we just heard about Brother Nelson and the Win-with-Win idea (I like the sound of that!) give me an opportunity to talk with you about my brother."

He said that the last time he had talked politics with Nelson was in 1962, and that he found out then that the New York governor wouldn't be "my political adviser."

In Arkansas, he said, he had been working on "a completely revolutionary idea—a two-party system," which wasn't very popular at first because people just didn't understand it.

"The last Republican they'd heard about was Alf Landon."

But out of curiosity, he said, they turned out, "perhaps in the mistaken idea that a carnival was coming to town." When he told Nelson about this later, the reply he received was, "Don't let this go to your head. Half of those people that showed up had never seen a millionaire."

He was also vexed with the idea that Nelson was the nation's highest paid governor, while he was the lowest, at a mere $10,000. "It's a sort of riches to rags story," he commented.

He denied the "rampant rumor of a Rockefeller and Rockefeller ticket."

"My PR people tell me it won't work," he said. "The bumper stickers would be too long. . . .

"And if you think we Rockefellers don't believe in the right of honorable dissent," he went on, "remember we have one known Democrat in the family [John D. Rockefeller IV of West Virginia]. Don't underestimate our true family loyalty. We hedged that one by marrying [him] into Chuck Percy's family."

He spoke of Senator Fulbright, and told how back in 1962, when he had his first opponent in a general election, "he broke down and actually opened a campaign headquarters."

Then the governor put a finger on the political weakness of Senator Fulbright, who, seven years later, was retired from the Senate by failing to win renomination.

"He got out and made speeches," said Rockefeller, "some of them derogatory about me and the minority party. But as I pointed out in the campaign, he was getting to see more of the state than he'd ever seen before.

"Now, despite all this, I like Bill, but he doesn't seem to appreciate me.

"So lately, I've been thinking of trying to work out a deal with my brother in Albany. The next time I get a peace feeler from Nelson, I think I'll propose that we swap junior senators.

"He can send me Bobby—and I'll send him Bill, a baseball bat, a ball, and three neckties.

"I think I can handle Bobby better in my ball park than Nelson can in his.

"And I believe Bill would be more at home in New York.

"Then, too, Bobby and I could fly to New York together for our haircuts."[4]

This was the dinner at which Herblock, the *Washington Post* cartoonist, was initiated into the club. He was introduced by Carleton Kent of the *Chicago Sun Times* as "that gentle delineator of our favorite politicians . . . perhaps better known as kindly Herblock."

Richard L. Wilson and Julius Frandsen did their usual guest skit, which was preceded by Wilson's statement:

"Mr. President, the great issue of the pre–revolutionary period was taxation without representation. Things haven't changed much. Today the issue is taxation with representation."

One of the guests at this dinner was Katharine Graham, publisher of the *Washington Post*. She was asked to stand, and Julius Frandsen commented:

"Mrs. Graham reports that when CBS moved Walter Cronkite back-to-back with the 6:30 P.M. spot of NBC's Huntley-Brinkley show, Mr. Brinkley wrote to Mr. Cronkite, Goodnight, Walter."

The Democratic skit was in the atmosphere of Colonial Williamsburg. The idea was to show how our modern-day statesmen would have organized the nation. The scene was the House of Burgesses in Johnsonburg, Virginia.

It was noted that "here in Virginia we have what? Land, tobacco, Indians, that's all," and the first idea proposed was to tax the land, abolish the tobacco, and turn the Indians over to Sargent Shriver—one Indian, one vote.

"All those Indians for me?" shouted "Shriver." "Whoopee!" And he sang:

> One little vote for one little Indian.
> Two little votes for two little Indians.
> Three little votes for three little Indians.
> Votes for the Kennedy boys.
> Poverty jobs for good little Indians.
> Cash for the mob of Kennedy Indians.
> Corn on the cob for right-votin' Indians.
> Votes for the Kennedy boys.
> New tee-pees for our little Indians.
> Firewater free for tame little Indians.
> All to please the Kennedy Indians.
> Vote for the Kennedy boys.

The word was brought that there'd been a ship in Boston Harbor with two tons of marijuana on board. "Secretary of Defense McNamara" announced that "some of the chicks and hippies rowed out there and, boy, did they have a party! They called it the Boston Pot party."

Lord William Fulbright had good ideas, it was said, on running an indigenous revolution, and he was asked to explain them. To the tune of "Button Up Your Overcoat," Fulbright's impersonator sang:

> Stay away from Lexington.
> Don't set Boston free.
> Take good care of yourself—
> Let the Red Coats be.
>
> Massachusetts can't be saved,
> Anyone can see.
> Take good care of yourself—
> Let the Red Coats be.
>
> Beware of Valley Forge, oh, oh.
> Brandywine, oh, oh.
> Bunker Hill, oh, oh.
> Try to get along with Lord Cornwallis.
>
> Don't you cross that Delaware
> When the wind blows free.
> Take good care of yourself—
> Let the Red Coats be.

"The Kennedy boys" appeared with their idea on how to organize the country, and "Bobby," pointing at the picture of President Johnson, "grandfather of his country, harrumph!" sang:

> We could make believe we're with him.
> We could make believe Lyndon's our man.
> You will find—all our kind—good pretenders,
> In the groove—
> For any move—
> Just you see.
> Make believe we really praise him
> In a clever speech between us two.
> Might as well make believe we're with him
> For there's nothing else to do.

The "credibility gap" was being talked about a great deal in the newspapers, and an impersonator of George Christian, press secretary to the President, sang:

> The news that I feed you is meant to mislead you,
> It ain't necessarily so.
> The President he wants a good press.
>
> When he plants a rumor it's all in good humor,

The President he *needs* a good press.

When you seek a story it's not mandatory
That I come clean with you.
Oh, I will be truthful whenever it's useful
To give the White House view.

But each time I'm forced to say no,
It ain't necessarily so.

An impersonator of Vice President Humphrey, dressed as Paul Revere, complete with ringing bell, appeared and yelled, "The ADA are coming! The ADA are coming! They're after me. Bobby's after me. Teddy's after me. Galbraith's after me. Schlesinger's after me. Everybody from Boston is out after me. The ADA are coming! The ADA are coming!"

"McNamara" told him to calm down; "Gramps will save you."

Humphrey: Do you really think so?
Rusk: That's what he said, didn't he?
Humphrey: That's what bothers me.

"Here's what bothers Hubert," announced a singer:

Will he ask for me the second time around?
Will I be up front when LBJ's recrowned?
Life's so wonderful these days in Washington,
Being Number Two
Is better far than being Number None.

The skit closed with "Secretary of State Rusk" proclaiming that "now our work is done. Our great country has been founded. Russell Long, will you lead us in a hymn of praise for our great leader, the grandfather of his country."

And "Long" sang:

The help Lyndon's getting from Fulbright and Wayne [Morse]
Is touching his heart as an oft-heard refrain.
He dares not repeat all that he's thinking of—
His cup runneth over with love.

Suggestions he welcomes from Schlesinger too—
Or Galbraith or Hartke, or Stennis or Stu.
And don't you believe he's resenting the above,
His cup runneth over with love.

His poverty program is loaded with frills.

The taxes are needed but he has his Mills.
The deficits soaring to heaven above.
As cups runneth over with love.

Oh, Bobby and Teddy don't seem to belong
And leader Mike Mansfield's not singing his song.
He loves the dissenters—the hawk or the dove.
His cup runneth over with love.

Governor Mills E. Godwin, Jr. of Virginia was introduced as "a successor to Patrick Henry, Thomas Jefferson and Harry Flood Byrd," to speak for the Democrats. This was before he had achieved the distinction of being first a Democratic governor and then a Republican governor of Virginia.

Governor Godwin, as the "host governor," welcomed everybody to the "repository of tradition which is Williamsburg," and said he was especially pleased at the "reverence for tradition" demonstrated by the President of the United States."

He recalled the story of George Washington throwing a dollar across the Potomac and said that one of the more ardent traditionalists in Virginia had suggested that we might repay the current President "by applying an historic eighteenth century reception to some of the distinguished senators here present, but I find that it is illegal to shoot hawks in Virginia, and the dove season ended on November the fourth."

Turning to Governor Rockefeller, he said he didn't really take him seriously about his "Win with Win" movement.

"I do think maybe Winthrop has started a new political trend with his cattleman's boots," he declared. "Footwear could take on powerful new significance for Republican non-candidates. If they wore spurs, too, it would be almost impossible to get the foot in the mouth."

Then he praised the four generations of Rockefellers, not only for giving "an example of the opportunity America offers, but of how opportunity's dividends can be plowed back into the public good. . . .

"Williamsburg gives us our thought for today," Godwin continued. "Those early Virginians were not just zealots, advocating what they believed regardless of the consequences. They were concerned with consequences. They were interested in means, as well as ends. And they were ready with a workable alternative when the time came to put their ideals into practice.

"We face something of the same problem now. . . . It is not an easy process, and when it gets particularly burdensome, we come to Williamsburg to get our bearings. In this historical city, present-day problems shrink in the perspective of two centuries."[5]

Trohan introduced Chief Justice Warren for a few brief words, and quoted the chief justice as saying to him beforehand about his introduction: "Be as generous as you like. You're not under oath."

The dinner closed with the customary toast to the President, whose first line was, "I have enjoyed the skits—I think." Johnson commented that he'd been glad to hear Winthrop Rockefeller say that he was not running for President, and that the last time he saw Nelson he was not running for President either.

"I hope that starts a trend in the Republican party," he said. . . . "I've been out with the troops for the last two days, and I didn't know until I got in tonight that as a result of that new automobile safety regulation they put out in Washington in my absence, that the Rambler had already called in George Romney.

"Ever since I ran off to California when I was a boy, and I operated an elevator and I washed cars out there for a living— that was before I ever met either Romney or Nixon—it seems like I've always been having lots of trouble with these used-car fellows.

"I said to Lady Bird the other night, though, 'Tell me, if they're fair, why won't Nixon have a credibility problem if he should be President, not ever being able to hold another press conference?'

"But reflecting on all the aspirants, past and present, I couldn't help thinking the other evening, after spending a part of the day in the office, how much I'd enjoyed my visits that day with Abba Eban and King Hussein. And I'd gone over two messages from Bunker, three from Ky, and one from Thieu, and then Dean Rusk stopped in on his way home to tell me about a flight he'd made out to the University of Indiana and said, 'And by the way, Mr. President, I'll review with you tomorrow the newest foreign policy suggestions that I've received from Senators Fulbright and Percy and Morse and the new mayor of Lansing.'

"And then someone came in to tell me that Mr. Mills had already stepped out of his office and just doesn't answer the phone any more.

"And then Lady Bird came in after I'd got home and waiting

to put the dinner on the table, with another one of those Herblock cartoons.

"And I just thought to myself about all those things that Nixon had said in '60, and more recently, what Goldwater had said in '64, and I said, 'Darling, if they could have only won and had just one day like this, it would have served them right.' . . .

"But tonight we're back here in Old Williamsburg. And that's more bad news, when Walter Trohan kept talking about the courtesies of Colonial Williamsburg. I just wonder if he was reminding Lady Bird and me that we ought to colonialize Johnson City, if we are to keep up with the Rockefellers.

"This is an old political town, you know. Dean Rusk was telling me the other afternoon that the archeologists recently discovered an old plank here on which only two words were written: 'Dump Jefferson.'

"This is the place where the *Virginia Gazette* started a number of great traditions in American journalism, because its owner was also the public printer and the postmaster. It was among the first newspapers to print government press handouts. Because it was always short of news, the *Gazette* ran whole stories picked up from other newspapers. And today that tradition lives on.

"In 1775 the *Gazette* picked up a story from a Boston paper. Paul Revere, it seems, used lanterns to send a message: One if by land, two if by sea.

"You see, even in those days they didn't trust telegrams.

"Not only journalistic tradition but political tradition began in this city. The parallels with modern times are many. It was in Williamsburg, as well as in Boston, that the politicians in America first learned of the hazards of recommending a tax increase.

"It was here in Williamsburg that George Washington, our first President, constantly reminded about his credibility, made the first news leak in American history. It was a story about a boy and a cherry tree and Mrs. Washington's beautification program. And it ended with a line that no White House reporter would ever buy today. He said, 'I just cannot tell a lie.'

"And it was near Williamsburg, just up the road a way, that a great Vice President, later a greater President, Thomas Jefferson, first began his public career as the principal of a small Mexican-American school.

"The statesmen of Williamsburg were some of our first political animals—larger than life—and it was here, Governor Godwin reminded me, that a special courier first delivered the advance release which referred to Patrick Henry's private poll from his home district: '46 percent for liberty, 39 percent for death.'

"And George Christian wanted '15 percent undecided.'

"Incidentally, I've been reading a lot about my own polls in the newspapers [which were pretty dismal]. And I'm worried. It could be I've peaked too soon!

"I appreciate your tolerance of the references this evening to my grandson. As a matter of fact, I had thought about bringing little Lyn Nugent along with me tonight, because I've always heard that Virginia was the cradle of the Presidency.

"So as Walter Trohan brings us here tonight to launch the third century in the American adventure, it is good to enjoy that great American tradition of kidding ourselves, but it's much more important, in the days that are immediately ahead, for us not to kid ourselves. The great English statesman Gladstone has said, 'You cannot fight against the future. Time is on our side.' His statement was made almost a century ago in a speech on the Reform Bill of 1866.

"Man has undertaken many advances in the century that has passed since Gladstone spoke those words. Men have taken giant strides across the face of the earth and also the heavens. Generation after generation has been blessed with fortune after fortune, despite the wars and the plagues and the persecutions and the natural disasters, the setbacks and the sins. Despite all the years and all the dangers, reform and improvement has been the password to man's future. And so it must be our password now.

"All that we won in the last century is but the measure of what we must achieve in the next century. And that century starts very soon. It is already upon us in the rush of change and the challenges that are flung at us every day by science and by technology, by population increases, by 40 percent of the people in the world that can't write 'cat,' and 40 percent of the people in the world that can't read 'dog,' by the unexplored oceans, by the untamed weather, by the unexplored and the unknown that wait around the next sudden corner of our lives.

"Was Gladstone really right? I wonder. Is time really on our side now, or is this already so different a century that even time is ticking against us? Does the enormity and the complexity and the vast variety of modern life in the world in which we live overwhelm any future that we might reach for?

"There are those among us who would answer 'Yes' with their obstruction or with their silence. There are some who would retreat rather than advance. But there are not many of those among us, I hope, tonight.

"America is not one of those nations. We are not going to retreat before the future. We will move to meet the new challenges and to transform them into new triumphs. We do believe that time is on our side, and I promise you this night that in the time allowed us we are going to put every last second of it to strong and to timely—and I hope and pray very much to wise—purpose. And the time to start is now.

"Thank you and good night."[6]

It was Johnson's last speech to the Gridiron Club.

• • •

The 1968 dinner was held on March 9, several weeks before President Johnson made his announcement that he would not be a candidate for reelection. As is usual in a campaign year, the emphasis of the dinner was on the Presidential race, but President Johnson was not present at this dinner.

Nat Finney, correspondent of the *Buffalo Evening News*, was president of the Gridiron Club that year, and be began his speech in the dark by describing the current situation.

"The Democrats are fighting each other because they want peace," he said. "The Johnsoncrats are worried about their leader's image. . . . The Kennedycrats want a leader with Go-Go. . . . The McCarthycrats claim their boy is the last of the New Dealers because he says, 'I hate war!'

"And George Wallace? . . . He's the spoiler."

The GOP was in similar disunity.

"The Ev and Jerry show sounds like a duet between a bass drum and a peanut whistle. [He didn't distinguish which was which.] There may not be much discord, but they're so far apart, who can tell?

"We've got a new, new Nixon. He's worried about a loser image. So the word for the new, new Nixon is winsome."

For other potential GOP candidates he had similar comments.

"Sometimes you almost get the feeling," he said, "that this may be the year the office seeks the man—and can't find one . . . Candidates used to promise free love, free liquor and free lunch. The magic word was free. President Johnson changed that. Now the magic word is fresh. Fresh water, fresh air and fresh fish! The fresh air is what LBJ will give Humphrey if he keeps calling us at 6 A.M. to ask how the President is. . . .

"Our national pastime is still making trouble for each other. The remedy is laughter. If we couldn't laugh at each other, what a dreary place this would be. So let us all relax in the friendly glow of the Gridiron."

The opener was a chorus of candidates who sang:

We love a campaign!
We are candidates
Who tour all the states
And places remote.

We love a campaign!
We're for motherhood,
Whatever is good
For winning a vote.

The scene for the Republican skit was a racetrack, and all the racetrack touts were pushing their various candidates.

The Gallup pick, they sang, was "sure to click with every city slicker and country hick," and Roper's man was "bright, and though he may be wrong, never too far right." And Lou Harris's idea was that we needed "a face that's new, and not the same old image of you-know-who."

Each of them had the winning name, "unless, of course, his horse later on goes lame."

Senator's Percy's escort officer sang that Percy "wants his picture snapped ere it's over, over there."

And former "Republican Chairman Hall" lamented, in a parody on "Pore Jud Is Daid":

Pore George is daid!
George Romney's daid. . . .
We all knew at a glance
That he never had a chance:
His campaign was so moral and so clean.

"Goldwater" was pushing Nixon, "a restless chap," and John Duvall, impersonating him, sang:

I've got it under my skin,
The White House deep in the heart of me,
So deep in my heart, it's really a part of me,
I've got it under my skin.

I'd sacrifice anything, come what might,
For the sake of winning this year.
In spite of a warning voice
That comes in the night

And repeats and repeats in my ear:
"Don't you know in your heart you never can win,
Use your mentality, wake up to reality."
But although I pause,
It won't work because
I can't stop before I begin,
'Cause I've got it under my skin.

"Lindsay" and "Rockefeller" were other candidates at the racetrack, and Lindsay commented that the latter was wearing that track suit to show, with his customary sincerity, that he's not running this year." Rockefeller, to the tune of "I Won't Dance," sang:

I won't run, even for you.
My instinct tells me running's not what to do.

You know what? I'm learning
A few things concerning
A new kind of campaign style:
I simply sit like Mona Lisa and smile;
Though Lindsay's garbage set me back for awhile.

I won't run, how could I?
I won't run, why should I?
I won't run, that's understood.
But if you want a winner there's only one:
Since I can win it in a walk—*I won't run!*

A character representing Harold Stassen, "the oldest established permanent boy wonder in the world," fought his way through the crowd and told everybody to step to the rear:

Will ev'ryone here kindly step to the rear,
And let a winner lead the way, he sang.

Then "Jerry Ford," who was "drilling the wooden soldiers that Lyndon praised so highly," sang:

Backward, wooden soldiers, to the *status quo*,
With old Ev and Jerry, let no progress show.
We have got some sinners, forward they would move,
Forward to McKinley, let's get in the groove!
Come now, wooden soldiers, this way we must go—
Backward, backward, backward, to the *status quo*.

Ford, as the House Minority Leader, was introduced to speak for the Republicans. "And if the electoral fates are in his favor," said Finney, "he may be the next Speaker of the House."

Referring to the last song, Ford said that "what the President calls us in public, 'wooden soldiers,' is nothing compared to what he calls us in private.

"Let me tell you a little inside story. I've heard that President Johnson tells his visitors, 'There's nothing wrong with Jerry Ford except he played football too long—without a helmet.'

"Now I don't mind a little joke. But like so many other things you hear nowadays, that just isn't true.

"And I can prove it. On the Gridiron, I always wear my helmet."

He pulled out a helmet from under the table and put it on.

"This is really my helmet," Ford said, "it used to fit."

Humphrey was to be the Democratic speaker, and Ford paid his respects to him.

"Why did I ever tell Nat Finney I wanted to be the next Republican Speaker? Matching me against Hubert Humphrey for laughs is like putting Twiggy up against Zsa Zsa Gabor.

"Nat told me how it would go tonight. He said first he'd give a little talk—and next I'd give a little talk—and then the Vice President would follow.

"I said, 'Who follows the Vice President?'

"He said, 'Hardly anybody.'

"It's good to see so many great political writers here tonight. More and more lately, you gentlemen have been the zipper on the Credibility Gap.

"Now where else in Washington can you bask in the warm glow of good fellowship—and see Bill Fulbright toast President Johnson's health in Charlie de Gaulle's wine?"

After some references to the "Garbage Gap" in New York City, which had supplanted the Missile Gap, Ford noted that "Presidents are not always considerate of their Vice Presidents."

"Remember when Nixon returned from South America—stoned?

"Remember when Johnson had to fly 26,000 miles—for a camel? [A reference to his having been given a camel in Saudi Arabia].

"Frankly, if I were Vice President Humphrey, and just got home from a backbreaking tour of Africa, and the next day my President put a stop to all foreign travel—well, I'd lead a pretty good riot myself.

"But what a full public career Vice President Humphrey has had—just one long struggle against McCarthyism.

"He's been birched red by the Old Right, and rapped brown by the New Left.

"But Hubert always comes up smiling. He's really the Pagliacci of politics."

Ford remarked that "Bobby [Kennedy]'s now at the awkward age. He's too young to be President—and he's really too old for that haircut."

He commented that "if George [Wallace] sneaks off with just a few little ol' electoral votes, we may have to pick the next President in the House of Representatives."

Of Nelson Rockefeller: "He still won't volunteer, but last week he installed a hot line to his draft board."

Concerning President Johnson, he recalled that Henry Clay always said he'd rather be right than President.

"Now President Johnson has proved once and for all," he said, "it really is a choice.

"You know, I nearly didn't get here on time tonight. When I heard it was to be a bi-partisan affair, I went straight to the President's Club.

"Isn't that where you go to *buy* partisans?"

But partisanship, Ford said, had to stop somewhere, and it does, for "the things that unite us as Americans are far more enduring than the things that divide us, and one of these is our national sense of humor. . . .

"Our unwritten compact of respect for the convictions of others and faith in the decency of others, allows Americans the luxury of rugged political competition. Let's all work to banish war from our shrinking world and hate from our expanding hearts—to make this whole planet as full of friendship and felicity as this room tonight.

"In this spirit, let me assure the distinguished Vice President of the United States, before all of you, that I have absolutely no designs on his job.

"How many others in this room can make that statement?

"I'm serious. I'm not at all interested in the Vice Presidency.

"I love the House of Representatives, despite the long, irregular hours.

"Sometimes, though, when it's late and I'm tired and hungry—on that long drive home to Alexandria, as I go past 1600 Pennsylvania Avenue, I do seem to hear a little voice saying, 'If you lived here, you'd be home now.' "[7]

The Democratic skit was set at the Alamo, where "132 years

ago tonight," said the announcer, "in the war for Texas independence, 4,000 Mexicans at the Alamo had Lyndon B. Johnson's grandfather surrounded. Since then, things haven't changed much. Once again the Alamo is under siege, and once again its defender is the head of the Johnson family."

A long list of Democratic senators were among the defenders, and an impersonator of John Bailey, chairman of the Democratic Party, thought them "a likely bunch of defenders! Look at them!" He named seven or eight. "I'd feel safer with the Viet Cong."

An impersonator of Senator Everett Dirksen asked that Bailey not forget him, and Bailey inquired, "Aren't you in the wrong skit?"

"Possibly I am," replied Dirksen. "But when anybody knows as much about me as does Lyndon Baines Johnson, I stalwartly and graciously rush to his defense. He is my Commander-in-Chief—so long as he doesn't begin to tell all he knows."

Bailey decided that in order to make a proper defense of the citadel, they would have to call in the reserves. The reserves proved to be "Bobby Kennedy" with an entourage including "John Kenneth Galbraith" and "Arthur Schlesinger, Jr."

This led Bailey to comment of Kennedy, "He may be ready, but he's not about to be called."

Schlesinger said that Bobby was a changed man; "He's got the faith." And Bobby's impersonator, John Bigbee, sang:

Stand up, stand up for Lyndon,
We must be firm and true.

I will stand up for Lyndon,
There's nothing else to do.

Stand up, stand up for Lyndon,
Shame on the traitorous few.
How can the lib'rals doubt him?
He seeks out every view.
Some men are so deceptive,
Chameleons changing hue,
Principle says support him,
My interests also do.

Stand up, stand up for Lyndon,
I am for Hubert too.
It's shocking how reporters
Show that it's just not true.

I never would oppose him—
Friend Lyndon's matchless taste.
Besides, the private polls say
I wouldn't reach his waist.

But Schlesinger and Galbraith objected, and to the tune of "Silver Threads among the Gold," Galbraith sang:

Bobby you are growing old,
Strike before the iron grows cold.
You must run in sixty-eight,
Seventy-two could be too late.
Though your long hair hints of youth,
    of youth,
Silver threads betray the truth.
Time will mar your magic hue,
You're no kid at forty-two.
Bobby we are growing, growing old.
Four more years and we might fold.
Help the dovish ADA.
Bring defeat to LBJ.

Then the "real reserves" were brought on, such as "Clark Clifford," Secretary of Defense, who was "so used to dealing with General Electric that he demanded a retainer from General Wheeler."

"George Christian," President Johnson's press secretary at the time, announced that Clifford had dictated a memo to his clients about what to do during his brief leave of absence at the Pentagon and was urged to go ahead and tell us what he told GE and Du Pont. To the melody of "Please Don't Talk about Me When I'm Gone," Clifford sang:

Please don't get arrested while I'm gone.
Remember, I can't spring you, from the Pentagon.
And if you find your enterprises on thin ice,
Don't panic—I'll be back 'fore long with my advice.

We're parting, You go your way, I'll go mine,
It's what we must do.
Au 'voir, Du Pont; bye-bye, GE;
But I don't mean adieu.
Duty drives me to the Pentagon,
But *please* don't learn to do without me while I'm gone!

"George Wallace" was also among the reserves, costumed as Yankee Doodle, and Bailey remarked that "he doesn't look like the kind of man who would carry the South," which elicited the reply from George Christian: "The South? He's going to carry the North. Tell them, George who you really are." And Wallace sang:

> Ah'm a Dixie Yankee Doodle,
> In the North I strut my stuff.
> Just as the voters did in Alabam'
> You Yankees will love my guff.
>
> If it will help me win the White House,
> Ah'll let Bobby run with me.
> Dixie Doodle from Montgom'ry.
> Ah'll throw out the pseudos,
> And set all you damnyankees free.

The most vocal opponent of the Vietnamese War at this time was Senator Eugene McCarthy, who came on the stage as Don Quixote, with Sancho Panza and a donkey, to sing a parody of "Man of La Mancha."

> Hear, me, Hubert and Lyndon and serpents of sin,
> All your dastardly doings are past;
> For a holy endeavor is now to begin
> And Virtue shall triumph at last.
> I, am I, Gene McCarthy,
> Lord of Minnesota,
> A name flower people all know.
>
> I had a peace vision,
> We doves shared the glory,
> But we could not sell it to Ho.
> Even our Bobby said no.
> (Still) Onward to glory we go.

The last of the reserves was Hubert Humphrey, dressed as Davy Crockett and introduced as "Hubert Horatio Humphrey in disguise."

"You'd go around in disguise, too," said Humphrey, "if you were in this administration."

Humphrey knew who would save the Alamo, "the real Davy Crockett over there in the big white house," and to "The Ballad of Davy Crockett," he sang:

> Born in a cabin on the brown prairie,
> Learned Texas politics at Old Sam's knee.
> Got him a medal for one Navy spree,
> Built himself a fortune through the FCC.
> Lyndon, Lyndon Johnson,

The Buckskin buccaneer.
Lyndon, Lyndon Johnson,
King of the wild frontier.

Ran for the Senate,
The records say.
Winner by a whisker
Was young LBJ.
Connally and Fortas
Made the crucial play.
Eighty-seven votes and
He was on his way.
Lyndon, Lyndon Johnson,
He seen his duty clear.
Lyndon, Lyndon Johnson,
King of the wild frontier.

A wheelin' dealin' leader
In a poli-tick-in' town.
Always helpful to his friends,
Especially Root and Brown.
Wealth and fame went to the men
Who never let him down.
He settled for the White House
'Cause there wasn't any crown.
Lyndon, Lyndon Johnson,
The buckskin buccaneer.
Lyndon, Lyndon Johnson,
Seein' his duty clear.

Polls were agin' him though
He shoveled out the dough.
His private pollster says
It just ain't so.
Swears he'll be winnin'
And they'll all eat crow.
Calls on the spirit of the Alamo.
Lyndon, Lyndon Johnson,
King of the wild frontier.
Lyndon, Lyndon Johnson,
Seein' his duty clear.

With a reference to the man from Minnesota who had been accompanied in the skit by Sancho Panza and the donkey, Finney then introduced "another man from Minnesota" as the Democratic speaker, Vice President Humphrey.

Mindful of what had happened two years before when President Johnson popped in unexpectedly, Humphrey said at the outset that he wanted to get rid of the preliminaries: "Is he coming?" He followed with a suggestion that they lock the doors, because "tonight we close the Credibility Gap."

Concerning the upcoming campaign, he remarked that "the office seeks the man. Don't tempt me. Loyalty oath or not, I could be tempted!"

Speaking of the Vice Presidency, Humphrey described it as "the only office designed by the mind of man with a constitutionally enforced humility. The President," he said, "is always thinking of me. His messages are full of talk about the disadvantaged and the forgotten. . . .

"But you may have noticed," he continued, "I have been more independent these days.

"In Boston, I attacked the Congress for inaction on legislation.

"In Detroit I called for a Marshall Plan for the cities.

"In Washington I discussed in some detail the report of the Kerner Commission.

"And each time I was happy to see that George Christian clearly spelled it out. 'The Vice President was speaking on his own.'

"I'm glad to be speaking to those who understand the American language of my boyhood," he said. "I was born of an oppressed minority. We were Democrats!

"Those were the good old days when to be 'far out' meant living on a farm away from town.

"A picket was a fence post. And when you 'took a trip,' you went over to your grandmother's house.

"As you all know, my father was in drugs. He never dreamed what a potential market he had at the nearby land-grant college."

Speculating on the forthcoming conventions, and where the Democratic conclave should be held, Humphrey said that the President was holding out for the Houston Astrodome, but that he was for the St. Paul Auditorium.

"We just couldn't agree, so we called Bobby to ask his preference. Really, I expected him to say the Boston Garden. But no, he said 'Las Vegas.'

"Why Las Vegas? The wiretaps are already installed."

Then he told about having a meeting with the President to talk about the campaign, and Johnson had said, "Hubert, we've got to divide the campaign duties.

"You take Berkeley, Cambridge, Harlem, downtown Detroit, the farm states and Alabama. I'll take Fort Bragg, the Space Center, and Johnson City."

About a week before, he continued, when the governors came to Washington, the President and Mrs. Johnson asked them to the White House. He thought it was pretty big of the President, too, particularly when he noticed, during cocktails, that several of the wives were measuring the furniture and feeling the draperies.

"Well, it's a wonderful house—a good address in a nice neighborhood. The plumbing works. The garbage is collected regularly. And when it's cold, you can count on a hot blast from Capitol Hill."

He noted that it was quite common for political personalities to appear on the Johnny Carson show and said that "what isn't so well known is that many of them plan to appear later this year in regular roles on other shows. For instance:

"Barry Goldwater in 'Snap Judgment.'

"George Romney in 'Get Smart.'

"George Wallace in 'Let's Make a Deal.'

"Bobby Kennedy and Chuck Percy in 'The Little Rascals.'

"Gene McCarthy in 'Sunrise Semester.'

"Lyndon Johnson and Hubert Humphrey in 'Run for Your Life.'

"Have you seen the buttons kids are wearing these days? The political ones are especially interesting.

" 'Romney's a Dropout.'

" 'Don't Walk—Buy a Used Car from Nixon.'

" 'Draft Rocky: He Looks Good in Khaki.'

"I'm told they're coming out with one that says: 'I'm a Lousy Listener—Unleash Hubert!'

"Now a word about the opposition," Humphrey went on. "We see across this great land hundreds of billboards proclaiming: 'Ford has a better idea.'

"Well, Jerry, if you have *any* idea, I wish you'd give it to the House."

In a peroration about America, he noted that "size is not grandeur" and "territory does not make a nation." Humphrey then recalled the words of Edmund Burke more than a century before that "the only thing necessary for the triumph of evil is for good men to do nothing," and of Calvin Coolidge, that "the business of America is business."

"But we know," he said, "the business of America is America, and the greatest gift of free enterprise to our nation is not what is on the balance sheet but what is in the communities."

It was business at work, producing a prosperous economy, a strong nation, and "the determination to see that America is not only rich but just."[8]

Prior to the dinner, President Johnson had asked people to restrict foreign travel, and this became the vehicle for the foreign affairs skit. The scene was set in the interior of the Passport Office, which had been transformed into a travel agency, with foreign travel posters overlaid with signs such as "Forbidden," and "Verboten."

The order to issue passports only for necessary business had gone to the State Department, it was pointed out by the announcer, "by decree of the President after he got back from his trip around the world."

"Averell Harriman," ambassador at large, was the first applicant to renew his passport, because he was "trouble shooting for the President." He was told to do his trouble shooting in this country—Los Angeles, Detroit, Newark, Cleveland, Chicago, Milwaukee, where there had been riots.

"We've just changed your ticket," he was told, "from Angkor Wat to Angry Watts."

An impersonator of Under Secretary of State Nicholas Katzenbach tried to explain the new foreign travel ban and sang, to the tune of "Cabaret":

Don't go to Paris
To London
Or Rome—
Not even for a day.

Altoona's got
What France has not,
Scrapple from York, Pa.
No Moulin Rouge,
Just Newport News—
No Indonesian Xanadus
Who serve booze
With your koochie koos.

Deal out the Casbah
And castles in Spain,
Ta-ta to old Norway,
Maybe it's not
An Angkor Wat,

But Newark sure is gay.

Get mugged in Harlem,
In Watts
Or Detroit—
Call it a holiday.

Pack up the kiddies,
Your maw and your paw—
And dine out at Joe's Cafe.

See all the sights
In Brooklyn Heights—
And travel the U.S.A.

The Middle East situation, which had become tense because of the stinging Israeli defeat of Egypt in the 1967 war, was handled by the club in a double parody, with the first verse sung by "President Nasser" of the United Arab Republic, and the second verse by "General Moshe Dayan," Defense Minister of Israel. Nassar sang:

I'm the Sheik of Araby,
Israel belongs to me.
At night when they're asleep
In their Kibbutz I'll creep.
I'll mow them down when in—
My tanks from Kosygin.
And if I lose, I'll win.
I'm the Sheik of Araby.

Dayan came in with:

I'm the Sneak of Araby,
Sinai belongs to me.
Jerusalem and Jordan
Are all inside my cordon.
My aircraft left at dawn,
And now your tanks are gone.
I've set the deserts free.
I'm the Sneak of Araby.

"Prime Minister Harold Wilson" of Great Britain and his aides arrived on the scene and started looking through their luggage. Asked if something was missing, Wilson's impersonator replied, "I think I have mislaid, or forgotten, or misplaced, I might just as well admit it, I seem to have lost an empire." Then, to the tune of "On the Road to Mandalay," he sang:

Find me some place west of Suez
Of a size within our purse.
To contain our mini-empire,
Lest the worst become still worse.
Let the temple bells keep calling.
There'll be no one there to hear.
For the curtain's finally falling
On Britannia's ancient sphere.

So-o-o good-bye to Mandalay.
We're retiring from the fray.
'Cause the chaps who keep our ledgers,
Say we can't afford to stay.
We are handing Mandalay
To the good old U.S.A.
It's all yours, complete with thunder
Out of China 'crost the bay.

At the conclusion of this song "Walter Rostow," special assistant to the President, noted the arrival of "Dean Acheson," former secretary of state, and remarked to Wilson that as he and Dean were walking past the British Embassy the day before, they saw "the statue of your great predecessor with his fingers held up in his famous victory sign. Dean will tell you what we thought we heard him say." Then Adon Phillips, as Acheson, sang:

There'll always be an England,
While there's a man who's free;
Wherever there's a spirit bold
Who dares upon the sea.

There'll always be an England,
Some dawn will end the night;
The sun will shine on fair green fields
And Dover's cliffs gleam white.

There'll always be an England,
Where courage still is shown,
As long as men remember when
Old England stood alone.

Incidentally, Gridiron files contain copies of correspondence between William Benton, then Ambassador to UNESCO in Paris, and Prime Minister Wilson, in which Benton sent him a newspaper story carrying the lyrics of the dinner and noting that he thought Wilson would be amused at the song attributed to him and at the response of the stage Acheson. Wilson replied by thanking him and commenting, "I greatly enjoyed the press accounts of the Gridiron Club dinner. Reading through them, I am not quite sure whether I should welcome or regret the fact that we have no equivalent here. At all events, it was clearly a very lively evening."[9]

With the last line of the song, "Old England Stood Alone," Gridiron President Finney banged the gavel, stopped the show, and said that Secretary of State Dean Rusk, "personifies a national commitment to the international search for a decent and peaceful world." He asked Dean Rusk to rise and take the spotlight, "while the Gridiron chorus honors him with our closing song."

> What the world needs now is peace, sweet peace.
> Let aggression halt, freedom grow, so war will cease.
> What the world needs now is peace, sweet peace.
> No, not just for some, but for everyone.
>
> For no one needs more lands to conquer.
> There are mountains and valleys enough to spare.
> There can be jobs and good homes enough for all,
> With peace on earth, bounties we'll all share.

The dinner was concluded with the Gridiron Club drinking a toast for the last time to President Johnson.

XXI

Richard M. Nixon

.

🍴 *1969-1971*
"The primary duty of the
President
is to preserve, bring, and
keep the peace. . . ."

And Hubert Humphrey, Edward Kennedy,
George Wallace, Spiro Agnew, Edmund Muskie,
and John Mitchell also Speak

The new administration of President Nixon and Vice President Agnew had been in office for two months at the time of the March 15, 1969 dinner. Both attended, along with the two losing candidates for the Presidency, Hubert H. Humphrey and George C. Wallace. All four made speeches.

Gridiron President John Hightower of the Associated Press pointed out in his speech in the dark that "the fog of the campaign has long since lifted. The ship of state is creaking off on another four-year voyage. . . .

"They're sailing under a bold banner," he said, "Forward Together. But they're still trying to figure out: Which way is forward? . . .

"In Congress, the accent is on youth. Senator Edward Kennedy has taken over as majority whip from Russell Long."

But he noted that Senator Kennedy couldn't tell "whether his colleagues are following him or chasing him." .

Youth, he said, was the great problem of the Democratic party, and both Lyndon Johnson and Hubert Humphrey "have gone back to college to try to win friends among the campus protesters."

But George Wallace had little interest in the academic life.

"What he wants to do," said Hightower, "is broaden his base in the electoral college."

Hightower noted that President Nixon was a veteran of these occasions, but "now and then a funny thing happened to him on the way to the White House—and we commented on it. But in twenty years of public life he has shown he could take it."

The opener was a nostalgic and pleasant reference to the President. The chorus came on stage in their full dress suits, each wearing a Nixon mask. The masks were removed when the announcer said that the Gridiron Club had celebrated the ups and downs of "tonight's most illustrious guest." Then they resang many of the Nixon songs from previous dinners, including "On a perch in the Senate a Dicky Bird sat," "Running's wonderful the second time around," and "I'll sacrifice in San Francisco."

The first skit, entitled "High Noon on the Moon," was a Gridiron tribute to the leading figures in the National Aeronautics and Space Administration, and to four of the top astronauts: John H. Glenn, Frank Borman, James A. Lovell, and William A. Anders.

Impersonators of each were characters in the skit, which began with the raising of the flag on the moon, while Borman claimed "this vast lunar wasteland for the United States."

Then a strange conglomeration of men entered, saying they had been hijacked while flying from Paris to Miami: impersonators of Henry Cabot Lodge, Henry Kissinger, Secretary of State Rogers, Chief Justice Warren, Supreme Court Justice Abe Fortas, and Governor George Wallace.

"Lodge," who was involved in Vietnam peace talks in Paris sang:

> The next time I see Paris,
> All peace talks I'll foreswear,
> I'll not sit at the table round,
> Not for the Croix de Guerre.

> The next time I see Paris,
> Give me the Place Pigalle,
> Without those Commies singing the
> Internationale.

I hear of Tet and North Tibet,
Of Mao and DMZ,
Of NLF and Viet Cong,
Of Ho Chi Minh and Ky.

The next time I see Paris,
I'll can-can in the aisles,
Toujour l'amour—and I'll make sure
That Mona Lisa smiles.

An impersonator of Secretary Rogers sang:

I wonder who's Kissinger now,
A dove or a hawk like Rostow?
I wonder who's filling him full of dope,
Just soft soap,
Without hope.
I wonder if he'll overhaul
The Harvard approach to de Gaulle?
I wonder just how—he'll react to Moscow?
I wonder who's kidding him now?

"Brezhnev" arrived and said that things weren't going too well in Russia those days and that he'd like to hitch a ride right back down to America. Then he sang a parody of "Taking a Chance on Love."

Take us along to the U.S.A.,
Let's sail along, down the Milky Way—
Take us along with you!
We'll swap the moon, and its dirty sand
For just a small piece of Disneyland—
Take us along with you.
We'll risk Siberia
For a night on the town, champagne and a song
If you will take us along with you.

Take us along—you can have the Czechs—
Please help us get Castro off our necks.
We'll give you Ho Chi Minh—
And a special treat—throw in Mao Tse-tung,
If you will take us along with you.

Impersonators of Chief Justice Warren and Associate Justice Fortas, the latter under attack for taking speaking fees, strolled in, and "Warren" sang:

I came from California,
With my law books on my knees,

Ain't used them since I got here
'Cause I rule just as I please.

I always, mostly, gently tried
For unanimity,
But when we split, you must admit
We did it brilliantly.

I tried to quit, but Lyndon said
First let's get Abe okayed.
But Abe forgot and took that fee,
So my partin's been delayed.

He coulda talked for free, I guess,
Though Senators seldom do—
That fifteen grand turned things around;
Now to Dick I'll say adieu.

The skit ended with a supporter of George Wallace, "Lloyd W. Bailey" of Rocky Mount, North Carolina, who had voted for him in the electoral college, singing:

We shall ovahcome, we shall ovahcome
All you pointy-haids some day.
Oh, deep in mah boots, ah do believe
We shall ovahcome some day.

Carpetbaggin' cohts, briefcase totin' types,
Beatniks, kooks and free speech folks,
Oh, deep in mah boots, ah do believe
We shall ovahcome some day.

Gridiron President Hightower introduced Wallace with a comment that "our speaker is a man who said that between the Democrats and the Republicans there's not a dime's worth of difference."

Wallace spoke of Mr. Nixon's problems in South America.

"I have the same problems in North America," he said, "and feel like I've been run over."

He referred to "standing in the school house door," and to his idea of having a balloon test for the news media with "a pink balloon."

The campaign, he said, had been tough, but "Mr. Humphrey and I believe it was even tougher on election day."

He said he had been swamped by letters indicating "that I probably misled the American people by using the expression 'dime's worth'—indicating there was a dime's worth. It seems that with the inflationary spiral we have seen, there is probably not over two cents worth of difference."

Then Wallace turned to Chief Justice Warren and the Supreme Court.

"After having read some of the dissenting opinions by the Supreme Court and what they said about one another, I feel that what I have said in the past might be moderate and mild indeed. At least, I have, except on one occasion involving the Ohio case, brought the court together in unanimous opinions."

He followed this with a story about himself: When he was a trial judge in Alabama, learned lawyers were involved in a case and one of them argued the case should be dismissed on the doctrine of *"res ajudicata."*

"My courtroom," he said, "was filled with good southern Alabamians that listened to the new judge perform before some of the top notch lawyers. Well, I just wasn't sure about this *res ajudicata*, so I just said, 'Well, I am going to file a writ of *error corum nobis* and tell you that *nunc pro tunc* and *ipso dixit*, and that settles that.'

"And they said, 'Well, he sho told them off.' So I hope that I can get out of this meeting without some writ being slapped on me by this court."

Turning to the President, Wallace noted, in what years later turned out to be a super understatement, that "it looks like Mr. Nixon may have trouble with the Congress."

"Well, if I were President," he said, "I would tell them that I'd be the last President that the Congress ever got in front of."

This is a great nation, Wallace added, and "I hope Mr. Nixon can unify the American dream—a better life for all people, which I subscribe to, domestic and foreign."[1]

The riots at the Democratic National Convention in Chicago in 1968 had been a disaster for the Democratic party. Because of the political effect of the elaborate documentation of these riots to the American people on television, it was logical that the Democratic skit at this dinner would be entitled "Riot on the Campus." The skit began with a discourse between "Dean Lyndon Baines Johnson" and "Professor Hubert Horatio Humphrey," who were "molding the minds of youth and rewriting history—telling it like it wasn't."

The skit moved on to a confrontation in the dean's office, where young revolutionaries had "unconditional, non-negotiable demands." The revolutionaries, impersonators of

Senator George McGovern, Senator Abraham Ribicoff, Senator
Edward M. Kennedy, and others, led by Ribicoff, sang:

> We grew our hair and learned to gain
>   attention in the press.
> Upset the establishment with our
>   mod flower power dress,
> Stormed the citadels of politics
>   and made a lot of news,
> And we haven't read too many books,
>   but we'll still be glad to give our views.
>
> We're experts on the bomb and the war in Vietnam.
> Yes we are, Yes we are.
> The new morality and police brutality
> and more, and more.
> Just pick a subject and we'll take a stand,
> 'Cause we're the young electric, psychedelic,
>   hippie, dippie, opposition, democratic,
>   turned-on, groovy, new Senate band.

Dean Johnson called them upstarts and whippersnappers.
Then he summoned the janitor, "Russell Long," to get them out
of the dean's office.

Long set about his job, remarking, when McGovern introduced Teddy Kennedy, that "I just cleans up after him now."
Then Teddy sang to the melody of "Gentle on My Mind":

> The thing I did to Russell Long,
> The job we did on Lyndon,
> Set our style.
> And I have just begun to prove
> That Teddy Boy can beat them
> By a mile.
>
> Now
> We bow a bit to Mansfield
> And we captured George McGovern,
> He's our toy.
> But the arrogance of Fulbright
> And the Gene McCarthy antics
> Still annoy.
> But I'm showing I'm not shackled
> By traditions moves and measures
> And my glamour has a brilliance that can blind.
> It keeps me in the spotlight,
> In the headlines, on the TV,

And not so very gentle on your mind.

McGovern recited one of the alleged poems of "that master of iambic pentameter, Eugene McCarthy":

I am a sweet statesman named Gene,
Whose ideals are so sweet and so clean
That I lured all our youth,
Unwashed and uncouth,
To the muddiest muddle you've seen.

"McCarthy" sang:

Roll out those lazy, hazy, crazy days last summer,
That big convention where I did my thing.
Bring back those hippy, dippy, lippy psycho-de-lics
In old Chicago where I had my biggest fling.
Just what they did and what they said I cannot mention,
Our highest court backs their excess gall.
Then out in Grant Park they created such dissension,
They practiced free speech with the poet from St. Paul.

"Jack Valenti" and "Clark Clifford" stepped forward, described by Humphrey as "faithful public servants. All they ever asked was to have their pictures printed on the dollar bill."

And a nostalgic Valenti sang:

Those were the days, my friend,
We thought they'd never end—
We'd hit the top,
Con-sen-sus was in flower.
You pulled the ears of Him
And on a simp-le whim
You drove your car at ninety miles an hour—
The voters had no say,
They simply paid our way.
Those were the days,
Oh, yes, those were the days.

McGovern shouted that "you can't get rid of us with all that old sentimental twaddle." At this point "Mayor Richard Daley" entered, leading four Keystone Cops, "the gentlest ones who ever cracked a skull," to end the riot. Daley sang:

Give my regards to Lindsay,
Garbage and school strikes plagued him,
Should-a let the billy club rule.
If Lindsay wants to learn the trade,
Sug-gest he come to Dal-eys school.

McGovern agreed to stop the riot on one condition: that they "kick Professor Hubert Humphrey out of this university and make him commander of our forces in Vietnam."

But the group thought that would be too cruel to Professor Humphrey, and it was decided that they would bring the riot to an end with memories of Humphrey's "campaign of happiness."

Humphrey, the Democratic speaker, said it wasn't the results on election night or even the verdict of the electoral college, but that "it's when you have been invited to speak at the Gridiron that you know it's official—then you know you have lost. . . .

"This is a night for reminiscing. When a man loses a Presidential election, he keeps thinking about what went wrong. I want to share those thoughts with you—because of the great support I got from the publishers and newspapers of this country. . . .

"But the defeat was not without some blessings. Each morning, as a professor, I grade a few term papers; in the afternoon, as a druggist, I fill a few prescriptions; and in the evening, as a husband, Muriel and I work on my collection of campaign buttons. The one I prize most says: 'Almost all the way *without* LBJ.'

"As a matter of fact, it's been rather easy for me to switch from political life to academic life—involuntarily, I might add—especially since I had my riot training last fall. My only complaint is, I don't get combat pay! . . .

"I teach at two schools and this gives me the unusual and historic opportunity to be held hostage on two campuses simultaneously. No other ex-Vice President or professor can make that claim!"

After several other remarks about college students, "The Love Poems of Eugene McCarthy," and Eric Goldman's book, he continued, "But enough of the past. Let us turn to the present. The last time I saw President Nixon was on Inauguration Day. He was taking his oath, and I was muttering a few of my own."

Since then, he said, it had been a fast-moving Presidency. President Nixon had withdrawn "nominations for 451 postmasters, twenty-six judges, retired more than a dozen ambassadors, rescinded the Trans-Pacific route decision, sent Governor Rockefeller to Latin America, and exiled Murray Chotiner to Bethesda."

Then, speaking very slowly and seriously, Humphrey said: "I know you all share with me an enormous sympathy for the man who holds the loneliest office in the land, the most sensitive office within the gift of the people, the man who walks a tight rope between what is right and what is wrong, buffetted by one force or another.

"We honor this man tonight and I want to pay my special respects to—the Vice President of the United States, Spiro T. Agnew.

"You know, Vice President Agnew and I are soul brothers! We have both occupied the office space allotted to the Vice President. So we both understand the meaning of that immortal phrase, from Aristotle, or was it Socrates, 'If you've seen one slum, you've seem them all.'

"It is traditional at the Gridiron Club to end on a serious note. You all know how I feel. I ran. I lost. I was disappointed. But I have recovered, and perhaps I will return."

Then, turning to Nixon, who had been Vice President for eight years and then out of office for eight, he said, "Mr. President, your own life has inspired me. May I be so fortunate."

"I have been close enough to high office over these past twenty years to know the pressures and problems that our President and Vice President must bear, day after day—the splendid‐ misery. Winning the peace is a lonely battle.

"Our hopes and prayers are with them. May good fortune smile upon them—until November 6, 1972."[2]

With a note that the cabana had replaced the ranch, and that lights burn again in the White House at night, the Republican skit was set at "Rebozo's Hideaway" on the beach at Key Biscayne.

When an impersonator of Secretary of Defense Melvin Laird inquired of a couple of natives what they thought about the winter White House being there, they replied that "Bebe says it don't hurt the real estate values hardly at all."

"Interior Secretary Walter J. Hickel," who was under a cloud because he had been critical of President Nixon, and because he wanted immediate development of the Alaska oil pipeline, led off with a song based on "The Punishment Fits the Crime," from *The Mikado*.

I fell in with evil companions;
The things they proposed were a crime;
Those oil men had schemes that gave me wild dreams—
And I had a wonderful time!

Among the many Republicans gathered at Key Biscayne was

"Deputy Secretary of Defense David Packard," who inquired naively, with the President setting up so many new commissions, "how about one to try sneaking some Republicans into the administration?"

This brought a severe rebuke just as "Governor Rockefeller" and "Ray Bliss," came on stage. Bliss, it was explained, "lost the only job he had, and the governor lost two he wanted, like President or secretary of state." Rockefeller sang, "Do you ever think of me?"

Congress had just voted an increase in congressional salaries, and a character representing Senator Everett Dirksen, "just back from fighting the fires of the high cost of living," sang:

> There was sure a lot of fussin'
> And Congress got a cussin'
> We ought to have been praised.
> Folks should be more forgivin'
> 'Cause we wanted some high livin'—
> It was just a little raise.
>
> Forty-one percent it figgered;
> A ruckus it sure triggered
> That left us in a daze.
> They said it was inflation
> And attacked our reputation—
> It was just a little raise.

"Congressman H. R. Gross" of Iowa, described as "the most conservative man in the world," was among the Key Biscayne group, and to the tune of "There'll Be Some Changes Made," he lamented that he didn't like what was going on at the White House.

> I guess he's gone and changed his plan—
> I should have known he wouldn't stay Republican.
> Each day he's switching more completely;
> He's not the same guy that we ran.
> He's getting strong for civil rights,
> And tougher taxes on the rich—that's dynamite.
>
> He's tried to give our patronage all away,
> He gets more progressive each day,
> The hero of our fattest cats
> Is just like all Democrats.

The final principal to come on the stage was "Vice President Agnew," who was to speak immediately after the skit. When

Republican leader "Gerald Ford" asked him how he was feeling, Agnew started to answer, but "Herb Klein," director of communications, interrupted, "That's a no-no, Mr. Agnew." Then Klein sang a parody of "A Bird in a Gilded Cage."

> The East Room was filled with fashion's throng,
> The White House a-gleam with lights.
> And there the Vice President passed along;
> The bravest of all the sights.
> A wife to her husband then softly sighed:
> "He has power at his command."
> "But he really has got no status," he cried,
> "Though he works in a mansion grand."
>
> He's only a bird in a gilded cage,
> A pitiful sight to see.
> You may think he's happy and free from care;
> He's not though he seems to be.
> He did his campaigning with bounce and flair,
> Though he was not always sage.
> That is why, no doubt,
> They won't let him out;
> He's a bird in a gilded cage.

Agnew responded by saying that the President had "spared no effort to keep me fully abreast of foreign policy. He has specifically requested Secretary Rogers and Dr. Kissinger to remind me whenever his press conferences are televised."

Besides seeing that he received important information, Agnew said that the President had encouraged him to initiate action.

"He suggested, as a beginning," said Agnew, "bilateral talks to determine if there is any way this administration could sign a nonaggression pact with Bill Fulbright."

There had been widespread comment at the time the Maryland governor had been selected by Nixon to be his running mate that this was an effort to placate the South.

"I would like to straighten out all those rumors as to how the Nixon-Agnew ticket was put together in Miami. Gentlemen, it was not due to Strom Thurmond's intervention! It is true that Strom was consulted, but I swear to you—I wanted Mr. Nixon on my ticket before Strom even mentioned him to me."

Then Agnew referred to some flubs he had made in public statements which had gotten into the newspapers.

"Speaking of the press," he said, "I am not going to complain to this distinguished Gridiron audience about the treatment I have received in the press. But I do think it's high time in this country for men who are supposed to be honest and truthful to make some decent effort to start reporting what I *meant* to say and *not* what I said.

"However, I learned a long time ago not to believe everything I read in the papers.

"Only the other day, I read a newspaper article which predicted I would not be on the ticket in 1972.

"Well, I want to dispense with that nonsense here tonight.

"I will be on the ticket with him again in 1972.

"Or Rose Woods [Nixon's personal secretary] doesn't get her jewels back."

Discussing the Vice Presidency, he commented that it was "a rare opportunity in politics for a man to move from a potential unknown to an actual unknown. "As Mr. Nixon well knows," Agnew continued, "the Vice Presidency can be an important stumbling stone to the Presidency.

"I must tell you, there's a feeling that comes over a man when he becomes Vice President. It's the same feeling that comes over a turkey the day before Thanksgiving. . . .

"I am fortunate to serve under a man who has himself been a Vice President and who is thus aware of the pitfalls of the office. And I must say, President Nixon has gone out of his way to show me every understanding and courtesy.

"For one thing, due to his insistence, I have my own plane, Air Force thirteen—it's a glider.

"And when I go to the White House, I don't have to use the back door. I go right in through the front—with the regular tour."

He said that the President had encouraged him to appear on various newsmaking programs, "where I can reach a wide audience with my own views," and that the Presidential staff had assembled some appearances for him.

"I'll be on 'Meet the Press' opposite the Army-Navy game.

"I'll be on 'Face the Nation' opposite General de Gaulle's arrival at the White House.

"And I'll be on 'Issues and Answers' opposite live coverage of Julie and David's surprise party for Ted Kennedy at the ranch."

Agnew commented about having slipped on the ice and fallen at the airport on one occasion when he had arrived to meet the President.

"I don't know how many of you have ever reviewed troops with the President at an icy airport. But when he slips on the ice and says, 'You fall,' you'd better fall!"

His final words were about the press, and they gave perhaps some indication of the role he was to assume, as time went on, as its chief critic.

"When the President went to Europe, it became my job to help solidify the grand alliance of columnists here in America. As you know, this alliance, once as closely united as Evans and Novak, has been showing signs of strain lately. The generation gap is growing between Walter Lippmann and Joseph Kraft; Max Lerner no longer likes the taste of Mary McGrory's cheesecake; Bill White and Dick Wilson are drifting apart; Charlie Bartlett is threatening to throw Alan Otten out of the Federal City Club.

"And you can imagine the disastrous 'domino effect' if Joseph Alsop decided to go it alone.

"Let me make one thing very clear: This administration will listen and learn, but it is not for us to unite the columnists—the columnists must unite themselves.

"And only if we have a strong alliance of Western press powers can we hope to enter an era of negotiation with Reston and Wicker." [3]

The dessert and coffee were served, the President was toasted, and Nixon rose to reply in his first Gridiron speech as President of the United States.

He reminisced at considerable length about previous dinners he had attended, the first one as a young Congressman twenty-one years before, another when he had been invited to speak after he had been defeated for the Presidency by John F. Kennedy, and the one in 1954 when Earl Warren attended for the first time as chief justice of the United States.

Noting that in the fifteen intervening years Chief Justice Warren had attended every Gridiron dinner except one, and that this was his last Gridiron dinner as chief justice [he had already announced his retirement], the President suggested that they all drink a toast to him.

"With that bit of historical reminiscing," he continued, "I now wish to evaluate the program of the evening. I have never commented on the skits. I have learned how to get along with the press."

He was doing quite well with the press at that time, but noted that he had been in office for almost eight weeks and that the columnists were beginning to write how his honeymoon had ended.

"I would like to be permitted just a serious note as we conclude the dinner," Nixon said, outlining his conception of how a President and a Congress, though of different parties, should work together.

"The honeymoon must always end where a new administration comes in. But that does not, of course, mean that the marriage is over. In our American political system when that great awesome day occurs and the transfer of power is made between the outgoing President and the new President, there is, in effect, a marriage ceremony not between parties, but between the executive power and the legislative power, not with the suggestion that they will always agree, because there are not always agreements in marriages, but with the thought that for the next four years at least after that ceremony occurs, they are together.

"And whether the nation goes forward will depend on the extent to which they are able to work together. And there's responsibility on both sides in that respect. I am keenly aware of that. And I have been most grateful for the fact that in these first eight weeks we have had somewhat of a honeymoon. And I'm also aware of the fact that for the balance of the next four years, it will be necessary for us to work out within this very delicate relationship between the executive and the legislative the kinds of programs that this nation needs and that the world expects from America."

Then he launched upon the subject of world peace.

He noted that during the dinner he had had to leave the room for half an hour to make a brief appearance at another hotel at a meeting of the American Legion on its fiftieth anniversary, that contributions had been made from all over the country to a fund for the purpose of lighting the Tomb of the Unknown Soldier, and that he had pressed the button that provided that lighting.

He spoke of the three who were buried there and of all the other young Americans who had given their lives for their country, and of the French boys, the Belgian boys, the British boys, the Italian boys, and the Russian boys.

"And Vice President Humphrey was altogether correct," he said, "when he reminded me in his own very eloquent remarks that the primary duty of the President of the United States, working with the Congress of the United States, is to preserve the peace; to bring peace where we do not have it; and to keep peace where we do have it.

"That is our goal. And in working toward that goal we need your criticism; we need your assistance; we need your prayers; we need also your support whenever we deserve that support.

"I stand for the first time before you as President of the United States. I hope to be here again on several occasions. But I can tell that as I stand here, I feel that truly while the honeymoon is over—and this Gridiron Dinner rather marks the end of the honeymoon—the marriage really begins.

"And the marriage vow, as I recall it, says for better or for worse. I hope that it's for better. It might be for worse. But if at times we can go forward together it could be for the best.

"Thank you." 4

• • •

The March 14, 1970 dinner was one of the great Gridiron dinners. Not only were speeches made by three of the leading figures in American public life at the time, Senator Edmund S. Muskie, Chief Justice Warren E. Burger, and Attorney General John N. Mitchell, but it was also the dinner at which President Nixon and Vice President Agnew put on their famous piano skit (described in Chapter I)—the first time a President of the United States had ever appeared on the Gridiron stage.

This skit was initiated not by the Gridiron Club but by President Nixon, who wanted to do something special for his old friend Jack Steele, then president of the Gridiron Club, who, as a *Herald-Tribune* correspondent in Nixon's early years in the House, had covered the future President's investigation of Alger Hiss.

Steele opened his speech in the dark by stating his regrets that former President Johnson wasn't able to be present.

"Even before his illness he sent regrets. But he did offer to send as a substitute his book-writing brother, Sam Houston Johnson. Lyndon said Sam Houston and those other fiction writers of the Washington press corps deserved each other.

"Speaking of fiction, Mr. Johnson has put the Nixon administration on the spot. It now has to convince the country it can *make* history as fast as LBJ can *rewrite* it.

"It was nice of Vice President Agnew to come tonight to get better acquainted with the instant analysts and other kooks of the news media.

"We're not going to try to convert you this evening, Mr. Vice

President. We only want to ask if you would mind lowering your voice.

"Between the Vice President and Attorney General Mitchell, a newspaperman's lot is not a happy one these days. Now a reporter has to worry that, if he doesn't get a subpoena, his boss will think he is lying down on the job."

Then, referring to the President, he pointed out that Nixon had been "upset by recent court orders requiring the busing of school children.

"But," said Steele, "the President has available an easy solution to the busing problem. All he has to do is get Ralph Nader to get General Motors to recall all the school buses.

"The President does have some problems. In his first year in the White House he has been surprised to find that things are just as bad as he said they were before he got there."

Some American soldiers were being brought before military tribunals and Steele commented that "at least the administration is keeping its pledge to bring the troops home from Vietnam—as fast as it can courtmartial them."

President Nixon had authorized elegant, new uniforms for the White House police, and the opener was based on this. Jerald F. terHorst of the *Detroit News,* and music chairman of the Gridiron Club, announced that we are "drinking with the Russians, smiling at the Chinese and apologetic to the French. Out of all this, our Chief of State has fashioned one great decision, so notable that it commands the attention of the entire world," and the Gridiron chorus would tell them about it.

The curtain opened and revealed the Gridiron chorus in the new uniforms of the White House police. A reporter entered, gazed with amazement, and went to the center mike to sing an adaptation of the "Drinking Song" from *The Student Prince.*

> Hail! Hail! Hail
> The Chief who has dressed his cops in such gay fin-er-y!

Then a police soloist stepped up and sang:

> Hail! Hail! Hail
> The Fuzz, for we are the sym-bol of de-moc-ra-cy!
> Here's a hope that our el-e-gance rates
> With all the mon-archs that bang on the gates!
> And those im-pu-dent snobs ef-fete
> Tonight with joy our clubs will beat!

Chorus:

Eyes right! In review pass!
We're together at last!
Hail! Hail! Hail!
The si-lent ma-jor-i-ty's
    trav-'ling first class!

The Democratic skit was set in the Enchanted Forest, with a chorus of elves, leprechauns and winged fairies carrying little electric candles. Puck announced that Hubert Humphrey was in the shade and sang:

Just hum a mer-ry song,
For-get we lost, for-get the cost,
And sing like nothing's wrong!

There were lots of "strange characters" in these woods, among them "Tweedledum George McGovern" and "Tweedledee Gene McCarthy." McGovern denied a suggestion that he had dropped out and said that he was just getting into the Kiddie Crusade.

"But let me say farewell—I hope—to my dear friend Eugene McCarthy."

Good night, Eugene! Good night, Eugene!
We'll leave you with your dreams.

My dov-ish credentials are greatest;
'Gainst hunger I lead the good fight.
And party reform is my latest;
At least the New Left thinks I'm right.

"Humphrey" appeared and sang, "I won't run, don't ask me," in a song that ended:

I won't run, unless you ask.
Taking a new whirl at it might be great fun—
And I just talked myself into it—I'll run!

An impersonator of House Speaker John McCormack, who had had trouble because of improper actions by some of the people in his office, and who was also under pressure to step aside because of his age, gave his reactions in song.

This old House is in rebellion
With Dick Bolling and Udall
Goo-goo eye-ing my position;
No respect for age at all.
"Out of touch" say these young upstarts,

Where I used to rule alone,
And it's all because some people
Rather freely used my phone.

I'm a-gonna run this House some longer,
Ain't a-gonna leave this House just yet.
I got tricks they never heard of,
That those boys won't soon forget.
And before I get through with them
Brash young leaders of the mob,
They're a-gonna be almighty sorry
That they ever tried for the Speaker's job.

"Teddy Kennedy" appeared next as a skier, introduced as "the champion uphill racer of our time."

"You fellows keep saying I can't make it," said Teddy. "Well, just you listen." And to the tune of "Yes, We Have No Bananas," he enthused:

Yes, I have a mañana!
I'll have my mañana some day.
You've Humphrey and Harris,
And Shriver from Paris,
And all kinds of losers today.
We have an old, out-of-date line-up;
Nooooo voters will sign up—
So wait! I've got a mañana!
I'll be top banana some day!

An impersonator of Fred R. Harris, former chairman of the Democratic National Committee thought they should come up with a new model, someone who would "look like a Republican and talk like a Democrat, a Prince Charming." "Mayor Lindsay" of New York, who had announced his departure from the Republican party and his new role as a Democrat, came on, saying "It's more fun to switch than fight!" Then, in a parody of "On the Sunny Side of the Street," he sang:

Guess you know the GOP,
Has revoked my party permit;
So I've switched my beat
To the sunny side of the street.
Somehow, never cared to be
Trainer for a pachy-derm—It
Seems life's more complete
On the donkey's side of the street!

Now I'm sure t'will be sayed

I'm a boorish renegade—
But I'm not afraid:
This Rover
Smells clover!

In the race for Pres-i-dent,
Got an edge on Rock-e-feller;
Future looks real sweet
On the donkey's side of the street!

An impersonator of Sam Houston Johnson, the former President's "book-writing brother," sang to the tune of "Casey Jones":

Come all you chillun, I will document
A story 'bout a brave President;
LBJ, that's mah brother's name;
Since I boarded in the White House, life just ain't the same.

The pee-pul called Lyndon in sixty-four,
He kissed his wife at the ranch house door,
Mounted to the platform with his program in his hand,
And he rode that big consensus to the Promised Land.

"Larry O'Brien," back again as Democratic chairman and having trouble raising money to make up the Democratic deficit, appeared as a mendicant with a large tin cup and sang a parody on "Bringing in the Sheaves."

Beggars can't be choosers,
When they do, they're losers;
(We're) sticking to the old faith,
Bringing in the sheaves.

Then, to typify the problems of pollution, on to the stage came a chimney sweep, a sewer worker, a street cleaner, a man in a gas mask, and a man with a garbage can, followed briskly by an impersonator of Edmund Muskie as the plumed White Knight. To the tune of "Chloe," Muskie sang:

Muskie! . . .
Muskie! . . .
Hear them calling—I sure can;
Let's quit stalling,
I'm your man.
Muskie! . . .
Muskie! . . .
The party's broke, I don't care;
I'll make my campaign on bad air.

Through the smoke and smog,
I want to go where it's at!
One big monologue,
Pollution will see to that!
Though Nixon is trying to make votes on that score,
My plan's the better one—
Spend ten billion more!
Call me Mister Clean, Bon Ami of seventy-two!
I am re-ally too good—to be true!
Our en-vir'n-ment dusky
Is just made for Muskie,
I see vic-to-ry,
Although it's a murky view.

Steele then introduced Muskie, the 1968 running mate of Hubert Humphrey, as the Democratic speaker, describing him as "the man who anticipated that ecology would be a major issue of the 1970s before the Republicans could even pronounce it."

"When the Gridiron Club says, 'We would like to have you for our speaker this year,' said Muskie, "it's like a cannibal saying to the missionary, 'We would like to have you for dinner this week.'"

The evening, he said, had reminded him of the Coliseum in ancient Rome. "The only difference," he said, "is in those days, the senators watched while the Christians were fed to the lions. It's great fun tonight—for the Christians."

But nevertheless he was delighted to be there, and one reason was that he received "very few invitations to address a Republican audience.

"Also," he continued, "this is a unique opportunity to speak to a group of newspapermen, without their constantly interrupting. Only the Vice President seems to be able to silence them altogether."

He cautioned the audience against selling the Democratic party short.

"The donkey," he said, "is an admirable animal. He is stubborn, patient, tenacious, long-lived—and, as you may have observed, long-winded."

Of course, the Democrats had problems, he admitted. But they would have fewer of them "if, in 1972, we can put one of them in the White House."

"Now, solely in the interest of my party, I find myself, from time to time, thinking of 1972. . . .

"I have prepared a program of action, a set of principles to guide us," Muskie said, and I have given a memo to our party's chairman, Larry O'Brien.

"*First:* We will adopt a Democratic no-knock policy. Our campaign must be conducted with dignity, and on the highest ethical plane, except in certain special circumstances.
"*Second:* Campaign contributions will be invited, but high pressure methods will not be used, except on weekdays. . . .
"*Third:* No contribution will be accepted from any person or organization suspected of ulterior motives, unless the contribution is very large, indeed."

Then he turned to the Republicans. "They have had much anguish this year with three major problems: inflation, the war in Vietnam, and what to say on Lincoln's Birthday."

"How about inflation?" he asked. "The Republicans say they have a program for controlling inflation, and they talk at length of preventing a recession, but when all is said and done—much has been said.

"In the 1920's, it took the Republicans *eight* years to substitute recession for prosperity. Now they have learned to do it in *one.*

"I don't mind the Nixon team passing the buck—but every time it goes through their fingers, it's worth ten cents less."

About Vice President Agnew, Muskie had but "one comment.

"According to the Constitution of the United States, Vice President Agnew has an inalienable right to talk. That may be; the United States has a Constitution that can stand it—but mine cannot."

Down South, he said, the situation had changed.

"A young lawyer friend of mine in Maine was interested in locating in the South. He wrote a friend in Alabama, who replied, 'If you are an honest lawyer, you will have no competition. If you are a Democrat, the game laws will protect you.'"

Picking up the phrase of Daniel Moynihan's in a memorandum to the President, Muskie said he had been fascinated with the new expression the Republicans had given to the nation: "benign neglect."

"I would define it," he said, "as a bold, new program of dynamic apathy."

Then he described benign neglect in the terms used by a

farmer in Maine: "If you stood on a bridge and watched a man drown, and you did nothing—that is 'neglect.'

"But, if, as you were watching, you smiled, that is 'benign neglect.' "

Striking out at Attorney General Mitchell, who was to follow him as the Republican speaker, Muskie commented that this was an "interesting pairing," because "our jobs appear to be quite complementary.

"For instance," he said, "he suggests Supreme Court justices—then I vote against them.

"We also constitute a fair balance on construing the Constitution, that noble document created by our Founding Fathers.

"He interprets it *his* way and I interpret it *their* way.

"I do this despite the risk of being charged with being guilty of 'instant analysis.'

"Although the attorney general was born in Detroit, he grew up on a farm in New York State.

"He can plow a furrow, shoe a horse and milk a cow. Later this evening the Gridiron Club is going to give him the chance to see if he can also lay an egg."

Seriously, Muskie said that he listened to many questions from Americans of all descriptions, and increasingly he was struck by their frustration. Most Americans, he said, wanted to build "a whole country and not a divided one," and most Americans who disapprove of present policies and conditions "do so because they love their country and want to improve it. . . .

"It has been said: 'The essential ingredient in a democracy is the identification, the instinctual trust that flows in thousands of minute and invisible currents through a society. It is this that makes a man feel that he belongs, that allows him to live at ease with his fellows without having to be watchful, competitive and tough.'

"That ingredient is threatened today.

"That threat poses a challenge to our political leadership and to the news media.

"We who have been entrusted with the responsibility of leadership must do our best to 'heal.'

"You [speaking to the newsmen] must do your best to inform and enlighten—in the critical, analytical, comprehensive, unintimidated way which is your best tradition." [5]

Senator Muskie's speech was followed by the guest skit, ending with the stand-up of the seven members of the Supreme

Court who were present, and by a brief speech by Chief Justice
Warren Burger.

The scene for the Republican skit was a football locker room,
with an impersonator of Representative Rogers C. B. Morton,
chairman of the Republican National Committee, singing, "We
always call him Mr. Touchdown." Then the coach introduced an
impersonator of the Reverend Billy Graham, "our friendly
neighborhood chaplain," who was a guest at the dinner and who
had frequently conducted Sunday morning church services at the
White House. In a rewording of "The Little Brown Church in the
Vale," Graham sang:

> There's a church in the East Room of the White House,
> A love-ly Establishment shrine.
> I give briefings Sunday at the Whi-ite House;
> They're on pol-i-cy matters divine.
>
> Here I help any high-ranking sin-ner.
> I slip him my switch-hitting prayer.
> And if that doesn't make him a wi-inner—
> Well, you can't win 'em all—Way Up There!

Among the others at the Republican team rally were "Ralph
Nader, the uncrowned king of General Motors," and three of his
raiders. "Labor Secretary George P. Shultz" assured the crowd
that he hadn't come to take over the government, "not yet—not
until it makes a profit." In a Gilbert and Sullivan parody,
"Nader" sang:

> I'm Captain Nader of the Raiding Crew,
> And a right good Captain too!
> I'm exceedingly adroit at need-ling Detroit—
> I know just how to turn the screw.

But it remained for "Robert Finch," secretary of health, education and welfare, to bring up the so-called "southern strategy,"
which was to be the focus of the Nixon-Agnew act that closed the
dinner. He sang, to the tune of "A Dixie Melody":

> Rock-a-bye the voters with a southern strategy;
> Don't you fuss; we won't bus children in ol' Dixie!
> We'll put George Wallace in decline
> Below the Mason-Dixon line.
> We'll help you save the nation
> From things like civil rights and inte-gra-tion!
> Weep no more, John Stennis!
> We'll pack that court for sure.

We will fight for voting rights—
To keep them white and pure!
A zillion Southern votes we will deliver;
Move Washington down on the Swanee River!
Rock-a-bye with Ol' Massa Nixon and his Dixie strategy!

March 1970, was a period of economic decline and an impersonator of Arthur Burns, chairman of the Federal Reserve Board, told them all how the economic program worked.

There's no business like slow business,
New-low business is swell;
Let's cool off this fever of employment,
Let's cut back to nineteen twenty-nine!
Daily bread's a low form of enjoyment—
If you get laid off—
Try not to dine!

There's no business like slow business,
No-dough business is swell!
When the market indices drop through the floor,
We boost the bank rate
A little more!
Ever-rising profits are a bloody bore,
Say farewell to your cash—
Let's get on with the Crash!

The nomination of Judge Clement Haynsworth to the Supreme Court had already been refused confirmation by the Senate, and Judge G. Harrold Carswell's name was before the Senate at the time of the dinner and was under heavy attack. "Carswell" sang:

Nobody knows the trouble I've seen,
Nobody knows but Haynsworth.

An impersonator of Secretary of State William P. Rogers, who was just back from a trip abroad in which he had been trying to promote disarmament agreements, came on the stage at this point along with a couple of minor State Department officials, and described his activities:

Seventy-six jet planes for the Libyans,
With a hundred and ten from us for Dayan.
To be followed by still more jets
From the friendly Soviets;
That's our new disarmamental plan!

The team's coach thought that about wrapped it up for this

season, but, ah, they had forgotten about "our friendly security officer, Attorney General John Mitchell." His wife Martha Mitchell had already created considerable consternation in Washington by her midnight telephone calls to newspaper friends, and "Mitchell" sang:

> I'm an ordinary man who desires nothing more
> Than just the ordinary chance to practice justice as he likes,
> And rule precisely as he wants.
> A kindly man am I, of no eccentric whim,
> Who likes to time a clerk, at his work—
> Keeping things tight and well to the right of him.
> Just a law-and-order man.
>
> But—let a woman in your life,
> And your serenity is through,
> For, whatever you preferred,
> She's become a household word;
> And the columnists are noting
> She's been busy quoting you.
>
> Oh, let a woman in your life
> And she will make you seem a dunce.
> You play soft on civil rights:
> She'll say something else that bites.
> Moratoriums are trouble
> That with her help seems to double
> All at once.

That closed the skit, and Mitchell was introduced by Steele as "a man who puffs unperturbably on his pipe while some of the hottest controversies in Washington swirl about his head."

Mitchell took it all in good grace and told the Gridiron members and guests that "we shall always remember the generous attention you have paid to both the Mitchells since we came to Washington. . . . However, any time you gentlemen are in a mood to indulge in some of that 'benign neglect' we've been hearing about, it will be all right with the Mitchells if you send a little our way."

He had been criticized by liberals for authorizing the use of wiretapping on occasion, and he told the Gridiron Club that "your privacy tonight is absolutely guaranteed. Purely as a precaution, however, I do suggest that, if you have anything really confidential to say at the dinner table, don't speak too close to the salt shakers."

He said that he wanted to speak candidly about his work as

attorney general. He'd been called a lot of things, but, he said, "I can point with the most pride to the role I have played in helping the President hold the Supreme Court down to eight members."

"At least we can't be charged with court-packing—by 1973, we may be down to five."

Remarking that politics was not off limits at Gridiron dinners, Mitchell said that he was proud to share the platform "with the distinguished Democratic spokesman, Senator Muskie.

"I bring Republican greetings to him and his Democratic colleagues, and I congratulate them on the good news that Larry O'Brien has become their national chairman.

"This is an important step as, under the rules of OEO, any organization making application for a poverty grant must have a chief executive to sign the forms. . . .

"And now, Senator, for those eggs.

"Senator Muskie, if you find yourself at the head of the Democratic ticket, may I offer a suggestion or two from our own experience—a few trade secrets, if you will.

"First, every campaign needs a good slogan. We had one in 1968 which you might find attractive and even useful. Say it early and say it often: 'If I am elected President—I promise you—there will be a new attorney general of the United States.'

"And, Senator, if you do make that pledge, and if by any chance you are elected, that would be one campaign promise I implore you to keep.

"Second, television is extremely important, but you have to use it right. Concentrate all your TV programs in the key states where the votes are. That's what we did—and that's how we carried New York, Massachusetts, Pennsylvania, Michigan, and Texas. [They had lost all these states.]

"Finally, a suggestion to you personally. If you ever hope to become a national figure in the Democratic party, you have got to get out of a Republican state like Maine. Senator Muskie, why don't you try moving to New York?"

In a brief, serious closing, Mitchell said he would like to express "a conviction that I feel most deeply: that everyone in this room, including all those on the dais and both sides of the aisle, are equal, truly equal, in their devotion to our American liberties, to our right to exercise them and our duty to protect them.

"And so, in the spirit of reciprocity, may I close with this promise: 'If you'll stop bugging me, I'll stop bugging you.'

"Now I must take my leave—Ramsey Clark has promised to walk me safely back to the Watergate [his Washington residence]."[6]

Mitchell's speech was warmly received, and he proved that despite his farm boy background, as a speaker he didn't lay an egg.

Finally, President Nixon and Vice President Agnew put on their extraordinary piano skit. It was Nixon's last appearance, as President, at a Gridiron dinner.

The Gridiron files contain a memorandum by President Jack Steele about the origin of the famous act. Steele said that at the after-dinner reception in the Wilson-Cowles suite in 1969, the President had told him that he would like to do something special at the next Gridiron dinner. When Steele went to invite the President in January 1970, to the March dinner, he reminded him of his remarks of the previous March and suggested that, since Gridiron dinners are heavily planned and scheduled right down to the minute, it would be of great aid to them if they could know in advance what the President had in mind.

Nixon told him to go ahead and plan the dinner in the usual way and that he would prefer to do whatever developed at the end of the dinner in response to the toast. He revealed nothing further.

Steele had learned from the White House early in the week before the dinner that the President wanted to visit some of the predinner receptions, and the next word he had was a call from the White House at 5:00 P.M. on Saturday, the day of the dinner, from Dwight Chapin, a White House aide, who requested that they have two grand pianos on the stage for Nixon and Agnew at the end of the dinner, plus microphones. He said the President had asked this be kept as secret as possible, and that he would fill Steele in on the details after he arrived at the dinner.

The Statler Hilton Hotel didn't have two grand pianos available, so they had to settle hurriedly for two uprights.

During the dinner, President Nixon told Steele a bit more of what he wanted, and they discussed the techniques. The floor manager was called to the head table, spotlight operators were alerted, and it was decided that before the toast to the President was proposed, he would leave the head table and wait behind the screen of greenery to the right of the stage, and that Agnew would be going to the same spot, so that he would be waiting at the foot of the ramp when the President summoned him.

All Nixon told Steele about the act was that they would wind it up by playing "God Bless America," and he hoped the guests would join in singing it, and that Steele might have to invite them to do so over the sound system.

The rest of the story can be told in Steele's own words:

"When I saw that coffee had been served, I suggested to the President it was time for him to leave the head table. I waited about half a minute and then signaled the Vice President to follow.

"Then I signaled for the fanfare. As I started proposing the toast, I noticed the President starting up the stage ramp. He was delayed slightly because members of the chorus had gathered around the bottom of the ramp, so I tried to slow down the toast to give him time to reach the stage.

"It may have been imagination, but I thought there was a buzz of puzzlement from the guests when they noticed the President was not in his seat after the toast. But it quickly stopped as the President's voice came over the mike saying he would respond from the stage, and all heads turned in that direction. . . .

"Secretary of State Rogers, who was not aware of the plans, told me later that Soviet Ambassador Dobrynin, when he saw Nixon leave the head table, asked where the President was going. Rogers replied that he undoubtedly was going to the men's room. When Dobrynin saw Agnew also leave, he turned to Rogers and asked, 'Is it the custom in your country, when the President goes to the men's room the Vice President has to accompany him?' "[7]

• • •

At the March dinner, Women's Liberation organizations had picketed the hotel, demanding admission to the dinner and admission to membership in the Gridiron Club. On November 21 the Gridiron Club held a dinner at The Greenbrier in White Sulphur Springs, West Virginia, at which the principal guests were Secretary of State Rogers and Governor Arch B. Moore, Jr. of West Virginia, and the two independents in the United States Senate, Harry F. Byrd, Jr. and James L. Buckley.

Steele took note of the "revolutionary" fact that a large number of women, including wives of guests and Gridiron members, were invited to this dinner. He said the club was honored that the ladies were willing "to eat, drink and be merry with mere men in a spirit of fraternity and equality," and added that

"we hope that, when you take over this club along with everything else, someday you'll invite us back."

But these were revolutionary times also for politicians. In
1970 President Nixon had campaigned extensively for the election of Republicans to Congress, without success, and Steele
quipped of the President, "In 1960 he campaigned in all fifty
states and lost. In 1970 he achieved the same result by campaigning in only twenty-three states."

As for the Democrats, he thought they might have gloated a
little too much about the reelection of all their Presidential hopefuls.

"With Muskie, Humphrey, Kennedy, McGovern and all the
other candidates, the Senate's sessions for the next two years may
be like a continuous TV rerun of the 1968 Chicago convention."

There were four speakers: Senators Byrd and Buckley and
two women members of the House, Martha W. Griffiths, Democrat of Michigan and sponsor of an equal rights amendment, and
Margaret Heckler, Republican of Massachusetts, who had won
former Speaker Martin's old seat.

Byrd commented that it was "nice of you in the Gridiron
Club" to invite him to this party.

"I haven't had much to do with parties this year," he said. "I
have been debating what I should do about party affiliation. But I
cannot decide with whom I have the greater rapport—Ted Kennedy or Jack Javits."[8]

Mrs. Griffiths congratulated the club on "shattering your
solid male tradition of speakers" and gibed her colleagues in the
Congress a bit by telling the story of an American tourist who
had come to Washington and finally looked down on Congress
from the gallery. She claimed to have heard a bright young page
explaining to her, "But, madam, these are the winners. You
should see the losers."[9]

There was one music skit at this dinner, featuring two songs.
The first was the chorus singing to the ladies:

Hello Darlings, well, Hello Darlings,
It's so nice to have you here to see our show.
No groc'ry shops, darling; no dust mops, darling,
Time for sing-in', time for swing'in in the Grid-ir'n glow.

Then an impersonator of Martha Mitchell sang:

I'm just a gal who can't keep still,
Talkin's my favorite sport;

I always say such outrageous things—
Things that I hadn't ort.

• • •

The March 13, 1971 dinner was an unusual one in several ways. It was the first one in which a group of unhappy women who called themselves "Journalists for Professional Equality" made a serious effort to disrupt the dinner.

It was the first annual that President Nixon did not attend since his election to the Presidency. His relations with the Washington press corps were already strained, and while he did not attribute his absence to this, most members believed that if he wanted to come he could have arranged it, since the invitation had been given months in advance.

It was also the dinner at which Spiro Agnew pulled out a bow and arrow to shoot at CBS, and the one at which a rousing demonstration was given to the first three prisoners of war repatriated from North Vietnam.

The Gridiron president that year was Jack Bell, political writer for the Gannett newspapers, who quipped at the outset that "if anyone thinks for a minute that he knows what the White House crowd is up to—he has it timed about right.

"We have been told time and again," he said, "what the administration stands for. The trouble is that we don't know what it won't stand for.

"Mr. Nixon says the economy is sound as a dollar," he continued. "No wonder everybody's scared."

Of the Democrats he commented that "Larry O'Brien is taking a nonmemory course to help forget that $9 million debt [from the '68 campaign]. Larry wants equal time on TV. What he needs more is an equal chance at the fat cats."

For the opener, the chorus was divided into two groups, Republicans and Democrats, and both sang about the Nixon administration's "New American Revolution," to the rousing anthem from the French Revolution, "The Marseillaise."

Republicans:
Come on and join our rev-o-lu-u-tion
Dick Nixon calls you out of bed.
With for-ward thrust and great el-o-cu-tion
The fed-'ral mon-ster we will be-head.
Oh, let the streets run with ink that is red!
We will re-store all pow'r to the pee-pul,

John May-nard Keynes, we'll ne'er for-sake.
The Dem-o-crats may all eat cake,
Rev-'nue sharing—shout it from each stee-pul.

Chorus:

To arms, Re-pub-li-cans!
We're pro-le-tar-i-ans,
Fight on, fight on,
Go marching through
To *win* in sev'n-ty two!

Democrats:

Don't let them steal the re-vo-lu-u-tion
From un-der our poor par-ty's nose.
The public debt is our in-sti-tu-tion,
With give-a-ways the voters we ca-joled,
The newest Nix-on is just like the old!
The New Fron-tier and Great So-o-ci-e-ty,
In-fla-tion curbed by spend-i-ing more.
We start-ed and we'll stop the war,
Ne-ver guil-ty of an im-propri-e-ty.

Chorus:

Stand fast, ye Dem-o-crats!
Put on your hard-est hats,
Fight on, fight on,
Go march-ing through
To *win* in sev'n-ty two!

The first skit in the dinner was the club's reply to the efforts of women journalists to gain admission to the club and to the dinner.

While there had been sporadic picketing before, this year the women went all-out for admission to the club.

They had enlisted the support of the American Newspaper Guild, and letters were sent to the President and Mrs. Nixon, to members of the cabinet, the Supreme Court, and various other distinguished individuals, urging them not to attend the dinner.

President Nixon had already declined his invitation before their campaign started. Elsewhere, their pressure also seemed to have had little effect, because there were only a very few accept-ances withdrawn that year.

Most notable of those to respond was Senator George McGovern, described by John S. Knight as "that shining example of knight-errantry,"[10] who had previously accepted an invitation but withdrew it after the protest.

His action led Senate Minority Leader Hugh Scott to comment, "Anybody that scared of Women's Lib should stay away from all-male functions. I like Women's Lib, but I'm not scared of any woman, except my wife."[11]

The Gridiron Club replied in its own manner, through a skit with an assorted list of characters, beginning with Adam and Eve. Lucian Warren, from the stage, noted that from time to time Women's Lib "pops up in the news."

"In a spirit of levity, we'd like to present a more or less historical version of Women's Lib. It all started in the Garden of Eden."

The curtain opened on the garden with a spotlight on Adam and Eve, and the general tenor of it was immediately evident.

"You're so smart, Eve," said Adam. "See what you can make out of this." He handed her an oversized rib.

"Don't you rib me, Adam," Eve shouted, as she whacked him over the head with it.

He fell to the floor. She picked an apple, pressed one foot on Adam's prostrate body, and said, "The devil made me do that."

There were similar quick stage flashes involving Joan of Arc, Betsy Ross, *Mr*. Carrie Nation, and finally, Martha Mitchell, who was on the hot line to Moscow, talking with Madame Kosygin.

"Martha" suddenly interrupted her conversation to ask, "What's that clickety-clack on the phone?"

She pulled aside the curtain, showing "John Mitchell" smoking his pipe and wearing earphones, with elaborate wiretapping apparatus fastened on Martha's phone line.

"Quit bugging me, John Mitchell," she yelled. "How many times have I told you that wire taps are for Democrats only?"

"Gentlemen, if there's a moral here," said Lucian Warren, "it's *lib* and *let lib*."

The curtain closed and the orchestra swung into "I Want a Girl Just Like the Girl that Married Dear Old Dad."

This bit of horseplay about the Women's Libbers, who were picketing in large numbers outside the hotel that night, was followed by the usual initiation and inauguration, and then by a guest skit and the diplomatic and Supreme Court stand-ups.

Alf M. Landon, 1936 Republican candidate for President, Thomas E. Dewey, 1940 and 1944 candidate, who was to die suddenly three days later, the ambassadors of the Soviet Union, Great Britain and several other countries, and all the justices of the Supreme Court except one were present. Chief Justice Burger made a very pleasant and gracious response to the stand-up.

The Democratic skit took on a Louisiana hayride atmosphere, with various Democratic characters lounging around the central hay wagon and deciding that what they needed was youth.

An impersonator of Larry O'Brien put it in song:

Hello, young voters, wherever you are.
Right on!—you chicks and you cats.
Please make our party your permanent pad.
Groove with the Democrats.

Our sideburns are long and we're wearing wide ties;
We're with it, believe it or not.
We're ending the draft, and we're building communes,
And we'll even legalize pot!

Turn on! Young voters, just look at our dudes;
Hubert and Teddy and Ed;
And George and then Harold and Birch and lots more—
Our party's moving ahead.
Old Left and New Left all make the scene,
Who says this party is dead?

Some of the "younger" members of this youth movement, like "Averell Harriman" and "Senator Ellender," actually one of the older Senate members, met with some scorn from "Russell Long." "I ain't going on nothing but a little old Louisiana Hayride. Meet my Louisiana friends," he said as he introduced them and triumphantly announced that "we run Congress."

Harriman scornfully denounced them as "the Crawfish Mafia."

Senator Ellender sang:

Medicare we don't need,
We're a durable breed
'Cause we're young at heart.

We won't get too senile
To run Congress in style,
And we'll rule a long while
On both sides of the aisle.

An impersonator of George McGovern was costumed in a long nightgown and nightcap and carried a candle. He came on the stage sleepwalking.

But someone commented that he wasn't really sleeping, "He just dreams all day—about possibilities."

McGovern sang:

It's impossible
Without me to lead the way,
It's just impossible.

We must throw off
All repression,
Law and Order's
An obsession.
Constitution-al
Objections never cease,
They're just impossible.

Can the party
Keep from rushing to my door?
It's just impossible.

And, tomorrow,
When it's nomination time,
Somehow I'll get it—
I would sell my very soul and not regret it.
For to live without that job
Is just impossible.

No Democratic skit in those days would have been complete without former President Johnson and Hubert Humphrey. So an impersonator of LBJ, costumed as a rich Texas rancher, accompanied by "Hubert Humphrey," his wrangler, appeared, and LBJ observed that the way things look around here, "they gonna need us again." Then he sang a new version of "I Did It My Way."

They say I blew the game
And that I wrecked your dreams of vict'ry. . . .

Yes, there were times all over town
When Nervous Nellies were hunkered down,
But everytime I faced your doubt
I bit the bullet 'n spit it out.
I took it all 'n I stood tall,
And I did it my way.

The Arkansas pair, "Senator J. William Fulbright," chairman of the Foreign Relations Committee, and "Martha Mitchell," came on stage. Fulbright sang:

She's just a lit-tle gal from Lit-tle Rock
And no one had e-ver heard her name,
Till she cornered me on the phone one night,

And after she taught me left from right
I knew I would never be the same.

Martha:

So one time after midnight
I put in that call to Fulbright,
Though I kept it a secret from my mate—
I holl-ered at him that I don't like war
But I didn't stop there, I said much more.

He's the one who done us wrong.

This was followed by "Muskie," who sang, somewhat prophetically, to the tune of "Get Me to the Church on Time":

Let's hold the e-lection in the morning,
This kind of foresight is no crime;
Before you know it
I just might blow it,
So open up the polls—
Open up the polls,
For *my* sake, open up the polls in time.

The skit closed with a song by an impersonator of Edward M. Kennedy, who had been deposed as majority whip by Senator Robert Byrd of West Virginia. One of the arguments against Kennedy was that he had been away so much and had missed so many roll calls, which in the Senate are always signaled by bells ringing throughout all committee rooms and senators' offices.

In a parody of "Till There Was You," Kennedy sang:

There were bells, on the hill,
But I never heard them ringing.
No, I never heard them at all
Till I was through!

There were friends, on the fly,
But I never saw them winging.
No, I never saw them at all
Till I was through.

There'll be love, all around,
Handsome Ted will set them swinging,
And the Senate won't count at all
When I get through.

Bell introduced Kennedy as "an avowed noncandidate for the Democratic Presidential nomination," and he spoke for the Democratic party.

Kennedy began by proclaiming his regard for Jack Bell and saying that the Gridiron Club had "realized long ago something that many of us have realized only lately—that the best President is a one-term President.

"We are disappointed, of course," he said, "that President Nixon couldn't be with us tonight. But we understand that he had an important previous engagement at the Bijou Theater in Key Biscayne. It's the last night he can see *Patton*—for the forty-third time."

Referring to his Senate contest with Senator Byrd, he noted that Jack Bell had invited him to this dinner over a year ago and had said at the time that it would be "appropriate for the majority whip to attend.

"So I hope Senator Byrd is with us as well," Kennedy said. "I want to assure you, I have nothing against the man who beat me in that whip fight, Bobby Byrd. But you have to admit, he wouldn't even have been elected to the Senate if he hadn't run for office on the strength of a famous name.

"I want to take this opportunity to thank the twenty-eight Democratic senators who pledged to vote for me for whip—and especially the twenty-four who actually did.

"According to a story in the *Washington Post*, the Secret Service says I receive more anonymous threatening letters than anyone else on Capitol Hill. It wasn't until January that I realized most of them came from my colleagues in the Senate."

Kennedy said he had "some misgivings about attending [the dinner] because of the outspoken opposition from the ladies of the press. I talked to some of my colleagues to see how they were going to handle the situation.

"George McGovern said straight out that the dinner was discriminatory and he wouldn't attend.

"Hubert Humphrey said he'd be pleased as Punch to attend, as long as he could be out in time to do 'Face the Nation,' 'Meet the Press,' and 'Issues and Answers'—and perhaps shake a few hands down at the Greyhound bus station.

"Scoop Jackson said he'd come if he could sit with the Joint Chiefs of Staff. . . .

"When I asked Ed Muskie, he took the longest time to reply. He considered the arguments of the women's group. And then he pondered the prestige of the Gridiron Club. And finally he made his decision: He'd attend, but he'd only stay for half the dinner."

For Senator Robert Dole of Kansas, who was to be the Republican speaker, Kennedy also had a word.

"Bob Dole and I have disagreements from time to time on the issues that confront our nation. But these disagreements are always kept on a professional level.

"I think it is safe to say that, on a personal basis, Bob Dole and I are as close to each other in our line of work as Joe Alsop and Art Buchwald are in yours."

His next gibe was at Secretary of the Treasury John Connally, whom he quoted in a press conference as having said, "When I tell you something today, that does not necessarily mean it will be true ninety days from now."

"I think," said Kennedy, "with that attitude, Secretary Connally can hold any job in this administration. . . .

"I don't want to seem too critical of the administration, but once in a while even its friendliest observers have to stand up and protest. For instance, can you imagine a President of the United States trying to get away with appointing to the Securities and Exchange Commission, in fact to the chairmanship of that commission, a man who has been involved in all kinds of litigation, investigations, and alleged manipulations? Nothing like that has happened sincce 1934, when FDR appointed my father to the chairmanship of the SEC."

Kennedy pointed out that two of his brothers had had the privilege of speaking at Gridiron dinners during their years in public life.

"They counted it an honor to appear before you," he said, "as I do tonight. I share their vision, as do you, of a wondrous land—proud of its strengths, proud of its accomplishments, concerned about its unmet needs and eager, always eager, to challenge the future.

"And I share with all of you the knowledge that the leader of our country, and the men who assist him in his work, bear impossible burdens, and bear them with honor and with grace.

"This evening is set aside to look at our country's leadership in a spirit of high good humor. But none of us ever doubts that the task of leading this vast nation is an awesome one, a task that no man can ever take lightly.

"So we meet in tribute to our country and our leaders, and as we look to the future, I think we all share a goal put down in the words of Aeschylus, words which my brothers used to quote: 'To tame the savageness of man and make gentle the life of the world.' "[12]

The Republican skit was entitled "Revolution in Suburbia."

The scene was a barbecue set-up, with picnic tables and the cast dressed in typical suburban sports clothes. It was described as "really the headquarters of Richard Nixon's New American Revolution which, he tells us, will be 'as profound, as far reaching, as exciting as that first revolution nearly 200 years ago.' "

The first speaking lines were those of "Hugh Scott" and Republican House Leader "Jerry Ford," who carried a bottle of catsup.

"What's that you've got there," said Scott, "catsup?"

"No, red ink," replied Ford. "It's our new Republican victory recipe."

They asked "Herb Klein" how things were going and Klein sang, a parody of "Everything's Coming up Roses":

> Things look great—well, almost,
> Muskie's leading the polls coast to coast,
> In the House, we lost seats,
> Baby, everything's coming up roses.
> We're awash in red ink,
> Balanced budgets have gone down the sink.
> Jobs decline, prices rise,
> Baby, everything's coming up roses.
>
> We're okay, no tin cup.
> We've got no place to go but go up.
> Nixon's swell, Agnew's great,
> Long as he don't orate.
> I take an oath of cred-i-bil-i-tee,
> Baby, everything's coming up roses for the GOP

"Walter J. Hickel" of Alaska, who had been secretary of the interior and had been sacked by Nixon because of a critical letter he wrote, came on the scene as a headless torso, carrying his head tucked under his arm.

Scott commented that the President had warned him to be quiet but he was heedless, and Ford said, "Yes, and now he's headless."

Hickel sang, to the tune of "Raindrops Are Fallin' on My Head":

> Something has happened to my head,
> I qui-et-ly wrote the boss a let-ter, now I'm dead.
> What could I have said; he
> Answered by choppin' off my head
> Just for writin'. . . .

Take some Excedrin if you get thoughts of meddlin'
You, too, can shed
Your one and only head.

There was press comment at the time about the supposed coolness between Secretary of State Rogers and the President's chief foreign adviser, Henry Kissinger. To the tune of "I'll Never Fall in Love Again," an impersonator of Rogers sang:

What do you get when you try to help?
A Kiss-in-ger to steal your thunder,
He's got a rug to sweep you under,
I'll never be in charge again.

A character representing Treasury Secretary John Connally, "a new recruit for the New American Revolution," described his problems in a rewording of "I'm Called Little Buttercup."

He called me to butter up,
Yes, sir, to butter up
Congress and teach them finance.
Their minds I will clutter up,
Then I will butter up,
Show them our deficit dance.

My knowledge financial
Is less than substantial,
In fact, it is all Greek to me.
But what does it matter?
I'll soothe and I'll flatter,
And maybe I'll wind up VP.

The Democrats had been raising indelicate hints about the desirability of retirement for J. Edgar Hoover of the FBI, so "Hoover" was a participant in the skit and he sang:

I'll run the FBI, always.
Be your super spy, always.
G-men all salute,
Or they get the boot,
I'm ab-sol-ute, always, always.

In tribute to his appearance at the dinner for the first time in several years, former Presidential candidate Alf Landon, then eighty-three, "the grand old revolutionary of the Republican Party," was a character in the skit.

He'd come by "to see how my shoot-'em-up boy from Kansas, Senator Bob Dole, is doing as national chairman."

The skit closed with "Vice President Agnew" as a golfer in old-fashioned, baggy plus fours coming on stage with "Dole." Dole was in a cowboy suit with a dog collar around his neck and a leash hanging from it. To the tune of "You Can't Get a Man with a Gun," he sang:

> I am cool, brave and daring—
> This is Checkers' leash I'm wearing,
> My devotion is second to none.
> While there's no way of knowing
> Which direction Nixon's going
> I will fight every foe just as though I did know—
> Ridin' shotgun for Dick is such fun!

Agnew, presented as that "ferocious, fulminating, fireball of the far-flung fairways," closed the skit by singing to "Mack the Knife":

> Politics is
> A rough game, boys,
> But I've never
> Dodged a fight.
> When effete snobs
> Ruled the air, boys,
> Someone had to
> Set things right.
>
> Ah, those were the
> Happy moments,
> When I slashed the
> Eastern press;
> Walter Cronkite
> And the networks
> Quailed before my
> Righteousness.

Dole, the Republican speaker, began by saying that he was glad to be at the dinner because he felt at home, "as most Republicans do, in a place where there are no reporters present. It reminds me of my press conferences."

He noted that "we are competing tonight with the opening of *Hair* at the Kennedy Center.

"This production looks like the National Theater Branch of the McGovern Campaign Headquarters," he said.

"It's great that eighteen-year-olds will have the right to vote; they're really bright. Yesterday I heard a McGovern 'youth leader' order pizza, and when asked if he would like it cut in six or eight pieces, he replied, 'Six—I don't think I could eat eight.' "

He described Henry Kissinger as one of the hardest people to reach at the White House.

"I think Bill Rogers can confirm that. Even my friend Bill Fulbright has trouble. He keeps getting recordings of Lyndon Johnson reciting the Gulf of Tonkin Resolution. . . .

"One of the President's six goals is to make America a healthy nation. He's absolutely dedicated," said Dole, "to finding a cure for the Common Cause.

"Incidentally, the White House is hiring a lot of people these days, but there's one thing they don't need—another Gardner."

For Wilbur Mills, then the powerful chairman of the House Ways and Means Committee, he had this quip: "There's talk that some Democrats want Wilbur Mills to run for President, but Wilbur is reluctant to step down."

He noted a difference between England and the United States: "In England, the Union Jack is the flag they fly. In America, the union jack is what they elect Democrats with."

Of the Democratic candidates for President, he commented that "the press is listing so many Democrat senators as dark horse Presidential candidates that there's a move afoot to rename the Senate the Jockey Club."[13]

Vice President Agnew responded to the toast to the President and said that the President had asked him to express his regrets that he was unable to be there.

"As you know," he continued, "he had to leave for a working vacation in Key Biscayne because Martha Mitchell is using the Oval Office."

Paying his satiric respects to various members present, he said it was always an honor to be with the Supreme Court, "the men who've made it safe to do anything you want in a movie theater as long as you don't pray in school."

Referring to the Gridiron show, he said that they'd had a lot of fun at his expense and that "it's evenings like this that make me miss Baltimore.

"However, in the spirit of complete forgiveness," he said, "I'll be glad to give you a dispassionate analysis of your program. . . .

"I'd like to congratulate that fellow who impersonated me. Really, he was very funny. . . .

"And that was a clever little skit when you had John Connally singing, 'Maybe I will end up VP.' I know it's part of your game of psychological warfare. Dave Broder has explained it to me many times. But even if he hadn't, I wouldn't worry about John Connally replacing me in 1972. Have you ever heard a Texan trying to pronounce 'pusillanimous?'

"And besides, the President's deeply indebted to me. After all, I was the one who recommended Judge Haynsworth, Judge Carswell and Wally Hickel."

He referred to the Rogers song and said he wanted to set the Gridiron Club straight about the respective roles of Rogers and Kissinger.

"The President talks to Secretary Rogers every day at least two or three times. He sees him at least one or two days a week. it just so happens that many foreign policy crises arise at night, and in that case, when that happens—they do arise at night—the Situation Room immediately phones Henry Kissinger, who then nudges the President, who gets up and calls Bill."

He thought they'd been "a little irreverent" with President Nixon's New Revolution and commented that the President had told him just the other day there would be certain hardships "for us who were carrying out that theme.

"And mind you," Agnew said, "I agree with most everything he has proposed for the Second American Revolution. But I'll be damned if I'll take the White House Staff's advice and move my winter headquarters to Valley Forge."

For each of the two previous speakers he had a line.

"I must say that Senator Kennedy was brilliant this evening. Of course, he'll never be as funny as Senator McGovern.

"And my compliments to Senator Dole. He certainly is an outspoken and refreshingly partisan Republican. Who the hell does he think he is—me?"

Agnew closed with comments about his relations with the press, which he had been criticizing so severely.

"Now, I don't have a thing against the media—particularly CBS. I have a forgiving nature. I still tune in Eric Sevareid. And perhaps in a few months I'll even turn on the sound.

"Let me straighten out a couple of my other views about the press.

"For one thing, I thoroughly enjoy Herblock's work. He gives fresh meaning to the expression, 'One word is worth a thousand pictures.'

"Now I'm going to close with just a few tips about sports.

But first I want you to know how grateful I am to the Gridiron Club for a very interesting evening. In fact, I shall thank each of you personally. The FBI has already handed me the address and fingerprints of everyone involved.

"Now for a final word about my golf game. Gentlemen, I'm fed up with all the advice and criticism and kidding. I'm getting advice from everyone. Henry Kissinger says I don't swing enough. Bill Buckley wants me to move more to the right. And George McGovern thinks I should choke up.

"I think this audience ought to know that this will be the last Gridiron—absolutely the last—at which we'll be hearing Agnew golf jokes. Because, as of tomorrow, I intend to give up golf and take up the challenge of another, and older field of American endeavor—despite the objections, I might say, of the President, my family and the National Safety Council . . .

"May I have my weapon please."

A Secret Service man handed Agnew a bow and arrow from behind the table and, as he pointed it toward the stage he said, "Gentlemen, the target please," while the curtains opened, revealing the big CBS monogram. [14]

Vice President Agnew, as he demonstrated so well in this speech, had a great sense of humor and was personally liked by many of the Gridiron members, even though most of them disagreed with his criticisms of the press and the TV.

XXII

Richard M. Nixon

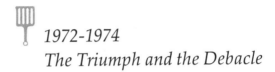

1972-1974
The Triumph and the Debacle

Hubert Humphrey, George McGovern,
and Barry Goldwater Speak

The date of the spring dinner for 1972, originally scheduled for March 11, was changed to April 3, because March 11 was regarded as too close to the time of President Nixon's visit to China in late February, when he was accompanied by many Gridiron members.

The club had responded to the rising pressure on behalf of women journalists by voting to include "a number of prominent women" for invitation to the spring dinner. Sponsors of the resolution told the club that they felt it was unfair to deny dinner invitations to women who were becoming increasingly prominent in government, business and journalism.

The point was made by those opposed that the proposal would create a special class of guests to be invited only by the executive committee, and that it would not quiet the advocates of Women's Liberation.

However, it was the consensus of the club that a dozen or fifteen women guests, prominent in public life, should be included, but the events that were to follow demonstrated the correctness of the view that this would not satisfy the advocates of Women's Lib.

Early in February, the "Journalists for Professional Equality" announced that it had urged all public figures to refuse to attend the April dinner. Some of the women who were invited scornfully declined, among them announced Presidential candidate Shirley Chisholm, who replied to the club in a public statement:

"Gentlemen of the Gridiron Club—guess who's *not* coming to dinner."

Among the men who responded promptly to the request of the Journalists for Professional Equality by declining their invitations were Senators George McGovern and Edmund Muskie. Other women who declined included Senator Margaret Chase Smith of Maine; Coretta King, the widow of the Rev. Dr. Martin Luther King, Jr.; the anthropologist Margaret Mead; and Katharine Graham, publisher of the *Washington Post.* But Alice Roosevelt Longworth and a host of others did attend.

However, the destination did not bother members of the Gridiron Club too much, because the club had been giving dinners since 1885 and would, they thought, still be going long after those who had scorned their invitation were no longer in public life.

Neither President Nixon nor Vice President Agnew came to that dinner, so the ranking guests were Chief Justice Warren Burger and Speaker Carl Albert.

The club created a dinner skit lampooning the action of its critics. Newbold Noyes and Rudolph Kauffmann of the *Washington Star* and three Gridiron members dressed as Women's Libbers came on stage to a big spotlight and a fanfare from the Marine Band. A postman came on and delivered three cards to the "women." They opened the invitations, looked at them for a moment, then tore them up, threw them down, stomped on them and walked angrily offstage.

Noyes and Kauffmann looked at each other in perplexity and then sang a parody of "Hymn to Him" from *My Fair Lady.*

Noyes:
> What in all of heaven can have caused them to decline
> The gracious invitation that we sent?
> What can have distressed them? What can have possessed them?
> I cannot fathom what the sweet things meant!
> Rudy, old friend, why can't a woman be more like a man?

Kauffmann:
> Eh?

Noyes:
> Why can't a woman be more like a man?
> Men are so solid, so thoroughly square,
> Perfectly willing their pleasures to share
> With anything in tails and top hat!
> Why can't a woman—be like that?

The song continued in this tone, with some banter back and forth between Noyes and Kauffmann, and ended with Noyes addressing Representatives Martha Griffiths and Margaret Heckler, who had accepted invitations and were to speak briefly:

> Why can't a woman behave like a man?
> If I were a woman invited tonight
> To brighten the glow of the Gridiron's light,
> Would I start squawking like a record that is broken?
> Would I insist that all my sisters join the spree?
> Would I dismiss myself as nothing but a token?
> Well, why can't a woman—be like me?

The Woman's Libbers, rushed back on the stage through a parted curtain, beat Noyes and Kauffmann over the head with a rolling pin, and pulled them offstage down the ramp.

Mrs. Griffiths' speech in response to this act is not in the Gridiron records, but Mrs. Heckler began hers by saying she was really very glad to be there, "although I do feel a little like Pete McCloskey at Camp David."*

Mayor John Lindsay of New York had bowed out of the race for the Democratic Presidential nomination after some poor showings, which led her to comment, "Despite the fact that John Lindsay has become a wallflower, they're still playing, 'The Sidewalks of New York.' Fiorella LaGuardia proved that an Italian can be mayor, Robert Wagner proved that anybody can be mayor, and John Lindsay proved that nobody can be mayor.

"George McGovern is showing himself as a man of courage. In Catholic wards, he has supported abortion; in VFW meetings, he has called for amnesty; before the B'nai B'rith he supported Sadat; and if he were here tonight, he would announce Gloria Steinem as his running mate."[1]

The skit on the women and the two responses came in the

---

*McCloskey, although a Republican, had become a strong critic of President Nixon.

early part of the dinner, which was opened by the customary speech in the dark by Gridiron President Edgar A. Poe, correspondent of the *New Orleans Times-Picayune*, who began with the non-traditional salutation: "Ladies and Gentlemen."

Busing, he said, was a burning issue.

"Down in the country I come from, some kids are being bused so far, they don't even get to school in time for recess.

"Many Mamas and Papas are so dad-blamed mad, they are keeping the kids at home and paying the teachers to make house calls."

This was a Presidential election year, and he described the candidates as "just as honest as the times will permit.

"George Wallace," he said, "four or more years ago, was promising to stand in the schoolhouse door. This year he says he's merely going to lie down in front of the bus.

"Senator Muskie recently publicly spanked the Gridiron Club for you know what. Nevertheless, I have a kind feeling toward him. He became the first Presidential candidate in history to shed tears over a newspaperman.

"Senator Humphrey, right after the 1968 Presidential election, came to breakfast every morning singing: 'This Nearly Was Mine.'. . .

"Scoop Jackson won't disclose the names of his campaign contributors. He says it would embarrass them. You can't blame him, the way he's been running so far.

"Ted Kennedy says he's not going to the Democratic convention in Miami Beach. Instead, he's going to stop off in Palm Beach, where he will be *all alone*—by the telephone."

But in Washington there was lots going on, according to Poe, and confusion had become "better organized.

"A proposal has been filed with the FCC to merge ITT with the GOP.

"Martha Mitchell is no longer in the cabinet. . . .

"President Nixon is concerned because the Hotel Pierre in New York charged John Connally five dollars for two eggs—while poultrymen are getting only thirty cents a dozen."

Then the chorus marched onstage dressed in white robes and halos, singing to the tune of "When the Saints Go Marching In."

There were umpteen saints in number,
At the start of this great race;

Only two will reach the finish,
Cause the rest won't stand the pace.

Let's begin with Big St. Richard
Who's already knocked off Paul—
Poor St. John wants to supplant him
As the candidate next fall.

But the slogan's "On to Moscow,"
And he's winding down the war,
And we just might have the pleasure
Of his comp'ny four years more.

Now the Democratic party,
As convention time draws near,
Is a trifle disunited;
They got saints right up to here.

There is "Left" George and there's ·
"Right" George,
Hubert, Scoop, John, Sam and Ed;
Wilbur, Gene and Vance and Shirley,
Not to mention young Saint Ted.

They have blown the starting whistle;
And there's only one can win,
On that fateful Day of Judgment
When the saints go marchin' in.

The Democratic problems were such, according to the Gridiron Club, that there had been a last-minute news announcement
that the 1972 convention "has been shifted from Miami to a more
appropriate place in Florida—the newly opened Disney World.
We take you now to the wonderful, Democratic world of Disney,
where Mickey Mouse Larry O'Brien [then chairman of the Democratic National Committee] reigns supreme."

The principals were all Disney characters, and Snow White,
in song, commented on the various candidates in a parody on
"The Real Thing," in which she talked about "teaching our
dwarfs to sing against the GOP." In her song, "Ed Muskie"
started as number one, but now "we wonder, as we watch, if Ed
can really run."

"Humphrey" was back again, "talking up a storm," and
singing:

In George McGovern we have got
A great man for our choir.

He'll get the votes of those who want
A quiet prairie fire.

Minnie Mouse came on the stage, revealed as "Shirley Chisholm," who said she'd "hit the Chisholm trail to the White House and won't be cowed." To the tune of "That's a No-No," she sang:

Yes, my name is Shirley Chisholm;
I am fighting chauvinism.

For the White House I am running,
A black woman could be stunning;
All our other candidates are only so-so.

So give your vote to Shirley Chisholm;
Win with female *terrorism*.
Tokenism, you should know, is a no-no.

The "Red Baron of South Dakota, George McGovern," commented that they were giving him "a lot of flak." To the tune of "Orange Colored Sky," he sang:

I was flying too high
In Florida sunshine,
When out of an orange colored sky,
Flash! Zam! Ol' Al-a-bam!
That other George flew by.

He was followed by "Wallace," who, to the tune of "That Old-Time Religion," sang:

I'll give 'em that old-time religion,
That old-time religion,
That pitch for law and order
And for white soo-pre-ma-cee.

I'll out-cuss 'em on school busin',
An' when I gets through fussin',
The winners will be us'n—
That's good enough for me.

Give 'em that old-time religion,
That old-time religion,
That message that the *pointy* heads
Call Dem-a-go-gue-ry.

"Muskie" sang:

I cried for you,
Now it's your turn to cry over me.

Ev'ry road has its turning;
Bill Loeb left me burning.
I cried for you.

"Kennedy" came on stage dressed as Superman and took all
the other characters by storm, in his song parody written by
Allan Cromley.

Superstar, Superstar.
Who will it be for our Superstar?
Wunderbar, Superstar.
We need a guy who's spectacular.

Where is he—Superstar?
I hear a call for a Lochinvar.
Kennedy, Superstar.
It could be me, and the door's ajar.

Ev'ry time I look around at each candidate
I get such a feelin' that they're all second-rate.
What the party needs is a real heavyweight.
Maybe I should do much more than just meditate.

Chorus:
Superstar. Duperstar.
He'll bring that old magic from afar.
Kennedy Superstar.
He really could be our *Superstar!*

The skit closed with Hubert Humphrey wanting "one more
ride on the merry-go-round."

Look at the worlds I have conquered—
I've won many spins of the wheel.
There's just one thing I have missed out on,
And they ask me, "How does it feel?"
I tell them that I'd trade my eyeteeth
To run for that top spot again—
And notice they really are my teeth—
I'm as good as I was way back then!

Give me one more chance at the midway,
Let me laugh and be gay as a clown,
Give me back the world I remember,
One more ride on the merry-go-round.

I run my campaign by myself now,
There's no LBJ in the wings.
McGovern, Scoop Jackson and Muskie

Cut deep with their arrows and slings.
I think of that old drugstore counter,
Then I promise them pie in the sky;
My eye is on Dick's oval office,
I plead for that big second try.

Give me one more chance at the midway,
Let "*Hail* to the Chief" be the sound;
I am on an old trail I remember,
One more ride on the merry-go-round.

Hubert Humphrey was introduced as the Democratic speaker by the Gridiron president, who presented him as the titular head of the Democratic party, and announced that "there is an old proverb in Washington: 'To make a long story short, don't let Hubert Humphrey tell it.' "

Humphrey commented on his being introduced as titular leader by saying, "I don't know whether any pun was intended by that introduction, given the circumstances surrounding this meeting."

But, in any event, he felt that night, he said, "like Hubert Horatio Hamlet: To be here or not to be here: that was my question. Whether t'would be nobler in the mind to suffer slings and arrows of the picket line *outside*, or take arms against the sea of troubles *inside*, and, by opposing, end them."

W. C. Fields had once been asked, he commented, whether he favored clubs for women, and his classic reply was: "Sure I do, when all other means of persuasion fail."

Gridiron speakers, he said, were supposed to present political jokes.

"Unfortunately," Humphrey said, "most of the political jokes I know are still in office."

Referring to the Republican speaker who was to follow him later, he mentioned the "handsome and distinguished Barry Goldwater" and announced that he had heard he was negotiating a movie contract "with Eighteenth Century Fox."

"Barry and I are good friends," he said, "because we have so much in common. We were both worked over by Lyndon Johnson.

"As a matter of fact," Humphrey continued, "this coming fall while I campaign for the Presidency in all fifty states, Barry, true to his style, and determined to prove his friendship for me, intends to do his campaigning for Richard Nixon in the original thirteen colonies.

"But one thing I'll say about Barry and me. He is clearly on the Republican side and I'm clearly on the Democratic side—now if we could only find out whose side Nixon is on!"

But he wanted to give the President credit.

"He did give the dollar back to its rightful owner—the banks. In fact, he has a charismatic, magical quality about him. He almost made the dollar disappear! . . .

"I won't say that Mr. Nixon hasn't had some success. Look at it this way—at least he kept us out of Northern Ireland."

And he'd just received a late bulletin: "President Nixon just ordered the bombing of Jack Anderson."

As for the Vice President, he assured his audience that it wasn't true that Agnew was opposed to newsmen expressing their views.

"He's only opposed to people reading those views!

"And another silly rumor is that Mr. Agnew is at odds with the young people. Actually, he feels about them as he feels about news commentators—they should be seen and not heard."

The Republicans, Humphrey thought, were irretrievably committed to controls: "Control the press, control the money and control the White House—if only they would control prices too!"

It was obviously "a nostalgic evening" for him, he said, with a gibe first at ITT, which had shredded some papers in its Washington office.

"There is a great deal to be said about the old politics and the old ways. Do you remember those good old days when all that was shredded was wheat?

"When the Republicans came into office they reminded us that a new broom sweeps clean. I just don't think anyone expected the new broom to sweep so much under the rug. . . .

"Do you remember the good old days when all you had to remember was ATT—now the Republicans want to forget ITT.

"And do you remember when we Democrats initiated a war on poverty? That was just before the Republicans started their war on prosperity.

"I remember when you called a plumber after a leak developed. Now you call J. Edgar Hoover, and have Jack Anderson following him.

"And remember when George Wallace was content to just block the door to the schoolhouse? Now he wants to block the door to the White House, again.

"Finally, do you remember Hubert Humphrey before he learned to be brief? Well, don't rely on it!

"Seriously, though, there is vitality in the Democratic party. Every mother's son and daughter that ever wanted to be President is running for the office. And, of course, it's all Nixon's fault—he's made the job so attractive—Key Biscayne, San Clemente, Camp David, Peking, Moscow and an occasional visit to the White House. Now that's living! I tell you, it beats going to the ranch. . . .

"Having been brought up in the belief that anyone can run for the Presidency at least twice, I am now too determined to add a platform plank that recommends a new Presidential election system. You can't blame me for being dissatisfied with the old one."

He ended his speech by making a plea that the Gridiron Club change its constitution by adding, in the section covering membership, after the word "men," the two words "and women."

"You can call it the Poe amendment," he suggested, and he sang, "Two little words—that's all I live for—those two little words."

Former President Johnson, just a few days prior to the dinner had been taken ill, and Humphrey closed his speech by saying:

"Tonight a former President lies ill in a hospital at Charlottesville, Virginia. I ask you to join me in wishing him a full and speedy recovery."[2]

The guest skit has traditionally been done by the secretary and treasurer of the Gridiron Club, and for years Richard L. Wilson, club treasurer has written it. At this dinner, he and Jack Steele asked two of President Nixon's closest campanions to stand, Charles G. ("Bebe") Rebozo and Robert H. Abplanalp.

"Mr. Abplanalp says that Bebe wishes fewer reporters knew how to spell Rebozo," commented Steele.

But though they took a crack at these two, they also balanced it off, "according to the best FCC fairness traditions," by presenting "the Counsel to the Democratic National Committee and, by coincidence, also the *Washington Post*, Mr. Joseph A. Califano."

Even though Nixon and Agnew were not present, the chief justice and seven of the eight associate justices of the Supreme Court were there, and several ambassadors, including those of Great Britain, France and the Soviet Union, all of whom were asked to stand as is customary.

Many a Gridiron member would give his editor's eye teeth to

see the reports of these dinners the Soviet and other Ambassadors send back to their Foreign Offices, because in none of the countries except Australia would such a thing as Gridiron spoofing of top government figures be tolerated.

Since this dinner came five weeks after President Nixon had returned from his historic visit to China, the Republican skit was set among pagoda arches, a plush Oriental villa, and a chorus in Mao suits and caps, with Mao buttons on their tunics.

This skit was introduced by Robert Roth of the *Philadelphia Bulletin*, who noted that election year had come around again and mentioned the "restless and frequently traveling Chief Executive," who had "discovered an even more exotic site for his headquarters."

"We take you now to the location where two of his leading helpers are organizing the 1972 reelection campaign—San Clemente East!"

The curtain opened with impersonators of Attorney General John Mitchell and Chou En-lai on stage.

"And you're John Mitchell," said Chou, "the big boss of the Nixon campaign. They tell me you tighten up everything that's loose—and Henry Kissinger loosens up everything that's tight."

Mitchell replied, "They tell me you really got law 'n order in China."

Chou shot back, "Not much law—but a lot of order."

Mitchell introduced "Bob Haldeman, a member of our Politburo," who was compiling a new campaign manual, and Haldeman sang the Gridiron version of a song from *South Pacific*.

> *Bally hoo* will con you
> In the news, on TV,
> It will lure you into voting
> GOP, GOP!
>
> *Bally hoo* will grab you
> As election day nears,
> We've got speeches and commercials
> Coming out of our ears.
>
> His trips and his dreams,
> Our star-spangled schemes,
> We'll boost his ratings
> Till victory gleams!
>
> *Bally Hoo*'s the game plan

And when our race is done,
Democrats will discover
Mister Nixon's the one.

The dollar had already had its first devaluation, and "Treasury Secretary John Connally" was brought forward by Mitchell to explain to Premier Chou how we'd solved all our money problems. To the tune of "It's De-Lovely," he sang:

Oh! Gold is up, the dollar's down,
Integrity is a worn-out noun—
It's delicious, it's delightful, to de-value!

Though thee-o-retic'lly we're dead broke,
I'll make us rich with a master stroke—
It's delicious, it's delightful, it's deflationist,
It's desirable, it's distinctive, it's deceptive,
It's de-way
To de-value!

An impersonator of Vice President Agnew, was introduced as "our alliterating apostle of agitation," and when the Chinese Premier asked him what was bothering him, Agnew sang, to the tune of "High Noon":

Do not forsake me, Richard Nixon,
On nomination day.
Do not forsake me, oh my leader,
Please——let me stay!
I'm still a better man than Con-lee,
I say the things you cannot say.
I take the high road or the lowly,
Or take the middle,
Play second fiddle,
While I await my turn some day.
I terrify the TV tyrants,
I make the paunchy pundits sore.
And, though you chose me for my brilliance,
I am a fighter,
A fearless fighter,
Don't send me back to Baltimore!

Two men were standing over at a wailing wall. They were identified as "William Buckley," the columnist who didn't want Nixon to go to China, and "Chiang Kai-shek" from Taiwan. Chiang sang:

O'er the hills far away runs that old China Wall,

The symbol of our ancient fame.
And I loved that old wall, where Dick made his call,
'Till he pulled up the stakes to my claim.

Yes, he gave us the old Double Cross.

Buckley: Double Cross.
Chiang: After all we had fought for in vain,
Buckley: For in vain.
Chiang: Chairman Mao's big gain is our loss;
Buckley: Is our loss,
Chiang: Now I'll never rule China again.

"Barry Goldwater" came rushing forward to the center and, after suitable introductory lines, sang:

Try *not* to remember those days of November,
In Sixty-eight, how right his speaking.
Try *not* to remember that kind of November—
Cuz loyalty is what we're seeking.
Please don't remember that far-off November
When he backed Chiang and blasted Peking.
Please *don't* remember, oh, please *don't* remember—
Just sah-wallow, sah-wallow, sah-wallow!

Mitchell assured Chou that he hadn't heard anything yet, that "we've got voters to woo—and in the White House there isn't a better man at pitching woo than Henry Kissinger." "Kissinger" sang in reply:

Summit-time, and the headlines are easy,
Tee-Vee's watchin' and our ratings are high;
Peking was great, now we're heading to Moscow,
So hush, lil'l starlets, don't you cry.

Some of these days, now, you'll find that you're feelin' queasy,
As we toast a Red or we dump an ally;
But just remember, the e-lec-tion's a shoo-in
With Nix-on our champ-ion sum-mit guy!

Summit-time and the dealin' is sleazy,
Those Chinese and the Russians are sly.
But Henry's shrewd and we get what we go for—
So here are the pan-das from Cho-ou-En-lai!

As the chorus finished, a boy panda chased a girl panda up the ramp, both turning somersaults as they reached center stage. Who said Gridironers couldn't perform?

There was considerable press and political comment about the settlement of the ITT antitrust suit, and a reported contribution pledged to the Republican party if its convention were held in San Diego, where ITT's subsidiary, Sheraton, had the leading hotel. The embarrassment later became sufficiently great that the Republicans transferred their convention to Miami.

In the skit, Harold Geneen, chief executive officer of ITT, was impersonated by a soloist who sang a parody of Vincent Youmans's "Tea for Two":

> Picture you upon my knee
> Just GOP and ITT;
> A quid for you,
> A teensie quo for me.
>
> Nobody near us
> To see us or hear us,
> And no secret memos
> To stir up the Demos,
> And presto, you may go
> To Old San Diego
> Free—ee!
>
> Antitrust
> Is so unjust,
> Let's you and me
> Somehow agree
> There'd better be
> A nice consent decree!
>
> Republicans can congregate
> And we'll keep our con-glom-er-ate,
> And don't you see how happy we will be!

The skit ended with the appearance of an impersonator of the Reverend Billy Graham, dressed as a Russian churchman. Chou was very suspicious.

"He looks Russian to me. I don't mind helping Nixon get reelected, but Mao don't 'low no Russian music played round here."

Mitchell assured him this was no Kremlin spy but was the Reverend Billy Graham.

"So why does he look like Rasputin?" asked Chou.

"Because he's orthodox. And he's the chaplain of our Nixon Republican army, with good advice for everybody. Try it! You'll like it!" counseled Mitchell.

Graham sang:

Put your hand in the hand of the man who used the chopsticks,
Just rely on the guy who's a re-jugglin his-to-ry;
Make your pick, stick with Dick and-a
You can share our-a landslide vic-to-ry,
By puttin' your hand in the hand of the boss of the GOP!

Ev'ry time I scan his super bowl plan I start to tremble,
When I see the tricky part where the quarterback has to scramble;
So I say a little prayer to the man upstairs for a winning stra-te-gy
For-a beatin' them Democrats and even Teddy Kennedy.

The Presidential candidate of the Republican party eight years before, Senator Barry Goldwater, was the Republican speaker.

He began with a reference to the ladies picketing outside. "You know, when I walked in here tonight, I was shocked to see a handful of you fellows dressed up as women. . . .

"It's been quite a day for me. I started out with breakfast this morning in the Executive Suite at ITT. They all had their regular breakfast—*shredded* wheat."

Goldwater went on to say that it was good to be among so many old friends.

"Before dinner," he said, "I had a nice chat with Earl Warren. Of course, I had to advise him of his rights first.

"And there was John Tunney. He just got back from his elocution lessons in Hyannisport. . . .

"It's good to see John Mitchell here—you know he's the 'Godfather' of law and order. Poor John. I bet that's the last time he'll ever receive a call from Dita Beard—and ask Martha to take the message.

"I am also happy to see many members of the Supreme Court here tonight. I saw their bus parked outside."

And then, in a delightful jab at the romanticism which some columnists were attributing to Henry Kissinger:

"I wish my son could be here tonight, but as some of you know, he's on his honeymoon. I sure hope that marriage works out. She's a liberal and he's a conservative, and it's murder for a guy whose wife is always wrong.

"Incidentally, there's no truth to the rumor that Henry Kissinger was invited to go along on the honeymoon as a technical adviser."

Then Goldwater remarked that since "we're going to be talking about politics tonight, I think you should know where I stand."

"My political philosophy," he said, "has never changed: considerably to the right of President Nixon and slightly to the left of Vice President Nixon.

"We kid about the President but it's not an easy job. Just look at all the leaks in this administration. The other day I telephoned the White House, got the Oval Room on the President's private line, told one of my best jokes and the only one who laughed was Jack Anderson."

This was the period after the New Hampshire primary had been held, and Presidential primaries in other states were getting hot.

"Of course," said Goldwater, "the primaries are making the big news in the Presidential picture. I'd say the next big one comes on May 23, the Moscow primaries. [The date President Nixon was scheduled to hold his summit conference with Brezhnev.]

"I'll tell you one thing, I'm glad John Lindsay has stopped running. Now he can get back to what he does best—the 'Johnny Carson Show.'

"And speaking of the other candidates, there's Wilbur Mills. I'm afraid he peaked too early.

"Muskie—even while he's slipping, people keep comparing him to Lincoln. I say that's a good comparison. I ought to know; I drive one and it takes forever to get it started, then it stalls a lot, and then it gets overheated. Sometimes, I get so mad at it I could just cry.

"I don't know whether to believe Teddy when he says he's not running for the nomination. I heard the other day that he called Dial-a-Prayer and asked if there were any messages.

"McGovern is coming up and I think it's because the only time he opens his mouth is to change his feet. Speaking about McGovern he and Nixon share one thing in common—they've each gone about as far in politics as they're ever likely to get.

"There's one thing about the Democratic candidates: All of them are self-made men—and this takes a load off the Almighty, saves him a lot of embarrassment. . . .

"A lot of you think Nixon is pretty confident about the election. Believe me, he's concerned. Just the other day, he talked with Billy Graham for an hour, asking advice on what he could do to get a big vote. I don't know what Billy told him, but I do know that at one point Graham turned his head skyward and said, 'Don't just look down—help us.'

"Then, of course, Nelson Rockefeller is promising New York, John Connally is delivering Texas, and Kosygin is guaranteeing the Oregon primary.

"So much for politics. Now about the President's trip to China. . . .

"I'll never forget, when the President announced his trip on TV, he made the most important foreign policy statement in thirty years in a minute and a half. And it took Eric Sevareid twenty minutes to say he was stunned by it. . . .

"But it was a great show. I'll never forget watching on TV while the President, glass in hand, walked around introducing himself to the Chinese. I sure wish he would come over to the Senate and do that some day. . . .

"But Nixon has broken some campaign promises. He said he was going to bring us together. But how can he when he's always waving good-bye?

"Another thing I would like to straighten out is all this hogwash about President Nixon isolating himself. I have *always* been able to get an appointment if I called for one. Of course, I guess it helped a little to have Chou En Lai place the call for me."[3]

The dessert and coffee were served, and the Gridiron members closed the show by having the entire chorus assemble on the stage again, lined up as in the opener, but this time in their white ties and with the saints' gowns but no halos, to sing a parody by Paul Martin on Vincent Youmans' "Great Day":

> There's no easy way,
> Let us close ranks and say:
> We're gonna make it OK.
> We'll end war and strife,
> We'll build a bet-ter life,
> We're gonna have a new day.
> Though e-vents have torn you,
> Some fu-ture morn you
> Will see the dawn.
> Hal-le-lu-jah!
>
> Peace—not far away,
> Lift up your hands and say
> There's gonna be a great day!

In the absence of both the President and the Vice President,

Carl Albert, Speaker of the House, and next in line of succession, was introduced as the final speaker, prior to the customary toast to the President.

• • •

President Nixon's 1972 triumph culminated in his reelection by one of the most overwhelming majorities in the country's history. He failed to carry only Massachusetts and the District of Columbia.

The only other comparable election since the days of James Monroe was President Roosevelt's in 1936, when he carried every state but Maine and Vermont. The debate over how much the Nixon victory was due to his strength and how much to McGovern's weakness will probably never be satisfactorily concluded, but, at any rate, his victory did not carry over to the Congressional elections.

But four months later, at the time of the March 10, 1973 dinner, the President's relations with the press were definitely deteriorating. His relations with Congress were equally unsatisfactory.

Gridiron president Robert Roth of the *Philadelphia Bulletin* opened the dinner by asking the audience to "be quiet, please, and stop asking silly questions."

"And don't take any notes," he continued. "You may be subpoenaed."

There was speculation about what Henry Kissinger would do when his leave of absence from Harvard expired, and Roth thought he might return to Massachusetts, "provided Harvard will grant him amnesty."

He noted that "the President and the Congress have agreed that the country isn't big enough for both of them," and that "it remains only to decide which one is going to get out."

He remarked that the cold war between the press and the White House was beginning to thaw.

"There was a major breakthrough last week," he said, "when the President held a news conference. Most of our press corps prisoners have been returned."

But, on the whole, the outlook was bright, according to Roth. George Meany's detente with the Nixon administration would be complete "as soon as the administration agrees to freeze prices and let wages float." McGovern wasn't mad at anybody "except the press, the administration and the 46,719,133 voters who voted wrong." We were on the threshold of a new Golden Age.

"Those who have many dollars will be *no* better off than those who have few. Neither will be able to buy anything."

The opener was based on the overwhelming election results, which had "left but one pocket of seditious and rebellious resistance—Massachusetts."

"So the Nixon government of national unity," said the announcer, "has sent federal troops to occupy Boston and impose unanimity on the damn-Yankee elitists."

The chorus was divided into two groups, one the triumphant Republicans, carrying a Confederate flag superimposed on a fat-cat elephant wearing a top hat, and the other composed of Hippie-Puritans. To the tune of "Marching through Georgia," the Confederates sang:

> Forty-nine to one we scored a famous victoree,
> We'll preserve the Union for the good old Gee-O-Pee!
> Lib'rals run for cover now from sea to shining sea,
> As we go marching through Boston.
>
> Hurray! Hurrah! Let's make it crystal clear!
> What we—proclaim—all hands had better cheer!
> We've got special remedies for them as ain't sincere,
> As we go marching through Boston.

And the Hippie chorus sang:

> Four more years will do the trick,
> Bring about defection.
> We'll keep saying, "Nix to Dick"
> And win the next election.

The act closed with the Confederates singing:

> Hurrah! Hurrah! For un-an-im-i-tee!
> Like Sherman from Atlanta to the sea
> We'll hang George McGovern from a sour apple tree,
> As we go marching through Boston.

The bitterness of many in the Washington press corps toward the White House was handled in a special skit envisaging a news "pool" system [frequently used by Nixon], under which only selected reporters would cover Nixon's activities. To a tune from *The Music Man*, Newbold Noyes wrote and sang of administration troubles, impersonating White House Press Secretary Ronald Ziegler.

> Well, we got trouble, my friends,
> Right here, I say trouble right here in the White House.

But, just as I say it takes judgment, brains
     and maturity to see the news our way,
I say that any boob can take and shove his nose
     in our affairs,
And I call that cheek—the first big step on the
     road to insubordina . . .

I wanta be perfectly clear.
Would you like to know what kind of
     conversation goes on while they're [the press]
     loafin' around that room?
They're talkin' 'bout Percy, talkin' 'bout Mondale,
     talkin' 'bout Wilbur Mills in seventy-six,
And braggin' all about how they're gonna swamp
     us at the polls with good old Teddy!

Friends, the Eastern press is the Devil's
     playground!
Trouble! Right here in the White House!
With a capital T, and that rhymes with P—
     and that stands for Pool!
We've surely got trouble! Right here in
     the White House!
Gotta figure out a way to send reporters to
     obedience school!

The break-in at Democratic headquarters at the Watergate
had occurred on June 17, 1972, just about nine months before this
dinner. The scene for the Democratic skit was a darkened Republican headquarters, in which a Democratic task force carrying
flashlights was sneaking around trying to reclaim evidence taken
from the Watergate.

As the flashlight was turned on an impersonator of Chicago's
Mayor Daley, the lights came up, and to the theme song from the
TV show "All in the Family," he sang:

Tax and tax and spend and spend,
Reelected without end
Brother we could use a statesman like
Sam Rayburn again.
All we've got is Common Cause,
Women's Libs all burning bras,
From the hard hats no applause,

These are sad days.

George McGovern's long-haired boys,
Acid rock and obscene joys,

Brotherhood and all that noise,

These are sad days.

Meanwhile, impersonators of former Democratic Chairman Lawrence O'Brien and House Speaker Carl Albert had succeeded in opening the safe, but what they found in it, according to Albert, was "a mess worse than a tax reform bill."

Prior to the campaign, the McGovern forces had installed Jean Westwood as chairman of the Democratic National Committee and revised the rules of the convention, introducing quotas for various minorities. This led to a song by her impersonator, based on "Makin' Whoopee":

Another black,
Another youth,
Another broad—
And here's the truth,
Reform is fair, boys,
Each gets a share, boys;
We're makin' quotas.

Picture the perfect party,
Just what it ought to be,
The demo*graphic* party—
One big minority!

As they continued to dig through the debris, O'Brien asked "Sargent Shriver" if he really expected to find anything there.

"Larry, I'll take anything I can find," replied Shriver. "There must be something important here."

Albert: Are you sure you'd know it was important?
Shriver: Sure, if Teddy said so.

As this was going on, "Senator Thomas F. Eagleton" reminisced in song:

Who——stole my job away?
Who——in his unc-tuous way?
Who backed me one-thousand percent?
Then dumped me for Vice President?
Who tore me all to bits?
Who? Don't blame Man-kie-wicz—
Who wears the shoe that fits?
    Who? Who? No one but you!
    (*Points at McGovern*)

An impersonator of Senator Kennedy perched himself upon a stool, as the spotlight picked him up and the stage lights dimmed to darkness.

"To run or not to run," he said. "Play it, Sam."

To the tune of "As Times Goes By," he sang:

It's still the same old story,
A lust for fame and glory,
A taste for flying high.
But still the nagging question comes,
Can I get by?

Wealth and charisma
Might not be enough.
Public reaction
Could be kind of rough;
That my credentials are not quite up to snuff
I surely can't deny.

Ambition could misguide me,
My thoughts confiict inside me;
I cannot prophesy
The answer to that great big question,
Can I get by?

The Democratic searchers in the Republican headquarters came up with "George McGovern's hospital record," which showed that "George was hospitalized three times for impaired hindsight. No wonder he doesn't know what hit him." This was the introduction for a McGovern song, a parody of "They Call the Wind Maria," written by Allan Cromley.

I still remember when last year
Our campaign was on fi-ah;
Wher-'er I went, without a cent,
Kids called me their Messiah.
I preached and preached for de-cen-cy,
And legal mari-juana,
And amnesty, and women's rights,
They called me their bwana.
    Messiah, Messiah,
    And I was the Messiah.
A thousand bucks for everyone,
I should have bid it higher,
And Women's Lib, we sang it well,
Abortions for the choir.

Then McGovern, the Democratic speaker, noted that in the

last election he had opened the door to the Democratic party—and all the Democrats walked out. He admitted that he wanted to run for President in the worst possible way, and that he did, and that he wanted to be President very badly but that now Nixon was doing it for him. Ideas and gibes such as these were spread through the speech, and it went over very well with the Gridiron audience.[4]

However, by agreement between the officers of the Gridiron Club and the author of this book, it has been decided to keep all "current" speeches off the record, and "current" has been defined as since 1972.

At the beginning of the guest skit, James A. Farley, who was attending his fortieth Gridiron dinner, was asked to stand.

Then, in view of subsequent events, there was a startling bit to follow. Richard L. Wilson asked H. R. Haldeman and Dwight Chapin of the White House entourage to rise. Jack Steele turned to Wilson and said, "Now permit me to introduce Mr. Chapin and Mr. Haldeman to a gentleman they will probably have to meet sooner or later—U.S. District Judge John J. Sirica."

The club had some fun with Chief Justice Warren Burger, who had been in the news because while riding the Metroliner between New York and Washington he had revealed some annoyance with the smoking of other passengers.

The curtain opened to show a mock-up of a Metroliner club car, with passengers smoking giant-sized cigars. The conductor came down the aisle, followed by a man wearing a black judicial robe and a white wig, who sang to the melody of "Humoresque":

> Passengers will please refrain
> From puffing stogies on the train.
> The U.S. Constitution tells me so. . . .
> Smoking rights between each station
> I'll outlaw throughout the nation.
> There is no appeal from me, you know.

The scene for the Republican skit was "the court of Royal Richard," with a throne on one side of the stage and a guillotine on the other. The announcer said that 'the landslide of November has produced a monarchy in March." As the curtain opened, the chorus of "serfs" was shouting gaily, "We won! We won! We won!" and a chaplain led them in singing:

> All hail the pow-wer of Nix-on's name!
> Let pink-o pun-dits crawl!
> Hail Nixon! Nixon! Loud and clear!

And he will lo-ove us all!

He'll rule with i-ron four more years!
Let Congress grov'ling fall!
Bring forth the royal di-a-dem
And crown him king of all!

Pretty rough for the Gridiron Club, but it reflected the strong feelings in the Washington newspaper corps.

Impersonators of all the familiar characters, John Ehrlichman, Bob Haldeman, Herbert Klein, Ron Ziegler, were prominent. Klein announced that he had "chanced upon the publicity coup of the century." He carried a sign inscribed "U.S.A." and to the roll of snare drums, he turned it to the opposite side, reading "NIXXON."

"We've changed our name," he proudly proclaimed, "but not our stripes."

There had been quite a few changes in the Executive branch of the government since the election, and the club came up with a new version of "The Whiffenpoof Song." This time it was written by Charles McDowell and sung by an impersonator of Peter G. Peterson, former secretary of commerce.

To the old administration,
To Dick Nixon's first four years,
To the dear old boys our Leader now rejects,
Sing the nincompoops assembled,
Tho' it's hard to sing too well,
For our heads are disconnected from our necks.

At this point, the guillotine dropped, and the song went on:

Yes we signed our resignations
As a mere formality,
But he *took* 'em and replaced us in the fold;
We'll remember Richard Nixon,
How he smiled in days gone by,
As we join old Wally Hickel in the cold.

We're old Nixon sheep who have lost our way:
Baa! Baa! Baa! (*The guillotine fell again.*)
We're little black sheep who have gone astray:
Baa! Baa! Baa!

Bureaucrats suddenly absentee,
Banished for nonconformity;
Lord, have mercy on such as we—
Baa! Baa! Baa! (*More guillotine.*)

Then the good new people stepped forward and sang:

We're *new* Nixon sheep who have *found* our way:
Ja! Ja! Ja!
We're good little sheep who know how to say:
Ja! Ja! Ja!

Sheep of impeccable loyalty,
Wagging our tails obediently,
He has faith in such as we—
Ja! Ja! Ja!

Inflation was becoming a major issue, and the club picked an impersonator of Secretary of Agriculture Earl Butz to express the farmers' joy at rising food prices, in a parody of "On the Banks of the Wabash Far Away," written by Ben Cole, a representative of a newspaper in a heavy agricultural area, the *Indianapolis Star*.

Round and 'round the old in-fla-tion spir'l keeps turn-ing,
And a bag of gro-c'ries costs more ev-ry day;
You may never taste that steak for which you're yearn-ing,
The ad-min-i-stra-tion's phased it all a-way.
For ev-ry-thing you buy you've got to pay more,
And for ev-ry-thing you sell, you're get-tin' less;
The rich are get-tin' rich-er and vice ver-sa,
Our e-con-o-my is real-ly in a mess—
But the price of corn is high a-long the Wa-bash
And old ag-ri-biz is real-ly mak-ing hay;
Through the syc-a-mores the Cad-il-lacs are gleam-ing
And the bankers of the Wa-bash shout hoo-ray!

There was also a song about Vice President Agnew, who was to respond to the toast to the President. Gridiron members sang of "the Agnew man, the hatchet man":

The Agnew man can because he's
    mellowed and he's sweet
And looks so doggone neat.

Then impersonators of Chou En-lai and Ambassador Dobrynin of the Soviet Union entered, and "Secretary of State Rogers" announced that "under the Nixon doctrine, a Commie is man's best friend," whereupon Chou and Dobrynin sang a duet to the tune of "Abdul Abulbul Amir":

The sons of the Dra-gon who rule in Pek-ing
Are in-spired by the say-ings of Mao;
When Dick Nix-on was young, he want-ed us hung,
But we are re-spec-ta-ble now.

At least to some correspondents at that time, Henry Kissinger was perhaps the only hero in government. With a grand Wagnerian fanfare, his impersonator came on stage and sang:

> Riding herd on the world,
> Being global cowboy is fun;
> I will drink two or three to the wonder of me
> And the wonderful things I've done.
>
> *Wunderbar! Wunderbar!*
>
> What a brilliant guy I am—
> What a high riding star—
> All this fame is *Wunderbar!*
> Oh, I'm trusted by Mister Nixon,
>
> All the ladies pine for me;
> And wherever things need fixin'—
> Turn on Tee-Vee—That's where I'll be!
> *Wunderbar! Wunderbar!*
>
> I'm the pride of Un-cle Sam!
> Like a bright, shining star
> I'm your Henry *Wunderbar!*

The skit ended on a pleasant note with an impersonator of George Bush, chairman of the Republican National Committee, and the Republican speaker, who sang that:

> With Nixon as our ruler,
> Here's what we're gonna do—
> Gonna help all the people who will help themselves
> And we'll bring sweet peace to you;
> Yes, we'll bring sweet peace to you!
>
> Singing, *Joy to the world!*
> Nixon's guys and girls!
> Joy to the countries from A to Z,
> Joy to you and me!

The dinner closed with the entire Gridiron chorus back in white tie and tails to sing a parody on John Philip Sousa's "The Stars and Stripes Forever":

> We think that it's time to return
> To an old-fashioned flag-waving finish,
> Three cheers, boys, before we adjourn
> And let's throw in a Hip Hoo Ray.
>
> It won't break your arm to salute
> And to hail Betsy Ross's bright creation,

(At this point an American flag was raised in stage center and spotlighted.)

Take a recess from dispute
So now let's hear it
For the emblem of our
Nation.

Vice President Agnew responded to the toast to the President.

• • •

Gasoline lines were long as a result of the Arab embargo when the 1974 dinner was held on April 6. Inflationary pressures were increasing, the dollar had been devalued a second time in two years. Spiro Agnew had resigned as Vice President, Gerald Ford had been confirmed as his successor, and Congress was hotly attacking President Nixon.

Walter T. Ridder, head of the Washington bureau of the Ridder Publications, was president of the Gridiron Club, and he began his speech with an undisguised gibe at President Nixon, by announcing that at the end of it, "I shall turn the original version over to the National Archives and take a tax deduction of fifteen cents."

Referring to the "turbulent times," he said inflation was so rampant in the land that one aroused citizen had recently told him, "I couldn't even make a down payment on a fried egg."

Our coins, he pointed out, were being cast in aluminum rather than silver, and the number of Latin words on them were being cut back from the traditional *"e pluribus unum"* to *"nolo contendere."*

"But that's in keeping with our times," he said. "Reductions are the order of the day. Why I am informed that here in the District of Columbia school system, children before they are taught to write, are taught to erase."

Former Vice President Agnew was supposed to be writing a novel at that time, and Ridder suggested a dedication for it: "To Elliot L. Richardson, without whose help I would not have had time enough to write this book."

Concerning Gerald Ford, he noted that the Vice President had said repeatedly that he did not intend to run for President in 1976.

"Perhaps I have been around Washington too long," commented Ridder, "but my in-built skepticism tells me that by two years hence Ford will have had a better idea. . . . So, let us proceed, ladies and gentlemen. I do make the announcement that when the lights go on and you discover with horror whom you are sitting next to, the Gridiron Club has mercifully scheduled during the course of this dinner an eighteen minute and seven second conversational gap."

In an ironic opener, introduced by Jerald terHorst, chairman of the music committee, the results of a supposed public opinion survey made by the Gridiron Club were revealed. The chorus was garbed as ordinary folk from assorted walks of life: mechanics, hardhats, farmers, white collar types, housewives, some long-haired youths—and two people wearing barrels and carrying gasoline cans. Two soloists parodied a duet from *Li'l Abner*.

Soloist One:
   Both gasoline and food are short and prices are sky high;
Soloist Two:
   Inflation is no problem when there's nothin' you can buy.
Duet:
   Adversity's the bestest way to strengthen you and I
   And teach us to cut back on our demands.
   The country's in the very best of hands!
Chorus:
   The country's in the very best of hands,
   The best of ha-a-a-a-nds!
   The best of ha-a-a-a-nds!
Soloist One:
   The cabinet's a happy place and loyal to the core;
Soloist Two:
   Instructions to each member read: 'Please use revolving door.'
Duet:
   A real good place to meet some folks you never met before,
   Obedient to the President's commands.
Chorus:
   The country's in the very best of ha-a-a-a-nds!
   The country's in the very best of hands,
   The best of hands, the best of ha-a-a-a-nds!

Immediately afterward, Warren Rogers, chairman of the entertainment committee, did a talk skit in which he explained the economic situation about oil to the audience. One of his solutions was to "subtract sixty-seven million gallons saved by the new method of student travel—streaking."

For seventeen years the Democratic skit had been planned, organized and partially written by Richard L. Wilson. The scene for the one at this dinner was the "Happy Days Truck Stop" on Interstate 76, where, according to the announcer, Edgar A. Poe, "the proprietor 'Mike Mansfield' is having a rap session with his chief waitress, 'Bella Abzug,' and the fry cook, 'Pete Rodino,' and a customer who just likes to hang around truck stops, 'Governor Shapp' of Pennsylvania."*

There was a "big rig with a load of dynamite highballin' down Interstate 76," but before it arrived another truck driver, "George Wallace," came on the stage to sing:

> They're Alabamy bound—
> See Ted and Scoop and Dick come hangin' 'round;
> They know who's got the most persuasive mix,
> Pop 'list tricks,
> Who's got the winning deal for sev'n-ty six!
> Just hear that campaign bell!
> I know they used to give us Holy Hell,
> I'll blitz them pointy-head boys one and all,
> Have a ball,
> 'Cause I am vic-t'ry bound.

> I blocked the school house door—
> But I don't act that way—not any more;
> The Democrats, they like my mod'rate stance,
> Song and dance,
> But I suspect them northern fancy pants.
> So I am riding free;
> It's great to have the big shots courtin' me;
> But I'll just tell the party, short and sweet—
> I'm in the catbird seat.

He was followed by the next truck, which had a fancy French horn that played "Camelot, Camelot, Camelot." An impersonator of Senator Birch Bayh wanted a road map, because "Ted don't know which way he's going." That led to a "Kennedy" song, a parody of "Tie a Yellow Ribbon 'Round the Old Oak Tree."

> As senator, I'm marking time,
> And I'm on this dreary job though in my prime;
> I went to see George Wallace
> Just to share his company;
> I can't imagine what I'd do
> If you still want me,
> If you still want me.

---

*This was a reference to Governor Shapp's visit to a truck stop during the truckers' slowdown in protest against reduced speed limits.

Tie a campaign ribbon 'round our fam-'ly tree;
Down through all these years, they must still want me. . . .

At Cam-o-lot, the question's hot—
Should I save the Democrats, or should I not?
But standing still's not suited
To my style or van'i'tee,
And so I might just have to run;
It comes natch-ur-'lly
For a Ken-ne-dee.

And although the party's cheering, I will
make 'em wait, you see.
Until we tie more ribbons 'round his old fa-am-'ly tree.

An old-fashioned car Klaxon sounded offstage, and Gene Archer, a Gridiron vocalist since 1946, impersonating Senator Sam Ervin, in a Colonel Sanders outfit, entered carrying a gavel. He had big eyebrows which wiggled, and as he entered he declaimed, "When in the course of human events, these truths are held to be self-evident: life, liberty and the pursuit of Richard Nixon."

Ervin then sang a song which is an ideal example of the way most Gridiron songs are written—the collaborative effort of a number of people. At least seven or eight of the Gridiron producers had a hand in this one, which proved to be the big hit of that dinner, not only because of the words but also because of the excellent impersonation of Ervin.

It ain't necessarily so,
It ain't necessarily so—
The things I was li'ble
To pull from the Bible,
They ain't necessarily so.

Now our Constitution is grand—
De bestest ol' book in de land—
De way dat ah quote it
Folks think dat ah wrote it;
Dat's kinda like what I had planned.

Dey loved me as Senator Sam—
Dat wunnerful ol' country ham—
But now Judge Sirica,
That big city slickah,
Done left me no gavel to slam.

Jaworski and Rodino, too—

Dey think what dey got is all true—
De stuff dey's purveyin'
Is what Ah been sayin'
It ain't necessarily new.

Ah grilled Haldeman on TV—
Gave Ehrlichman de third degree—
Mah eyebrows was poppin',
Mah tongue malaproppin',
Yeah! What a publicity spree!

Some say dat mah hearin'
Was jes' interferin'
With more important folks.
But this country lawyer
Knows how to destroy-ya
Wiff Carolina jokes.

Please give back mah hearin's to me—
Day made me a star, don't you see?
A matinee idol
Who spouted de Bible
An' knocked Lucy off the TV.

Chorus:

He's preachin' dis sermon to show
It ain't nessa, ain't nessa, ain't nessa, ain't nessa,
Ain't necessarily so.

At the conclusion, a drummer began his steady beat for the
entry of serious Democratic 1976 dark horses, who appeared as
vaudeville hoofers. "Birch Bayh" called out their names as they
trooped in one by one:

Here's Lloyd Bentsen, a Texas Ranger;
'n Adlai Stevenson, he's no stranger;
'n Reubin Askew, they had him hidden;
'n Dale Bumpers—ya gotta be kiddin'!
'n Wendell Anderson, a Minnesota prize;
'n John Gilligan, cut down to size!
'n Fritz Mondale, the would-be king;
Hubert Humphrey wouldn't do *his* thing!

Then all together they sang:

We're only shad-ows
On the White House av-en-ue;
We're only shad-ows
Even though we try for ballyhoo.

Each day we sell our souls
For headline space;
We watch the polls,
Can't get in the race.
'Cuz we're only shad-ows
Waiting for our big de-but.

It ended with two lines:

We'll dance from the shad-ows—
Maybe wind up as VP!

The next arrival at the truck stop was an impersonator of "the biggest little truck driver on Capitol Hill—Carl Albert." He was pulling a U-Haul trailer. "Mansfield" greeted him, "I like your car. It's a peach." And "Bella Abzug" shouted, "Not a peach. Impeach! Impeach! That's the issue."
"Albert" sang a love song:

The Lord above gave us a Richard Nixon,
On him our party's campaign hopes are pinned. . . .

The Lord gave us an awful burden—
It sends the shivers up and down our spine;
Impeachment is a job cut out for statesmen, *but*
With a little bit of luck,
With a little bit of luck,
He'll take pity on us and resign.

At the time of this dinner, Senator Henry M. Jackson of Washington, an active Democratic Presidential candidate, cognizant of the people's gasoline problems, was attacking the oil companies with much gusto. So, when the big rig loaded with dynamite arrived at the Happy Days Truck Stop, the driver turned out to be "Scoop Jackson." He entered with bandoliers of ammunition on his shoulders, carrying a packet marked TNT, and with hand grenades attached to his belt. Mansfield stepped up and fingered the explosives.
"You know Scoop," he said. "He's got a blast for every purpose. You name it, Scoop'll blow it."
And Jackson sang, to the tune of "Jericho":

Jackson fit the battle of Texaco, Amoco, Sunoco;
Jackson fit 'em fiercely on his TV show,
So they'd all come tumblin' down.
    He talked about the foes of Is-ra-el,
    He told Sadat just where to go;

> There's votes in good old Golda
> And his battle with Texaco.

Fightin' oil and Rooskies is a sure-fire show, voters know, blow by
    blow;
He will sing it like an o-ra-to-ri-o
When détente comes tumblin' down.

> Up to the halls of the Senate
> He called dat oily band;
> Roll back your pric-es, Jackson cried,
> For he could see the promised land.
> De pe-tro-le-um barons began to blow,
> Trumpets began to sound;
> Jackson—commanded the headlines to shout,
> Got his campaign off the ground!

Re-mem-ber . . .
Jackson fit the battle of Texaco, Amoco, all those co's,
De Exxon profits—they grows and grows,
But Scoop, they'll never bring down!

Jackson was introduced as the Democratic speaker.

In the guest skit, Richard L. Wilson asked a group of governors who were present at the dinner to stand, and then introduced to them the man who "may, in fact, know something about some of you already, the Commissioner of Internal Revenue, Mr. Donald C. Alexander."

Jack Steele reported that Governor Daniel J. Evans of Washington, chairman of the Governors Conference, "says that Commissioner Alexander's Internal Revenue Service has indeed been looking into the tax returns of some governors, and has given them the Good Taxpayers Seal of Approval—just as he did for Richard Nixon."

Newbold Noyes of the *Washington Star* did a bit on how a White House press briefing would go "if Noel Coward were President Nixon's press secretary."

> The Watergate mess
> May be something less
> Than great,
> And yet the question that I raise
> Is who keeps it alive these days?
> Who keeps us immersed
> In the endless cursed
> Debate,
> While our reactions grow more bitter,

And we force ourselves to sit a-
round and wait?
Life in Washington
Is not much fun
Alack!
Since certain parties won't get off our leader's back.
Mad dogs and activists are out to impeach Nixon!

Pearl Bailey doesn't care to—
Republicans don't dare to—
The Democrats
Wear various hats,
But when all is said and done
They end up feeling wary
Of Jerry.
The trouble comes
From those media bums
All jumping through their hoops;
From liberal types
With more gripes
And similar nincompoops.
The thinking man
Knows the ouster plan
Is one he ought to shun,
But mad dogs and activists are out to impeach Nixon!

The Republican skit was "Watergate Wonderland," and it was announced by Lucian Warren, vice president of the Gridiron Club, in this language:

The Nixon Team has chalked up yet another dandy year!
Shortage, debt and trouble may seem to overflow,
While Jaworski and Rodino simply multiply their woe.
How can they keep on smiling? Perhaps you'll understand
When Alice takes us on a tour of *Nixon Wonderland!*

"Alice" asked how she entered "your enchanted realm," and "Pat Buchanan," the White Rabbit, replied, "Easy! Simply believe 18½ incredible things before breakfast." "I do! I do!" Alice replied, "I read the Eastern Establishment press!"

At this point the chorus came in and sang:

'S wonderful! 'S marvelous!
We're the GOP!
Nixon's great! Watergate
'S ancient histor-ee!

Who cares what those indictments mean?

Or if we line up to get gasoline?

Oh, 'S wonderful! 'S marvelous!
Inside the GOP!

Various characters representing the White House staff and Nixon's close friends peopled the stage, and "Robert Abplanalp" led off by singing:

He has only two shanties in two shanty towns—
Nothing more or less really than two hand-me-downs.
But they needed repair,
For this poor millionaire,
So the government helped him
And call'd it all square.
He sure loves those shanties,
They're fit for a king,
No sweat about taxes
He scarce pays a thing.

An impersonator of Rose Mary Woods, asked by "Ron Ziegler" what she could do "to save us from Leon Jabberwocky," replied that she'd deal with matters in her own efficient way and then sang, to the tune of "Rose Marie":

I'm Rose Mary with pencils
And memo books and stencils;
My White House job I do with dedication,
I've even learn'd the art of obfuscation.
So when those tapes were brought me,
I did what just came natur'lly:
I tapped a dainty toe upon the treadle—
I'm a loyal Rose Mary!

With legal writs and papers,
And lots of courtroom capers,
They ask'd me how I lost those eighteen minutes—
They act'ed like an awful bunch of dimwits!
And if they didn't b'lieve me,
I guess what is to be must be—
But all the same my President approves me—
Resourceful Rose Mary!

Gridiron members portraying two Presidential aspirants at that time, Governor Ronald Reagan of California and John Connally of Texas, sang a duet to the tune of "Strangers in the Night":

Reagan:
> Stranger on the right,
> don't try to stop me!

Connally:
> Ronny, let's not fight—
> You'll be my VP

Reagan:
> Stranger on the right,
> you just switch'd parties last year!

Connally:
> Ronnie, keep in sight, a lowly
> sinner can repent and see the light.

Reagan:
> But it just ain't right—for a rookie
> to aspire to step right up
> and lead the choir!

Connally:
> Well, buddie, we are in this thing together,

Reagan:
> Former Democrats, birds of a feather;

Unison:
> Ev'rything's up-tight
> For strangers on the right!

Although no one at that time foresaw that Nelson Rockefeller would be Vice President in less than a year, some did foresee him as a Presidential candidate again if Vice President Ford did not run. One of the arguments against him by Republicans was his age, since he would be 68 in 1976. "Rockefeller" sang an adaptation of "Rock of Ages."

> Rocky's aging, people say,
> 'Cause my locks are turning gray.
> But no need to feel alarm,
> I have kept my boyish charm.
> And the longer that I live,
> I grow more conservative.

> Rocky's aging, sure enough,
> But I've still got lots of stuff.
> Ray-gan, Ford and Connally—
> I am richer than all three!
> In the contest that's ahead,
> I'm the kid to tackle Ted.

> Rocky's aging, I'll admit,
> But I vow I'll never quit

'Til my fortune I have spent
Trying to be President.
'Though my vic'try may come late,
Grandpa lived to ninety-eight.

The outstanding figure in the Nixon administration was
Henry Kissinger, who had been promoted to secretary of state
and whose ability as a negotiator at that time was winning the
praises of practically everyone. Kissinger had just persuaded the
Arabs to lift the oil embargo, and had been married only a few
days before the dinner. An impersonator came on the stage
dressed in an Arab costume and sang:

I'm the Sheik of Araby,
A chronic absentee;
The sign outside my tent
Reads "Diplomat for Rent."
I've coaxed my Arab kith
To join B'nai B'rith,
My miracle technique
Makes me one busy Sheik.

My mystique in Araby
Makes oil wells gush for thee;
The car in your garage
Gets gas through my massage,
But still I pound my beat,
Despite my aching feet,
'Cause something in me cries
For one more Nobel Prize.

While living on the wing
I still found time to swing;
At singles I surpassed
Until . . . until at last
I was led by female wile
Right down that middle aisle;
And thus, one day last week
Became a married sheik!

On the last line, the chorus showered him with confetti and
rice.

At this point Alice turned upon all the other characters and
said that if they were going to be saved from the Jabberwocky it
was time to stop talking about the bad things and start saying
what's right about America. "Hear, hear," called the chorus and,
led by Alice, they began to sing "America."

During the song an impersonator of Vice President Ford in football gear moved surreptitiously into the front row of the chorus. Then, as Alice finished the solo, "Ford" moved up to the center mike. The White Rabbit moved to the other side of Alice, and they joined hands and sang a parody on "America the Beautiful":

O beautiful for Tel and Tel,
Du Pont and Sperry Rand,
For U.S. Steel and Honeywell
And Continental Can;
American Cyanamid,
Three M's and A and P,
And Standard Brands and Ho-Jo Stands
From sea to shining sea!

O beautiful for Friendly skies,
Anheuser Busch and Schlitz,
For Howard Hughes—tools and dies
And for the Statler's Ritz;
Americard! and Diner's Club!
Sears and Montgom'ry Ward,
And Pontiac and Cadillac
And good old Jerry Ford!

The skit ended on this note and Vice President Ford spoke off the record. For a closer, a soloist and the chorus sang, without parody, "This Land Is Your Land."

The toast to the absent President was proposed, and the dinner, one of the most tuneful on record, ended with the customary singing by everyone of "Auld Lang Syne."

XXIII

Gerald R. Ford

1975–
*"How much of a life-saving medicine
a little laughter is for
Presidents."*

In the interval between the 1974 and 1975 dinners, there occurred one of the greatest political upheavals in American history.

Richard Nixon, who had carried forty-nine of the fifty states in the 1972 elections, less than two years later, was forced by a hostile Congress to face the dilemma of resignation or certain impeachment. These events brought into power a new administration, headed by Gerald Ford and Nelson Rockefeller.

As a result of the changes, the heavy new Democratic majorities which had been elected to the Congress the previous November were feeling their oats, and Lucian Warren of the *Buffalo Evening News*, Gridiron president on its ninetieth anniversary, noted in his speech in the dark that "nobody here is taking the crisis lying down.

"Congress is revolting," he said, "even more revolting than usual, and in the process is dethroning old leaders and violating time honored traditions.

"Vice President Rockefeller is writing a new manual on the

Senate filibuster rule.* It is called Catch 22, or how to antagonize conservatives by really trying. . . .

"The Republicans in Congress aren't doing much, but that's because there are so few of them—fewer, all told, than there are Democrats running for President.

"But that is a dismal subject, the Democratic candidates. They're even worse than the state of the economy—which is merely terrible."

Then came a quick twist on President Ford's "Whip Inflation Now" program, which was being phased out at the time of the dinner.

"President Ford is on the right track. He has an ingenious program to whip the recession so we can afford inflation."

Gridiron President Warren then pointed out that over the Gridiron Club's ninety years it had had three rules that never changed:

"Ladies are always present, reporters are never present, and the Gridiron may singe, but it never burns.

"But," he added, "if the energy crisis continues, it may not even be able to singe next year."

Just as there had been a political upheaval in Washington, so had there been one in the Gridiron Club. A month before this dinner held on March 22, 1975, the club had elected to membership its first woman member, Helen Thomas, who covers the White House for the United Press International. There were also more women on the guest list that night than ever before, including Mrs. Ford and Mrs. Rockefeller, both of whom participated from the head table in the initiation skit.

There were seven initiates, the last of whom was Miss Thomas. Clark Mollenhoff, chairman of the initiation committee, called upon Mrs. Ford and Mrs. Rockefeller to help swear them in.

"Gridiron Class of 1975," said Mrs. Ford, "raise your right hand and give forthright answers to our questions."

"Do you solemnly swear," asked Mrs. Rockefeller, "to uphold the constitution of The Gridiron Club, discharge your responsibilities as a member and respect your seniors?"

"Do you promise," said Mrs. Ford, "to love, honor and obey the rules and traditions of The Gridiron Club?"

---

*As presiding officer of the Senate, Rockefeller had made a very controversial ruling in the debate on the filibuster rule change.

In order, as Mollenhoff pointed to each, they answered, "I do."

Finally, he pointed to the latest elected member, Miss Thomas, who said nothing.

Mrs. Ford: Answer the question, Helen.
Helen (in disgust): Oh, all right, I do.

In recognition of the Gridiron capitulation to the pressure to admit women, the initiation was followed by a song to the tune of "Stout Hearted Men":

Girls!
Sisters mine!
We can win
By hanging tough.
Pearls
Before swine
We have been
Quiet long enough!
Let our adversaries all be male—
Any female
Can call their bluff!
We're
On our way!
Give a cheer—
Hip hurray!
Now our might is loosed,
We will show them who rules the roost!

Chorus:
Give me a hen who's a stout-hearted hen,
Who will fight for her right to the sun—
Add in some frails disenchanted with males,
And before long the war has begun—Oh!
Bring on the masses of matrons and lasses—
The battle like that'll be won!
Then there's no one in the world won't get our message quick,
When stout-hearted hens can stick together chick to chick!

Immediately afterward, Ella Grasso, who had vanquished all males and won the governorship of Connecticut, was introduced as the "Women's Liberator of state houses," and the first Democratic speaker.

The scene for the Democratic skit was a meeting of the Committee of Public Safety of the French Revolution, and Robert

Roth introduced it by noting that "the spirit on Capitol Hill these days is downright revolutionary," and that it reminded him of the French Revolution.

"Here in Paris-on-the-Potomac," he said, "upstart Democrats have guillotined their elders. They have denuded one emperor and are lusting after the crown of another. Only the motto of the Revolution has changed over the years—now it's Liberté, Égalité, and Fratricide."

In French Revolutionary costumes, some bloody and tattered, the chorus held aloft the tricolor, and in place of Madame DeFarge, the scene opened with "Madam DeFoxe, the French Firecracker,"* singing:

Let me entertain you,
Let me tell you how
A Congressman relaxes
From legislating taxes
And other things highbrow.

As she vanished, the music shifted to "The Marseillaise," and a singer exhorted the chorus:

Ye Democrats, awake to glo-o-ry,

(Though some would call it—catastrophe!)

Behead the GOP,
Red ink, from sea to sea!
Spend on! Spend on!
We'll make it pay
On next election day.

At this point, "Tip 'Robespierre' O'Neill," majority leader of the House, took over, banging his gavel loudly and announcing that he was going to get this revolution organized. "Citizen Humphrey" was asked to tell them about it, and to the tune of "Love Is Sweeping the Country," he sang:

We are running the country,
We are pulling the strings,
Swinging axes on guns and taxes,
Just having one of our mad flings.
See us pushing and shoving,
Grabbing time on TV;
Each Democrat alike picks his place to strike.

*A reference to the nightclub stripper whose escapades with Wilbur Mills ended his career as a congressional leader.

Thinking national is irrational;
We are running the country,
Yes, we are off on a spree!

We already run Congress
Now we're moving downtown;
Ford can't balk us—we'll rule by caucus—
We're turning things all upside down.
We are running the whole show,
Jerry's running behind;
We listen for applause while we're making laws,
Playing diplomats, bossing bureaucrats;
We are running the country,
Yes, running it out of its mind!

The transfer of the real power in the House from the Speaker and the majority leader to the Democratic caucus was bemoaned by three of the victims who had been deposed from their committee chairmanships, and an impersonator of F. Edward Hebert, former chairman of the House Services Committee, expressed their viewpoints in this song, to the tune of "The Sting":

We got hit by a deadly sting,
See what happens when caucus is king.
Whip-per snap-pers are full of sting,
And the freshmen no longer kiss your ring.
Must have learned it in eastern schools,
They made us look like a bunch of durn fools,
We old timers play fair-ly, yes,
We always shoot square-ly,
But reformers don-t go by the rules.

Another revolutionary character, "Sidney Carton Jackson," sang of himself:

Oh, I believe in you—I believe in you.

You make those oil men sweat, yes,
    they tremble whenever you talk;
Com-mies and Ay-rabs dread to
    confront you, you high-flying hawk.
Oh, I believe in you—I believe in you.

Senator Mondale quit, when the fire
    in his belly went out;
Kennedy holds back too, but with Scoop
    there is never a doubt.
Oh, he believes in Scoop—he believes in Scoop!

Another Democratic potential who was posing a strong threat to the unity of the party, "George Wallace," was told by O'Neill that if he wanted to join he'd have to recant in public. This he was willing to do, if they'd just let him "through the schoolhouse door," and he sang:

> There is a Brotherhood of Man,
> I'm a-joinin' that Brotherhood of Man,
> A lofty tent that spreads
> O'er blacks and pointy-heads,
> All in one Brotherhood of Man.
> Yes, I believe in liberty;
> Stop a-foolin' 'round with the Ku Klux Klan;
> Give me equality
> In that fraternity
> The great big Brotherhood of Man.

Since the Gridiron Club wanted both President Ford and Vice President Rockefeller to be speakers at this dinner, in order to achieve balance it was necessary to have two Democratic speakers. Therefore, in addition to Mrs. Grasso, they invited Democratic National Chairman Robert Strauss.

In the Democratic skit "Citizen Bob Strauss" was the last to enter, announcing he was going to tell them all about the many candidates. He overlooked none except Senator Kennedy, who had publicly taken the position that he wouldn't run. In a song written by Charles McDowell, Bob Stranahan, impersonating Strauss, characterized all the rest.

> We've got a loverly bunch of coconuts,
> There they are a-standing' in a row,
> Small ones, smaller ones, smaller ones than that;
> Some of 'em dumb, and some of 'em numb,
> Who don't know where they're at;
> We've got a loverly bunch of coconuts,
> And frankly, friends, they all have got the itch,
> Please take a chance,
> Step up and take a chance,
> On our candidates for just a penny a pitch:
>
> Bumpers, Bentsen, Bobby Byrd—
>   a penny a pitch,
> Scoop and Mo and Adlai Third—
>   a penny a pitch,
> Humphrey, Muskie, Bayh!
> Carter, Wallace, aye!

Any coconut you want, a penny a pitch.

Harris, Hartke, Hart and Church—
    a penny a pitch,
Reubin, Terry, Hugh and Birch—
    a penny a pitch,
Lawton, William, Joe,
Larry, Curly, Mo—
Any coconut you want, a penny a pitch.

Tunney, Cranston, Bond and Brown—
    a penny a pitch,
Any Democrat in town—a penny a pitch,
Grasso, Glenn and Strauss,
(Had you thought of Strauss?)
Any coconut you want, a penny a pitch.

As the curtain closed, Strauss was introduced and made a very witty off-the-record speech, which ended with some gracious words about President Ford.

The guest skit chided some of the President's economic advisers. Jack Steele called to their feet Arthur Burns, chairman of the Federal Reserve Board, Dr. Paul McCracken and Dr. Herbert Stein, former heads of the Council of Economic Advisers, and William Seidman, chief economic consultant to President Ford. While they were standing, he called for advice from "the answer lady for all seasons, Miss Ann Landers."

And Richard Wilson commented, "Ann Landers gives this advice to the designers of President Ford's economic policy— Dear Boobs: Keep your traps shut and nobody'll know who fathered the child."

Secretary of State Henry Kissinger was the subject of a special skit written by Warren Rogers, in which Kissinger was depicted as a salesman running "Henry the K's Bazaar," answering numerous telephones on his desk one after the other, telling Anwar Sadat that he'd come back but first he'd have to stop off in Korea, Japan, Taiwan, the Soviet Union, India, Greece, Turkey, Italy, France, Germany, England and Georgetown, and "I can't get to Cairo before 10 o'clock tomorrow morning."

Three sheiks entered, singing:

First Sheik:
    We three kings of Orient are
    Growing rich on gas for your car.
    Hot in summer, winter's a bummer.

We are your energy czars.
Second Sheik:
> Kings of oil for profit we are,
> Trading gas for weapons of war.
> Send us jetplanes, end your chilblains.
> Bow to your creditors.
Third Sheik:
> Greedy kings of oil are we.
> Petrobucks will pay any fee.
> Our loans fatten Chase Manhattan.
> What price is liberty?
All Three:
> O-oh, Star of Exxon,
> Star of Shell,
> Star of David
Third Sheik:
> *(Spoken)* Rockefell',
> You proclaim your independence.
> We will buy it if you'll sell.

Kissinger finally explained his position:

> A wandering merchant, I,
> Who deals in confrontation,
> Detente and consternation
> And schemes that mystify.
> Bismarck and Metternich
> And me and Machiavelli
> I'm not a Nervous Nelly!
> I've slippery rhetoric—
> Yes, slippery rhetoric.

Kissinger, who was in the Middle East, had planned to speak at the conclusion of the skit, but the problems there forced him to stay longer than he had planned, and he did not return in time for the dinner.

Some people may have thought that the Democratic skit singed the members of that party; if so, the Republican skit came very close to burning the Republicans. But the genial President Ford didn't seem to mind.

The scene was the quadrangle of "Hoover University," dominated by a huge portrait of Herbert Hoover, and the chorus and soloist opened the skit by singing:

> Hoover days are here again,
> Millionaires are drinking beer again,

Fear is all we have to fear again,
Hoover days are here again.

Hard luck times are back again,
The economy is slack again,
The country's out of whack again,
Hoover days are here again.

Gloom and doom are all about.
The Statler's serving sauerkraut.
Where's the RFC to bail us out?
Hoover days are here again.

Detroit has layoffs galore
And Ford will lay off some more.
Brother, show you care again,
Do you have a dime to spare again?
Laissez faire is in the air again,
Hoover days are here again.

Hoover University was in trouble. Robert S. Boyd, chairman
of the music committee, explained in his announcement that "Big
Jerry, the star center and captain of the team, is flunking
economics—and he may not be able to play in the Big Game
against Hoover's traditional enemy, Roosevelt Academy. To
boost morale, the chairman of the Hoover Pep Club, John
Rhodes, has organized a rally on campus."

The chorus of students was worried about pulling Big Jerry
through his economics exam, but an impersonator of Ron Nessen
was sure he was going to do all right: "He's gonna buckle down
and *WIN*." The cheerleaders came forth and sang:

Trickle down, Winsocki,
    trickle down,
You can win, Winsocki, if you
    trickle down,
Give a tax rebate
To the highest rate,
Let it gravitate
And trickle down.

"Ron Nessen," Press Secretary to the President, advised Secretary of the Treasury Simon what to do:

Tough it out, Bill Simon,
    tough it out,
You can win, Bill Simon,
    if you tough it out;

Let your fatter cats
Eat in Automats
With the Democrats;
They've got to learn
To tough it out.

Cheerleaders:

Play it cool, Bill Seidman,
      play it cool,
You can win, Bill Seidman,
      if you play it cool;
On the burning deck
Of a fiscal wreck,
Write a rubber check,
And play it cool.

Give 'em hell, Winsocki,
      give 'em hell,
You can win, Winsocki
      if you give 'em hell;
When the pump won't prime
And the Dow won't climb
And it's panic time,
It's Congress' fault,
So give 'em hell!

Nessen, incidentally, was played by Jerald F. terHorst, who had resigned as press secretary to the President after a month. At the conclusion of the song a student said, "Gee, have you noticed how Ron Nessen is getting to look more like Jerry terHorst all the time?"

As the rally trotted out various members of the economics faculty, impersonators of Simon, Greenspan, Seidman and Zarb, Helen Thomas, "star reporter of the Hoover Campus Crier," announced that "Big Jerry's in the study hall walking up and down and chewing gum like crazy," and worrying because some "second stringers," Reagan, Baker, Percy, and others, were figuring on grabbing his spot in the lineup. So impersonators of the second stringers sang:

Reagan:

Standing on the corner, watching Jerry Ford go by,
Standing on the corner, knowing I'm the better guy.
I've got the right-wingers solidly behind me,
And they love me like apple pie—
(So I'm) Standing on the corner,

> Cherishing my dreams,
> Polishing my schemes,
Watching Jerry Ford go by.

Baker:

> Sitting in the Senate, watching Jerry Ford go by,
> Sitting in the Senate, knowing I'm the better guy.
> So if you're hoping to capture votes in Dixie,
> Ronnie and Chuck needn't apply.
> (So I'm) Sitting in the Senate,
> Waiting for my chance,
> Sitting out the dance,
Watching Jerry Ford go by.

Percy:

> Looking at the White House, I see Jerry Ford and sigh,
> Looking at the White House hurts so much I want to cry,
> Reagan and Baker are terribly old-fashioned
> Not even Ford's modern as I.
> (So I'm) Standing on the sidelines
> Trying hard to smile,
> Knowing all the while
Jerry Ford will pass me by.

Then, as the rally warmed up, "Mel Laird," the coach, came on the scene with good news for everybody—he had found the answer to the problem:

"Our richest alumni, Nelson Rockefeller, has just agreed to give the economics department a billion-dollar endowment and a year-long sabbatical for every faculty member—provided they let Jerry pass the course."

"Hooray! Yippee! We love Rocky. We love Rocky," shouted both students and faculty, and Gene Archer, impersonating Rockefeller, came on and sang a song written by Henry Gemmill, editor of the *National Observer*, which was the big hit of the dinner.

> If I were a poor man,
> Daidle, deedle, daidle, digguh, digguh,
> deedle, daidle dum.

> I'd sit on my bid-dy, bid-dy bum,
> If I were a poor-ish man.

> Wouldn't have to work hard,
> Daidle, deedle, daidle, digguh, digguh,
> deedle, daidle dum.

If I were a-biddy, biddy-*poor*—digguh,
    digguh, deedle—*man*.

I'd drive a beat-up Ford with low gas consumption,
No Jerry Ford a-driving me.

Quit grabbing folks to say, "Hi-ya, fe-ell-ah!"

That no-rent Naval shack would suit me just fine and
With food stamps we'd eat almost free.

Fill up on fatback, turnips and jell-ah.

I'd never have to smile at jokes about dimes,
Or friends at the Chase Manhattan bank.

Any one jokes, I sp-it in his eye.

I'd finance no Gold-berg books; to Kissinger I
    would give a stare so cold and blank,

That he'd know I'm an impecunious guy . . . (*sigh*)

I see my Happy wearing a Republican cloth coat,
    plastic curlers in her hair.

Thawing casseroles for me ev'ry night.

I see her pushing her own cart in the supermarket,
Playing a game of solitaire.

That would be a poor man's wife's delight!

And I would fire my experts, say just what occurs to-o-o to me.

Sociologists will test me, like Solomon the Wise,

"If you please, dear Rocky; if you please, dear Rocky."

Asking questions that would cross an egg-head's eyes.
Boi boi boi, boi boi boi, boi boi boi.

And it won't make one bit of diff'rence
    If I answer yes or no;

When you're poor they think you really know.

If I were poor I would stop talking about such guff
As the Brotherhood of man.

I could cut corners in my-y income tax.

And I'd discuss the racing form with the boys out back,
Checking how my horses ran;

If I were on welfare I'd relax.

If I were a poor man,
Daidle, deedle, daidle, digguh, digguh,
    deedle, daidle, dum.

I'd sit on my biddy, biddy bum,
    If I were a poor-ish man. . . .

Lord, who made the vulture and the bat,

You decreed my wallet should be fat.

Would it spoil some vast eternal plan,
    If I were a poor, poor man?

Vice President Rockefeller was introduced as the "poor man's Vice President, and made a terrific speech, briefly summarized with his permission.

He said that he wanted everybody to know that his appearance was made possible by the "Ford Foundation." He was delighted to speak for the Republican party in Washington, because that had never happened to him before. His selection as Vice President proved that the White House was an equal opportunity employer. He learned in his confirmation hearings that he would have been better off if, like his grandfather, he'd only given away dimes.

Washington was having trouble with the starlings at the time and was spraying and using chemical "bombs" to get rid of them. Referring to his confirmation hearings, Rockefeller said that now he knew what it was like to be a starling. And he liked presiding over the Senate, because where else could he be called "Mr. President" by Barry Goldwater. He spoke for about ten minutes in this vein, and the audience loved it!

After the dessert was served, the Gridiron chorus closed the musical part of the show "with an expression of the feelings all of us have about this country and its hopes for the world."

We can walk through the storm
    with our heads held high,
And not be afraid of the night.
For the stars we have followed
Still ride the sky,
And still show us the way back to light.

The times may be hard,
    the road may be long,
But our destiny's our own.

We'll all join hands with the rest
of the world,
And we'll never walk alone—
We'll never walk alone.

The toast was offered to President Ford, and he responded with good grace and closed with a tribute to the Gridiron Club, which, with his permission, is reproduced here.

Since he had moved into the White House, he said, "I've learned how much of a life-saving medicine a little laughter is for Presidents. So, if a fine evening of fun and friendship like this is good for Presidents, it must also be good for America.

"The Gridiron Club nurtures this great national asset. And I'm very glad we can all poke gentle jokes at ourselves and one another just this way—singeing without really burning—and I hope it will always stay that way.

"Americans are a very diverse people, living together in many different styles and many different places. We are united more by the way we look at things than by the traditional ties of blood or belief or battles long forgotten. And when we are able to look at the brighter side of our troubles and the lighter side of our struggles, and see the smile that lies just below the surface of our neighbor's face, I think we Americans are at our very best.

"Thank you and goodnight."

• • •

Thus ended ninety years of Gridiron history, during which fifteen Presidents, hundreds of distinguished Americans who never made the Presidency, and thousands of guests heard and saw themselves satirized, and often answered with great wit.

Abba Eban once said that "men and nations do behave wisely, once all other alternatives have been exhausted." Perhaps the Gridiron Club and the wit of its speakers have contributed something, through its ninety years of satire and ribbing, to the more rapid exhaustion of the other alternatives.

SOURCE NOTES

CHAPTER I
1. *Wall Street Journal*, 16 May 1975.
2. *New York Times*, 5 February 1905.
3. Sara Mayfield, *The Constant Circle; H. L. Mencken and His Friends* (New York: Delacorte Press, 1968), p. 210.

CHAPTER II
1. *Gridiron Club Annals; Twentieth Anniversary Dinner*, p. 13.
2. *Washington Post*, 27 January 1889.
3. Chalmers M. Roberts, *Washington Post*, 7 March 1972.
4. Arthur Wallace Dunn, *Gridiron Nights*, p. 32.
5. *Gridiron Record*, 1940.
6. *Gridiron Club Annals; Twentieth Anniversary Dinner*, p. 41.
7. Much later, Col. Oscar O. Stealey, a charter member, verified this in a speech at a Gridiron Club meeting April 9, 1927 (Oscar O. Stealey, *Birth of the Gridiron Club*).
8. Dunn, *Gridiron Nights*, pp. 19-20.
9. Ibid., p. 16.

CHAPTER III
1. *Gridiron Record*, 1909.
2. Arthur Wallace Dunn, *Gridiron Nights*, pp. 71-72.
3. Clipping from the *Washington Star*, in the *Gridiron Record*, 1899.
4. Dunn, *Gridiron Nights*, p. 90.
5. *Gridiron Club Annals; Twentieth Anniversary Dinner*, pp. 66-67.
6. Dunn, *Gridiron Nights*, p. 98.
7. Ibid., pp. 113-114.
8. Ibid., p. 116.

CHAPTER IV
1. *Washington Post*, 28 January 1907.
2. *New York Evening Post*, 27 January 1907.
3. *Gridiron Club Scrapbook B* (1895-1898), pp. 80-87.
4. James E. Watson, *As I Knew Them*, p. 71.
5. Mark Sullivan, *Our Times*, Vol. 2, p. 225.

6. Arthur Wallace Dunn, *Gridiron Nights*, 148.
7. Ibid.
8. Ibid., p. 122.
9. Bill Adler, ed., *Presidential Wit*, p. 92.
10. Dunn, *Gridiron Nights*, p. 134.
11. Ibid., p. 139.
12. Ibid., pp. 155-156.
13. *New York Times*, 5 February 1905.
14. *Gridiron Record*, 1905.
15. Dunn, *Gridiron Nights*, pp. 157-159.
16. *Washington Star*, 28 January 1906.
17. Address by Theodore Roosevelt in Washington, D.C., April 14, 1906, found in *The Works of Theodore Roosevelt*, Memorial ed., Vol. 13, *American Problems* (New York: Charles Scribner's Sons, 1925), p. 574.
18. Charles Willis Thompson, *Presidents I've Known*, p. 160.
19. *New York Times*, 26 September 1909.
20. *Gridiron Record*, 1919.

CHAPTER V
1. Harold Brayman, "The Gay Humors of Taft," *New York Evening Post*, 8 February 1930.
2. Arthur Wallace Dunn, *Gridiron Nights*, p. 237.
3. Ibid., p. 242.
4. Letter from President Taft to Oulahan dated June 28, 1911, in *Gridiron Record* of the same year.
5. Dunn, *Gridiron Nights*, 258-259.
6. *Saturday Evening Post*, 28 February 1914.
7. Bill Adler, ed., *Presidential Wit*, p. 100.

CHAPTER VI
1. *Gridiron Record*, 1913.
2. Ibid.
3. Ibid.
4. *Washington Star*, 12 December 1915.
5. Woodrow Wilson Collection, Princeton University Library, Princeton, New Jersey.
6. *Gridiron Record*, 1916.
7. Microfilm Reel #495, Woodrow Wilson Papers, Manuscript Division, U.S. Li-

brary of Congress, Washington, D.C.
8. *Gridiron Club Scrapbook F* (1912-1917), pp. 226-227.
9. Woodrow Wilson Collection, Princeton University Library.
10. William Bolitho, *Twelve against the Gods*, pp. 345-346.
11. *Gridiron Record*, 1920.
12. Undated clipping preserved in *Gridiron Record* for 1943, marked "Washington, D.C., Thursday, N"—which would place it in November 1943, after the death of her husband. I believe the paper was the *Washington Times*, a publication which no longer exists.

CHAPTER VIII
1. *Gridiron Record*, 1925.

CHAPTER IX
1. Herbert Clark Hoover, *Hoover after Dinner*, pp. 3-12.
2. Ibid., pp. 13-23.
3. Ibid., pp. 29-31.
4. Ibid., pp. 41-46.
5. *Commuter* (Great Neck, New York), 2 May 1931.
6. Hoover, *Hoover after Dinner*, pp. 53-63.
7. Ibid., pp. 65-72.
8. Ibid., pp. 73-80.
9. Ibid., pp. 81-88.

CHAPTER X
1. *Washington Times*, 1 May 1933.
2. Ibid.
3. *Gridiron Record*, 1933.
4. Franklin D. Roosevelt Library, Hyde Park, New York.
5. *Gridiron Record*, 1934.
6. Gridiron Club files for 1934.
7. Roosevelt Library, Hyde Park.
8. *Gridiron Record*, 1934.
9. Roosevelt was quoting from Henry Louis Mencken, *Prejudices: Sixth Series* (New York: A. A. Knopf [c1927]), p. 15.
10. Roosevelt Library, Hyde Park.

CHAPTER XI
1. From transcript of Hill commentary, *Gridiron Record*, 1955.
2. Franklin D. Roosevelt Library, Hyde Park, New York.
3. Franklin D. Roosevelt, *The Public Papers and Addresses of Franklin D. Roosevelt*, Vol. 5 (New York: Random House, 1936), pp. 568-569.
4. *Gridiron Record*, 1937.
5. Roosevelt Library, Hyde Park.
6. *Gridiron Record*, 1936.

7. Harold L. Ickes, *Secret Diary*, Vol. I, pp. 559-560.
8. Roosevelt Library, Hyde Park.
9. *Gridiron Record*, 1936.
10. *Washington Times*, 21 December 1937.
11. Roosevelt Library, Hyde Park.

CHAPTER XII
1. *Gridiron Record*, 1937.
2. Franklin D. Roosevelt Library, Hyde Park, New York.
3. Harold L. Ickes, *Secret Diary*, Vol. II, pp. 285-286.
4. Ibid., pp. 271-272.
5. Roosevelt Library, Hyde Park.
6. *Gridiron Record*, 1938.
7. Ibid.
8. Roosevelt Library, Hyde Park.
9. *Gridiron Record*, 1938.
10. Ibid.
11. Ibid.

CHAPTER XIII
1. *Gridiron Record*, 1939.
2. Franklin D. Roosevelt Library, Hyde Park, New York.
3. Harold L. Ickes, *Secret Diary*, Vol. III, pp. 90-91.
4. *Gridiron Record*, 1939.
5. Ibid., 1940.
6. Roosevelt Library, Hyde Park.
7. *Gridiron Record*, 1940.
8. Ibid., 1941.
9. Roosevelt Library, Hyde Park.
10. *Gridiron Record*, 1941.
11. Ibid., 1945.
12. All materials about Eleanor Roosevelt's "Widows Parties" come from the *Gridiron Record*, 1933-1941.

CHAPTER XIV
1. *Gridiron Record*, 1945.
2. Charles G. Ross papers, Gridiron Club file, Harry S. Truman Library, Independence, Missouri. Charles G. Ross was a member of the Gridiron Club, and was Truman's press secretary during much of his Presidency. The typed version of the speech signed by Truman with the Biblical phrase "in fear and trembling" (*see* pp. 410-412), is apparently the final version delivered before the Gridiron Club, since 12/15/45 was the date of the dinner.
3. *Gridiron Record*, 1946.
4. Herbert Hoover, *Addresses upon the American Road*, pp. 152-155.
5. *Gridiron Record*, 1947.
6. Charles G. Ross papers, Gridiron Club file, Truman Library.

7. *Gridiron Record,* 1947.
8. *McNaughton Reports,* Gridiron Club file, Truman Library.
9. *Gridiron Record,* 1947
10. *Gridiron Record,* 1948.
11. Ibid.

CHAPTER XV
1. Letter by Adams commenting on both dinners, *Gridiron Record,* 1948.
2. *Gridiron Record,* 1948.
3. Ibid.
4. Letter, Harry S. Truman to Ralph McGill, November 26, 1948, PPF 1109, Truman Papers, Harry S. Truman Library, Independence, Missouri.
5. *Gridiron Record,* 1949.
6. Ibid., 1950.
7. Ibid.
8. Ibid.
9. Ibid., 1951.
10. Herbert Hoover, *Addresses upon the American Road,* pp. 323-327.
11. *Gridiron Record,* 1952.

CHAPTER XVI
1. *Gridiron Record,* 1953.
2. Ibid.
3. Ibid., 1955.
4. Ibid., 1956.
5. Ibid.

CHAPTER XVII
1. *Gridiron Record,* 1957.
2. Ibid., 1958.
3. Ibid.
4. Ibid.
5. Ibid., 1959.
6. Ibid.
7. Ibid., 1960.
8. Ibid.
9. Ibid.
10. *Washington Post,* 3 June 1974.

CHAPTER XVIII
1. *Gridiron Record,* 1961.
2. Ibid.
3. Ibid.
4. Ibid., 1962.
5. Ibid.
6. Ibid.

7. Ibid., 1963.
8. Ibid.
9. Ibid.

CHAPTER XIX
1. *Gridiron Record,* 1964.
2. Ibid.
3. Ibid.
4. Ibid., 1965.
5. *Washington Star,* 24 March 1965.
6. *Gridiron Record,* 1965.
7. Ibid., 1966.
8. Ibid.
9. Ibid.

CHAPTER XX
1. *Gridiron Record,* 1967.
2. Ibid.
3. Ibid.
4. Ibid.
5. Ibid.
6. Ibid.
7. Ibid., 1968.
8. Ibid.
9. Ibid.

CHAPTER XXI
1. *Gridiron Record,* 1969.
2. Ibid.
3. Ibid.
4. Ibid.
5. Ibid., 1970.
6. Ibid.
7. Ibid.
8. Ibid.
9. Ibid.
10. Ibid., 1971.
11. *Washington Post,* 26 February 1971.
12. *Gridiron Record,* 1971.
13. Ibid.
14. Ibid.

CHAPTER XXII
1. *Gridiron Record,* 1972.
2. Ibid.
3. Ibid.
4. Ibid., 1973.

CHAPTER XXIII
1. *Gridiron Record,* 1975.
2. Ibid.

BIBLIOGRAPHY

ARCHIVAL SOURCES

Libraries
Dwight D. Eisenhower Library, Abilene, Kansas.
Woodrow Wilson Manuscript Collection, Princeton University Library, Princeton, New Jersey.
Franklin D. Roosevelt Library, Hyde Park, New York.
Harry S. Truman Library, Independence, Missouri.
Manuscript Division, U.S. Library of Congress, Washington, D.C.

Gridiron Club
Gridiron Club . . . Scrapbooks, 1885-1929.
Gridiron Records, 1885-1975.
Bound and loose-leaf volumes, arranged by year, containing speeches, newspaper clippings, letters, minutes of meetings, and other Gridiron Club memorabilia.
Gridiron Club Show Scripts, 1914-1975.
Stage directions and dialogue for all the scheduled events at each dinner. The scripts include the text of the speech in the dark, the toast to the President, all other introductions, and of course, all the skits and songs that take place throughout each dinner.

PUBLISHED SOURCES

Gridiron Club
Dunn, Arthur Wallace. *Gridiron Nights: Humorous and Satirical Views of Politics and Statesmen as presented by the Famous Dining Club.* New York: Frederick A. Stokes, 1915 (Reprinted, Arno Press: New York, 1974).
Dunn had been Gridiron Club President.
Gridiron Club, Washington, D.C. *The Barkis Club.* Washington, D.C.: Menu Committee of the Gridiron Club, 1924.
———. *The Bunk Book.* Washington, D.C.: Menu Committee of the Gridiron Club, 1925.
———. *Forty-eight Gridiron Years: A Chronicle written from Its Records for the Use of Members of the Gridiron Club, by Ernest George Walker. . . .* Washington, D.C.: Privately Printed [°1933].
———. *Gridiron Almanac for Statesmen, Journalists, Real Newspaper Men, Mollycoddles, Malefactors of Great Wealth, and General Family Use.* [Washington, D.C.: Gridiron Press, 1909].
———. *Gridiron Club Campaign Song Book.* [Washington, D.C.: Gridiron Press, 1908].
———. *The Gridiron Club, 1885-XX-1905, Annals: Twentieth Anniversary Dinner, Saturday, January 28, 1905, the New Willard, Washington.* [Washington, D.C.: Gridiron Press, 1905].
———. *The Gridiron Club of Washington, D.C. Organized January 24, 1885. Fifteenth Anniversary, January 27, 1900.* [Washington, D.C., 1900].

———. *The Gridiron Sporting Guide 1926.* [Washington, D.C.: Menu and Souvenir Committee of the Gridiron Club, 1926].

———. *The I-Did-It Club, Published by the Menu Committee, the Gridiron Club of Washington, D.C., the New Willard, December Ninth, 1916.* [Washington, D.C.: W. F. Roberts Co., 1916].

———. *Mother Goose in Gridiron Rhyme: A Collection of Alphabets, Rhymes, Tales and Jingles. . . . December Dinner of the Gridiron Club, Washington, D.C., December 9, 1911.* [Washington, D.C.: Gridiron Press, 1911].

———. *One Evening on Newspaper Row: An Idyl of the Long-ago. Forty-fifth Anniversary, 1885-1930.* Washington, D.C.: Gridiron Club [°1930].

———. *Standard Guide for Office-Seekers in Washington.* [Washington: Gridiron Press, 1912].

———. *Tenth Annual Dinner . . . January 26, 1895 [at the Arlington].* [Washington, D.C., 1895].

———. *Thirtieth Anniversary Dinner of the Gridiron Club. The Book of Plays and a Few Words about Ourselves.* Washington [Gridiron Press] 1915.

———. *A Truthful Statement of the Transactions of the Gridiron Club, from Its Origin to the Present Time.* [Washington: W. F. Roberts, 1895].

———. *XXth Century Gridiron Primer, Wherein Are Laid down in Easy Characters, Adapted to the Most Senile Understanding, the Principles of Patriotic Politics. . . .* [Washington, D.C.: W. F. Roberts, 1901].

———. *Washington As It Really Is, A Guide for Gridiron Guests: The Capitol To-day. . . .* [Washington, 1906?].

———. *Who's Who in Gridiron Prose and Rhyme: Historic Characters Portrayed with a Profusion of Cuts, Published at the Annual Winter Dinner . . . January 26, 1907.* [Washington, D.C.: W. F. Roberts, 1907].

Stealey, Oscar O. *The Birth of the Gridiron Club, Washington, D.C.* Washington, D.C.: W. F. Roberts, 1927.
Stealey was a charter member of the Gridiron Club.

Other Books

Adler, Bill, ed. *Presidential Wit from Washington to Johnson.* New York: Simon and Schuster, Trident Press, 1966.

Bolitho, William. *Twelve against the Gods: The Story of Adventure.* New York: Simon and Schuster, 1929.

Hoover, Herbert Clark. *Addresses upon the American Road, 1950-1955.* Stanford: Stanford University Press, 1955.

———. *Hoover after Dinner: Addresses Delivered by Herbert Hoover before the Gridiron Club of Washington, D.C., with Other Informal Speeches; with an Introduction by Theodore G. Joslin.* New York: Charles Scribner's Sons, 1933.
For many years, Theodore Joslin was correspondent for the *Boston Transcript.* During the last two years of Hoover's administration, Joslin was his press secretary, and after his retirement from the Presidency, Hoover gave Joslin permission to do a limited edition book, consisting of all the President's Gridiron speeches and four others.

Ickes, Harold Le Claire. *The Secret Diary of Harold L. Ickes.* 3 vols. New York: Simon and Schuster, 1953-1954.
Vol. 1: *The First Thousand Days, 1933-1936.*
Vol. 2: *The Inside Struggle, 1936-1939.*
Vol. 3: *The Lowering Clouds, 1939-1941.*

Sullivan, Mark. *Our Times: The United States 1900-1925.* 6 vols. New York: Charles Scribner's Sons, 1926-1935.
Vol 1: *The Turn of the Century, 1900-1904.*
Vol. 2: *America Finding Herself.*
Vol. 3: *Pre-War America.*
Vol. 4: *The War Begins, 1904-1919.*
Vol. 5: *Over Here, 1914-1918.*
Vol. 6: *The Twenties.*
Thompson, Charles Willis. *Presidents I've Known and Two Near Presidents.* Indianapolis: Bobbs-Merrill, 1929.
Watson, James E. *As I Knew Them: Memoirs of James Eli Watson, Former United States Senator from Indiana.* New York: Bobbs-Merrill, 1936.

THE GRIDIRON CLUB of Washington, D.C.

Officers for 1976

President, Peter Lisagor
Vice President, Jerald F. terHorst
Secretary, Jack Steele
Treasurer, Richard L. Wilson
Historian, Robert Roth

Executive Committee (In Addition to the Officers)

Grant Dillman, Charles McDowell, Jr., Alan L. Otten, Lucian Warren

Active Members

Arrowsmith, Marvin, *Associated Press*
Barnett, David L., *Hearst Newspapers*
Bartlett, Charles L., *Chicago Daily News*
Block, Herbert, *Washington Post*
Boyd, Robert S., *Knight Newspapers*
Broder, David S., *Washington Post*
Broom, William W., *Ridder Publications*
Childs, Marquis W., *St. Louis Post-Dispatch*
Cleland, John A., *Houston Chronicle*
Cole, Benjamin R., *Indianapolis Star*
Cormier, Frank, *Associated Press*
Cromley, Alan W., *Daily Oklahoman and Times*
Dillman, Grant, *United Press International*
Drummond, Roscoe, *Los Angeles Times Syndicate*
Dudman, Richard, *St. Louis Post-Dispatch*
Emory, Alan S., *Watertown Daily Times*
Free, James, *Birmingham News*
Germond, Jack W., *Washington Star*
Geyelin, Philip L., *Washington Post*
Greene, Charles J., *New York Daily News*
Irwin, Don, *Los Angeles Times*
Kilpatrick, Carroll, *Washington Post*
Kole, John W., *Milwaukee Journal*
Kraslow, David, *Cox Newspapers*
Larrabee, Donald R., *Griffin-Larrabee News Bureau*
Lastelic, Joseph A., *Kansas City Star*
Lewine, Frances L., *Associated Press*
Lisagor, Peter, *Chicago Daily News*
McCartney, James H., *Knight Newspapers*
McDowell, Charles, Jr., *Richmond Times-Dispatch*
McNeil, Marshall, *Scripps-Howard Newspapers*
Mears, Walter R., *Associated Press*
Mollenhoff, Clark, *Des Moines Register and Tribune*
O'Brien, Edward W., *St. Louis Globe-Democrat*
Olofson, Darwin R., *Omaha World-Herald*
O'Rourke, Lawrence M., *Philadelphia Bulletin*
Otten, Alan L., *Wall Street Journal*
Poe, Edgar A., *New Orleans Times-Picayune*
Reed, Dean, *Newhouse News Service*
Richert, Earl H., *Scripps-Howard Newspapers*
Ridder, Walter T., *Ridder Publications*
Ross, Thomas B., *Chicago Sun-Times*
Roth, Robert, *Philadelphia Bulletin*
Rowan, Carl T., *Chicago Daily News*
Sperling, Godfrey, Jr., *Christian Science Monitor*
Steele, Jack, *Scripps-Howard Newspapers*

853

terHorst, Jerald F., *Detroit News*
Thomas, Helen, *United Press International*
Thomasson, Dan K., *Scripps-Howard Newspapers*
Warren, Lucian, *Buffalo Evening News*
Wieghart, James G., *New York Daily News*
Wilson, Richard L., *Des Moines Register and Tribune*

Limited Members

Archer, Gene W., *Brookeville, Md. 20729*
Bigbee, John C., *3320 Senator Ave., Washington, D.C. 20028*
Bourgeois, Lt. John R., *Marine Bks., Washington, D.C. 20390*
Duvall, John H., *2004 Fort Dr., Alexandria, Va. 22307*
Kline, Lt. Col. Jack T., *Marine Bks., Washington, D.C. 20390*
Koop, Theo. F., *2737 Devonshire Pl., N.W., Washington, D.C. 20008*
Matarrese, Anthony F., *2601 Cool Spring Rd., Adelphi, Md. 20783*
Myers, George A., *4400 East-West Hwy., Bethesda, Md. 20014*
Ritter, William O., *Fairchild Industries, Germantown, Md. 20767*
Ryan, Michael S., *6153 So. Maryland Blvd., Lothian, Md. 20820*
Santelmann, Lt. Col. William F. (Ret.), *7414 Admiral Dr., Alexandria, Va. 22307*
Stranahan, Robt. P. Jr., *5316 Cardinal Ct., Washington, D.C. 20016*
Sult, Ernest P., *6808 Grey Fox Dr., Springfield, Va. 22152*
Waring, James D., *Catholic University, Washington, D.C. 20064*

Associated Members

Adams, Phelps H., *Box 881, Litchfield Park, Ariz. 85340*
Bailey, Charles W. II, *Minn. Tribune, Minneapolis, Minn. 55415*
Beale, William L. Jr., *4040 51st St., N.W., Washington, D.C. 20016*
Brayman, Harold, *Wilm. Trust Bldg., Wilmington, Del. 19801*
Canham, Erwin D., *Chr. Science Monitor, Boston, Mass. 02115*
Catledge, Turner, *2316 Prytania St., New Orleans, La. 70130*
Cauley, John R., *4901 Wornall Rd., Kansas City, Mo. 64112*
Collins, Frederic W., *3929 Jenifer St., N.W., Wash., D.C. 20015*
Donovan, Robert J., *Los Angeles Times, Washington, D.C. 20006*
Eklund, Laurence C., *5602 York Lane, Bethesda, Md. 20014*
Finney, Nat S., *3376 Chiswick Ct., Rossmoor, Md. 20906*
Folliard, Edward T., *3200 4th St., N.W., Washington, D.C. 20016*
Frandsen, Julius, *5134 Worthington Dr., Washington, D.C. 20016*
Frankel, Max, *New York Times, New York, N.Y. 10036*
Freeburg, Russell W., *1617 Courtland Rd., Alexandria, Va. 22306*
Friendly, Alfred, *47 Cheyne Place, London SW3, England*
Gemmill, Henry, *National Observer, Silver Spring, Md. 20910*
Griffin, Gerald E., *Rt. 2, Box 50, Emmitsburg, Md. 21727*
Harkness, R. L., *3035 Dumbarton Ave., N.W., Wash., D.C. 20007*
Harpham, Lt. Col. Dale L. (Ret.), *3816 Mil. Rd., Wash., D.C. 20015*
Hayden, Martin S., *Detroit News, Detroit, Mich. 48231*
Hightower, John M., *916 Old S. Fe Trail, Santa Fe, N.M. 87501*
Jarrell, John W., *1002 Don Cubero Ave., Santa Fe, N.M. 87501*
Jones, Wm. D., *909 Lyndell Dr., Kissimmee, Fla. 32741*
Kauffmann, Rudolph II, *11 Quincy St., Chevy Chase, Md. 20015*
Kent, Carleton, *Shorecliff House, Glandore, Ireland*
Kirchhofer, A. H., *925 Delaware Ave., Buffalo, N.Y. 14209*
Knebel, Fletcher, *208 Edgerstoune Rd., Princeton, N.J. 08540*
Kumpa, Peter J., *14 Gough Sq., Fleet St., London EC4A 3DE*
Leacacos, John P., *2401 Ft. Scott Dr., Arlington, Va. 22202*
Leach, Paul R., *220 Lynnhurst Dr., Ormond Beach, Fla. 32074*
Lewis, Edward W., *1515 28th St., N.W., Washington, D.C. 20007*

Lucey, Charles T., *Rt. 2, Thurmont, Md. 21788*
Martin, Paul, *U.S. News & World Report, Wash., D.C. 20037*
McKelway, Benj. M., *Washington Star, Washington, D.C. 20003*
Miller, Paul, *Gannett Newspaper, Rochester, N.Y. 14614*
Mylander, William H., *1008 Kent Rd., Wilmington, Del. 19807*
Noyes, Newbold, *5015 Garfield St., N.W., Washington, D.C. 20016*
Perry, Glen, *10 Lighthouse Way, Darien, Conn. 06820*
Phillips, Adon W., *5024 Gramont Ave., Orlando, Fla. 32809*
Potter, Philip, *1421 Nut Tree Lane, Sonoma, Calif. 95476*
Price, Byron, *Box 206, Chestertown, Md. 21620*
Reston, James B., *New York Times, Washington, D.C. 20036*
Riggs, Robert L., *5412 Duvall Dr., Washington, D.C. 20016*
Rogers, Warren, *1622 30th St., N.W., Washington, D.C. 20007*
Schoepper, Col. Albert F. (Ret.), *4013 N. Woodstock St., Arlington, Va. 22207*
Silverman, Alvin, *1125 17th St., N.W., Washington, D.C. 20036*
Steffe, Edwin C., *145 W. 55 St., New York, N.Y. 10019*
Sylvester, Arthur, *2 Belvedere St., Cold Spring, N.Y. 10516*
Theis, J. William, *705 Winhall Way, Silver Spring, Md. 20904*
Thompson, Glenn, *4716 Fawnwood Rd., Dayton, Ohio 45429*
Timmons, B. N., *1316 30th St., N.W., Washington, D.C. 20007*
Trohan, W., *Carrowmeer House, Newmarket-on-Fergus, Eire*
Waltman, Franklyn, *Warwick Hotel, Philadelphia, Pa. 19103*
Wheaton, Warren, *360 Wyatt Rd., Harrisburg, Pa. 17104*
Whitehead, Don, *3636 Talituna Ave., Knoxville, Tenn. 37919*
Wicker, Thomas G., *New York Times, New York, N.Y. 10036*
Wiggins, J. Russell, *Brooklyn, Maine 04616*
Wise, David, *3434 Ashley Ter., N.W., Washington, D.C. 20008*

INDEX

Abplanalp, Robert H., 804, 829
Abzug, Bella, 823, 826
Acheson, Dean, 409, 487, 491-492, 507, 517, 530, 559, 593, 696-697, 750
Adams, Charles Francis, 334
Adams, John, 271, 289
Adams, John Quincy, 271, 289
Adams, Phelps H., 5, 17, 356, 382, 398, 444, 454-455, 459, 467, 675
Adams, Sherman, 531, 544, 578, 583-587, 599
Adenauer, Konrad, 606, 658
Adonis, Joe, 481
Adzhubei, Aleksei I., 658
Aeschylus, 788
Agnew, Spiro T., 4, 11-13, 27, 129, 752, 760-764, 766-767, 772, 774, 778-779, 781, 789, 791-794, 796, 803-804, 806, 811, 819, 821
Aguinaldo, Emilio, 42-43
Albert, Carl, 664-668, 796, 812, 815, 826
Alcorn, Meade, 571, 594
Aldrich, Nelson W., 55-56, 78, 257
Aldrich, Winthrop, 353
Alexander, Donald C., 827
Allen, George E., 612, 621
Allen, Henry, 296-297
Alsop, Joseph W., 515, 704, 764, 788
Anders, William A., 753
Andersen, Hans Christian, 211
Anderson, Clinton P., 700
Anderson, Jack, 17, 803, 810
Anderson, Robert B., 603
Anderson, Wendell R., 825
Archer, Gene W., 458, 463, 477, 556, 606, 721, 824, 843
Armstrong, Robert, 159
Arthur, Chester A., 25, 33, 272
Arvey, Jacob M. ("Jake"), 449, 460, 463, 510, 559, 607, 627-628
Ashurst, Henry Fountain, 128-129

Askew, Reubin O., 825, 839
Astor, Lady Nancy, 342
Astor, Vincent, 234, 245, 247
Atlee, Clement, 402, 410
Austin, Warren, 297
Avery, Sewall, 411

Bacall, Lauren, 423, 489
Bailey, Charles W., II, 676
Bailey, John, 677, 697, 742-743
Bailey, Lloyd W., 755
Bailey, Pearl, 828
Baker, Howard H., Jr., 842-843
Baker, Robert G. ("Bobby"), 662, 665-667, 675, 685, 697, 714
Balfour, Lord Arthur James, 141-142, 390
Ball, George, 676
Barkley, Alben W., 329, 422-423, 462, 470, 478, 480-483, 488, 503-504, 510, 651
Barnes, William, 110
Barnum, Phineas T., 202, 266
Barry, Robert, 158, 209
Bartlett, Charles L., 764
Barton, Bruce, 174, 376, 439
Baruch, Bernard, 227, 234, 381
Bayh, Birch, 784, 823, 825, 838-839
Beale, Betty, 683
Beale, William L., 646
Beame, Abraham, 697, 715
Beard, Dita, 809
Beck, Dave, 581
Bedford, A. C., 121
Bell, Jack, xvii, 781, 786-787
Bell, Ulric, 264-265, 276, 360-361
Bender, George, 623-624
Ben Gurion, David, 577
Benn, Anthony Wedgwood, 17
Bennett, Frank V., 30
Bennett, Ira, 119-121, 124
Bennett, James Gordon, 348

Bennett, James O'Donnell, xiii
Benson, Ezra Taft, 535, 566, 584, 596,
    612-613, 615
Benton, William, 750
Bentsen, Lloyd M., Jr., 825, 838
Bergen, Edgar, 433
Berryman, Clifford K., 49-50, 78, 83, 170,
    175, 264, 554
Beveridge, Alfred J., 77
Bevin, Ernest, 411, 417, 419, 427, 467
Bidault, Georges, 537-538
Bigbee, John, 742
Bingham, Hiram, 206
Black, Hugo L., 316, 318
Black, Shirley Temple, 726
Blaine, James G., 29
Bliss, Ray C., 623-624, 679-680, 695, 708,
    761
Block, Herbert (Herblock), 670, 729-730,
    735, 793
Blough, Roger, 647, 686, 698
Blount, James H., 30
Blythe, Samuel G., 50-54, 555
Bohlen, Charles E. ("Chip"), 526
Bolitho, William, 124
Bolling, Richard W., 768
Bond, Julian, 839
Bone, Scott C., 74
Borah, William E., 97-98, 102, 109, 125,
    127-128, 138, 142, 145, 151-152, 163,
    171, 174, 181, 185, 188-189, 206, 212,
    227, 267, 269, 279, 289
Borman, Frank, 753
Bowes, "Major" (Edward), 309
Bowles, Chester, 415, 633, 637, 642
Boyd, Robert S., 841
Boynton, Charles A., 41
Boynton, H. V., 25
Brahany, Thomas W., 145
Brandegee, Frank B., 151
Brandt, Raymond P., 395, 412, 414, 418, 518
Brannan, Charles F., 472
Branson, Taylor, 265, 371
Brayman, Harold, xii-xv, 380, 393
Brennan, George E., 155
Brewster, Owen, 485, 487
Brezhnev, Leonid I., 754, 810
Bricker, John W., 413, 421, 429-430, 623-624
Bridges, Styles, 498, 529, 572
Brigham, William E., 6, 120, 145, 153, 159
Brinkley, David, 270, 668, 730
Broder, David, 793
Brookhart, Smith W., 201, 218
Brooks, Ned, 458, 488, 572, 593
Broun, Heywood, 317
Browder, Earl, 293
Brown, Ashmun, 128, 179, 183

Brown, Edmund G., 595-597, 610, 665,
    694-695, 715
Brown, Edmund G., Jr. ("Jerry"), 839
Brown, George Rothwell, 554
Brown, Harry J., 155
Brownell, Herbert, 458, 506, 580
Bryan, Charles W., 155, 158-160
Bryan, William Jennings, 17, 39, 43-46,
    59-60, 66-68, 73, 78, 82-85, 91-92, 96,
    98-101, 103, 110, 114, 127, 155, 159-160,
    189, 248, 273, 524, 574
Bryant, William Cullen, 348
Bryce, James, 349
Brynner, Yul, 593
Buchanan, Patrick J., 828
Buchwald, Art, 788
Buck, Gene, 216, 336, 338-339, 378, 452
Buckley, James L., 779-780
Buckley, William F., Jr., 794, 806-807
Buel, Walker S., 5, 212, 214, 222, 228-229,
    257, 296, 322, 330, 381, 395, 405, 437,
    477, 531, 555
Buffalo Bill (William F. Cody), 265, 273
Bulganin, Nikolai A., 564
Bumpers, Dale L., 825, 838
Bundy, McGeorge, 621, 658
Bunker, Ellsworth, 734
Burch, Dean, 677, 680
Burger, Warren E., 766, 774, 783, 796, 804,
    817
Burke, Arleigh, 590-591
Burke, Edmund, 747
Burns, Arthur, 775, 839
Bush, George, 820
Butcher, Harry, 338
Butler, Nicholas, 250
Butler, Paul, 574, 582, 615
Butler, William M., 173-175, 187
Butz, Earl, 819
Bynum, William D., 35-36
Byrd, Harry F., 368-369, 465, 480, 487-491,
    493, 626, 639, 662, 733
Byrd, Harry F., Jr., 638, 779-780
Byrd, Richard Evelyn, 182, 369
Byrd, Robert C., 786-787, 838
Byrnes, James F., 347, 409, 417, 423, 427,
    472, 518, 532, 541-542, 626

Cagney, James, 276
Califano, Joseph A., 804
Cannon, Bishop James, 250
Cannon, Joseph G., 53-54, 58, 60-61, 67,
    72-73, 76, 78-79, 99, 106, 114, 273, 421,
    582
Capehart, Homer, 536, 563
Caplin, Mortimer, 655

Capone, Al, 215, 217, 250
Caraway, Thaddeus, 202, 266-267
Carnegie, Andrew, 273
Carnegie, Dale, 411
Carson, John M., 25-27, 61
Carson, Johnny, 705, 747, 810
Carswell, G. Harrold, 775, 793
Carter, James Earl, Jr. (Jimmy), 838
Case, Francis H., 561-563
Castro, Fidel, 593, 643, 650, 656-657, 662, 675, 754
Catledge, Turner, 5, 234, 330, 340, 388-389, 396, 429
Celebrezze, Anthony J., 691
Celler, Emanuel, 713
Chamberlain, Neville, 342
Chambers, Whittaker, 456
Chapin, Charles, 324
Chapin, Dwight, 778, 817
Chaplin, Charles S., 144, 276
Chiang Kai-shek, 394-395, 806-807
Chiari, Roberto F., 675
Childs, Marquis, 569-570
Chiles, Lawton M., 839
Ching, Cyrus, 481
Chisholm, Shirley, 796, 799-800
Chotiner, Murray, 759
Chou En-lai, 552-553, 805-808, 811, 819
Christian, George, 731-732, 736, 743-744, 746
Church, Frank, 839
Churchill, Winston, 379, 388, 390, 394-395, 402, 537, 658, 706, 750
Clapper, Raymond, 22, 344-348, 352, 357, 360-361, 395
Clark, D. Worth, 494
Clark, James B. ("Champ"), 78-80, 82-85, 92, 96, 100, 102, 126
Clark, Ramsey, 778
Clark, Tom C., 404-406, 442, 452
Clay, Henry, 741
Clayton, William L., 409
Clémenceau, Georges, 125, 131
Cleveland, Grover, 25-37, 44, 161, 265, 271-273, 281, 349-350, 473, 499, 616
Cleveland, Mrs. Grover, 28
Cleveland, Richard Folsom, 265
Clifford, Clark M., 5, 24, 433, 441, 556-557, 596, 609, 684-685, 743, 758
Cockran, W. Bourke, 31
Cohen, Benjamin V., 340-341, 355, 360
Cole, Benjamin R., 819
Collingwood, Charles, 494-495
Collins, Frederic W., 674, 677-678, 681, 686, 702
Columbus, Christopher, 270
Confucius, 362, 395

Connally, John, 628, 745, 788, 790, 792-793, 798-799, 806, 811, 829-830
Connally, Thomas T., 309
Cook, Frederick A., 211
Coolidge, Calvin, 140, 149-193, 202, 207, 212, 214-215, 224, 272-273, 279, 281, 500, 616, 654, 747
Coolidge, Louis Arthur, 99
Coolidge, Marcus A., 212
Copeland, Royal S., 206, 211, 219, 247
Corcoran, Thomas G. ("Tommy"), 340-341, 355, 360, 405, 684
Costello, Frank, 481, 525
Couzens, James, 163-164, 219
Coward, Noel, 827
Cowles, Gardner (Mike), 519, 723, 778
Cowles, John, 519, 778
Cox, James M., 126, 129, 132, 137, 189
Coxey, Jacob Sechler, 95, 248, 265, 273
Craig, May, 654
Cranston, Alan, 839
Crawford, Joan, 651
Creel, George, 120-121
Crisp, Charles F., 35
Croker, Richard, 41-42, 45, 265, 273
Cromley, Allan W., 801, 816
Cronkite, Walter, 730, 791
Crossley, Archibald M., 457
Crump, Ed, 378, 449
Cummings, Homer S., 266, 277-278, 313, 531
Cummins, Albert B., 79
Cunningham, J. Harry, 87-88
Curry, John F., 227-228
Curtis, Charles, 166, 170, 183-185, 190-191, 196-197, 214, 223
Curley, James M., 385, 449, 510
Curtis, Cyrus H. K., xiii
Cutting, Bronson M., 247

Daley, Richard J., 628, 657, 758, 814-815
Dalzell, John, 78
Daniel, Price, 728
Daniels, Josephus, 100, 132
Daugherty, Harry M., 132, 136, 142, 146, 186
Davies, Joseph E., 309
Davis, Henry G., 60
Davis, John W., 155-158, 160, 184, 280, 302
Dawes, Charles G., 58, 140, 160-161, 166-167, 169-170, 172-174, 176, 182-185, 191, 193, 219, 334
Dayan, Moshe, 749, 775
deGaulle, Charles, 605-606, 615, 654, 657-658, 675-676, 690, 740, 754, 763
De Murville, Maurice Couve, 675

Denfeld, Louis E., 466, 472, 474
Depew, Chauncey M., 44, 58, 161-163
De Sapio, Carmine, 541, 548-549, 559, 593, 607
Dewey, Thomas E., 4, 14-15, 17, 320, 340, 344, 346-347, 361, 363, 372, 376-377, 397, 402, 406-408, 410, 413, 421, 429-430, 434, 437-438, 446, 453-462, 475, 485, 507, 511-512, 524, 536, 598, 600, 609, 783
Diefenbaker, John George, 654
Dies, Martin, 345
Dietrich, Marlene, 356
Dillon, C. Douglas, 630, 651-652, 661
Dirksen, Everett McKinley, 10, 530, 539, 543, 612-615, 617, 626, 634, 648, 656, 663, 668, 670, 679, 694-695, 707-709, 737, 739, 742, 761
DiSalle, Michael V., 607
Dobrynin, Anatoly F., 779, 819
Dobson, Austin, 274
Dodge, Arthur, 495
Doheny, Edward L., 185-186
Doherty, Henry L., 278
Dole, Robert J., 787-788, 790-793
Donaldson, Jess, 522
Donovan, James, 650
Donovan, Robert J., 633
Douglas, Paul H., 503, 709, 715
Douglas, Stephen A., 610, 626
Douglas, William O., 317
Douglas-Home, Sir Alec, 675
Drummond, Roscoe, 24, 408, 517, 557, 560, 567, 678
Dulles, Allen, 605, 617
Dulles, John Foster, 507, 526-527, 529, 531, 537, 545-546, 552-553, 564, 577-578, 591
Dunn, Arthur Wallace, 45, 56, 495
Dunraven, Lord, 32
Du Pont, Pierre S., 234, 258, 329, 364, 476
Duvall, John, 738

Eagleton, Thomas F., 815
Early, Stephen T., 245-246, 275, 319, 327, 360, 367-368
Eastland, James O., 573
Eban, Abba, 734, 846
Eden, Anthony, 537, 552-553, 577
Edmunds, George Franklin, 36
Edward VII (Prince of Wales, 1841-1901), 32
Ehrlichman, John D., 818, 825
Einstein, Albert, 144
Eisenhower, Dwight D., 3, 5, 9, 13-16, 20, 27, 36, 57, 408, 434, 437-438, 447-448, 463-464, 469, 473, 477-478, 483, 485, 498-500, 505-511, 513, 515, 517,

520-619, 621-622, 626, 630, 634, 636, 641, 654, 658, 668, 671-672, 708
Eisenhower, Mrs. Dwight D., 531
Eisenhower, Dwight David, II, 763
Eisenhower, Mrs. Dwight David, II, 763
Eisenhower, Milton S., 594
Ellender, Allen Joseph, 784
Elson, E. L. E., 594
Erhard, Ludwig, 689
Ervin, Samuel J., Jr., 700, 824-825
Essary, Helen, 133-134
Essary, J. Fred, 95-96, 133-134, 158, 161, 166, 330
Esterhazy, Prince, 427-428
Evans, Daniel J., 827
Evans, Rowland, Jr., 764

Fairbanks, Charles Warren, 61, 66-67, 69
Fairless, Benn, 3, 476, 522
Fall, Albert B., 146, 185-186
Farley, James A., 2, 227, 260, 266, 287, 293, 296, 305, 317, 321, 339, 341, 355, 358, 360-362, 366, 372, 382-383, 432, 451, 522, 531, 817
Faubus, Orval, 579-580, 583
Ferguson, Miriam A. ("Ma"), 159
Fern, Richard Lee, 63
Fess, Simeon D., 206, 212, 215, 218-219, 226
Field, Carter, 158
Fields, W. C., 802
Finch, Robert, 774-775
Finney, Nat, 737-740, 745, 751
Fish, Hamilton, 376, 439
Fitzgerald, F. Scott, 90
Fleeson, Doris, 659
Fletcher, Duncan U., 211
Fletcher, Henry P., 257, 262, 275, 360
Flynn, Edward J., 379, 405-406, 449
Foch, Ferdinand, 125
Folliard, Edward T., 517-519, 547, 554-556
Folsom, Marion B., 586
Foote, Mark, 361-362, 375, 378
Foraker, Joseph B., 18, 48-57, 67, 79, 162, 555
Ford, Gerald R., xviii, 2-4, 9-10, 21, 526, 648, 679, 694, 707, 726, 737, 739-741, 747, 762, 789, 821, 828, 830, 832, 833-846
Ford, Mrs. Gerald R., 3, 834-835
Ford, Henry, 110, 115, 121, 144, 158, 160, 163, 241, 259-260, 262, 381
Ford, Henry, II, 478-480, 483, 686
Ford, Jules Howard, 150
Forrestal, James, 456
Fortas, Abe, 684-685, 745, 753-755
Fox, Fanne, 836

France, Anatole, 250
Franco, Francisco, 417
Frandsen, Julius, 622, 632-633, 644-645, 730
Frank, Glenn, 330-331, 333-336, 372
Frankfurter, Felix, 405
Franklin, Benjamin, 105, 314, 522
Freeman, Orville L., 626-627
Frelinghuysen, Joseph S., 139, 334
Freud, Sigmund, 153-154
Froehlke, Robert F., 49
Frost, Robert, 627
Fulbright, J. William, 424, 603, 631, 637, 639, 700-704, 729-732, 734, 740, 757, 762, 785-786, 792

Gableman, Edwin W., 212, 283, 293-294, 298
Gabor, Zsa Zsa, 740
Gabrielson, Guy G., 476-477, 484-485, 498-499
Galbraith, John Kenneth, 622, 637, 642-643, 732, 742-743
Gallup, George H., 377, 411, 443, 457, 476, 593, 635, 676, 738
Gandhi, Mohandas (Mahatma), 212
Gardner, John W., 792
Garfield, James A., 28, 150
Garfield, James R., 72
Garner, John N., 217, 234, 238-239, 247, 251, 308, 327, 347-348, 355-356, 358, 361-362, 366, 374-375
Garst, Roswell, 641
Garthe, Louis, 82, 85
Gay, Charles R., 317
Gemmill, Henry, 843
Geneen, Harold, 808
George, Walter F., 339, 551-553, 560
Gilbert, Clinton W., 131
Gilligan, John J., 825
Girdler, Tom, 353-354, 379, 476
Gladstone, William E., 736
Glass, Carter, 189, 211
Glenn, John H., Jr., 633, 644, 753, 839
Godwin, Mills E., Jr., 733-735
Goldberg, Arthur, 622, 720, 844
Goldman, Eric, 759
Goldwater, Barry M., 4, 15-16, 598, 624, 626, 633-634, 636-638, 640-642, 645, 647-648, 662, 667, 669, 671, 680-683, 686-687, 689, 694, 701, 704, 708, 725, 735, 738, 747, 802-803, 807, 809-811, 845
Goldwater, Mrs. Barry M., 682, 725
Gorman, Arthur P., 36, 55-56
Gould, Jay, 243
Gouzenko, Igor, 537

Grace Patricia, Princess of Monaco, 688
Graham, Billy, 565, 704, 774, 808-811
Graham, Katharine, 730, 796
Grant, Ulysses S., 281, 421
Grasso, Ella T., 3, 835, 838-839
Greeley, Horace, 348
Green, Theodore F., 462, 592
Green, William, 259-260, 262, 317
Greenewalt, Crawford H., xiv, 622, 698
Greenspan, Alan, 842
Griffith, Clark, 515
Griffiths, Martha W., 780, 797
Gromyko, Andrei A., 417, 436-437, 468, 717, 720
Gross, H. R., 761
Groves, Charles S., 205, 228-229
Gruening, Ernest, 700
Grundy, Joseph R., 201-202, 421, 476
Guffey, Joseph F., 422

Hagerty, James C., 57, 531, 544, 550, 556-557, 578, 598, 668
Hague, Frank, 378-379, 460, 463
Haldeman, H. R. ("Bob"), 805, 817-818, 825
Halifax, Lord Edward, 342
Hall, Henry, 58, 69, 121, 139
Hall, Leonard, 550, 566, 571, 577, 738
Halleck, Charles A., 457, 597-598, 600-602, 626, 634, 648, 656, 707
Halsey, William F., 474
Hamilton, Alexander, 169, 271
Hamilton, John, 297, 305, 360, 372
Hammarskjold, Dag, 553
Hanford, Charles B., 83
Hanna, Marcus A., 18, 38-40, 42, 44, 46, 48, 55-56, 59, 162, 243, 273, 292, 421, 722-723
Hannegan, Robert E., 405, 422, 433
Harding, Warren G., 109, 112, 129-132, 136-148, 152, 162, 186, 271-273, 421
Harmon, Judson, 79, 82-83
Harper, John, 698
Harriman, E. H., 18, 48, 50, 56
Harriman, W. Averell, 18, 56, 502, 504, 510, 540-542, 547-549, 554-556, 559, 579, 630, 748, 784
Harris, Fred R., 700, 769, 839
Harris, Lou, 738
Harrison, Benjamin, 2, 21, 27, 29, 33-37, 39, 45, 132, 161, 272, 289, 348, 616
Harrison, Byron Patton ("Pat"), 178, 189, 339, 347, 368-369
Harrison, William Henry, 289
Hartke, Rupert Vance, 700, 703, 732, 799, 839
Harvey, "Coin", 248

Harvey, George, 142
Hassett, William D., 293
Hatfield, Mark O., 613
Hatton, Frank, 30-31
Hawes, Harry, 189
Hawley, Joseph R., 421
Hay, John, 40
Hayden, Carl, 664
Hayden, Jay G., 158, 183, 210, 217, 228
Hayden, Mrs. Jay G., 401
Hayden, Martin, 248-249, 482-483
Haynsworth, Clement, 775, 793
Hays, Will H., 186
Hayworth, Rita, 465
Hearst, William Randolph, 55, 96, 276, 284
Heath, Perry S., 34
Heatter, Gabriel, 621
Hebert, F. Edward, 837
Heckler, Margaret, 780, 797
Heflin, James T., 196
Helms, Richard S., 720
Hendricks, Thomas A., 26
Henle, Ray, 395
Henning, Arthur Sears, 145, 149, 158, 186, 207
Henry, Patrick, 398, 733, 736
Herblock, see Block, Herbert
Herrick, Genevieve Forbes, 200
Herschell, Lord Farrer, 40-41
Herter, Christian A., 564, 567, 577, 603, 606-607
Hickel, Walter J., 760, 789-790, 793, 818
Hickenlooper, Bourke B., 635
Hightower, John, 708, 725, 752-753, 755
Hill, David B., 31-32
Hill, Edwin C., 270
Hilles, Charles D., 360
Hillman, Sidney, 381, 415
Hindenburg, Paul von, 212
Hiss, Alger, 766
Hitchcock, Frank H., 72
Hitchcock, Gilbert M., 126, 130
Hitler, Adolph, 9, 212, 237, 268, 308, 327, 337, 341-342, 344-345, 361, 379, 381, 383, 393, 402
Ho Chi Minh, 744, 754
Hoar, George F., 41
Hobby, Oveta Culp, 507-508
Hoffa, James R., 652
Hogan, Frank J., 186, 280
Holmes, George R., 219, 327-328, 331, 337, 340-341
Hoover, Herbert, xiii, xviii, 4, 10, 33, 118, 120, 137, 147, 166-167, 172, 183-185, 188-191, 193, 194-232, 236, 240-241, 250, 271-274, 281, 320, 330, 334, 366-367, 377, 379, 396, 420-421,

427-429, 434, 446, 458, 473, 475, 484, 498-501, 508, 616, 840-841
Hoover, Herbert, Jr., 545, 553, 572
Hoover, J. Edgar, 715, 790, 803
Hope, Bob, 6
Hopkins, Harry L., 251, 275, 285-286, 339-340, 378
Hosford, Franklin H., 32, 34, 40
Houdini, Harry, 144
House, E. M., 195
Houston, Sam, 663
Howard, Roy, 216, 377, 425
Howard, Sir Esme, 159
Howe, Louis, 255
Hoxha, Enver, 657
Huerta, Victoriano, 96
Hughes, Charles Evans, 22, 102-103, 109-110, 112-113, 137, 139-140, 142, 166, 174-175, 233-234, 279, 284, 290, 293, 296, 306-308, 337, 369, 392
Hughes, Don, 519
Hughes, Emmet John, 619
Hull, Cordell, 277, 323, 363, 380, 393
Humphrey, George, 506, 535, 549, 562, 570, 598, 651
Humphrey, Hubert H., 4, 15-17, 21, 463, 502, 523, 542, 559, 572, 574, 579-580, 596, 602-604, 607-608, 610, 614-615, 627, 649, 652-656, 664-665, 682, 685-689, 696-699, 701-702, 705-706, 714-715, 721-724, 732, 737, 740-742, 744-748, 752-753, 755-756, 758-760, 765, 768-769, 771, 780, 784-785, 787, 798-799, 801-804, 825, 836-838
Humphrey, Mrs. Hubert H., 687, 759
Huntley, Chet, 668, 730
Hurley, Patrick J., 411
Hussein I, 734
Hyde, Arthur M., 214

Ickes, Harold L., 15, 22-23, 266, 277, 285-286, 288-289, 321, 328, 339, 341, 353-354, 358, 362, 366, 370, 379, 388, 416, 421, 460
Inouye, Daniel K., 700
Insull, Samuel, 174

Jackson, Andrew, 78, 249, 271, 314, 481
Jackson, Henry M., 787, 798-799, 801, 823, 826-827, 837-838
Jackson, Robert H., 340
Javits, Jacob K., 626, 780
Jaworski, Leon, 824, 828
Jefferson, Joseph, 273
Jefferson, Thomas, 169, 237, 271, 286, 314, 367, 412, 733, 735
Jenner, William E., 487, 529

Jermane, W. W., 129, 133, 145
Johnson, Andrew, 281
Johnson, Hiram W., 136, 145, 151-152, 185, 201, 218, 226-227, 289, 379
Johnson, Hugh S., 239, 246-247, 255, 269, 277-278, 317-318, 354
Johnson, Jack, 95
Johnson, John A., 66-67
Johnson, Louis, 474
Johnson, Luci Baines (Mrs. Patrick J. Nugent), 701, 704
Johnson, Lyndon, 4, 9-10, 12, 15-16, 18, 20, 456, 505, 518, 523-524, 526-530, 532, 539-540, 542, 548, 556, 559-562, 567, 572, 578-581, 583, 588-589, 593-596, 601, 604, 607-608, 610, 614-615, 628, 639, 652-653, 659, 661-751, 753, 755-757, 759, 766, 770, 785, 792, 801-802, 804
Johnson, Mrs. Lyndon B., 677, 701, 704, 725, 734-735
Johnson, Sam Houston, 766, 770
Jones, Jesse H., 242, 384, 531
Jones, John Paul, 249
Jones, William D., 719
Jordan, B. Everett, 665-666
Joslin, Theodore G., xiii, 172, 214
Judd, Walter, 491
Jusserand, Jules, 141

Kaiser, Henry, 482
Kappel, Fred, 686
Karig, Walter, 382, 396
Katzenbach, Nicholas deB., 748
Kaufmann, Rudolph, 42-43, 87, 91-92, 95, 156
Kauffmann, Rudolph, II, 580, 639, 651, 796-797
Keating, Kenneth, 598, 626, 659
Keck, Howard, 561, 563
Keeler, Christine, 675
Kefauver, Estes, 503-504, 510, 525, 549, 558-559, 579-580, 582
Kellogg, Frank B., 181, 188, 392
Kelly, Edward J., 378-379
Kemal Pasha, Mustafa, 237
Kennedy, Caroline, 620, 632, 635, 652
Kennedy, Edward M., 4, 641, 644, 646, 649, 651, 653, 655, 697, 700, 715, 730-733, 752, 757, 763, 769, 780, 784, 786-788, 793, 798-799, 801, 809-810, 814-816, 823-824, 830, 837-838
Kennedy, John F., xiv, 1, 3-5, 10, 27, 33, 129, 572-573, 579, 581-585, 589, 592-597, 602, 604, 607-608, 610, 614-615, 620-660, 672, 712, 764, 788

Kennedy, Mrs. John F., 632-633, 645, 647, 652
Kennedy, Joseph P., 10, 279, 340-341, 573, 581-582, 594-596, 602, 607-608, 610, 723, 788
Kennedy, Robert F., 1, 4, 581, 594, 620, 625, 627-629, 632-633, 640, 646-647, 649, 651-652, 656, 665, 671, 685, 697-700, 703, 708-709, 711-712, 714-717, 722-724, 729-733, 737, 741-744, 746-747, 788
Kennedy, Mrs. Robert F., 715
Kennedy, Robert F., Jr., 645
Kent, Carleton, 729
Kent, Frank R., 286-289, 292, 302, 411
Kerr, Clark, 710
Kerr, Robert S., 504, 563
Keynes, John Maynard, 782
Khan, Ali Shah, 465
Khanh, Nguyen, 691
Khrushchev, Nikita S., 552, 556, 564, 591, 593, 596, 602, 606, 614, 625, 637, 643-644, 650, 656, 658-659, 671-672, 680
Kilgore, Bernard, 5, 344, 353
King, Martin Luther, Jr., 796
King, Mrs. Martin Luther, Jr., 796
Kirchhofer, Alfred H., 173-174
Kissinger, Henry, 3, 363, 519, 753-754, 762, 790, 792-794, 805, 807, 809, 812, 820, 831, 839-840, 844
Kleberg, Richard M., 526
Klein, Herbert, 622, 762, 789, 818
Knebel, Fletcher, 5, 518, 566, 594, 621, 661-662, 666, 670, 673-674, 676
Knight, Goodwin, 551, 554, 556, 569, 586, 595-596
Knight, John S., 782
Knowland, William F., 534, 536, 539, 545-547, 550, 553, 555, 565, 569, 572, 586, 595-597, 669, 679
Knox, Frank, 279, 289, 296, 360
Knox, Philander C., 61, 109, 131
Knudsen, William S., 380-381
Kosygin, Alexsei N., 717-719, 724, 749, 811
Kraft, Joseph, 764
Krock, Arthur, xviii, 5, 9-10, 19, 54, 89, 95-96, 234, 248, 291, 380, 393, 396, 409, 495-496, 518, 539, 616, 645, 659, 722-723
Ky, Nguyen Cao, 734, 754

La Follette, Robert M., 82, 84, 96, 122, 142, 145, 151-152, 156-158, 160, 163
La Guardia, Fiorello, 223, 239-241, 316, 320-321, 325, 334, 379, 797
Laird, Melvin, 760, 843

Lamont, Daniel Scott, 27, 31-32
Landers, Ann, 839
Landon, Alfred M., 4, 15, 23, 279, 285, 289, 293, 296-301, 304, 306, 320, 325, 333, 338, 360-361, 375, 421, 475, 596, 609, 708, 728, 783, 790
Lansing, Robert, 113, 122, 127
Larson, Arthur, 570, 572, 575
Laughton, Charles, 510
Laurier, Sir Wilfrid, 390
Lausanne, Stephane, 141
Lausche, Frank, 559, 700
Laval, Pierre, 268
Lawford, Peter, 651-652
Lawrence, David, 19, 288, 290, 302, 318
Leach, Paul R., 24, 353-354, 408, 416, 496, 505
Lehman, Herbert, 340
Lemnitzer, Lyman, 631
Lenin, Vladimir I., 718
Lerner, Max, 764
Lewis, John L., 3, 312, 317, 355, 366, 379, 501, 622
Lewis, Sir Willmott, 216, 496
Liberace (Walter Valentino Liberace), 542
Lilienthal, David, 331, 429
Liliuokalani, Queen, 30-31
Lin Piao, 717
Lincoln, Abraham, 249, 311, 484, 526, 584, 610, 612, 614, 625-626, 656, 705, 772
Lincoln, G. Gould, xviii, 33, 39, 57, 308, 315-317, 321
Lincoln, Robert Todd, 150
Lindbergh, Charles A., 182
Lindsay, John, 696, 739, 758, 769-770, 797, 810
Lippmann, Walter, 19, 290, 302, 317-318, 411, 515, 637, 764
Litvinoff, Maxim, 268, 442
Livingstone, David, 348
Lloyd, Selwyn, 606
Lloyd George, David, 125, 131
Lodge, Henry Cabot, 41, 61, 77, 125, 131, 133, 151
Lodge, Henry Cabot, Jr., 385-387, 475, 529, 553, 591, 668-671, 719-720, 724, 753-754
Loeb, Will, 72
Loeb, William, 801
Long, Huey P., 127, 234, 236, 239, 264, 700-701
Long, Russell B., 700-701, 711-712, 732, 752, 757, 784
Longworth, Alice Roosevelt, 57, 99, 301-302, 796
Longworth, Nicholas, 77, 79, 99, 166, 174, 214
Lovell, James A., 753

Lowden, Frank O., 136, 174, 185, 193
Lucas, Robert H., 214
Luce, Clare Boothe, 416
Luce, Henry R., 410, 560, 676
Lundberg, Ferdinand, 329
Luther, Martin, 629

McAdoo, William G., 91-92, 100, 121, 126, 145, 152, 155, 157, 160, 166, 172, 182, 247
MacArthur, Douglas, 403-404, 446-447, 457, 498, 560
McCarran, Patrick A., 247, 269
McCarthy, Eugene J., 629-630, 665, 737, 744-745, 747, 757-759, 768, 799
McCarthy, Joseph R., 492, 527, 529, 531, 536, 539
McClendon, Sarah, 646
McCloskey, Paul N., 726, 797, 799
McCone, John, 656
McCooey, "Uncle John," 227
McCormack, Edward J., Jr., 644
McCormack, John, 471, 664, 768-769
McCormick, Robert R., 276, 305, 414, 555
McCormick, Vance C., 116
McCracken, Paul, 839
McDowell, Charles, 818, 838
McElroy, Neil, 590-591
McGill, Ralph, 465
McGovern, George, 757-759, 768, 780, 782, 784-785, 787, 791, 793-794, 796-797, 799-801, 810, 812-817
McGrath, J. Howard, 441-443, 452, 463, 470, 497
McGrory, Mary, 764
McIntyre, Marvin, 275
McKay, Douglas, 506
McKellar, Kenneth, 247, 429
McKelway, Benjamin M., 578-579, 592
McKinley, William, 2, 36, 38-46, 75, 161, 272-273, 484, 616, 624, 641, 739
MacMillan, Harold, 657
McNamara, Patrick, 542
McNamara, Robert S., 631, 639, 691, 711, 730, 732
McNamee, Graham, 183
McNary, Charles L., 376-377
McNeil, Marshall, xviii, 5, 445, 455-456, 458, 465, 504, 523, 539-540, 585
McNutt, Paul, 323, 328-329, 356-358, 361-362, 374
McPherson, Aimee Semple, 250, 276
McReynolds, James Clark, 400
Machado, Gerardo, 180
Malenkov, Georgi, 537-538, 546

Manchester, William, 712, 714, 723
Mankiewicz, Frank F., 815
Mann, Thomas C., 675
Mansfield, Jayne, 683
Mansfield, Michael J. ("Mike"), 627, 708, 733, 757, 823, 826
Mao Tse-tung, 546, 625, 657, 675, 708, 717-719, 754, 805, 807-808, 819
Marks, Leonard, 719
Marriott, J. Willard, 710
Marshall, George C., 426, 436, 445, 517
Marshall John, 169
Marshall, Thomas R., 95-96, 98, 101, 118, 120, 125-126, 133-135, 161
Martin, Joseph W., Jr., 376, 420, 437, 439-441, 444, 446, 507, 543, 598-599, 780
Martin, Paul L., 719, 721, 811
Martine, James, 119
Marx, Karl, 718
Mason, Frank E., xviii
Massey, Vincent, 180
Mayfield, Sara, 19
Mazo, Earl, 517
Mead, Margaret, 796
Meany, George, 563, 607, 812
Meir, Golda, 827
Mellon, Andrew W., 137, 143, 147, 154, 164, 169, 187, 212, 224, 258, 262, 314
Mencken, Henry L., xiii, 19, 255-257, 260-262
Menjou, Adolph, 437
Menshikov, Mikhail A., 588
Menzies, Robert G., 670
Messenger, North O., 138
Mesta, Perle, 547-548, 567
Michelson, Charles, 201, 210-213, 240, 286-288, 317
Mikoyan, Anastas I., 596, 602, 606
Miles, Nelson A., 56
Miller, George Edmund, 78
Miller, Harlan, 336-337, 347
Miller, William E., 662, 672
Millikin, Eugene D., 469
Mills, Ogden, 175, 236, 238-239, 249, 258, 262
Mills, Wilbur D., 733-734, 792, 799, 810, 814
Mitchell, John, 57
Mitchell, John N., 766-767, 773, 776-778, 783, 805-809
Mitchell, Martha, 776, 780-781, 783, 785-786, 792, 798, 809
Mitchell, Stephen A., 523
Moley, Raymond, 233, 235, 247, 255, 358
Mollenhoff, Clark, 834-835
Mollet, Guy, 577

Molotov, V. M., 410-411, 427, 436-437, 442, 552, 644
Mondale, Walter F., 814, 825, 837
Monroe, James, 293, 812
Monroney, A. S. ("Mike"), 700
Montgomery, Robert, 574
Moore, Arch B., Jr., 779
More, Sir Thomas, 126
Morgan, Arthur E., 331
Morgan, J. P., 2, 18, 48, 50-51, 53, 57, 250, 276, 329
Morgenthau, Henry, Jr., 275-276, 368, 442
Morley, John, 94
Morse, Wayne, 429, 446, 472, 485-487, 493, 508, 523, 527, 536, 588, 614-615, 700, 702, 732, 734
Morsell, Herndon, 46, 54
Morsell, Tudor, 119, 143, 176-177, 198, 200
Morton, Rogers, C. B., 774
Morton, Thruston, 622, 625-626, 671
Moses, George H., 151, 154, 212, 218, 296
Moyers, Bill D., 685, 699, 703, 723
Moynihan, Daniel, 772
Murphy, Charles F., 95-96, 98, 114, 155, 227
Murphy, Frank, 22, 360, 369-370
Murphy, George, 695, 710
Murray, Arthur, 613
Murray, Philip, 411
Murrow, Edward R., 621, 642
Muskie, Edmund S., 572-573, 766, 770-773, 777, 780, 784, 786-787, 789, 796, 798-801, 810, 838
Mussolini, Benito, 237, 268, 341, 383, 385, 402
Myers, George, 297, 433, 438, 633, 651
Mylander, William H., xiv, 485, 498, 522

Nader, Ralph, 767, 774
Nash, Pat, 378
Nasser, Gamal Adbal, 564, 577-578, 689, 691, 749
Nation, Carrie, 248, 273
Nehru, Jawaharlal, 564, 643
Nessen, Ronald H., 841-842
Newsom, Earl, 483
Nimitz, Chester W., 403-404, 408, 473
Nixon, Richard M., 1, 4, 9, 11-17, 49, 363, 456, 505, 509, 517-519, 526, 551, 556, 565-567, 569, 571-572, 574, 577, 579, 583-584, 587, 591-600, 604, 610-611, 613, 617, 620, 622-624, 626, 632, 635-636, 638, 641-642, 655-656, 662, 667, 670-674, 676-677, 679, 687, 694-695, 698, 708-709, 727, 734-735, 737-740, 747, 752-832, 833
Nkrumah, Kwame, 701

Norris, George W., 79, 178, 212, 214, 218, 267, 379
Northcliffe, Lord, 141-142
Novak, Robert, 764
Noyes, Crosby, 42
Noyes, Frank, 188
Noyes, Newbold, 796-797, 813, 827
Nugent, Patrick Lyndon, 736
Nurmi, Paavo, 673
Nye, Gerald P., xiv, 351

O'Brien, Jimmy "The Famous," 227
O'Brien, John C., 604
O'Brien, Larry, 770, 772, 777, 781, 784, 799, 815
O'Brien, Robert Lincoln, 28, 473
O'Connor, Frank, 715
O'Connor, John J., 337
O'Donnell, Kenneth, 621
O'Dwyer, William, 405, 463-464
O'Leary, Jeremiah A., 122
Olvany, George W., 187, 227
O'Mahoney, Joseph C., 340
Onassis, Mrs. Aristotle, see Kennedy, Mrs. John F.
O'Neill, Lillian W., xviii
O'Neill, Thomas P., Jr. ("Tip"), 836, 838
Otis, Harrison Gray, 43
Otten, Alan, 764
Oulahan, Richard V., xiii, 48, 72, 79, 81, 100, 138, 157-159, 183, 189, 192, 201, 205
Oxnam, G. Bromley, 10, 582

Paar, Jack, 609
Packard, David, 761
Palmer, A. Mitchell, 126
Parker, Alton B., 59-60
Parker, John J., 205
Payne, Sereno E., 78
Peale, Norman Vincent, 623
Pearson, Drew, 589
Pearson, Lester, 537
Pecora, Ferdinand, 151, 250
Pegler, Westbrook, 318
Pendergast, Thomas J., 488
Penrose, Boies, 92, 140, 142, 206, 257, 292, 421, 649
Pepper, Claude, 422, 432, 442, 449
Percy, Charles H., 696, 709, 727, 729, 734, 738, 747, 814, 842-843
Perkins, Frances, 246-247, 255, 269, 277, 303, 353, 399, 405
Peron, Juan, 417
Perry, Glen C. H., xviii

Pershing, John J., 127, 183, 209, 239, 276
Peterson, Peter G., 818
Pew, Joseph N., Jr., 364, 430, 476, 531
Phillips, Adon, 720, 750
Pierce, Arthur, 176-177, 259, 459, 469
Pilsudski, Joseph, 237
Pinchot, Gifford, 73, 77, 83-85, 297
Pine, David A., 501-502
Pittman, Key, 189
Platt, Orville H., 61
Platt, Thomas C., 41, 206
Poe, Edgar A., xvii, 798, 804, 823
Pomerene, Atlee, 126
Poore, Ben: Perley, 26
Poteet, Cemetery, 522
Pound, Roscoe, 334
Powell, Adam Clayton, 659, 661-662, 696, 713
Powell, Wesley, 610
Powell, William, 276
Powers, David F., 651-652
Powers, Gary, 650
Pressman, Lee, 415
Preston, James, 354
Price, Byron, 327
Procopé, Hjalmar, 352
Profumo, John, 675
Proxmire, William, 596, 601
Pulitzer, Joseph, 32, 216, 234, 435

Quay, Matthew S., 421
Quesada, Elwood ("Pete"), 622
Quezon, Manuel Luis, 323
Quill, Mike, 696

Radford, Arthur W., 546
Radziwill, Princess Lee, 645, 652
Rainey, Henry T., 247
Rand, Sally, 309
Raskob, John J., 189, 211, 218, 258, 292, 302, 353
Rasputin, Grigori Y., 808
Rayburn, Sam, 267, 309, 423, 462, 471, 505, 540, 542, 548-549, 559, 572, 581-582, 588, 627, 744, 814
Raymond, William F., 276, 423, 633
Reagan, Ronald, 695, 707, 710-711, 716, 724, 726-727, 829-830, 842-843
Rebozo, Charles G. ("Bebe"), 760, 804
Reece, Carroll, 432, 437, 443
Reed, Daniel A., 535
Reed, David A., 248-249, 257, 260, 280
Reed, James A., 125, 147, 171, 187-188
Reed, Thomas B., 36
Reedy, George, 663, 685, 688

Reid, Whitelaw, 36, 61
Reston, James B., 764
Reuther, Walter, 479, 559, 563, 579-580, 593, 686
Revere, Paul, 284, 388-389, 732, 735
Reynolds, Stanley M., 131
Rhodes, James, A., 703
Rhodes, John J., 841
Ribicoff, Abraham A., 607, 638, 640-642, 645, 757
Richardson, Elliot L., 821
Richberg, Donald R., 255, 269, 277
Ridder, Walter T., xvii, 635, 679, 685, 821-822
Riggs, Robert L., 494, 620-621
Roberts, Roy, 131-132, 194, 200, 228, 285, 444
Robinson, Joseph T., 215
Rockefeller, David, 2, 656, 840
Rockefeller, John D., 48
Rockefeller, John D., Jr., 98
Rockefeller, John D., IV, 729
Rockefeller, Lawrence, 656
Rockefeller, Nelson A., 3, 593-594, 596-597, 599-600, 613, 623-624, 626, 634-636, 638, 641-642, 647-648, 650, 668-671, 680, 694, 696, 709, 727-729, 734, 739, 741, 747, 759, 761, 770, 811, 830-831, 833-834, 838, 843-845
Rockefeller, Mrs. Nelson A., 3, 834, 844
Rockefeller, Winthrop, 656, 709, 727-729, 733-734
Rodino, Peter W., Jr., 823, 825, 828
Rogers, H. H., 18, 49-50
Rogers, Warren, 822, 839
Rogers, Will, 237, 238
Rogers, William P., 519, 587-590, 753-754, 762, 775, 779, 790, 792-793, 819
Romney, George, 635-636, 641-642, 648-651, 654, 668-669, 671, 680, 694-695, 708, 710, 716, 727, 734, 738, 747
Romney, Mrs. George, 649
Rooney, John J., 630
Roosevelt, Elliott, 422
Roosevelt, Franklin D., 3, 5, 9, 12-13, 15, 18-19, 21-23, 27, 33, 89, 118, 165-166, 197-198, 205, 211-212, 214, 218, 222-223, 226-228, 233-401, 402, 404-405, 411, 415-416, 427, 439, 452, 473, 509, 517, 533, 558, 612, 616, 633, 788, 812
Roosevelt, Mrs. Franklin D., 399-401, 596, 609
Roosevelt, Franklin D., Jr., 330, 533-535, 541, 548
Roosevelt, James, 245, 265, 322, 541

Roosevelt, John, 534
Roosevelt, Theodore, xv, 3, 17-18, 40, 44-78, 81, 83-85, 96, 99, 109-110, 145, 162, 236, 272-273, 281, 289, 386, 396, 452, 499-500, 529, 554-555, 660
Roosevelt, Theodore, Jr., 158
Root, Elihu, 58-59, 67, 73, 109, 139, 257
Roper, Daniel C., 277-278
Roper, Elmo, 457, 476, 738
Rorer, Dwight, 469, 593
Rosenman, Sam, 340
Ross, Charles G., xiii, 158, 201, 234, 238, 396, 494, 556
Ross, Nellie Tayloe, 159
Rostow, Walter, 750, 754
Roth, Robert, xvii, 805, 812-813, 835-836
Rowan, Carl, 690-691
Rusk, Dean, 631, 639, 642, 657-658, 674-676, 682, 690-691, 702, 717, 721, 725, 732, 734-735, 751
Russell, Richard B., 469, 480, 503-504, 523-524, 639

Sabath, Adolph J., 462
Sadat, Anwar, 797, 826, 839
St. Laurent, Louis, 537
Salinger, Pierre, 646, 653, 662
Saltonstall, Leverett, 475, 572
Sanders, Everett, 249-250
Sanford, Terry, 839
Sanger, Margaret, 250
Santelmann, William F., 540
Sargent, John, 177
Sawyer, Charles, 501-502
Sawyer, Dr. Charles, 140
Schlesinger, Arthur M., Jr., 621, 697, 712, 732, 742-743
Schuman, Robert, 467
Scott, Hugh, 782-783, 789
Scott, N. B., 59
Scranton, William, 647, 669-671, 680
Seidman, William, 839, 842
Sevareid, Eric, 793, 811
Shapiro, Irving S., xiv
Shapp, Milton J., 823
Sherman, James S., 67
Sherman, William T., 412, 679, 813
Shivers, Alan, 626
Shoop, Duke, 444, 520, 531
Shouse, Jouett, 189, 258, 280, 301, 332-334
Shriver, Eunice Kennedy, 629, 652
Shriver, R. Sargent, 642-643, 649, 652, 657, 664-665, 684, 692, 696-697, 730, 769, 815
Shultz, George P., 774
Sickler, Gerald W., 278

Simon, Sir John, 268
Simon, William E., 841-842
Simpson, "Sockless" Jerry, 248
Sinatra, Frank, 627
Sinclair, Harry F., 186-187
Sinclair, Upton, 284
Sinnott, Arthur, 188
Sirica, John J., 817, 824
Slemp, C. Bascom, 151-152
Smith, Alfred E., xiii, 146, 152, 157-158,
   160, 164, 166, 177, 184, 187-189, 191,
   217-218, 222, 227, 242, 287, 302, 379,
   449, 582, 632
Smith, Charles Emory, 46
Smith, Ellison D. ("Cotton Ed"), 247,
   339-340
Smith, Frank L., 178
Smith, Hubbard T., 27
Smith, Jesse W., 146
Smith, Margaret Chase, 635, 671, 796
Smoot, Reed, 78, 92, 206, 226, 421, 649
Smuts, Jan Christiaan, 390
Snell, Bertrand, 223
Snyder, Edgar C., 101-102
Snyder, John W., 426, 433, 491
Socrates, 512
Sorensen, Theodore C., 621, 638-639,
   653-654, 696-697
Sousa, John Philip, 24, 27, 173, 209, 820
Sparkman, John J., 422, 558
Spellman, Francis J., 645
Stalin, Joseph V., 23, 237, 394-395, 402, 417,
   420, 426, 435-437, 442, 445, 468, 472,
   507, 537, 565, 644, 718
Stanley, Sir Henry Morton, 348
Stanton, Frank, 703
Stassen, Harold E., 357-361, 413-416,
   429-430, 437-438, 446, 475, 498, 500,
   552, 569, 572, 574, 578, 583, 586, 588,
   596, 609, 613, 668, 671, 695, 710-711,
   739
Stearns, Frank W., 171, 174
Steed, H. Wickham, 141
Steele, Jack, xi, xvii, 11-12, 766-767, 771,
   776, 778-780, 804, 817, 827, 839
Steelman, John, 501
Steffe, Edwin C., 379
Steffens, Lincoln, 65
Stein, Herbert, 839
Steinem, Gloria, 797
Stennis, John, 639, 732, 774
Stepin Fetchit, 319
Stettinius, Edward R., Jr., 404
Stevenson, Adlai Ewing, 36, 44
Stevenson, Adlai E., 4, 15-16, 36, 504-505,
   510-517, 524-525, 532-533, 542, 547,
   549, 557-559, 570, 573-577, 579-580,

588-589, 594, 596, 602, 609, 614-615,
   629, 654
Stevenson, Adlai E., III, 825, 838
Stewart, Potter, 648
Stimson, Henry L., 9, 392, 411
Stofer, Alfred J., 46
Stokes, Thomas L., 483, 494
Stone, Harlan F., 186
Stranahan, Robert P., Jr., 838
Straus, Oscar S., 273
Strauss, Robert S., 3, 838-839
Strayer, Louis W., 109-110
Sukarno, 689
Sullivan, Gael, 432-433
Sullivan, Mark, 19, 55, 173-174, 250, 288,
   290, 302, 318, 396
Sulzer, William, 95-96
Summerfield, Arthur, 506
Suydam, Henry, 5, 279, 293, 395
Swope, Girard, 145
Sylvester, Arthur, 494, 631, 646, 653
Symington, Stuart, 474, 525, 532, 539, 559,
   579-581, 583, 593, 596, 604, 608-613,
   615, 617, 639, 732

Taft, Lorado, 274
Taft, Robert A., 4-5, 14, 289, 346-347,
   349-350, 361, 363, 371-372, 376-377,
   413, 420, 424, 429-430, 434, 436-438,
   446-450, 457, 468, 475, 477, 498-499,
   508, 513, 515-516, 527, 529
Taft, William Howard, xv, 59, 64, 67-68,
   71-88, 109, 137, 142-143, 161-162, 197,
   272-273, 281, 289, 349, 363, 438
Taft, Mrs. William Howard, 81
Taggart, Thomas, 155
Talburt, Harold M., 424-425, 436
Talmadge, Herman, 572
Tarbell, Ida M., 65
Taylor, Glen, 451, 472, 494
Taylor, Maxwell D., 590-591, 674-675, 691
Taylor, Myron C., 308-312, 314
terHorst, Jerald F., 767, 822, 842
Thant, U., 689
Thatcher, Margaret, 17
Thaw, Harry K., 95
Thieu, Nguyen Van, 734
Thomas, Elmer, 242
Thomas, Helen, 3, 834-835, 842
Thomas, Norman, 278, 280-283, 293
Thompson, Charles Willis, 17, 60, 65
Thompson, Dorothy, 318, 411
Thompson, Llewellyn, 671
Thurber, Henry T., 31-32
Thurmond, J. Strom, 17, 453-455, 463,
   541-542, 639-640, 654, 762

Thurston, Lorin A., 30-31
Tillman, Benjamin R., 49
Timmons, Bascom N., 374-375
Tito, Josip Broz, 445, 637, 643
Tower, John G., 642
Townsend, Francis E., 264, 347, 350
Trohan, Walter, 5, 605, 703, 707, 710, 714,
    721-723, 725, 734-736
Truman, Harry S., 1, 3, 5, 9-10, 12, 14-15,
    17, 23, 33, 397, 402-519, 522-523, 525,
    529, 532-533, 542, 547-548, 554, 556,
    559-560, 579-580, 588-589, 594, 607,
    609, 613, 616, 673-674, 724
Truman, Mrs. Harry S., 519
Truman, Margaret (Mrs. E. Clifton Daniel,
    Jr.), 444, 579
Tshombe, Moise K., 10, 645
Tugwell, Rexford G., 235, 247, 330
Tumulty, Joseph P., 130, 134
Tunney, John V., 809, 839
Twain, Mark, 667
Twiggy (Leslie Hornby), 740
Tydings, Millard, 337, 339, 464

Udall, Morris K., 768, 838
Udall, Stewart L., 626
Underwood, Oscar W., 80, 82-84, 92, 98,
    146, 157, 177-178

Valenti, Jack, 664, 685, 699, 704, 723, 758
Vandenberg, Arthur H., 4, 240, 257,
    261-262, 267, 279, 289, 291, 325, 347,
    361, 363-367, 371-372, 376-378, 417,
    429-430, 437-438, 446, 467
Vandenberg, Hoyt, 474
Vanderlip, Frank A., 121
Vare, William S., 178
Vaughan, Harry, 412, 481
Vernon, Roy, 54, 99-100
Villard, Oswald Garrison, 290
Vinson, Fred M., 470, 493-494
Vishinsky, Andrei Y., 436-437
Volstead, Andrew J., 139, 191
vonBernstorff, Count J. H., 98

Wadsworth, James W., Jr., 175
Wagner, Robert F., 321, 549, 559, 797
Walker, Ernest G., 238, 246
Walker, Frank, 522
Walker, James J., 218, 250
Wallace, George, 712-713, 737, 741,
    743-744, 747, 752-753, 755-756, 774,
    798-800, 803, 823, 838
Wallace, Henry A., 247, 266, 278, 286, 347,

358, 366, 374-375, 380, 382-384, 397,
    407, 413-415, 421-423, 426, 431, 435,
    441-442, 445, 448-449, 451-455
Wallace, Jonathan H., 38
Wallace, Lurleen, 712-713
Walsh, Thomas J., 163, 186-187, 211, 219,
    247
Warren, Charles B., 166, 173, 176
Warren, Earl, 22, 429-432, 434-435, 461,
    475, 498, 500, 555, 567, 569, 579, 585,
    641, 646, 648, 666, 720, 725, 734,
    753-756, 764, 809
Warren, Lucian, xvii, 783, 828, 833-834
Washington, George, 169, 192, 195, 203,
    249, 271, 367, 389, 465, 683, 726, 733,
    735
Watson, James E., 54, 174, 196-197, 207,
    211, 219, 226-227, 240, 512
Watson, Marvin, 728
Watson, "Pa," 368
Webb, James E., 644
Weeks, John W., 133, 151
Weeks, Sinclair, 475, 507
Welch, Robert, 634, 648
Welles, Orson, 338-339
Welles, Sumner, 362-363
Wells, H. G., 141
West, Henry Litchfield, 43-45
Westmoreland, William C., 724
Westwood, Jean, 815
Wheeler, Earle G., 691, 743
Whelan, Grover, 641
Wherry, Kenneth S., 469, 476, 487
White, Paul Dudley, 565
White, Stanford, 95
White, Thomas, 590-591
White, Wallace H., 297
White, William Allen, 296-297, 379
White, William S., 764
Whiteman, Paul, 309
Whitman, Charles S., 98
Whitney, Richard, 234
Whitney, William C., 30
Wicker, Thomas G., 764
Wickersham, George W., 74, 90, 215, 250,
    280
Wiggins, J. Russell, 689, 692, 696, 703
Wiley, Alexander, 487, 530
Wilhelm II (Kaiser), 81, 122, 127
Wilkerson, James H., 217
Wilkins, Beriah, 42
Willcox, William R., 116
Williams, Edward Bennett, 186, 665
Williams, G. Mennan ("Soapy"), 541, 543,
    573, 579-580, 583, 593, 621, 625, 632,
    637, 662, 674, 715
Williams, John J., 497

Willkie, Wendell L., 343, 346, 357-358, 362,
374-378, 381, 385, 388, 393-394
Wilson, Charles E., 506, 521, 571
Wilson, Harold, 749-751
Wilson, Lyle C., 396-397, 402, 531, 555, 594,
621-622
Wilson, Richard L., xvii, 13, 340, 408, 417,
437, 465, 469, 472, 594, 610, 621-622,
696, 699, 705, 730, 764, 778, 804, 817,
822, 827, 839
Wilson, William L., 35
Wilson, Woodrow, 3, 8, 21, 61, 73, 84-86,
89-135, 137, 162, 271-272, 290, 342, 495,
585, 689
Windsor, Edward, Duke of, 319, 418, 569
Windsor, Wallis Warfield, Duchess of, 418
Wister, Owen, 57
Wood, Leonard, 136
Wood, Lewis, 316, 355, 394, 397

Woodin, William H., 236
Woods, Rose Mary, 763, 829
Wooton, Paul, 592, 600, 604
Wright, Harold Bell, 207
Wright, James L., 245-246, 248, 254, 256,
298, 360
Wright, Orville, 273
Wright, Wilbur, 273

Xander, Henry, 489

Youmans, Vincent, 4, 419, 624, 808, 811

Zarb, Frank G., 842
Zhukov, Goergi, 552, 556
Ziegler, Ronald, 813-814, 818, 829

THE PRESIDENT SPEAKS OFF-THE-RECORD

Designed by Helen Barrow

Set in Palatino by Waldman Graphics, Inc.
    Philadelphia, Pennsylvania

Printed on Warren's 1854 Text by Port City Press
    Baltimore, Maryland

Bound by Port City Press